Fodor's

P9-AFX-806

COLORADO

10th Edition

Where to Stay and Eat
for All Budgets

Must-See Sights
and Local Secrets

Ratings You Can Trust

Fodor's Travel Publications   New York, Toronto, London, Sydney, Auckland
www.fodors.com

FODOR'S COLORADO

Writers: Ricardo Baca, Jad Davenport, Martha Schindler Connors, Kyle Wagner

Editors: Salwa Jabado, Matt Lombardi
Editorial Contributors: Andrew Collins, John Rambow, Mark Sullivan

Production Editor: Jennifer DePrima
Maps & Illustrations: David Lindroth and Mark Stroud, *cartographers;* Bob Blake, Rebecca Baer, *map editors;* William Wu, *information graphics*
Design: Fabrizio La Rocca, *creative director;* Guido Caroti, *art director;* Tina Malaney, Chie Ushio, Nora Rosansky, Jessica Walsh, *designers;* Melanie Marin, *associate director of photography*
Cover Photo: Cumbres and Toltec Railroad: Ron Ruhoff/Index Stock/Photolibrary
Production Manager: Angela L. McLean

10th Edition

ISBN 978–0–307–92842–9

ISSN 0276–9018

SPECIAL SALES
This book is available at special discounts for bulk purchases for sales promotions or premiums. Special editions, including personalized covers, excerpts of existing books, and corporate imprints, can be created in large quantities for special needs. For more information, write to Special Markets/Premium Sales, 1745 Broadway, MD 3-1, New York, NY 10019, or e-mail specialmarkets@randomhouse.com.

AN IMPORTANT TIP & AN INVITATION
Although all prices, opening times, and other details in this book are based on information supplied to us at press time, changes occur all the time in the travel world, and Fodor's cannot accept responsibility for facts that become outdated or for inadvertent errors or omissions. So **always confirm information when it matters,** especially if you're making a detour to visit a specific place. Your experiences—positive and negative— matter to us. If we have missed or misstated something, **please write to us.** Share your opinion instantly through our online feedback center at fodors.com/contact-us.

PRINTED IN THE UNITED STATES OF AMERICA

10 9 8 7 6 5 4 3 2 1

CONTENTS

CONTENTS

MAPS

ABOUT
THIS BOOK

Our Ratings

As travelers we've all discovered a place so wonderful that its worthiness is obvious. And sometimes that place is so unique that superlatives don't do it justice: you just have to be there to know. These sights, properties, and experiences get our highest rating, **Fodor's Choice,** indicated by orange stars throughout this book. Black stars highlight sights and properties we deem **Highly Recommended.** By default, there's another category: any place we include in this book is by definition worth your time, unless we say otherwise. And we will. Disagree with any of our choices? Care to nominate a place or suggest that we rate one more highly? Visit our feedback center at www.fodors.com/feedback.

Hotels

Hotels have private bath, phone, TV, and air-conditioning, and do not offer meals unless we specify that in the review. We always list facilities but not whether you'll be charged an extra fee to use them.

> For expanded hotel reviews, visit **Fodors.com**

Restaurants

Unless we state otherwise, restaurants are open for lunch and dinner daily. We mention dress only when there's a specific requirement and reservations only when they're essential or not accepted—it's always best to book ahead.

Credit Cards

We assume that restaurants and hotels accept credit cards. If not, we'll note it in the review.

Budget Well

Hotel and restaurant price categories from ¢ to $$$$ are defined in the opening pages of the respective chapters. For attractions, we always give standard adult admission fees; reductions are usually available for children, students, and senior citizens.

Listings		Hotels & Restaurants	Outdoors
★ Fodor's Choice	✍ E-mail	🏨 Hotel	⛳ Golf
★ Highly recommended	🎫 Admission fee	⇄ Number of rooms	⛺ Camping
✉ Physical address	☺ Open/closed times	⌾ Facilities	**Other**
✛ Directions or Map coordinates	Ⓜ Metro stations	⍾ Meal plans	☾ Family-friendly
⌂ Mailing address	▭ No credit cards	✗ Restaurant	⇨ See also
☏ Telephone		⊡ Reservations	✉ Branch address
🖷 Fax		🏛 Dress code	☞ Take note
⊕ On the Web		↘ Smoking	

1

Experience Colorado

WORD OF MOUTH

"It sounds like you like the feel of Colorado ski towns, the beauty of staying right in the middle of the mountains with access to a small picturesque town. I would use Rocky Mountain National Park, Aspen, Telluride and Crested Butte for my bases. You will have spectacular scenery, and endless hiking, biking and rafting options. In addition they are all connected by scenic byways with interesting stops along the way . . . Seriously you cannot make a wrong choice when it comes to Colorado, I was just thinking those options make a nice circle trip. Have fun!"

—Barblab

WHAT'S WHERE

The following numbers refer to chapters.

2 Denver. Colorado's capital and largest city, Denver is unmatched in its combination of urban pleasures and easy access to outdoor recreation.

3 The Rockies near Denver. Scenic highway I–70 ascends into the foothills through historic towns Idaho Springs and Georgetown. Feeling lucky? Try the gambling at Central City and Black Hawk.

4 Summit County. The ski resorts of Keystone, Breckenridge, Copper Mountain, and Arapahoe Basin cluster near I–70 as it rises in the Rockies. Lake Dillon and its port towns attract summer visitors.

5 Vail Valley. Vail, the world's largest single-mountain ski resort, sits in a narrow corridor bounded by steep peaks. Also in the valley: upscale ski area Beaver Creek and sleepy Minturn.

6 Aspen and the Roaring Fork Valley. Glitzy Aspen is a serious skiing draw. Farther west, Victorian charmer Glenwood Springs centers on a massive hot springs pool.

7 Boulder and North Central Colorado. College town Boulder balances high-tech with bohemia. Estes Park abuts Rocky Mountain National Park's eastern entrance, while Grand Lake is its quieter western gateway.

8 Rocky Mountain National Park. The wilderness and alpine tundra here welcome wildlife and outdoor enthusiasts year-round.

9 Northwest Colorado and Steamboat Springs. Where the Rockies transition into an arid desert, Grand Junction is the region's hub. Nearby are the Colorado and Dinosaur National Monuments. Steamboat Springs offers skiing with cowboy charm.

10 Southwest Colorado.
Evergreen-clad peaks and red desert beckon outdoor enthusiasts to mountain-biking birthplace Crested Butte, Black Canyon of the Gunnison, idyllic Telluride, and historic Durango.

11 Mesa Verde National Park. Designated a park in 1906, this protected series of canyons provides a peek into the lives of the Ancestral Puebloan people who made their homes among the cliffs.

12 South Central Colorado.
Next to Pikes Peak, Colorado Springs' mineral waters still flow. Cañon City is a rafting hub; Buena Vista and Salida are two artists' colonies. To the south, explore Great Sand Dunes National Park and Preserve.

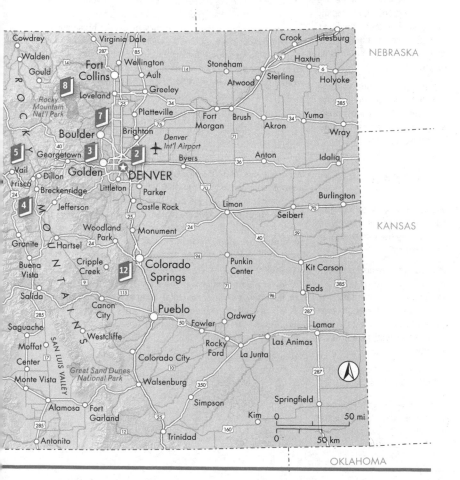

WELCOME TO COLORADO

What to Bring?

Colorado is famous for its "Rocky Mountain formal" dress code, which means cowboy attire is accepted everywhere, even in the fanciest restaurants, so bring your jeans and leave your formalwear at home. It's wise to be prepared for rapidly changing weather, however, as well as cooler nights (even when daytime temperatures hit summer highs).

If your plans include outdoor activities such as golf, skiing, or mountain biking, most major towns and cities have rental equipment available.

High Altitude Tips

The three things to consider with high-altitude travel are altitude sickness, dehydration, and sunburn.

■ If you are coming from sea level and plan to visit the mountains, it's worth taking a day or two in Denver or other lower-elevation area to acclimate. Either way, take it easier than usual.

■ Drink plenty of water and avoid alcohol.

■ Always wear sunscreen and protective clothing. Sunglasses and a hat also are must-haves at higher elevation.

When to Go

The Colorado you experience will depend on the season you visit. Summer is a busy time. Hotels in tourist destinations book up early, especially in July and August, and hikers crowd the backcountry. Ski resorts buzz from December to early April, especially around Christmas and Presidents' Day. Many big resorts are popular summer destinations.

If you don't mind capricious weather, rates drop and crowds are nonexistent in spring and fall. Spring's pleasures are somewhat limited, since snow usually blocks the high country—and mountain-pass roads—well into June. But spring is a good time for fishing, rafting, birding, and wildlife-viewing. In fall, aspens splash the mountainsides with gold, wildlife comes down to lower elevations, and the angling is excellent.

How's the Weather?

Summer in the Rocky Mountains begins in late June or early July. Days are warm, with highs often in the 80s; nighttime temperatures fall to the 40s and 50s. Afternoon thunderstorms are common over the higher peaks. Fall begins in September; winter creeps in during November, and deep snows arrive by December. Temperatures usually hover near freezing by day, thanks to the warm mountain sun, and drop overnight, occasionally as low as -60°F. Winter tapers off in March, though snow lingers into April on valley bottoms and into July on mountain passes.

At lower elevations (Denver, the eastern plains, and the southwestern corner of the state), summertime highs above 100°F are not uncommon, and winters are still cold, with highs in the 20s and 30s. The entire state sees snowy winters, even on the plains.

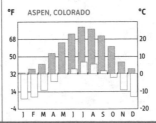

Getting Here and Around

For more detailed information, see Travel Smart Colorado.

Modern and busy, **Denver International Airport** (DEN ☎ 800/247–2336 ⊕ www.flydenver.com) moves travelers in and out efficiently. There's also **Colorado Springs Airport** (COS ☎ 719/550–1972 ⊕ www.flycos.com) and a number of smaller airports near resorts—Steamboat Springs, Aspen, and Telluride.

In Denver some of the hotels provide free shuttles, and the free Mall shuttle and light rail make it easy to get around the metro area. You can travel to some major ski areas by prearranged shuttle van. **Amtrak** (☎ 303/825–2583 ⊕ www.amtrak.com) has stops in Denver, Winter Park, Glenwood Springs, Grand Junction, Trinidad, and La Junta.

Any other travel requires a car. Always check on road conditions, as the weather can be unpredictable. **Colorado Road Condition Hotline** (☎ 303/639–1111 near Denver, 303/639–1234 statewide ⊕ www.cotrip.org).

Dining

Dining in Colorado has evolved, and there are now more options than ever. However, the dress code remains casual. Reservations are recommended in most areas, and are essential in the high country, especially during the winter ski season, and in places where golf, mountain biking, and water sports are popular during the summer.

Lodging

Plan well ahead for lodging in resort towns, particularly during ski season and midsummer, when festivals dominate. Condos can be a value during high season, especially if you have a group or family, because you can save money on dining or share expenses. While ski-area lodges can offer the closest access, they also will be the most expensive.

DINING AND LODGING PRICE CATEGORIES

	¢	$	$$	$$$	$$$$
Restaurants	under $8	$8–$12	$13–$18	$19–$25	over $25
Hotels	under $80	$80–$120	$121–$170	$171–$230	over $230

Restaurant prices are for a main course at dinner, excluding tax. Hotel prices are for two people in a standard double room in high season, excluding service charges and tax.

Festivals and Events

Summer in Colorado is full of food and culture celebrations. Here are some highlights:

June Country Jam. The likes of Keith Urban and Blake Shelton party in Grand Junction. ☎ 800/780–0526 ⊕ www.countryjam.com.

Telluride Bluegrass Festival. The top acts in bluegrass take the music to new levels in a stunning setting. ☎ 800/624–2422 ⊕ www.bluegrass.com.

June–Aug. Bravo! Vail Valley Music Festival. This festival brings national orchestras to venues around the Valley. ☎ 877/812–5700 ⊕ www.vailmusicfestival.org.

Strings in the Mountains Music Festival. Chamber music, jazz, rock, and country shows take place in Steamboat Springs. ☎ 970/879–5056 ⊕ www.stringsmusicfestival.com.

July and Aug. Crested Butte Music Festival. A variety of genres are played among the wildflowers at this festival. ☎ 970/349–0619 ⊕ www.crestedbuttemusicfestival.com.

Sept. Telluride Film Festival. You'll find movie premieres, workshops, and the chance to rub elbows with celebs at this film fest. ☎ 510/665–9494 ⊕ www.telluridefilmfestival.com.

COLORADO TOP ATTRACTIONS

Aspen and Glenwood Springs
(E) Stop by Glenwood Springs for a rejuvenating dip in the mineral springs–fed pool before continuing on to the glitzy-but-relaxing scene that is Aspen. The historic mining town has top-notch dining, the beautiful Maroon Bells mountains, and unparalleled skiing.

Black Canyon of the Gunnison National Park
(H) It's hard to say who appreciates this natural wonder more: anglers, river rafters, hikers, or photographers. All are drawn to the glorious narrow canyon with its dramatic, jagged walls and enormous surrounding recreation area.

Boulder
(D) A college town with dramatic environs nestled up against the Flatirons, Boulder has a reputation for being the most outdoors-oriented of all of Colorado's towns. With its commitment to preserving open space and wilderness, the city abuts so many nonurbanized zones that you can be on a trail to a mountain peak in no time. Terrific restaurants and a vibrant arts scene add to the allure.

Mesa Verde National Park
(F) Home to the Ancestral Puebloans more than 700 years ago, Mesa Verde allows visitors to walk among the mesmerizing cliff dwellings built into alcoves perched hundreds of feet above and below level ground. Drive through the 80-square-mi park, stopping along the way to climb down into the dwellings, which tuck into the dramatic sandstone formations.

Mile-High Denver
(C) The state's capital and largest city, Denver boasts of a diverse population with a rich mix of cultural offerings, and most of the 2.7 million metro area residents are intense sports fans and serious outdoors enthusiasts. The lively downtown area has a baseball stadium, an amusement park, historic neighborhoods, and a vast park

system. Denver also claims the Denver Art Museum, the Denver Museum of Nature & Science, and the Denver Performing Arts Complex.

Pikes Peak

(A) There are 54 peaks topping 14,000 feet in Colorado, but only here can you drive the switchbacks or take the Cog Railway to the top. The inspiration for Katharine Bates' song "America the Beautiful," Pikes Peak looms a few miles west of Colorado Springs.

Rocky Mountain National Park and Estes Park

(B) Estes Park is the gateway town to Rocky Mountain National Park, which is full of lush forests, high-alpine lakes, snowcapped peaks, wildflower-covered meadows, and 355 mi of trails. Abundant wildlife like black bear, elk, and bighorn sheep, and even more abundant crowds are drawn to this year-round paradise.

Summit County

(G) One of Colorado's premier giant playgrounds, Summit County is a year-round destination. Choose from a number of ski resorts—Copper Mountain, Keystone, Breckenridge, or local favorite Arapahoe Basin. The towns of Dillon, Silverthorne, and Frisco cluster around Dillon Reservoir, connected by an extensive paved bike path and rimmed by the looming peaks of the Continental Divide that border the east and south of the county. The old mining town of Leadville, with its exceptional greenway and historic buildings, has become a destination for families.

QUINTESSENTIAL COLORADO

The Great Outdoors

Colorado gets more than 300 sunny days per year, and that's a big part of why the natives get restless when forced to spend too much time inside. On any given day you'll find folks figuring out ways to get out there, from biking to work along the intricate veins of multiuse paths to hiking with the dog around expanses of open space, to soccer and jogging at the well-planned parks scattered around cities. In fact, Coloradans talk about the outdoors the way some people elsewhere talk about meals. They want to know where you just skied, hiked, biked, or rafted, and then, while they're in the middle of those adventures themselves, they'll discuss in-depth the next places on the list.

Hot Springs

In the late 1800s people came to Colorado not for gold or skiing, but for the legendary restorative powers of the mineral-rich hot springs that had been discovered all over the state. Doc Holliday was one such patient. Suffering from consumption, he spent his final days breathing the sulfurous fumes in Glenwood Springs. To this day there are nearly two-dozen commercial hot-springs resorts, most with lodging or other activities attached, and many more pools have been identified where people can hike in for the private backcountry experience. Some hot springs have been left in their natural state, while others are channeled into Olympic-size swimming pools and hot tubs. Either way, they have become destinations for all who long to take advantage of their therapeutic benefits.

Summits Without the Sweat

As fanatic as the famous "Fourteeners" bunch can be—folks who have climbed or are in the process of "bagging" or summiting all 54 of the state's 14,000-foot peaks—not everyone is as enthusiastic about spending entire days to get the good

Colorado is famous as one big playground, from snowcapped ski resorts and biking and hiking trails to white-water rivers and hot springs. So do as the locals do and experience some of the allure of Colorado.

views. The good news is that there are other ways to get, well, if not to 14,000 feet, then at least Rocky Mountain high enough to see something spectacular. In summer a ride on the gondola in Telluride between town and Mountain Village is free and provides magnificent views. Any road trip through the Rockies will give you great views. You can drive to the tops of Mount Evans and Pikes Peak or take the Pikes Peak Cog Railway to the summit, or take a road trip to Aspen and drive the route over Independence Pass. Another terrific drive is Shrine Pass—Exit 180 off I–70 toward Vail Pass—especially in fall, which allows you to see the Mount of the Holy Cross and the Tenmile, Gore, and Sawatch ranges.

Land of the Lost
Colorado definitely has a thing for dinosaurs—no surprise, considering that the state sits on prime dino real estate, with plenty of sandstone and shale perfect for preservation and the Rocky Mountains pushing the fossils closer to the surface for easier discovery. Dinosaur Ridge, close to Morrison, features a trail where you can see, touch, and easily photograph Jurassic-period bones and Cretaceous footprints and participate in a simulated dig. Both the Denver Museum of Nature & Science and the University of Colorado Museum of Natural History have extensive collections of fossil specimens, the former offering views into its working laboratory where volunteers process fossil specimens. Other attractions, such as the Denver Botanic Gardens and Red Rocks Amphitheatre, offer regular dino-theme events. There's even a town called Dinosaur, which sits near Dinosaur National Monument in the southwest part of the state, and Parfet Prehistoric Reserve east of Golden and Picketwire Canyonlands south of La Junta have hiking trails with extensive sets of dinosaur tracks.

OUTDOOR ADVENTURES

HORSEBACK RIDING

Horseback riding in the Rocky Mountains can mean a quick trot on a paved trail through craggy red rocks or a week-long stay at a working dude ranch, where guests rise at dawn and herd cattle from one mountain range to another. Horse-pack trips are great ways to visit the backcountry, because horses can travel distances and carry supplies that would be impossible for hikers.

What to Wear

Clothing requirements are minimal. A sturdy pair of pants, a wide-brim sun hat, and outerwear to protect against rain are about the only necessities. Ask your outfitter for a list of things you'll need. June through August is the peak period for horse-pack trips.

Choosing a Dude Ranch

Dude ranches fall roughly into two categories: working ranches and guest ranches. Working ranches, where you participate in such activities as roundups and cattle movements, sometimes require experienced horsemanship. Guest ranches offer a wide range of activities in addition to horseback riding, including fishing, four-wheeling, spa services, and cooking classes. At a typical dude ranch you stay in log cabins and are served meals family style in a lodge or ranch house; some ranches now have upscale restaurants on-site, too. For winter, many ranches have now added snow-oriented amenities.

When choosing a ranch, consider whether the place is family-oriented or adults only, and check on the length-of-stay requirements and what gear, if any, you are expected to bring. Working ranches plan around the needs of the business, and thus often require full-week stays for a fixed price, while regular guest ranches operate more like hotels.

Contacts Colorado Dude Ranch Association ⊕ *www.coloradoranch.com.*

Best Horseback Rides

Academy Riding Stables, Colorado Springs. Ideal for visitors who have only a short time in the area but long to do a half-day trail ride, Academy brings red-rock country up close at the Garden of the Gods, with pony rides for kids and hay wagon or stagecoach rides for groups.

C Lazy U Guest Ranch, Granby. One of the finest ranches in the state, C Lazy U offers a relaxing upscale experience, from daily horseback rides with a horse chosen for the duration of the visit to supervised kids' activities and chef-prepared meals, deluxe accommodations, a spring-fed pool, and an on-site spa.

Colorado Cattle Company & Guest Ranch, New Raymer (near Fort Collins). The real deal, the adults-only Colorado Cattle Company is two hours from Denver International Airport and seconds from turning you on to a true Western experience, with continual cattle drives, branding, fencing, and roping on a 7,000-acre ranch with 1,000 head of cattle.

Devil's Thumb Ranch, Tabernash (near Winter Park). Their commitment to the environment, use of renewable resources, and focus on the finest quality, from the organic ingredients in the restaurant to the luxurious bed linens in the rustic yet upscale cabins, makes Suzanne and Bob Fanch's spread a deluxe getaway. They continue to update the ranch, with a new spa and lodge added to the superior horseback-riding, cross-country skiing, and ice-skating programs already in place.

SKIING AND SNOWBOARDING

The champagne powder of the Rocky Mountains can be a revelation for newcomers. Forget treacherous sheets of rock-hard ice, single-note hills where the bottom can be seen from the top, and mountains that offer only one kind of terrain from every angle. In the Rockies the snow builds up quickly, leaving a solid base that hangs tough all season, only to be layered upon by thick, fluffy powder that holds an edge, ready to be groomed into rippling corduroy or left in giddy stashes along the sides and through the trees. Volkswagen-size moguls and half-pipe–studded terrain parks are the norm, not the special attractions.

Many resorts have a wide variety of terrain at all levels, from beginner (green circle) to expert (double black diamond). Turn yourself over to the rental shops, which provide expert help in planning your day and outfitting you with the right equipment. Renting is also a great chance for experienced skiers and snowboarders to sample the latest technology.

Lift Tickets

Shop around for lift tickets before you leave home. Look for package deals, multiple-day passes, and online discounts. The traditional ski season usually runs from mid-December until early April, with Christmas, New Year's, and the month of March being the busiest times at the resorts.

What to Wear

Skiing the Rockies means preparing for all kinds of weather, sometimes in the same day, because the high altitudes can start a day off sunny and bright but kick in a blizzard by afternoon. Layers help, as well as plenty of polypropylene to wick away sweat in the sun, and a water-resistant outer layer to keep off the powdery wetness that's sure to accumulate—especially if you're a beginner snowboarder certain to spend time on the ground. Must-haves: plenty of sunscreen, because the sun is closer than you think, and a helmet, because so are the trees.

Contacts Colorado Association of Ski Towns ⊕ *www.coloradoskitowns.org*. **Colorado Ski** ⊕ *www.coloradoski.com*.

Best Slopes

Aspen. Part "Lifestyles of the Rich and Famous" and part sleepy ski town, picturesque Aspen offers four mountains of widely varied terrain within easy access and some of the best dining in the state.

Breckenridge. Five terrain parks, each designed to target a skill level and promote advancement, give snowboarders the edge at this hip resort, which manages to make skiers feel just as welcome on its big, exposed bowls.

Keystone. Near Breckenridge and Copper Mountain, Keystone has a high percentage of beginner and intermediate offerings and is small enough to navigate easily.

Vail. Those looking for the big-resort experience head to Vail, where modern comforts and multiple bowls mean a dizzying variety of runs and every possible convenience, all laid out in a series of contemporary European-style villages.

Winter Park. Winter Park has retained the laid-back vibe of a locals' mountain, and is still one of the better values on the Front Range. Mary Jane offers a mogul a minute, while the gentler Winter Park side gives cruisers a run for their money.

HIKING

Hiking is easily the least expensive and most accessible recreational pursuit. Sure, you could spend a few hundred dollars on high-tech hiking boots, a so-called personal hydration system, and a collapsible walking staff made of space-age materials, but there's no need for such expenditure. All that's really essential are sturdy athletic shoes, water, and the desire to see the landscape under your own power.

Hiking in the Rockies is a three-season sport that extends as far into fall as you're willing to tromp through snow, though in the arid desert regions it's possible to hike year-round without snowshoes. One of the greatest aspects of this region is the wide range of hiking terrain, from high-alpine scrambles that require stamina to flowered meadows that invite a relaxed pace to confining slot canyons where flash floods are a real danger.

Safety

There are few real hazards to hiking, but a little preparedness goes a long way. Know your limits, and make sure the terrain you are about to embark on does not exceed your abilities. It's a good idea to check the elevation change on a trail before you set out—a 1-mi trail might sound easy, until you realize how steep it is—and be careful not to get caught on exposed trails at elevation during afternoon thunderstorms in summer. Bring layers of clothing to accommodate changing weather, and always carry enough drinking water. Make sure someone knows where you're going and when to expect your return.

Contacts Colorado Mountain Club ⊕ *www. cmc.org.*

Best Hikes

Bear Lake Road, Rocky Mountain National Park. A network of trails threads past alpine lakes, waterfalls, aspens, and pines. Stroll 1 mi to Sprague Lake on a wheelchair-accessible path, or take a four-hour hike past two waterfalls to Mills Lake, with its views of mighty Longs Peak.

Black Canyon of the Gunnison National Park. These are serious trails for serious hikers. There are six routes down into the canyon, which can be hot and slippery, and super steep. But the payoff is stunning: a rare look into the canyon's heart and the fast-moving Gunnison River.

Chautauqua Park, Boulder. Meet the locals (and their dogs) as you head up into the mountains to look back down at the city or to get up close and personal with the Flatirons. There's even a grassy slope perfect for a picnic.

Colorado National Monument, Grand Junction. Breathe in the smell of sagebrush and juniper as you wander amid red-rock cliffs, canyons, and monoliths.

The Colorado Trail. The beauty of this epic hike, which starts just north of Durango and goes 500 mi all the way to Denver, is that you can do it all or just pieces of it.

Green Mountain Trail, Lakewood. Part of Jefferson County Open Space, the easy, mostly exposed trail affords panoramic views of downtown Denver, Table Mesa, Pikes Peak, and the Continental Divide from the top. You must share with bikers and dogs, as well as other critters.

Maroon Bells, Aspen. Bring your camera and take your shot at the twin, mineral-streaked peaks that are one of the most-photographed spots in the state.

BICYCLING

The Rockies are a favorite destination for bikers. Wide-open roads with great gains and losses in elevation test (and form) the stamina for road cyclists, while riders who prefer pedaling fat tires have plenty of mountain and desert trails to test their skills. Many bicyclers travel between towns (or backcountry huts or campsites) in summer. Unmatched views often make it difficult to keep your eyes on the road.

Bike Paths

Most streets in the larger cities have bike lanes and separated bike paths, and Denver, Boulder, Fort Collins, Durango, Crested Butte, and Colorado Springs are especially bike-friendly. Cities and biking organizations often offer free maps.

Bike Rentals

Thanks to the popularity of the sport here, it's usually easy to find a place that rents bicycles, both entry-level and high-end. Bike shops are also a good bet for information on local rides and group tours.

Safety

On the road, watch for trucks and stay as close as possible to the side of the road, in single file. On the trail, ride within your limits and keep your eyes peeled for hikers and horses (both of which have the right of way), as well as dogs. Always wear a helmet and carry plenty of water.

Contacts Bicycle Colorado ☎ *303/417–1544* ⊕ *bicyclecolo.org.*

Best Rides

Breckenridge. Groups of mixed-skill level bikers make for Summit County, where beginners stick to the paved paths, the buffs take on Vail Pass, and single-track types test their technical muscles in the backcountry.

Cherry Creek Bike Path, LoDo, and Cherry Creek. The ultimate urban trek, the paved trail along the burbling creek is part of 400 mi of linked Denver greenway.

Crested Butte. Pearl Pass is the storied birthplace of mountain-biking (check out the museum devoted to it in town). If your legs are not quite ready for that 40-mi, 12,700-foot challenge, there are plenty of paths more suitable to mere mortals.

Durango. Bikes seem to be more popular than cars in Durango, another fabled biking center. You can bike around town or into the mountains with equal ease.

Grand Junction/Fruita. With epic rides such as Over the Edge and Kokopelli Trail, these areas beckon single-track fanatics with their wavy-gravy loop-de-loops and screaming downhill payoffs. Beware: the heat can be intense.

Keystone. Serious downhillers head to Keystone's Drop Zone, the resort's expert section packed with rock gardens and high-speed jumps. Don't like the grunt-filled climb? Hop on a chairlift and smile away the sweet downhill.

Matthews/Winters Park, Morrison. With expansive views of the Red Rocks Park, the moderate to challenging combination of double-track and single-track mountain biking is crowded at sunrise and sunset.

Rangely. From the Raven Rims, you can see the town from nearly every point along this fun mountain-bike ride that starts in the corrals at Chase Draw.

Winter Park. Home to the fabled Fat Tire Classic bike ride, Winter Park features tree-lined single-track trails that vary from gentle, meandering jaunts to screaming roller-coaster rides.

RAFTING

Rafting brings on emotions as varied as the calm induced by flat waters surrounded with stunning scenery and wildlife and the thrill and excitement of charging a raging torrent of foam. Beginners and novices should use guides, but experienced rafters may rent watercraft.

Choosing a Guide

Seasoned outfitters know their routes and their waters as well as you know the road between home and work. Many guides offer multiday trips in which they do everything, including searing your steak and rolling out your sleeping bag. Waters are ranked from Class I (the easiest) to Class VI (think Niagara Falls).

Select an outfitter based on recommendations from the local chamber, experience, and word of mouth. Ask your guide about the rating on your route before you book. Remember, ratings can vary greatly throughout the season due to runoff and weather events.

"Raft" can mean any number of things: an inflated raft in which passengers do the paddling; an inflated raft or wooden dory in which a licensed professional does the work; a motorized raft on which some oar work might be required. Be sure you know what kind of raft you'll be riding—or paddling—before booking.

What to Wear

Wear a swimsuit or shorts and sandals and bring along sunscreen and sunglasses. Outfitters are required to supply a life jacket for each passenger that must be worn. Most have moved to requiring helmets, as well. Early summer, when the water is highest, is the ideal time to raft, although many outfitters stretch the season, particularly on calmer routes.

Contacts Colorado River Outfitters Association ☎ *303/280-2554* ⊕ *www.croa.org.*

Best River Runs

Animas River, Durango. Even at high water, the Lower Animas stays at Class III, which makes for a great way to see the Durango area. Meanwhile, the Upper Animas runs between Class III and Class IV, hits a few at V, and gives little time to appreciate the mountain scenery and canyon views that race by.

Arkansas River, Buena Vista, and Salida. The Arkansas rages as a Class V or murmurs as a Class II, depending on the season. It's *the* white-water rafting destination in the state.

Blue River, Silverthorne. The Class I–III stretches of the Blue that run between Silverthorne and Columbine Landing are ideal for first-time paddlers. Be sure to check the flows; there is a short season.

Colorado River in Glenwood Canyon, Glenwood Springs. Choose a wild ride through the Shoshone Rapids (up to Class IV) or a mellow float down the lower Colorado.

Eagle River, Vail. Three sections offer fun for beginners to expert paddlers. The water levels vary, as this alpine river is not dam-controlled and rises and falls according to snow melt.

Gunnison River, north of Black Canyon of the Gunnison National Monument. Packhorses carry your equipment into this wild area that leads into Gunnison Gorge, where Class I–III waters take you past granite walls while bald eagles fly overhead.

Yampa and Green Rivers, Grand Junction. Ride the Yampa and Green rivers through the remote, rugged canyons of Dinosaur National Monument.

FISHING

Trout do not live in ugly places.

And so it is in Colorado, where you'll discover unbridled beauty, towering pines, rippling mountain streams, and bottomless pools. It's here that blue-ribbon trout streams remain much as they were when Native American tribes, French fur trappers, and a few thousand miners, muleskinners, and sodbusters first placed a muddy footprint along their banks.

Make the Most of Your Time

To make the best use of that limited vacation, consider hiring a guide. You could spend days locating a great fishing spot, learning the water currents and fish behavior, and determining what flies, lures, or bait the fish are following. A good guide will cut through the options, get you into fish, and turn your excursion into an adventure complete with a full creel.

If you're not inclined to fork over the $250-plus that most quality guides charge per day for two anglers and a boat, your best bet is a stop at a reputable fly shop. They'll shorten your learning curve, tell you where the fish are, what they're biting on, and whether you should be "skittering" your dry fly on top of the water or "dead-drifting" a nymph.

What to Bring

If you're comfortable with your fishing gear, bring it along, though most guides loan or rent equipment. Bring a rod and reel, waders, vest, hat, sunglasses, net, tackle, hemostats, and sunscreen.

Know the Rules

Fishing licenses, available at tackle shops and a variety of stores, are required in Colorado for anyone over the age of 16. Famed fisherman Lee Wolff wrote that "catching fish is a sport. Eating fish is not a sport." Most anglers practice "catch and release" to maintain productive fisheries and to protect native species. A few streams are considered "private," in that they are stocked by a local club; other rivers are fly-fishing or catch-and-release only.

When to Go

The season is always a concern when fishing. But as many fishing guides will attest, the best time to come and wet a line is whenever you can make it.

Contacts **Colorado Division of Wildlife** ☎ *303/297–1192* ⊕ *www.wildlife.state. co.us.*

Best Fishing

Arkansas River, Buena Vista, and Cotopaxi. Fly-fish for brown or rainbow trout through Browns or Bighorn Sheep Canyon, or combine white-water rafting with fishing by floating on a raft through the Royal Gorge.

Gunnison River, Almont. In a tiny hamlet near Crested Butte and, more importantly, near the headwaters of the Gunnison, they *live* fly-fishing.

Lake Dillon, Dillon. Pick your spot along 26 mi of shoreline and cast away for brown and rainbow trout and kokanee salmon. The marina has rental boats and a fully stocked store.

Lake Granby, Grand Lake. Can't wait for summer? Try ice fishing on Lake Granby, on the western side of the Rockies.

Roaring Fork River, Aspen. Uninterrupted by dams from its headwaters to its junction with the Colorado, the Roaring Fork is one of the last free-flowing rivers in the state, plus it has a healthy population of 12- to 18-inch trout.

FLAVORS OF COLORADO

Despite a short growing season in much of the state, Colorado enjoys a strong culinary reputation for its commitment to organic, sustainable farming practices, farmers' markets, and chef-fueled focus on buying and dining locally. Locally produced microbrews and wine, a robust agricultural foundation, and a continual roster of food-theme festivals make it easy for the traveler to snag a taste of Colorado while passing through. The region also is known for its many steak houses that keep the state's reputation as cattle country thriving.

Festivals of Local Bounty
Nearly every region of Colorado has some kind of fruit or vegetable that grows so well it makes a name for itself—which inevitably leads to a festival. The alternating swathes of high altitude and low valley are credited with providing a head start or a late blast of sun that in turn pumps that produce with extra flavor.

Peach Festival, Palisade. The small town of Palisade, which also is blessed with a climate ideal for growing wine grapes, is noted for several types of fruits, including their famous peaches, which are celebrated in August.

Wild Mushroom Festival, Crested Butte. The climate above 9,000 feet in Crested Butte is just right for fungi, which leads to a celebration of the result every August.

Stream-Raised and Grass-Fed
Colorado is famous for its trout, beef, bison, and lamb, so much so that vegetarian restaurants have been slower in proliferating than in other parts of the country. The state also offers visitors the chance to pluck the trout right from its many rivers and lakes—rainbow, cutthroat, brook, brown and, of course, lake—although so many get shipped out that it's as likely to

be frozen as not at restaurants—be sure to ask. Meanwhile, whether or not the beef and bison seen grazing across the West are natural (meaning no hormones, steroids, or antibiotics), every town, large or small, boasts a steak house. And it's the grasses in their mountain diet that have been credited with the superior flavor and texture of the Colorado lamb.

Buckhorn Exchange, Denver. More than 500 pairs of eyes stare down at you during the meal, but it's what's on your plate that will keep your attention: dry-aged, prime-grade Colorado steaks served with hearty sides. Since 1893 this has been one of the state's game-meat specialists, as well.

The Fort Restaurant, Morrison. Bison is a particular specialty at this replica of Bent's Fort, a former Colorado fur-trade mecca, but the steaks, trout, elk, and other meats are delicious, as well.

Game Creek Club, Vail. With the word "game" in the name, it's not hard to imagine that the tony eatery does a good job with meats. The Bavarian-style lodge is open to the public for dinner.

Green Chile
Not the pepper itself but a gravy-like stew is what Coloradans refer to when they talk about *chile verde,* the heady mixture that migrated with families who made their way from Mexico up through New Mexico and Texas and over from California to settle the high country. Its recipes vary as much across the state as minestrone does across Italy and pot-au-feu across France, but you can usually count on a pork-based concoction with jalapeños, sometimes tomatoes, and maybe tomatillos, the heat ranging from mellow to sinus-clearing. Green chile can smother just about anything—from enchiladas to huevos—but a plain bowlful with

a warmed tortilla is all the purist requires, and it's the best hangover cure ever.

Dos Hombres, Grand Junction. The regular green chile at this cheerful spot is tomato-based, with a variety of chilies and pork for a thick, colorful mixture. They also offer milder, vegetarian, and New Mexican-style versions.

Fiesta Jalisco, Frisco. Light on chilies but packed with pork, the green here is medium-spicy and perfect on a burrito. The margaritas are special, too.

Jack 'n' Grill, Denver. This family-run joint pulls its chilies from New Mexico and makes its green chile stew into a fire-breathing brew made of cooked-down, chopped green chilies that they roast themselves, so hot it separates the serious from the simply curious.

Topical Microbrews

Although fancy cocktails and wine continue to make headway against beer elsewhere in the country, Colorado is still the land of microbrews. Pool tables, multiple televisions for sports viewing, and live music make the brewpub an essential part of the weekend scene in most major cities and towns. Many of the best Denver brewpubs are in LoDo, or lower downtown. These offer tasting flights much like wineries, served with food that runs the gamut from pub grub to upscale. Many microbreweries also have tasting rooms open to the public, where growlers (half-gallon glass jugs) of fresh beer can be purchased for takeout, perfect for picnics and tailgate parties.

Boulder Beer Company, Boulder. Colorado's first microbrewery (it started in 1979) offers a British-style ale, amber, pale, golden, and India pale ales and a stout, to name a few—and has a pub attached that offers a solid roster of grub. Catch a tour weekdays at 2 pm.

New Belgium Brewing Company, Fort Collins. Fat Tire Amber Ale resonates with Coloradans because of its mountain-biking history, and is this microbrewery's most popular beer. It's readily available around the state, but a visit to the 100% wind-powered brewery is the best way to check it out.

Wynkoop Brewing Co., Denver. You can see part of the brewing operation through large glass windows at this popular brew-pub in LoDo. The Railyard Ale is one of the signature beers, but the spicy chili beer is a local favorite.

Local Wines

Microbrews may rule, but Colorado's wine country continues to get kudos for producing reasonably priced, award-winning vino. The wines run the gamut, from lightweight whites to heavy-duty reds, and Colorado varietals as well as wines made from California grapes that don't grow well in the short season (such as red zinfandel). Cabernet sauvignon, merlot, and chardonnay are the most popular, but the viognier and Riesling offerings have gotten good press, too. Another of Colorado's best-kept secrets is its winery tours through Palisade and Grand Junction.

Two Rivers Winery & Chateau, Grand Junction. With its setting evocative of rural France, this inn set among the vines is the ideal spot for a sip of Burgundian-style chardonnay after a tour of the Colorado national monuments.

Trail Ridge Winery, Fort Collins. In an atmospheric feed-and-grain barn, the tasting room for Trail Ridge sets out sips of their spicy Gewürztraminer, buttery chardonnays, oakey merlots, creamy Rieslings, and smooth cabernet sauvignons.

GREAT ITINERARIES

CONNECTING THE DOTS IN COLORFUL COLORADO

Arriving in Denver

Denver is filled with folks who stopped to visit and never left. After a few days in the Mile High City and surrounding metro area it's easy to see why: Colorado's capital has much to recommend it, including a thriving cultural scene, restaurants representing every ethnicity, plenty of sunshine, outdoor options galore, and snowcapped peaks for visual variety.

The Old West still holds sway in visitors' imaginations, and there are plenty of throwback trappings to check out, but the reality is that Denver is a modern metropolis that offers cosmopolitan amenities and state-of-the-art amusements.

Logistics: There are myriad well-marked ground transportation options near baggage claim at the sprawling Denver International Airport (DEN). Head to the taxi stand to pay about $55–$65 to get downtown, or visit the RTD desk for bus schedules (SkyRide operates multiple routes starting at $9 one-way). Several independent companies operate shuttles from desks within the airport for about $22 one-way, and many hotels have complimentary shuttles for their guests.

All of the major car-rental companies operate at DEN. The rental-car counters that you see in the main terminal are there merely to point you toward the shuttles that take you to the car-rental center. Depending on time of day and traffic, it will take 30 minutes to an hour to reach downtown Denver and another 30 minutes for Boulder and the foothills.

DAYS 1–2: DENVER AND BOULDER

Option 1: Metro Denver

After you've settled into your hotel, head downtown, or if you're already staying there—always a good option to truly explore the city—make your way to Lower Downtown, or LoDo. The historic district is home to many of the city's famous brewpubs, art galleries, and Coors Field, as well as popular restaurants and some of the area's oldest architecture.

Hop on the free MallRide, the shuttle bus run by RTD, to head up the 16th Street Mall, a pedestrian-friendly, shopping-oriented strip that runs through the center of downtown. From there you can walk to Larimer Square for more shopping and restaurants, as well as the Denver Art Museum, the History Colorado Center, the Colorado State Capitol, the Molly Brown House, and the U.S. Mint.

Logistics: Vending machines at each station for TheRide, Denver's light-rail, show destinations and calculate your fare ($2.25–$4 depending on the number of zones crossed). The machines accept bills of $20 or less and any coin except pennies. Children under age 5 ride free when accompanied by a fare-paying adult. RTD buses also provide an excellent way to get around; schedules are posted inside shelters and are available at Civic Center Station at the south end of the 16th Street Mall and Market Street Station toward the north end. Fares are $2.25 one-way.

Option 2: Boulder

Boulder takes its fair share of ribbing for being a Birkenstock-wearing, tofu-eating, latter-day hippie kind of town, but the truth is that it is one healthy, wealthy area, exceedingly popular and rapidly

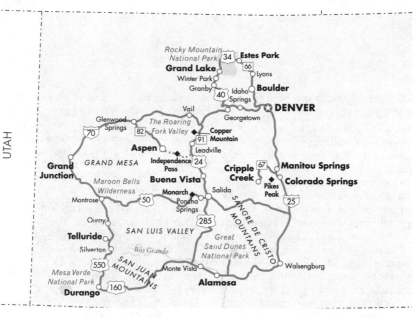

UTAH

Rocky Mountain National Park — 34 — **Estes Park**
Grand Lake — 66 — Lyons
Winter Park — **Boulder**
Granby — 40 — Idaho Springs
Vail — **DENVER**
Georgetown
Glenwood Springs — 70 — 82 — *The Roaring Fork Valley* — **Copper Mountain** — 91
Aspen — Leadville
Grand Junction — GRAND MESA — Independence Pass — 24 — **Cripple Creek** — 67 — **Manitou Springs**
Maroon Bells Wilderness — **Buena Vista** — Salida — Pikes Peak — **Colorado Springs** — 25
Montrose — 50 — **Monarch** — Poncha Springs
Ouray — 285 — **Great Sand Dunes National Park**
Telluride — SAN LUIS VALLEY
Silverton — *Rio Grande* — SANGRE DE CRISTO MOUNTAINS — Walsenburg
Mesa Verde National Park — 550 — SAN JUAN MOUNTAINS — Monte Vista — **Alamosa**
Durango — 160

heading toward overdevelopment. For now, though, it's still a groovy place to visit. Stroll along the Pearl Street Mall and sample the excellent restaurants and shops, catching one of the dozens of street performers; or head just outside the city to tour Celestial Seasonings, the tea manufacturer; or to Chautauqua Park to hike in the shadow of the dramatic Flatiron Mountains. In winter, Eldora Mountain Resort is a 21-mi jaunt up a steep, switchback-laden road with no lift lines as payoff. The University of Colorado campus here means there is a high hip quotient in much of the nightlife.

Logistics: You can take an RTD bus to Boulder from Denver, but it's just as easy to drive up U.S. 36, and if you're going to go beyond the Pearl Street Mall, it's nice to have a car once you're there. Parking, though, can be quite tight.

DAYS 3–7: THE ROCKIES

Option 1: Estes Park, Rocky Mountain National Park, and Grand Lake

Rocky Mountain National Park (RMNP) is a year-round marvel, a park for every season: summer's hiking, fall's elk-mating ritual, winter's snowcapped peaks, and spring's wildflowers. Estes Park is the gateway to RMNP but a worthwhile destination itself, a small town swelling to a large one with the tourists who flock to its Western-theme shops and art galleries. The alpine-surrounded Grand Lake is a rustic charmer, a mecca for the sports person, and an idyllic locale for a family vacation.

Logistics: Estes Park is a hop-skip from Denver and Boulder, about 65 mi northwest of Denver via Interstate 25 and then CO–66 and U.S. 36. To get to RMNP, simply take U.S. 34 or U.S. 36 into the park. Grand Lake is on the other side of RMNP via U.S. 34, or from Denver, it's 100 mi by taking I–70 to U.S. 40 over Berthoud Pass through Winter Park, Fraser, and Granby, and then turning onto U.S.

34 to Grand Lake. It can be a bit more challenging in winter.

Option 2: Aspen and the Roaring Fork Valley

The drive to Aspen sends you straight through the heart of the Rocky Mountains, from the foothills to the peaks, with plenty of highs and lows between. Along the way there are several possible stops, including small-town diversions in places such as Idaho Springs and Georgetown, outlet shopping in Silverthorne, high-alpine mountain biking and hiking in Vail, and a dip in the hot springs in Glenwood Springs. Once in Aspen, world-class dining, upscale shopping, and celebrity-sighting await, while, depending on the season, the slopes will serve up wildflower-covered meadows or some of the best skiing in North America. Do not miss a pilgrimage to the Maroon Bells Wilderness area for a glimpse of the famous peaks.

Logistics: There are several flights in and out of Aspen/Pitkin County Airport daily, most routing through Denver. Many travelers drive to Aspen, however, making the 220-mi journey west on I–70 from Denver to Glenwood Springs, then taking U.S. 82 to Aspen. From May until about mid-October, Independence Pass, a more scenic option, is open; from I–70 take U.S. 91 at Copper Mountain south through Leadville to U.S. 82 and then use Independence Pass.

Option 3: Colorado Springs, Manitou Springs, and Cripple Creek

The Pikes Peak area may be dominated by 14,115-foot Pikes Peak itself—long ago the inspiration for "America the Beautiful"—and certainly getting to its summit, whether by cog railway, foot, or car, is a worthy goal. But there are other options along this popular corridor, such as strolling through the red rocks of the Garden of the Gods, peeking at the tunnel in Cave of the Winds, checking out the animals at the Cheyenne Mountain Zoo, taking advantage of the healing vibes in the artists' community that is Manitou Springs, or exploring the old gold-mining town of Cripple Creek.

Logistics: Colorado Springs sits 70 mi south of Denver on Interstate 25. You'll enjoy mountain views on most of the drive; Pikes Peak is visible on clear days. Take U.S. 24 west from Interstate 25 to reach Manitou Springs; follow CO–67 south from U.S. 24 west to visit Cripple Creek.

DAYS 8–14: THE SOUTHWEST

Option 1: Salida and Buena Vista

The way the Collegiate Peaks open up in magnificent panorama as you come around the bend on U.S. 285 is only one of the draws of a trip from Denver to Buena Vista and Salida. The plethora of outdoor activities available in this mountain- and river-rich region adds to the appeal. Salida has become a haven for its bevy of artists making a national name for their Western-oriented themes and grassroots sensibilities, and the banana-belt weather makes it all the more alluring.

Logistics: Take U.S. 285 south to Buena Vista. To reach Salida, continue on to Poncha Springs, then follow U.S. 50 east. Winter sports enthusiasts will want to make a side trip to Monarch Mountain, while mountain bikers won't want to miss the Monarch Crest Trail at Monarch Pass, both about 18 mi west of Salida on U.S. 50.

Option 2: Alamosa, San Luis Valley, and Great Sand Dunes National Park and Preserve

The sand dunes dominate this sleepy, agriculturally abundant area, though they are only one of the natural playgrounds available to visitors. Alamosa National Wildlife Refuge is famous for its crane migrations, the fishing is superior in the Rio Grande, and the Sangre de Cristo Wilderness has its peaks and trails. Hop aboard the Cumbres & Toltec Scenic Railroad for a 64-mi trip back in time; the area, not to mention the train itself, has changed little since the 1880s.

Logistics: The round-trip is a worthwhile excursion alone, because the corridor between the Sangre de Cristo Mountains and the San Juans is one of the largest intermountain valleys in the world. Take Interstate 25 south to Walsenburg, then head west on U.S. 160 to Alamosa and north on CO–150.

Option 3: Telluride, Mesa Verde, and Durango

Durango is about an eight-hour drive from Denver, and well worth the effort. Mountain bikers make it a mission to try their mettle on the tough trails, and the Old West feel and small-town charm put this energetic spot high on the list for tourists. Telluride, though second home to several notable celebrities and famous for its film festival and other national events, presents a less glitzy face than other ski resorts like Aspen; and the San Juan Skyway, a 236-mi loop that connects Durango, Telluride, Ouray, and Silverton, is a gloriously scenic tour of mountains, alpine forests, and wildflower meadows. Mesa Verde National Park, meanwhile, safeguards the 1,400-year-old cliff dwellings of the Ancestral Puebloans.

TIPS

■ Guard against the effects of altitude. Drink lots of water, slather on the sunscreen, and watch your alcohol intake. And pace yourself, especially when hiking or engaging in other outdoor pursuits.

■ Pack a lunch for your day in Rocky Mountain National Park. You'll have your pick of jaw-droppingly gorgeous spots for a picnic.

■ For the night in Aspen, consider reserving a room down-valley in Basalt or Carbondale if the rates in Aspen proper look too steep.

■ Denver and Aspen are the places to splurge on meals.

■ If you have a morning flight, consider staying the final night in Denver.

Logistics: To go straight to Durango, take U.S. 285 southwest to Monte Vista and then head west on U.S. 160. Mesa Verde is a 1½-hour drive from Durango, heading west on U.S. 160. For Telluride, take I–70 to Grand Junction and go south on U.S. 50 to Montrose; continue south on CO–550 to Ridgway, then turn right onto CO–62. Follow this to CO–145 and turn left. Follow the signs into Telluride. Telluride and Durango also have regional airports with limited service from major carriers.

MOUNTAIN FINDER

To help you decide which of Colorado's ski slopes are best for you, we've rated each major mountain according to several categories. To give some sense of cost, we have included the price of a peak-season one-day adult lift ticket at the time of covers affordable lodging options. Don't think this chart is only for winter visitors though—we've also rated the mountain areas on their summer offerings. *You should also consult the regional chapters and Outdoor Adventures.*

	LIFT TICKET COST	VARIETY OF TERRAIN	SNOWBOARDER FRIENDLY	OTHER SNOW SPORTS	FAMILY FRIENDLY	DINING VARIETY	NIGHTLIFE	AFFORDABLE LODGING	OFF-SLOPE ACTIVITIES	SUMMER ACTIVITIES	CONVENIENCE FACTOR
Arapahoe Basin	$49	◑	●	○	◑	○	○	●	○	○	●
Aspen	$96	●	◐	●	◑	●	●	●	●	●	◑
Beaver Creek	$98	◐	◐	◐	●	◑	◑	●	◑	◐	◑
Breckenridge	$94	◐	●	●	●	◑	◐	◐	●	●	◑
Copper Mountain	$79	●	●	◑	●	◑	◐	◐	◑	○	◑
Crested Butte	$59	◐	●	◑	●	○	◑	◐	◑	●	○
Purgatory at Durango	$67	◑	◐	●	◐	○	○	●	○	○	○
Eldora	$69	◑	●	◑	◐	○	○	●	○	○	◑
Keystone	$98	●	◐	◐	●	◑	◐	◐	◐	◑	●
Loveland	$59	◑	●	○	●	○	○	●	○	○	◑
Monarch	$56	◐	◐	○	●	○	○	●	○	○	○
Ski Cooper	$44	○	◐	○	●	○	○	●	○	○	◑
Snowmass	$96	◐	◑	◑	●	◑	◑	◐	◐	◑	◑
Steamboat	$99	◐	●	●	●	◑	◑	◐	●	●	◑
Telluride	$98	◐	◐	◑	◐	◑	◑	◑	◐	●	○
Vail	$98	●	◐	◑	●	●	●	◑	◑	●	◑
Winter Park	$92	●	●	◑	●	○	○	◐	○	◑	●
Wolf Creek	$52	◐	◐	○	●	○	○	●	○	○	○

KEY: ○ few or none   ◐ moderate   ◑ substantial   ● noteworthy

Denver

WORD OF MOUTH

"Great shopping in Denver. The Botanic Gardens are very nice and the Denver Art Museum is VERY nice with excellent collections. I am particularly fond of their Native American collections."

—Gretchen

"I love Denver! I'll second the recommendation for the art museum and add that I thought the Molly Brown mansion was interesting."

—Birdie

Updated by
Kyle Wagner

You can tell from its skyline alone that Denver is a major metropolis, with a Major League Baseball stadium at one end of downtown and the State Capitol building at the other. But look to the west to see where Denver distinguishes itself in the majestic Rocky Mountains, snow-peaked and breathtakingly huge, looming in the distance. This combination of urban sprawl and proximity to nature is what gives the city character and sets it apart as a destination.

Throughout the 1960s and 1970s, when the city mushroomed on a huge surge of oil and energy revenues, Denver worked on the transition from Old West "cow town" to a comfortable, modern place to live. The city demolished its large downtown Skid Row area, paving the way for developments such as the Tabor Center and the Auraria multicollege campus. In the early 1990s mayors Federico Peña and Wellington Webb championed a massive new airport to replace the rickety Stapleton. Then the city lured major-league baseball, in the form of the purple-and-black Colorado Rockies, and built Coors Field in the heart of downtown. Around the stadium planners developed LoDo, a business-and-shopping area including hip nightclubs, Larimer Square boutiques, and bike and walking paths.

Since the mid-1990s Denver has caught the attention of several major national corporations looking to move their operations to a thriving city that enjoys a relatively stable economy and a healthy business climate. The fact that the Democratic National Party chose Denver for the 2008 national convention made it clear that the city had finally arrived. And win or lose, the sports teams continue to imbue the city with a sense of pride.

Many Denverites are unabashed nature lovers who can also enjoy the outdoors within the city limits, walking along the park-lined river paths downtown. (Perhaps as a result of their active lifestyle, Denverites are the "thinnest" city residents in the United States, with only 20% of the adult population overweight.) For Denverites, preserving the environment and the city's rich mining and ranching heritage are of equally vital importance to the quality of life. LoDo buzzes with jazz clubs, restaurants, and art galleries housed in carefully restored century-old buildings. The culturally diverse populace avidly supports the Denver Art Museum, the Denver Museum of Nature & Science, the Museo de las Americas, and the new History Colorado Center (formerly the Colorado History Museum). The Denver Performing Arts Complex is the nation's second-largest theatrical venue, bested in capacity only by New York's Lincoln Center. An excellent public transportation system, including a popular, growing light-rail system and 400 mi of bike paths, makes getting around easy.

2

TOP REASONS TO GO

Denver Art Museum: Visitors are treated to Asian, pre-Columbian, and Spanish Colonial works along with a world-famous collection of Native American pieces.

Denver Botanic Gardens: Creatively arranged displays of more than 15,000 plant species from around the world draw garden enthusiasts year-round.

Larimer Square: Specialty stores, superior people-watching, and some of the city's top restaurants and

nightlife bring tourists and locals alike to the city's oldest street.

LoDo: Lower downtown's appeal lies in its proximity to Coors Field and the convenient and free 16th Street Mall shuttle. Shops and galleries are busy during the day, and it's also a hot spot at night.

Red Rocks Park and Amphitheatre: Even if you aren't attending a concert, the awe-inspiring red rocks of this formation-turned-venue are worth a look and there are hiking trails nearby.

ORIENTATION AND PLANNING

GETTING ORIENTED

Denver's downtown is laid out at a 45-degree angle to the rest of the metro area. Interstate 25 bisects Denver north to south, and I–70 runs east to west. University Boulevard is a major north–south road and Speer Boulevard is a busy diagonal street. Most Denverites are tied to their vehicles, but the light-rail works well if you're going to certain areas.

If you're staying downtown, you can visit LoDo, Capitol Hill, and Larimer Square by walking or using light-rail or the free Mall shuttle. The Central Platte Valley can be accessed by taking the Mall shuttle all the way north to the end and then walking across the pedestrian-only Millennium Bridge. You will need a car to get to Cherry Creek or City Park, however, but once there, those sections also are easy to explore on foot.

Downtown. With its pedestrian-friendly numbered streets, free Mall shuttle, and plethora of restaurants, galleries, and museums within easy walking distance, downtown is a logical starting point for exploring.

Central Platte Valley. Just west of downtown, the Central Platte Valley is a destination for daytime activities along the Platte River and evening pursuits such as dining, music, and dancing.

City Park and Environs. East of downtown, the 370-acre oasis that is City Park also serves as a jumping-off point for the Denver Zoo and the Denver Museum of Nature & Science.

PLANNING

WHEN TO GO

Denver defies easy weather predictions. Although its blizzards are infamous, snowstorms are often followed by beautiful spring weather just a day or two later. Ski resorts are packed from roughly October to April, and Denver itself often bears the traffic. Summers are festival-happy, with a rock-concert slate at nearby Red Rocks Park and Amphitheatre and big names at the tent-covered Universal Lending Pavilion (also known as CityLights), in the parking lot outside the Pepsi Center downtown. Perhaps the best times to visit, though, are spring and fall, when the heat isn't so intense, the snow isn't so plentiful, and crowds are relatively thin. Ski resorts are still as scenic, but less expensive.

GETTING HERE AND AROUND

AIR TRAVEL

Denver International Airport (DEN) is 15 mi northeast of downtown, but it usually takes about a half-hour to 45 minutes to travel between them, depending on time of day. It's served by most major domestic carriers and many international ones. Arrive at the airport with plenty of time before your flight, preferably two hours; the airport's check-in and security-check lines are particularly long.

TRANSFERS Between the airport and downtown, Super Shuttle makes door-to-door trips. The region's public bus service, Regional Transportation District (RTD), runs SkyRide to and from the airport; the trip takes 50 minutes, and the fare is $8–$12 each way. There's a transportation center in the airport just outside baggage claim. A taxi ride to downtown costs $60–$70.

Airport Denver International Airport (DEN) ☎ *800/247–2336* ⊕ *www. flydenver.com.*

Airport Transfers Regional Transportation District/SkyRide ☎ *303/299–6000 for route and schedule information* ⊕ *www.rtd-denver.com.* **Super Shuttle** ☎ *303/370–1300* ⊕ *www.supershuttle.com.*

BUS TRAVEL

In downtown Denver free shuttle-bus service operates about every 10 minutes until 1:35 am, running the length of the 16th Street Mall (which bisects downtown) and stopping at one-block intervals. If you plan to spend much time outside downtown, a car is advised, although Denver has one of the best city bus systems in the country.

The region's public bus service, RTD, is comprehensive, with routes throughout the metropolitan area. The service also links Denver to outlying towns such as Boulder, Longmont, and Nederland. You can buy bus tokens at grocery stores or pay with exact change on the bus. Fares vary according to time and zone. Within the city limits, buses cost $2.25.

Bus Contacts RTD ☎ *303/299–6000, 800/366–7433* ⊕ *www.rtd-denver.com.*

2

CAR TRAVEL

Rental-car companies include Advantage, Alamo, Avis, Budget, Dollar, Enterprise, Hertz, and National. All have airport and downtown representatives.

Reaching Denver by car is fairly easy, except during rush hour. Interstate highways 70 and 25 intersect near downtown; an entrance to I–70 is just outside the airport.

■TIP➜ When you're looking for an address within Denver, make sure you know whether it's a street or avenue. Speer Boulevard runs alongside Cherry Creek from northwest to southeast through downtown; numbered streets run parallel to Speer and most are one-way. Colfax Avenue (U.S. 287) runs east–west through downtown; numbered avenues run parallel to Colfax. Broadway runs north–south. Other main thoroughfares include Colorado Boulevard (north–south) and Alameda Avenue (east–west). Try to avoid driving in the area during rush hour, when traffic gets heavy. Interstates 25 and 225 are particularly slow during those times; although the Transportation Expansion Project (T-REX) added extra lanes, a light-rail system along the highways, bicycle lanes, and other improvements, expansion in the metro area outpaced the project.

PARKING Finding an open meter has become increasingly difficult in downtown Denver, especially during peak times such as Rockies games and weekend nights. Additionally, most meters have two-hour limits until 10 pm, and at 25¢ for 10 minutes in some downtown areas, parking in Denver is currently more expensive than in New York or Chicago. However, there's no shortage of pay lots for $5 to $25 per day.

TAXI TRAVEL

Taxis can be costly and difficult to simply flag down as in some major metropolitan areas; instead, you usually must call ahead to arrange for one. Cabs are $1.80–$2.50 minimum, $1.80–$2.60 per mile depending on the company. However, at peak times—during major events, and at 2 am when the bars close—taxis are very hard to come by.

Taxi Companies **Freedom Cab** ☎ *303/444-4444.* **Metro Taxi** ☎ *303/333-3333.* **Yellow Cab** ☎ *303/777-7777.*

TRAIN TRAVEL

Historic Union Station in the heart of downtown is undergoing extensive redevelopment through 2014 that has forced Amtrak service to relocate temporarily several blocks away.

RTD's Light Rail service's 5.3-mi track links southwest, southern, and northeast Denver to downtown, including new service from Union Station. The peak fare is $2.25 within the city limits.

Contacts **Amtrak** ☎ *800/872-7245* ⊕ *www.amtrak.com.* **RTD Light Rail** ☎ *303/299-6000* ⊕ *www.rtd-denver.com.* **Temporary Amtrak Station** ✉ *1800 21st St., at Wewatta St., LoDo* ☎ *303/825-2583.*

SAFETY

Although Denver is a generally peaceful city, the crime rate has increased slightly in recent years as the population has boomed. There are a few shadier areas on the outskirts of downtown, but violent crimes are few and far between. As always, paying attention to your surroundings is your best defense.

VISITOR AND TOUR INFORMATION

The Visitors and Information Center, operated by VISIT Denver, the Convention and Visitors Bureau, is open weekdays 9–6, Saturday 9–5, and Sunday 11–3, and is located downtown at the corner of 16th and California. They also have self-guided walking-tour brochures and offer free guided walking tours at 9:30 am on Thursday and Saturday June–August.

The Denver Microbrew Tour is a guided walking tour in LoDo that includes beer sampling at several microbreweries and a comprehensive history of local beer-making as well as Denver's history. Fees are $25–$29. Denver History Tours runs guided tours of historic Denver; prices vary according to the tour.

Gray Line Colorado runs the usual expansive and exhaustive coach tours of anything and everything, from shopping in Cherry Creek to visiting Rocky Mountain National Park. Fees range from $17 to $135.

Tours Denver History Tours ☎ 720/234–7929 ⊕ www.denverhistorytours.com. **Denver Microbrew Tour** ☎ 303/578–9548 ⊕ denvermicrobrewtour.com. **Gray Line** ☎ 800/966–8125, 303/394–6920 ⊕ grayline.com.

Visitor Information Lower Downtown District, Inc. ☎ 303/628–5428. **VISIT Denver, The Convention and Visitors Bureau** ✉ 1600 California St., LoDo ☎ 303/892–1112, 800/393–8559 ⊕ www.denver.org.

EXPLORING DENVER

For many out-of-state travelers Denver is a gateway city, a transitional stop before heading into the nearby Rocky Mountains. Often, visitors will simply fly into Denver International Airport, rent a car, ask for directions to I–70, and head west into the mountains. But it's worth scheduling an extra few days, or even a few hours, to delve into the city itself. The city is an easy place to maneuver, with prominent hotels such as the Brown Palace, excellent shopping at Cherry Creek and Larimer Square, a full range of professional sports teams, and plenty of (expensive) parking.

DOWNTOWN

Denver's downtown is an intriguing mix of well-preserved monuments from the state's frontier past and modern high-tech marvels. You can often catch the reflection of an elegant Victorian building in the mirrored glass of a skyscraper. Hundreds of millions of dollars were poured into the city in the 1990s in such projects as Coors Field, the downtown home of Denver's baseball Rockies; the relocation of Elitch Gardens, the first amusement park in the country to move into a downtown urban area; and an expansion of the light-rail system to run from downtown into the southern suburbs. Lower downtown, or LoDo, is a Victorian warehouse district revitalized by the ballpark, loft condominiums, and numerous brewpubs, nightclubs, and restaurants.

TIMING Downtown is compact and can be toured on foot in an hour or less, but a car is recommended for exploring outside of downtown proper. The Denver Art Museum merits at least two to three hours, and the Colorado History Museum, renamed the History Colorado Center in spring 2012 after moving to a new three-story building a few blocks from the previous location, can be covered in an hour or two. Save some time for browsing and people-watching along the 16th Street Mall and Larimer Square. LoDo is a 30-block-square area that takes a few hours to meander through.

LODO

TOP ATTRACTIONS

Fodor'sChoice **Larimer Square.** Larimer Square is on the oldest street in the city, immor-
★ talized by Jack Kerouac in his seminal book *On the Road*. It was saved from the wrecker's ball by a determined preservationist in the 1960s, when the city went demolition-crazy in its eagerness to present a more youthful image. Much has changed since Kerouac's wanderings; Larimer Square's rough edges have been cleaned up in favor of upscale retail and chic restaurants. The Square has become a serious late-night party district thanks to spillover from the expanded LoDo neighborhood and Rockies fans flowing out from the baseball stadium. Shops line the arched redbrick courtyards of **Writer Square**, Denver's most charming shopping district. ⊠ *Larimer and 15th Sts., LoDo* ☎ *303/685–8143* ⊕ *www.larimersquare.com.*

★ **LoDo.** Officially, the Lower Downtown Historic District, the 25-plus square-block area that was the site of the original 1858 settlement of Denver City, is nicknamed LoDo. It's home to art galleries, chic shops, nightclubs, and restaurants ranging from Denver's most upscale to its most down-home. This part of town was once the city's thriving retail center, then it fell into disuse and slid into slums. Since the early 1990s LoDo has been transformed into the city's cultural center, thanks to its resident artists, retailers, and loft dwellers who have taken over the old warehouses and redbricks.

Coors Field. The handsome field, home of baseball's Colorado Rockies, has helped galvanize the LoDo area. Its old-fashioned brick and grillwork facade was designed to blend in with the surrounding Victorian warehouses. As with cuddly Wrigley Field, on the north side of Chicago, Coors Field has engendered a nightlife scene of sports bars, restaurants, and dance clubs. ⊠ *Blake and 20th Sts., LoDo* ⊠ *From Larimer St. to South Platte River, between 14th and 22nd Sts., LoDo* ⊕ *www.lodo.org.*

OFF THE
BEATEN
PATH
  Forney Museum of Transportation. Inside a converted warehouse are an 1898 Renault coupe, Amelia Earhart's immaculately maintained "Goldbug," and a Big Boy steam locomotive, among other historic vehicles. Other exhibits in this eccentric museum consist of antique bicycles, cable cars, and even experimental car-planes. This trivia-laden showcase is outside of the downtown loop: Go north on Brighton Boulevard; the museum is adjacent to the Denver Coliseum on the south side of I–70. ⊠ *4303 Brighton Blvd., Globeville* ☎ *303/297–1113* ⊕ *www. forneymuseum.org* ⊠ *$8* ☉ *Mon.–Sat. 10–4.*

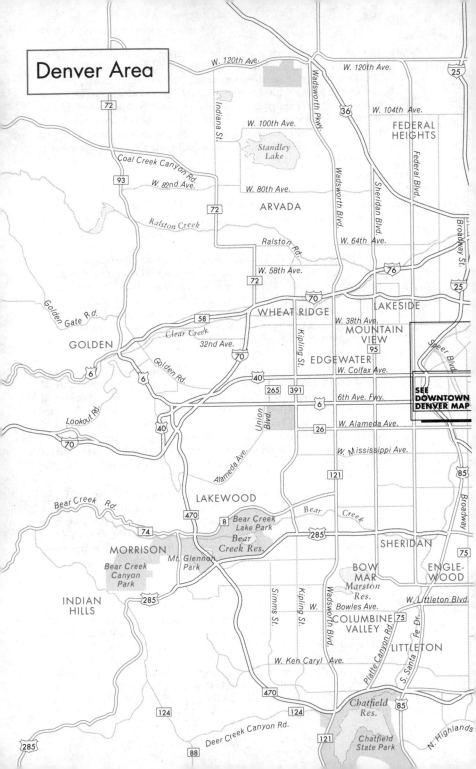

Denver Area

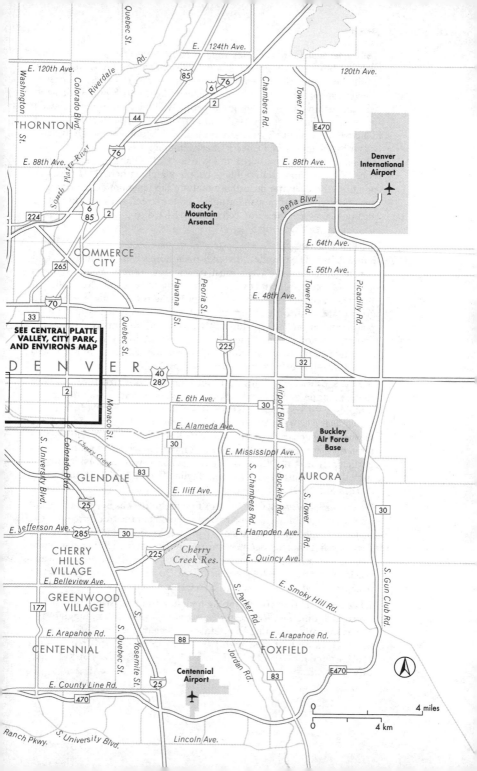

★   **16th Street Mall.** Outdoor cafés and tempting shops line this pedestrians-only 12-block thoroughfare, shaded by red-oak and locust trees. The Mall's businesses run the entire socioeconomic range. There are popular meeting spots for business types at places like the Irish pub Katie Mullen's in the Sheraton Hotel; great people-watching from the sidewalk patio at the Paramount Cafe, around the corner from the Paramount Theatre; and plenty of fast-food chains. Although some Denverites swear by the higher-end Cherry Cheek Shopping District, the 16th Street Mall covers every retail area and is a more affordable, diverse experience. You can find Denver's best people-watching here. ■ TIP→ **Catch one of the free shuttle buses here that run the length of downtown.** Pay attention when you're wandering across the street, as the walking area and bus lanes are the same color and are hard to distinguish. ⊠ *From Broadway to Wynkoop St., LoDo.*

WORTH NOTING

Brown Palace. The grande dame of Denver hotels was built in 1892, and is still considered the city's most prestigious address. Famous guests have included President Dwight D. Eisenhower, Winston Churchill, and Beyoncé. Even if you aren't staying here, the Brown Palace lobby is a great place to sit on comfortable old couches, drink tea, and listen to piano standards (or harp, during afternoon tea). Reputedly this was the first atrium hotel in the United States; its ornate lobby and nine stories are crowned by a Tiffany stained-glass window. ⊠ *321 17th St., LoDo* ☎ *303/297–3111* ⊕ *www.brownpalace.com.*

Daniels & Fisher Tower. This 330-foot-high, 20-floor structure emulates the campanile of St. Mark's Square in Venice, and it was the tallest building west of the Mississippi when it was built in 1909. William Cooke Daniels originally commissioned the tower to stand adjacent to his five-story department store. Today it's an office building with a cabaret in the basement as well as the city's most convenient clock tower. It's particularly striking—the clock is 16 feet high—when viewed in concert with the fountains in the adjacent Skyline Park. ⊠ *1601 Arapahoe St., at 16th St., LoDo.*

☾   **Denver Firefighters Museum.** Denver's first firehouse was built in 1909 and now serves as a museum where original items of the trade are on view, including uniforms, nets, fire carts and trucks, bells, and switchboards. Artifacts and photos document the progression of firefighting machinery from horses and carriages in the early 1900s to the flashy red-and-white trucks of today. ⊠ *1326 Tremont Pl., LoDo* ☎ *303/892–1436* ⊕ *www. denverfirefightersmuseum.org* ⊠ *$6* ⊙ *Mon.–Sat. 10–4.*

Tabor Center. This festive shopping mall has about 55 stores and attractions, including fast-food eateries, strolling troubadours, jugglers and fire-eaters, and splashing fountains. A concierge desk at the Lawrence Street entrance is staffed with friendly people who lead free walking tours around the city. ⊠ *1200 17th St., LoDo* ☎ *303/572–6868* ⊕ *www. taborcenter.com.*

CIVIC CENTER

Byers-Evans House Museum. Sprawling and detailed, red and black, this elaborate Victorian went up in 1883 as the home of *Rocky Mountain News* publisher William Byers. Restored to its pre–World War I condition, the historic landmark has occasional exhibitions and regular tours. Its main appeal is the glimpse it provides into Denver's past, specifically 1912 through 1924. The furnishings are those the Evans family acquired over the 80-some years they lived here. ⊠ *1310 Bannock St., Civic Center* ☎ *303/620–4933* ⊕ *www.historycolorado.org* ✎ *$6* ⊗ *Mon.–Sat. 10–4.*

Civic Center. A peaceful respite awaits in this three-block park in the cultural heart of downtown, site of the State Capitol. A 1919 Greek amphitheater is in the middle of one of the city's largest flower gardens. Two of the park's statues, *Bronco Buster* and *On the War Trail,* depicting a cowboy and an Indian on horseback, were commissioned in the '20s. Festivals such as Cinco de Mayo, Taste of Colorado, and the People's Fair keep things lively here in spring and summer. The park was born in 1906, when Mayor Robert Speer asked New York architect Charles Robinson to expand on his vision of a "Paris on the Platte." ⊠ *Bannock St. to Broadway south of Colfax Ave. and north of 14th Ave., Civic Center.*

Ⅽ **Denver Art Museum.** Unique displays of Asian, pre-Columbian, Spanish
Fodor's Choice   Colonial, and Native American art are the hallmarks of this model
★   of museum design. Among the museum's regular holdings are John DeAndrea's sexy, soothing, life-size polyvinyl painting *Linda* (1983); Claude Monet's dreamy flowerscape *Le Bassin des Nympheas* (1904); and Charles Deas's red-cowboy-on-horseback *Long Jakes, The Rocky Mountain Man* (1844). The works are thoughtfully lighted, though dazzling mountain views through hallway windows sometimes steal your attention. Imaginative hands-on exhibits, game and puzzle-filled Family Backpacks, and video corners will appeal to children; the Adventures in Art Center has hands-on art classes and exploration for children and adults. With the 2007 opening of the Frederic C. Hamilton building, the museum doubled in size. Designed by architect Daniel Libeskind, the 146,000-square-foot addition prompts debate: Some say the glass and titanium design has ruined the view, while others think the building is a work of art in its own right. To the east of the museum is an outdoor plaza—you'll know it by the huge orange metal sculpture—that leads to the Denver Public Library next door. ⊠ *100 W. 14th Ave. Pkwy., Civic Center* ☎ *720/865–5000* ⊕ *www.denverartmuseum.org* ✎ *$13* ⊗ *Tues., Thurs., Sat., Sun. 10–5; Fri. 10–8.*

QUICK BITES   **Palettes.** The Denver Art Museum's restaurant, Palettes, is the product of a culinary artist. Chef Kevin Taylor, a local fixture who also runs Prima Ristorante, fills the menu with colorful dishes like fruit-stuffed pork and flash-fried calamari. There's also a coffee shop, **Novo Coffee**, on the second floor of the museum, as well as **Mad Greens Inspired Eats**, a sandwich and salad spot on Martin Plaza across from the museum's main entrance, with

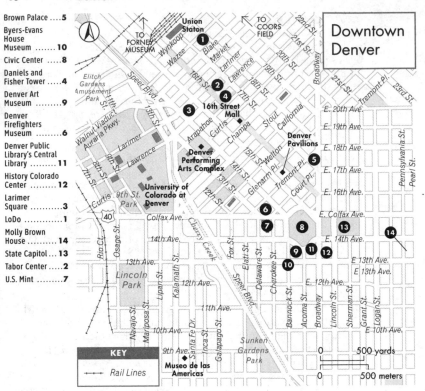

outdoor tables on the plaza between the museum and the Denver Public
Library. ⊠ **100 W. 14th Ave. Pkwy.** ☎ **303/534–0889.**

Denver Public Library's Central Library. A life-size horse on a 20-foot-tall
chair and other sculptures decorate the expansive lawn of this sprawling complex with round towers and tall, oblong windows. Built in the
mid-'50s, the Central Library underwent a massive, Michael Graves–
designed renovation in 1995. The map and manuscript rooms, Gates
Western History Reading Room (with amazing views of the mountains),
and Schlessman Hall (with its three-story atrium) merit a visit. The
library houses a world-renowned collection of books, photographs,
and newspapers that chronicle the American West, as well as original
paintings by Remington, Russell, Audubon, and Bierstadt. The children's library is notable for its captivating design and its unique, child-
friendly multimedia computer catalog. ⊠ *10 W. 14th Ave. Pkwy., Civic
Center* ☎ *720/865–1111* ⊕ *www.denver.lib.co.us* ☉ *Mon.–Tues. 10–8,
Wed.–Fri. 10–6, weekends 1–5.*

**OFF THE
BEATEN
PATH**

Museo de las Americas. The region's first museum dedicated to the
achievements of Latinos in the Americas has a permanent collection as
well as rotating exhibits that cover everything from Hispanics in the
state legislature to Latin American women artists in the 20th century.
Among the permanent pieces are the oil painting *Virgin of Solitude*

(circa 1730) and a Mayan polychrome jar (circa 650–950), in addition to contemporary works. In addition to the regular hours, the museum is open, with free admission, the first Friday evening of each month from 5 to 9. ✉ *861 Santa Fe Dr., Lincoln Park* ☎ *303/571–4401* ⊕ *www.museo.org* ▭ *$5* ☉ *Tues.–Fri. 10–5, weekends noon–5.*

History Colorado Center. The three-story, interactive History Colorado Center is scheduled to open spring 2012 and replaces the flagship museum of the Colorado Historical Society that sat two blocks away. In addition to revamped versions of the previous collections depicting state history from 1800 to the present, new exhibitions combine technology, artifacts, and multimedia presentations, and visitors can expect virtual displays that include experiencing the state in a "time machine," a Model T Ford and on skis. ✉ *1560 Broadway, Civic Center* ☎ *303/447–8679.*

U.S. Mint. Tour this facility to catch a glimpse of the coin-making process, as presses spit out thousands of coins a minute. There are also exhibits on the history of money and a restored version of Denver's original mint prior to numerous expansions. More than 14 billion coins are minted yearly, and the nation's second-largest hoard of gold is stashed away here. ■ TIP➡ **To schedule a tour and prepare for your visit (there are strict security guidelines) visit the Mint's Web site.** Reservations are required for all tours, which are guided, free, and available weekdays from 8 to 2. The gift shop, which sells authentic coins and currency, is in the Tremont Center, across Colfax Avenue from the Mint. ✉ *320 W. Colfax Ave., Civic Center* ☎ *303/405–4761* ⊕ *www.usmint.gov/mint_tours/* ▭ *Free* ☉ *Gift shop weekdays 9–3:30, tours by reservation weekdays 8–2.*

CAPITOL HILL

Molly Brown House. This Victorian celebrates the life and times of the scandalous, "unsinkable" Molly Brown. The heroine of the *Titanic* courageously saved several lives and continued to provide assistance to survivors back on terra firma. Costumed guides and period furnishings in the museum, including flamboyant gilt-edge wallpaper, lace curtains, tile fireplaces, and tapestries, evoke bygone days. The museum collects and displays artifacts that belonged to Brown, as well as period items dating to 1894–1912, when the Browns lived in the house. Tours run every half-hour; you won't need much more than that to see the whole place. A bit of trivia: Margaret Tobin Brown was known as Maggie, not Molly, during her lifetime. Meredith Willson, the composer–lyricist of the musical *The Unsinkable Molly Brown*, based on Brown's life, thought Molly was easier to sing. ✉ *1340 Pennsylvania St., Capitol Hill* ☎ *303/832–4092* ⊕ *www.mollybrown.org* ▭ *$8* ☉ *Tues.–Sat. 10–3:30, Sun. noon–3:30.*

State Capitol. Built in 1886, the capitol was constructed mostly of materials indigenous to Colorado, including marble, granite, and rose onyx. Especially inspiring is the gold-leaf dome, a reminder of the state's mining heritage. The dome is open for tours by appointment on the hour; 30 people at a time can go to the top (using a 99-step staircase from the third floor) to take in the 360-degree view of the Rockies. Historical tours are also available. Outside, a marker on the 13th step indicates where the elevation is exactly 1 mi high (above sea level). The legislature is generally in session from January through May, and visitors are welcome to sit in third-floor viewing galleries above the House and Senate chambers. ✉ *200 E. Colfax Ave., Capitol Hill* ☎ *303/866–2604, 303/866–3834 for dome tours* ⊕ *www.state.co.us/gov* ✉ *Free* ☉ *Weekdays 7–5. Tours Sept.–May, weekdays 9–2:30; June–Aug., weekdays 9–3:30.*

CENTRAL PLATTE VALLEY

Less than a mile west of downtown is the booming Central Platte Valley. Once the cluttered heart of Denver's railroad system, it's now overflowing with attractions. The imposing glass facade of the NFL Broncos' Sports Authority Field at Mile High, the stately Pepsi Center sports arena, the Downtown Aquarium, and the flagship REI outdoors store are four of the biggest attractions. New restaurants, a couple of coffeehouses, and a few small, locally owned shops, including a wine boutique, make it appealing to wander around. The sights in this area are so popular that the light-rail line was extended to connect the attractions with downtown.

The South Platte River valley concrete path, which extends several miles from downtown to the east and west, snakes along the water through out-of-the-way parks and trails. The 15th Street Bridge is particularly cyclist- and pedestrian-friendly, connecting LoDo with growing northwest Denver in a seamless way. The most relaxed, and easiest, way to see the area is on one of the half-hour or hour-long tours on the **Platte Valley Trolley** (☎ *303/458–6255* ⊕ *www.denvertrolley.org* ✉ *$4*), which can be accessed by parking at the Children's Museum and catching the streetcar east of the lot by the river.

TIMING You can easily spend a full day in this area, especially if you have kids or would like to explore the Greenway. Older kids tend to blaze through the Children's Museum in a morning or afternoon, but the under-6 set can spend all day here. The Aquarium can make a good four- to six-hour stop. If you want to do both the Elitch Garden water park and main park, plan on spending a full day there.

TOP ATTRACTIONS

♻ ★ **Children's Museum of Denver.** This is one of the finest museums of its kind in North America, with constantly changing hands-on exhibits that engage children up to about age 8 in discovery. The Maze-eum is a walk-through musical maze. Children can build a car on an assembly line and send it careening down a test ramp at the Inventions display, or enter the Bubbles Playscape, where science and soap collide in kid-made bubbles up to six feet long. One of the biggest attractions is the Center for the Young Child, a 3,700-square-foot playscape aimed at newborns through four-year-olds and their caregivers. ✉ *2121 Children's Museum Dr., off Exit 211 of I–25, Jefferson Park* ☎ *303/433–7444* ⊕ *www. mychildsmuseum.org* ✉ *$8* ☉ *Weekdays 9–4, Wed. open until 7:30, weekends 10–5.*

Central Platte Valley, City Park, and Environs

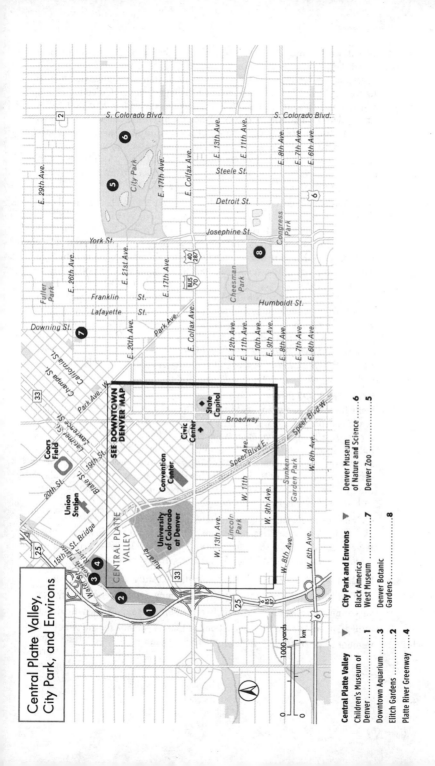

Central Platte Valley ▶

Children's Museum of
Denver 1

Downtown Aquarium 3

Elitch Gardens 2

Platte River Greenway 4

City Park and Environs ▶

Black America
West Museum 7

Denver Botanic
Gardens 8

Denver Museum
of Nature and Science 6

Denver Zoo 5

○ **Downtown Aquarium.** On the north side of the South Platte across from
★ Elitch Gardens, this is the only million-gallon aquarium between Chicago and the West Coast. It has four sections that show aquatic life in all its forms, from the seas to the river's headwaters in the Colorado mountains. The 250-seat Aquarium Restaurant surrounds a 150,000-gallon tank filled with sharks and fish. Other highlights include an expanded stingray touch pool, a gold-panning area, animatronic creatures, and an interactive shipwreck. The aquarium also has a lounge with a weeknight happy hour. ✉ *700 Water St., off Exit 211 of I–25, Jefferson Park* ☎ *303/561–4450* ⊕ *www.aquariumrestaurants.com* 🎫 *$15.99; $9.95 after 6 pm* ☉ *Sun.–Thurs. 10–9, Fri. and Sat. 10–9:30.*

○ **Elitch Gardens.** This elaborate and thrilling park was a Denver family tra-
★ dition long before its 1995 relocation from northwest Denver to its current home on the outskirts of downtown. The park's highlights include hair-raising roller coasters and thrill rides; for younger kids and squeamish parents there are also plenty of gentler attractions such as bumper cars and tea cups. Twister II, an update of the classic, wooden Mister Twister, is from the original Elitch Gardens, as is a 100-foot-high Ferris wheel that provides sensational views of downtown. A 10-acre water-adventure park is included in the standard entry fee. You can spend a whole day at either the water park or the main park. Locker and stroller rentals are available; discounted tickets are available online. ✉ *I–25 and Speer Blvd., Auraria* ☎ *303/595–4386* ⊕ *www.elitchgardens.com* 🎫 *$42.99 unlimited-ride pass* ☉ *June–Aug., daily; Apr., May, Sept., and Oct., Fri.–Sun.; hrs vary so call ahead.*

WORTH NOTING

Platte River Greenway. Just behind the REI flagship store, this serene park is at the center of the South Platte River valley path. Its rocks and rapids are especially attractive in summer for kayakers, bicyclists, and hikers. Sidewalks extend down the South Platte to the east toward the suburbs and west toward Invesco Field at Mile High. A pathway in yet another direction leads to LoDo. From the park it's about a 20-minute walk to the 16th Street Mall and Coors Field, which makes it a healthy way to sightsee when the weather is good.

Confluence Kayaks. You can rent a kayak from Confluence Kayaks and take a quick lesson before paddling yourself down the Platte River. ✉ *2373 15th St., Jefferson Park* ☎ *303/433–3676* ⊕ *www. confluencekayaks.com* ✉ *1615 Platte St., Jefferson Park.*

QUICK BITES

My Brother's Bar. Down the street from the REI store, along the bicycle path on 15th Street, My Brother's Bar is a homey neighborhood tavern that serves microbrews, burgers—buffalo and beef—and sandwiches of all kinds until 1:30 am. The bar's name isn't on the facade, so look for the street number. ✉ *2376 15th St., Highland* ☎ *303/455–9991.*

DENVER INVENTIONS

Every city likes to claim inventions, and Denver is no different. At the top of the city's list of accomplishments is the cheeseburger, for which resident Louis Ballast received a patent in 1935 after he accidentally spilled cheddar on his grill at the Humpty-Dumpty Drive-In on Speer Boulevard. The Denver boot, a bright yellow lock that attaches to a car tire and can only be removed with a special key, was invented by Frank Marugg as a way to keep people from stealing tires during World War II, when rubber snagged big bucks; in 1955 the boot came back to halt scofflaws. The Barnes Dance, a way for pedestrians to cross a four-way street diagonally, was named after Denver traffic engineer Henry Barnes in the 1930s, and although he didn't invent it, he was the first to use it on a large scale. And the Denver omelet, with green peppers, onions, and diced ham, has so many theories of inception it's almost impossible to track, but the best explanation is its evolution from the Western sandwich, with similar ingredients slapped inside bread by Chinese cooks who translated egg foo yong while working on the railroads.

CITY PARK AND ENVIRONS

Acquired by the city in 1881, City Park, Denver's largest public space (370 acres), contains rose gardens, lakes, a golf course, tennis courts, and a huge playground. A shuttle runs between two of the city's most popular attractions: the Denver Zoo and the Denver Museum of Nature & Science, both on the site. City Park is east of downtown Denver, and runs from East 17th Avenue to East 26th Avenue, between York Street and Colorado Boulevard.

TIMING   If you have children or are an animal lover, you could easily spend half a day in City Park. Plan to arrive early on weekends, as parking can be difficult to obtain (it's free at the attractions, but goes fast), and in warm-weather months pack a picnic, as the park itself is a delightful daytime rest area, with plenty of room to stretch.

TOP ATTRACTIONS

Denver Museum of Nature & Science. Founded in 1900, the museum has
Fodor's Choice   amassed more than 775,000 objects, making it the largest natural history museum in the western United States. It houses a rich combination of traditional collections—dinosaur remains, animal dioramas, a mineralogy display, an Egyptology wing—and intriguing hands-on exhibits. In the Hall of Life you can test your health and fitness on a variety of contraptions and receive a personalized health profile. The Prehistoric Journey exhibit covers the seven stages of earth's development. The massive complex also includes an IMAX movie theater and a planetarium whose Space Odyssey exhibit simulates a trip to Mars. An impressive eating-and-relaxation area has a full-window panoramic view of the Rocky Mountains. ✉ *2001 Colorado Blvd., City Park* ☎ *303/370–6000, 800/925–2250* ⊕ *www.dmns.org* ✉ *Museum $12, IMAX $10; $19 for combined pass (IMAX or planetarium)* ☉ *Daily 9–5, IMAX showtimes vary.*

Pete's Kitchen. This old-fashioned greasy-spoon diner specializes in Greek food, huge pancakes, and spicy huevos rancheros. It's a short drive from the Denver Museum of Nature & Science, and it's often packed, particularly on Sunday mornings. ✉ *1962 E. Colfax Ave.* ☎ *303/321–3139.*

★ **Denver Botanic Gardens.** The horticultural displays in thoughtfully laid-out theme gardens—more than 15,000 plant species from Australia, South Africa, and the Himalayas, and especially the western United States—are at their peak in July and August, when garden enthusiasts could spend half a day here. The tropical conservatory alone is worth an hour's visit in the off-season. Spring brings a brilliant display of wildflowers to the world-renowned rock alpine garden, primarily in late May and early June. The new OmniGlobe simulates the climate and atmospheric changes on earth; other environmental additions include a "green roof" atop the new bistro. Tea ceremonies take place some summer weekends in the tranquil Japanese garden, and artists such as folk-rocker Richard Thompson, singer–songwriter Jewel, and blues legend B.B. King have performed as part of the summer concert series. ✉ *1005 York St., Cheesman Park* ☎ *720/865–3500* ⊕ *www.botanicgardens.org* ✆ *$12.50* ☉ *May–Sept., daily 9–9; Oct.–Apr., daily 9–5.*

☾ ★ **Denver Zoo.** A bright peacock greets you at the door to the state's most popular cultural attraction, whose best-known exhibit showcases man-eating Komodo dragons in a lush re-creation of a cavernous riverbank. The Conservation Carousel ($2) rotates in the center of the 80-acre zoo, with handcrafted endangered species as mounts. A 7-acre Primate Panorama houses 31 species of primates in state-of-the-art environments that simulate the animals' natural habitats. Other highlights include a nursery for baby animals; seal shows; the world's only painting rhinoceros, Mshindi; the electric Safari Shuttle, which snakes through the property as you are treated to a lesson on the zoo's inhabitants; and the usual lions, tigers, bears, giraffes, and monkeys, and one extremely hairy elephant. The exhibits are spaced far apart along sprawling concrete paths, so build in plenty of time to visit. ✉ *2300 Steele St., City Park* ☎ *303/376–4800* ⊕ *www.denverzoo.org* ✆ *$10 Nov.–Feb., $13 Mar.–Oct.* ☉ *Nov.–Feb., daily 10–4; Mar.–Oct., daily 9–5.*

WORTH NOTING

Black American West Museum. The revealing documents and artifacts here depict the vast contributions that African-Americans made to opening up the West. Nearly a third of the cowboys and many pioneer teachers and doctors were African-Americans. One floor is devoted to black cowboys; another to military troops such as the Buffalo Soldiers. Changing exhibits focus on topics such as the history of black churches in the West. ✉ *3091 California St., Five Points* ☎ *720/242–7428* ⊕ *www. blackamericanwestmuseum.com* ✆ *$8* ☉ *Thurs.–Sat. 10–2, Sun. 1–4.*

SPORTS AND THE OUTDOORS

Denver is a city that can consistently, enthusiastically support three professional sports teams. Unfortunately, it has more than that—the Colorado Rockies, Colorado Avalanche, Denver Broncos, Denver Nuggets, and Colorado Rapids (soccer). Until recently, the Nuggets and Rapids had been the odd teams out, as the Rockies, Avalanche, and Broncos have all reached or won championships in their respective sports. But the Nuggets have come close to catching up, and fans eagerly await the next chapter.

What's great about Denverites is that most aren't just spectators. After a game, they go out and do stuff—hiking, bicycling, kayaking, and, yes, playing team sports themselves. The city and its proximity to outdoor pursuits encourage a fit lifestyle.

BASEBALL

Coors Field. The Colorado Rockies, Denver's National League baseball team, play April–October in Coors Field. Because of high altitude and thin air, the park is among the best in the major leagues for home run hitters—and one of the worst for pitchers. ✉ *2001 Blake St., LoDo* ☎ *303/292–0200, 800/388–7625* ⊕ *www.coloradorockies.com.*

BASKETBALL

Pepsi Center. The Denver Nuggets of the National Basketball Association were the ugly duckling in Denver's professional-sports scene for years, but some success on the court has brought an increase in fan interest. From November to April the Nuggets play at the Pepsi Center. The 19,000-seat arena, which opened in 1999, is also the primary indoor venue for large musical acts such as U2 and the Black Eyed Peas. ✉ *1000 Chopper Circle, Auraria* ☎ *303/405–8555* ⊕ *www.nba.com/nuggets.*

BICYCLING AND JOGGING

Denver Parks Department. The Parks Department has suggestions for bicycling and jogging paths throughout the metropolitan area's 250 parks, including the popular Cherry Creek and Chatfield Reservoir State Recreation areas. With more than 400 mi of off-road paths in and around the city to choose from, cyclists can move easily between urban and rural settings. ☎ *720/913–0696* ⊕ *www.denvergov.org/parks.*

Bicycle Doctor/Edgeworks. Just south of downtown, this facility repairs street and mountain bikes and rents them for $15 to $50 a day. ✉ *860 Broadway, Golden Triangle* ☎ *303/831–7228, 877/245–3362* ⊕ *www.bicycledr.com.*

Cherry Creek Bike Path. A well-kept path runs from Cherry Creek Shopping Center to Larimer Square downtown alongside the peaceful creek of its name. ✉ *Cherry Creek, LoDo.*

Highline Canal. The scenic canal has 70 mi of mostly dirt paths through the metro area running at almost completely level grade. ✉ *Auraria, Cherry Creek, LoDo.*

South Platte River. There are 12 mi of paved paths along the river heading into downtown. ✉ *Central Platte Valley, LoDo.*

Matthews/Winters Park. West of the city, paved paths wind through Matthews/Winters Park near both Golden and Morrison. It's dotted with plaintive pioneer graves amid the sun-bleached grasses, thistle, and columbine. ⊠ *South of I–70 on CO 26, Golden.*

Deer Creek Canyon. The Deer Creek Canyon trail system is popular with mountain bikers, running through forested foothills southwest of Denver near the intersection of C–470 and Wadsworth Avenue. ⊠ *Littleton* ⊕ *www.co.jefferson.co.us/openspace.*

FOOTBALL

Sports Authority Field at Mile High. The National Football League's Denver Broncos play September–December at Sports Authority Field at Mile High. Every game has sold out for 30 years, so tickets are not easy to come by. ⊠ *1701 Bryant St., Exit 210B off I–25, Sun Valley* ☎ *720/ 258–3000* ⊕ *www.denverbroncos.com.*

GOLF

With their sprawling layouts and impressively appointed greens, these four private clubs merit a special look over their city-operated counterparts simply because of their more rural settings. On any Denver-area course, though, out-of-town golfers should keep in mind that the high altitude affects golf balls like it does baseballs—which is why the Rockies have so many more home runs when they bat at home. It's generally agreed that your golf ball will go about 10%–15% farther in the thin air here than it would at sea level.

Arrowhead Golf Club. Designed by Robert Trent Jones Jr., this course is set impressively among red sandstone spires. It's 45 minutes from downtown in Roxborough State Park, which means that any members of your group who don't want to golf can hike nearby. ⊠ *10850 W. Sundown Trail, Littleton* ☎ *303/973–9614* ⊕ *www.arrowheadcolorado. com* ⅃ *18 holes. Yards: 6682/5465. Par: 70/72. Green fee: $29/$139.*

Buffalo Run. A Keith Foster–designed course and the site for the 2004 Denver Open, the bargain-priced Buffalo Run counts wide-open views of the plains surrounding its lake-studded course among its charms, which also include streams running through it and the Bison Grill Restaurant. ⊠ *15700 E. 112th Ave., Commerce City* ☎ *303/289–1500* ⊕ *www.buffalorungolfcourse.com* ⅃ *18 holes. Yards: 7411/5277. Par: 72/71. Green fee: $25/$40.*

Ridge at Castle Pines North. Tom Weiskopf designed this 18-hole course with great mountain views and dramatic elevation changes. It's ranked among the nation's top 100 public courses. It's in Castle Rock, about 45 minutes south of Denver on I–25. ⊠ *1414 Castle Pines Pkwy., Castle Rock* ☎ *303/688–0100* ⊕ *www.playtheridge.com* ⌁ *Reservations essential* ⅃ *18 holes. Yards: 7013/5001. Par: 71/71. Green fee: $60/$125.*

Riverdale Golf Courses. It's two golf courses in one: Riverdale has the Dunes, a Scottish-style links course designed by Pete and Perry Dye that sits on the South Platte River and offers railroad ties, plenty of bunkers, and water, while the Knolls has a more-gnarly, park-inspired layout. Both courses are shaded by plenty of trees, and you can't beat the green fee. ⊠ *13300 Riverdale Rd., Brighton* ☎ *303/659–6700* ⊕ *www.*

riverdalegolf.com 🏌 *Knolls: 18 holes. Yards: 6771/5891. Par: 71/72. Dunes: 18 holes. Yards: 7064/4903. Par: 73/70. Green fee: $23/$42.*

City of Denver Golf Reservation System. Seven courses—City Park, Harvard Gulch, Evergreen, Kennedy, Overland Park, Wellshire, and Willis Case—are operated by the City of Denver and are open to the public. Green fee for all ranges from $22 to $35. For advance reservations golfers must use the City of Denver Golf Reservation System (on the Web or by phone) up to three days in advance. For same-day tee times you can call the starters at an individual course. ☎ *303/784–4000* ⊕ *www. cityofdenvergolf.com* ✉ *City Park, 2500 York St.* ☎ *303/295–2096* ✉ *Evergreen, 29614 Upper Bear Creek Rd.* ☎ *303/674–6351* ✉ *Harvard Gulch, 660 Iliff Ave.* ☎ *303/698–4078* ✉ *Kennedy, 10500 E. Hampden Ave.* ☎ *720/865–0720* ✉ *Overland Park, 1801 S. Huron St.* ☎ *303/698–4975* ✉ *Wellshire, 3333 S. Colorado Blvd.* ☎ *303/692–5636* ✉ *Willis Case, 4999 Vrain St.* ☎ *720/865–0700.*

HIKING

Barr Lake State Park. The 9-mile, multi-use Lake Perimeter Trail at Barr Lake State Park (about 24 mi northeast of Denver) circles the lake and passes by several wildlife viewing stations and the park's wildlife refuge. More than 350 species of birds have been spotted in the park, including bald eagles. ✉ *13401 Picadilly Rd., Brighton* ✛ *Take U.S. 36 east about 20 mi., then take I-76 east for about 17 mi to the Bromley Ln. exit. Go east about 1 mi, then turn left onto Picadilly Rd. Go north on Picadilly Rd. 2.1 mi. The park entrance will be on your left* ⊕ *parks. state.co.us/Parks/barrlake* 🎟 *$7 for a day pass.*

Mount Falcon Park. This park looks down on Denver and across at Red Rocks. It's amazingly tranquil, laced with meadows and streams, and shaded by conifers. The trails are well marked. ✉ *Off Rte. 8, Morrison exit, or U.S. 285, Parmalee exit, Aurora.*

Fodor's Choice ★ **Red Rocks Park and Amphitheatre.** Fifteen miles southwest of Denver, Red Rocks Park and Amphitheatre is a breathtaking, 70-million-year-old wonderland of vaulting oxblood-and-cinnamon-color sandstone spires. The outdoor music stage is in a natural 9,000-seat amphitheater (with perfect acoustics, as only nature could have designed). Just want a look? The 5-mile scenic drive offers a glorious glimpse of the 868 acres of sandstone, and there are picnic and parking areas along the way for photos and a rest. If you're feeling particularly spunky, follow the locals' lead and run the steps for a real workout. The Trading Post loop hiking trail, at 6,280 feet, is 1.4 mi long and quite narrow with drop-offs and steep grades. The trail closes one-half hour before sunset. The park is open from 5 am to 11 pm daily. ✉ *17598 W. Alameda Pkwy., Morrison* ✛ *I–70 west to Exit 259, turn left to park entrance* ⊕ *www. redrocksonline.com.*

Roxborough State Park. This park has an easy 2-mi loop trail through rugged rock formations, offering striking vistas and a unique look at metro Denver and the plains. This trail is wheelchair accessible. ✉ *I–25 south to Santa Fe exit, take Santa Fe Blvd. south to Titan Rd., turn right and follow signs, Littleton.*

Green Mountain. Green Mountain is the first named foothill as you head west from Denver toward the mountains. Part of Jefferson County Open Space and a piece of William Frederick Hayden Park (City of Lakewood), the easy, mostly exposed trail affords panoramic views of downtown Denver, Table Mesa, Pikes Peak, and the Continental Divide from the top (895 feet in elevation gain). You must share with bikers and dogs, as well as other critters. There are multiple trails from several trailheads, including a 6.4-mi loop and a 3.1-mi loop. Open 5 am to 10 pm daily. ⊠ *I–70 west to CO 470 to W. Alameda Pkwy., turn left to trailhead entrance, Lakewood* ⊕ *www.lakewood.org.*

HOCKEY

Colorado Avalanche. The Colorado Avalanche of the National Hockey League are wildly popular in Denver; the team won the Stanley Cup in 1996 and beat the New Jersey Devils for an encore in 2001. Although they've been relatively disappointing since, and legendary goalie Patrick Roy retired after the 2003 season, the still-exciting team plays October to April at the 19,000-seat Pepsi Center arena. ⊠ *1000 Chopper Pl., Auraria* ☎ *303/405–8555* ⊕ *www.coloradoavalanche.com.*

STOCK SHOWS

National Western Stock Show. Thousands of cowpokes retrieve their string ties and worn boots and indulge in two weeks of hootin', hollerin', and celebratin' the beef industry during the National Western Stock Show every January.

Whether you're a professional rancher or bull rider, or just plan to show up for the people-watching, the Stock Show is a rich, colorful glimpse of Western culture. The pros arrive to make industry connections, show off their livestock, and perhaps land a few sales. The entertainment involves nightly rodeo events, presentations of prized cattle (some going for thousands of dollars), and "Mutton Bustin'." The latter is one of those rowdy rodeo concepts that usually has no place in a genteel metropolis like Denver: kids, six years old and younger, don huge hockey-goalie helmets and hold for dear life onto the backs of bucking baby sheep. At the trade show you can buy hats and boots as well as yards of beef jerky and quirky gift items.

Denver Coliseum. The yearly event is held at the Denver Coliseum. Just be sure to call first and ask for directions; although parking is plentiful, the Coliseum, usually home of straightforward sporting and entertainment events, becomes a labyrinth of lots and shuttles during the Stock Show. ⊠ *4600 Humboldt St., east of I–25 on I–70, Elyria* ☎ *303/865–2475* ⊠ *Denver Coliseum, 4600 Humboldt St., east of I–25 on I–70, Elyria* ☎ *303/297–1166* ⊕ *www.nationalwestern.com.*

WHERE TO EAT

As befits a multiethnic crossroads, Denver lays out a dizzying range of eateries. Head for LoDo, 32nd Avenue in the Highland District, or south of the city for the more inventive kitchens. Try Federal Street for cheap ethnic eats—especially Mexican and Vietnamese—and expect more authentic takes on classic Italian, French, and Asian cuisines than the city has offered in the past. Throughout Denver, menus at trendy restaurants are pairing international flavors with regional products in unique ways; Denver's top chefs are gaining the attention of national food magazines and winning culinary competitions.

WHAT IT COSTS				
	¢	$	$$	$$$	$$$$
Restaurants	under $8	$8–$12	$13–$18	$19–$25	over $25

Prices are per person for a main course, excluding 8.22% tax.

Use the coordinate (✛ B2) at the end of each listing to locate a site on the corresponding map.

DOWNTOWN

LODO

$$$ ✕ **Denver ChopHouse & Brewery.** This is the best of the LoDo brewpubs
STEAKHOUSE and restaurants surrounding the Coors Field ballpark. Housed in the old Union Pacific Railroad warehouse, the restaurant, similar to the ones in Washington, D.C., Cleveland, and Boulder, is clubby, with dark-wood paneling and exposed brick. The food is basic American, and there's plenty of it: steaks, seafood, pizzas, and chicken served with hot corn bread and honey butter, and "bottomless" salads tossed at the table. ✉ *1735 19th St.* ☎ *303/296–0800* ⊕ *www.chophouse.com* ⚠ *Reservations essential* ✛ *B4.*

$$ ✕ **India House.** Diners get to see their food being prepared in the tandoor
INDIAN in this handsome space complete with luxurious wall treatments, comfy upholstery, and interesting art. The spicing is gentle—unless you request that it not be—and the preparations are skillful on the lengthy, well-chosen menu, which includes vegetarian options. A local favorite is the *shahi sabz,* vegetables in a nut-strewn cream sauce, and the house-made ice creams are delicious. The market-price lobster dishes are standouts, too. ✉ *1514 Blake St.* ☎ *303/595–0680* ⊕ *www.indiahouse.us* ✛ *A5.*

$$$ ✕ **Jax Fish House.** A popular oyster bar serves as the foyer to the ever-
SEAFOOD busy Jax, whose brick-lined back dining room packs in the crowds, especially when there's a ball game at Coors Field three blocks away. A dozen different types of oysters are freshly shucked each day, and they can be paired with one of the house-made, fruit-infused vodkas or chili-fired shooters. Main courses make use of fresh catches flown in from both coasts such as ahi tuna, scallops, snapper, and shrimp, and although there are a couple of meat dishes, only the truly fish-phobic should not go there. The sides are fun, too: buckwheat waffles, zucchini

BEST BETS FOR DENVER DINING

Fodor's Choice ★	$$	Restaurant Kevin Taylor, p. 59
The Fort, p. 64	Domo, p.60	
LoLa Mexican Seafood, p. 62	Little India, p. 61	**By Cuisine**
Mizuna, p. 61	$$$	MEXICAN
Restaurant Kevin Taylor, p. 59	Fruition, p. 60	LoLa, p. 62
Sushi Den, p. 63	LoLa Mexican Seafood, p. 62	Jack-n-Grill, p. 62
	New Saigon, p. 63	NEW AMERICAN
By Price	Olivéa, p. 57	Fruition, p. 60
	Panzano, p. 58	Highland's Garden Café, p. 61
¢	Rioja, p. 56	
Anthony's Pizza, p. 57	Sushi Den, p. 63	Mizuna, p. 61
Spicy Pickle Sub Shop, p. 59	$$$$	Potager, p. 57
	Elway's, p. 62	Vesta Dipping Grill, p.53
$	The Fort, p. 64	STEAK
Jack-n-Grill, p. 62	Highland's Garden Café, p. 61	Capital Grille, p. 53
Sam's No. 3, p. 59	Mizuna, p. 61	Elway's, p. 62
WaterCourse, p. 57		Sullivan's, p. 52

fritters, buttery noodles. ✉ 1539 17th St. ☎ 303/292–5767 ⊕ www.jaxfishhousedenver.com ♙ Reservations essential ⊘ No lunch ✛ A5.

$$$$ STEAKHOUSE ✕ **Morton's of Chicago.** The Denver outpost of this nationally revered steak house is as swanky and overwhelming as the rest, with dark woods, white linens, and the signature steak knives at each place setting. Diners are greeted by expert staff wielding the cuts of the day and their accompaniments, and once choices are made the experience is almost always seamless. The steaks themselves are superb—prime, well aged, and unadorned. All sides cost extra, but they're big enough to feed two or three. The extensive wine list is pricey, and the delicious desserts are enormous. ✉ 1710 Wynkoop St. ☎ 303/825–3353 ⊕ www.mortons.com ♙ Reservations essential ⊘ No lunch ✛ A4.

$$$$ STEAKHOUSE ✕ **Sullivan's Steakhouse.** Sullivan's bills itself as a more affordable steak house, and although technically that may be true, it's easy to spend just as much here as at any other top-tier steak joint. Still, it's worth it, because the hand-carved, aged Black Angus beef is of high quality, well grilled, and accompanied by stellar sides such as grill-greasy onion rings and chunky mashed potatoes. The wood-lined barroom is filled with high tables and makes for a fun gathering place, especially when there's live jazz. It's reminiscent of a 1940s club. Swing by early for the reasonably priced happy-hour prix-fixe menu before 6 pm. ✉ 1745 Wazee

St. ☎ *303/295–2664* ⊕ *www.sullivanssteakhouse.com* ⌂ *Reservations essential* ⊘ *No lunch* ⊹ *A4.*

$$$$ ✕**Vesta Dipping Grill.** Both the remodeled building and the interior space
MODERN   designed to house this modern grill, named after Vesta, the Roman
AMERICAN   hearth goddess, have won national architectural awards, and it's easy
to see why: the sensual swirls of fabric and copper throughout the room
make diners feel as though they're inside a giant work of art, and the
clever, secluded banquettes are among the most sought-after seats in
town. The menu is clever, too, and the competent grill masters in the
kitchen put out expertly cooked meats, fish, and vegetables, all of which
can be paired with some of the three dozen dipping sauces that get their
inspiration from chutneys, salsas, mother sauces, and barbecue. The
wine list is as cool as the clientele. ✉ *1822 Blake St.* ☎ *303/296–1970*
⊕ *www.vestagrill.com* ⌂ *Reservations essential* ⊘ *No lunch* ⊹ *B5.*

$$ ✕**Wynkoop Brewing Co.** This trendy yet unpretentious local institution
AMERICAN   was Denver's first brewpub, and now its owner, John Hickenlooper, is
Colorado's governor. Different crowds frequent its pool-hall, cabaret,
and dining-room levels—with the younger crowd on the top floor enjoy-
ing drinks and bar snacks during happy hour or down in the lower caba-
ret level for improv or live music, and families and urban professionals
dining on the main level. Try the terrific buffalo meatloaf or venison
served over mashed potatoes with fried onions. Wash it down with one
of the Wynkoop's trademark microbrews—try either the exemplary
Railyard Ale or the spicy chili beer. ✉ *1634 18th St.* ☎ *303/297–2700*
⊕ *www.wynkoop.com* ⊹ *A4.*

LARIMER SQUARE

$$$$ ✕**Capital Grille.** In a town that loves its steaks, the Rhode Island–based
STEAKHOUSE   chain was taking a chance moving in and pretending to offer anything
different from the other high-end big-boy steak houses. That said, Capi-
tal Grille—housed in a dark, noisy, broodingly decorated room typical
of the genre—has much to recommend it, including a drop-dead Delmo-
nico, textbook French onion soup, and terrific skin-on mashed potatoes.
If you were ever to try steak tartare, this would be the place to do it, and
the lobster is one of the best in town. The wine list is long, important,
and expensive, but the service is remarkably fresh-faced and eager to
please. ✉ *1450 Larimer St.* ☎ *303/539–2500* ⊕ *www.thecapitalgrille.*
com ⌂ *Reservations essential* ⊘ *No lunch Sat., Sun.* ⊹ *A6.*

$$ ✕**Lime.** Hidden at basement-level, ultracasual Lime is always happen-
MEXICAN   ing, especially for the younger, hipper crowd whose pockets aren't deep
enough for more upscale LoDo spots. The made-to-order deep-fried
tortilla chips arrive at the table when you do, and the salsas are zippy
and well crafted. Imbibers are treated to a half-shot in a lime shell,
and the Mighty Margarita is the only way to go from there. Shrimp
stuffed with jalapeños and cream cheese—two of these "scorpions"
can be added to any plate for $4—the tamales, and chiles rellenos are
all winners, and the green-and-white bar is a fun place for late-night
snacking. ✉ *1424-C Larimer St.* ☎ *303/893–5463* ⊕ *www.eatatlime.*
com ⊘ *Closed Sun. No lunch* ⊹ *A6.*

$$ ✕**Osteria Marco.** The Bonannos, whose Mizuna and Luca d'Italia are
ITALIAN   among the best restaurants in town, continue their success with this

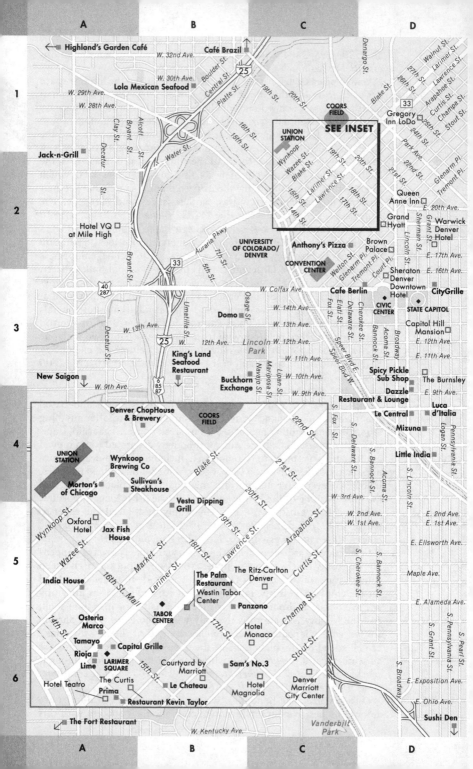

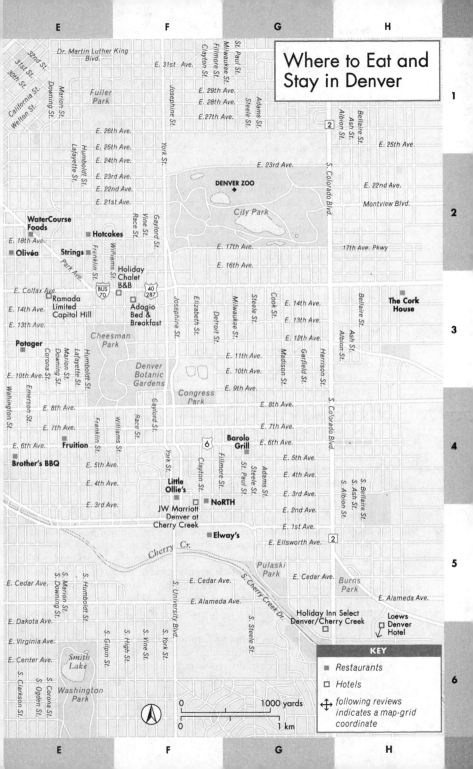

Where to Eat and Stay in Denver

Map labels (streets and avenues):

3rd St., 31st St., 30th St.
California St., Downing St., Welton St.
Dr. Martin Luther King Blvd.
E. 31st Ave.
Clayton St., Fillmore St., Milwaukee St., St. Paul St.
Fuller Park
E. 29th Ave.
E. 28th Ave.
E. 27th Ave.
Marion St., Humboldt St., Lafayette St.
E. 26th Ave.
E. 25th Ave.
E. 24th Ave.
E. 23rd Ave.
E. 22nd Ave.
E. 21st Ave.
York St.
Josephine St.
Adams St., Steele St.
Bellaire St., Ash St., Albion St.
2
E. 25th Ave.
E. 23rd Ave.
DENVER ZOO
E. 22nd Ave.
Montview Blvd.
S. Colorado Blvd.
City Park
WaterCourse Foods
Hotcakes
Gaylord St., Vine St., Race St.
E. 18th Ave.
Olivéa
Strings
Franklin St., Williams St.
Park Ave.
E. 17th Ave.
E. 16th Ave.
17th Ave. Pkwy
Holiday Chalet B&B
E. Colfax Ave.
BUS 70
40 287
Ramada Limited Capitol Hill
E. 14th Ave.
Adagio Bed & Breakfast
E. 13th Ave.
Josephine St.
Elizabeth St., Detroit St.
Milwaukee St., Steele St.
Cook St.
E. 14th Ave.
E. 13th Ave.
E. 12th Ave.
Garfield St., Madison St., Harrison St.
Bellaire St., Ash St., Albion St.
The Cork House
3
Cheesman Park
Potager
Humboldt St., Lafayette St., Marion St., Corona St., Downing St.
E. 10th Ave.
Denver Botanic Gardens
E. 11th Ave.
E. 10th Ave.
E. 9th Ave.
Washington St., Emerson St.
Congress Park
E. 8th Ave.
E. 7th Ave.
Franklin St., Williams St., Race St., Gaylord St.
E. 8th Ave.
E. 7th Ave.
S. Colorado Blvd.
E. 6th Ave.
Fruition
E. 5th Ave.
Brother's BBQ
E. 4th Ave.
6
York St.
Clayton St., Fillmore St., St. Paul St., Steele St., Adams St.
Barolo Grill
E. 6th Ave.
E. 5th Ave.
E. 4th Ave.
E. 3rd Ave.
S. Bellaire St., S. Ash St., S. Albion St.
4
Little Ollie's
NoRTH
JW Marriott Denver at Cherry Creek
E. 3rd Ave.
E. 2nd Ave.
E. 1st Ave.
Elway's
E. Ellsworth Ave.
2
Cherry Cr.
Pulaski Park
S. Cherry Creek Dr.
E. Cedar Ave.
Burns Park
5
E. Cedar Ave.
E. Cedar Ave.
E. Alameda Ave.
S. University Blvd.
E. Alameda Ave.
S. Steele St.
Holiday Inn Select Denver/Cherry Creek
Loews Denver Hotel
E. Cedar Ave.
S. Marion St., S. Downing St., S. Humboldt St.
E. Dakota Ave.
E. Virginia Ave.
E. Center Ave.
S. Clarkson St., S. Ogden St., S. Corona St., S. Gilpin St., S. High St., S. Vine St., S. York St.
Smith Lake
Washington Park
0 — 1000 yards
0 — 1 km

KEY
- ■ Restaurants
- □ Hotels
- ⊕ following reviews indicates a map-grid coordinate

E   F   G   H

reasonably priced, casual eatery. High-backed wooden booths, dish towels as napkins, and exposed-brick walls provide a hip, urban setting below street level for wood-fired pizzas topped with Frank Bonanno's homemade or imported cheeses and house-cured meats. Or try one of the sampler trays from the formaggi and salumi (fresh cheese and meats) bar, the Italian version of an artisan deli that greets you at the entrance. Salads are large enough to eat as entrées. The mostly locally sourced meat dishes shine—especially Sunday night's roast suckling pig special. ✉ *1453 Larimer St.* ☎ *303/534–5855* ⊕ *www.osteriamarco. com* ⚱ *Reservations essential* ✛ *A6.*

$$$
MEDITERRANEAN

✕ **Rioja.** Chef Jennifer Jasinski's intense attention to detail is evident in her tribute to Mediterranean food with contemporary flair. Formerly of Panzano, she partners in this venture with two other women: Beth Gruitch runs the front of the house while sous chef Dana Rodriguez helps in the back, and together this trio makes intriguing and compelling combinations like seared bigeye tuna with saffron-tangerine vinaigrette and Colorado lamb with preserved lemon yogurt. The restaurant is hip and artsy, with exposed brick and blown-glass lighting, arched doorways, and textured draperies. The wine list presents riojas galore, and is well priced for Larimer Square. ✉ *1431 Larimer St.* ☎ *303/820–2282* ⊕ *www.riojadenver.com* ⚱ *Reservations essential* ☉ *No lunch Mon. and Tues.* ✛ *A6.*

$$$
MEXICAN

✕ **Tamayo.** Chef–owner Richard Sandoval brought his popular concept of modern, upscale Mexican cuisine from New York to Denver, and it's just as welcome here. The food is classic Mexican with a twist, such as seafood tacos, *huitlacoche* (edible fungus) dumpling soup, elaborate moles, and empanadas for dessert. The tequila flights are a favorite at the large, inviting bar, which is highlighted by a mural made of semiprecious stones made by artist and restaurant namesake Rufino Tamayo. Screens made from blond wood and Spanish art fill the interior, and in season the outdoor patio supplies a rare view of the mountains. ✉ *1400 Larimer St.* ☎ *720/946–1433* ⊕ *www.modernmexican.com* ⚱ *Reservations essential* ☉ *No lunch weekends* ✛ *A6.*

CAPITOL HILL

$
AMERICAN

✕ **CityGrille.** Politicians and construction workers rub shoulders while chowing down on the well-crafted sandwiches, soups, and salads at this casual eatery across the street from the State Capitol. CityGrille has earned national attention for both the burger, a half-pounder of ground sirloin, and the chili, a gringo stew of pork, jalapeños, and tomatoes that's spicy and addictive. The three-martini lunch lives on in this power-packed spot, and you can get a meal here until 11 pm (midnight on weekends). ✉ *321 E. Colfax Ave.* ☎ *303/861–0726* ⊕ *www. citygrille.com* ✛ *D3.*

¢
DINER

✕ **Hotcakes Diner.** This jumping Capitol Hill spot is a breakfast and lunch hangout. Weekend brunch draws crowds of bicyclists and newspaper readers in search of the croissant French toast, "health nut" pancakes, and colossal omelets. Even bigger are the scrumptious one-dish skillets; a popular one tops grilled pork chops with home fries, chili, cheddar, and eggs. They're open weekdays at 6 am and weekends at

7 am; closed each day at 2 pm. ⊠ *1400 E. 18th Ave.* ☎ *303/832–4351* ⌲ *Reservations not accepted* ⊘ *No dinner* ✛ *E2.*

$$$
MEDITERRANEAN
✗ **Olivéa.** At this casual but cozy eatery that serves a Mediterranean menu filled with affordable and memorable dishes, it makes sense to start with a tasting plate of charcuterie—$16 for three such tidbits as lamb sausage, duck liver mousse, and boudin blanc (white sausage)—and then try the house-made cavatelli (ricotta dumplings) or the duck meatballs on creamy polenta as an entrée. It's hard to save room for dessert, but it's equally hard to choose between the elegant concoctions (the chocolate and fleur de sel caramel tart is outstanding) and the house-made ice creams and sorbets. Service is friendly but snappy, and although the wine list is short, it's filled with well-chosen low-priced bottles. Still, it's the innovative happy-hour cocktails that truly have the town talking, along with the elaborate weekend brunches. ⊠ *719 E. 17th Ave.* ☎ *303/861–5050* ⊕ *www.olivearestaurant.com* ⌲ *Reservations essential* ⊘ *No lunch weekdays* ✛ *E2.*

$$$
MODERN
AMERICAN
✗ **Potager.** The menu changes monthly at this industrial-designed restaurant, whose name, French for "kitchen garden," refers to the herb-rimmed back patio. Exposed ducts and a high ceiling make for a trendy dining room, and the floor-to-ceiling front windows allow the hip to be seen and the twinkling lights outside and in to be reflected for a warm glow. The menu always includes a risotto of the day along with fish dishes and the ever-popular goat-cheese soufflé. The wine list is all over the map but well priced, and the servers are among the most savvy in town. ⊠ *1109 Ogden St.* ☎ *303/832–5788* ⊕ *www.potagerrestaurant.com* ⌲ *Reservations not accepted* ⊘ *Closed Sun. and Mon. No lunch* ✛ *E3.*

$$$
MODERN
AMERICAN
✗ **Strings.** This light, airy restaurant with its wide-open kitchen resembles an artist's loft. It's a preferred hangout for Denver's movers and shakers as well as for visiting celebs, whose autographs on head shots, napkins, and program notes hang on the walls. The specialties include seafood dishes such as butter-poached monkfish and pasta dishes such as a mesmerizing lamb ravioli with sausage, preserved lemon, harissa and crispy leeks. Desserts are amazingly intricate and well crafted, and the elaborate salads and a rich lobster omelet have made Sunday brunch as popular as the rest of the week. ⊠ *1700 Humboldt St.* ☎ *303/831–7310* ⊕ *www.stringsrestaurant.com* ⌲ *Reservations essential* ✛ *E2.*

$
VEGETARIAN
✗ **WaterCourse Foods.** In a town known for its beef, WaterCourse stands out as a devoted vegetarian eatery in spacious digs uptown. This casual, low-key place serves herbivores three meals a day, most of which are based on fruits, vegetables, whole grains, and meatlike soy substitutes. There are vegan and macrobiotic dishes available, along with choices for those who eat cheese and eggs. The Reuben, with sauerkraut, portobellos, and Swiss on grilled rye, is amazing, as are the seitan-based faux Buffalo wings. ⊠ *837 E. 17th Ave.* ☎ *303/832–7313* ⊕ *www.watercoursefoods.com* ✛ *E2.*

CENTRAL DOWNTOWN

¢
PIZZA
✗ **Anthony's Pizza & Pasta.** This two-story dive, with a standing counter as well as a sit-down dining area upstairs crammed with ramshackle chairs and tables in various stages of disrepair, is the closest Denver gets to a New York slice. Fold each triangle in half, tilt it to let it drip,

and inhale. Sweet- and-spicy-sauced spaghetti with a side of meatballs offers an alternative for those who don't want pizza. ✉ *1550 California St.* ☎ *303/573–6236* ⊕ *www.anthonyspizzaandpasta.com* ♥ *Closed Sun.* ✤ *C2.*

$$
GERMAN
✕ **Cafe Berlin.** A beloved German eatery in an inviting spot that sports a somewhat contemporary feel and a small bar that serves an extensive Schnaps roster. No fake beer-house stuff here, just traditional German fare: the potato pancakes taste like your (German) grandma made them, and the liver pâté and homemade German bread are as authentic as it gets. The kitchen attempts to lighten up heavy items such as dumplings, spaetzle, and Wiener schnitzel, and the sweet-and-sour cabbage is amazing. Check out the German beer roster, and finish off with an apple strudel. ✉ *323 14th St.* ☎ *303/377–5896* ⊕ *www.cafeberlindenver.com* ♥ *No lunch weekends* ✤ *D3.*

$$$
FRENCH
✕ **Le Chateau/La Fondue.** The former La Fondue has been transformed into a bright, open, airy space with a dual name that works well for pretheater dining considering the location, as long as you leave plenty of time for the experience. The pretheater prix-fixe menu is always $52.80 per person and includes salad, two entrée choices, and dessert, and there's a three-course prix-fixe menu for $18 per person that includes cheese and chocolate fondues and is particularly well suited to families. Service is snappy, friendly, and helpful, and the valet will hold your car until after the show. ✉ *1040 15th St.* ☎ *303/534–0404* ⊕ *www. lafonduedenver.com* ⌂ *Reservations essential* ♥ *No lunch* ✤ *B6.*

$$$$
STEAKHOUSE
✕ **Palm Restaurant.** This Denver outpost of the longtime New York steak house serves meat, seafood, pork chops, and other American dishes à la carte. The walls are bedecked with caricatures of local celebrities, and there's a chance you might see one in person—the restaurant is a favorite of local politicians, executives, and athletes, and with good reason: The steaks and the portions are both superlative. ✉ *1672 Lawrence St.* ☎ *303/825–7256* ⊕ *www.thepalm.com* ♥ *No lunch weekends* ✤ *B6.*

$$$
ITALIAN
✕ **Panzano.** This dining room in Hotel Monaco is filled with fresh flowers and windows that let in natural light, making the space cheerful and bright. Three meals a day are served, but it's lunch and dinner that focus on true Italian cuisine. Everything on the menu is multilayered, such as grilled flatbread topped with cheese, prosciutto, truffle oil and balsamic vinegar; or risotto made with an ever-changing and ever-pleasing variety of cheeses and fresh produce. The breads are baked in-house. The superior service and accommodating staff make for a pleasant dining experience. The large, roomy bar is available for dining, too. ✉ *909 17th St.* ☎ *303/296–3525* ⊕ *www.panzano-denver.com* ⌂ *Reservations essential* ✤ *B5.*

$$$
ITALIAN
✕ **Prima Ristorante.** The less expensive, whimsically decorated little sister of the upscale Restaurant Kevin Taylor also resides in the Hotel Teatro. With its Italian opera prints, curvaceous mezzanine, and black-granite bar, Prima appeals to lovers of modern Italian fare. The menu focuses on upscale renditions of contemporary classics, such as roasted garlic chicken with toasted farro and Angus sirloin with Gorgonzola potato gratin, and theatergoers love the one-block proximity to the Denver Performing Arts Complex. The weekend champagne brunch, which begins

2

with a full line of crudo and continues through an astounding selection of northern Italian specialties such as soft egg ravioli with truffle butter, draws a crowd. ✉ *1106 14th St.* ☎ *303/228–0770* ⊕ *www.ktrg.net* ♣ *Reservations essential* ✛ *A6.*

$$$$
MEDITERRANEAN
Fodor's Choice
★

✕ **Restaurant Kevin Taylor.** Elegant doesn't do justice to this restaurant's dining room, a classy, soothing space done in tones of gold and hunter green. Exclusive upholstery, flatware, and dishes add to the upscale attitude, as does the formal service style and a top-shelf wine list. The contemporary menu has an updated Mediterranean bent underscored by French techniques, with such classics as roasted lamb with sweet bread fricassee and roasted lobster tail with a foie gras emulsion. The tasting menu, geared to theatergoers heading to the Denver Performing Arts Complex a block away, provides a rare chance to try chef Taylor's eclectic creations, and the stone-lined wine cellar makes for intimate private dining. ✉ *1106 14th St.* ☎ *303/820–2600* ⊕ *www.ktrg.com* ♣ *Reservations essential* ☉ *Closed Sun. No lunch* ✛ *A6.*

$
DINER
☻

✕ **Sam's No. 3.** Greek immigrant Sam Armatas opened his first eatery in Denver in 1927, and his three sons use the same recipes Pop did in their updated version of his all-American diner, from the famous red and green chiles to the Coney Island–style hot dogs and the creamy rice pudding. The room is a combination of retro diner and a fancy Denny's, and the bar is crowded with theatergoers and hipsters after dark. Good luck choosing: the menu is 10 pages long, with Greek and Mexican favorites as well as diner classics. The chunky mashed potatoes rule, and breakfast, which is served all day, comes fast. ✉ *1500 Curtis St.* ☎ *303/534–1927* ⊕ *www.samsno3.com* ♣ *Reservations not accepted* ✛ *B6.*

¢
CAFÉ
☻

✕ **Spicy Pickle Sub Shop.** A spicy pickle does indeed come with every order at this hopping deli, which makes giant subs and panini, all filled with Boar's Head meats and house-made spreads. The breads are baked locally, and the side salads are good quality. Sit and eat in the casual space or take it to go. Come for lunch or an early dinner; they are open until 7 Monday to Thursday and 6 Friday to Sunday. Other locations are scattered around the Denver area. ✉ *988 Lincoln St.* ☎ *303/860–0730* ⊕ *www.spicypickle.com* ♣ *Reservations not accepted* ✛ *D3.*

CITY PARK AND ENVIRONS

$$$$
ITALIAN

✕ **Barolo Grill.** This restaurant looks like a chichi Italian farmhouse, with dried flowers in brass urns, hand-painted porcelain, and straw baskets everywhere. The food isn't pretentious in the least, however. It's more like Santa Monica meets San Stefano—bold yet classic, healthful yet flavorful. Duckling stewed in red wine; fresh pastas, including tagliatelle tossed with beef, veal and pork ragu; and risotto with lobster and shrimp, are all well made and fairly priced. The reasonably priced five-course tasting menu is a smart way to sample more of the kitchen's talents; although adding the wine pairings ups the cost, it also improves the value. ✉ *3030 E. 6th Ave.* ☎ *303/393–1040* ⊕ *www.barologrilldenver. com* ♣ *Reservations essential* ☉ *Closed Sun. and Mon. No lunch* ✛ *G4.*

$
SOUTHERN

✕ **Brother's BBQ.** Two brothers from England traveled the southern United States on a quest to learn everything there is to know about barbecue, and they decided to share the information with Denver. The result is some of the best 'cue in town, from St. Louis–style ribs to beef brisket, pulled pork, and chicken. The sauces are a mishmash of their favorites, including a vinegary one and a sweet one, and the baked beans use their smoked meats for extra flavor. Eat at one of the metal tables amid license plates and knickknacks from the boys' travels, or get it packed up nicely to go. ✉ *568 N. Washington St.* ☎ *720/570–4227* ⊕ *www.brothers-bbq.com* ⌖ *Reservations not accepted* ✢ *E4.*

$$$$
STEAKHOUSE

✕ **Buckhorn Exchange.** If hunting makes you queasy, don't enter this Denver landmark and taxidermy shrine, where 500 pairs of eyes stare down at you from the walls. The handsome men's-club look—with pressed-tin ceilings, burgundy walls, red-checker tablecloths, rodeo photos, shotguns, and those trophies—probably hasn't changed much since the Buckhorn first opened in 1893. Rumor has it that Buffalo Bill was to the Buckhorn what Norm Peterson was to *Cheers.* The dry-aged, prime-grade Colorado steaks are huge, juicy, and magnificent, as is the game. Try the smoked buffalo sausage or navy-bean soup to start. ✉ *1000 Osage St.* ☎ *303/534–9505* ⊕ *www.buckhornexchange.com* ⊘ *No lunch weekends* ✢ *C3.*

$$
AMERICAN

✕ **Dazzle Restaurant and Lounge.** If it's martinis and jazz you're after, come to this Art Deco space that allows for a groovy bar scene on one side and groovy dining on the other. The menu is as retro as the atmosphere, with an emphasis on comfort foods with a twist (check out the updated macaroni and cheese or the baked casserole dips) and small plates, and live music most nights makes this a laid-back spot. The cocktail roster, printed inside old jazz albums, is one of the most intricate around, and the Sunday jazz brunch swings. ✉ *930 Lincoln St.* ☎ *303/839–5100* ⊕ *www.dazzlejazz.com* ⊘ *No lunch Mon.–Thurs.* ✢ *D4.*

$$
JAPANESE

✕ **Domo.** Domo's owners pride themselves on fresh flavors and the painstaking preparation of Japanese country foods, as well as one of the largest sake selections in town. Everything is prepared to order, and it's worth the wait: this is where you can find some of Denver's best seafood, curry dishes, and vegetarian fare. The house specialty is *wankosushi*—three to five courses of sushi accompanied by rice, soup, and six of Domo's tantalizing side dishes. The restaurant also houses a cultural-education center, a museum, and a Japanese garden. ✉ *1365 Osage St.* ☎ *303/595–3666* ⊕ *www.domorestaurant.com* ✢ *B3.*

$$$
MODERN
AMERICAN

✕ **Fruition.** Well-crafted, elegant comfort food made from seasonal ingredients is served in compelling combinations, like grilled pork chops with a sweet corn and goat cheese pancake and prosciutto-wrapped scallops with shrimp toast. A nightly offering of two courses of delightful dishes includes many vegetarian options, but many diners choose to make a meal from the amazing appetizer roster. The two small but nicely spaced dining rooms are gently lighted for a warm-toned atmosphere that fades into the background, allowing the evening to focus on the food and the expertly chosen and fairly priced wine list. ✉ *1313 E. 6th Ave.* ☎ *303/831–1962* ⊕ *www.fruitionrestaurant.com* ⊘ *No lunch* ✢ *E4.*

$$
FRENCH

✕ **Le Central.** A real find, this homey bistro serves excellent mussel dishes and provincial French specialties, including beef bourguignonne (braised in red wine and garnished with mushrooms and onions), salmon *en croûte* (wrapped in pastry and baked), and steak au poivre. You can depend on Le Central for fabulous food, great service, and a surprisingly low tab. Weekend brunch is a big favorite. ✉ *112 E. 8th Ave.* ☎ *303/863–8094* ⊕ *www.lecentral.com* ✚ *D4.*

$$ ✕ **Little India.** The all-you-can-eat lunch buffet ($8.99), with dozens of
INDIAN well-prepared Indian dishes, is the big draw for Denverites at this casually elegant restaurant between downtown and Cherry Creek. Little India's menu has nearly 100 items, but it specializes in curries, vindaloos, and *biryanis,* all of which are expertly spiced. Be sure to try one of the specialty naans (tandoori-baked flat bread). The sweet mango *lassi,* a yogurt drink, is delightfully rich. ✉ *330 E. 6th Ave.* ☎ *303/871–9777* ⊕ *www.littleindiadenver.com* ✚ *D4.*

$$$$ ✕ **Luca d'Italia.** The restaurant's steel-gray, orange-and-red contemporary
ITALIAN decor belies the fact that it's one of the most authentic Italian restaurants in the city. Chef-owner Frank Bonanno summons the memory of his Italian grandmother to re-create small-town Italy through wild boar with pappardelle, goat-stuffed caramelle (pasta shaped like candy wrappers), and house-cured capocollo and homemade cheeses. His tiramisu and chocolate sorbet have to be tasted to be believed. Service, overseen by Jacqueline Bonanno, is as impeccable as at Bonanno's other restaurants, Mizuna and Osteria Marco, and the wine list is agreeably priced and heavy on interesting Italians. ✉ *711 Grant St.* ☎ *303/832–6600* ⊕ *www.lucadenver.com* ⌦ *Reservations essential* ☉ *Closed Sun. and Mon. No lunch* ✚ *D4.*

$$$$ ✕ **Mizuna.** Chef-owner Frank Bonanno knows how to transform butter
MODERN and cream into comforting masterpieces at this cozy eatery with warm
AMERICAN colors and intimate seating. His menu is reminiscent of California's
Fodor's Choice French Laundry—witness the foie gras tourchon and butter-poached
★ lobster—but his Italian heritage has given him the ability to work wonders with red sauce, such as in his inimitable ragout. Be sure to try the peanut butter cup for dessert, and expect to be served by the most professional staff, trained by Jacqueline Bonanno, in town. ✉ *225 E. 7th Ave.* ☎ *303/832–4778* ⊕ *www.mizunadenver.com* ⌦ *Reservations essential* ☉ *Closed Sun. and Mon. No lunch* ✚ *D4.*

GREATER DENVER

HIGHLAND

$$$ ✕ **Café Brazil.** This always-packed spot is worth the trip to Highland for
BRAZILIAN shrimp and scallops sautéed with fresh herbs, coconut milk, and hot chilis; *feijoda completa,* the Brazilian national dish of black-bean stew and smoked meats, accompanied with fried bananas; or grilled chicken breast in a sauce of palm oil, red chili, shallots, and coconut milk. There's a party style in this festive café with its vivid paintings and colorful traditional masks, and it's frequented by locals in the know. ✉ *4408 Lowell Blvd.* ☎ *303/480–1877* ⌦ *Reservations essential* ☉ *Closed Sun. and Mon. No lunch* ✚ *B1.*

$$$$ ✕ **Highland's Garden Café.** Chef-owner Pat Perry follows the philoso-
MODERN phy of Alice Waters and her famous Chez Panisse: use what's fresh
AMERICAN that day. The result is an ever-changing menu that takes advantage of Colorado's unique produce and meats, and Perry puts them together

in interesting and refreshing ways, as in her sea scallops with passion fruit glaze and grilled pineapple, kiwi and mango. And as the name implies, the outdoor patio is surrounded by elaborate gardens, and the inside dining rooms, which occupy two Victorian houses, are painted with trompe-l'oeil views into gardens as well. ⊠ *3927 W. 32nd Ave.* ☎ *303/458–5920* ⊕ *www.highlandsgardencafe.com* ⚐ *Reservations essential* ⊗ *Closed Mon.* ✛ *A1.*

$$$
MEXICAN
Fodor's Choice
★

✕ **LoLa Mexican Seafood.** This casual seafood eatery brings in a young, hip clientele, and provides a spectacular view of the city skyline from most of the sunny dining room, the bar, and the patio. Tableside guacamole, more than 90 tequilas, superior margaritas, and a clever, glass-lined bar area are just a few of the reasons the lovely LoLa remains a locals' hangout. The food is modern Mexican, with fresh seafood in *escabeche* (marinated, poached fish), *ceviche* (lime-cooked fish), and salads, as well as smoked rib eye and chicken *frito* (fried chicken). A Mexican-style brunch is served Saturday and Sunday. ⊠ *1575 Boulder St.* ☎ *720/570–8686* ⊕ *www.loladenver.com* ⚐ *Reservations essential* ⊗ *No lunch* ✛ *B1.*

NORTH DENVER

$
MEXICAN
☺

✕ **Jack-n-Grill.** The friendly family that runs this small, pepper-decorated place moved to Denver from New Mexico, and they brought their love of chilies with them. The green chile is fire-breathing spicy, and the red is a smoky, complex brew. The best item, though, is the plate of chicken or beef *vaquero* tacos, slathered with a sticky-sweet barbecue sauce and served on buttery tortillas. Get it with a bowl of freshly roasted corn off the cob. Lunch is always packed, so arrive early, and don't be afraid to tackle a gigantic breakfast burrito, either. There's a mean margarita and there are cervezas, too. ⊠ *2424 Federal Blvd.* ☎ *303/964–9544* ⊕ *www. jackngrill.com* ⚐ *Reservations essential* ✛ *A1.*

CHERRY CREEK

$$$$
STEAKHOUSE

✕ **Elway's.** You won't see the big guy here very often—or at the newer Ritz-Carlton-Denver location, either—but that doesn't keep hopeful sports fans from packing it in. But when the toothy-grinned former Broncos QB John Elway doesn't show, diners console themselves with some of the best steak-house fare in town, particularly the porterhouse (big enough for half a football team) and the huge side of chunky-creamy Yukon gold mashed potatoes. While you eat, ease back into the intimately set-up, camel-color suede booths and watch waterfalls cascade over granite slabs, choose from the pricey but appealing wine list, and save room for make-your-own s'mores. There's a second location in the Ritz-Carlton. ⊠ *2500 E. 1st Ave.* ☎ *303/399–5353* ⊕ *www. elways.com* ⚐ *Reservations essential* ✛ *F4.*

$$$
CHINESE

✕ **Little Ollie's.** Black dominates the glossy interior of the swank Ollie's, which has a large outdoor patio and exceptionally well-crafted Chinese food. The whole steamed sea bass in black-bean sauce is one of the menu's highlights, along with mu shu pork and crispy duck. Lunch specials make this a popular midday spot, and the wine list is unusually well chosen for a Chinese restaurant. Reservations are taken for parties of six or more. ✉ *2364 E. 3rd Ave., Cherry Creek North* ☎ *303/316–8888* ⊕ *www.littleolliescherrycreek.com* ✛ *F4.*

$$$
ITALIAN

✕ **NoRTH.** The beautiful people of Cherry Creek, young and old, flock to this jazzy space, the entire front of which opens to the sidewalk in nice weather. The space is decorated in what sound like food-themed Crayola colors: vanilla-white and sherbet-orange, lime-green and cocoa-brown, all setting diners up for a parade of savory dishes. Start with the paper-thin zucca chips—faintly oily, addictively crispy, deep-fried zucchini—and then move on to an entrée; pasta, fish, and meat are each kissed with just the right amounts of Mediterranean herbs and sauces. The staff is smiley and reflects the cheerful exuberance of the atmosphere, and the lively bar is usually packed three deep. ✉ *190 Clayton La.* ☎ *720/941–7700* ⊕ *www.foxrc.com* ⌫ *Reservations essential* ✛ *F4.*

SOUTH DENVER

$$$
JAPANESE
Fodor'sChoice
★

✕ **Sushi Den.** With a sister restaurant in Japan and owners who import sushi-grade seafood to the United States, it's easy to see why this chic sushi bar is the one Denverites count on to provide the best quality available. The sushi chefs here can meet your every request, and the cooked dishes are just as well prepared—don't miss the steamed fish baskets. Check out the tony crowd and feast your eyes on the luxurious fabrics and well-designed furniture. There's almost always a wait to get in, and parking can be a hassle, but for serious sushi-heads this is the place to be. From Sunday through Thursday they'll accept a reservation for parties of five or more. ✉ *1487 S. Pearl St.* ☎ *303/777–0826* ⊕ *www.sushiden.net* ⊘ *No lunch weekends* ✛ *D6.*

EAST DENVER

$$
ECLECTIC

✕ **Cork House Wine Restaurant.** Two veteran Denver restaurateurs took over the beloved, 30-year-old Tante Louise and turned it into a popular small-plate place (they also serve plenty of large plates, too), gently renovating it into a slightly-more-contemporary space that invites snacking with a glass of wine from the lengthy, well-priced roster. The wine bar offers 25 to 30 cheeses a night, with fresh breads, pâtés, and other appetizers, and the staff is adept at matching the international vino with the eclectic victuals. ✉ *4900 E. Colfax Ave.* ☎ *303/355–4488* ⊕ *www.corkhousedenver.com* ⊘ *Closed Sunday. No lunch* ✛ *H3.*

WEST DENVER

$
CHINESE

✕ **King's Land Seafood Restaurant.** Like a Chinese eatery in New York or San Francisco, King's Land does dim sum to perfection, serving it daily during the week for lunch and during their crazy, jam-packed weekends. Choose from dozens of dumplings, buns, and steamed dishes that are wheeled to you on carts, or go with the regular menu, also available at night, which includes delectable duck and seafood specialties. The dining room is huge and always noisy, and the staff doesn't speak much English. Just close your eyes and point. Reservations are accepted for parties of six or more. ✉ *2200 W. Alameda Ave.* ☎ *303/975–2399* ✛ *B3.*

$$$
VIETNAMESE

✕ **New Saigon.** Denver's best Vietnamese, New Saigon is always crowded with folks trying to get at their crispy egg rolls, shrimp-filled spring rolls, and cheap but hefty noodle bowls. With nearly 200 dishes on the menu, this vast, avocado-color eatery has everything Vietnamese covered, including 30-some vegetarian dishes and 10 with succulent frogs' legs. Service can be spotty, and not much English is spoken, but the staff goes overboard trying to help and never steers anyone wrong. It's best to go at off times to ensure a seat. Reservations are accepted for parties of six or more. ✉ *630 S. Federal Blvd.* ☎ *303/936–4954* ⊕ *www. newsaigon.com* ✿ *Closed Mon.* ✛ *A3.*

MORRISON

$$$$
STEAKHOUSE
Fodor's Choice
★

✕ **The Fort Restaurant.** This adobe structure, complete with flickering luminarias and a pinyon-pine bonfire in the courtyard, is a perfect reproduction of Bent's Fort, a Colorado fur-trade center. Buffalo meat and game are the specialties; the elk with huckleberry sauce and tequila-marinated quail are especially good. Intrepid eaters might try the buffalo bone-marrow appetizer, fiery peanut-butter–stuffed jalapeños, or Rocky Mountain oysters. Costumed characters from the fur trade wander the restaurant, playing the mandolin and telling tall tales. ✉ *19192 Hwy. 8, Morrison* ☎ *303/697–4771* ⊕ *www.thefort.com* ⚔ *Reservations essential* ✿ *No lunch* ✛ *A6.*

WHERE TO STAY

For expanded hotel reviews, visit Fodors.com.

Denver's lodging choices include the stately Brown Palace, bed-and-breakfasts, and business hotels. Unless you're planning a quick escape to the mountains, consider staying in or around downtown, where most of the city's attractions are within walking distance. Many of the hotels cater to business travelers, with accordingly lower rates on weekends—many establishments slash their rates in half on Friday and Saturday. The three hotels in the vicinity of Cherry Creek are about a 10- to 15-minute drive from downtown.

WHAT IT COSTS				
	¢	$	$$	$$$	$$$$
For two people	under $80	$80–$120	$121–$170	$171–$230	over $230

Prices are for two people in a standard double room in high season, excluding service charges and 14.85% tax.

Use the coordinate (✛ B2) at the end of each listing to locate a site on the corresponding map.

DOWNTOWN

LODO

$$$$
HOTEL
Fodor's Choice
★

⌖ **Brown Palace.** This grande dame of Colorado lodging has hosted public figures from President Eisenhower to the Beatles since it first opened its doors in 1892, and the details are exquisite: a dramatic nine-story lobby is topped with a glorious stained-glass ceiling, and the Victorian rooms have sophisticated wainscoting and Art Deco fixtures. **Pros:** sleeping here feels like being part of history; exceptional service; spacious and comfortable rooms. **Cons:** one of the most expensive hotels in

2

Denver; parking costs extra. ⊠ *321 17th St.* ☎ *303/297–3111, 800/321–2599* ⊕ *www.brownpalace.com* ⊃ *205 rooms, 36 suites* ⚎ *In-room: Internet. In-hotel: restaurant, bar, gym, spa, business center, parking* ⦵ *No meals* ✛ *D2.*

$$
B&B/INN

🏨 **Gregory Inn LoDo.** Decorated to resemble an old English inn, the Gregory in the Curtis Park neighborhood captures Old World charm through the use of mossy colors and exquisite linens and accents. **Pros:** a few blocks removed from downtown's bustle; inviting setting; excellent breakfasts. **Cons:** extra blocks from downtown center mean more walking; no young children. ⊠ *2500 Arapahoe St.* ☎ *303/295–6570, 800/925–6570* ⊕ *www.gregoryinn.com* ⊃ *8 rooms, 1 suite* ⚎ *In-room: Wi-Fi. In-hotel: business center, some age restrictions* ⦵ *Breakfast* ✛ *D1.*

$$$
HOTEL
Fodor'sChoice
★

🏨 **Oxford Hotel.** During the Victorian era this hotel was an elegant fixture on the Denver landscape, and civilized touches like complimentary shoe shines, afternoon sherry, and morning coffee remain. **Pros:** prime LoDo location; gorgeous historic setting; great restaurants on-site and nearby. **Cons:** noisy ballpark crowds in-season turn LoDo area into a big party. ⊠ *1600 17th St.* ☎ *303/628–5400, 800/228–5838* ⊕ *www.theoxfordhotel.com* ⊃ *79 rooms, 1 suite* ⚎ *In-room: Internet, Wi-Fi. In-hotel: restaurant, bar, gym, spa, business center, parking* ⦵ *No meals* ✛ *A5.*

CAPITOL HILL

$
B&B/INN

🏨 **Adagio Bed & Breakfast.** The music room of this 1892 Victorian mansion has a grand piano, and rooms are named after composers. **Pros:** breakfast available when you want it; pretty, cozy rooms; within driving distance of major attractions. **Cons:** not within walking distance of downtown or Cherry Creek; limited amenities due to size. ⊠ *1430 Race St.* ☎ *303/370–6911, 800/533–4640* ⊕ *www.adagiobb.com* ⊃ *6 rooms, 1 suite* ⚎ *In-room: Internet, Wi-Fi. In-hotel: business center* ⦵ *Some meals* ✛ *F3.*

$$
HOTEL
☾

🏨 **The Burnsley.** This 16-story Bauhaus-style tower is a haven for visitors seeking peace and quiet; it's a few blocks south of the State Capitol. **Pros:** family-friendly; good for business travelers; convenient location. **Cons:** rooms are somewhat plain. ⊠ *1000 Grant St.* ☎ *303/830–1000, 800/231–3915* ⊕ *www.burnsley.com* ⊃ *80 suites* ⚎ *In-room: kitchen, Internet. In-hotel: restaurant, bar, pool, business center, parking, some pets allowed* ⦵ *No meals* ✛ *D3.*

$
B&B/INN

🏨 **Capitol Hill Mansion Bed & Breakfast Inn.** The dramatic turret and intense rust color of this Richardson Romanesque Victorian mansion built in 1891 is enough to draw you into the eight elegantly appointed rooms done in varying themes, such as Rocky Mountain, Victorian, and Colonial. **Pros:** welcoming hosts; inviting rooms. **Cons:** walls are thin; place feels remote compared to rest of downtown. ⊠ *1207 Pennsylvania St.* ☎ *303/839–5221, 800/839–9329* ⊕ *www.capitolhillmansion.com* ⊃ *5 rooms, 3 suites* ⚎ *In-room: Internet, Wi-Fi. In-hotel: business center* ⦵ *Breakfast* ✛ *D3.*

$
B&B/INN
☾

🏨 **Holiday Chalet B&B.** Stained-glass windows and homey accents throughout make this 1896 Victorian brownstone in Capitol Hill, the neighborhood immediately east of downtown, exceptionally appealing. **Pros:** welcoming staff; delightful teas; enchanting style. **Cons:** parking can be a challenge. ✉ *1820 E. Colfax Ave.* ☎ *303/437–8245* ⊕ *www. denver-bed-breakfast.com* ➷ *10 rooms* ♿ *In-room: kitchen, Internet, Wi-Fi. In-hotel: business center, some pets allowed* ⭕ *Breakfast* ✛ *F3.*

$ 🏨 **Ramada Limited Capitol Hill.** As the name suggests, this Ramada is HOTEL within walking distance of the State Capitol, as well as nine blocks east of downtown and the 16th Street Mall. **Pros:** very reasonable rates; easy to get downtown. **Cons:** not the safest part of Colfax Avenue late at night. ✉ *1150 E. Colfax Ave.* ☎ *303/831–7700, 800/272–6232* ⊕ *www.ramada.com* ➷ *135 rooms, 8 suites* ♿ *In-room: safe, Internet, Wi-Fi. In-hotel: restaurant, bar, pool, gym, parking, some pets allowed* ⭕ *No meals* ✛ *E3.*

CENTRAL DOWNTOWN

$$$$ 🏨 **Courtyard by Marriott.** This stunning building (it used to be Joslins HOTEL Department Store) sits right on the 16th Street Mall, which means everything downtown is a few blocks or a free Mall shuttle away. **Pros:** great location and views; deluxe rooms have sofabeds. **Cons:** pricey; rooms nothing fancy. ✉ *934 16th St.* ☎ *303/571–1114, 888/249–1810* ⊕ *www.marriott.com* ➷ *166 rooms, 11 suites* ♿ *In-room: Internet, Wi-Fi. In-hotel: restaurant, bar, pool, gym, business center, parking* ⭕ *No meals* ✛ *B6.*

$$$ 🏨 **The Curtis.** Each floor here has a pop-culture theme, from classic HOTEL cars to TV to science fiction, and the rooms are spacious and groovy, ☾ with speakers for your MP3 player and comfy, mod furnishings. **Pros:** across the street from Denver Performing Arts Complex; kid-friendly; reasonably priced for location. **Cons:** can be noisy; high-traffic area; staff not always helpful. ✉ *1405 Curtis St.* ☎ *303/571–0300, 800/525–6651* ⊕ *www.thecurtis.com* ➷ *334 rooms, 2 suites* ♿ *In-room: Internet, Wi-Fi. In-hotel: restaurant, bar, pool, business center, parking, some pets allowed* ✛ *B6.*

$$$$ 🏨 **Denver Marriott City Center.** Definitely geared toward the business trav- HOTEL eler, the Denver Marriott is a three-block walk from the Denver Convention Complex and has 25,000 square feet of meeting space of its own. **Pros:** nice gym and pool; close to the convention center. **Cons:** not much maneuvering space in the rooms; prices have gone up. ✉ *1701 California St.* ☎ *303/297–1300, 800/228–9290* ⊕ *www.denvermarriott. com* ➷ *601 rooms, 14 suites* ♿ *In-room: Internet, Wi-Fi. In-hotel: restaurant, bar, pool, gym, spa, business center, parking* ⭕ *No meals* ✛ *C6.*

$$$$ 🏨 **Grand Hyatt.** Close to Larimer Square, the theaters, the 16th Street HOTEL Mall, and the Colorado Convention Center—downtown locations don't ☾ get much better than this. **Pros:** great views from top floors; prime location; top-notch gym; lavish concierge lounge services. **Cons:** restaurant is inconsistent. ✉ *1750 Welton St.* ☎ *303/295–1234, 800/233–1234* ⊕ *www.grandhyattdenver.com* ➷ *473 rooms, 43 suites* ♿ *In-room: Internet. In-hotel: restaurant, pool, gym, business center, parking, some pets allowed* ✛ *D2.*

$$$ 🏨 **Hotel Monaco.** Celebrities and business travelers check into this hip HOTEL property, which occupies the historic 1917 Railway Exchange Building ★ and the 1937 Art Moderne Title Building, for the modern perks and Art Deco–meets–classic French style. **Pros:** one of the pet-friendliest hotels in town; welcoming complimentary wine hour; central location.

Cons: may be too pet-friendly; hotel has decidedly business rather than romantic feel. ✉ *1717 Champa St.* ☎ *303/296–1717, 800/990–1303* ⊕ *www.monaco-denver.com* ⤸ *157 rooms, 32 suites* ⚒ *In-room: Internet, Wi-Fi. In-hotel: restaurant, bar, gym, spa, business center, parking, some pets allowed* �‖�‖ *No meals* ✛ *C6.*

$$$$
HOTEL
★

⬚ Hotel Teatro. Black-and-white photographs, costumes, and scenery from plays that were staged in the Denver Performing Arts Complex across the street decorate the grand public areas of this hotel. **Pros:** great location for theater and other downtown pursuits; excellent restaurants; lovely rooms and hotel spaces. **Cons:** noisy and chaotic area; costly parking; some rooms are tiny. ✉ *1100 14th St.* ☎ *303/228–1100, 888/727–1200* ⊕ *www.hotelteatro.com* ⤸ *104 rooms, 6 suites* ⚒ *In-room: Internet, Wi-Fi. In-hotel: restaurant, bar, gym, parking, some pets allowed* ✛ *A6.*

$$$
HOTEL

⬚ Magnolia Hotel. The Denver outpost of this Texas-based chain has spacious, elegant rooms with sophisticated furnishings—some with fireplaces—and warm colors, all built within the confines of the 1906 former American Bank Building. **Pros:** pretty, comfortable rooms; nice complimentary breakfast buffet; good restaurants. **Cons:** although classy, can feel like a generic chain hotel. ✉ *818 17th St.* ☎ *303/607–9000, 888/915–1110* ⊕ *www.magnoliahoteldenver.com* ⤸ *127 rooms, 119 suites* ⚒ *In-room: Internet, Wi-Fi. In-hotel: restaurant, room service, bar, gym, business center, parking* �‖�‖ *Breakfast* ✛ *C6.*

$$
B&B/INN

⬚ Queen Anne Inn. Just north of downtown in the regentrified Clements historic district (some of the neighboring blocks have yet to be reclaimed), this inn made up of adjacent Victorians is a delightful, romantic getaway. **Pros:** lovely rooms; welcoming hosts; hearty fare. **Cons:** not right downtown. ✉ *2147 Tremont Pl., Central Downtown* ☎ *303/296–6666, 800/432–4667* ⊕ *www.queenannebnb.com* ⤸ *10 rooms, 4 suites* ⚒ *In-room: Internet. In-hotel: business center* �‖�‖ *Breakfast* ✛ *D2.*

$$$$
HOTEL

⬚ The Ritz-Carlton, Denver. This beautiful property features warm woods, elaborate glass fixtures, and luxurious details, and the pampering service is typical of the chain. **Pros:** gracious service; room-service fare delicious and prompt; inviting public spaces. **Cons:** fitness-center staff not as service oriented as hotel's; pricey; feels away from the action. ✉ *1881 Curtis St.* ☎ *303/312–3800* ⊕ *www.ritzcarlton.com* ⤸ *155 rooms, 47 suites* ⚒ *In-room: safe, Wi-Fi. In-hotel: restaurant, room service, bar, pool, gym, spa, business center, parking, some pets allowed* ✛ *B5.*

$$$
HOTEL

⬚ Sheraton Denver Downtown Hotel. Guest rooms at the ever-bustling Sheraton are roomy and streamlined, with unfussy furniture and nice workstations that appeal primarily to the business traveler. **Pros:** great location; many amenities; friendly and accommodating staff. **Cons:** front area where cars come in is chaos central; feels like nothing but conventions. ✉ *1550 Court Pl.* ☎ *303/893–3333, 866/716–8134* ⊕ *www.sheratondenverhotel.com* ⤸ *1,149 rooms, 82 suites* ⚒ *In-room: Internet. In-hotel: restaurants, bar, pool, gym, business center, parking* ✛ *D3.*

$$
HOTEL

⬚ Warwick Denver Hotel. This stylish midsize business hotel is ideally located on the edge of downtown, and the last touches from a long-term remodel finds the spacious rooms further updated with comfortable beds and the latest in high-tech perks to complement the brass and mahogany furnishings and roomy marble bathrooms. **Pros:** reasonable rates; motivated and friendly staff; oversize rooms. **Cons:** more than walking distance from the business district; low rates sometimes attract large, noisy groups. ⊠ *1776 Grant St.* ☎ *303/861–2000, 800/525–2888* ⊕ *www.warwickdenver.com* ⤴ *103 rooms, 58 suites* ⚭ *In-room: safe, Wi-Fi. In-hotel: restaurant, bar, pool, gym, business center, parking, some pets allowed* ⊕ *D2.*

$$$
HOTEL
★

⬚ **Westin Tabor Center.** This sleek, luxurious high-rise opens right onto the 16th Street Mall and all the downtown action. **Pros:** convenient location on Mall; contemporary rooms; nice pool with great city view. **Cons:** the Palm is pricey; breakfast options are also expensive. ⊠ *1672 Lawrence St.* ☎ *303/572–9100, 800/937–8461* ⊕ *www.westin.com* ⤴ *430 rooms* ⚭ *In-room: Internet. In-hotel: restaurant, bar, pool, gym, business center, parking* ⦿ *No meals* ⊕ *B5.*

GREATER DENVER

CHERRY CREEK

$
HOTEL

⬚ **Holiday Inn Select Denver/Cherry Creek.** The Cherry Creek shopping district is 4 mi away, and the major museums and the zoo a five-minute drive from this bustling hotel, which provides coveted mountain views from many of its rooms. **Pros:** good for business travelers; Starbucks on-site; location bridges gap for folks who want both museums and downtown. **Cons:** not walking distance to any attractions; far from downtown. ⊠ *455 S. Colorado Blvd.* ☎ *303/388–5561, 800/388–6129* ⊕ *www.cherrycreekhoteldenver.com* ⤴ *269 rooms, 7 suites* ⚭ *In-room: Internet. In-hotel: restaurant, bar, pool, gym, parking* ⦿ *No meals* ⊕ *G6.*

$$$$
HOTEL

⬚ **JW Marriott Denver at Cherry Creek.** The hip atmosphere and location smack in the middle of Cherry Creek's shopping district has made this upscale outpost of the Marriott family popular with tourists and locals alike. **Pros:** friendly staff; great location for shopping; bus to downtown a block away. **Cons:** feels very much like a chain; feels far from downtown; pricey. ⊠ *150 Clayton La.* ☎ *303/316–2700* ⊕ *www.marriott.com* ⤴ *191 rooms, 5 suites* ⚭ *In-room: safe, Internet, Wi-Fi. In-hotel: restaurant, bar, pool, gym, spa, laundry facilities, parking, some pets allowed* ⦿ *No meals* ⊕ *F4.*

$$
HOTEL

⬚ **Loews Denver Hotel.** The 12-story steel-and-black-glass facade conceals the unexpected and delightful Italian baroque motif within; spacious rooms are done in earth tones and blond wood and garnished with fresh flowers, fruit baskets, and Renaissance-style portraits. **Pros:** gorgeous rooms and public spaces; wonderful restaurant; gracious staff. **Cons:** not near downtown; eatery pricey. ⊠ *4150 E. Mississippi Ave., Southeast Denver* ☎ *303/782–9300, 800/345–9172* ⊕ *www.loewshotels.com* ⤴ *183 rooms, 17 suites* ⚭ *In-room: safe, Internet. In-hotel: restaurant, bar, gym, business center, parking* ⦿ *Breakfast* ⊕ *H6.*

WEST DENVER

$ Hotel VQ at Mile High. A stone's throw from Sports Authority Field
HOTEL   at Mile High, the Hotel VQ provides free parking and complimentary
shuttles to downtown, half a mile away. **Pros:** reasonable rates; easy
highway access; spacious rooms. **Cons:** rooms feel dated; traffic during rush hours can be a nightmare. ⊠ *1975 Mile High Stadium Cir.*
☎ *303/433–8331, 800/388–5381* ⊕ *www.hotelvq.com* ⮭ *169 rooms*
⚘ *In-room: Wi-Fi. In-hotel: restaurant, bar, pool, gym, laundry facilities, parking, some pets allowed* �📶 *No meals* ✛ *A2.*

NIGHTLIFE AND THE ARTS

Friday's *Denver Post* (⊕ *www.denverpost.com*) publishes a calendar of
the week's events, as does the slightly alternative *Westword* (⊕ *www.
westword.com*), which is free and published on Thursday. Downtown
and LoDo are where most Denverites go at night. Downtown has more
mainstream entertainment, whereas LoDo is home to fun, funky rock
clubs and small theaters. Remember that Denver's altitude can intensify
your reaction to alcohol.

TicketMaster. The ubiquitous TicketMaster is Denver's prime agency,
selling tickets to almost all concerts, sporting events, and plays that
take place in the Denver area. ☎ *800/745–3000* ⊕ *ticketmaster.com.*

THE ARTS

PERFORMANCE VENUES

★   **Denver Performing Arts Complex.** The Denver Performing Arts Complex
is a huge, impressively high-tech group of theaters connected by a soaring glass archway to a futuristic symphony hall. The complex, which
occupies a four-block area, hosts more events than any other performing
arts center in the world. Run by the Denver Center for the Performing
Arts since 1972, the complex's anchors are the round, relaxing Temple
Hoyne Buell Theatre, built in 1991, and the more impressive, ornate
Auditorium Theatre, built in 1908. Both host large events, from classical orchestras to Jay Leno to *Wicked*. Some of the other five theaters
include the small Garner Galleria Theatre, where the comedy *I Love
You, You're Perfect, Now Change* once packed the house for more than
four years running, and the midsize Space Theatre. Both the ballet and
opera have their seasons here. Guided tours for groups of five or more
are available by appointment only. ⊠ *Box office, 1101 13th St., LoDo*
☎ *303/893–4100, 800/641–1222* ⊕ *www.denvercenter.org.*

Paramount Theatre. Downtown, the Paramount Theatre is the venue for
large-scale rock concerts. Designed by renowned local architect Temple
H. Buell in the Art Deco style in 1930, the lovingly maintained Paramount is both an elegant place to see shows and a rowdy, beer-serving
party location for rock fans. ⊠ *1631 Glenarm Pl., LoDo* ☎ *303/623–
0106* ⊕ *www.denverparamount.com.*

Fodor's Choice   **Red Rocks Amphitheatre.** The exquisite 9,000-seat Red Rocks Amphi-
★   theatre, amid majestic geological formations in nearby Morrison,
is renowned for its natural acoustics, which have awed the likes of

Leopold Stokowski and the Beatles. Although Red Rocks is one of the best places in the country to hear live music, be sure to leave extra time when visiting—parking is sparse, crowds are thick, paths are long and extremely uphill, and seating is usually general admission. ⊠ *17598 W. Alameda Pkwy., Morrison ✛ off U.S. 285 or I–70* ☎ *303/640–2637* ⊕ *www.redrocksonline.com.*

SYMPHONY, OPERA, AND DANCE

Colorado's premier orchestra, opera company, and ballet company are all in residence at the Denver Performing Arts Complex.

Colorado Symphony Orchestra. The Colorado Symphony Orchestra performs September to June in the Boettcher Concert Hall. ⊠ *13th and Curtis Sts., LoDo* ☎ *303/623–7876.*

Opera Colorado. Opera Colorado has a spring season, often with internationally renowned artists, in the magnificent Ellie Caulkins Opera House in the renovated Newton Auditorium. Already world-renowned for its superior acoustics and a Figaro seat-back titling system that allows attendees to follow the text of the opera, the cherrywood-accented theater has red-velvet seating and a lyre shape, ideal for full-bodied sound travel. ⊠ *950 13th St., Downtown* ☎ *303/778–1500* ⊕ *www.operacolorado.org.*

Colorado Ballet. The Colorado Ballet specializes in the classics with performances from September to April, primarily at the Ellie Caulkins Opera House. ⊠ *1278 Lincoln St., Downtown* ☎ *303/837–8888* ⊕ *www.coloradoballet.org.*

THEATER

Bug Theatre Company. This company produces primarily cutting-edge, original works in Denver's Highland neighborhood. ⊠ *3654 Navajo St., Highland* ☎ *303/477–9984.*

Denver Center Attractions. Denver Center Attractions brings Broadway road companies to town. ⊠ *14th and Curtis Sts., at DPCA's Temple Hoyne Buell and Auditorium theaters, LoDo* ☎ *303/893–4100.*

Denver Center Theater Company. This company presents high-caliber repertory theater, including new works by promising playwrights, at the Bonfils Theatre Complex, part of the Denver Performing Arts Complex. ⊠ *14th and Curtis Sts., LoDo* ☎ *303/893–4100, 800/641–1222.*

El Centro Su Teatro. El Centro Su Teatro is a Latino-Chicano company that puts on mostly original works and festivals during its May to September season at the Denver Civic Theater. ⊠ *721 Santa Fe Dr., Lincoln Park* ☎ *303/296–0219.*

Theatre Productions. Theatre Productions has made a name for itself locally by presenting top-notch adaptations of nationally regarded comedies and dramas, such as *Angels in America*. ⊠ *Vintage Theatre, 2119 E. 17th Ave., City Park* ☎ *303/839–1361.*

NIGHTLIFE

BARS AND BREWPUBS

Denver ChopHouse & Brewery. This high-end microbrewery is on the site of the old Union Pacific Railroad headhouse—with the train paraphernalia to prove it. It's a bit expensive for a brewpub, but if you hang out after Broncos games you might encounter local sports celebrities celebrating or commiserating. ✉ *1735 19th St., LoDo* ☎ *303/296–0800* ⊕ *www.chophouse.com.*

Mynt Mojito Lounge. Mynt Mojito Lounge has established a chichi reputation with its namesake mojitos, Miami-style pastel colors, and fruity martinis—try the Strawberry Banana. ✉ *1424 Market St., LoDo* ☎ *303/825–6968* ⊕ *www.myntmojitolounge.com.*

PS Lounge. Considered by some Denverites as the best bar in town, the laid-back, casual, slightly divey PS Lounge has a well-stocked jukebox and an owner, known to all simply as Pete, who hands out a free shot to anyone who behaves and seems to be having a good time. ✉ *3416 E. Colfax Ave.* ☎ *303/320–1200.*

Rock Bottom Brewery. Rock Bottom Brewery is a perennial favorite, thanks to its rotating special brews and reasonably priced pub grub. ✉ *1001 16th St., LoDo* ☎ *303/534–7616* ⊕ *www.rockbottom.com.*

Skylark Lounge. A vintage-style poolroom is just one reason to stop by the beloved Skylark Lounge, which counts live music, pinball machines, comfortable seating, and friendly staffers among its many charms. ✉ *140 S. Broadway, South Denver* ☎ *303/722–7844* ⊕ *www.skylarklounge.com.*

Wynkoop Brewing Co. The Wynkoop Brewing Co. is now more famous for its founder—Colorado governor and former Denver mayor John Hickenlooper—than for its brews, food, or ambience. But it remains one of the city's best-known bars—a relaxing, slightly upscale, two-story joint filled with halfway-decent bar food, the usual pool tables, and games and beers of all types. It has anchored LoDo since it was a pre-Coors Field warehouse district. ✉ *1634 18th St., LoDo* ☎ *303/297–2700* ⊕ *www.wynkoop.com.*

BEERDRINKER OF THE YEAR

Though it's a title many have tried to usurp, only one person (at a time) can truly be the Beerdrinker of the Year, as determined by Wynkoop Brewing Company and its panel of local and national judges, who wear British wigs and robes during the finals. Begun in 1997 by then-owner and current Colorado governor John Hickenlooper, the annual event draws contestants from all over the country, who are required to submit beer résumés and undergo a rigorous battery of tests and contests to determine their beery worthiness. Winners receive free beer for life at Wynkoop, not to mention bragging rights.

COMEDY CLUBS

Bovine Metropolis Theater. Eight times a week, a rotating cast of characters offers improv at Bovine Metropolis Theater, which also stages satirical productions and teaches classes in the genre. ✉ *1527 Champa St., LoDo* ☎ *303/758–4722* ⊕ *www.bovinemetropolis.com.*

Comedy Works. Denver comics have honed their skills at Comedy Works for more than 20 years. Well-known performers often drop by. ✉ *1226 15th St., LoDo* ☎ *303/595–3637* ⊕ *www.comedyworks.com.*

Impulse Theater. Downstairs in the Wynkoop brewpub, at the Impulse Theater, the audience is invited to participate in interactive improv comedy and theater, and touring stand-up comics and local acts provide entertainment through physical comedy and other routines. ✉ *1634 18th St., LoDo* ☎ *303/297–2111* ⊕ *www.impulsetheater.com.*

COUNTRY MUSIC CLUBS

Grizzly Rose. The Grizzly Rose has miles of dance floor, national bands, and gives two-step dancing lessons—and sells plenty of Western wear, from cowboy boots to spurs. Classic-rock bands are big, in addition to country acts big and small. Sunday nights are for all ages. ✉ *5450 N. Valley Hwy., I–25 at Exit 215, Globeville* ☎ *303/295–1330* ⊕ *www. grizzlyrose.com.*

Stampede Grill & Dance Emporium. The suburban Stampede Grill & Dance Emporium is another cavernous boot-scooting spot, with dance lessons and a restaurant. ✉ *2430 S. Havana St., Aurora* ☎ *303/696–7986* ⊕ *www.stampedeclub.net.*

DANCE CLUBS

The Church. Multiple rooms on three floors in a decommissioned church offer up DJ-spun techno, trance, rave and other dance music four nights a week. ✉ *1160 Lincoln St., Capitol Hill* ☎ *303/832–3528.*

Funky Buddha Lounge. The Funky Buddha Lounge distinguishes itself with two outdoor rooftop bars for dancing and mingling, with live DJs six nights a week. ✉ *776 Lincoln St., Capitol Hill* ☎ *303/832–5075.*

La Rumba. La Rumba offers up "Lipgloss," a DJ-spun frenzy of Brit-pop, soul, and rock on Friday nights in its cavernous industrial space, while Thursday and Saturday nights find salsa, meringue, and other Mambo King moves happening. ✉ *99 W. 9th Ave., Golden Triangle* ☎ *303/572–8006* ⊕ *www.larumba-denver.com.*

GAY BARS

Charlie's. Charlie's has country-western atmosphere and music. ✉ *900 E. Colfax Ave., Capitol Hill* ☎ *303/839–8890* ⊕ *www.charliesdenver.com.*

JR's Bar & Grill. JR's Bar & Grill features theme nights like retro and trivia, a raucous atmosphere, and a huge, long patio—with neighborhood people-watching—in nice weather. ✉ *777 E. 17th Ave., Central Denver* ☎ *303/831–0459.*

JAZZ CLUBS

El Chapultepec. El Chapultepec is a cramped, fluorescent-lighted, bargain-basement Mexican dive. Still, the limos parked outside hint at its enduring popularity: this is where Ol' Blue Eyes used to pop in, and where

CLOSE UP

Denver Rock History

Colorado's moments of pop-music history have been spectacular. Many happened at Red Rocks Amphitheatre, where the Beatles performed in 1964 and U2's Bono made his famous "this song is not a rebel song—this song is 'Sunday Bloody Sunday'" speech in 1983. The Denver–Boulder area was a huge hub for country-rock in the 1970s, and members of the Eagles, Poco, Firefall, and others lived here, at least briefly. Some of the most famous spots have closed, but rock fans can tour the hallowed ground—Ebbets Field, where Steve Martin and Lynyrd Skynyrd made early-career appearances in the 1970s, at 15th and Curtis; and the original Auditorium Theatre, where Led Zeppelin performed its first U.S. show in 1968, at 14th and Curtis. The local scene remains strong, with the Fray, the Flobots, the Samples, Big Head Todd and the Monsters, Leftover Salmon, String Cheese Incident, Apples In Stereo, and Dressy Bessy attracting audiences. Check *Westword* or *the Denver Post* for show listings.

visiting musicians, including the Marsalis brothers, continue to jam after hours. Cash only. ⊠ *1962 Market St., LoDo* ☎ *303/295–9126.*

★ **Dazzle Restaurant and Lounge.** Dazzle Restaurant and Lounge is a cozy, casual spot for nightly live jazz in the Golden Triangle. *Downbeat* magazine has named it one of the 100 best jazz clubs in the world; it offers acoustically treated walls in the dining room and the lounge, where the audience is up close and personal with the musicians. ⊠ *930 Lincoln St., Central Denver* ☎ *303/839–5100* ⊕ *www.dazzlejazz.com.*

Herb's Hideout. Hidden in the back of a parking lot, the hipster favorite Herb's Hideout is a gloriously nostalgic bar with dim lighting and checkerboard floors. ⊠ *2057 Larimer St., LoDo* ☎ *303/299–9555* ⊕ *www.herbsbar.com.*

ROCK CLUBS

Bluebird Theater. Of Denver's numerous old-school music hangouts, the most popular is the regally restored Bluebird Theater, which showcases local and national acts, emphasizing rock, hip-hop, ambient, and the occasional evening of cinema. ⊠ *3317 E. Colfax Ave., Capitol Hill* ☎ *303/377–1666* ⊕ *www.bluebirdtheater.net.*

Fillmore Auditorium. The Fillmore Auditorium, Denver's classic San Francisco concert hall spin-off, looks dumpy on the outside but is elegant and impressive inside. Before catching a big-name act such as Coldplay, Snoop Dogg or Mumford & Sons, scan the walls for color photographs of past club performers. ⊠ *1510 Clarkson St., Capitol Hill* ☎ *303/837–1482* ⊕ *www.livenation.com.*

Gothic Theatre. The Gothic Theatre came of age in the early '90s, with a steady stream of soon-to-be-famous alternative-rock acts such as Nirvana and the Red Hot Chili Peppers. It has since reinvented itself as a community venue for theater, music, and charity events, and sits south of downtown. ⊠ *3263 S. Broadway, Englewood* ☎ *303/788–0984* ⊕ *www.gothictheatre.com.*

Herman's Hideaway. Down-home Herman's Hideaway showcases mostly local rock in a south Denver neighborhood, with a smattering of reggae and blues thrown in. ✉ *1578 S. Broadway, Overland* ☎ *303/777–5840* ⊕ *www.hermanshideaway.com.*

Hi-Dive. The Hi-Dive is an energetic, hip club that books a diverse and eclectic range of talent. The crowd is young, likes Red Bull, and tends to revel in the discovery of obscure underground music. ✉ *7 S. Broadway, Capitol Hill* ☎ *720/570–4500* ⊕ *www.hi-dive.com.*

Lions Lair. The Lions Lair is a dive where punk-rock bands and occasional name acts like British rocker Graham Parker perform on a tiny stage just above a huge, square, central bar. ✉ *2022 E. Colfax Ave., Capitol Hill* ☎ *303/320–9200.*

Mercury Café. The Mercury Café triples as a health-food restaurant with sublime tofu fettuccine, fringe theater, and rock club in a downtown neighborhood specializing in acoustic sets, progressive, and newer wave music. ✉ *2199 California St., Five Points* ☎ *303/294–9281* ⊕ *www.mercurycafe.com.*

Ogden Theatre. The Ogden Theatre is a classic old theater that showcases alternative-rock acts such as Band of Horses and the Flaming Lips. ✉ *935 E. Colfax Ave., Capitol Hill* ☎ *800/745–3000* ⊕ *www.ogdentheatre.net.*

SHOPPING

Denver may be the best place in the country for shopping for recreational gear. Sporting-goods stores hold legendary ski sales around Labor Day. The city's selection of books and Western fashion is also noteworthy.

MALLS AND SHOPPING DISTRICTS

Cherry Creek. In a pleasant, predominantly residential neighborhood 2 mi from downtown, the Cherry Creek shopping district has retail blocks and an enclosed mall.

Cherry Creek Shopping Center. At Milwaukee Street, the granite-and-glass behemoth Cherry Creek Shopping Center holds some of the nation's top retailers. Its 160 stores include Abercrombie & Fitch, Banana Republic, Burberry, Tiffany & Co., Louis Vuitton, Neiman Marcus, and Macy's. ✉ *3000 E. 1st Ave., Cherry Creek* ☎ *303/388–3900* ⊕ *www.shopcherrycreek.com*

Cherry Creek North. Just north of the Cherry Creek Shopping Mall is the district Cherry Creek North, an open-air development of tree-lined streets and shady plazas with art galleries, specialty shops, and fashionable restaurants. ✉ *Between 1st and 3rd Aves. from University Blvd. to Steele St., Cherry Creek* ☎ *303/394–2904* .

Denver Pavilions. The Denver Pavilions in downtown Denver is a three-story, open-air retail and entertainment complex that houses national chain store like Barnes & Noble, Forever 21, Ann Taylor, and Gap. There are also restaurants, including Denver's Hard Rock Cafe, and a 15-screen movie theater, the UA Denver Pavilions. Don't expect distinctive local flavor, but it's a practical complement to Larimer Square a few blocks away. ⊠ *16th St. Mall between Tremont and Welton Sts., LoDo* ☎ *303/260–6000* ⊕ *www.denverpavilions.com.*

Larimer Square. Historic Larimer Square houses distinctive shops and restaurants. Some of the square's retail highlights are Dog Savvy, a boutique devoted to pets complete with spa treatments; Cry Baby Ranch, which specializes in all things Western and cowboy-nostalgic; and John Atencio Designer Jewelry. ⊠ *14th and Larimer Sts., LoDo* ⊕ *www.larimersquare.com.*

Park Meadows. The upscale Park Meadows is a mall designed to resemble a ski resort, with a 120-foot-high log-beam ceiling anchored by two massive stone fireplaces. The center includes more than 100 specialty shops. On snowy days "ambassadors" scrape your windshield while free hot chocolate is served inside. ⊠ *I–25, 5 mi south of Denver at County Line Rd., Littleton* ⊕ *www.parkmeadows.com.*

Tabor Center. Tabor Center is a light-filled atrium whose 20 specialty shops and restaurants lean heavily toward the latter and include the ESPN Zone–theme restaurant and the Cheesecake Factory. ⊠ *16th St. Mall, LoDo* ⊕ *www.taborcenter.com.*

Writer Square. Writer Square is a small but charming and pedestrian-friendly gathering place with shops and restaurants popular with downtown business types on their lunch breaks. The quirky galleries make for amusing window-shopping. ⊠ *1512 Larimer St., LoDo* ⊕ *www. wsdenver.com.*

SPECIALTY SHOPS

ANTIQUES

South Broadway between 1st Avenue and Evans Street, as well as the surrounding side streets, is chockablock with dusty antiques stores.

Brass Armadillo Antique Mall. More than 600 dealers are crammed into a treasure-hunter's paradise, where prices and quality vary. Plan to spend the day if you're serious about searching. ⊠ *11301 W. I–70 Frontage Rd.* ☎ *303/403–1677.*

BOOKSTORES

Fodor's Choice ★ **Tattered Cover.** A must for all bibliophiles, the Tattered Cover may be the best bookstore in the United States, not only for the near-endless selection (more than 400,000 books on two floors at the newer Colfax Avenue location and 300,000 in LoDo) and helpful, knowledgeable staff, but also for the incomparably refined atmosphere. Treat yourself to the overstuffed armchairs, reading nooks, and afternoon readings and lectures, but be prepared for a less cozy environment at the Capitol Hill site in the renovated historic Lowenstein Theater than at the original Cherry Creek location. ⊠ *2526 E. Colfax Ave., Capitol Hill* ☎ *303/322–7727* ⊕ *www.tatteredcover.com* ⊠ *1628 16th St., LoDo* ☎ *303/436–1070.*

CRAFTS AND ART GALLERIES

LoDo has the trendiest galleries, many in splendidly and stylishly restored Victorian warehouses.

David Cook. David Cook specializes in historic Native American art and regional paintings, particularly Santa Fe modernists. ✉ *1637 Wazee St., LoDo* ☎ *303/623–8181* ⊕ *www.davidcookfineart.com.*

John Fielder's Colorado. Few photographers capture the state's magnificent landscape the way John Fielder does, and his work is displayed along with a rotating roster of noted world photographers. ✉ *833 Santa Fe Dr., Lincoln Park* ☎ *303/744–7979.*

Mudhead Gallery. This gallery sells museum-quality Southwestern art, with an especially fine selection of Santa Clara and San Ildefonso pottery and Hopi kachinas. ✉ *555 17th St., across from the Grand Hyatt, LoDo* ☎ *303/293–0007* ⊕ *www.mudheadgallery.net.*

Native American Trading Company. The collection of crafts, jewelry, and regional paintings is outstanding. ✉ *213 W. 13th Ave., Golden Triangle* ☎ *303/534–0771* ⊕ *www.nativeamericantradingco.com.*

Old Santa Fe Pottery. The 20 rooms are crammed with Mexican masks, pottery, and rustic Mexican furniture—and there's even a chip dip and salsa room. ✉ *2485 S. Santa Fe Dr., Overland* ☎ *303/871–9434* ⊕ *www.oldsantafevillage.com.*

Pismo. Cherry Creek has its share of chic galleries, including Pismo, which showcases exquisite handblown-glass art. ✉ *2770 E. 2nd Ave., Cherry Creek* ☎ *303/333–2879* ⊕ *www.pismoglass.com.*

SPORTING GOODS

★ **REI.** Denver's REI flagship store, one of three such shops in the country, is yet another testament to the city's adventurous spirit. The store's 94,000 square feet are packed with all stripes of outdoors gear and some special extras: a climbing wall, a mountain-bike track, a whitewater chute, and a "cold room" for gauging the protection provided by coats and sleeping bags. There's also a Starbucks inside. Behind the store is the Platte River Greenway, a park path and water area that's accessible to dogs, kids, and kayakers. ✉ *1416 Platte St., Jefferson Park* ☎ *303/756–3100* ⊕ *www.rei.com.*

Sports Authority. At this huge, multistory shrine to Colorado's love of the outdoors, entire floors are given over to a single sport. There are other branches throughout Denver. ✉ *1000 Broadway, Civic Center* ☎ *303/863–2260* ⊕ *www.sportsauthority.com.*

WESTERN PARAPHERNALIA

Cry Baby Ranch. This rambunctious assortment of 1940s and '50s cowboy kitsch is at Larimer Square. ✉ *1421 Larimer St., LoDo* ☎ *303/623–3979* ⊕ *www.crybabyranch.com.*

The Rockies
Near Denver

WORD OF MOUTH

"We have owned a home in Winter Park for over 30 years, so needless to say, it is our favorite mountain destination. And we have been to most all of them. The WP ski mountain is awesome. The scenery is gorgeous. It is certainly not glitzy; more a home-spun atmosphere. The people are friendly. Restaurants and shops are reasonably priced. But, to be honest, it is lacking in that cozy town feeling that Aspen has, for example. . . . There is now a new village at the base of the mountain, which I think is a huge improvement. It is very cute, with a 'contemporary' Old West look to it, heated cobblestone walks, a parking garage, and a free gondola to take you to the upper parking lots."

—PeaceOut

www.fodors.com/community

Updated by
Kyle Wagner

If you ever wondered why folks living along the Front Range—as the area west of Denver and east of the Continental Divide is known—continually brag about their lifestyles, you need only look at the western horizon where the peaks of snow-capped Rocky Mountains rise just a 35-minute drive from downtown. For those drawn to the Front Range, a morning workout might mean an hour-long single-track mountain-bike ride at Winter Park, a half-hour kayak session in Golden's Clear Creek, or a 40-minute hike in Mount Falcon Park.

The allure of this area, which rises from the red-rock foothills cloaked in lodgepole pine and white-barked aspens to the steep mountainsides draped with the occasional summer snowfields, has brought increasing recreational pressures as mountain bikers, equestrians, hikers, dog lovers, hunters, and conservationists all vie for real estate that is increasingly gobbled up by McMansion sprawl. On the Front Range the days of the elitist "Native" bumper stickers are long since gone; almost everyone here is from somewhere else. Finding an outdoor paddling, climbing, or skiing partner is about as difficult as saying hello to the next person you meet on the trail.

ORIENTATION AND PLANNING

GETTING ORIENTED

The Front Range Mountains, the easternmost mountains in Colorado, stretch more than 180 mi from the Wyoming border to Cañon City. The Continental Divide flows along much of the northern portion of this spine, which includes several "Fourteeners," 14,000-foot or higher peaks. A boon for high-country lovers, the Rockies near Denver are easily accessed from the metro area via Interstate 70, Colorado's major east–west interstate, or U.S. 285, the major route heading southwest into the mountains toward Fairplay in the now infamous South Park, one of the largest high-altitude valleys in the country. (Trey Parker, co-creator of the animated sit-com South Park, went to Evergreen high school.) I–70 stitches together Denver, Golden, Idaho Springs, and Georgetown before crossing the Continental Divide through the Eisenhower Tunnel, right next to Loveland Ski Resort.

Foothills Near Denver. Less than 40 minutes from the city's heart, there are fast, cooling escapes in the mountain towns of Golden, Morrison, and Evergreen. Try your luck at the gaming towns of Central City and Black Hawk, or explore the former mining town of Idaho Springs.

TOP REASONS TO GO

Explore the Rockies: This section of mountains butts up against the Denver metro area, so it's easy to explore interesting towns and enjoy the mountain lifestyle.

Hit the slopes at Winter Park Resort: There's a blocked-off area for beginners, an outstanding children's program, and chutes and inbounds off piste–style terrain for experts.

Ride the Georgetown Loop Railroad: Peering out the window at the raw, steep mountainside and the rickety trestle bridge on the vintage train ride from Georgetown to Silverplume provides an eye-opening lesson in 1800s transportation.

Tour the MillerCoors Brewery: An entertaining (and free) tour ends in a sudsy stop at the end for an informal tasting. You'll see the steeping, roasting, and milling of the barley, then tour the Brew House where the "malt mash" is cooked in massive copper kettles.

3

Continental Divide Area. Colorado's gold and silver mining heritage is the highlight of Georgetown, within an hour's drive of Denver along I–70. Highway 40 climbs northwest from I–70, west of Idaho Springs, making a switchback ascent up Berthoud Pass before dropping into the resort town of Winter Park.

PLANNING

WHEN TO GO
Summers are hot in the city, but when you go higher up in the Front Range the days may be warm but the nights are cool. It's a time of year when many hikers and bikers head for the higher peaks. Heavy traffic on I–70 during weekends and holidays has become a sad fact of life for those wanting to explore the Front Range and Colorado's High Country. Slowdowns peak on Friday and Sunday afternoon when stop-and-go jams are the norm, particularly around Idaho Springs and Georgetown. Winter weekend and holiday traffic fares little better, with regular slowdowns in the morning rush to the Summit County ski resorts and afternoon returns. Many locals claim that the best times to visit Colorado are the spring "mud season" and autumn, when the tourists are gone and the trails are empty. In spring the Front Range mountains are carpeted with fresh new growth, while late September brings the shimmering gold of turning aspens. The interstate is well maintained. It's rare, but atop the mountain passes and at the Eisenhower Tunnel it's possible to see a bit of snow during the summer.

GETTING HERE AND AROUND
AIR TRAVEL
Denver International Airport is east of Denver, about a 35-minute taxi ride from the city center and a two-hour drive from the Continental Divide when the roads are clear and traffic is normal.

Airport Denver International Airport (DEN) ☎ 800/247–2336 ⊕ www.flydenver.com.

Airport Transfers Home James ☎ 800/359–7503 shuttle service from Denver International Airport to Winter Park and Grand County ⊕ www.ridehj.com.

CAR TRAVEL

The most convenient place to rent a car is at Denver International Airport. You can save money if you rent from the other offices of major car companies, but you'll have to take a shuttle or taxi to the city locations.

The hardest part about driving in the High Rockies is keeping your eyes on the road, what with canyons, mountain ridges, and animals to distract your attention. Some of the most scenic routes aren't necessarily the most direct, like the spectacular Loveland Pass.

Although it is often severely overcrowded on weekends and holidays, I–70 is still the quickest and most direct route from Denver to the High Rockies. It slices through the state, separating it into northern and southern halves. Idaho Springs is along I–70. Winter Park is north of I–70, on U.S. 40 and over Berthoud Pass, which has gorgeous views but also has several hairpin turns. U.S. 285 is the southwest route to Buena Vista, Salida, and the High Rockies. Any mountain road or highway can be treacherous when a winter storm blows in. Drive defensively, especially downhill to Denver and Dillon where runaway truck ramps see a fair bit of use.

Gasoline is readily available along I–70 and U.S. 285, but not so in more-remote areas like Mount Evans and Guanella Pass. Blinding snowstorms can appear out of nowhere on the high passes at any time of the year. In the fall, winter, and early spring, it's a good idea to bring chains and a shovel along. Road reports and signage on the highways will indicate whether chains or four-wheel-drive vehicles are required. Keep your eyes peeled for wildlife, especially along the stretch of I–70 from Idaho Springs to the Eisenhower Tunnel. Bighorn sheep, elk, and deer frequently graze along the north side of the highway.

TRAIN TRAVEL

Amtrak has service from a temporary kiosk near Denver's Union Station (which is under renovation construction slated to continue until 2014) to Fraser, where shuttles to the Winter Park Ski Area are available.

PARKS AND RECREATION AREAS

Arapaho-Roosevelt National Forest. Much of the northern Front Range region is within Arapaho-Roosevelt National Forest. The **Indian Peaks Wilderness Area** is northwest of Denver and encompasses a rugged area of permanent snowfields, alpine lakes, and peaks reaching 13,000 feet and higher. It's a popular wilderness area for Denver and Front Range residents because it's easily reachable for overnight trips. Some of the trailheads on the eastern side are about one hour from Boulder and almost two hours from Denver. Because 90% of the people enter from the east side of the forests, visitors entering from the west side will find more solitude. *For more information about the Indian Peaks, see the Boulder and North Central Colorado section.* ☎ 303/541–2500 ⊕ *www.fs.fed.us.*

Clear Creek. For Class II to IV rafting and kayaking, try Clear Creek, which offers rafting on Clear Creek near Idaho Springs and on the Arkansas during the early spring snowmelt season and throughout the summer. ☎ *800/353–9901* ⊕ *www.clearcreekrafting.com.*

Golden Gate Canyon State Park. Golden Gate Canyon State Park, just west of Golden, has great hiking and wildlife-viewing, and offers some of the best car camping in the metro area. ☎ *303/582–3707* ⊕ *www. parks.state.co.us.*

Jefferson County Open Space Parks. Most recreational lands in the foothills west of Denver are protected by Jefferson County Open Space Parks. These relatively small county parks are heavily used and have excellent hiking, mountain-biking, and horse-riding trails. ☎ *303/271–5925* ⊕ *www.co.jefferson.co.us/openspace/index.htm.*

RESTAURANTS

Front Range dining draws primarily from the Denver metro area; you'll find standard chains, mom-and-pop restaurants, upscale dining, and good ethnic food choices like Mexican and Thai with the occasional Middle Eastern restaurant thrown in.

HOTELS

In summertime, out-of-state and regional visitors flock to Georgetown and Idaho Springs to explore the rustic ambience, tour a mine, and hike or mountain bike on trails that thread the mountainsides; or to Golden to tour the MillerCoors Brewery. You won't find megaresorts or grand old lodges; but there are bed-and-breakfasts, condominiums, a few nice hotels in Golden, and some chain properties. Winter Park Resort has a mix of hotels and motels, plus a few upscale ranches. In Black Hawk and Central City, where gambling is allowed, there are several big hotels with casinos on the main floor, plus a few smaller casinos tucked into historical storefronts.

WHAT IT COSTS				
¢	$	$$	$$$	$$$$
Restaurants	under $8	$8–$12	$13–$18	$19–$25	over $25
Hotels	under $80	$80–$120	$121–$170	$171–$230	over $230

Restaurant prices are for a main course at dinner, excluding 7.1%–8.9% tax. Hotel prices are for two people in a standard double room in high season, excluding service charges and 8.9% tax.

VISITOR INFORMATION

Contacts Chamber and Tourism Bureau of Clear Creek County 🖃 *Box 100, Idaho Springs 80452* ☎ *303/567–4660, 866/674–9237* ⊕ *www.clearcreekcounty. org.*

FOOTHILLS NEAR DENVER

If you want to head into the High Country for a few hours, take the MillerCoors tour in Golden, then head up to the Buffalo Bill Museum. If you want to climb even higher, take a walk around the lake in the center of Evergreen and visit some of the local shops in the tiny downtown area.

GOLDEN

15 mi west of Denver via I–70 or U.S. 6 (W. 6th Ave.).

Golden was once the territorial capital of Colorado. City residents have smarted ever since losing that distinction to Denver by "dubious" vote in 1867, but in 1994 then-Governor Roy Romer restored "ceremonial" territorial-capital status to Golden. Today it is one of Colorado's fastest-growing cities, boosted by the high-tech industry as well as MillerCoors Brewery and Colorado School of Mines. Locals love to kayak along Clear Creek as it runs through Golden; there's even a race course on the water.

GETTING HERE AND AROUND

Golden is a 30-minute drive from downtown Denver via U.S. 6. Downtown Golden is compact and easily walkable. You may want to drive to the Colorado School of Mines area of town; it's about a mile away from the downtown area, and you'll want a car to reach the Buffalo Bill Museum, which is several miles away. The parking area for the MillerCoors tours is within walking distance of downtown.

TIMING

You can explore downtown and tour the MillerCoors Brewery in three hours or so.

ESSENTIALS

Visitor Information Greater Golden Chamber of Commerce ⊠ *1010 Washington Ave.* ☎ *303/279–3113* ⊕ *www.goldencochamber.org.*

EXPLORING
TOP ATTRACTIONS

12th Street. Golden's 12th Street, a National Historic District, has a row of handsome 1860s brick buildings.

   Golden History Museums. Three properties—the Astor House, the Golden History Center, and Clear Creek History Park—have combined under the name of Golden History Museums, and are all available on a $5 combination ticket. The Astor House Museum, which explores the material culture and local life of the era, is a restored late-Victorian–era Western hotel and boardinghouse. ⊠ *822 12th St.* ☎ *303/278–3557* ⊕ *www.goldenhistorymuseums.org* ⊠ *$5* ⊙ *Tues.–Sat. 10–4:30; also June–Aug., Sun. 11–3 .*

★ **American Mountaineering Museum.** Even if you never intend to go climbing, you may enjoy learning about lofty adventures showcased at the American Mountaineering Museum here. Visual exhibits display experiences climbing some of the world's highest mountains. Artifacts from famous climbs are alongside exhibits about the 10th Mountain

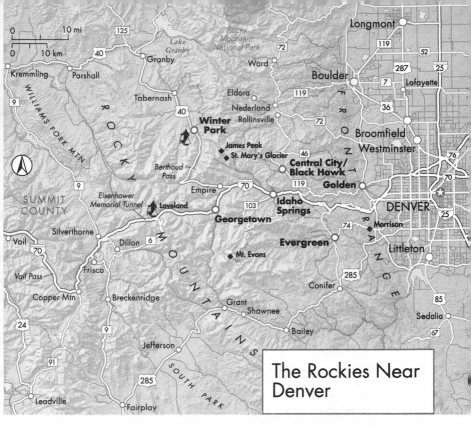

The Rockies Near Denver

Division—men who fought in Italy in World War II, some of whom founded several of Colorado's ski resorts. ⊠ *710 10th St.* ☎ *303/996–2755* ⊕ *www.mountaineeringmuseum.org* ☖ *$5* ⊙ *Mon. and Wed.–Thurs. 9–6, Tues. 9–7, Fri. 9–4, Sat. noon–5.*

⟳ **Buffalo Bill Museum and Grave.** The drive up **Lookout Mountain** to the
★ Buffalo Bill Museum and Grave provides a sensational panoramic view of Denver that alone is worth the price of admission. It was this view that encouraged Bill Cody, Pony Express rider, cavalry scout, and tireless promoter of the West, to request Lookout Mountain as his burial site. Adjacent to the grave is a small museum with art and artifacts detailing Cody's life and times, as well as a souvenir shop. The grave is 100 yards past the gift shop on a paved walkway. ⊠ *Rte. 5 off I–70 Exit 256, or 19th Ave. out of Golden, 987½ Lookout Mountain Rd.* ☎ *303/526–0744* ⊕ *www.buffalobill.org* ☖ *$5* ⊙ *Museum May–Oct., daily 9–5; Nov.–Apr., Tues.–Sun. 9–4; grave daily dawn–dusk.*

Clear Creek History Park. Clear Creek History Park interprets the Golden area circa 1843–1900 via restored structures and reproductions, including a tepee, prospector's camp, one-room schoolhouse, and cabins, and is populated with live chickens and bees. On select days, guides in period clothing lead 45-minute tours, but you can stroll the park and peek into the buildings anytime. ⊠ *11th and Arapahoe Sts.* ☎ *303/278–3557*

✉ *$5 (includes admission to Golden Museums)* ⊗ *Daily dawn–dusk; call for tour times.*

★ **MillerCoors Brewery.** Thousands of beer lovers make the pilgrimage to the venerable MillerCoors Brewery each year. Founded in 1873 by Adolph Coors, a 21-year-old German stowaway, today it's the largest single-site brewery in the world and part of MillerCoors. The free self-paced tour explains the malting, brewing, and packaging processes. Informal tastings are held at the end of the tour, and you can buy souvenirs in the gift shop. A free shuttle runs from the parking lot to the brewery. ✉ *13th and Ford Sts.* ☎ *303/277–2337, 866/812–2337* ⊕ *www.millercoors. com* ✉ *Free* ⊗ *June–early Sept., Mon.–Sat. 10–4 and Sun. noon–4; early Sept.–May, Thurs.–Mon. 10–4 and Sun. noon–4* ☞ *Children under 18 must be accompanied by an adult.*

WORTH NOTING

☾ **Colorado Railroad Museum.** Just outside Golden is a must-visit for any choo-choo lover. More than 100 vintage locomotives and cars are displayed outside the Colorado Railroad Museum. Inside the replica-1880 masonry depot are historical photos and memorabilia of Puffing Billy (the nickname for steam trains), along with an astounding model train set that steams through a miniature-scale version of Golden. In the Roundhouse you can witness a train's restoration in progress. ✉ *17155 W. 44th Ave.* ☎ *303/279–4591, 800/365–6263* ⊕ *www.crrm.org* ✉ *$8* ⊗ *June–Aug., daily 9–6; Sept.–May 9–5.*

☾ **Heritage Square.** Heritage Square, a colorful re-creation of an 1880s frontier town, has a music hall, a rip slide, an alpine slide, and some specialty shops. A vaudeville-style review ends each evening's entertainment. ✉ *Off the Golden I–70 exit on Colfax/U.S. 40 north 1 mi, 18301 W. Colfax Ave.* ☎ *303/279–2789* ⊕ *www.heritagesquare.info* ✉ *Entrance to park is free; admission varies per ride* ⊗ *Shops: Daily. Rides: June–Oct., daily, hrs vary.*

SPORTS AND THE OUTDOORS

GOLF

Fodor's Choice **Fossil Trace Golf Club.** Created by James Engh, this spectacular 18-hole
★ course is set into an old quarry. You play along fairways that have been set into deep gouges in the earth created when the quarry was mined and hit past pillars of sandstone to reach some of the greens. Along the way, players can stop to look at fossils of triceratops' footprints in an aeons-old rock wall, and relics of old clay-mining equipment. The course is consistently ranked among the top courses by ESPN, *Golf Digest,* and local publications. ✉ *3050 Illinois St.* ☎ *303/277–8750* ⊕ *www.fossiltrace.com* ⚐ *18 holes. Yards: 6833. Par 72. Green fee: $79 with cart, $62 walking.*

HIKING

Mount Falcon Park. Mount Falcon Park is a great way to explore the true foothills of the Front Range, and the comparatively low elevation makes it a good warm-up for higher ventures. Early in the morning mule deer can be seen grazing on the adjacent slopes. Take the **Turkey Trot Trail** from the east parking lot in the Morrison Town Park marked with a "hikers only" sign. The trail winds 1.7 mi up the east face of Mount Falcon through brushy slopes before curving behind the mountain up a forested draw to top out at around 7,000 feet. The trail loops back around and connects to the Castle Trail for a 1.3-mi easy return to the parking lot. Allow about 90 minutes. ⚠ **CAUTION: Stay on the path to avoid critters, including rattlesnakes, that lie in the grass.** ✉ *Jefferson County Open Space, start at east parking lot* ⊕ *www. co.jefferson.co.us.*

WHERE TO EAT AND STAY

For expanded hotel reviews, visit Fodors.com.

$$ ⤬ **Woody's Wood Fired Pizza.** Woody's has a full menu, with pastas, chicken, calzones, and burgers, but it's more fun to choose the $9.49 all-you-can-eat pizza, soup, and salad bar. The choices on the pizza bar range from classic to It's Greek to Me and Margherita, and the salad is always fresh. Woody's is so popular that the choices are always just out of the oven. Don't be surprised if you have to join the throng of families and college students waiting outside for a table on a busy night. ✉ *1305 Washington Ave.* ☏ *303/277–0443* ⊕ *www. woodysgolden.com.*

AMERICAN

Fodor'sChoice

★

$$ ⌂ **Golden Hotel.** Right in the heart of Golden, this hotel was renovated in early 2009, and is now a comfortable place to stay midway between downtown Denver and the mountains. **Pros:** downtown and riverside setting. **Cons:** this hotel caters to businesspeople, so you may see many suits. ✉ *800 11th St.* ☏ *800/233–7214, 303/279–0100* ⊕ *www. TheGoldenHotel.com* ⤺ *62 room* ⌂ *In-room: a/c, Wi-Fi. In-hotel: restaurant, bar, gym, parking, some pets allowed.*

HOTEL

EVERGREEN

20 mi southwest of Golden via U.S. 6 east, Hwy. 470, I–70 west, and Hwy. 74 (Evergreen Pkwy.); 28 mi west of Denver.

Once a quiet mountain town, today Evergreen is a tony community filled with upscale to extravagantly designed homes. The downtown core remains rustic in feel, however, and on warm-weather weekends it's filled with tourists and Denverites escaping the city heat. Visitors browse the eclectic mix of shops and mingle with locals walking their dogs on the path, which circles Lake Evergreen.

GETTING HERE AND AROUND

It's 45 minutes' drive from downtown Denver. Once you're in the heart of town, it's easy to find parking and explore on foot.

WHEN TO GO

Evergreen Jazz Fest. The annual multiday Evergreen Jazz Fest in July features musicians from around the country. ⊕ *www.evergreenjazz.org.*

EXPLORING

Hiwan Homestead Museum. The Hiwan Homestead Museum is a restored log cabin built between 1890 and 1930 that shows a popular and relaxed mountain summertime lifestyle. The museum, which includes three other buildings, has an exceptional collection of Southwestern Indian artifacts. ✉ *4208 S. Timbervale Dr.* ☏ *720/497–7650*

⊕ *www.co.jefferson.co.us/openspace/openspace_T56_R10.htm* 🖃 *Free* ⊙ *June–Aug., daily 11–5; Sept.–May, daily noon–5.*

WHERE TO STAY

For expanded hotel reviews, visit Fodors.com.

$$$
B&B/INN
Fodor's Choice
★

Highland Haven Creekside Inn. Walking distance from downtown Evergreen, the inn has a combination of standard and luxury rooms, suites, and cottages set alongside Bear Creek, where guests can go trout fishing. **Pros:** ideally located for travelers who want to stay in a mountain town but be 35 minutes from downtown Denver or Georgetown; very quiet; romantic. **Cons:** bathrooms tend to be small; you'll have to stroll into Evergreen or drive for dinner. ⊠ *4395 Independence Trail* ☎ *303/674–3577, 800/459–2406* ⊕ *www.highlandhaven.com* 🛏 *6 rooms, 5 suites, 7 cottages* ♿ *In-room: kitchen, Wi-Fi. In-hotel: some pets allowed* ⦿ *Breakfast.*

SHOPPING

★ **Evergreen Gallery.** The Evergreen Gallery has an excellent collection of contemporary decorative and useful ceramics, art glass, photographs, and other fine craft work. ⊠ *28195 Hwy. 74* ☎ *303/674–4871.*

CENTRAL CITY AND BLACK HAWK

18 mi west of Golden via U.S. 6 and Hwy 119; 38 mi west of Denver.

Recent changes in the gambling laws have created a "gold rush" to Black Hawk and Central City. As of 2009 the casinos stay open 24/7 and offer craps and roulette, and the betting limit has been raised to $100. The two former mining towns edge up against each other with more than 20 casinos, several that are topped by big hotels. Central City offers a fleeting sense of what the original mining town looked like.

GETTING HERE AND AROUND

Both towns are about a 45-minute drive from Denver. If you want to start in Black Hawk, take the narrow and winding Highway 119. If you'd rather start in Central City, head up I–70 and take the wide Central City Parkway. Bus transportation is also available from Denver and Golden through most of the casinos and the Opera House.

TIMING

You can cover Central City and Black Hawk's main attractions in a few hours on foot, although they're hard to find amid the crowds of gamblers.

TOP EXPERIENCE: GAMBLING

There are more than 20 casinos in Black Hawk and Central City. Many of the casinos in Central City are in buildings dating from the 1860s—from jails to mansions—and their plush interiors have been lavishly decorated to re-create the Old West era—a period when this town was known as the "Richest Square Mile on Earth." Black Hawk looks like builders stuck a load of glitzy hotels and casinos right in the middle of once-quiet mountainous terrain. Virtually every casino has a restaurant with the usual all-you-can-eat buffet. The biggest casinos are in newer buildings in Black Hawk. Hotel deals are common.

Ameristar Casino Resort Spa. Opened in 2009, Ameristar upped the ante for size and amenities—it has a Starbucks, is filled with TVs, plays contemporary house music, and offers several top-notch eateries. There's also an upscale hotel with a rooftop pool. ⊠ *111 Richman St., Black Hawk* ☎ *720/946–4000, 866/667–3386* ⊕ *www.ameristar.com/Black_Hawk.aspx.*

Doc Holliday Casino. Doc Holliday Casino is set in one of the historic buildings in Central City. ⊠ *131 Main St.* ☎ *303/582–1400* ⊕ *www.dochollidaycasino.net.*

Isle Casino and Hotel and Lady Luck Hotel and Casino. Among the largest casinos, owned by the same company and topped with hotel rooms, are Isle Casino and Hotel and Lady Luck Hotel and Casino. ⊠ *401 Main St. and 340 Main St., Black Hawk* ☎ *800/843–4753* ⊕ *black-hawk.isleofcapricasinos.com/.*

EXPLORING

★ **Central City Opera House.** Opera has been staged at the Central City Opera House, the nation's fifth-oldest opera, almost every year since opening night in 1878. Lillian Gish has acted, Beverly Sills has sung, and many other greats have performed in the Opera House. Performances are held in summer only. ⊠ *124 Eureka St.* ☎ *303/292–6700, 800/851–8175 Denver box office* ⊕ *www.centralcityopera.org* ☉ *Late June–early Aug.*

Gilpin History Museum. At the Gilpin History Museum, photos and reproductions, as well as vintage pieces from different periods of Gilpin County history, paint a richly detailed portrait of life in a typical rowdy mining community. ⊠ *228 High St.* ☎ *303/582–5283* ⊕ *www.gilpinhistory.org* 🔖 *$5; $8 includes admission to Thomas House Museum* ☉ *Late May–early Sept., Tues.–Fri. 10–4, weekends 9–4; early Sept.–late May, by appointment only.*

WHERE TO EAT AND STAY

For expanded hotel reviews, visit Fodors.com.

$$$
STEAKHOUSE
✕ **White Buffalo Grille.** Inside Black Hawk's Lodge Casino, this upscale spot focuses on steaks, seafood such as honey-bourbon glazed salmon, and Colorado rack of lamb. Garlic-herb mashed potatoes, creamed corn, and rice pilaf can be ordered as sides. For something lighter, try the tenderloin salad with beef tips pan-seared in a teriyaki sauce, jasmine rice, mixed greens, and an Asian vinaigrette. The views from the all-glass enclosure on a bridge above Richmond Street are divine. ⊠ *Lodge Casino, 240 Main St., Black Hawk* ☎ *303/582–6375* ☉ *No lunch.*

$
B&B/INN
🏠 **Chase Creek B&B.** This small historic house was nearly a casualty of a planned casino before owners Hal and Karen Midcap had it moved to the banks of namesake Chase Creek. **Pros:** two rooms have private hot tubs; in a quiet area. **Cons:** almost all of the nearby restaurants are in big casinos; a drive to Central City; only three rooms, so book far in advance. ⊠ *250 Chase St., Black Hawk* ☎ *303/582–3550* ⊕ *www.chasecreekinn.com* 🛏 *3 rooms* ⚭ *In-room: no a/c, Wi-Fi. In-hotel: some age restrictions* ⦿ *Breakfast.*

IDAHO SPRINGS

11 mi south of Central City via Central City Pkwy. and I–70; 33 mi west of Denver via I–70.

Colorado prospectors struck their first major vein of gold here on January 7, 1859. That year local mines dispatched half of all the gold used by the U.S. Mint—ore worth a whopping $2 million. Today the quaint town recalls its mining days, especially along portions of Colorado Boulevard, where pastel Victorians will transport you back to a century giddy with all that glitters.

GETTING HERE AND AROUND

After taking one of the I–70 Idaho Springs exits, it's hard to get lost, because the central part of this small town is bordered by the highway on one side and landlocked by a steep mountainside just a few blocks away. Head to the center of town, park, and walk around.

EXPLORING

TOP ATTRACTIONS

Ⓒ **Argo Gold Mill.** During gold-rush days the Argo Gold Mill processed
★ more than $100 million worth of the precious metal. To transport the ore from mines in Central City, workers dug through solid rock to construct a tunnel to Central City, 4½ mi away. When completed in 1910 the Argo Tunnel was the longest in the world. During a tour of the mine and mill, guides explain how this monumental engineering feat was accomplished. Admission includes the small museum and a gold-panning lesson. This tour focuses more on the processing of gold than visiting a gold mine. ⊠ *2350 Riverside Dr.* ☎ *303/567–2421* ⊕ *www.historicargotours.com* ⊠ *$15* ⊙ *Mid-Apr.–mid-Oct., daily 9–6, weather permitting.*

Phoenix Gold Mine. At the Phoenix Gold Mine a seasoned miner leads tours underground, where you can wield 19th-century excavating tools or pan for gold. Whatever riches you find are yours to keep. ⊠ *Off Trail Creek Rd.* ☎ *303/567–0422* ⊕ *www.phoenixgoldmine.com* ⊠ *$15; $10 for tour only* ⊙ *May–Oct., daily 10–5; Nov.–Apr., daily 10–4, weather permitting.*

WORTH NOTING

Charlie Tayler Water Wheel. Within sight of Indian Springs Resort is a 600-foot waterfall, Bridal Veil Falls. The imposing Charlie Tayler Water Wheel—the largest in the state—was constructed in the 1890s by a miner who attributed his strong constitution to the fact that he never shaved, took baths, or kissed women. ⊠ *South of Idaho Springs on I–70.*

Indian Hot Springs Resort. Idaho Springs presently prospers from the hot springs at Indian Hot Springs Resort. Around the springs, known to the Ute natives as the "healing waters of the Great Spirit," are geothermal caves that were used by tribes as a neutral meeting site. The hot springs, a translucent dome–covered mineral-water swimming pool, mud baths, and geothermal caves are the primary draws for the resort. You don't need to be an overnight guest to soak in the mineral-rich waters; day rates start at $18 for the geothermal cave baths (depending on type of bath and day of week), outdoor Jacuzzi baths $21.50, and $14 for the pool. ✉ *302 Soda Creek Rd.* ☎ *303/989–6666* ⊕ *www. indianhotsprings.com* ✍ *Varies by bath and pool; prices higher on weekends* ⊘ *Daily 7:30 am–10:30 pm.*

Fodor's Choice ★ **Mount Evans Scenic and Historic Byway.** The incomparable Mount Evans Scenic and Historic Byway—the highest paved road in the United States—leads to the summit of 14,264-foot-high Mount Evans. This is one of only two Fourteeners in the United States that you can drive up (the other is her southern sister, Pikes Peak). More than 7,000 feet are climbed in 28 mi, and the road tops out at 14,134 feet, 130 feet shy of the summit, which is a ¼-mi stroll from the parking lot. The toll road winds past placid lakes and through stands of towering Douglas firs and bristlecone pines. This is one of the best places in the state to catch a glimpse of shaggy white mountain goats and regal bighorn sheep. Small herds of the nimble creatures stroll from car to car looking for handouts. Feeding them is prohibited, however. Keep your eyes peeled for other animals, including deer, elk, and feather-footed ptarmigans. ✉ *From Idaho Springs, State Road 103 leads south 14 mi to the entrance to Hwy 5, which is the beginning of the scenic byway. The U.S. Forest Service fee station is here on State Rd. 3* ☎ *303/567–3000* ⊕ *www.mountevans.com* ✍ *$10* ⊘ *The road is open only when road conditions are safe. Generally, the last 5 mi to summit, Memorial Day–Labor Day.*

★ **Oh-My-Gawd Road.** Although most travelers heading to Central City take the new highway from I–70, adventurous souls can take the Oh-My-Gawd Road. Built in the 1870s to transfer ore, this challenging drive climbs nearly 2,000 feet above Idaho Springs to Central City. After traveling along a series of hairpin curves you arrive at the summit, where you are treated to sweeping views of Mount Evans. The dusty road is often busy with mining traffic, so keep your windows up and your eyes open. From Idaho Springs (Exit 240), drive west through town on Colorado Boulevard. Turn right on 23rd Avenue, left on Virginia Street, and right at Virginia Canyon Road (279). ✉ *Hwy. 279.*

Fodor's Choice ★ **St. Mary's Glacier.** St. Mary's Glacier is a great place to enjoy a mountain hike and the outdoors for a few hours. From the exit, it's a beautiful 10-mi drive up to a forested hanging valley to the glacier trailhead. The glacier, technically a large snowfield compacted in a mountain saddle at the timberline, is thought to be the southernmost glacier in the United States. During drought years it all but vanishes; a wet winter creates a wonderful Ice Age playground throughout the following summer. Most visitors are content to make the steep 0.75-mi hike on a rock-strewn path up to the base of the glacier to admire the snowfield and sparkling sapphire lake. The intrepid hiker, with the right type of gear, can climb up the rocky right-hand side of the snowfield to a plateau less than a mile above for sweeping views of the Continental Divide. Because of its proximity to Denver, St. Mary's Glacier is a popular weekend getaway for summer hikers, snowboarders, and skiers. There are no facilities or parking, except for a rough pull-out area near the base of the trail, and you risk a ticket if you park on private property. Don't look for a St.

Mary's Glacier sign on I–70; it's off the Fall River Road sign. ⊠ *I–70 Exit 238, west of Idaho Springs.*

WHERE TO EAT AND STAY
For expanded hotel reviews, visit Fodors.com.

$
PIZZA
✕ **Beau Jo's Pizza.** This always-hopping pizzeria is the area's original après-ski destination. Be prepared for a wait on winter weekends, because Denverites often stop in Idaho Springs for dinner until the traffic thins down. Topping choices for the famous olive oil–and-honey pizza crust range from traditional to exotic, and they've added a decent version of a gluten-free crust, as well. ⊠ *1517 Miner St.* ☎ *303/567–4376* ⊕ *www.beaujos.com.*

$$
AMERICAN
✕ **Buffalo Bar & Restaurant.** No surprise as to the specialties here: burgers, fajitas, chili, and steak sandwiches, all made with heart-healthy bison meat. American Buffalo, or bison, is raised at local ranches, and the light red meat is popular because of its low fat content. A Western theme dominates the dining room, where the walls are jam-packed with frontier memorabilia. The ornate bar dates from 1886. ⊠ *1617 Miner St.* ☎ *303/567–2729* ⊕ *www.buffalorestaurant.com.*

$$
AMERICAN
✕ **Tommyknocker Brewery & Pub.** Harking back to gold-rush days, this casual bar and restaurant is usually filled with skiers in winter and travelers or Denverites year-round who want to meet High Country friends halfway. The suds have a distinctly local flavor and sporty names like Alpine Glacier Pilsner and Pick Axe IPA. In addition to fare such as buffalo burritos, the brewery has plenty of vegetarian options. ⊠ *1401 Miner St.* ☎ *303/567–2688* ⊕ *www.tommyknocker.com.*

¢
B&B/INN
⊡ **Peck House.** About a 10-minute drive from either Georgetown or Idaho Springs via I–70, this red-roof inn in Empire is Colorado's oldest continually operating hostelry. **Pros:** classic lodging experience with nice restaurant; a few fun shops nearby. **Cons:** remote location: Winter Park is still 35 minutes away in good weather; Idaho Springs and Georgetown are 10 to 20 minutes away in opposite directions on I–70. ⊠ *83 Sunny Ave., Empire* ⟿ *Box 428, Empire 80438* ☎ *303/569–9870* ⊕ *www.thepeckhouse.com* ⟿ *10 rooms* ♿ *In-room: no a/c, no TV, Wi-Fi. In-hotel: restaurant* ❙◯❙ *Breakfast.*

SHOPPING
Ramblin' Rose Ranch. Ramblin' Rose Ranch sells all things Western, from attractive clothing and jewelry to housewares. ⊠ *1430 Miner St.* ☎ *303/567–1582.*

Wild Grape. Wild Grape is filled with an eclectic collection of gift items and souvenirs and an outstanding collection of greeting cards. ⊠ *1435 Miner St.* ☎ *303/567–4670.*

CONTINENTAL DIVIDE AREA

As I–70 climbs higher into the Rockies, the population and air begin to thin. Georgetown is a former mining town; Winter Park is a mountain resort town with a more recent history. Nearby Loveland is smaller, but one of the locals' favorite ski areas because of its proximity to Denver.

WINTER PARK

36 mi west of Idaho Springs; 67 mi west of Denver via I–70 and U.S. 40.

Winter Park Resort has made some dramatic changes recently, and now there's a small village at the base anchored by Zephyr Mountain Lodge and the Fraser Crossing and Founders Pointe condominiums. The Village Cabriolet—an open gondola—takes day skiers from a big parking lot to one end of the village, and they must walk past most of the shops, restaurants, and bars before reaching the lifts at the base of the resort.

GETTING HERE AND AROUND

In winter you can catch a ride on shuttle buses that move between the resort and the town of Winter Park, a few miles away. But in summer you'll need a car to vacation here. Valley Taxi is the local taxi service. Home James provides shuttle service between Denver Airport and the resort. Amtrak stops at nearby Fraser and Granby.

WHEN TO GO

From late November to mid-April good snow attracts winter sports lovers. Winter Park is equally popular in summer with hikers, bicyclists, and golfers, but has few tourist attractions besides its natural beauty. Mountain bikers flock here because of the diversity of the trails and the growing emphasis on downhill mountain biking.

ESSENTIALS

Visitor Information Winter Park/Fraser Valley Chamber of Commerce
⌂ *Box 3236, 80482* ☎ *970/726–4118, 800/903–7275* ⊕ *www.playwinterpark. com.* **Winter Park Resort** ☎ *800/729–5813, 970/726–1564* ⊕ *www. winterparkresort.com.*

DOWNHILL SKIING AND SNOWBOARDING

★ **Winter Park.** Winter Park is really two interconnected ski areas: Winter Park and Mary Jane, both open to skiers and snowboarders. Between the two peaks there are four distinct skiable sections: Winter Park; the "Jane"; Vasquez Ridge, which is primarily intermediate cruising; and Vasquez Cirque, which has seriously steep inbounds off-piste terrain. Pick a meeting place for lunch in case you and your friends get separated.

The skiing on the Winter Park and Vasquez Ridge trails is generally family-friendly, and there are segregated areas for beginners. Winter Park's runs promise lots of learning terrain for beginners and easy cruising for intermediates. On busy weekends Vasquez Ridge is a good place for escaping crowds, partly because this area is a bit more difficult to find, but the run-outs can be long.

Mary Jane is famous for her bumps and chutes, delivering 2,610 vertical feet of unrelenting moguls on a variety of trails, although there are a couple of groomed intermediate runs. Experts gravitate toward the far end of the Jane to runs like Trestle and Derailer, or to Hole-in-the-Wall, Awe, and other chutes. Expert skiers and riders seeking inbound off piste–style terrain hike over to the Vasquez Cirque.

The resort's Eagle Wind terrain has advanced steeps and deeps tucked among the trees. Panoramic Express, the highest six-person lift in

North America, provides access to above-the-tree-line skiing at Parsenn Bowl, Perry's Peak, and Forever Eva, as well as terrain and gladed sections. The pitch in many areas of Parsenn's is moderate, making the bowl a terrific place for intermediate skiers to try powder and crud-snow skiing.

The resort's Rail Yard, with its superpipe and terrain parks, is specially designed for freestylers. A progressive park system allows skiers and snowboarders to start small and work their way up to the bigger and more difficult features. There is also a limited access park, the Dark Territory, which is for experts only and requires an additional fee. ☎ 800/729–5813, 970/726–5587 ⊕ www.winterparkresort.com.

FACILITIES 2,610-foot vertical drop; 3,078 skiable acres; 143 trails; 7% beginner, 17% intermediate, 73% advanced, 3% expert; 25 lifts; 1 gondola, 2 high-speed six-person chairs, 7 high-speed quad chairs, 4 triple chairs, 6 double chairs, 5 surface lifts.

LESSONS AND PROGRAMS **Winter Park Ski and Ride School.** For adult skiers and snowboarders, the Winter Park Ski and Ride School has half-day lessons starting at $99. Daylong children's programs, which include lunch, start at $139. ⊠ Balcony House ☎ 800/729–7907.

National Sports Center for the Disabled. Winter Park is home to the National Sports Center for the Disabled, one of the country's largest and best programs for skiers with disabilities. ⊿ Box 1290, Winter Park 80482 ☎ 303/726–1540.

LIFT TICKETS The walk-up rate is $92, but you can save on multiday tickets, and many lodging packages include discounted tickets.

RENTALS **Winter Park Resort Rentals.** Winter Park Resort Rentals rents skiing and snowboarding gear from Village location (☎ 970/726–1664) and west Portal location (☎ 970/726–1662) and includes free overnight storage. Rental equipment is also available from shops downtown. ⊠ Zephyr Mountain Lodge.

NORDIC SKIING
TRACK SKIING
Devil's Thumb Ranch. About 8 mi northwest of Winter Park, Devil's Thumb Ranch grooms about 100 mi of cross-country trails. Some skiing is along fairly level tree-lined trails; some is with more ups and downs and wide-open views. The ranch has rentals, lessons, and backcountry tours. ⊠ 3530 County Rd. 83, Tabernash ☎ 970/726–5632, 800/933–4339 ⊕ www.devilsthumbranch.com 🎿 Trail fee $18.

Snow Mountain Ranch. Snow Mountain Ranch, 12 mi northwest of Winter Park, has a 62-mi track system that includes almost 3 mi of trails lighted for night skiing. The ranch is a YMCA facility (with discounts for members) and has added bonuses such as a sauna and an indoor pool. Lessons, rentals, and on-site lodging are available. ⊠ 1101 Hwy. 53, Granby ☎ 970/887–2152, 800/777–9622 ⊕ www.ymcarockies.org 🎿 Trail fee $15.

BACKCOUNTRY SKIING

Berthoud Pass. South of Winter Park, Berthoud Pass is a hard place to define. At the top of the pass there is a former downhill skiing area— its lifts have been removed—which is popular with some backcountry skiers. There's no regular avalanche control on these former runs. Skiers and snowboarders venturing in must have their own rescue equipment, including beacons, shovels, and probes. Backcountry skiing on the slopes from the former ski area or anywhere else on Berthoud Pass is only for very experienced, well-conditioned, and properly prepared skiers and riders. You must check current avalanche conditions before starting out, although that's no guarantee. In addition to skiing the slopes of the former ski areas, many people pull into parking areas elsewhere alongside the highway over Berthoud Pass and go cross-country or backcountry skiing. At many spots along the highway you'll see signs warning of avalanche blasting at any time with long-range weaponry. (This blasting is done to help prevent avalanches from covering the highway.) ⊠ *U.S. 40* ⊕ *www.berthoudpass.com.*

OTHER SPORTS AND THE OUTDOORS

GOLF

Headwaters. Headwaters is an 18-hole course laid out through a natural landscape passing very few buildings. The original course by Micheal Asmundson was redesigned by the Nicklaus Design firm to turn it into a more walkable course; two "family holes" were added to offer a golf experience for novices. The back nine is fraught with interesting challenges and fast greens. ⊠ *1000 Village Rd., Granby* ☎ *970/887–2709* ⊕ *www.granbyranch.com/golf* ⅄. *7210 yards. Green fee: $75–$90, plus $15 for cart.*

Pole Creek Golf Club. Designed by Denis Griffiths, Pole Creek has three 9-hole, par-36 courses and fantastic views of the mountains. You can play any combination of 18 holes, but try to get on the Ridge 9, which has particularly challenging holes with slippery greens and one of the best views in the state. ⊠ *5827 Hwy. 51* ☎ *970/887–9195* ⊕ *www. polecreekgolf.com* ⅄. *Meadow: 3497 yards. Ranch: 3609 yards. Ridge: 3603 yards. Green fee: $73–$99.*

HIKING

Byers Peak. At 12,804 feet, Byers Peak is one of the tallest mountains overlooking Fraser, and the highest point in the Byers Peak Wilderness Area. The trail climbs the northern ridge of Byers through lodgepole pine and Engelmann spruce forests before entering the spaciousness of the alpine tundra at around 11,200 feet. Climbers are rewarded with views of the Indian Peaks Wilderness, the Gore Range, and Middle Park. The trail is only 1.5 mi, but it climbs 2,400 feet. ∎ **TIP➔ If you aren't used to it, high altitude can catch you off guard.** Take plenty of water with you and slather on the sunscreen. In summer an early morning start is best. Afternoon thunderstorms are frequent, and you should never be above the tree line during a storm with lightning. Plan on three hours for the round-trip hike. ⊠ *Sulphur Ranger District, Arapaho-Roosevelt National Forest* ☎ *970/887–4100* ⊕ *www. fs.fed.us/r2/arnf.*

HORSEBACK RIDING

Cabin Creek Stables at Devil's Thumb Ranch. For leisurely horseback-riding tours of the Fraser Valley, your best bet is Cabin Creek Stables at Devil's Thumb Ranch. ✉ *3530 Hwy. 83, Tabernash* ☎ *800/933–4339* ⊕ *www. devilsthumbranch.com.*

MOUNTAIN BIKING

★ **Vazquez Creek.** Winter Park is one of the leading mountain-biking destinations in the Rockies, with some 30 mi of trails crisscrossing the main part of the resort and 600 more mi off the beaten path. Vazquez Creek is an easy but fun 4.5-mi trail that runs along a forest of blue spruce, fir, and aspen. The trail sticks to dirt roads with easy grades; the elevation gain is barely 600 feet. For more serious bikers the side trails have challenging climbs and rewarding vistas. ✉ *Trailhead: parking garage next to the visitor center at the junction of U.S. 40 and Vazquez Rd.*

SNOWMOBILING

Grand Adventures. Rentals and guided tours are available from Grand Adventures. Rates range from $65 per hour to $200 for a full-day tour. ✉ *81699 U.S. 40 S* ☎ *970/726–9247, 800/726–9247.*

SNOW TUBING

Fraser Snow Tubing Hill. Slide downhill on an oversize inner tube; hold onto the tow-lift for a ride up to the top to do it all over again and again. When you get cold, head into the warming hut at Fraser Snow Tubing Hill. The hill is lighted at night, and the rate is $16 per hour. ✉ *Hwy. 72 and Fraser Valley Pkwy.* ☎ *970/726–5954.*

WHERE TO EAT

$ ✕ **Carver's.** Long a local and Denverite favorite for breakfast, this casual
AMERICAN joint makes Belgian waffles that are as delicious as the variety of Bene-
★ dicts and scrambles with fresh orange or grapefruit juice. Lunch is also served. ✉ *93 Cooper Creek Way, behind Cooper Creek Sq.* ☎ *970/726–8202* ☾ *No dinner.*

$$$ ✕ **Deno's Mountain Bistro.** A sizable selection of beers from around the
AMERICAN world helps make this casual establishment the liveliest spot in town. But what sets it apart is a wine list that's comprehensive and fairly priced—a rarity in low-key Winter Park. The cellar full of fine vintages is a labor of love for Deno and his son, the powerhouse duo behind the restaurant. The menu ranges from sesame-crusted seared ahi tuna to Kobe "wagyu" cap of rib eye, all expertly prepared and served by friendly staffers who know their stuff. ✉ *78911 U.S. 40* ☎ *970/726–5332* ⊕ *www.denoswp.com.*

$$$$ ✕ **Dining Room at Sunspot.** Reached via chairlift during the day and gon-
AMERICAN dola at night, this massive log-and-stone structure set at 10,700 feet
Fodor's Choice above sea level is a real stunner. Douglas-fir beams, Southwestern rugs on
★ the walls, and a huge stone fireplace in the bar add to the rustic charm. The real draw is the view of the surrounding mountains, including the peaks marching along the Continental Divide. A prix-fixe menu includes game and fish paired with side dishes such as wild rice and potatoes roasted in olive oil and herbs. Elk Tournedos, elk tenderloin with a sun-dried cherry demi-glace and red roasted potatoes, is one example

of the signature dishes. Wines can be chosen to complement your meal. ⊠ *Top of Zephyr Express Lift* ☎ *970/726–1446* ⊕ *www. winterparkresort.com* ⊜ *Reservations essential* ⊙ *Hrs vary with the season.*

$$ ✕ **Hernando's Pizza Pub.** Bring along a dollar bill that you're willing to leave on the wall. It will joins thousands of others that have been drawn on, written on, and tacked up in rows around and above the bar. Nothing fancy here, just good pasta and pizzas that keep locals and regular resort visitors coming back. If you're in a creative mood, build your own pie, with a combination of the ordinary toppings, from pepperoni to sausage, then add more unusual extras like almonds or jalapeños. ⊠ *78199 U.S. 40* ☎ *970/726–5409* ⊕ *www. hernandospizzapub.com.*

PIZZA

$$ ✕ **Smokin' Moe's Ribhouse & Saloon.** You'll fill up on delicious spicy smoky ribs, smoked BBQ chicken, or Southern-fried catfish served in huge portions, plus a choice of sides including creamy coleslaw, mashers and gravy, or smoky beans. Diners are served at long tables covered with checkered tablecloths, and there's a salad bar for a lighter option. Check out "Moe," a lifelike mannequin slouched down on a bar stool hiding behind sunglasses. ⊠ *78930 U.S. 40* ☎ *970/726–4600* ⊕ *www. smokinmoes.com.*

SOUTHERN
☺

WHERE TO STAY
For expanded hotel reviews, visit Fodors.com.

$$ ▥ **Devil's Thumb Ranch.** Many visitors come to this 5,000-acre ranch outside Winter Park for the unrivaled cross-country skiing, with 100 km of groomed trails, but they wind up staying for the resort's comfort and privacy. **Pros:** terrific cross-country skiing and horseback riding; top-notch restaurant. **Cons:** in winter getting there can be rough; one of the pricier properties in the state; must drive to eat in any other restaurant or cook your own meals. ⊠ *3530 Hwy. 83, Tabernash* ☎ *800/933–4339* ⊕ *www.devilsthumbranch.com* ⇆ *52 rooms, 16 cabins* ⚲ *In-room: no a/c, no TV, Wi-Fi. In-hotel: restaurant, bar, pool, spa, business center, parking, some pets allowed* |⦿| *No meals.*

RESORT
Fodor's Choice
★

$$ ▥ **Gasthaus Eichler.** Antler chandeliers cast a cheery glow as Strauss waltzes lilt softly in the background at this little guesthouse. **Pros:** dreamy setting; great dining options. **Cons:** you're right in the middle of town, and on busy weekends the streets in front of the hotel can be busy. ⊠ *78786 U.S. 40* ☎ *970/726–5133, 800/543–3899* ⊕ *www. gasthauseichler.com* ⇆ *15 rooms* ⚲ *In-room: Wi-Fi. In-hotel: restaurant* |⦿| *Some meals.*

B&B/INN

WINTER PARK LODGING ALTERNATIVES

Destinations West. Destinations West is the premier source for luxury condos, town homes, and multi-bedroom, million-dollar homes on the fairways at Pole Creek and at the base of Winter Park. Price-wise, if you're bringing a family or a group of friends, it's worth comparing these luxury homes against regular condos. Concierge services are available. ⌂ *Box 3478 80482* ☎ *800/545–9378* ⊕ *www.mtnlodging.com* ⇆ *127.*

$$$$ ⊡ **Iron Horse Resort.** On the banks of the Fraser River, this condo-style
HOTEL   hotel is ski-in ski-out, but it's removed from the resort's base village.
Pros: truly ski-in ski-out; set in a quiet location. **Cons:** isolated area,
so you must drive to the base village or to town for all the restaurants and shops; must create your own nightlife. ⊠ *101 Iron Horse
Way* ☎ *970/726–8851, 800/621–8190* ⊕ *www.ironhorse-resort.com*
↪ *85 rooms* ⚷ *In-room: kitchen, Wi-Fi. In-hotel: restaurant, bar,
pool, gym.*

$$$ ⊡ **Vintage Hotel.** Right next to the Village Cabriolet lift, the Vintage is
HOTEL   the best value if you want to be close to the resort base. **Pros:** from door
to base village in five minutes on the cabriolet; pet-friendly property.
Cons: its popularity means it might get a bit noisy at times; you'll need
to drive or take a shuttle to the town of Winter Park. ⊠ *100 Winter Park
Dr.* ☎ *970/726–8801, 800/472–7017* ⊕ *www.vintagehotel.com* ↪ *118
rooms* ⚷ *In-room: no a/c, kitchen, Internet. In-hotel: restaurant, bar,
pool, gym, laundry facilities, some pets allowed.*

$$ ⊡ **Wild Horse Inn.** Tucked into the woods on the way to Devil's Thumb
B&B/INN   Ranch, this mountain retreat is a bit off the beaten path. **Pros:** very
★   quiet at night; after an exhausting day of skiing you can book an hour
with the on-site massage therapist. **Cons:** it's a 10- to 15-minute drive
to get into Winter Park; must create your own nightlife; the largest,
loveliest room is on the first floor near the entrance area. ⊠ *1536 Hwy.
83* ☎ *970/726–0456* ⊕ *www.wildhorseinncolorado.com* ↪ *7 rooms, 3
cabins* ⚷ *In-room: no a/c, Wi-Fi. In-hotel: some pets allowed, some age
restrictions* ⊠|*Breakfast.*

$$$$ ⊡ **Zephyr Mountain Lodge, Frasier Crossing, and Founders Pointe.** These are
HOTEL   all condo complexes, some with individual hotel rooms, too, that are
in the village at the base a short walk from the base lifts. **Pros:** all of
these are nice places to stay in the wintertime, because they are so
close to the lifts, and there are fireplaces in most units; walk out the
door and there are a few restaurants and bars. **Cons:** choose other
lodging in the summertime, because there is no air-conditioning and
only limited circulation in the units; if you want to head into the town
of Winter Park in the winter for nightlife or restaurants, you'll need
to take a shuttle or have a car. ⊠ *201 Zephyr Way* ☎ *866/433–3908*
⊕ *www.zephyrmountainlodge.com* ↪ *175 rooms* ⚷ *In-room: no a/c,
kitchen, Wi-Fi. In-hotel: restaurant, gym, laundry facilities.*

NIGHTLIFE

Cheeky Monk. One of the hot spots in the base village is the colorful
Cheeky Monk, which bills itself as a Belgian beer café. ⊠ *Base of lifts,
Winter Park Village* ☎ *970/726–6871* ⊕ *www.thecheekymonk.com.*

Crooked Creek Saloon. For a bit of local color, head down the road a few
miles to Fraser and the Crooked Creek Saloon. The motto here is "Eat
till it hurts, drink till it feels better." Locals show up for the cheap beer
during happy hour. ⊠ *401 Zerex St., Fraser* ☎ *970/726–9250.*

Pub. The under-30 crowd hangs out at the Pub, grooving to local bands.
⊠ *78260 U.S. 40* ☎ *970/726–4929.*

Ullrs Tavern. In the space that was the popular locals hangout Buckets,
Ullrs provides the closest thing to real nightlife in the area, with live

CLOSE UP

Eisenhower Memorial Tunnel

As you travel west along I–70 you'll reach one of the world's engineering marvels, the 8,941-foot-long Eisenhower Memorial Tunnel. Most people who drive through take its presence for granted, but until the first lanes were opened in 1973 the only route west through the mountains was the perilous Loveland Pass, a heart-pounding roller-coaster ride. In truly inclement weather the eastern and western slopes were completely cut off from each other. Authorities first proposed the tunnel in 1937. Geologists warned about unstable rock, and through more than three decades of construction, their direst predictions came true as rock walls crumbled, steel girders buckled, and gas pockets caused mysterious explosions. When the project was finally completed, more than 500,000 cubic yards of solid granite had been removed from Mount Trelease. The original cost estimate was $1 million. By the time the second bore was completed in 1979 the tunnel's cost had skyrocketed to $340 million. Today there can be a long wait during busy weekends because so many travelers use I–70.

3

music on the weekends, a DJ other nights, and a handful of pool tables. ⊠ *78415 U.S. 40* ☎ *970/726–3026.*

SHOPPING

Cooper Creek Square. Cooper Creek Square is filled with inexpensive souvenir shops and fine jewelers, upscale eateries and local cafés, plus live entertainment all summer in the courtyard. ⊠ *47 Cooper Creek Way* ☎ *970/726–8891.*

GEORGETOWN

32 mi southwest of Winter Park via U.S. 40 and I–70; 50 mi west of Denver via I–70.

Georgetown rode the crest of the silver boom during the second half of the 19th century. Most of the impeccably maintained brick buildings that make up the town's historic district date from that period. Georgetown hasn't been tarted up, so it provides a true sense of what living was like in those rough-and-tumble times. It's a popular tourist stop in the summertime. Be sure to keep an eye out for the state's largest herd of rare bighorn sheep that often grazes alongside I–70 in this region.

GETTING HERE AND AROUND

Just west of where I–70 and U.S. 40 intersect, the downtown historic area is just a few blocks long and a few blocks wide, so park and start walking.

TIMING

Georgetown is close enough to attract day-trippers from Denver, but much of the summer the town is filled with vacationers who have come here to ride the Georgetown Loop Railroad. Weekdays are quieter than weekends.

ESSENTIALS

Visitor Information Georgetown
⊕ town.georgetown.co.us/ ☎ 303/569–
2555. **Loveland Snow Report**
☎ 800/736–3754 ⊕ www.skiloveland.
com.

EXPLORING

♺ **Georgetown Loop Railroad.** Hop on
FodorsChoice the Georgetown Loop Railroad,
★ a 1920s narrow-gauge train that
connects Georgetown with the
equally historic community of
Silver Plume. The 6-mi round-
trip excursion takes about 70
minutes, and winds through vast
stands of pine and fir before crossing the 95-foot-high Devil's Gate
Bridge, where the track actually
loops back over itself as it gains
elevation. You can add on a tour
of the **Lebanon Silver Mill and
Mine,** which is a separate stop

> **HIKING THE
> CONTINENTAL DIVIDE**
>
> The Continental Divide, that iconic
> geographic division that sends
> raindrops to either the Atlantic or
> Pacific Ocean, makes a worthy pil-
> grimage for day hikers and back-
> packers alike in summer. Although
> it doesn't look dangerous to the
> untrained eye, the slopes off the
> Divide are avalanche prone, so it
> is an extremely dangerous place
> to ski in winter. The easiest way
> to reach the divide is to drive up
> U.S. Highway 6 over Loveland Pass
> at the Eisenhower Tunnel on I–70
> and park on top of the divide. Hik-
> ing trails lead both east and west
> along the divide.

between the two towns. ✉ *100 Loop Dr.* ☎ *888/456–6777* ⊕ *www.
georgetownlooprr.com* ✆ *$24.95 for train; $32.95 with mine tour*
⊙ *May–Oct., daily 10:25–2:55.*

Guanella Pass Scenic Byway. South of Georgetown, the Guanella Pass
Scenic Byway treats you to marvelous views of the Mount Evans Wil-
derness Area. Along the way—while negotiating some tight curves,
especially as you head down to Grant—you'll get close views of
Mount Evans as well as Grays and Torrey's peaks—two Fourteeners.
It takes about 40 minutes to cross the 22-mi dirt and asphalt road.
✉ *Hwy. 381.*

Hamill House. Dating from 1869, Hamill House once was the home of
silver magnate William Arthur Hamill. The Gothic Revival beauty displays most of its original wall coverings and furnishings. Don't miss the
gleaming white structure's unique curved-glass conservatory. ✉ *3rd and
Argentine Sts.* ☎ *303/569–2840* ⊕ *www.historicgeorgetown.org* ✆ *$4*
⊙ *Memorial Day–Labor Day, daily 10–4; Sept.–mid-Dec., weekends
10–4; Jan.–May, by appointment.*

Hotel de Paris. The elaborate Hotel de Paris, built almost single-hand-
edly by Frenchman Louis Dupuy in 1878, was one of the Old West's
preeminent hostelries. Now a museum, the hotel depicts how luxu-
riously the rich were accommodated: Tiffany fixtures, lace curtains,
and hand-carved furniture re-create an era of opulence. ✉ *409 6th St.*
☎ *303/569–2311* ⊕ *www.hoteldeparismuseum.org* ✆ *$5* ⊙ *June–Aug.,
daily 10–4:30; May and Sept.–Dec., Sat. 10–5, Sun. noon–5.*

3

DOWNHILL SKIING AND SNOWBOARDING

Loveland Ski Area. Because of its proximity to Denver (an hour's drive), lack of resort facilities and hotels, and few high-speed lifts, Loveland Ski Area is often overlooked by out-of-staters, but that's just the way locals like it. Loveland has some of the highest runs in Colorado spread across a respectable 1,670 acres serviced by 10 lifts. It's split between Loveland Valley, a good place for beginners, and Loveland Basin, a good bet for everyone else. Loveland Basin has excellent glade and open-bowl skiing and snowboarding, especially on the 2,210-foot vertical drop. Best of all, it opens early and usually stays open later than any other ski area except Arapahoe Basin. ⊠ *I–70 Exit 216, 12 mi west of Georgetown* ☎ *303/571–5580, 800/736–3754* ⊕ *www. skiloveland.com* ☼ *Mid-Oct.–May, weekdays 9–4, weekends 8:30–4.*

FACILITIES   2,210-foot vertical drop; 1,670 skiable acres; 93 runs; 13% beginner, 41% intermediate, 46% advanced; 10 lifts; 3 doubles, 2 triples, 3 quads, 1 surface, and 1 magic carpet (ski school only).

LESSONS AND **Loveland Ski School.** Loveland Ski School offers 2½-hour group "New-
PROGRAMS comer Packages" beginning at 10 am and 1 pm for $84 including all rental gear and an all-day lift ticket; advanced half-day lessons (a maximum of four people per group) are $57 or $85 with rental gear. ☎ *303/571–5580.*

LIFT TICKETS   In the early season, from opening to December 14, tickets are $47, but $59 is the regular season price. Discount tickets are on sale at local Safeway and King Soopers stores.

RENTALS   **Loveland Rentals.** Loveland Rentals has two on-mountain locations. Sport packages are $30, and performance packages are $45. Snowboard packages are $35; helmets run $15. ☎ *303/569–3203.*

WHERE TO EAT AND STAY

For expanded hotel reviews, visit Fodors.com.

$ ✕ **Euro Grill.** Hearty portions of reasonably priced Eastern European
EUROPEAN dishes are served in this sparsely decorated but roomy eatery with alpine views. Menu options include goulash, sauerbraten, and potato pancakes, as well as superb chicken, veal, and pork schnitzels. The apple schnitzel is also worth saving room for at the end. The selection of Czech beers is ideal for the menu, and the patio is a welcome warm-weather option. ⊠ *1025 Rose St.* ☎ *303/569–2126* ⊕ *www. eurogrillrestaurant.com.*

¢   ⛨ **Georgetown Mountain Inn.** Next door to the Old Georgetown Rail-
HOTEL road, this step up from a basic motel has rooms decorated with Western-style wood furniture and Southwestern blankets. **Pros:** right by the station for the Georgetown Loop railroad; Colorado rooms enhanced with pine-paneled walls and hand-hewn log headboards and bedside tables are particularly nice. **Cons:** several blocks away from the historic downtown; some guests have complained about noise. ⊠ *1100 Rose St.* ☎ *303/569–3201, 800/884–3201* ⊕ *www. georgetownmountaininn.com* ⬅ *33 rooms* ⬧ *In-room: Wi-Fi. In hotel: pool, some pets allowed.*

$$ 🏨 **Hotel Chateau Chamonix.** This hotel, with its log exterior and green
HOTEL   roof, doesn't look exceptional for the region outside, but inside it's a
★   lovely property put together by local owners. **Pros:** some rooms over-
look a stream and have a two-person hot tub on a porch; extras like
espresso-cappuccino machines in the rooms. **Cons:** on one of the town's
busy main streets; not quite within easy walking distance of the historic
downtown area. ✉ *1414 Argentine St.* ☎ *303/569–1109, 888/569–1109*
⊕ *www.HotelChateauChamonix.com* 🛏 *10 rooms* ⚘ *In-room: a/c,
Wi-Fi. In-hotel: some age restrictions* ⦿ *Breakfast.*

SHOPPING

★   **Canyon Wind.** For a break from the I–70 weekend traffic or just a bit
of local flavor, stop by Canyon Wind, just off the Georgetown exit.
You can sample Colorado wines from the family-owned Canyon Wind
Cellars, which owns the shop, order a cheese plate, and sit by the
fireplace for a bit. ✉ *1500 Argentine St.* ☎ *303/569–3152* ⊕ *www.
canyonwindcellars.com.*

Grizzly Creek Gallery. The Grizzly Creek Gallery has wonderful scenic
large-scale photographs of the Rockies and wildlife. ✉ *512 6th St.*
☎ *303/569–0433.*

Summit County

WORD OF MOUTH

"With two sons to entertain, I would suggest something like Breckenridge—Cowboy mine, Alpine Slide, Bike trails, etc. For an out-of-the-way place to stay, you might consider Leadville—a mine to tour, a short train ride, the Mineral Belt Trail."

—fmpden

"We were in Breckenridge and drove Swan Mountain Road between Keystone and Breckenridge. [It] is really pretty. We loved our hike at Lower Cataract Lake. It is about a 40-minute drive but a pretty one and well worth it. Frisco is a very cute little town, and we enjoyed walking around it and going to the marina. Dillon and Silverthorne are good for grocery shopping."

—AustinTraveler

Updated by
Jad Davenport

Summit County, a mere hour's drive from the Denver Metro Area on a straight shot up Interstate 70, is Denver's playground. The wide-open mountain park ringed by 13,000- to 14,000-foot peaks greets westbound travelers minutes after they pop out the west portal of the Eisenhower Tunnel. The sharp-toothed Gore Range rises to the northwest and the Tenmile Range gathers up behind Breckenridge. Resting in the center of this bowl are the sapphire waters of Dillon Reservoir, an artificial lake fed by Blue River.

In winter Summit County is packed with tourists and Front Range day-trippers skiing the steeps at Breckenridge, Keystone, Arapahoe Basin, and Copper Mountain. The high density of first-rate ski resorts generally keeps lift lines low, particularly on weekdays. In summer the steady westbound traffic is mostly SUVs stacked high with kayaks and mountain bikes.

Summit County, as its name implies, is relatively high. The town of Breckenridge sits at 9,603 feet (Aspen by comparison is at 7,908 feet), and the resort's highest ski lift tops out just shy of 13,000 feet. Visitors from sea level should take their time getting acclimated. Even Denverites find themselves breathless in the thin air. Drink lots of water and rest your first few days. There will be plenty of time to play.

ORIENTATION AND PLANNING

GETTING ORIENTED

The great east–west Colorado corridor I–70 cleaves through the heart of Summit County, punching west from Denver past Idaho Springs and Georgetown. The traffic here can be heavy and fast; everyone is in a hurry to make it through the Eisenhower Tunnel, the traditional gateway to Summit County. Those with an extra half hour and a yearning for hairpin turns, shaggy mountain goats, and 100-mi views opt for U.S. 6 over Loveland Pass and the Continental Divide. As it drops into the Summit County Basin on the west side of the divide, U.S. 6 passes Arapahoe Basin and Keystone Ski Resort before merging with I–70. Both roads skirt Dillon Reservoir with its shoreline communities of Dillon and Frisco. The highway quickly disappears back into a narrow mountain valley and climbs to Copper Mountain and then up and over Vail Pass.

Keystone and Arapahoe Basin. Tucked up a western valley off the Continental Divide, Keystone and Arapahoe Basin tend to attract more of

TOP REASONS TO GO

Festival fun: Breckenridge hosts numerous festivals, including the aptly named Spring Massive Festival in April, and the weeklong Ullr Festival in January.

Mining heritage: It was gold that built Colorado in the 1800s, and this legacy is alive and well in the rejuvenated mining town of Leadville.

Mountain waters: Nothing beats a day of lake kayaking or fishing among the many wooded islets on Lake Dillon, the reservoir that is the heart of Summit County.

Skiing choices: You won't find more choices to ski and ride within snowball-throw's distance of one another than in Summit County, many a mere hour's drive from the Denver Metro Area.

Trail biking: Sure, there are plenty of single-track rides, but the real draw is the glorious paved bike trail that runs from Dillon up and over the mountains to Vail.

a local—and hardier—ski crowd; and hikers in summer. Keystone is an intimate resort town but "A-Basin" is little more than a ski area.

Lake Dillon and Breckenridge. Dillon and Frisco are twin towns hugging the shores of Dillon Reservoir, a sparkling man-made lake. Skiers will bypass both for Breckenridge, the largest ski area in Summit County. "Breck" has a blend of authentic Colorado character with a flashy dose of upscale lodges and high-end condos.

Copper Mountain and Leadville. Farther west on I–70, Copper Mountain makes up for a lack of mountain charm with its near-perfect ski mountain. The high-altitude mountain town of Leadville will leave you breathless, both from the thin air and from the gorgeous views of Colorado's highest peak, 14,440-foot Mount Elbert.

PLANNING

WHEN TO GO

Summit County is a haven for winter enthusiasts: the resorts of Arapahoe Basin and Breckenridge—and nearby Loveland in Clear Creek County—are so high that the ski season often dawns here weeks before it does in the rest of the state, with Arapahoe Basin and Loveland competing to see who has the longest season, which can begin as early as October and end as late as July. The altitude also means that it can snow on any day of the year, so be prepared. Traffic, particularly on the I–70 approaches to the Eisenhower Tunnel and the Georgetown-to–Idaho Springs stretch, moves at a snail's pace around weekend rush hours—noon to 10 pm on Friday and all day Sunday.

GETTING HERE AND AROUND
AIR TRAVEL

Denver International Airport (DEN) is the gateway to the attractions and ski resorts in Summit County. The airport is an hour's drive from the Continental Divide along I–70.

TRANSFERS   To and from Summit County (Breckenridge, Copper Mountain, Dillon, Frisco, and Keystone), use Colorado Mountain Express and 453 Taxi, which have regular service to and from the Denver airport.

Airport Denver International Airport (DEN) ☎ *800/247–2336* ⊕ *www. flydenver.com.*

Airport Transfer Colorado Mountain Express ☎ *970/926–9800, 800/525– 6363.* **453-Taxi** ☎ *970/453–8294.*

BUS OR SHUTTLE TRAVEL

All the resorts run free or inexpensive shuttles between the ski villages and the slopes. Summit Stage provides free public transportation to town and ski areas, in and between ski areas in Summit County.

Shuttles Summit Stage ☎ *970/668–0999.*

CAR TRAVEL

The hardest part about driving in the High Rockies is keeping your eyes on the road. A glacier-carved canyon off to your left, a soaring mountain ridge to your right, and there, standing on the shoulder, a bull elk. Some of the most scenic routes aren't necessarily the most direct. The Eisenhower Tunnel sweeps thousands of cars daily beneath the mantle of the Continental Divide, whereas only several hundred drivers choose the slower, but more spectacular, Loveland Pass. Some of the most beautiful byways, like the Mount Evans Scenic and Historic Drive, are one-way roads.

Although it is severely overcrowded, I–70 is still the quickest and most direct route from Denver to Summit County. The interstate slices through the state, separating it into northern and southern halves. Breckenridge is south of I–70 on Highway 9; Leadville and Ski Cooper are south of I–70 along U.S. 24 and Highway 91.

The most convenient place for visitors to rent a car is at the Denver International Airport. Gasoline is readily available along I–70 and its arteries, but when venturing into more remote areas be sure that you have enough fuel to get there and back. Blinding snowstorms can appear out of nowhere on the high passes at any time of the year. Chains aren't normally required for passenger vehicles on highways, but it's a good idea to carry them. A shovel isn't a bad idea, either. The highway shuts down during severe snowstorms and blizzards. Keep your eyes peeled for mule deer and for bighorn sheep, especially along the stretch of I–70 from Idaho Springs to the Eisenhower Tunnel.

PARKS AND RECREATION AREAS

Summit County is perched in a 9,000-foot-high park (a wide valley surrounded by peaks) with Lake Dillon at its recreational heart.

Arapaho National Forest. The wild Gore Range northwest of Lake Dillon is protected within the Eagles Nest Wilderness Area, administered by the Arapaho National Forest. As in all wilderness areas in Colorado, motorized or mechanized vehicles (forestry-speak for mountain bikes) are prohibited. You can tackle the backcountry peaks on your own two feet or on horseback.

White River National Forest. ☎ 970/945–2521 ⊕ www.fs.usda.gov/ whiteriver ☎ 970/295–6600 ⊕ www.fs.fed.us.

The Blue River, which bisects the county south to north and is the lifeblood of Lake Dillon, has gold-medal fishing beginning below Lake Dillon to the Green Mountain Reservoir.

RESTAURANTS

Whereas the restaurants in the celeb resorts of Aspen and Vail mimic the sophistication and style of New York and Los Angeles, Summit County eateries specialize in pub food and Mexican cuisine for calorie-hungry hikers, skiers, and boaters, with the exception of a few more urbane spots in Breckenridge. You won't find much sushi here, but you will find fish tacos, shepherd's pies, and burgers with every imaginable topping. Hearty, reasonably priced comfort food is served at a number of cozy brewpubs along with handcrafted local suds like Dam Straight Lager, Avalanche Amber, and Ptarmigan Pilsner.

HOTELS

Summit County is a great place for history buffs looking for redone Victorian mining mansions–cum–bed-and-breakfasts and budget hunters who want affordable rooms close to the slopes. The county probably has the highest density of condominium units in the state. The competition tends to keep prices lower than in other resort towns. Note that staff at hotels in the region are sometimes young and inexperienced, which may result in less-than-desirable service at some otherwise excellent properties. Also note that many accommodations do not have air-conditioning—beware that rooms with southern exposure warm up quickly. Summer nights, however, are often cool enough in the mountains that opening the windows will do the trick.

WHAT IT COSTS					
	¢	$	$$	$$$	$$$$
Restaurants	under $8	$8–$12	$13–$18	$19–$25	over $25
Hotels	under $80	$80–$120	$121–$170	$171–$230	over $230

Restaurant prices are for a main course at dinner, excluding 7.75%–12.7% tax. Hotel prices are for two people in a standard double room in high season, excluding service charges and 8.8%–12.1% tax.

KEYSTONE AND ARAPAHOE BASIN

Just 90 mi west of Denver over Loveland Pass or through the Eisenhower Tunnel, Keystone and Arapahoe Basin are among the closest ski resorts to the Front Range. Given their location hugging the Continental Divide's western flank—both are surrounded by high-altitude peaks topping 12,000 feet—they are also among the highest resorts in the state. You can reach both by taking I-70 across the Divide to Dillon and then following U.S. 6 south and east up the narrow valley.

KEYSTONE

8 mi southeast of Dillon via U.S. 6.

Fodor's Choice
★
One of the region's most laid-back destinations, Keystone is understandably popular with families, and as the state's only large resort to offer seasonal night skiing (with lifts running until 9 pm), has long been a local favorite. Its trails are spread across three adjoining peaks: Dercum Mountain, North Peak, and the Outback. Through the years, as the resort added more runs, it morphed from a beginner's paradise on Keystone Mountain to an early-season training stop for the national ski teams that practice on the tougher and bumpier terrain on North Peak. Keystone now also has full-day guided snowcat tours ($225; backcountry ski gear like avalanche beacons, shovels, and probes are provided). Today it's a resort for all types of skiers and riders, whether they prefer gentle slopes, cruising, or high-adrenaline challenges on the Outback's steep bowls.

The planners were sensitive to the environment, favoring colors and materials that blend inconspicuously with the natural surroundings. Lodging, shops, and restaurants are in Lakeside Village, the older part of the resort, and in River Run, a newer area at the base of the gondola that has become the heart of Keystone. Everything here operated by Keystone, which makes planning a vacation one-stop shopping.

GETTING HERE AND AROUND

The easiest way to travel to and around Summit County is to rent a car at Denver International Airport. Catching one of the numerous shuttles up to the ski areas and then taking advantage of the free transportation by Summit Stage (taxi service is also available) is a more economical route, but requires patience and a good timetable. You'll want a car to reach both resorts, but once there both Keystone and A-Basin are easily navigated on foot.

WHEN TO GO

From late October to late April winter sports rule. But Keystone is quickly becoming a magnet in summer, with a small lake for water sports, mountain biking and hiking trails, two highly respected golf courses, and outdoor concerts and special events.

ESSENTIALS

Transportation Rainbow Taxi ☎ *970/453–8294.* **Summit Stage** ☎ *970/668–0999.*

Visitor Information Keystone Resort ☎ *970/496–2316, 877/625–1556* ⊕ *www.keystone.snow.com.* **Keystone Snow Report** ☎ *970/496–4111, 800/934–2485.*

DOWNHILL SKIING AND SNOWBOARDING

Keystone. What you see from the base of the mountain is only a fraction of the terrain you can enjoy when you ski or snowboard at Keystone. There's plenty more to Keystone Mountain, and much of it is geared to novice and intermediate skiers. The Schoolmarm Trail has 3.5 mi of runs where you can practice turns. Dercum Mountain is easily reached from the base via high-speed chairs or the River Run gondola. You can

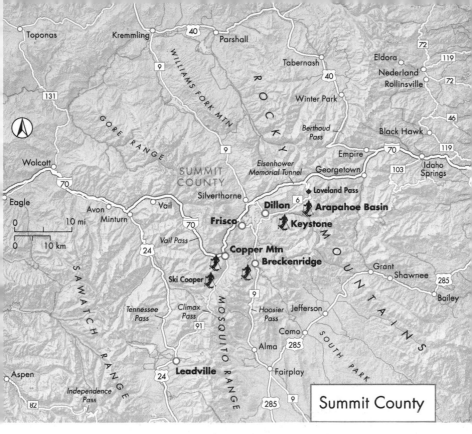

Summit County

ski or ride down the back side of Dercum Mountain to reach North Peak, a mix of groomed cruising trails and ungroomed bump runs.

If you prefer to bypass North Peak, the River Run gondola is a short walk from the Outpost gondola, which takes you to the Outpost Lodge (home to the Alpenglow Stube, which at 11,444 feet above sea level is advertised as the "highest gourmet restaurant in the country"). From here it's an easy downhill run to the third mountain, appropriately named the Outback because of its wilderness setting. Some glades have trees thinned just enough for skiers and riders who are learning to explore gladed terrain; other sections are reserved for advanced skiers. Weather permitting, the resort also has snowcat tours that whisk you up to powder skiing on some of the state's steepest terrain.

One of the most popular nonskiing or boarding sports at Keystone is tubing. Both Adventure Point at the summit of Dercum Mountain and the Keystone Nordic Center have tube rentals and runs, but reserve a day or two ahead of time. Personal sleds and tubes are not allowed. ⊠ *U.S. 6* ☎ *800/239–1639* ⊕ *www.keystoneresort.com* ☉ *Early Nov.– early Apr.; call for hrs.*

FACILITIES 3,128-foot vertical drop; 3,148 skiable acres; 19% beginner, 32% intermediate, 49% advanced; 20 lifts; 2 gondolas, 1 super six lift, 5 high-

speed quad chairs, 1 quad chair, 1 triple chair, 3 double chairs, 1 surface lift, and 6 carpets.

LESSONS AND PROGRAMS
Keystone has a variety of instructional programs, from half-day group lessons to specialty clinics, including mogul classes and women's seminars.

LIFT TICKETS
With prices in high season starting around $100 for a one-day lift ticket, few skiers pay the walk-up rate. Season passes, which range from 10 days of skiing to unlimited access, are available through Vail Resorts, which owns Keystone, Breckenridge, Vail, and Beaver Creek. Most vacationers purchase lift-and-lodging packages or multiday lift passes at discounted rates online and at local Safeway and King Soopers grocery stores.

RENTALS
Rental packages (skis, boots, and poles, or snowboards and boots) start at around $35 per day for a basic package but increase quickly for high-performance gear. Cheaper ski and snowboard stores are in Breckenridge, Dillon, and Frisco.

CHILD CARE
Keystone has children's centers at the base of River Run and at the Mountain House for children three months to six years. The resort also has private classes for families.

> ### BIGHORN SHEEP
>
> Keep your eyes peeled on the northern slopes of I–70 as you drive up to Summit County from Denver (your right side). Herds of bighorn sheep congregate around Georgetown, often right off the highway.

NORDIC SKIING
Keystone Nordic Center. The Keystone Nordic Center has 9 mi of groomed trails and access to 35 mi of trails available for skiing and snowshoeing. Lessons and rentals of cross-country skis and snowshoes are available. ⊠ *155 River Course Dr.* ☎ *970/496–4275.*

OTHER SPORTS AND THE OUTDOORS
FISHING
Summit Fly Fishing. Summit Fly Fishing has a shop and full- and half-day fishing trips throughout Summit, Grand, and Eagle counties. They also lead fly-fishing float trips on several rivers. ⊠ *Lakeside Village at Keystone* ☎ *970/468–8945* ⊕ *www.summitflyfish.com.*

GOLF
Keystone Golf. With 36 challenging holes, Keystone lures golfers as soon as the snow melts. **Keystone Ranch,** designed by Robert Trent Jones Jr., has a links-style front nine; the back nine has a traditional mountain-valley layout. Holes play past lodgepole pines, meander around sage meadows, and include some carries across water. **The River Course** is a par-71 stunner designed by Michael Hurdzan and Dana Fry. The front nine runs around the Snake River, whereas the back nine threads through a stand of lodgepole pines. Dramatic elevation changes, bunkers, and water hazards combine to test golfers of all abilities. Add magnificent views of the Continental Divide and Lake Dillon, and it's easy to see why this course is so popular. ⊠ *1239 Keystone Ranch Rd.* ☎ *800/464–3494* ⊕ *www.keystonegolf.com* ⚑ *Reservations essential*

🏌. *Keystone Ranch*: 18 holes. *Yards*: 7090. *Par*: 72. *Green fee*: $140. *The River Course*: 18 holes. *Yards*: 6886. *Par*: 71. *Green fee*: $170.

ICE-SKATING

🛷 **Ice-Skating Rink.** In winter 5-acre Keystone Lake freezes to become the country's largest outdoor ice-skating rink. You can rent skates, sleds, or even hockey sticks for an impromptu game. Lessons in figure skating and hockey are available. Weather permitting, skating runs from late November to early March. Another smaller ice rink is also available in River Run. ⊠ *Lakeside Village* ☎ *800/354–4386.*

WHERE TO EAT

$$$$

AMERICAN

★

✕ **Alpenglow Stube.** The competition has heated up in recent years, but Alpenglow Stube remains one of the finest mountaintop restaurants in Colorado. The exposed wood beams, stone fireplace, and floral upholstery make it elegant and cozy. At night the gondola ride to get here alone is worth the cost of the meal. Dinner is a six- or four-course extravaganza, starting perhaps with the signature pinecone pâté, and followed by delights such as the white truffle honeyglazed elk chop. Lunch is equally delectable, with excellent pasta specials. Remove your ski boots and put on the plush slippers reserved for diners. ⊠ *North Peak, 21996 U.S. 6* ☎ *970/496–4386* ⊕ *www. keystoneresort.com* 🍴 *Reservations essential* ☾ *Closed late Apr.–early June and mid-Sept.–late Nov.*

$

IRISH

✕ **Cala Inn.** A street sign noting the distance to Galway is the first clue that you've entered an Irish pub. It's a scruffy but entertaining place where diners and drinkers sit around wood tables inhaling pub fries, bangers and mash, and steak-and-kidney pie. If you're brave enough, down a "Nessie" shot—layered Midori and Bailey's with a floater of Jägermeister. ⊠ *40 Cove Blvd.* ☎ *970/468–1899* ⊕ *www.calainn.com.*

$$$$

AMERICAN

✕ **Keystone Ranch.** This 1930s homestead was once part of a working cattle ranch, and cowboy memorabilia is strewn throughout, nicely blending with stylish throw rugs and Western crafts. The gorgeous and massive stone fireplace is a cozy backdrop for sipping an aperitif or after-dinner coffee. The seasonal five-course menu emphasizes local ingredients, including farm-raised game and fresh fish. You're in luck if the menu includes elk with wild mushrooms in juniper sauce with quince relish. ⊠ *Keystone Ranch Golf Course, 1239 Keystone Ranch Rd.* ☎ *970/496–4386* ⊕ *www.keystoneresort.com* 🍴 *Reservations essential* ☾ *No lunch Oct.–May.*

$$

AMERICAN

✕ **Kickapoo Tavern.** This rustic bar and grill in Jackpine Lodge has local microbrews on tap and big portions of homestyle dishes such as Cajun pasta, hearty two-mile-high meatloaf, and burritos said to be "as big as a barn." The central location, pleasant patio, and TVs tuned to sporting events keep the place hopping both après ski and après night ski. ⊠ *129 River Run Rd., River Run Village* ⊕ *www.kickapootavern.com.*

$$$$

MODERN
AMERICAN

✕ **Ski Tip Lodge.** In this ski lodge dating from the 1880s almost everything on the menu melts in your mouth. The four-course, prix-fixe dinner is a favorite for Colorado-spun American cuisine. Main courses have included wood-grilled pork tenderloin, roast pheasant with game sausage, and seafood fricassee with coconut and lime. Adjourn to the cozy lounge for the decadent desserts and specialty coffees. It's closed during the fall and spring shoulder seasons. ✉ *764 Montezuma Rd., 1 mi off U.S. 6* ☎ *970/496–4386, 800/354–4386* ⊘ *Closed Tues. and Wed. in summer.*

WHERE TO STAY

For expanded hotel reviews, visit Fodors.com.

$$$ 🖫 **Keystone Lodge & Spa, a Rock Resort.**
RESORT The cinder-block structure gives no hint of the gracious, pampered living just inside the door. **Pros:** one of the larger properties in the resort; spa; ski valet. **Cons:** iffy service; rooms are small; hot tubs get crowded. 🕮 *Keystone Resort, 22101 U.S. 6, Keystone80435* ☎ *877/753–9786, 970/496–4500* ⊕ *www.keystoneresort.com* ⇔ *152 rooms* ♿ *In-room: no a/c, Internet. In-hotel: restaurant, bar, pool, tennis court, gym, spa, children's programs, laundry facilities, business center, parking.*

$$ 🖫 **Ski Tip Lodge.** Opened as a stop along the stagecoach route back in
HOTEL the 1880s, this property was turned into the state's first ski lodge in the 1940s by skiing pioneers Max and Edna Dercum. **Pros:** good location for the price; on-site restaurant; romantic. **Cons:** small rooms; not near the lifts. 🕮 *764 Montezuma Rd., 80435* ☎ *970/496–4500, 877/753–9786* ⊕ *www.keystoneresort.com* ⇔ *7 rooms, 3 suites* ♿ *In-room: no a/c, no TV, Wi-Fi. In-hotel: restaurant, bar, parking* ⎜⎝ *Breakfast.*

NIGHTLIFE

Goat Soup and Whiskey. Across from Mountain View Plaza, the Goat Soup and Whiskey has two bars filled with twenty- and thirty-somethings drinking whiskey and beer. There's live music during ski season. ✉ *22954 U.S. 6* ☎ *970/513–9344.*

Snake River Saloon. Live music with rockabilly leanings makes the Snake River Saloon a good spot to stop for a beer. The fun-loving crowd is mostly under 35. ✉ *23074 U.S. 6* ☎ *970/468–2788.*

KEYSTONE LODGING ALTERNATIVES

Keystone Resort Corporation.
Keystone Resort Corporation operates most of the lodgings at the resort, which range from hotel-style rooms at Keystone Lodge and the Inn at Keystone to a wide range of condominiums. The condos are in Lakeside Village, River Run, and Ski Tip. Free shuttles ferry visitors to other parts of the resort. ☎ *877/753–9786* ⊕ *www.keystoneresort.com.*

ARAPAHOE BASIN

6 mi northeast of Keystone via U.S. 6.

Arapahoe Basin was the first ski area to be built in Summit County. It has changed—but not too much—since its construction in the 1940s, and most of A-Basin's dedicated skiers like it that way. It's America's highest ski area, with a base elevation of 10,780 feet and a summit of 13,050 feet. Many of the runs start above the timberline, ensuring breathtaking views (and the need for some extra breaths). Aficionados love the seemingly endless intermediate and expert terrain and the wide-open bowls that stay open into June (sometimes July). "Beachin' at the Basin" has long been one of the area's most popular summer activities. If you've got your heart set on slope-side accommodations or fine dining, look elsewhere: A-Basin has no rooms and serves only the most basic cafeteria food. You'll have to set up your base camp in nearby Keystone, Breckenridge, Frisco, or Dillon, and shuttle in for the day.

GETTING HERE AND AROUND
Given the remoteness of Arapahoe Basin, a car is the best way to go.

WHEN TO GO
This is truly a winter destination, skiing being the only attraction. That said, winter in this high-country spot can begin in early October and last into June.

ESSENTIALS
Visitor Information Arapahoe Basin Ski Area ☎ *970/468–0718, 888/272–7246* ⊕ *www.arapahoebasin.com.* **Arapahoe Basin Snow Report** ☎ *970/468–0718.*

DOWNHILL SKIING AND SNOWBOARDING

Arapahoe Basin. What makes Arapahoe Basin delightful is also what makes it dreadful in bad weather: its elevation. Much of Arapahoe's skiing is above the tree line, and when a storm moves in, you can't tell up from down.

If that sounds unpleasant, consider the other side of the coin: on sunny spring days Arapahoe is a wonderful place, because the tundra surrounded by craggy peaks is reminiscent of the Alps. Intermediate-level skiers can have a great time here on the easier trails. But A-Basin is best known for its expert challenges: the East Wall, a steep face with great powder-skiing possibilities; Pallavicini, a wide tree-lined run; and the West Wall, from which skiers of varying degrees of bravado like to launch themselves. After a long battle with the U.S. Forest Service, A-Basin won permission to install a snowmaking machine for certain trails. ☎ *970/468–0718, 888/272–7246* ⊕ *www.arapahoebasin.com* ☉ *Late Oct.–mid-June or early July.*

FACILITIES 2,270-foot vertical drop; 900 skiable acres; 10% beginner, 40% intermediate, 25% advanced, 25% expert; 1 quad, 2 triple chairs, 3 double chairs, 1 carpet.

LESSONS AND **Arapahoe Basin Central Reservations.** Contact Arapahoe Basin Central
PROGRAMS Reservations for information on regular classes and ski clinics. ☎ *970/468–0718.*

LIFT TICKETS Depending on the season, lift tickets are $68. Multiday tickets can save you as much as 20%.

RENTALS Daily ski-rental packages (skis, boots, and poles) start at $29, and snowboard packages at $37. Ski stores in Breckenridge, Dillon, and Frisco are even cheaper.

LAKE DILLON AND BRECKENRIDGE

Lake Dillon, a 2,300-acre artificial reservoir with four narrow arms and 25 mi of shoreline, sits at the heart of Summit County. The lake is guarded on the northwest by the steep Gore Range and on the southwest by the Tenmile Range (a part of the Mosquito Range), and to the east by the Continental Divide. Along the northern shore sit Dillon and her sister town Silverthorne, while Frisco hugs a southwest arm of the lake. Breckenridge is roughly 5 mi south of Lake Dillon, backed up against the Tenmile Range.

DILLON

73 mi west of Denver via I–70.

Dillon can't seem to sit still. Founded in 1883 as a stagecoach stop and trading post for men working in the mines, Dillon has had to pack up and move three times since. It was first relocated to be closer to the Utah and Northern Railroad, and then to take advantage of the nearby rivers. Finally, in 1955, bigwigs in Denver drew up plans to dam the Blue River so they could quench the capital's growing thirst. The reservoir would submerge Dillon under more than 150 feet of water. Once again the town was dismantled and moved, this time to pine-blanketed hills mirrored in sapphire water. Residents agreed that no building in the new location would be taller than 30 feet, so as not to obstruct the view of the reservoir, which is appropriately called Lake Dillon.

Dillon now blends with neighboring Silverthorne, where dozens of factory outlets are frequented by locals and travelers vying for bargains. Combined, the two towns have hotels, restaurants, and stores galore.

GETTING HERE AND AROUND

Private car is the best way to explore Dillon, although in summer a network of bicycle trails around the reservoir makes pedaling an attractive option.

WHEN TO GO

Dillon is a hub for all seasons. In winter, during ski season, Dillon is the place to get gas, groceries, and directions before heading to Keystone, A-Basin, Breck, or Copper. Beginning with the snowmelt in May, Dillon unfolds as a center for hiking, biking, and water sports.

ESSENTIALS

Visitor Information Summit Information Center *246 Rainbow Dr., Silverthorne 80498 970/668–2051, 800/530–3099 www.summitchamber.org.*

EXPLORING

Fodor's Choice ★ **Lake Dillon.** Resting in the heart of Summit County at 9,017 feet is the Front Range's answer to a day at the beach—beautiful Lake Dillon and her two ports, Dillon, just off I–70 on the south, and Frisco, off I–70 and Highway 9 on the west. The lake is actually backed up by a 231-foot earth-filled dam that fills the valley where Dillon once sat. During the frequent Western droughts, when water levels can drop dramatically, collectors wander along the exposed shores hunting for artifacts from this Rocky Mountain Atlantis.

It was these droughts that inspired the Denver Water Board to construct the reservoir and divert the water through the Harold D. Roberts Tunnel, beneath the Continental Divide. Below the mile-long dam the Blue River babbles past the outlet shopping haven and turns into miles of gold-medal fly-fishing waters on its journey north.

The lake has been a boon to both the Front Range and the exploding Summit County population. There are more than 27 mi of gravel beaches, marshes, peninsulas, and wooded islets for picnickers to enjoy, many accessible from a 7.5-mi paved trail along the northern shores, or from the informal dirt paths elsewhere. Gaze out at the deep blue waters from Sapphire Point Lookout (a ½-mi hike on the south side of the lake) any nice day, and you'll see a flotilla of motorboats, sailboats, canoes, kayaks, and sailboarders dancing in the waves. In winter the frozen waters are enjoyed by ice anglers and cross-country skiers.

Because the lake is considered a drinking-water source, swimming is not permitted, and the lake is patrolled vigorously by Summit County sheriffs. Just because you don't see a patrol boat doesn't mean they can't see you; their surveillance is done with binoculars.

SPORTS AND THE OUTDOORS

BICYCLING

Summit County attracts cyclists with its 40 mi of paved bike paths and extensive network of backcountry trails. There are dozens of trailheads from which you can travel through gentle rolling terrain, up the sides of mountains, and along ridges for spectacular views. Starting in Dillon, you could bike around the reservoir to Frisco. From there you could ride the Blue River Pathway, largely along the river, to Breckenridge. Or you could ride through beautiful Tenmile Canyon all the way to Copper Mountain. If you're really fit, you could even continue your ride over Vail Pass and down into Vail Village.

Summit County Chamber of Commerce Information Center. The Summit County Chamber of Commerce Information Center has detailed information about bike trails in the area. Ask for a free Summit County Bike Trail Guide that outlines, with great detail, your options. Listings include distance, difficulty, and elevation changes. ⊠ *216 Rainbow Dr., Silverthorne* ☎ *970/668–2051* ⊕ *www.summitchamber.org.*

BOATING

Dillon Marina. At Dillon Marina you can rent a rowboat, sailboat, or just about anything else that floats. Reserve ahead in high season. Take I–70 Exit 205 to U.S. 6, and follow the signs to the marina. ⊠ *Lake Dillon* ☎ *970/468–5100* ⊕ *www.dillonmarina.com.*

Frisco Bay Marina. The Frisco Bay Marina is less crowded than Dillon and has quick access to the numerous pine-cloaked islands along the western shores. Here you can rent powerboats, canoes, and kayaks. Take I–70 Exit 203 to Highway 9 to Main Street, and follow signs to the marina. ⊠ *902 E. Main St., Frisco* ☎ *970/668–4334* ⊕ *www.friscobaymarina.com.*

Boats rented from the Frisco Bay and Dillon marinas are not permitted to beach; the aluminum pontoons are easily damaged on the rock and gravel shores.

FISHING

Cutthroat Anglers. A favorite with locals, Cutthroat Anglers has a pro shop chock-full of gear for avid fly-fishermen. Their wade trips are best for beginners; full-day float-trip adventures are for those with a bit more experience. The wade trip is available in half-day and full-day versions.

✉ *400 Blue River Pkwy., Silverthorne* ☎ *970/262–2878, 888/876–8818* ⊕ *www.fishcolorado.com.*

GOLF

Raven Golf Club at Three Peaks. *Colorado Avid Golfer* magazine named this 18-hole beauty the best mountain course and the best golf experience in Colorado, both for its technically challenging layout and for its rich, natural beauty including stands of pine and aspen trees and visiting elk and deer herds. Each hole on the par-72 course has dramatic views of the Gore Mountain range. ✉ *2929 N. Golden Eagle Rd., Silverthorne* ☎ *970/262–3636* ⊕ *www.raventhreepeaks.com* ⚐ *Reservations essential* **↑** *18 holes. Yards: 7413/5235. Par: 72. Green fee: $165.*

WHERE TO EAT

$$
AMERICAN

✕ **Dillon Dam Brewery.** Belly up to the horseshoe-shape bar and sample the ales and lagers while you munch on burgers, sandwiches, or pub grub. The menu is steps above average bar food. Try the pan-seared tuna encrusted with sesame seeds, which is available in a salad, sandwich, or wrap. Other tasty options include the sweet-jalapeño salmon entrée and the Pilsner chicken with portobello mushrooms deglazed with beer. Carnivores and vegetarians alike have plenty to choose from, including the Ptarmigan Portobella, a char-grilled mushroom-stuffed whole wheat bun topped with melted pepper jack. ✉ *100 Little Dam St.* ☎ *970/262–7777* ⊕ *www.dambrewery.com.*

$$
STEAKHOUSE

✕ **Historic Mint.** Built in 1862, this raucous eatery originally served as a bar and brothel. The olden days are still evident in the brass handles and hand-carved wood, as well as in the antiques and vintage photographs covering the walls. Red meat reigns supreme, although you'll also find chicken and fish on the menu. Either way, you cook your own meal on lava rocks sizzling at 1,100°F. If you prefer to leave the cooking to the chef, there's a prime rib special. A well-stocked salad bar complements your entrée. ✉ *347 Blue River Pkwy., Silverthorne* ☎ *970/468–5247* ⊕ *www.mintsteakhouse.com* ☉ *No lunch.*

NIGHTLIFE

The bars and clubs in Dillon rock well after midnight, especially on winter nights when the towns are packed with skiers and snowboarders.

Bootleggers. Bootleggers serves pizzas, gyros, grinders, and some of the area's best calzones. ✉ *119 La Bonte* ☎ *970/468–2006.*

Pug Ryan's Steak House & Brewery. Across from the post office, Pug Ryan's Steak House & Brewery is popular for slow-roasted prime rib and well-crafted microbeers. ✉ *104 Village Pl.* ☎ *970/468–2145* ⊕ *www.pugryans.com.*

SHOPPING

Outlets at Silverthorne. A sprawling complex with more than 50 discount factory outlets, the clusters of shops here are color-coded for your shopping convenience. The Red Village has Calvin Klein, Tommy Hilfiger, Polo Ralph Lauren, and other upscale clothing shops. If you need sneakers, the Blue Village is home to the Nike Factory Store. For dishes, head to the Kitchen Collection in the Green Village. ✉ *246-V Rainbow Dr., I–70 Exit 205* ☎ *970/468–9440* ⊕ *www.outletsatsilverthorne.com.*

CLOSE UP

Colorado Golf

It isn't easy to define "golf" in Colorado, because the topography varies so dramatically, from the rolling plains near the Kansas state line to the flat-top buttes and mesas at the western end of the state. In the Rockies, the state's central spine, the courses climb up and down mountainsides; in the foothills the fairways roll over more gentle terrain and over canyons; and down in the cities many layouts march back and forth in confined spaces.

ROCKY MOUNTAIN COURSES

Mountain golf has unique challenges, but vacationers flock to the high-country golf courses because of their dramatic scenery. "Aim for that peak" is an oft-repeated phrase. It doesn't matter whether you are playing the Jack Nicklaus–designed 27-hole municipal course in Breckenridge, the Club at Crested Butte, or the golf course at the Snowmass Club, there's bound to be a hole where that description fits.

Resort courses, often available only to guests, are spread around mountain towns from Snowmass and Steamboat to Vail and Telluride. For example, if you stay at certain properties in Vail and Beaver Creek, you get access to the Tom Fazio course (woven through sagebrush-covered hills) and the Greg Norman course (spread around a broad valley with shots across ravines) at the posh, private Red Sky Golf Club in Edwards, 15 minutes west of Beaver Creek. Even if you're not staying in a hotel that has preferred tee times at specific resort courses, a good concierge (or your own Web search) will obtain tee times at many entertaining courses, such as the Raven at Three Peaks in Summit County and Sheraton Steamboat Golf Club in Steamboat.

When playing high-altitude golf, you do have to deal with mountain lies and illusions. The thrill of a clean hit and watching the ball fly 300 yards downhill may be deflected by the agony of seeing a putt topple off the back edge of a green because you "knew" that the green tilted left, although it actually sloped right. Lowland golfers who come to the mountains to play golf quickly learn they may have to change club lengths and lofts, because balls fly 10%–15% farther in the thinner air and land on never-level terrain. Greens are especially difficult to read, because the ball will try to roll from the highest mountain peak to the nearest valley—unless the course architect foxes players by building up the green's lower end to counterbalance that pull. Ask the pro in the golf shop for tips before setting out.

CITY COURSES

If you aren't heading up to the mountains, there are plenty of public and semiprivate courses in and around the bigger cities. Some city-owned courses in Denver proper tend to be unimaginative layouts in confined spaces, but there's a variety of challenging and award-winning courses in the surrounding burbs, especially in Lakewood, Littleton, and Parker. On the western slopes, a big standout is the Golf Club at Redland Mesa in Grand Junction. This Jim Engh public course is woven among mesas and sand-color flat-top buttes.

—Lois Friedland

4

FRISCO

9 mi north of Breckenridge via Hwy. 9.

Keep going past the hodgepodge of strip malls near the interstate and you'll find that low-key Frisco has a downtown district trimmed with restored B&Bs. The town is removed from the ski lifts, but a low-cost lodging alternative to pricier resorts in the surrounding communities.

GETTING HERE AND AROUND

Private car is the best way to arrive in Frisco, but the town is compact enough for walking or biking.

EXPLORING

Historic Park & Museum. Historic Park & Museum re-creates the boom days. Stroll through 11 buildings dating from the 1880s, including a fully outfitted one-room schoolhouse, a trapper's cabin with snowshoes and pelts, the town's original log chapel, and a jail with exhibits on mining and skiing. ⊠ *120 Main St.* ☎ *970/668–3428* ☜ *Free* ☉ *May–Sept., Tues.–Sat. 9–5, Sun 9–3; Oct.–Apr., Tues.–Sat. 10–4, Sun. 10–2.*

SPORTS AND THE OUTDOORS

FISHING

Blue River Anglers. Blue River Anglers runs fly-fishing tours on the Blue, South Platte, and Williams Fork rivers, as well as various lakes and streams in the area. You can expect to catch 18- to 20-inch rainbow and brown trout. ⊠ *281 Main St.* ☎ *888/453–9171* ⊕ *www. blueriveranglers.com.*

WHERE TO EAT

$
MEXICAN
✗ **Fiesta Jalisco.** This casual eatery serves great margaritas and south-of-the-border specialties such as blackened fish tacos. ⊠ *269 Summit Pl.* ☎ *970/468–9552* ⊕ *www.fiestajalisco.net.*

$$$
AMERICAN
✗ **Silverheels at the Ore House.** At this longtime favorite you can join the locals who gather around the bar for margaritas and treat appetizers like entrées throughout the day. For lunch you can try lighter fare like the haddock tacos or Joel's Bowl, stir-fried chicken and vegetable over sushi rice. Kick dinner off with a tasty appetizer like snow-crab empanadas or Thai scallops and for the main course head right for the classic trout plates—trout stuffed with corn bread stuffing and crab smothered in hollandaise sauce or barbecue-sauce-rubbed trout. If fish isn't your thing, there's always a great stash of beef and pork plates. ⊠ *603 Main St.* ☎ *970/668–0345* ⊕ *www.silverheelsrestaurant.com.*

WHERE TO STAY

For expanded hotel reviews, visit Fodors.com.

$$
HOTEL
🔲 **Frisco Lodge.** This 1885 stagecoach stop has morphed into a European-style boutique hotel complete with a chalet facade and a garden courtyard. **Pros:** great location on Main Street; outdoor hot tub and fireplace; courtyard garden. **Cons:** street noise audible; thin walls. ⊠ *321 Main St.* ☎ *800/279–6000* ⊕ *www.friscolodge.com* ↩ *19 rooms, 15 with bath* ☖ *In-room: no a/c, Wi-Fi* ⎢◯⎢ *Breakfast.*

$$ **Hotel Frisco.** This Main Street HOTEL hostelry is a great home base for ★ skiers wanting to hit Breckenridge, Copper, Keystone, and Arapahoe Basin. **Pros:** centrally located; friendly owners. **Cons:** small bathrooms; no elevator. ✉ *308 Main St.* ☎ *970/668–5009, 800/262–1002* ⊕ *www.hotelfrisco.com* ⟿ *11 rooms, 2 suites* ⚘ *In-room: no a/c, kitchen, Wi-Fi. In-hotel: business center, parking, some pets allowed.*

> **FRISCO LODGING ALTERNATIVES**
>
> **Summit Mountain Rentals.** Summit Mountain Rentals, run by the owners of the Hotel Frisco, has a collection of medium and high-end condos throughout Summit County. ⌂ *308 Main St. 80443* ☎ *970/453–7370, 800/383–7382.*

$$ **Woods Inn.** The rooms are as distinctive as their names in this cedar-B&B/INN frame house one block from Frisco's Main Street. **Pros:** natural setting; outdoor hot tub; dog-friendly. **Cons:** can get noisy if teenage ski clubs are staying there; a bit worn around the edges. ✉ *205 S. 2nd Ave.* ☎ *970/668–2255, 877/664–3777* ⊕ *www.woodsinn.biz* ⟿ *12 rooms* ⚘ *In-room: no a/c, kitchen, Wi-Fi. In-hotel: laundry facilities, parking, some pets allowed.*

NIGHTLIFE

Backcountry Brewery. Boisterous Backcountry Brewery is home to Great American Beer Festival gold medal–winner Telemark IPA and other homemade brews. ✉ *720 Main St.* ☎ *970/668–2337* ⊕ *www. backcountrybrewery.com.*

Moose Jaw. The Moose Jaw is a locals' hangout. Pool tables beckon, and a plethora of old-time photographs, trophies, and newspaper articles makes the barn-wood walls all but invisible. ✉ *208 Main St.* ☎ *970/668–3931.*

BRECKENRIDGE

22 mi southwest of Keystone via U.S. 6, I–70, and Hwy. 9.

Breckenridge was founded in 1859, when gold was discovered in the surrounding hills. For the next several decades the town's fortunes rose and fell as its lodes of gold and silver were discovered and exhausted. Throughout the latter half of the 19th century and the early 20th century, Breckenridge was famous as a mining camp that "turned out more gold with less work than any camp in Colorado," according to the *Denver Post*. Dredging gold out of the rivers continued until World War II. Visitors today can still see evidence of the gold-dredging operations in the surrounding streams.

At 9,603 feet above sea level and surrounded by higher peaks, Breckenridge is the oldest continuously occupied town on the western slope. The town was originally dubbed Breckinridge, but the spelling was changed after its namesake, a former U.S. vice president, became a Confederate brigadier general in the Civil War. Due to an error by a cartographer, Breckenridge wasn't included on the official U.S. map until 1936, when the error was discovered by a member of the Breckenridge Women's Club.

Much of the town's architectural legacy from the mining era remains, so you'll find stores occupying authentic Victorian storefronts, restaurants, and bed-and-breakfasts in Victorian homes. Surrounding the town's historic core, condos and hotels are packed into the woods and along the roads threading the mountainsides toward the base of the Peak 8.

> **WORD OF MOUTH**
>
> "Breck is one of my favorite towns in CO. It is more laid back and far less upscale than Aspen and Vail." —Mrt

GETTING HERE AND AROUND

Most people arrive by car or a shuttle from Denver International Airport. Getting around is easiest by car, but can also be done by local shuttles and taxis.

TOURS
★

The **Breckenridge Heritage Alliance** leads lively tours of downtown Breckenridge, Colorado's largest National Historic District; the schedule varies seasonally.

WHEN TO GO

The ski season runs from November to April, but festivals and warm-weather activities attract visitors year-round.

FESTIVALS

Festivals run rampant here, and it's rare to show up when locals aren't celebrating. Among the best festivals are the annual U.S. Snowboard Grand Prix (⊕ *www.ussnowboarding.com*) and the International Snow Sculpture championships in winter, the Spring Massive Festival (⊕ *www.springmassive.com*) in April, and Genuine Jazz (⊕ *www.genuinejazz.com*) in June. Summer events include the Toast of Breckenridge food and wine festival and the National Repertory Orchestra (⊕ *www.nationalrepertoryorchestra.com*) performances at the Riverwalk Center near the center of town.

ESSENTIALS

Transportation Contacts Breckenridge Free Shuttle ☎ 970/547–3140.

Visitor and Tour Information Breckenridge Heritage Alliance ✉ 309 N. Main St. ☎ 800/980–1859 ⊕ www.breckheritage.com ☉ Year-round by appointment. **Breckenridge Resort Chamber** ✉ 111 Ski Hill Rd. ☎ 970/453–2918, 888/251–2417 ⊕ www.gobreck.com. **Breckenridge Snow Report** ☎ 970/496–4111, 800/934–2485.

EXPLORING

Country Boy Mine. Ever since gold was discovered here in 1887, the Country Boy Mine has been one of the region's top producers. During tours of the facility you can belly up to the stove in the restored blacksmith shop. The mine has hayrides and gold panning in summer and romantic dinner sleigh rides in winter. ✉ 0542 French Gulch Rd. ☎ 970/453–4405 ⊕ www.countryboymine.com ⌐ Mine tours $21, sleigh rides $55 ☉ Days and hrs vary seasonally; call ahead.

Edwin Carter Museum. Dating from 1875, the Edwin Carter Museum is dedicated to the "log cabin naturalist" who helped to create Denver's Museum of Nature and Science. Look for realistic stuffed animals, including a large buffalo and a burro carrying a miner's pack. ✉ 111

N. Ridge St. ☎ *800/980–1859* ⊕ *www.breckheritage.com* ✉ *$3* ⊙ *Hrs vary, call ahead.*

Historic District. Downtown Breckenridge's Historic District is one of Colorado's largest, with about 250 buildings on the National Register of Historic Places. The district is roughly a compact 12 square blocks, bounded by Main, High, and Washington streets and Wellington Road. There are some 171 buildings with points of historical interest, from simple log cabins to Victorians with lacy gingerbread trim.

DOWNHILL SKIING AND SNOWBOARDING

Breckenridge. With plenty of facilities for snowboarders, Breckenridge is popular with young people. There are several terrain parks and an area where you can learn to freeride. The resort's slopes are spread across four interconnected mountains in the Tenmile Range, named Peaks 7, 8, 9, and 10. The highest chairlift in North America—a high-speed quad lift on Peak 8—tops out at an air-gulping 12,840 feet. Peak 7 and Peak 8 have above-the-timberline bowls and chutes. The lower reaches of Peak 7 have some of the country's prettiest intermediate-level terrain accessible by a lift. Peak 8 and Peak 9 have trails for all skill levels. Peak 10 has long trails with roller-coaster runs.

In line with the town's proud heritage, some runs are named for the old mines, including Bonanza, Cashier, Gold King, and Wellington. During one week each January the town declares itself an "independent kingdom" during the wild revel called Ullr Fest, which honors the Norse god of snow. ☎ *970/453–5000* ⊕ *www.breckenridge.com* ⊙ *Nov.–Apr., daily 8:30–4.*

FACILITIES 4,337-foot vertical drop; 2,358 skiable acres; 14% beginner, 50% intermediate, 36% advanced; 29 lifts; 1 gondola, 2 high-speed six-person lifts, 7 high speed quad chairs, 1 triple chair, 6 double chairs, 12 surface lifts.

LESSONS AND **Breckenridge Ski & Ride School.** Contact the Breckenridge Ski & Ride
PROGRAMS School for information about lessons and specialty clinics. The Children's Ski and Ride School at Peak 8 has its own lift. ☎ *888/576–2754.*

LIFT TICKETS Few skiers and riders pay the high-season walk-up rate of around $100 for a one-day lift ticket. Breckenridge skiers use a variety of season passes sold by Vail Resorts, which owns Breckenridge, Beaver Creek, Keystone, and Vail. Most vacationers purchase lift and lodging packages, or buy advance multiday lift passes at discounted rates online.

RENTALS Rental packages (skis, boots, and poles; snowboards and boots) start around $30 per day. Prices vary, but not dramatically. If you can't find your brand of high-performance equipment in the first store you try, you're sure to find it elsewhere.

CHILD CARE Breckenridge has a number of child-care programs. All-day classes or half-day classes for kids are available. Early drop-off is an option if you want to get to the slopes before everyone else. Classes meet at the Kids' Castle at Peak 8, and Beaver Run and the Village on Peak 9.

NORDIC SKIING
BACKCOUNTRY SKIING

They don't call this place Summit County for nothing—mountain passes above 10,000 feet allow relatively easy access to high-country terrain and some of the area's best snow. But remember: avalanche-related deaths are all too common in Summit County. Don't judge an area solely on appearances or the fact that other skiers or snowmobilers have been there before, as even slopes that look gentle may slide. Never head into the backcountry without checking weather conditions, letting someone know where you're going, and wearing appropriate clothing. Always carry survival gear and travel with a buddy.

> **EPIC AND SUMMIT PASSES**
>
> For unlimited skiing at Keystone, Breckenridge, and Arapahoe Basin, consider the Summit Pass ($429), all for the cost of about four daily lift tickets. The Epic Pass ($669) also includes Vail and Heavenly in California.

Dillon Ranger District Office of the White River National Forest. For information on snow conditions and avalanche dangers, contact the Dillon Ranger District Office of the White River National Forest. ☎ 970/468–5400.

Summit County Huts Association. One popular touring route is the trip to Boreas Pass, just south of Breckenridge. The 12-mi-long trail follows the route of a former railroad, with good views of distant peaks along the way. The Summit County Huts Association has four backcountry cabins where skiers can spend the night (two are open for summer hikers). ☎ 970/453–8583 ⊕ www.summithuts.org.

10th Mountain Division Hut Association. If you're traveling farther afield, there are also cabins available through the 10th Mountain Division Hut Association. ☎ 970/925–5775 ⊕ www.huts.org.

TRACK SKIING

Breckenridge Nordic Center. The Breckenridge Nordic Center has 18.5 mi of groomed tracks for classic and skate skiing, as well as ungroomed trails in the Golden Horseshoe. There are also 6 mi of marked snowshoe trails. ☎ 970/453–6855 ⊕ www.breckenridgenordic.com.

OTHER SPORTS AND THE OUTDOORS

Alpine Events. Alpine Events has a full range of summer and winter activities. In warm weather there are ATV and Jeep tours of the backcountry, cattle drives, and even rafting after dark with night-vision goggles. In winter there's snowmobiling, snow-catting, dogsledding, and sleigh rides. ✉ 1516 Blue Ridge Rd. ☎ 970/262–0374.

FISHING

Mountain Angler. Mountain Angler organizes fishing trips, including float trips on the Colorado River, half-day trips on streams near Breckenridge, and all-day trips on rivers farther away. ✉ 311 S. Main St. ☎ 970/453–4665, 800/453–4669 ⊕ www.mountainangler.com.

FITNESS

Breckenridge Recreation Center. Breckenridge Recreation Center is a 62,000-square-foot facility with a fully equipped health club, two swimming pools, climbing walls, and indoor tennis and racquetball courts. Outdoor facilities include clay tennis courts, basketball courts, a skateboard park, and bike paths. ⊠ *880 Airport Rd.* ☎ *970/453–1734.*

GOLF

Breckenridge Golf Club. This is the world's only municipally owned course designed by Jack Nicklaus. You may play any combination of the three 9-hole sets: the Bear, the Beaver (with beaver ponds lining many of the fairways), or the Elk. The course resembles a nature reserve as it flows through mountainous terrain and fields full of wildflowers. ⊠ *200 Clubhouse Dr.* ☎ *970/453–9104* ⊕ *www.breckenridgegolfclub.com* ↖ *27 holes. Yards: 7276. Par: 72. Green fee: $130.*

RAFTING

Breckenridge Whitewater Rafting. This outfitter runs white-water rafting and fishing trips on stretches of the Colorado, Arkansas, Eagle, and Blue rivers in Summit County, and Clear Creek on the Front Range. They also offer zip-line and horseback tours. ⊠ *842 N. Summit Blvd., Frisco* ☎ *800/370–0581, 970/423–7031* ⊕ *www.breckenridgewhitewater.com.*

Performance Tours. Performance Tours leads expeditions on the Arkansas, Blue, and the upper Colorado rivers for newcomers looking for some action and experienced rafters ready for extremes. The company is based in Buena Vista, but will pick up groups in Breckenridge for all-day trips. ☎ *800/328–7238* ⊕ *www.performancetours.com.*

☪ **Whitewater Kayak Park.** Whitewater Kayak Park is a playground for kayakers, with splash rocks, eddy pools, and S-curves. This public park on the Blue River behind the Breckenridge Recreation Department is free and open from April through August. ⊠ *880 Airport Rd.* ☎ *970/453–1734.*

SNOWMOBILING

Good Times Adventures. Good Times Adventures runs snowmobile and dogsledding trips on more than 40 mi of groomed trails, through open meadows and along the Continental Divide to 11,585-foot-high Georgia Pass. ⊠ *6061 Tiger Rd.* ☎ *970/453–7604, 800/477–0144* ⊕ *www.snowmobilecolorado.com.*

WHERE TO EAT

$ ╳ **Downstairs at Eric's.** Loud, dark, and lots of fun for young partiers,
AMERICAN this place is video-game central. Kids hang out in the arcade while
☪ their folks watch sports on the big-screen TVs. Pizzas are popular here—try them topped with veggies, seafood, or "garbage" (the management's colorful term for everything). The sandwiches are just as good. Try the Philly Burger topped with sautéed green peppers, onions, and melted Swiss cheese. ⊠ *111 S. Main St.* ☎ *970/453–1401* ⊕ *www.downstairsaterics.com.*

$ ╳ **Giampietro Pasta & Pizzeria.** The smell of freshly baked pizza will draw
AMERICAN families to the door of this Italian eatery. Peek through the window and
☪ you'll see families gathered around tables covered with the ubiquitous red-checked tablecloths. There are lots of pastas on the menu, from classic baked ziti to tasty spaghetti with shrimp and pesto. Hungry diners gravitate toward the New York–style pizza with the works and the Sicilian-style deep-dish pizza. You can also build your own calzone or pizza from the huge list of ingredients. A take-out menu is available.

100 N. Main St. ☎ *970/453–3838* ⊕ *www.giampietropizza.com.*

WHERE TO STAY

For expanded hotel reviews, visit Fodors.com.

$$
B&B/INN

Allaire Timbers Inn. Nestled in a wooded area, this stone-and-timber log cabin has a living room dominated by a stone fireplace, as well as a reading loft and a sunroom with a green-slate floor and hand-crafted log furniture. **Pros:** great mountain views; friendly owners; tasty homemade breakfast. **Cons:** downstairs rooms can be noisy; no elevator. ⊠ *9511 S. Main St.* ☎ *970/453–7530, 800/624–4904* ⊕ *www.allairetimbers.com* ⇆ *8 rooms, 2 suites* ⚘ *In-room: no a/c, Wi-Fi. In-hotel: business center, parking* ⏐◎⏐ *Breakfast.*

BRECKENRIDGE LODGING ALTERNATIVES

Several companies handle condominiums in the area.

Breckenridge Central Lodging. Summit Mountain Rentals has 150 condos, private homes, and conventional hotel rooms for rent around the county. ☎ *970/453–2160, 800/383–7382* ⊕ *www.summitrentals.com.*

Resort Quest. Resort Quest manages Hyatt Main Street Station and other complexes. ☎ *970/453–4000, 800/661–7604* ⊕ *www.resortquest.com.*

$$$
B&B/INN
★

Barn on the River Bed and Breakfast. Innkeepers Fred Kinat and Diane Jaynes run this timber-frame B&B. **Pros:** all rooms are within earshot of the river; gas fireplaces; friendly owners. **Cons:** rooms fill fast; reservations are essential. ⊠ *303B N. Main St.* ☎ *970/453–2975, 800/795–2975* ⊕ *www.breckenridge-inn.com* ⇆ *4 rooms* ⚘ *In-room: no a/c, Wi-Fi. In-hotel: parking* ⏐◎⏐ *Breakfast.*

$$$
HOTEL
Fodor's Choice
★

Lodge & Spa at Breckenridge. This lodge more than compensates for its location on a mountainside beyond the downtown area with breathtaking views of the Tenmile Range from nearly every angle. **Pros:** great mountain views; complimentary Continental breakfast and shuttle to town or resort. **Cons:** a bit outdated; no room service. ⊠ *112 Overlook Dr.* ☎ *970/453–9300, 800/736–1607* ⊕ *www.thelodgeandspaatbreck.com* ⇆ *45 rooms, 2 houses* ⚘ *In-room: no a/c, kitchen, Wi-Fi. In-hotel: restaurant, bar, pool, gym, spa, parking, some pets allowed* ⏐◎⏐ *Breakfast.*

$$$$
HOTEL

Mountain Thunder Lodge. Rising above the trees, this lodge constructed from rough-hewn timber brings to mind old-fashioned ski lodges. **Pros:** family-sized suites; close to ski lifts; free Wi-Fi. **Cons:** short walk to main street. ⊠ *50 Mountain Thunder Dr.* ☎ *888/989–1269* ⊕ *www.breckresorts.com* ⇆ *88 rooms* ⚘ *In-room: no a/c, kitchen, Wi-Fi. In-hotel: pool, gym, spa, laundry facilities, parking.*

$$$
RESORT

Village at Breckenridge. The word "village" puts it mildly, as this sprawling resort is spread over 14 acres of mountainous terrain alongside the beautiful river and right across from the historic Main Street. **Pros:** great concierge; ski-in ski-out. **Cons:** some rooms have better style than others, decor depends on individual owners. ⊠ *535 S. Park Ave.* ☎ *970/453–5192, 888/400–9590* ⊕ *www.breckresorts.com* ⇆ *200 rooms* ⚘ *In-room: no a/c, kitchen, Wi-Fi. In-hotel: bar, pool, gym, spa, laundry facilities, business center, parking, some pets allowed.*

NIGHTLIFE
BARS AND LOUNGES

Breckenridge Brewery. Breckenridge Brewery serves 10 microbrews, from Avalanche Ale to Breck Lite, and has an extensive and kid-friendly pub menu. It's a great après-ski spot. ☒ *600 S. Main St.* ☎ *970/453–1550* ⊕ *www.breckbrew.com.*

Cecilia's. On the lower level of La Cima Mall, Cecilia's is a lounge with mouthwatering martinis. Smokers head to the cigar patio. ☒ *520 S. Main St.* ☎ *970/453–2243* ⊕ *www.cecilias.tv.*

Downstairs at Eric's. Downstairs at Eric's is standing-room only when there's a game. There are four big-screen TVs and 34 smaller ones scattered around the bar, so you don't have to worry about missing a touchdown. More than 120 brands of bottled beers and another 21 on tap make this a favorite of aficionados. ☒ *111 S. Main St.* ☎ *970/453–1401* ⊕ *www.downstairsaterics.com.*

Hearthstone. With maroon velour wallpaper and lacy curtains, Hearthstone hints at its roots as a bordello. Skiers and locals scarf down the happy-hour specials, including baked brie and chile rellenos. ☒ *130 S. Ridge St.* ☎ *970/453–1148* ⊕ *www.hearthstonerestaurant.biz.*

MUSIC CLUBS

Base 9 Bar. Base 9 Bar is a lively après-ski destination with two pool tables, three high-definition TVs, and a martini bar. ☒ *620 Village Rd.* ☎ *970/453–6000.*

SHOPPING

Main Street, stretching the entire length of Breckenridge, has an abundance of shopping, with T-shirt shacks, high-end boutiques, and art galleries. It's a good idea to spend an evening window-shopping before breaking out your wallet.

Bay Street Company. In a quaint Victorian house, the Bay Street Company carries colorful hand-painted furniture and collectibles. ☒ *232 S. Main St.* ☎ *970/453–6303.*

COPPER MOUNTAIN AND LEADVILLE

Skiers head to Copper Mountain because the runs make sense—you can start easy and progress to harder slopes without having to crisscross the mountain. It also offers the largest expanse of skiing in Summit County. Although nearby Leadville has a small ski resort (Ski Cooper) and plenty of snowmobiling trails, this rustic mining town is more popular as a summer base for hiking forays to nearby Mount Elbert, the highest peak in Colorado.

COPPER MOUNTAIN

7 mi south of Frisco via I–70.

Once little more than a series of strip malls, Copper Mountain is now a thriving resort with a bustling base. The resort's heart is a pedestrian-only village anchored by Burning Stones Plaza, which is prime people-watching turf. High-speed ski lifts march up the mountain on one side

CLOSE UP

Colorado's Fragile Wilderness

More than 1,500 peaks pierce the Colorado skyline, creating one of the most extensive and pristine alpine landscapes in the United States. It is a treeless landscape that has changed little in thousands of years; summer storms bury prehistoric glaciers, colorful wildflowers push up through snowy meadows, and ice-covered mountains fill 100-mi views.

GROWING THREATS

But time is catching up with this ice-age wilderness. The very characteristics that once preserved the panoramic heights from human impact—rugged peaks, polar weather, barren vistas—are the same ones that today threaten it. Growing environmental pressures from recreational use, industrial pollution, and changing land-use patterns are taking a toll on this surprisingly fragile ecosystem.

Colorado's burgeoning population is increasing at an annual rate of 2% to 3%, a rate not seen since the gold-rush days of 1859. Many who move to the Mile High State enjoy an outdoor lifestyle that includes hiking. A popular pastime for many has been tackling the Fourteeners, the state's 54 peaks that top 14,000 feet. As more and more hikers trample up these mountains, they gouge new trails, compact thin soil, and crush root systems. This damage can take a surprisingly long time to heal. Trails across the tundra near Rocky Mountain National Park that were carved out by Ute and Arapaho scouts hundreds of years ago are still visible today.

Less subtle than erosion, and equally devastating, is the harm caused by industrial pollution. Western Slope power plants in Craig and Hayden burn low-sulfur coal. Scientists believe the resulting sulfur and nitrogen emissions may be creating acid snow in the alpine watersheds, the same watersheds that pour forth several of the great American rivers, including the Colorado, Rio Grande, and Arkansas.

Ironically, one of the greatest threats to the alpine tundra comes from attempts at preserving native wildlife. With wolves and grizzlies extinct in Colorado and hunting banned in Rocky Mountain National Park, the elk population has exploded from a handful of over-hunted animals to more than 2,100. Their sharp hooves trample summer pastures above the timberline and destroy many of the arctic willow stands that provide food and shelter for other wildlife, including the white-tailed ptarmigan.

PINE BEETLES

Had you emerged from the west portal of Eisenhower Tunnel a dozen years ago you would have been greeted by a sweeping view of green lodgepole pine forests dressing the flanks of Summit County's peaks. But today that view is tinted an ugly rust-red. That's because a pine beetle infestation is killing Colorado's lodgepole. The infestation, which began in 1996, is the result of a perfect storm. Fire suppression and a regional drought created dense forests susceptible to attack, while global climate change and mellow winters allowed the beetles to expand their range south from Canada. Experts believe that by 2013 almost 90% of Summit County's pines will be dead. Spraying, selective cutting, and natural remedies are all being tried, so far in vain and the fire danger is increasing.

of the plaza, and the other three sides are flanked by condominiums with retail shops and restaurants on the ground floors. Lodgings extend west toward West Village and east to Center and East villages, where a six-pack high-speed lift ferries skiers.

In winter Burning Stones is filled with skiers on their way to and from the slopes and shoppers browsing for gifts to give to those left at home. In summer people relax on condo balconies or restaurant patios as they listen to free concerts on the plaza or watch athletes inch up the 37-foot-high climbing wall. Kids can also learn to kayak or float in paddleboats.

GETTING HERE AND AROUND
The easiest way to reach Copper Mountain is by car. The resort is foot-friendly, and there is also a free resort shuttle service around town.

WHEN TO GO
Skiing is from November to mid-April. In summer the resort tends to be quieter, as most visitors gravitate to the Lake Dillon area for hiking and biking.

ESSENTIALS
Visitor Information Copper Mountain Resort ☎ 970/968–2882, 800/458–8386 ⊕ www.coppercolorado.com. **Copper Mountain Snow Report** ☎ 970/968–2100.

DOWNHILL SKIING AND SNOWBOARDING
Copper Mountain. Copper Mountain is popular with locals because the resort's 2,465 acres are spread across several peaks where the terrain is naturally separated into areas for beginners, intermediates, and expert skiers and snowboarders, making it easy to pick your slope. The Union Creek area contains gentle, tree-lined trails for novices. The slopes above the Village at Copper and Copper Station are an invigorating blend of intermediate and advanced trails. Several steep mogul runs are clustered on the eastern side of the area, and have their own lift. At the top of the resort and in the vast Copper Bowl there's challenging above-tree-line skiing. Freeriders gravitate to the Woodward Central and the Bouncer Park. Weather permitting, on several days each week beginning in mid-February, expert skiers can grab a free first-come, first-served snow-cat ride up Tucker Mountain for an ungroomed, wilderness-style ski experience. ☎ 970/968–2882, 800/458–8386 ⊕ *www.coppercolorado.com* ☉ *Nov.–mid-Apr., daily 9–4.*

FACILITIES 2,601-foot vertical drop; 2,450 skiable acres; 21% beginner, 25% intermediate, 36% advanced, 18% expert; 1 high-speed six-person chair, 4 high-speed quad chairs, 5 triple chairs, 5 double chairs, 4 surface lifts, 3 conveyor lifts.

LESSONS AND PROGRAMS **Ski and Ride School.** Copper Mountain's Ski and Ride School has classes for skiers and snowboarders, private lessons, men- and women-only groups, and special competitive lessons (to help you make a quantum leap in skills). Copper's Kids Sessions, divided into groups based on age and skill level, are designed to both teach and entertain. There's also Kids' Night Out, popular among parents who want an evening without the children. ☎ 970/968–2318.

LIFT TICKETS   Early-season window tickets (through mid-December) are $70 and then jump to about $85 in high season. Few people pay the walk-up rate, however. Vacationers usually purchase lift-and-lodging packages, which include discounted lift rates. Copper Mountain has last-minute deals online at ⊕ *www.coppersavers.com*. Passes can save skiers and riders 20% or more. The best deal is Copper's four-pass program for $159 (with no blackout dates). If you want to short-circuit lift lines during busy times (like Christmas week and spring break), try the Bee Line Advantage—for $20 a day you can get on the lifts 15 minutes earlier in the morning and use a dedicated (and shorter) lift line. Ask about it when you book your hotel or condo; many properties have this as a free bonus.

RENTALS   Rental packages (skis, boots, and poles) start at $30 per day for sport ski packages and go as high as $45 per day for high-performance equipment. Snowboard rental packages (snowboard and boots) start at $42 for adults. Helmet rentals begin at $10.

CHILD CARE   Copper Mountain Resort has ski-school options for older kids and child care for youngsters. The smell of chocolate-chip cookies wafts from the Belly Button Bakery, day care for tots two to four years old. Belly Button Babies accepts kids six weeks to two years old. Children's programs are based in the Mountain Plaza at Center Village.

OTHER SPORTS AND THE OUTDOORS
BICYCLING
Gravitee. Hundreds of miles of bike paths weave around the resort, leading up and down mountainsides and through high-country communities. In summer there are weekly group rides for early risers. Gravitee has all the gear you need for cycling in the area. ⊠ *0164 Copper Rd., Tucker Mountain Lodge* ☎ *970/968–0171* ⊕ *www.gravitee.com*.

GOLF
Copper Mountain has reasonably priced golf and lodging packages. You can also take a shuttle from the resort to the Raven Golf Club at Three Peaks, about 15 minutes away in Dillon.

Copper Creek Golf Club. Right at the resort is a par-70, 6,057-yard course designed by Pete and Perry Dye. The highest-elevation 18-hole golf course in North America, it flows up and down some of the ski trails at the base of the mountain and between condos and town homes in the resort's East Village. ⊠ *104 Wheeler Pl.* ☎ *866/286–1663* ⊕ *www.coppercolorado.com* ⤢ *18 holes. Yards: 6057. Par: 70. Green fee: $69.*

WHERE TO EAT AND STAY
For expanded hotel reviews, visit Fodors.com.

$$
AMERICAN   ✕ **Endo's Adrenaline Café.** Just a few ski-boot steps from the American Eagle Lift, Endo's Adrenaline Café is one of the more hopping sports bar/restaurants. Enjoy rock music as you climb atop one of the high bar stools and catch a game on one of the TVs, or pick a table for a more intimate lunch or dinner at this high-energy establishment. Try the fish tacos or a mountainous plate of Endo's Mondo Nachos—a heaping portion of chips covered in melted cheddar, jalapeños, and guacamole. ⊠ *209 Ten Mile Circle* ☎ *970/968–3070* ⊕ *www.endoscafe.com*.

$$$
RESORT
☾

⊡ **Copper Mountain Resort.** The resort runs the majority of lodging in the area, ranging from standard hotel rooms to spacious condos and town homes. **Pros:** centrally located; wide range of accommodations. **Cons:** village can be noisy; quality of rooms varies greatly. ✉ *209 Tenmile Circle* ☎ *970/968–2882, 800/458–8386* ⊕ *www.coppercolorado.com* ⇪ *800 rooms* ♿ *In-room: no a/c, safe, kitchen, Internet, Wi-Fi. In-hotel: restaurant, bar, golf course, pool, tennis court, gym, children's programs, parking, some pets allowed.*

NIGHTLIFE

Whether it's a warm afternoon in winter or a cool evening in summer, one of the best places to kick back is at one of the tables spreading across Burning Stones Plaza.

Endo's Adrenaline Café. At the base of the American Eagle lift, Endo's Adrenaline Café is the place to be for après-ski cocktails. ✉ *209 Ten Mile Circle* ☎ *970/968–3070* ⊕ *www.endoscafe.com.*

SHOPPING

Retail shops fill the ground floors of the Village at Copper, a pedestrian-only plaza.

Mountain Adventure Center. Shop for ski and snowboard gear, book your ski lessons, and reserve rental equipment at Mountain Adventure Center. ✉ *0184 Copper Rd.* ☎ *970/968–2318.*

LEADVILLE

24 mi south of Copper Mountain via Hwy. 91.

Sitting in the mountains at 10,430 feet, Leadville is America's highest incorporated city. The 70 square blocks of Victorian architecture and adjacent mining district hint at its past as a rich silver-mining boomtown. In the history of Colorado mining, perhaps no town looms larger. Two of the state's most fascinating figures lived here: mining magnate Horace Tabor and his second wife, Elizabeth Doe McCourt (nicknamed Baby Doe), the central figures in John LaTouche's Pulitzer prize–winning opera *The Ballad of Baby Doe.*

Tabor amassed a fortune of $12 million, much of which he spent building monuments to himself and his mistress "Baby Doe." His power peaked when his money helped him secure a U.S. Senate seat in 1883. He married Baby Doe after divorcing his first wife, the faithful Augusta. The Tabors incurred the scorn of high society by throwing their money around in what was considered a vulgar fashion. After the price of silver plummeted, Tabor died a pauper in 1899 and Baby Doe became a recluse, rarely remerging from her tiny, unheated cabin beside the mine entrance. She froze to death in 1935.

GETTING HERE AND AROUND

A car is the only reasonable mode of transportation into Leadville. Once in town, the main street, lined with shops and restaurants, and the cozy surrounding neighborhoods make for pleasant walks in summer.

WHEN TO GO

It's not that summer never comes to Leadville, it's just that winter never really leaves. This high-altitude town can see snow almost any month, though really only a brief flurry in July and August. In winter Leadville hibernates (except for the nearby Ski Cooper and snowmobile trails), but in summer the town is a popular and cool respite from the heat.

FESTIVALS **Leadville Boom Town Days.** Eccentricity is still a Leadville trait, as witnessed by the 21-mile **International Pack Burro Race** over Mosquito Pass and a local parade. The annual event is part of Leadville Boom Town Days, held the first weekend of August. The event is immortalized with thousands of T-shirts and bumper stickers that read, "Get Your Ass Over the Pass." ⊕ *www.leadville.com/boomdays.*

ESSENTIALS

Visitor Information Leadville Chamber of Commerce ⊠ *809 Harrison St., Leadville* ☎ *719/486–3900* ⊕ *www.leadvilleusa.com.*

EXPLORING
TOP ATTRACTIONS

☾ **Leadville, Colorado & Southern Railroad Company.** Still chugging along is the Leadville, Colorado & Southern Railroad Company, which can take you on a breathtaking 2½-hour trip to the Continental Divide. The train leaves from Leadville's century-old depot and travels beside the Arkansas River to its headwaters at Freemont Pass. The return trip takes you down to French Gulch for views of Mount Elbert, Colorado's highest peak. ⊠ *326 E. 7th St.* ☎ *719/486–3936, 866/386–3936* ⊕ *www.leadville-train.com* ⊠ *$35* ☉ *June–early Oct., daily; call for hrs.*

★ **Mount Elbert.** The massive, snowcapped peak watching over Leadville is Mount Elbert. At 14,433 feet it's the highest mountain in Colorado and the tallest peak in the entire Rocky Mountain Range, second in height in the contiguous 48 states only to California's 14,495-foot Mount Whitney.

☾ **National Mining Hall of Fame and Museum.** The National Mining Hall of
★ Fame and Museum covers virtually every aspect of mining, from the discovery of precious ore to fashioning it into coins and other items. Dioramas in the beautiful brick building explain extraction processes. ⊠ *120 W. 9th St.* ☎ *719/486–1229* ⊕ *www.mininghalloffame.org* ⊠ *$7* ☉ *Nov.–Apr., daily 11–4; May–Oct., daily 9–5.*

Tabor Opera House. The three-story Tabor Opera House opened in 1879, when it was proclaimed the "largest and best west of the Mississippi." It hosted luminaries such as Harry Houdini, John Philip Sousa, and Oscar Wilde. Shows on the current schedule, like *Cowboys and Indian* and *The Silver Boom,* revisit the rags-to-riches characters of the Colorado golden days. ⊠ *308 Harrison Ave.* ☎ *719/486–8409* ⊕ *www. taboroperahouse.net* ⊠ *$15* ☉ *June–Aug., Mon.–Sat. 10–5.*

WORTH NOTING

Healy House and Dexter Cabin. On a tree-lined street in downtown Leadville you'll find the Healy House and Dexter Cabin, an 1878 Greek Revival house and an 1879 log cabin—two of Leadville's earliest residences. The lavishly decorated rooms of the clapboard house provide a sense of how the town's upper crust, such as the Tabors, lived and played. ✉ *912 Harrison Ave.* ☎ *719/486–0487* ⊕ *www.historycolorado. org/museums* ✉ *$6* ⊙ *Late Mar.–Aug., daily 10–4:30.*

Heritage Museum. The Heritage Museum paints a vivid portrait of life in Leadville at the turn of the last century, with dioramas depicting life in the mines. There's also furniture, clothing, and toys from the Victorian era. ✉ *104 E. 9th St.* ☎ *719/486–1878* ✉ *$6* ⊙ *mid May–Sept., daily 10–5.*

Matchless Mine. The Matchless Mine and Baby Doe's cabin are 1 mi east of downtown. Peer into the dark shaft, then pay a visit to the small museum with its tribute to the tragic love story of Horace and Baby Doe Tabor. ✉ *E. 7th St.* ☎ *719/486–1229* ⊕ *www.matchlessmine.com* ✉ *$7* ⊙ *Late May–Sept., daily 10–4.*

DOWNHILL SKIING AND SNOWBOARDING

⟳ **Ski Cooper.** Nine miles west of Leadville, Ski Cooper is one of those undiscovered boutique ski areas in the Rockies. It has 400 acres skiable via lift and another 2,400 acres of backcountry powder accessible by snow cat. The 26 groomed runs are perfect for beginning or intermediate skiers. ✉ *U.S. 24* ☎ *719/486–3684, 800/707–6114* ⊕ *www. skicooper.com* ⊙ *Late Nov.–early Apr., daily 9–4.*

FACILITIES 1,200-foot vertical drop; 400 skiable acres; 30% beginner, 40% more difficult, 30% advanced; 5 lifts; 1 triple chair, 1 double chair, 3 surface lifts.

LESSONS AND PROGRAMS **Chicago Ridge Snowcat Tours.** Chicago Ridge Snowcat Tours are for expert backcountry skiers who want the off-piste adventure of scripting their signature across acres of untracked powder. Tickets are $275, but you'll get your fill of phat snow. The terrain has tree glades and open bowls. You must be over 18 (or be accompanied by an adult) and fit; the runs are up to 10,000 feet long, and some vertical drops top 1,400 feet. Wide powder skis are available for rent for those who really want to float. ☎ *719/486–2277* ⊕ *www.skicooper.com/snow-cat-skiing.*

Ski Cooper Ski School. The Ski Cooper Ski School covers the gamut for skiers and snowboarders. A "Never Ever" two-hour group lesson with magic carpet lift ticket and rental gear is $50. You can also book private lessons, race and telemark clinics, and lessons for your children, which can be extended as part of the all-day child-care programs. Lessons for handicapped skiers are available by appointment.

Ski Cooper has a number of options for children, including their popular Panda Patrol for children ages 5 to 12. A full-day package (from 10 am to 3 pm) includes a group ski lesson, equipment rental, lunch, and full mountain lift ticket for $80. The Panda Cubs program caters to four-year-olds and provides a two-hour lesson, lift ticket, rental package, lunch, and afternoon daycare for $77. ☎ *719/486–2277.*

LIFT TICKETS At $44 for a full-day lift ticket, you'll be hard-pressed to find cheaper powder. Vacationers should still shop around for discounted rates at King Soopers and Safeway stores.

RENTALS Rental packages (skis, boots, and poles) start at $15 per day, among the cheapest in the state. Snowboarding packages start at $25. Performance packages and backcountry ski gear rentals are also available and start at $25.

OTHER SPORTS AND THE OUTDOORS
CANOEING AND KAYAKING

Twin Lakes Canoe & Kayak. There's no better way to see the high country than by exploring its alpine lakes. Twin Lakes Canoe & Kayak offers guided tours of Twin and Turquoise lakes to beginners, and equipment rental to more experienced paddlers. ⊠ *6451 Hwy. 82, about 20 mi south of Leadville* ☎ *719/251–9961.*

GOLF

★ **Mt. Massive Golf Course.** Play North America's highest 9-hole green at 9,680 feet—and watch your distance increase in the thin mountain air. Just west of Leadville in the Arkansas River valley, this public golf course was opened in the 1930s to the delight of the mining community. True green fairways replaced sagebrush flats after a $50,000 grant in the 1970s heralded an automated irrigation system. ⊠ *259 Hwy. 5* ☎ *719/486–2176* ⊕ *www.mtmassivegolf.com* ⌣ *Reservations essential* ⚐ *9 holes. Yards: 3150. Par: 36. Green fee: $23/$36.*

HORSEBACK RIDING

Mega Mountain Magic. If you're feeling like it's time to hit the trail, Mega Mountain Magic has a stable of horses ready for you. ⊠ *1100 Hwy. 18* ☎ *719/486–4570.*

SNOWMOBILING

Alpine Snowmobiles. Skiing extreme slopes isn't the only way to feel the blast of powder on your face. Fire up your own mechanical beast with Alpine Snowmobiles. ⊠ *21767 U.S. 24* ☎ *719/486–9899* ⊕ *www. alpineadventuresinc.com.*

2 Mile Hi Ski-Doo. Snowmobiling fans often head to 2 Mile Hi Ski-Doo. ⊠ *1719 N. Poplar St.* ☎ *719/486–1183* ⊕ *www.2milehiskidoo.com.*

WHERE TO EAT AND STAY

For expanded hotel reviews, visit Fodors.com.

$ ✕ **The Grill.** Run by the Martinez family since 1965, this local favorite
MEXICAN   draws a standing-room-only crowd. The service is sometimes slow,
↻   but that leaves time for another marvelous margarita. New Mexican cuisine is the specialty here, including dishes with hand-roasted green chilies. In summer you can retreat to the patio and dine with views of Colorado's two highest mountains. ⊠ *715 Elm St.* ☎ *719/486–9930* ⊕ *www.grillbarcafe.com* ⊙ *Closed Mon. and Tues. No lunch except June–Aug. weekends.*

$$ ▥ **Delaware Hotel.** This artfully restored 1886 hotel is one of the best
HOTEL   examples of high Victorian architecture in the area, so it's no surprise
★   that it's listed on the National Register of Historic Places. **Pros:** loaded with gold-rush character; great mountain views; very friendly staff. **Cons:** lobby is one large store; the altitude in Leadville can be tough if you're arriving from sea level. ⊠ *700 Harrison Ave.* ☎ *719/486–1418, 800/748–2004* ⊕ *www.delawarehotel.com* ⊅ *36 rooms, 4 suites* ⌂ *In-room: no a/c, Internet, Wi-Fi. In-hotel: restaurant, bar, business center, parking* ▯⊙▯ *Breakfast.*

Vail Valley

WORD OF MOUTH

"Basically just loved the town of Vail in general. It's very well planned out and easy to get around. Vail also didn't have the "look at me" crowd of Aspen although it still has a very upscale feel. I guess I found it to be the perfect combination of upscale and laid back."

—AustinTraveler

"Vail is fabulous and easy to get to from Denver (or you can fly into Vail), Their manufactured ski village is better than most towns! Larger, with excellent stores (some very upscale, like Loro Piano) and restaurants and bars. It's pedestrian-only once you're in the village and the ski lifts are in the village as well."

—sf7307

Updated by
Jad Davenport

If Aspen is Colorado's Hollywood East, then her rival Vail is Wall Street West. So popular is this ski resort with the monied East Coast crowd that locals sometimes refer to particularly crowded weeks as "212" weeks, in reference to the area code of their visitors. The attraction for vacationers from all over is the thin, aspen-cloaked Vail Valley, a narrow corridor slit by Interstate 70 and bounded by the rugged Gore Range to the north and east and the tabled Sawatch escarpments to the south. Through it all runs the sparkling Eagle River.

The resorts begin just west of Vail Pass, a saddle well below tree line, and stretch 20 mi through the communities of Vail, Eagle-Vail, Minturn, Avon, Beaver Creek, Arrowhead, and Edwards. The vibe in these places varies dramatically, from Beaver Creek, a gated community of second (and probably third) megahomes, to Edwards, a rapidly growing worker town, to Vail, filled with styles of lodging, dining, and shopping appealing to many tastes.

In winter this region is famous for the glittering resorts of Vail and Beaver Creek. Between these two areas skiers and snowboarders have almost 7,000 acres at their disposal, including the unforgettable Back Bowls far beyond the noise of I–70 traffic.

In summer these resorts are great bases from which you can explore the high country on foot, horseback, raft, or bike. But take heed: all trails go up—though you can cheat and catch the Eagle Bahn Gondola up and hike or ride down. Some trails are designated for bikers, others for hikers, and many for both. Always remember that bikers should yield to hikers, though in practice it's considered courteous to let them blow by. In addition, there are hundreds of miles of trails weaving through the White River National Forest. Warm-weather weekends are filled with an exciting range of cultural events, including performances by such groups as the New York Philharmonic and the Bolshoi Ballet.

ORIENTATION AND PLANNING

GETTING ORIENTED

Finding your way around the Vail Valley is relatively easy; the valley runs east and west, and everything you need is less than a mile off the I–70 corridor (and the constant drone of traffic), which parallels the Eagle River. The Gore Range to the north and east is one of the most rugged wilderness areas in Colorado—the peaks are jagged and broken, and any hiking here immediately involves a steep and sustained

TOP REASONS TO GO

High altitude golf: The thin air at this elevation lets your Titleist fly much farther—enjoy those hero swings at more than a dozen venues.

Romantic meals: A number of intimate restaurants are hidden away among the peaks, reachable by ski, on horseback, and even by horse-drawn sleigh.

Rugged scenery: The Gore Range presents some of the most sharp-spined backcountry in the state,

with ice-cold tarns, sheer cliffs, and shaggy white mountain goats.

The slopes: Vail is as real and challenging a ski mountain as you'll find anywhere in the western United States, with the steeps and back bowls to prove it.

Summer festivals: Check out some of Vail's many cultural activities—summer is full of music, culinary, and dance festivals.

5

climb. To the south, the tabled heights of the Sawatch Mountain Range are gentler, and give Vail her superb skiing, particularly in the famed Back Bowls. Beaver Creek feels more isolated, being set off the highway behind a series of gates that control access to the posh communities within.

Vail. European-style cafés and beautifully cobbled streets lined with boutiques are more than just window dressing—Vail is no longer just known for its serious skiing. The nearby town of Minturn is a much more modest burg.

Beaver Creek. As the entrance gates will remind you, Beaver Creek is the most exclusive skiing community in Colorado. This is resort-to-resort skiing set among gorgeous glades of aspens; it never seems to get crowded.

PLANNING

WHEN TO GO

Winter is by far the most crowded time in Vail Valley, with early spring seeing the highest number of visitors hoping to catch that blissful blend of thick powder and china-blue skies. Naturally, prices are highest then as well, though you can sometimes get pre- and postseason deals. Although summer is quickly gaining in popularity, the real deals can be had in the shoulder seasons—late autumn and late spring when the ski slopes are closed. Restaurants will often have two-for-one entrées with a bottle of wine, and hotels run deeply cut rates. Traffic through the I–70 corridor moves at a good clip unless snows have stacked up truckers putting on chains on either side of Vail Pass. The pass itself is low, and stays below tree line, affording it some protection from drifting and blowing snow.

GETTING HERE AND AROUND

AIR TRAVEL

Denver International Airport (DEN), the gateway to the High Rockies, is 119 mi east of Vail. It's a 90-minute drive from Vail, but ski traffic can double the time (expect it to take much longer if a blizzard hits). The Vail Valley is served by Eagle County Airport (EGE), 34 mi west of Vail. During ski season, American, Continental, Delta, and United have nonstop flights to Eagle County from several gateways. United and American fly here year-round.

If possible, try snagging a direct flight straight into the Eagle County Airport from your hometown. But if your trip involves a connection through Denver or another hub, it is often faster to rent a car and make the scenic 90-minute drive through the mountains or catch one of the many shuttle services. Although winter mountain weather can be fickle and delay flights, the two high passes on I–70 between Denver–Loveland and Summit County–Vail are rarely closed, though traffic might slow to a creep.

Airports Denver International Airport (DEN) ☎ 800/247–2336 ⊕ www.flydenver.com. **Eagle County Airport (EGE)** ☎ 970/328–8600 ⊕ www.eaglecounty.us/airport.

Airport Transfers Colorado Mountain Express ☎ 970/926–9800, 800/525–6363. **453-Taxi** ☎ 970/453–8294.

BUS AND SHUTTLE TRAVEL

All the resorts run free or inexpensive shuttles between the ski villages and the slopes. Locals and visitors alike hop the free Town of Vail buses up and down from East Vail to West Vail (a distance of nearly 6 mi, with Lionshead at the center). For trips to Beaver Creek, catch the ECO Transit bus from the Vail Transportation Center in Vail Village, beside the Vail Information Center.

Contacts Avon/Beaver Creek Transit ☎ 970/748–4120 ⊕ www.avon.org. **Colorado Mountain Express** ☎ 800/525–6363, 970/468–7600 ⊕ www.ridecme.com. **ECO Transit** ☎ 970/328–3520 ⊕ www.eaglecounty.us/Transit. **Town of Vail** ☎ 970/479–2100 ⊕ www.vailgov.com.

CAR TRAVEL

The most convenient place for visitors to rent a car is at Denver International Airport. Alamo, Avis, Budget, Dollar, Enterprise, Hertz, and National have offices in Eagle County Airport as well.

Although it is often severely overcrowded, I–70 is still the quickest and most direct route from Denver to Vail. For the first 45 minutes it climbs gradually through the dry Front Range mountains before ducking into the Eisenhower Tunnel. The last 45 minutes are through the high Summit County Basin and up and over the mellow grade of Vail Pass.

PARKS AND RECREATION AREAS

The Vail Valley has two wilderness areas in close proximity—the truly untrammeled Eagle's Nest Wilderness Area to the northeast in the Gore Range, and the more-popular Holy Cross Wilderness to the southwest.

White River National Forest. The land in between the Eagle's Nest Wilderness and the Holy Cross Wilderness, including much of the ski resorts' slopes, is part of the White River National Forest. ☎ *970/945–2521* ⊕ *www.fs.fed.us/r2/whiteriver*.

The Eagle River, whose headwaters are on the north side of Tennessee Pass, is an excellent fishing stream, mostly for brook and brown trout in the 6- to 12-inch range. Public access is easiest upriver of Red Cliff on Forest Service land. There's some superb rafting in Gore Canyon on the Colorado River west of Vail, particularly in spring when the river is boiling with snow runoff.

RESTAURANTS

Unlike the nearby Summit County ski resorts, which pride themselves on standard "mining fare" like surf and turf, Vail has a distinctly European dining experience. This is the town in which to sample creamed pheasant soup or bite into a good cut of venison. For the most romantic options, look into a slope-side restaurant like Beano's, where the fixed-course menus and unique transportation (horses in summer and sleighs in winter) make the experience more than just a meal. The farther down-valley you move, the more the prices drop.

HOTELS

Vail and Beaver Creek are purpose-built resorts, so you won't find any quaint historic Victorians converted into bed-and-breakfasts here as you will in Breckenridge and Aspen. Instead, Vail lodgings come in three flavors—European chalets that blend with the Bavarian architecture, posh chain resorts up side canyons, and loads of small but serviceable condominiums perfect for families. Down-valley in Edwards and Minturn you'll find that accommodation prices drop, but so does the accessibility to the slopes.

WHAT IT COSTS				
¢	$	$$	$$$	$$$$
Restaurants	under $8	$8–$12	$13–$18	$19–$25	over $25
Hotels	under $80	$80–$120	$121–$170	$171–$230	over $230

Restaurant prices are for a main course at dinner, excluding 4.4%–8.4% tax. Hotel prices are for two people in a standard double room in high season, excluding service charges and 5.4%–9.8% tax.

VAIL

100 mi west of Denver via I–70.

Consistently ranked as one of North America's leading ski destinations, Vail has a reputation few can match. The four-letter word means Valhalla for skiers of all skill levels. Vail has plenty of open areas where novices can learn the ropes. It can also be an ego-building mountain for intermediate and advanced skiers who hit the slopes only a week or two a season. Some areas, like Blue Sky Basin, can make you feel like a pro.

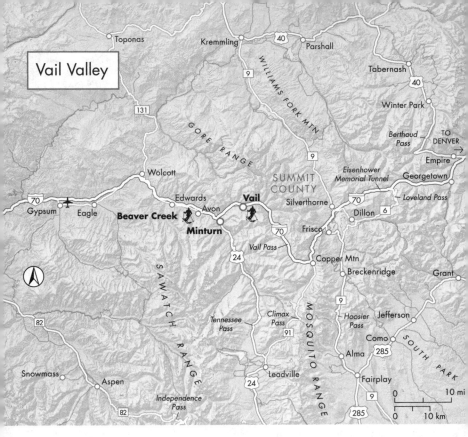

Although Vail is a long, thin town spread for several miles along the Eagle River and comprising East Vail, Vail Village, Lionshead in the center, and West Vail, the hub of activity in winter and summer revolves around Vail Village, and the recently redone Lionshead, which has shops, restaurants, a heated gondola, and even a glockenspiel tower. Vail Village is also a hub of retail and dining with direct lift access to the mountain.

Vail, along with most savvy ski resorts, actively courts families through special packages, classes for youngsters, and activities geared to people of all ages. At Vail kids can play in specially designed ski parks like Chaos Canyon and Fort Whippersnapper. After a day on the slopes, the whole family can get in on the action at Adventure Ridge, where activities range from kids' snowmobile rides to tubing and biking at night by headlamp.

In terms of size, Vail overwhelms nearly every other ski area in North America (only Whistler, in Canada, is larger). There are 5,289 acres popular with skiers and riders of all skill levels. Areas are clearly linked by a well-placed network of lifts and trails. The Front Side is draped with long trails; the infamous Back Bowls beckon powder skiers. A few hours of adventure skiing in Blue Sky Basin is a must for intermediate to advanced skiers and riders.

When the snows melt and two-for-one dinners are advertised in restaurant windows, you can be sure of two things—Vail is in the heart of the mud season, and the tranquillity won't last long. With the blooming of summer columbines come the culture crowds for music and culinary festivals and self-enrichment in writing workshops and health-food seminars. While the valley teems with visitors, hikers and mountain bikers stream up the steep slopes on foot and via the Eagle Bahn Gondola to head into the network of trails that web the seemingly endless backcountry.

GETTING HERE AND AROUND
The best way to get to the Vail Valley is with a rental car. Once in the valley, a free shuttle makes it's easy to get around town, and inexpensive bus service runs between Vail and Beaver Creek

TOURS Vail's Nova Guides runs jeep and all-terrain-vehicle tours, as well as rafting, fishing, snowmobiling, and hiking expeditions.

WHEN TO GO
Vail has grown into a year-round resort, skiing being the main attraction from December through March, and outdoor pursuits like hiking, biking, and fishing the rest of the year. While May and June have pleasant temperatures, many of the hiking and biking trails are still buried beneath snowdrifts. For those interested in seeing wildflowers, mid-July is the time to hit the peaks. The colorful aspen trees generally turn bright gold sometime in September.

FESTIVALS Vail hosts a wide variety of festivals, starting with the Teva Mountain Games (⊕ *www.tevamountaingames.com*), showcasing such sports as kayaking, rafting, and mountain biking. Then there are Taste of Vail (⊕ *www.tasteofvail.com*), Gourmet on Gore, Spring Back to Vail (⊕ *www.springbacktovail.com*), Snow Daze, CarniVail, Bravo!, and the Vail International Dance Festival, to name just a few. There are also free outdoor concerts by up-and-coming musicians, as well as concerts both on and off the mountain by some of the biggest names in the business.

Fodor's Choice **Bravo! Vail Valley Music Festival.** Stretching from late June through early
★ August, the annual Bravo! Vail Valley Music Festival is a month-and-a-half-long celebration of music. Among the performers in residence for a few days or more than a week are the New York Philharmonic and the Dallas Symphony Orchestra. Chamber-music concerts, many performed by the ensemble-in-residence, are popular events. There's also music from an American composer-in-residence. ☎ *877/812–5700* ⊕ *www.vailmusicfestival.org.*

★ **Vail International Dance Festival.** Held early in late July and early August, the annual Vail International Dance Festival hosts an unparalleled collection of ballet and modern dance groups from around the globe. The performers vary from year to year, but frequently include guest artists from the New York City Ballet, the Mark Morris Dance Group, and other world-class companies. In recent years visitors enjoyed Savion Glover of the Tony Award–winning *Bring in Da Noise, Bring in Da Funk.* Most performances are at the Gerald R. Ford Amphitheater, an outdoor venue where some people sit in the seats, but many more recline on blankets on the surrounding lawn. ☎ *970/777–2015* ⊕ *www. vaildance.org.*

ESSENTIALS

Tour Contacts Nova Guides ☎ *719/486–2656.* **Timberline Tours** ☎ *800/831–1414* ⊕ *timberlinetours.com.*

Visitor Information Vail Resorts, Inc. ☎ *800/404–3535* ⊕ *vail.com.* **Vail Snow Report** ☎ *970/754–4888.* **Vail Valley Partnership** ☎ *970/476–1000,* ⊕ *www.visitvailvalley.com.*

EXPLORING

★ **Betty Ford Alpine Gardens.** The Betty Ford Alpine Gardens, open daily from snowmelt (around Memorial Day) to snowfall (Labor Day or a bit later), are an oasis of forsythia, heather, and wild roses. These are the highest public botanical gardens in North America. ⊠ *Ford Park* ☎ *970/476–0103* ⊕ *www.bettyfordalpinegardens.org* 🎫 *Free* ☉ *May–Sept., daily dawn–dusk.*

Colorado Ski & Snowboard Museum and Hall of Fame. The Colorado Ski & Snowboard Museum and Hall of Fame traces the development of the sport throughout the world, with an emphasis on Colorado's contributions. On display are century-old skis and tows, early ski fashions, and an entire room devoted to the 10th Mountain Division, an Army division that trained nearby. Snowboard enthusiasts will get a kick out of two original "snurfers"—prehistoric boards from 1966 and 1967, along with some vintage Burton boards. ⊠ *231 S. Frontage Rd. E* ☎ *970/476–1876* ⊕ *www.skimuseum.net* 🎫 *Free* ☉ *Daily 10–6.*

DOWNHILL SKIING AND SNOWBOARDING

Vail. Year after year, Vail logs more than a million "skier days" (the ski industry's measure of ticket sales), perpetuating its ranking as one of the top two or three most-popular resorts in North America. From the top of China Bowl to the base of the Eagle Bahn Gondola at Lionshead, the resort is more than 7 mi across. The vast acreage is roughly divided into three sections: the Front Side, the Back Bowls, and Blue Sky Basin. Snowboarders will find plenty of steeps on the Front Side, and technical challenges at the Golden Peak or Bwana terrain parks, but they should avoid the Back Bowls, where long catwalks can get slow in the afternoon sun.

Vail is perhaps best known for its legendary **Back Bowls,** more than 3,000 acres of wide-open spaces that are sensational on sunny days. Standing in any one of them, it's difficult to get a visual perspective, as skiers on the far side resemble Lilliputians. These bowls stretch from the original Sun Up and Sun Down to Game Creek on one side and Teacup, China, Siberia, and Outer Mongolia bowls on the far side. The terrain ranges from wide, groomed swatches for intermediate skiers to seemingly endless bump fields to glades so tight that only an expert boarder can slither between the trees. When there's fresh powder, these bowls beckon to skiers intermediate and above. But after the fresh snow has been tracked up by skiers and pummeled by wind and sun, it may be wise for less-than-expert skiers to stay in the groomed sections of the bowls.

The **Front Side** of Vail Mountain delivers a markedly different experience. Here there's lots of wide-trail skiing, heavily skewed toward groomed intermediate runs, especially off the Northwood Express, Mountaintop Express, and Avanti Express lifts, as well as the slopes reachable via the Eagle Bahn Gondola. Pockets of advanced and expert terrain are tucked in and around the blue-marked slopes. The upper parts of Riva and the top of Look Ma are just a few of the places you'll find skilled skiers. The best show in town is on Highline (you can see it while riding Chair 10), where the experts groove through the moguls and those with a bit less experience careen around the bumps. The other two extremely difficult double-black-diamond trails off this slow lift are the best cruisers on the mountain for skilled skiers.

5

It takes time (as long as 45 minutes) to reach **Blue Sky Basin,** made up of three more bowls, but it's worth the effort. Tucked away in a secluded corner of Vail, this 645-acre area has been left in a wilder state, and the majority of the terrain is never groomed. Intermediate skiers will find a few open trails with spectacular views of rugged mountain peaks. For advanced and expert skiers, the real fun is playing in glades and terrain with names such as Heavy Metal, Lovers Leap, the Divide, and Champagne Glade. ☎ *970/476–5601* 🌐 *www.vail.com* 🕑 *Late Nov.–mid-Apr., daily 9–3:30.*

FACILITIES 3,450-foot vertical drop; 5,289 skiable acres; 18% beginner, 29% intermediate, 53% expert (the majority of this terrain is in the Back Bowls); 1 gondola, 16 high-speed quads, 1 fixed grip quad, 3 triples, 1 double, 3 surface lifts and 6 conveyors.

LESSONS AND PROGRAMS **Vail and Beaver Creek Ski and Snowboard School.** The Vail and Beaver Creek Ski and Snowboard School runs classes for skiers of all levels. The school at Vail has almost 1,000 instructors who teach in 30 languages. Afternoon-only group lessons are $131; all-day group lessons are $150, or $185 with a beginner lift ticket. Special workshops and clinics are offered throughout the year. Beginners take three-day courses that include equipment rental and lift passes. Workshops for women, teen sessions, and telemark courses are among the programs targeting specific groups. ☎ *970/754–5300.*

LIFT TICKETS Few skiers pay the high-season walk-up rate of $105 for a one-day lift ticket. Colorado's Front Range skiers purchase a variety of season passes. Most vacationers purchase lift-and-lodging packages, or go online to buy multiday lift passes at discounted rates. A lift ticket purchased at either Vail or Beaver Creek may also be used at Breckenridge, Keystone, and Arapahoe Basin.

RENTALS **One Track Mind Snowboard Shop.** At Lionshead, at One Track Mind Snowboard Shop you can rent everything you need for snowboarding. ✉ *610 W. Lionshead Circle* ☎ *970/476–1397.*

Vail Sports. Vail Sports is within steps of the lifts. The shop rents a wide range of ski gear, including high-end equipment. Prices for skis range from $42 to $62 a day. Book online and save up to 10% on daily rentals and up to 20% for rentals of five days or more. ⊠ *161 Vail Lane* ☎ *970/477–5740* ⊕ *www.vailsports.com.*

NORDIC SKIING

BACKCOUNTRY SKIING

Fodor's Choice
★
10th Mountain Division Hut and Trail System. The 10th Mountain Division Hut and Trail System is one of Colorado's outdoor gems. This network of 29 huts is in the mountains near Camp Hale, where the decorated namesake World War II division trained. Skiers and snowshoers in winter (snowmobiles are not permitted to approach the huts) and hikers and mountain bikers in summer tackle sections of the more than 350 mi of trails linking new and rustic cabins on day trips or weeklong expeditions. Apart from the joy of a self-reliant adventure among rugged mountains, travelers enjoy the camaraderie of communal living (there are very few private rooms in the huts), and evenings spent swapping stories by the glow of a wood-burning stove or the twinkle of summer stars.

10th Mountain Division Hut Association. Maps and other information are available through the 10th Mountain Division Hut Association. Hut reservations should be made at least a month in advance. ⊠ *1280 Ute Ave., Aspen* ☎ *970/925–5775* ⊕ *www.huts.org* .

Paragon Guides. If you aren't familiar with the area's backcountry trails, hiring a guide is a good idea. In Vail, contact Paragon Guides. ☎ *970/ 926–5299* ⊕ *www.paragonguides.com.*

TRACK SKIING

Vail Nordic Center. The cross-country skiing at the Vail Nordic Center is on a golf course. It's not the most beautiful terrain, but it's free. ⊠ *1778 Vail Valley Dr.* ☎ *970/476–8366* ⊕ *www.vailnordiccenter.com.*

OTHER SPORTS AND THE OUTDOORS

Adventure Ridge. In summer, Adventure Ridge, at Eagle's Nest high above Lionshead, is the hub of Vail Mountain activities. It's cool and high, and it has the views. It also has tons of activities like Friday Afternoon Club live bands, beer, sunset watching, the Dino Dig (a large sandbox with buried plastic dinosaur bones for kids), a gravity trampoline, horseshoe pits, volleyball nets, Frisbee golf, horseback riding, a climbing wall, and free guided nature hikes through the Gore Range Natural Science School's Discovery Center. In winter you can go tubing, play laser tag, ice-skate, or try a ski bike. ⊠ *Atop Front Side of Vail Mountain* ☎ *970/476–9090.*

Mountain Information Center. Mountain Information Center has the lowdown on events in the area. ☎ *800/503–8748.*

BICYCLING

A popular summer destination for both road bikers and mountain bikers, Vail has a variety of paved bike paths (including one that leads up to Vail Pass), plus dozens of miles of dirt mountain-bike trails. You can take bikes on lifts heading uphill, then head downhill on an array of routes.

Vail Recreation District. Each summer riders from around the region participate in races sponsored by the Vail Recreation District. ☎ 970/479–2279 ⊕ *www.vailrec. com.*

Vail Ski Tech. Vail Ski Tech rents and repairs bikes. Best of all, they are only steps from the Eagle Bahn Gondola, a summer gateway to the ski slope trails. ✉ *555 E. Lionshead Circle* ☎ *800/525–5995* ⊕ *www. vailskitech.com.*

> **KNOW YOUR SNOW**
>
> Vail is known for its "powder": slopes puffed with light, fluffy flakes that make you feel like you are gliding on silk. Ungroomed runs, however, can quickly turn to "crud" as they get "tracked out" (scarred with deep tracks). That's when it's time to hunt up the "corduroy"—freshly groomed runs.

FITNESS AND SPAS

Deciding to get a massage or spa treatment is the easy part—deciding where to get it is a bigger problem, because there are many outstanding spas and health clubs in the area.

Aria Spa & Club. The Aria Spa & Club is one of the best places to be pampered. If you're up for a full-spa experience, ask about the Songs of the Mountain packages. This 78,000-square-foot facility in the Vail Cascade Resort & Spa also has racquetball, basketball, and tennis courts. ✉ *1300 Westhaven Dr.* ☎ *970/476–7111* ⊕ *www.vailcascade.com.*

Sonnenalp Spa. In the Sonnenalp Resort the lovely Sonnenalp Spa is a European-style facility where you can relax on one of the lounge chairs around a big fireplace as you sip juice from the nearby bar. ✉ *20 Vail Rd.* ☎ *970/479–5404* ⊕ *www.sonnenalp.com.*

GOLF

Golfers who love to play mountain courses know that some of the best are in Vail Valley. These courses meander through the valleys dividing the area's soaring peaks. The region is home to more than a dozen courses, and there are another half-dozen within easy driving distance. It's all just a matter of where you're staying and how much you want to spend. Some courses are only open to members and to guests at certain lodges.

Sonnenalp Golf Course. This Robert Cupp–Jay Morrish design threads through an upscale neighborhood 13 mi west of Vail. There are some serious elevation changes. Guests at the Sonnenalp Resort get preferred tee times. ✉ *1265 Berry Creek Dr., Edwards* ☎ *970/477–5372* ⊕ *www. sonnenalp.com* ⚑ *Reservations essential* 🏌 *18 holes. Yards: 7100. Par: 71. Green fee: $155.*

Vail Golf Club. The area's municipal course rolls along between homes and condominiums in East Vail. ✉ *1778 Vail Valley Dr.* ☎ *970/479–2260* ⊕ *www.vailgolfclub.net* ⚑ *Reservations essential* 🏌 *18 holes. Yards: 7024. Par: 71. Green fee: $80.*

HIKING

If you aren't used to it, high altitude can catch you off guard. Drink plenty of water to help stave off the effects of altitude sickness—dizziness, shortness of breath, headache, and nausea. Slather on the sunscreen—it's easy to get sunburned up here. And in summer an early morning start is best, as afternoon thunderstorms are frequent and a danger above the tree line.

Fodor's Choice ★ **Booth Lake.** Booth Lake is one of Vail's most popular hikes, so get on the trail early or pick a weekday during the summer high season. This is a sustained 6-mi one-way climb from 8,400 feet to Booth Lake at 11,500 feet, right above the tree line. Fit hikers can do this in about seven hours. En route, hikers can cool off at the 60-foot Booth Creek Falls; at only 2 mi in, this is also a great spot to turn around if you're feeling winded (this should take about two to three hours round-trip, and is a great option for an easier hike). The reward for pushing on is a nice view of Booth Lake cradled among the alpine tundra. ⊠ *Trailhead: Take Exit 180 from I–70 to end of Booth Falls Rd.*

Eagle's Loop. Eagle's Loop starts from atop the Eagle Bahn Gondola at 10,350 feet, but it's a mellow, 1-mi stroll along the mountaintop ridge with panoramic views of the Mount of the Holy Cross. Allow about half an hour. ⊠ *Trailhead: Top of Eagle Bahn Gondola.*

OUTFIT-
TERS AND
EXPEDITIONS
Paragon Guides. Paragon Guides runs backcountry adventures. In summer there's rock climbing, mountain biking, and day and overnight llama treks in and around Vail Valley. In winter the company runs daylong ski trips through the backcountry, and three- to six-day trips along the 10th Mountain Division Hut System. ☎ 970/926–5299 ⊕ *www.paragonguides.com.*

HORSEBACK RIDING

One of the best ways to see Vail Valley is from the back of a horse.

A.J. Brink Outfitters. On scenic Sweetwater Lake A.J. Brink Outfitters has day and overnight horseback excursions high in the Flat Tops Wilderness. ⊠ *3406 Sweetwater Rd., Gypsum* ☎ 970/524–9301 ⊕ *www.brinkoutfitters.com.*

Piney River Ranch. This snowmobiling outfit runs 1½, 2½-hour, and custom guided tours into the White River National Forest. They have complimentary pickup in Vail, Avon, and Beaver Creek. ☎ 970/476–7749 ⊕ *www.vailvalleytours.com.*

NATURE CENTERS

Vail Nature Center. The Vail Nature Center occupies an old homestead just across from the Betty Ford Alpine Gardens. In summer, you can sign up for half-day and full-day backcountry hikes, wildflower walks, morning birding expeditions, and evening beaver-pond tours. ⊠ *Adjacent to Ford Park* ☎ 970/479–2291 ⊕ *www.vailrec.com.*

★ **Vail Nordic Center.** In winter backcountry snowshoe excursions and photography classes are available at the Vail Nordic Center. ⊠ *1778 Vail Valley Dr.* ☎ 970/476–8366.

SNOWMOBILING

Adventure Ridge. Adventure Ridge, at the top of Lionshead, leads twilight snowmobile excursions, as well as snowshoe, snow inner-tubing, and ice-skating trips. ⊠ *Atop Front Side of Vail Mountain* ☎ 970/476–9090.

Nova Guides. Nova Guides has snowmobile rentals and guided snow cat tours. ☎ 719/486–2656 ⊕ *www.novaguides.com.*

WHERE TO EAT

$$$
MODERN
AMERICAN
★
✕ Atwater on Gore Creek. This tavern in the Vail Cascade Resort has beautiful floor-to-ceiling windows, hardwood furniture, cream-color walls, and a nice gas fireplace. The Atwater stakes its reputation on organic and farm-fresh foods, and has a number of small tapas-style plates for lighter meals. Try the Moroccan lamb meatballs with house-made BBQ sauce for a starter followed by mushroom-encrusted white meatloaf with mashed potatoes and gravy. Save room for a vanilla-bean crème brûlée. ⊠ *Vail Cascade Resort, 1300 Westhaven Dr., Cascade Village* ☎ 970/479–7014 ⊕ *www.vailcascade.com.*

$
AMERICAN
✕ Bart & Yeti's. Grilled portobello-mushroom sandwiches, spicy South-western green chile, and Irish stew are among the choices at this laid-back, rustic restaurant. If you want a full meal, try the most popular entrée, barbecued baby back ribs. The deck is a gathering spot in warm weather. The place is in Lionshead, just north of the Eagle Bahn Gondola. ⊠ *553 E. Lionshead Circle, Lionshead* ☎ 970/476–2754.

$
AMERICAN
✕ Big Bear Bistro. Locals kick off their mornings with a pit stop at this joint near the Vista Bahn lift to grab a cup of java and a breakfast burrito—scrambled eggs, roast potatoes, cheddar cheese, and applewood smoked bacon (you can get them wrapped to go). The service is quick and there's a simple but decent range of baked goods, fresh fruit, and organic options. The cobbled patio with a picnic table is a great place to enjoy a sandwich for lunch and during winter the inside is decorated with evergreen trimmings like a Tyrolean bistro. ⊠ *304 Hanson Ranch Rd., Lionshead* ☎ 970/300–1394.

$$$$
AMERICAN
Fodor's Choice
★
✕ Game Creek Restaurant. Getting to this restaurant is certainly half the fun, as you must catch a gondola up the mountain, then hop on a snow cat to get across Game Creek Bowl during the winter. During the summer you can travel by shuttle or take a horseback ride one-way. The Bavarian-style lodge is members-only for lunch, but open to the public for dinner all year and for an outstanding Sunday brunch in summer. Be prepared to linger over a multicourse prix-fixe meal as you enjoy spectacular views of the slopes and the mountains beyond. You might start with butter-poached prawns with fried vermicelli followed by duo of dry-aged Black Angus beef. ⊠ *278 Hanson Ranch Rd.* ☎ 970/754–4275 ⊕ *www.gamecreekclub.com* ⌘ *Reservations essential* ☾ *No lunch.*

$$$
ITALIAN
✕ La Bottega. This casual, small restaurant has a loyal following that appreciates the creative northern Italian fare in a romantic setting with brick alcoves and blond-wood tables. Customers especially love the lunch specials, which include creative pizzas from the stone ovens and delicious pastas. Some people turn out for a glass of vino in the wine

bar, which takes up one side of the establishment. The cellar is one of the best in town. ⊠ *100 E. Meadow Dr., Vail Village* ☎ *970/476–0280* ⊕ *www.labottegavail.com.*

$$$$
MODERN
AMERICAN

✕**Larkspur Restaurant.** An open kitchen bustling with activity is the backdrop at Larkspur, popular with a parka-clad crowd at lunch and well-dressed diners in the evening. Owner and chef Thomas Salamunovich has a talent for blending cuisines, so the menu is filled with creative entrées such as house-made ricotta ravioli with Parmesan emulsion and certified organic chicken with "smashed" potatoes. Leave room for decadent desserts such as warm chocolate spice cake and petite doughnuts with chocolate and espresso sabayon. ⊠ *Golden Peak Lodge, 458 Vail Valley Dr., Vail Village* ☎ *970/754–8050* ⊕ *www. larkspurvail.com* ⌘ *Reservations essential.*

<table><tr><td></td></tr></table>

VAIL AND BEAVER CREEK LODGING ALTERNATIVES

Vail/Beaver Creek Reservations. Vail/Beaver Creek Reservations is the place for one-stop shopping. ☎ *800/525–2257.*

Vail Valley Partnership. Vail Valley Partnership operates a central reservations service for properties in Vail, Avon, and Beaver Creek. ☎ *800/653–4523.*

$$$$
MODERN
AMERICAN

✕**Sweet Basil.** The decor may be understated—blond-wood chairs and buff-color walls—but the contemporary cuisine is anything but. The freshest seasonal ingredients available are used, so the menu changes about once a month. You might find cardamom-spiced duck breast with duck confit and champagne-vanilla pickled cherries or 28-day dry-aged Heritage pork chop with grilled Colorado peaches. Pair these entrées with one of the hundreds of wines from the restaurant's expansive cellar. Leave room for luscious desserts such as caramel corn beignets with sweet-corn ice cream. ⊠ *193 E. Gore Creek Dr., Vail Village* ☎ *970/476–0125* ⊕ *www.sweetbasil-vail.com.*

$$$$
MODERN
AMERICAN
★

✕**Terra Bistro.** With spacious glass windows and track lighting, this sleek, sophisticated space in the Vail Mountain Lodge & Spa looks as if it belongs in a big city. Only the fireplace reminds you that this is Vail. The menu focuses on contemporary American cuisine that throws in a few Asian, Mediterranean, and Southwestern influences. Grilled Amish beef tenderloin with Yukon mashed potatoes and cornmeal-crusted Rocky Mountain trout with sweet-potato hash are headliners; organic produce and free-range meat and poultry are used whenever possible. ⊠ *Vail Mountain Lodge & Spa, 352 E. Meadow Dr., Vail Village* ☎ *970/476–6836* ⊕ *www.terrabistrovail.com.*

WHERE TO STAY

For expanded hotel reviews, visit Fodors.com.

$$$$
HOTEL

⌂**Arrabelle at Vail Square.** The Arrabelle is a star among Vail's collection of ski-in ski-out luxury lodges. **Pros:** ski valet; pet friendly; great location; fabulous on-site spa and restaurant. **Cons:** the valet parking entrance is hard to find. ⊠ *675 Lionshead Pl.* ☎ *970/754–7777, 866/662–7625* ⊕ *www.arrabelle.rockresorts.com* ⇗ *62 rooms, 25 condominiums* ⌂ *In-room: a/c, safe, kitchen, Wi-Fi. In-hotel: restaurant, pool, gym, spa, parking, some pets allowed* ⓘ *No meals.*

$$$$ 🏠**Four Seasons Resort Vail.** The newest luxury property in Vail, the
RESORT swank Four Seasons is the king of the village, despite its having just
121 rooms and suites. **Pros:** new property; alpine architecture; complimentary meals for children five and under. **Cons:** $30 daily resort fee;
occasionally inconsistent service. ⊠ *1 Vail Rd., Vail* ☎ *970/477–8600,
800/819–5053* ⊕ *www.fourseasons.com/vail/* ⤴ *97 rooms, 24 suites*
⚠ *In-room: a/c, safe, Internet, Wi-Fi. In-hotel: restaurant,
bar, pool, gym, spa, children's programs, business center, parking.*

$$$$ 🏠**Galatyn Lodge.** This luxury lodge in a quiet part of Vail Village main-
HOTEL tains a low profile, which is just the approach its hard-core skiing
regulars prefer. **Pros:** indoor-outdoor heated pool; high percentage of
return guests; apartment style. **Cons:** no children's programs; no restaurant or bar. ⊠ *365 Vail Valley Dr., Vail Village* ☎ *970/479–2418,
800/943–7322* ⊕ *www.thegalatynlodge.com* ⤴ *4 4-bedroom condos*
⚠ *In-room: safe, kitchen, Wi-Fi. In-hotel: pool, laundry facilities, business center, parking.*

$$$$ 🏠**Gasthof Gramshammer.** Pepi Gramshammer, a former Austrian Olym-
HOTEL pic ski racer who runs some of the country's best intensive ski programs,
operates this guesthouse. **Pros:** European flavor; village location. **Cons:**
no room service. ⊠ *231 E. Gore Creek Dr., Vail Village* ☎ *970/476–
5626, 800/610–7374* ⊕ *www.pepis.com* ⤴ *30 rooms, 9 suites and
apartments* ⚠ *In-room: no a/c, safe, kitchen, Wi-Fi. In-hotel: restaurant, bar, pool, parking.*

$$$$ 🏠**Lodge at Vail.** The first facility to open in Vail, in 1962, the sprawl-
RESORT ing lodge—modeled after the Lodge at Sun Valley—is popular with
skiers and families because of its fabulous location only 150 feet from
the village's main lift, the Vista Bahn. **Pros:** on-mountain ski storage; located near main ski lift. **Cons:** pricey; quality of rooms varies.
⊠ *174 E. Gore Creek Dr., Vail Village* ☎ *970/754–7800, 877/528–
7625* ⊕ *www.lodgeatvail.rockresorts.com* ⤴ *122 rooms, 46 suites*
⚠ *In-room: no a/c, safe, kitchen, Wi-Fi. In-hotel: restaurant, bar, golf
course, pool, gym, spa, laundry facilities, business center, parking,
some pets allowed.*

$$$$ 🏠**The Sebastian.** The Sebastian is what results when you slip a bit of
HOTEL Manhattan chic into a Colorado ski lodge—this boutique hotel is part
art museum (the halls and lobby are dedicated to Mexican abstract artist Manuel Felguérez), and part nightclub, with the Frost Bar featuring
a tapas menu and sparkling wine and popcorn served in the library
on Friday nights. **Pros:** great location; chic style; excellent restaurant.
Cons: many rooms overlook the freeway; minimum stays required
in high season. ⊠ *16 Vail Rd., Vail* ☎ *970/477–8000, 800/354–6908*
⊕ *www.thesebastianvail.com* ⤴ *100 rooms, 7 suites* ⚠ *In-room: a/c,
safe, kitchen, Internet, Wi-Fi. In-hotel: restaurant, bar, pool, gym, spa,
business center, parking, some pets allowed.*

$$$$ 🏠**Sitzmark Lodge.** This cozy family-run lodge buzzes with a dozen lan-
HOTEL guages, thanks to the international guests who return year after year.
Fodor's Choice **Pros:** friendly; easy access to ski lifts; international ambience. **Cons:** no
★ spa. ⊠ *183 Gore Creek Dr., Vail Village* ☎ *970/476–5001, 888/476–
5001* ⊕ *www.sitzmarklodge.com* ⤴ *35 rooms* ⚠ *In-room: no a/c,*

5

safe, kitchen, Wi-Fi. In-hotel: restaurant, bar, pool, laundry facilities, business center, parking.

$$$$
HOTEL
Fodor's Choice
★

🎿 **Sonnenalp Resort.** It's the sense of family tradition and European elegance that makes the Sonnenalp Resort the most romantic of all hotels in the faux-Tyrolean village of Vail. **Pros:** classic alpine ambience; incredible buffet breakfast; spa. **Cons:** removed from lifts; tough to regulate room temperature in winter. ⊠ *20 Vail Rd., Vail Village* ☎ *970/476–5656, 800/654–8312* ⊕ *www.sonnenalp.com* 🛏 *12 rooms, 115 suites* ♿ *In-room: safe, kitchen, Wi-Fi. In-hotel: restaurant, bar, golf course, pool, gym, spa, children's programs, business center, parking, some pets allowed* 🍽 *Breakfast.*

$$$$
HOTEL

🎿 **Vail Cascade Resort & Spa.** Down-to-earth yet luxurious is the best way to describe this family-oriented ski-in ski-out hotel. **Pros:** right on the slope; spa and health club; nice views of creek. **Cons:** staff can be hard to find; concrete exterior; expensive parking. ⊠ *1300 Westhaven Dr., Cascade Village* ☎ *970/476–7111, 800/420–2424* ⊕ *www.vailcascade.com* 🛏 *292 rooms, 27 suites, 80 condominiums* ♿ *In-room: safe, kitchen, Internet, Wi-Fi. In-hotel: restaurant, bar, pool, tennis court, gym, spa, children's programs, laundry facilities, business center, parking.*

NIGHTLIFE

Garfinkel's. Near the gondola in Lionshead, Garfinkel's has plenty of televisions where you can catch the game. It's open late, especially on weekends. ⊠ *333 E. Lionshead Circle* ☎ *970/476–3789* ⊕ *www.garfsvail.com.*

Red Lion. The Red Lion is a tradition in Vail. It's standing-room only in the afternoon, and a bit mellower in the evening. Most nights there's guitar or piano music. ⊠ *304 Bridge St.* ☎ *970/476–7676* ⊕ *www.theredlion.com.*

Sarah's Lounge. Sarah's Lounge showcases Helmut Fricker, a Vail institution who plays accordion while yodeling up a storm on Friday evening in ski season. ⊠ *356 E. Hanson Ranch Rd.* ☎ *970/476–5641.*

Vendetta's. A young crowd scarfs down excellent late-night pizzas at Vendetta's. ⊠ *291 Bridge St.* ☎ *970/476–5070* ⊕ *www.vendettasvail.com.*

SHOPPING

BOUTIQUES

Axel's. Across from the Children's Fountain, Axel's carries high-end European fashions including Italian suede pants, riding boots, and shearling coats. ⊠ *201 Gore Creek Dr.* ☎ *970/476–7625* ⊕ *www.axelsltd.com.*

Golden Bear. For years, a golden bear (papa-, mama-, or baby-size) on a chain has been a popular souvenir from this ski resort. The Golden Bear makes many versions of its namesake, as well as other popular items such as hammered-gold necklaces and bracelets. You can also purchase fashionable clothes and accessories. ⊠ *286 Bridge St.* ☎ *800/338-7782* ⊕ *thegoldenbear.com* ⊠ *Village Hall, Beaver Creek* ☎ *970/845–7881.*

Gorsuch. Stocking buffalo-hide coats and bowls filled with potpourri, Gorsuch is an odd combination of an upscale boutique and a sporting-goods store. ✉ *263 E. Gore Creek Dr.* ☎ *970/476–2294* ⊕ *www.gorsuch.com* ✉ *138 Beaver Creek Pl., Beaver Creek* ☎ *970/949–7115.*

Pepi Sports. Pepi Sports sells chic ski clothing and accessories from designers such as Bogner, Skea, Descente, and Spyder. ✉ *231 Bridge St.* ☎ *970/476–5206* ⊕ *pepisports. com.*

ART GALLERIES

Claggett/Rey Gallery. The Claggett/ Rey Gallery is the place to purchase canvases and sculptures by well-known Western artists. ✉ *100 E. Meadow Dr., Bldg. 10* ☎ *800/252–4438* ⊕ *www.claggettrey.com.*

Pismo Gallery. You'll be dazzled by handblown creations at the Pismo Gallery. The outstanding collection of handblown glass ranges from perfume bottles to paperweights. ✉ *122 E. Meadow Dr.* ☎ *970/476–2400* ⊕ *www.pismoglass.com.*

10TH MOUNTAIN DIVISION

A pair of red-crossed swords on a blue shield is the familiar insignia of the famed 10th Mountain Division, created to train soldiers in mountain and winter warfare during World War II. One of their first training centers, Camp Hale, was opened in 1942 in a small park between Red Cliff and Leadville. The high valley must have borne at least a passing resemblance to the Himalayas, because before it closed in 1966 the CIA also secretly trained Tibetan guerrillas there to wage a war of independence in their Chinese-occupied homeland.

5

SIDE TRIP: MINTURN

5 mi west of Vail; 105 mi west of Denver via I–70.

The Vail Valley stretches far beyond the town of Vail. Minturn began to thrive in 1987, when the Rio Grande Railway extended a narrow-gauge line into town to carry away the zinc, copper, silver, and lead extracted from nearby mines. The main street has an eclectic collection of antiques, curio, and other shops, plus popular restaurants housed in the old buildings. It's a good place to take a break from skiing and grab a bite.

GETTING HERE AND AROUND
As you travel west along I–70, Exit 171 leads to this quiet community.

EXPLORING
Minturn Cellars Winery. Minturn Cellars Winery is a wine-tasting room featuring some of the finest local wines. ✉ *107 Williams St.* ☎ *970/827–4065.*

WHERE TO EAT AND STAY
For expanded hotel reviews, visit Fodors.com.

$$$
STEAKHOUSE
✗ **Minturn Country Club.** This homey hangout is one of those "you've gotta go" places people talk about after returning home as much for the concept—you are your own chef—as the prime and choice cuts of

aged steak. Choose from steaks, poultry, and fish and head to one of several lava rock grills—heated to 1,100-degrees—and sear your meat (ask if you need some pointers). Sounds like too much work? Order some slow-cooked baby back ribs or the one-pound Alaskan king crab legs and let the chefs cook it for you. Favorite sides like sweet potato fries and shrimp kabobs are ordered from the kitchen. And don't miss the Minturn Tater for dessert—a cookie and ice cream loaf drizzled with chocolate. ⊠ *131 Main St.* ☎ *970/827–4114* ⊕ *www.minturn-country-club.com* ⚠ *Reservations not accepted* ☯ *No lunch.*

$$ ✗ **Minturn Saloon.** After a day on the slopes, reward yourself with mar-
MEXICAN garitas made with real lime juice and baskets of tortilla chips served
☯ with homemade salsa. No wonder the place is always packed with locals. In a dining room that calls to mind the Old West, you can feast on such specialties as chiles rellenos and a steak-and-quail plate. There's even a children's menu. ⊠ *146 N. Main St.* ☎ *970/827–5954* ⊕ *www.minturnsaloon.com* ⚠ *Reservations not accepted* ☯ *No lunch.*

$$ ☷ **Minturn Inn.** This three-story 1915 log home, one of the town's old-
B&B/INN est residences, was converted into an inn with hewn-log beds and ant-
ler chandeliers. **Pros:** historic lodgings; view of the river; fireplaces. **Cons:** removed from the ski resort; few room and hotel amenities. ⊠ *442 Main St.* ☎ *970/827–9647, 800/646–8876* ⊕ *www.minturninn.com* ⌁ *18 rooms, 1 cabin* ⚠ *In-room: no a/c, Wi-Fi. In-hotel: parking* ☷ *Breakfast.*

BEAVER CREEK

12 mi west of Vail; 110 mi west of Denver via I–70.

As with the majority of the area's resorts, the heart of Beaver Creek is a mountainside village. What sets Beaver Creek apart is that it's a series of cascading plazas connected by escalators. In this ultraposh enclave even boot-wearing skiers and snowboard-hauling riders ride the escalators from the hotels and shuttle stops on the lower levels. Opened in 1980 as a smaller version of Vail, Beaver Creek has over-shadowed its older sibling. In fact, its nearest rival in the luxury market is Utah's Deer Valley.

Locals know that Beaver Creek is the best place to ski on weekends, when Vail is too crowded, or anytime there's fresh powder. Beaver Creek is just far enough from Denver that it doesn't get the flood of day-trippers who flock to Vail and the other Front Range resorts. The slopes of Beaver Creek Mountain are connected to those of even ritzier Bachelor Gulch. These are close to Arrowhead, creating a village-to-village ski experience like those found in Europe.

Savvy travelers have learned that Beaver Creek is even lovelier in summer, when diners can enjoy a meal on a spacious patio, mountain bikers can hitch a ride uphill on the chairlift, and golfers can play on the beautiful Beaver Creek Course or on one of the dozen others in the Vail Valley. On special evenings you can attend concerts, get tickets to the theater, or head to a performance at the Beaver Creek Vilar Center for the Arts. In Beaver Creek you have easy access to all of the activities in Vail Valley.

Beaver Creek speaks loudly and clearly to a settled and affluent crowd, but visitors on a budget can also enjoy the resort's many attractions. Just drive past the pricier lodgings in the village and opt instead for a room in nearby Avon, Edwards, or even Vail.

GETTING HERE AND AROUND

Driving is the most convenient way to get around Beaver Creek, but there are private shuttles and public buses.

WHEN TO GO

Beaver Creek's seasons are the same as Vail; winter is great for snow sports and summer also attracts outdoor enthusiasts.

ESSENTIALS

Transportation Contacts Avon/Beaver Creek Transit ☎ *970/748–4120* ⊕ *www.avon.org.* **Colorado Mountain Express** ☎ *800/525–6363, 970/468–7600* ⊕ *www.ridecme.com.*

5

DOWNHILL SKIING AND SNOWBOARDING

Beaver Creek. Beaver Creek is a piece of nirvana, partly because of its system of trails and partly because of its enviable location two hours from Denver. Although only a third the size of Vail, Beaver Creek is seldom crowded. The skiable terrain extends from the runs down Beaver Creek to the slopes around Bachelor Gulch to the network of trails at Arrowhead. You can easily ski from one village to another. The omnipresent and helpful ambassadors are always willing to point you in the right direction, and even give you a lift back to your lodge if you forgot your goggles.

Beaver Creek has a little of everything, from smoother slopes for beginners to difficult trails used for international competitions. Grouse Mountain, in particular, is famed for its thigh-burning bump runs. Beginners have an entire peak, at the summit of Beaver Creek Mountain, where they can learn to ski or practice on novice trails. And newcomers can return to the village on one of the lifts if they are too tired to take the long trail all the way to the bottom. Intermediate-level skiers have several long cruising trails on the lower half of Beaver Creek Mountain and in Larkspur Bowl. Both locations also have black-diamond trails, so groups of skiers and snowboarders of varying abilities can ride uphill together. The Birds of Prey runs, like Peregrine and Redtail, are aptly named, because the steepness of the trails can be a surprise for skiers who mistakenly think they are skilled enough to take on this challenging terrain. The days of snowboarders getting snubbed in Beaver Creek are long gone, and shredders can tackle a series of terrain parks with increasing difficulty from Park 101 to the Zoom Room and on to the Moonshine half-pipe.

The slopes of neighboring **Bachelor Gulch** are a mix of beginner and intermediate trails. Here you can often find fresh powder hours after it's gone elsewhere. Many of the open slopes weave past multimillion-dollar homes; cost of real estate is even higher than in Beaver Creek.

CLOSE UP

Skiing and Snowboarding Tips

Although downhill skiing has long been the classic winter activity, snowboarding—once the bastion of teenage "riders" in baggy pants—is fast catching up as a mainstream sport. Telemarking and cross-country skiing still have loyal followings, though these skiers tend to prefer the wide-open backcountry to the more-populated resorts.

Although it snows somewhere in the Colorado high country every month—and resorts can open their lifts as early as October and close as late as the fourth of July—the traditional ski season usually runs from December until early April. Christmas through New Year's Day and the month of March (when spring-breakers arrive) tend to be the busiest periods for most ski areas. The slower months of January and February often yield good package deals, as do the early and late ends of the season.

EQUIPMENT RENTAL

Rental equipment is available at all ski areas and at ski shops around resorts or in nearby towns. It's often more expensive to rent at the resort where you'll be skiing, but then it's easier to go back to the shop if something doesn't fit. Experienced skiers can "demo" (try out) premium equipment to get a feel for new technology before upgrading.

LESSONS

In the United States the Professional Ski Instructors of America (PSIA) has devised a progressive teaching system that is used at most ski schools. This allows skiers to take lessons at different ski areas. Classes range in length from hour-long skill clinics to half- or full-day workshops. Deals can be had for first-time and beginner skiers and

snowboarders who attend morning clinics and then try out their new skills on beginner and intermediate slopes for the remainder of the day.

Most ski schools follow the PSIA teaching approach for children, and many also incorporate SKIwee, another standardized teaching technique. Classes for children are arranged by ability and age group; often the ski instructor chaperones a meal during the teaching session. Children's ski instruction has come a long way in the last 10 years; instructors specially trained in teaching children, and equipment designed for little bodies, mean that most children can now begin to ski successfully as young as three or four. Helmets are often de rigueur.

LIFT TICKETS

With some lift ticket prices increasing every year, the best advice is to shop around. Single-day, adult, holiday-weekend passes cost the most, but better bargains can be had through off-site purchase locations (check newspaper Sunday sections and local supermarkets, such as King Soopers and Safeway), online discounts, multiple-day passes, and season passes. You can always call a particular resort's central reservations line to ask where discount lift tickets can be purchased. With a little legwork you should never have to pay full price.

TRAIL RATING

Ski areas mark and rate trails and slopes—Easy (green circle), Intermediate (blue square), Advanced (black diamond), and Expert (double black diamond).

The Ritz-Carlton Bachelor Gulch, which sits at the base of the lift, is one of the region's most beautiful hotels. A stop here is a must for any architecture buff. Many skiers plan to arrive in time for a hearty lunch at Remington's or an après-ski cocktail in the Buffalo Bar or the Fly Fishing Library. There are shuttles handy to take you back to Beaver Creek.

The third village in the area, **Arrowhead,** has the best and usually the least crowded intermediate terrain. Locals take advantage of sunny days by sitting on the spacious deck at the Broken Arrow Café. It's not much more than a shack, but the burgers can't be beat. The European concept of skiing from village to village was introduced here in 1996, when the new owners, Vail Associates, decided to connect Arrowhead, Beaver Creek, and Bachelor Gulch via lifts and ski trails. ☎ *800/404–3535* ⊕ *www.beavercreek.com* ☾ *Late Nov.–mid-Apr., daily 9–4.*

FACILITIES 4,040-foot vertical drop; 1,805 skiable acres; 19% beginner, 43% intermediate, 38% advanced; 2 gondolas, 10 high-speed quads, 2 triples, 2 doubles, 1 surface lift.

LESSONS AND PROGRAMS **Vail and Beaver Creek Ski and Snowboard School.** The Vail and Beaver Creek Ski and Snowboard School runs classes at both resorts. At Beaver Creek there are about 600 instructors; lessons are available in more than 20 languages. Afternoon-only group lessons are $131; all-day lessons are $150. Special clinics run throughout the year, like workshops for women, teen sessions, and telemark courses. Beginners take three-day courses that include equipment rental and lift passes. ☎ *970/754–8245.*

LIFT TICKETS Few skiers pay the high-season walk-up rate of approximately $105 for a one-day lift ticket. Most vacationers purchase lift-and-lodging packages for Beaver Creek, or go online to ⊕ *www.snow.com* and purchase multiday lift passes at discounted rates. A lift ticket purchased at Beaver Creek may also be used at Vail, Breckenridge, Keystone, and Arapahoe Basin.

RENTALS **Beaver Creek Sports.** Beaver Creek Sports rents ski equipment for $50 to $75, depending upon whether you choose regular or high-performance gear. ⊠ *Beaver Creek Village* ☎ *970/754–5418.*

NORDIC SKIING

TRACK SKIING

Beaver Creek Nordic Sports Center. Lessons, equipment rentals, and guided tours are available through Beaver Creek Nordic Sports Center. ⊠ *Strawberry Park Condo Bldg., at the bottom of Chair 12* ☎ *970/745–5313* ☾ *Daily 9–4.*

★ **McCoy Park.** The prettiest place for cross-country skiing is McCoy Park, with more than 19 mi of trails groomed for traditional cross-country skiing, skate skiing, and snowshoeing, all laid out around a mountain peak. To reach McCoy Park, take the Strawberry Park chairlift—a plus because it gets you far enough from the village that you're in a pristine environment. The groomed tracks have a fair amount of ups and downs (or perhaps because the elevation rises to 9,840 feet, it just seems that way). ☎ *970/754–5313* ⊕ *www.beavercreek.com* ⊙ *Open Dec.–mid-Apr.*

OTHER SPORTS AND THE OUTDOORS

Activities Desk of Vail. The Activities Desk of Vail gives you the low-down on many of the activities in the region, summer or winter. ☎ *970/ 476–9090.*

BICYCLING

Colorado Bike Services. Colorado Bike Services is a great bike shop where you can get more information about the trails around Beaver Creek. ⊠ *41149 U.S. 6, at U.S. 24* ☎ *970/949–4641* ⊕ *www. coloradobikeservice.com.*

Vail Recreation District. Each summer, riders from around the region participate in races sponsored by the Vail Recreation District. ⊠ *700 S. Frontage Rd. E, Vail* ☎ *970/479–2279* ⊕ *www.vailrec.com.*

FITNESS AND SPAS

It's easy to find a full-body massage in Beaver Creek, as many hotels have full-service spas included.

Allegria Spa. In the Park Hyatt Beaver Creek, the Allegria Spa—inspired by Roman bathhouses—has a relaxing 105-degree mineral pool, steam rooms with soothing fiber-optic displays, and even a few tables for room-service meals (they're even happy to serve you cocktails and bar drinks). The spa offers a full range of services, including a wonderful "barefoot" massage. ■ TIP→ The signature "ginger peach cure" treatment comprises a scrub, full-body massage, wrap, and Swiss shower (with 12 jetted nozzles). ⊠ *136 E. Thomas Pl.* ☎ *970/748–7500* ⊕ *www.allegriaspa.com.*

GOLF

The Club at Cordillera. The Lodge & Spa at Cordillera has three 18-hole courses and a 10-hole course. Hotel guests can play the Jack Nicklaus–designed Summit Course, which surrounds a peak like a string of pearls. The Hale Irwin Mountain Course runs through aspen groves, past lakes, and through meadows surrounded by luxury homes. The Dave Pelz–designed 10-hole course lets you show off (or makes you practice) your short-game skills. ⊠ *2205 Cordillera Way, Edwards* ☎ *970/569–6480* ⊕ *www.cordillera-vail.com* ⚑ *Reservations essential* ⚲. *Mountain: 18 holes. Yards: 7413. Par: 72/72. Green fee: $175.*

★ **Eagle Ranch Golf Club.** This 6,600-foot-high course was landscaped in the lush wetlands of the Brush Creek valley. Caddies like to joke that the perfect club might actually be a fly rod. Arnold Palmer, who designed the 18-hole course, said, "The fairways are very playable and the roughs are not extremely rough." ⊠ *0050 Lime Park Dr.* ☎ *970/328–2882, 866/328–3232* ⊕ *www.eagleranchgolf.com* ⚑ *Reservations essential* ⚲. *18 holes. Yards: 7500. Par: 72. Green fee: $95.*

Red Sky Golf Club. At this tony private course a few miles west of Beaver Creek members alternate with guests on two courses designed by Tom Fazio and Greg Norman. The Tom Fazio Course's front nine are laid out on sagebrush-covered hills, but the back nine flows up and down a mountainside covered with groves of junipers and aspens. The Greg Norman Course sprawls through a broad valley. Some shots require carries across jagged ravines. Norman's signature bunkers abound, guarding slippery greens. In order to play at Red Sky Golf Club you must be staying in the Lodge at Vail, the Pines Lodge in Beaver Creek, the Ritz-Carlton Bachelor Gulch, other hotels owned by Vail Resorts, or other partner properties. ⊠ *376 Red Sky Rd.* ☎ *970/754–8425* ⊕ *www. redskygolfclub.com* ⬧ *Reservations essential* ⚑ *Greg Norman: 18 holes. Yards: 7580. Par: 72. Green fee: $250. Tom Fazio: 18 holes. Yards: 7113. Par: 72. Green fee: $250.*

HIKING

Beaver Creek Hiking Center. The Beaver Creek Hiking Center arranges everything from easy walks to difficult hikes. If you're traveling with kids, ask about educational programs. ⊠ *Beaver Creek Village* ☎ *970/ 754–5373.*

Holy Cross Wilderness Area. The Holy Cross Wilderness Area is southwest of Beaver Creek. **Eagle Lake** is a great trail for hikers who want to test their bodies at altitude without overdoing it. The trail starts at 9,100 feet (just slightly higher than Beaver Creek's base at 7,400 feet) and contours through a glacial valley for almost 2.5 mi around Woods Lake to Eagle Lake at 10,000 feet. Plan on a five-hour round-trip journey. You can continue up the valley to explore more lakes if you're feeling fit. ⊠ *Holy Cross Ranger District, White River National Forest* ☎ *970/827–5715* ⊕ *www.fs.fed.us/r2/whiteriver/recreation/wilderness/ holycross.*

HORSEBACK RIDING

Beaver Creek Stables. Beaver Creek Stable arranges outings ranging from one-hour rides to all-day excursions. Many trips include a tasty picnic lunch. In the evening there are hayrides and sunset rides. ⬧ *93 Elk Track Rd., Avon* ☎ *970/845–7770.*

WHERE TO EAT

$$$$
AMERICAN
✕ **8100 Mountainside Bar & Grill.** This altitude-inspired bistro in the Park Hyatt has a great slope-side location and hearty meals. The open kitchen with a massive wood-burning grill and the outdoor fire pit make this a favorite for après-ski diners. Chef Christian Apetz favors a local "mountain" menu that includes favorites like pan-seared river trout and free-range elk loin. The bar—with a full range of organic wines and the best of Colorado microbrews—seats 20 along a polished stone counter. ⊠ *Park Hyatt Beaver Creek Resort & Spa, 50 W. Thomas Pl.* ☎ *970/827–6600* ⊕ *www.8100barandgrill.com* ⬧ *Reservations essential.*

$$$$
MODERN
AMERICAN
✕ **Beano's Cabin.** One of the memorable experiences during a trip to Beaver Creek is traveling in a sleigh to this former hunting lodge. In summer you can get here on horseback or by shuttle van. During the journey, your driver will undoubtedly fill you in on some local history. The pine-log cabin, warmed by a crackling fire, is an unbeatable location for a romantic meal. Choose from among the entrées that change with the seasons. Pair pan-seared halibut with duo of venison, then top it

all off with a bourbon pecan torte. ⊠ *Larkspur Bowl* ☎ *970/754–3463* ⌕ *Reservations essential* ⊙ *Closed May and Nov.*

$$$$
AMERICAN
✕ **Beaver Creek Chophouse.** A ski-in ski-out restaurant right at the base of Centennial Lift, the Beaver Creek Chophouse is a favorite people-watching après-ski hangout. The food is hearty—the 18-ounce bone-in rib eye is the most popular plate followed by a decadent spin on comfort food: lobster mac-and-cheese. When the snow is blowing try some of the hot specialty drinks like a Bacardi Colorado Blizzard (rum and coffee) or a Mexican hot chocolate (with Tuaca and hot sauce). You can also select from more than 150 wines and a dozen beers on tap. You didn't hear it here, but show up at 3:30 for the free afternoon champagne toasts during ski season. ⊠ *15 W. Thomas Pl.* ☎ *970/845–0555* ⊕ *www.beavercreekchophouse.com* ⌕ *Reservations essential* ⊙ *Closed mid-Apr. through Memorial Day and early November.*

$$
MEXICAN FUSION
✕ **Fiesta's.** The Marquez sisters, Debbie and Susan, use old family recipes brought to Colorado by their great-grandparents to create great Southwestern cuisine. Among the favorites are chicken enchiladas in a white jalapeño sauce and blue-corn enchiladas served Santa Fe style with an egg on top. Handmade corn tamales are stuffed with pork and smothered in a classic New Mexican–chili sauce. The eatery in Edwards Plaza is brightly decorated with New Mexican folk art and paintings. More than 20 tequilas keep the bar—and patrons—hopping. ⊠ *57 Edwards Access Rd., Edwards* ☎ *970/926–2121.*

$$
SUSHI
✕ **Foxnut Sushi.** Right at the base of the Centennial Lift, Foxnut Sushi has a huge outdoor patio (underground heating during the winter) that's perfect for people-watching while you dine on the village's best sushi and down some Golden Dragon hot sake. Try the pork-and-vegetable pot stickers or the "dynamite kamikaze" shrimp. ⊠ *15 W. Thomas Pl.* ☎ *970/845–0700* ⊙ *Closed mid-Apr. through Memorial Day, and 1st few wks Nov.*

$$
AMERICAN
✕ **The Gashouse.** This longtime hangout set inside a 1930s-era log cabin has walls covered with hunting trophies. (If stuffed animal heads aren't your thing, think twice about eating here.) Locals swear by the buffalo, prime rib, and elk. Stop in for a brew and some buffalo wings and watch how some of the Vail Valley residents kick back. ⊠ *34185 U.S. 6, 4 mi west of Beaver Creek, Edwards* ☎ *970/926–3613* ⊕ *www. gashouse-restaurant.com.*

$
AMERICAN
✕ **Gore Range Brewery.** After a morning on the slopes or an afternoon playing a few rounds of golf, locals gravitate here for a burger or spicy ribs and a locally brewed beer. In the Edwards Village Center, the brewery blends high-tech styling with a laid-back aura on its spacious outdoor patio and in comfortable indoor booths. ⊠ *0105 Edwards Village Blvd., Bldg. H, Edwards* ☎ *970/926–2739* ⊕ *www. gorerangebrewery.com.*

$$$$
EUROPEAN
✕ **Mirabelle.** In a restored farmhouse at the entrance to Beaver Creek, Mirabelle is one of the area's loveliest restaurants. Owner and chef Daniel Joly serves superb Belgian–French cuisine. His preparations are a perfect blend of colors, flavors, and textures. The menu changes regularly, but if it's available, try hot foie gras with caramelized golden apples, and roasted elk fillet with rhubarb jam. Depending on your

point of view, the elaborate desserts are either heavenly or sinful. The wine list is roughly two-thirds European—to match the menu—and a third domestic. ⊠ *55 Village Rd., Avon* ☎ *970/949–7728* ⊕ *www. mirabelle1.com* ☉ *Closed Sun. No lunch.*

$$$$ ✕ **Spago.** At the Ritz Carlton, Wolfgang Puck's restaurant, is housed in
MODERN an expansive, dining room whose vegetable-dyed wood paneling and
AMERICAN enlarged black-and-white photographs achieves a sleekly modern look without contradicting the resort's rustic mountain sensibility. Puck's seasonal menu often favors Asian accents and regional ingredients. In late autumn the menu's butternut squash soup is deliciously intensified with cherry-balsamic, Romanesco and brown-butter shallots. The Colorado lamb chops spiced with Hunan eggplant and cilantro-mint vinaigrette is not to be missed and for dessert the *kaiserschmarren*, a souffléd crème fraîche pancake with strawberry sauce, is otherwordly. Service is impeccable, if a touch formal; those who prefer a low-key (or less bank-breaking) meal might consider dining in the bar area. ⊠ *0130 Daybreak Ridge, at the Ritz Carlton, Bachelor Gulch, Avon* ☎ *970/343–1555* ⊕ *www.wolfgangpuck.com* ♨ *Reservations essential.*

$$$$ ✕ **Splendido.** With elegant marble columns and custom-made Italian
MODERN linens, this posh eatery is the height of opulence. Owner and chef David
AMERICAN Walford is a master of New American cuisine, and he borrows freely from many traditions. He is equally adept at turning out rack of lamb with rosemary as he is grilling up an elk loin with braised elk osso buco. Retire for a nightcap to the classically elegant piano bar, where Peter Vavra entertains. ⊠ *17 Chateau La., Beaver Creek Village* ☎ *970/845– 8808* ⊕ *www.splendidobeavercreek.com* ☉ *No lunch.*

$$$$ ✕ **Toscanini.** You have a ringside seat at the ice rink in the heart of Bea-
ITALIAN ver Creek when you dine at this casual eatery. The menu is authentic Italian, starting with a variety of dipping oils for the fresh bread— you might then graduate to sliced octopus carpaccio with fried capers. Entrées include panfried gnocchi with basil pesto and house-made fettuccine with veal Bolognese. ⊠ *60 Avondale Rd., Beaver Creek Village* ☎ *970/754–5590* ⊕ *www.toscaninibeavercreek.com* ☉ *Closed May, June, Oct., Nov.*

WHERE TO STAY

For expanded hotel reviews, visit Fodors.com.

$$$$ ⛆ **Beaver Creek Lodge.** A large central atrium that doubles as an art
HOTEL gallery grabs all the attention at this modern hotel a few hundred
★ yards from the lifts. **Pros:** room layouts great for families; good value; friendly service. **Cons:** a short walk to the lifts; fee for parking; no spa. ⊠ *26 Avondale La., Beaver Creek Village* ☎ *970/845–9800* ⊕ *www. beavercreeklodge.net* ↩ *72 suites* ♨ *In-room: safe, kitchen, Wi-Fi. In-hotel: restaurant, bar, pool, gym, laundry facilities, business center, parking* ⭐ *No meals.*

$$$$ ⛆ **Charter at Beaver Creek.** With its elegantly angled blue-slate roof, this
HOTEL sprawling property is one of the area's largest accommodations. **Pros:** on-site spa; ski-in ski-out. **Cons:** small rooms; mediocre breakfasts;

pools can be noisy with children. ⊠ *120 Offerson Rd., Beaver Creek Village* ☎ *970/949–6660, 800/525–6660* ⊕ *www.thecharter.com* ⇗ *240 rooms* ⚬ *In-room: no a/c, safe, kitchen, Wi-Fi. In-hotel: restaurant, bar, pool, gym, spa, laundry facilities, business center, parking.*

$$$$
RESORT

🏨 **Lodge & Spa at Cordillera.** An aura of isolated luxury prevails at this ridge-top lodge with a style that calls to mind the finest alpine hotels, and is popular with return guests. **Pros:** spa; fireplaces in rooms. **Cons:** must take shuttle or drive to lifts or town; $30 daily resort fee. ⊠ *2205 Cordillera Way* ⌂ *Box 1110, Edwards 81632* ☎ *970/926–2200, 800/877–3529* ⊕ *www.cordilleralodge.com* ⇗ *56 rooms* ⚬ *In-room: Wi-Fi. In-hotel: restaurant, bar, golf course, pool, gym, spa, business center, parking.*

$$$$
RESORT
Fodor's Choice
★

🏨 **The Osprey at Beaver Creek, A Rock Resort.** You can't get any closer to a ski run in the U.S. than the Osprey, unless you sleep on the lift. **Pros:** best ski location at Beaver Creek; rooms are fresh and light; romantic. **Cons:** often sold out well in advance. ⊠ *10 Elk Track La.* ☎ *970/754–7400, 866/621–7625* ⊕ *www.ospreyatbeavercreek.rockresorts.com* ⇗ *40 rooms* ⚬ *In-room: Wi-Fi. In-hotel: restaurant, bar, pool, spa, parking* ⎟◎⎟ *Breakfast.*

$$$$
RESORT

🏨 **Park Hyatt Beaver Creek Resort & Spa.** With magnificent antler chandeliers, and towering windows opening out onto the mountain, the lobby of this slopeside hotel manages to be both cozy and grand. *136 E. Thomas Pl., Beaver Creek Village* ☎ *970/949–1234,* ⊕ *www. beavercreek.hyatt.com* ⇗ *190 rooms, 12 suites* ⚬ *In-room: safe, kitchen, Wi-Fi. In-hotel: restaurant, bar, pool, tennis court, gym, spa, children's programs, laundry facilities, business center, parking.*

$$$$
HOTEL

🏨 **Pines Lodge.** This Swiss-style ski-in ski-out lodge is a winner for skiers, combining upscale accommodations with an unpretentious attitude. **Pros:** traditional European chalet decor; slope-side; on-site ski shop and ski concierge. **Cons:** a short walk to the village; valet parking only. ⊠ *141 Scott Hill Rd., Beaver Creek Village* ☎ *970/754–7200, 888/959–6782* ⊕ *www.pineslodge.rockresorts.com* ⇗ *60 rooms, 5 condos, 5 townhouses* ⚬ *In-room: safe, kitchen, Wi-Fi. In-hotel: restaurant, bar, golf course, pool, gym, spa, laundry facilities, business center, parking.*

$$$$
RESORT
★

🏨 **Ritz-Carlton, Bachelor Gulch in Beaver Creek.** The stone-and-timber resort crowns Beaver Creek Mountain above the bustle of Vail Valley like one of King Ludwig's Bavarian castles. **Pros:** the most luxurious property on the mountain; excellent guest service; ski-in ski-out. **Cons:** high altitude (9,000 feet); removed from the Village. ⊠ *0130 Daybreak Ridge, Bachelor Gulch Village* ☎ *970/748–6200, 800/241–3333* ⊕ *www.ritzcarlton. com* ⇗ *140 rooms, 40 suites* ⚬ *In-room: safe, kitchen, Wi-Fi. In-hotel: restaurant, bar, golf course, pool, tennis court, gym, spa, children's programs, business center, parking, some pets allowed.*

$$$$
RESORT

🏨 **The Westin Riverfront Resort & Spa at Beaver Creek Mountain.** This rambling, contemporary resort isn't actually located in Beaver Creek but in the nearby town of Avon, just off the I–70 corridor, so getting up to the ski village requires a free shuttle trip (in winter you can also reach the slopes via a 15-minute ride on the Riverfront Express Gondola). **Pros:** smartly appointed rooms; good value; first-rate facilities, from the spa to the restaurant. **Cons:** located outside the ski village; steep resort and parking fees; staff may try to pitch you on timeshares. ⊠ *126 Riverfront La., Avon* ☎ *970/790–6000* ⟿ *289 rooms* ⚲ *In-room: a/c, safe, kitchen, Internet, Wi-Fi. In-hotel: restaurant, bar, golf course, pool, gym, spa, business center, parking, some pets allowed.*

NIGHTLIFE AND THE ARTS

THE ARTS

★ **Vilar Performing Arts Center.** Vilar Performing Arts Center is an artwork in itself, with gold-color wood paneling and an etched-glass mural re-creating with bold strokes the mountains outside. Seating more than 500, the horseshoe-shaped auditorium has great views from just about every seat. Throughout the year there's a stellar lineup of events, including concerts by orchestras and pop stars, great theater, and even a circus. In the surrounding plazas you'll find many art galleries. Just walking around Beaver Creek is a feast for the eyes, because sculptures are set almost everywhere you look. ⊠ *68 Avondale La.* ☎ *970/845–8497, 888/920–2787* ⊕ *www.vilarpac.org.*

NIGHTLIFE

Coyote Café. The boisterous Coyote Café is a kick-back-and-relax sort of place right on the pedestrian mall, where locals hang out at the bar and enjoy the patio. The kitchen doles out Mexican food, sandwiches, and burgers. ⊠ *210 The Plaza* ☎ *970/949–5001* ⊕ *www.coyotecafe.net.*

Dusty Boot Saloon. For the best après-ski scene among both visitors and locals, head to this rollicking saloon complete with Wild West decor, including cowboy hats and buffalo skulls over the pine-wood bar. When the ski slopes close, the bar is usually three-deep. ■TIP➜ **The $6 happy hour menu includes an appetizer and a draft beer. The dinner menu features hand-cut steaks and local barbecue. Tables fill fast and reservations aren't accepted.** ⊠ *210 Offerson Rd.* ☎ *970/748–1146* ⊕ *www.dustyboot.com.*

McCoy's Café. Right at the base of the mountain, McCoy's Café draws crowds most afternoons in the winter months with live music. ⊠ *136 East Thomas Pl., Village Hall* ☎ *970/949–1234.*

SHOPPING

Christopher & Co. Christopher & Co. has vintage poster art dating from the 1890s to the 1950s. Depictions of American and European ski resorts are among the more than 3,000 posters on display. ⊠ *105 Edwards Village Blvd., Edwards* ☎ *970/926–8191* ⊕ *www.christopherco.com.*

Shaggy Ram. Although the Shaggy Ram sounds like it would stock mostly Western items, this shop is filled with French and English antiques. Items range from fringed lamps to crystal decanters to elegant old desks. ⊠ *210 Edwards Village Blvd., Edwards Village Center, Edwards* ☎ *970/926–7377* ⊕ *www.theshaggyram.com.*

Aspen and the Roaring Fork Valley

WORD OF MOUTH

"Aspen is a great town, very vibrant, with lots of hotels, condos, restaurants, shopping. Lots of bling, but plenty of "regular" people too. When we ate out at one upscale steak place, customers were dressed in everything from ski clothes (actual ski clothes, as in they'd just come off the mountain) to furs and diamonds. We were wearing jeans and boots and were perfectly comfortable. Aspen is a lot farther from Denver, but also has its own airport. The one ski area in town is Ajax Mountain, which is geared to experts. Snowmass is the best area for intermediates—it's a 20-minute [free] shuttle ride from Aspen."

—sf7307

Updated by
Jad Davenport

The Roaring Fork Valley—and Aspen, its crown jewel—is the quintessential Colorado Rocky Mountain High. A row of the state's famed Fourteeners (peaks over 14,000 feet) guards this valley. There are only two ways in or out: over the precipitous Independence Pass in summer or up the four-lane highway through the booming Roaring Fork Valley, which stretches nearly 50 mi from Glenwood Springs to Aspen.

Outside Aspen, Colorado natives regard the city and its mix of longtime locals, newly arrived ski bums, hard-core mountaineers, laser-sculpted millionaires, and tanned celebs with a mixture of bemusement and envy. The "real Aspenites," who came for the snow and stayed for summers, have been squeezed out by seven-digit housing prices. Most have migrated down-valley to the bedroom communities of Basalt and Carbondale. In the words of one refugee, "the Aspen millionaires are making room for the billionaires."

The quest for wealth in the valley dates back to the mid-1800s, when the original inhabitants, the Ute people, were supplanted by gold prospectors and silver miners, who came to reap the region's mineral bounty. The demonetization of silver in 1893 brought the quiet years, as the population dwindled and ranching became a way of life. Nearly half a century later the tides turned again as downhill skiing gave new life to Aspen. Today the Roaring Fork Valley weaves together its past and present into a blend of small-town charm and luxurious amenities, all surrounded by the majestic beauty of central Colorado's 2-million-acre White River National Forest.

ORIENTATION AND PLANNING

GETTING ORIENTED

Wedged in a valley between the Elk Mountain palisades to the southwest and the high-altitude massifs of the Sawatch Range in the east, the Roaring Fork Valley is a Rocky Mountain Shangri-la. The charm and beauty of this isolation makes reaching Aspen a scenic journey, but also one that can be frustrating.

The only land-based way in or out of Aspen is Highway 82—heading either across the Roaring Fork Valley or (in summer) over Independence Pass across the eastern side of the mountains (the pass begins at the junction of U.S. 24 and Highway 82). Aspen's explosive growth hasn't come without some headaches. Despite expanded lanes, Highway 82 quickly clogs with skiers and day commuters.

TOP REASONS TO GO

Fine fare: Restaurants in Aspen, Carbondale, and Glenwood Springs are used to being praised for climbing gastronomic heights, and the dishes that many offer, from sushi Matsuhisa to lobster strudel, are as upscale as the clientele.

Historic hotels: Thanks to moneyed preservationists, the Victorian Hotel Jerome in Aspen and the Medici-inspired Hotel Colorado in Glenwood Springs still stand.

Hot springs: The 93°F mineral-water pool at Glenwood Springs has been a therapeutic retreat since the Ute Indians called it "healing waters."

The mountains: You'll find postcard Colorado in the 14,000-foot Maroon Bells, especially when these steep-faced peaks are reflected in Maroon Lake.

The scene: You'll see it all in Aspen—Hollywood celebs in cowboy boots, glamorous wives of Saudi royalty shopping, tanned European ski instructors, and fascinating and friendly locals.

Aspen. Head here for a dose of the high life in an almost too-pretty town. The aspen-draped Maroon Bells peaks are one of the state's iconic images.

The Roaring Fork Valley. Snowmass is a year-round family resort destination rather than a true town. The historic towns of Glenwood Springs, Redstone, and Marble offer a pleasant—and less expensive—alternative experience, and have great fly-fishing and rafting in summer.

PLANNING

WHEN TO GO

Aspen and the Roaring Fork Valley are a year-round destination. If it's skiing you're after, February and March have the best snow and warmest winter weather (and prices are lower than the peak Thanksgiving-to-Christmas season). Aspen summers are legendary for their food, art, and music festivals. Although only 6,000 locals call Aspen home, the population more than quadruples to 27,000 in summer and winter high seasons. June and early July are best for rafting (snowmelt makes for high-octane rapids), but many high-country hiking and mountain-biking trails are buried under snowdrifts until July, when the wildflowers peak. Mid-September brings hotel-room deals, cooler days, photogenic snow dustings on the Maroon Bells, and flame-orange aspen groves.

GETTING HERE AND AROUND
AIR TRAVEL

Aspen-Pitkin County Airport (ASE) is 3 mi from Aspen and 7 mi from Snowmass. It is served daily by United Express, Delta (from Salt Lake City and Atlanta), Frontier Airlines (from Denver), and has nonstop United service to Los Angeles. During ski season United also offers nonstop service from Chicago and San Francisco.

TRANSFERS If you aren't renting a car, your best bet for traveling to and from Aspen and Snowmass Village is Roaring Fork Transit Agency, which provides bus service from Aspen-Pitkin County Airport to the Rubey Park bus station right at the base of the ski mountain. Colorado Mountain Express, a shared-van shuttle service, connects Aspen with Denver, Grand Junction, and the Eagle County/Vail airport. High Mountain Taxi, a taxi company with four-wheel drive vehicles based in Aspen, can also provide charter service outside the Roaring Fork Valley.

Airports Aspen-Pitkin County Airport (ASE) ☎ 970/920–5384 ⊕ www. aspenairport.com. **Denver International Airport (DEN)** ☎ 800/247–2336 ⊕ www.flydenver.com.

Airport Transfers Colorado Mountain Express ☎ 970/926–9800, 800/525–6363 ⊕ www.ridecme.com. **High Mountain Taxi** ☎ 970/925–8294 ⊕ www. hmtaxi.com.

CAR TRAVEL

You can rent a car from half a dozen companies at Aspen's airport.

In summer the 160-mi, three-hour drive from Denver to Aspen is a delightful journey up the I–70 corridor and across the Continental Divide through the Eisenhower Tunnel (or by way of the slower, but more spectacular, Loveland Pass), down along the eastern ramparts of the Collegiate Peaks along State Highway 91 and U.S. Highway 24, with a final push on twisty State Highway 82 up and over 12,095-foot Independence Pass.

The scenery, particularly south of Leadville on U.S. 24, is among the best in Colorado, with views to the west of 14,433-foot Mount Elbert, the highest mountain in the state. Independence Pass is closed in winter (the timing depends on snowfall, typically late October–late May), but motorists should always drive cautiously. Blinding snowstorms— even in July—can erase visibility and make the pass treacherously icy. Be especially careful on the western side, where the road narrows and vertigo-inducing drop-offs plunge thousands of feet from hairpin curves. Both Route 82 and I–70, like all Colorado roads, should be driven with caution, especially at night when elk, bighorn sheep, and mule deer cross without warning.

Generally speaking, driving to Aspen from Denver in winter is more trouble than it's worth, unless you plan to stop along the way. The drive west on I–70 and east on Route 82 takes more than three hours at best, depending on weather conditions and, increasingly, ski traffic. On the other hand, the 3-mi drive from the Aspen-Pitkin County Airport is a breeze along the flat valley floor. The 70-mi drive from the Eagle County Airport-Vail—which doesn't cross any mountain passes—is another option. Whenever you visit, the traffic and parking may try your patience.

SHUTTLE TRAVEL

The Roaring Fork Transit Agency provides bus service up and down the valley; many resorts have free private shuttles.

Shuttles Roaring Fork Transportation Authority ☎ 970/925–8484 ⊕ www. rfta.com.

TRAIN TRAVEL

Glenwood Springs is on Amtrak's *California Zephyr* route, which runs from Emeryville, California to Chicago.

PARKS AND RECREATION AREAS

The Roaring Fork Valley is surrounded by recreational land, wilderness areas, and national forests. To the southeast, in the Collegiate Peaks Wilderness area, more 14,000-foot summits beckon hikers than anywhere else in the Lower 48.

The often-overlooked Hunter-Fryingpan Wilderness Area is one of Colorado's hidden secrets—a thin-air spine of unnamed peaks and excellent trout rivers in the Williams Mountains just east of Aspen. On the other side of the Continental Divide, the Hunter-Fryingpan becomes the Mount Massive Wilderness Area, named for Colorado's second-highest peak, which stands 14,421 feet tall. Most of these wilderness areas are encompassed within the much larger—and more fragmented—White River National Forest.

RESTAURANTS

Sushi? Coconut curry? Bison and lobster? Colorado's culinary repertoire is at its broadest in Aspen. With all the Hummers and designer handbags comes an equal number of menus with high-end ingredients and showy preparations. Plates can be pricey, particularly in Aspen, but many eateries have at least a few moderately priced entrées (usually pastas) and bar menus as a nod to the budget-conscious. For those who want a break from Aspen, there are good dining options down-valley in Basalt and Carbondale as well.

HOTELS

There's no shortage of lodging in Aspen and the Roaring Fork, but you'll pay the highest rates in the state. Downriver alternatives like Carbondale and Glenwood Springs are attractive for budget hunters—but you'll face heavy traffic when commuting to Aspen. Before booking down-valley, however, look for special deals in town that might include lift tickets and parking. If you're staying for more than a weekend or are traveling with a large group, condominiums are an affordable option and have the added bonus of a kitchen.

WHAT IT COSTS					
	¢	$	$$	$$$	$$$$
Restaurants	under $8	$8–$12	$13–$18	$19–$25	over $25
Hotels	under $80	$80–$120	$121–$170	$171–$230	over $230

Restaurant prices are for a main course at dinner, excluding 8.2%–8.6% tax. Hotel prices are for two people in a standard double room in high season, excluding service charges and 8.6%–10.7% tax.

CLOSE UP

Independence Pass

From Memorial Day to Labor Day, the most beautiful route to Aspen is over Independence Pass. From the Vail–Leadville–Buena Vista corridor on the east side of the Sawatch Mountains, Highway 82 climbs up and over 12,080-foot Independence Pass and switchbacks down to Aspen, along the way passing above tree line and making some spectacular white-knuckle hairpin turns (drive slowly to appreciate the scenery, and also because you might have to yield to oncoming traffic in narrow, one-lane sections). The pass divides the Mount Massive Wilderness to the north from the Collegiate Peaks to the south. The trip's not for the fainthearted, given the long exposed drops and the possibility for snow at any time of the year. Elk and mule deer herds can sometimes be seen at dawn and dusk, grazing in the willow thickets beside Lake Creek as it cascades down the eastern flank of the pass. As soon as the autumn snow flies, however, the pass closes and Aspen becomes a cul-de-sac town accessible only via Glenwood Springs.

ASPEN

220 mi west of Denver via I–70 and Hwy. 82.

One of the world's fabled resorts, Aspen practically defines glitz, glamour, and glorious skiing. To the uninitiated, Aspen and Vail might be synonymous. To residents, a rivalry exists, with locals of each claiming to have the state's most epic skiing, finest restaurants, and hottest nightlife. The most obvious distinction is the look: Vail is a Bavarian-inspired village, whereas Aspen is an overgrown mining town. Vail is full of politicians—it's where Gerald Ford, Dan Quayle, and John Sununu fled to escape the cares of state—whereas Aspen is popular with singers and movie stars like Mariah Carey, Melanie Griffith, and Jack Nicholson.

Between the galleries, museums, music festivals, and other glittering social events, there's so much going on in Aspen that even in winter many people come simply to "do the scene," and never make it to the slopes. High-end boutiques have been known to serve free Campari-and-sodas après-ski. At the same time, Aspen is a place where some people live average lives, sending their children to school and working at jobs that may or may not have to do with skiing. It is, arguably, America's original ski-bum destination, a fact that continues to give the town's character an underlying layer of humor and texture. You can come to Aspen and have a reasonably straightforward, enjoyable ski vacation, because once you've stripped away the preciousness, Aspen is simply a great place to ski.

Aspen has always been a magnet for cultural and countercultural types. The late bad-boy gonzo journalist Hunter S. Thompson was one of the more visible citizens of the nearby community of Woody Creek. One of Aspen's most amusing figures is Jon Barnes, who tools around in his "Ultimate Taxi" (it's plastered with 3-D glasses, crystal disco balls, and neon necklaces, and is redolent of dry ice and incense). You'll find

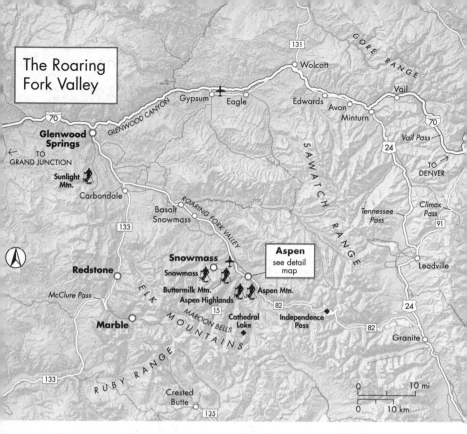

everyone from socialites with *Vogue* exteriors to long-haired musicians in combat boots and fatigues. Ultimately, it doesn't matter what you wear here, as long as you wear it with conviction.

GETTING HERE AND AROUND

The rich arrive by private planes, but almost everyone else arrives in Aspen by car or shuttle bus. Parking is a pricey pain, and traffic, especially on weekends, clogs the streets. The Roaring Fork Transit Agency has bus service connecting the resort with the rest of the valley. The easiest way to get around Aspen is on foot or by bike. For longer trips hop aboard the free Aspen Skiing Company Shuttle, which connects Aspen, Aspen Highlands, Buttermilk, and Snowmass base areas.

TOURS A romantic (albeit pricey) way to orient yourself to the backcountry is by taking a private sleigh ride with Aspen Carriage and Sleigh. Rates start around $300 for up to four adults. They also have carriage tours around downtown and the historic West End.

WHEN TO GO

The summer season in the Roaring Fork Valley runs from June to August, and winter season starts in November and lasts through March.

FESTIVALS **Aspen Music Festival and School.** The Aspen Music Festival and School,
Fodor's Choice focusing on chamber music to jazz, runs from late June to mid-August.
★ Musicians like Joshua Bell and Sarah Chang make pilgrimages here to

perform at more than 350 events held at the 2,050-seat Benedict Music Tent, the Victorian Wheeler Opera House, and the Harris Concert Hall. Tickets are readily available online. A quarter of the performances are free, and one of the great pleasures of the festival is showing up on the free-seating lawn outside the Benedict Music Tent with some friends, a blanket, and a bottle of something good. ☎ 970/925–3254 ⊕ *www. aspenmusicfestival.com.*

> **WORD OF MOUTH**
>
> "Aspen . . . has beautiful historic buildings, good restaurants, culture, and some very pretty mountain scenery nearby (check out the Maroon Bells area—there are some very short hikes if you aren't up for anything longer). You could stop at the Glenwood Hot Springs on the way."
>
> —christy1

ESSENTIALS

Tour Information Aspen Carriage and Sleigh ☎ *970/925–3394* ⊕ *www. aspencarriage.com.* **Maroon Bells bus tour** ☎ *970/925–8484* ⊕ *www.rfta.com.*

Visitor Information Aspen Chamber Resort Association ✉ *425 Rio Grande Pl.* ☎ *970/925–1940, 800/670–0792* ⊕ *aspenchamber.org.* **Aspen Snow Report** ☎ *907/925–1220* ⊕ *www.aspensnowmass.com.*

EXPLORING

TOP ATTRACTIONS

Aspen Art Museum. Works by top national and international artists are exhibited at the Aspen Art Museum. An endowment keeps admission to the museum free. ✉ *590 N. Mill St.* ☎ *970/925–8050* ⊕ *www. aspenartmuseum.org* 🎫 *Free* ⊗ *Tues., Wed., Fri., and Sat. 10–6; Thurs. 10–7; Sun. noon–6.*

Hotel Jerome. Many of Aspen's beautiful buildings were constructed in the 1880s, when the surrounding mines were overflowing with silver. Jerome Wheeler, one of the town's most prominent citizens, constructed the 1889 Hotel Jerome. Peek into the ornate lobby to get a sense of turn-of-the-20th-century living. ✉ *330 E. Main St.* ☎ *970/920–1000.*

QUICK BITES

Ink! Coffee. Follow the locals to Ink! Coffee, where you can sample hot and cold coffee, tea, and other drinks, including the signature Blended Black and White—iced espresso mixed with black and white chocolate. The café also serves pastries and snacks. In summer the patio is a nice place to relax. ✉ *520 E. Durant Ave.* ☎ *970/544–0588* ⊕ *www.inkcoffee.com.*

Fodor's Choice ★

Maroon Bells. The majestic Maroon Bells are twin peaks more than 14,000 feet high. The colorful peaks, thanks to mineral streaking, are so vivid you'd swear they were blanketed with primrose and Indian paintbrush. It's one of the most-photographed spots in the state. Before 9 am and after 5 pm cars can drive all the way up to the lake (and vehicles with children in car seats are permitted at any time). Otherwise, cars are allowed only partway, but the Roaring Fork Transportation Authority provides shuttle buses that leave regularly in summer months from the Aspen Highlands. A convenient pass, available for $27, includes one trip to the Maroon Bells and one ride up Aspen Mountain's Silver Queen Gondola, where concerts, nature walks, amazing hiking, and other activities await you. ⊠ *White River National Forest, Maroon Creek Rd., 10 mi west of Aspen.*

WORTH NOTING

Ute Cemetery. With a trail that winds through gravestones dating to the 1800s, Ute Cemetery is a reminder of Aspen's roots. ⊠ *Next to Ute Park off Ute Ave.*

Wheeler Opera House. Built in 1889, the elegant Wheeler Opera House

> ## WHEN DO THE WILDFLOWERS PEAK?
>
> The Maroon Bells Snowmass Wilderness Area southwest of Aspen is famed for dramatic cliffs and alpine meadows. The bloom will start first in the valleys and eventually climb above the 11,200-foot tree line. Most Colorado wildflowers reach their peak from just before the summer solstice until mid-July.

still serves as a concert venue. ⊠ *320 E. Hyman Ave.* ☎ *970/920–5770.*

Wheeler/Stallard House Museum. You can get a taste of Victorian high life at the Queen Anne–style Wheeler/Stallard House Museum, which displays memorabilia collected by the Aspen Historical Society. While you're there, ask about the organization's Holden–Marolt Ranching and Mining Museum, a hands-on exploration of Aspen's past housed in an old barn on the western edge of town. ⊠ *620 W. Bleeker St.* ☎ *970/925–3721* ⊕ *www.aspenhistorysociety.com* ⊠ *$6* ⊙ *Tues.–Sat. 1–5.*

DOWNHILL SKIING AND SNOWBOARDING

Aspen is really four ski areas rolled into one resort. Aspen Highlands, Aspen (or Ajax) Mountain, Buttermilk, and Snowmass can all be skied with the same ticket. Most are clustered close to downtown Aspen, but Snowmass is down the valley near Snowmass Village. A free shuttle system connects the four.

Aspen Highlands. Locals' favorite Aspen Highlands is essentially one long ridge with trails dropping off either side. Aspen Highlands has thrilling descents at Golden Horn, Olympic Bowl, and Highland Bowl, a hike-in experience unlike any in Colorado. The steep and often bumpy cluster of trails around Steeplechase and Highland Bowl makes this mountain one of the best places to be on a good-powder day. Aspen Highlands has a wide-open bowl called Thunder that's popular with intermediate skiers, as well as plenty of lower-mountain blue runs. The best overall downhill run is Highland Bowl. Besides the comparatively short lift lines and some heart-pounding runs, a highlight of Aspen Highlands is your first trip to the 12,500-foot summit. The view, which includes the Maroon Bells and Pyramid Peak, is the most dramatic in the area, and one of the best in the country. ⊠ *Maroon Creek Rd.* ☎ *970/925–1220, 800/525–6200* ⊕ *www. aspensnowmass.com* ⊙ *Early Dec.–early Apr., daily 9–4.*

Aspen Mountain. Open since 1947, Aspen Mountain is a dream destination for mogul and steep skiers. Nearby Bell Mountain provides some of the best bump skiing anywhere, followed by Walsh's (also a favorite for snowboarders), Hyrup's, and Kristi's. Those wanting long cruisers head to the ridges or valleys: Ruthie's Run, Ridge of the Bell, and International are the classics. There are no novice-level runs here: this is a resort where nearly half the trails are rated advanced or expert, and a black-diamond trail here might rank as a double-black diamond elsewhere. The narrow ski area is laid out on a series of steep, unforgiving ridges with little room for error. Most skiers spend much of the morning on intermediate trails off the upper-mountain quad. Then they head for lunch on the deck of Bonnie's, the mid-mountain restaurant that on sunny days is one of the great people-watching scenes in the skiing world. After a big storm there's snow cat skiing on the back side of the mountain. The biggest drawback to skiing at Aspen Mountain is that too many trails funnel into Spar Gulch, making the end-of-day rush to the bottom chaotic and often dangerous—a situation that has become increasingly tense because snowboarders are now part of the mix. ⊠ *Durant St.* ☎ *970/925–1220, 800/525–6200* ⊕ *www. aspensnowmass.com* ☉ *Late Nov.–mid-Apr., daily 9–4.*

Buttermilk. If you're looking for an escape from the hustle and bustle of Aspen, spend a day at Buttermilk—a family-friendly place where it's virtually impossible to get into trouble. Buttermilk is terrific for novices, intermediates, and, thanks to its half-pipe and Buttermilk Park (which has over 100 features), snowboarders. It's a low-key, lighthearted sort of place, and an antidote to the kind of hotdogging you might encounter at Aspen Mountain. Sterner Run is a favorite for its length and curves, while Racer's Edge appeals to speed demons. Among the featured attractions is a hangout for children named Fort Frog. The Tiehack section to the east, with sweeping views of Maroon Creek valley, has several advanced runs (though nothing truly expert). It also has superb powder, and the deep snow sticks around longer because many serious skiers overlook this mountain. Buttermilk's allure hasn't been lost on pros, however; it now hosts the Winter X Games. ⊠ *W. Buttermilk Rd.* ☎ *970/925–1220, 800/525–6200* ⊕ *www.aspensnowmass.com* ☉ *Early Dec.–mid-Apr., daily 9–4.*

FACILITIES **Aspen Highlands.** Aspen Highlands: 3,635-foot vertical drop; 1,028 skiable acres; 118 trails; 18% beginner, 30% intermediate, 16% advanced, 36% expert; 3 high-speed quad chairs, 2 triple chairs.

Aspen Mountain. Aspen Mountain: 3,267-foot vertical drop; 675 skiable acres; 76 trails; 48% intermediate, 26% advanced, 26% expert; 1 6-passenger gondola, 1 high-speed quad chair, 2 quad chairs, 1 high-speed double chair, 3 double chairs.

Buttermilk. Buttermilk: 2,030-foot vertical drop; 470 skiable acres; 44 trails; 35% beginner, 39% intermediate, 26% advanced; 3 high-speed quad chairs, 1 double chair, 4 surface lifts.

LESSONS AND PROGRAMS **Aspen Mountain Powder Tours.** Aspen Mountain Powder Tours provides access to 1,500 acres on the back side of Aspen Mountain via a 12-person snow cat. Most of the terrain can be handled by confident intermediates, with about 10,000 vertical feet constituting a typical day's skiing. Reservations are required at least a day in advance, but you should book as early as possible. Full-day trips—including a hot lunch, two guides and all the skiing you can do—cost $410. ☎ *970/920–0720.*

Aspen Skiing Company. Aspen Skiing Company gives lessons at all four mountains. Full-day group lessons start at $139, and a private half-day lesson for up to five other people will cost you $485. A noteworthy deal is the three-day guaranteed learn-to-ski or learn-to-snowboard package at Snowmass or Buttermilk, which includes lessons, rental

gear, and lift tickets for $405. The company also runs snow cat trips on Aspen Mountain. ☎ 970/925–1220, 800/525–6200.

LIFT TICKETS   Lift tickets are $87, but almost nobody pays full price, thanks to multiday savings, early- and late-season specials, and other discounts.

RENTALS   Numerous ski shops in Aspen rent equipment. Rental packages (skis, boots, and poles) start at around $45 per day and rise to $75 or more for the latest and greatest equipment. Snowboard packages (boots and boards) run about $50. Bargain shopping at stores around town may turn up better deals.

Aspen Sports. Aspen Sports has plenty of gear to choose from. ✉ 408 E. Cooper Ave. ☎ 970/925–6331 ⊕ www.aspensports.com.

Pomeroy Sports. Pomeroy Sports, at the base of Aspen Mountain across from the gondola, has good deals on equipment and rentals. ✉ 614 E. Durant Ave. ☎ 970/925–7875 ⊕ www.pomeroysports.com.

NORDIC SKIING

BACKCOUNTRY SKIING

★ **10th Mountain Hut & Trail System.** The 10th Mountain Hut & Trail System, named in honor of the U.S. Army's 10th Mountain Division, includes 10 huts along the trail connecting Aspen and Vail. The main trail follows a generally avalanche-safe route in altitudes from 8,000 feet to 12,000 feet. This translates to a fair amount of skiing along tree-lined trails and a good bit of high-alpine ups and downs. You must be in good shape, and some backcountry skiing experience is extremely helpful. Accommodations along the trail vary, but this system does include comfortable backcountry huts that are supplied with mattresses and pillows, precut logs for wood-burning stoves, and utensils for cooking. Huts sleep from 6 to 16 people (more if you're willing to cuddle). For a $25 membership fee you can enter a reservation lottery in March. Otherwise, reservations are accepted beginning in April; weekends in peak ski season fill up quickly. ✉ 1280 Ute Ave. ☎ 970/925–5775 ⊕ www.huts.org ✉ $30 and up per person per night.

Alfred A. Braun Hut System. The Alfred A. Braun Hut System is one of Aspen's major backcountry networks. The trailhead leads from the Ashcroft Ski Touring Center into the Maroon Bells–Snowmass Wilderness. Take the usual precautions, because the trails cover terrain that's prone to avalanche. Huts sleep 7 to 14 people. They're open in winter only, and reservations can be made beginning May 1. ✉ Box 7937,

Aspen 81612 ☎ *970/925–5775* ⊕ *www.huts.org* ✉ *$25 per person per night, 4-person minimum.*

Aspen Alpine Guides. If you're unfamiliar with the hut system or are inexperienced in backcountry travel, you should hire a guide. One reliable company is Aspen Alpine Guides. ☐ *Box 659, Aspen 81612* ☎ *970/925–6618* ⊕ *www.aspenalpine.com.*

Ute Mountaineer. In Aspen the best place for renting ski equipment, climbing skins, packs, sleeping bags, mountaineering supplies, and other backcountry gear is the Ute Mountaineer. ✉ *210 S. Galena St.* ☎ *970/925–2849* ⊕ *www.utemountaineer.com.*

TRACK SKIING

Ashcroft Ski Touring Center. About 12 mi from Aspen, the Ashcroft Ski Touring Center is sequestered in a high-alpine basin up Castle Creek, which runs between Aspen Mountain and Aspen Highlands. The 25 mi of groomed trails are surrounded by the high peaks of the Maroon Bells–Snowmass Wilderness, and crisscross the ghost town of Ashcroft. This is one of the most dramatic cross-country sites in the High Rockies. ✉ *11399 Castle Creek Rd.* ☎ *970/925–1971* ⊕ *www. pinecreekcookhouse.com/ashcroft.html.*

Aspen Cross-Country Center. Lessons and rentals are available at the Aspen Cross-Country Center. Diagonal, skating, racing, and light-touring set-ups are available. ✉ *39551 Hwy. 82* ☎ *970/925–2145.*

Aspen/Snowmass Nordic Council. Subsidized by local taxes, the Aspen/ Snowmass Nordic Council charges no fee for the 48 mi of maintained trails in the Roaring Fork Valley, making it the largest free groomed Nordic-trail system in North America. For a longer ski, try the Owl Creek Trail, connecting the Aspen Cross-Country Center trails with the Snowmass Club trail system. More than 10 mi long, the trail leads through some lovely scenery. ☐ *Box 10815, Aspen 81612* ☎ *970/429– 2039* ⊕ *www.aspennordic.com.*

OTHER SPORTS AND THE OUTDOORS

☾ ★ **Aspen Center for Environmental Studies.** Aspen Center for Environmental Studies is a research center that runs workshops that teach everything from how to create a small wildlife sanctuary in your own backyard to what animals you might find on local trails. The facility sponsors snow-shoe walks with naturalist guides in winter, and in summer there are bird-watching hikes and "special little naturalist" programs for four- to seven-year-olds, which include nature walks and arts and crafts. ✉ *100 Puppy Smith St.* ☎ *970/925–5756* ⊕ *www.aspennature.org.*

FISHING

Aspen Trout Guides. Aspen Trout Guides runs fly-fishing tours of local waterways. The company is in the Hamilton Sports Pro Shop. ✉ *520 E. Durant Ave.* ☎ *970/379–7963* ⊕ *aspentroutguides.com.*

★ **Roaring Fork River.** The Roaring Fork River, fast, deep, and uninterrupted by dams from its headwaters to its junction with the Colorado, is one of the last free-flowing rivers in the state. The healthy populations of rainbow and brown trout—of the hefty 12- to 18-inch variety—make the Roaring Fork a favorite with anglers. From the headwaters at Independence Pass to within 3 mi of Aspen most of the river access is on public lands, and is best fished in summer and early fall. Downstream from Aspen the river crosses through a checkerboard pattern of private and public land; it's fishable year-round. The river's rounded stones make felt soles or studs a good idea for waders. ⊕ *www.wildlife.state. co.us/fishing.*

Taylor Creek Fly Shop. Taylor Creek Fly Shop has the town's best selection of flies and other supplies. ⊠ *408 E. Cooper Ave.* ☎ *970/920–1128* ⊕ *www.taylorcreek.com.*

FITNESS

Aspen Club & Spa. The upscale Aspen Club & Spa has plenty of weight-training and cardiovascular equipment, as well as indoor squash courts and spinning and yoga classes. It's also home to John Clendenin's Ski Doctor indoor ski simulator. When you're finished getting all sweaty, you can relax in the luxurious full-service spa. ⊠ *1450 Ute Ave.* ☎ *970/925–8900* ⊕ *aspenclub.com.*

HIKING

If you aren't used to it, high altitude can pack a wallop. Drink plenty of water to remedy the effects of altitude sickness—dizziness, shortness of breath, headache, and nausea. And slather on the sunscreen—it's easy to get sunburned at high altitude even when the sky looks cloudy. In summer, plan to be back below timberline by noon; afternoon thunderstorms are frequent and sometimes deadly.

★ **Cathedral Lake.** You'll get a taste of several ecozones as you tackle Cathedral Lake, a 5.6-mi round-trip trail. The trail starts gently in aspen and pine groves, but you're likely to break out in a sweat during the long, steep climb into a high valley. Another series of steep, short switchbacks ascend a headwall. From there it's a short stroll to a shallow alpine lake cupped by a wall of granite cliffs. When the high-country snows melt off in mid-July the meadows and willow thickets surrounding the lake are colored with blooming wildflowers. ⊠ *Sopris Ranger District, White River National Forest* ☎ *970/963–2266* ⊕ *www.fs.fed.us/r2/whiteriver.*

Fodor'sChoice **Maroon Bells–Snowmass Wilderness Area.** Aspen excels at high-altitude
★ scenery (seven of the state's 54 Fourteeners are in the Elk Mountain range), and nowhere is the iconic image of the Colorado Rockies more breathtaking than in the Maroon Bells–Snowmass Wilderness Area. In summer, shuttle buses take visitors up Maroon Creek Road to Maroon Lake at the base of the peaks from 9 am until 5 pm. Private cars are allowed at all other times (there is a $10 recreational fee). More ambitious sightseers can select from a number of trails. ⊠ *Aspen/Sopris Ranger District, White River National Forest, Maroon Creek Rd., 10 mi west of Aspen* ☎ *970/925–3445* ⊕ *www.fs.fed.us/r2/whiteriver.*

HORSEBACK RIDING

Maroon Bell Outfitters. For day or overnight horseback tours into the spectacular Maroon Bells–Snowmass Wilderness, try Maroon Bell Outfitters. ⊠ *3133 Maroon Creek Rd.* ☎ *970/920–4677* ⊕ *maroonbellsaspen.com.*

ICE SKATING

Aspen Recreation Center. The Aspen Recreation Center is home to an indoor ice rink big enough for National Hockey League games. There's also an Olympic-size swimming pool. ⊠ *0861 Maroon Creek Rd.* ☎ *970/544–4100* ⊕ *www.aspenrecreation.com.*

Silver Circle Ice Rink. For outdoor ice-skating, try the Silver Circle, which is run by the CP Burger restaurant. ⊠ *433 E. Durant Ave.* ☎ *970/ 925–3056.*

MOUNTAIN BIKING

Aspen Sports. Aspen Sports has the area's widest selection of rental bikes and many types of carriers for kids. ⊠ *408 E. Cooper Ave.* ☎ *970/925– 6331* ⊕ *www.aspensports.com.*

Blazing Adventures. Blazing Adventures leads biking, hiking, jeep, and rafting tours through Aspen and the surrounding valleys. ⊠ *555 E. Durant Ave.* ☎ *970/923–4544, 800/282–7238* ⊕ *www.blazingadventures.com.*

★ **Crystal and Lead King Basin.** Crystal and Lead King Basin is a scenic 16-mi loop on four-wheel-drive roads surrounded by the Maroon Bells–Snowmass Wilderness. The first 6 moderate mi get you to the ghost mine of Crystal. You can turn back here, or tackle the rugged, remaining 2 mi and enjoy views from the 10,800-foot summit. Keep your eyes out for bouncing jeeps behind you. ⊠ *Trailhead: From north side of Beaver Lake in Marble, continue driving up Forest Service Rd. 314 (Daniel's Hill). The ride begins wherever you park.*

Hub of Aspen. Hub of Aspen has high-performance mountain and road bikes. ⊠ *315 E. Hyman Ave.* ☎ *970/925–7970* ⊕ *www.hubofaspen.com.*

PARAGLIDING

If you've ever considered paragliding, then Aspen—with its shining river and black-diamond ski slopes—is the place to do it. Though paragliders look like rectangular parachutes, they are actually classed as aircraft, and can fly high on warm thermals. After a short safety briefing, you'll be harnessed to an instructor for a mad dash down one of the steep ski slopes until the wind fills the "wing" and you are airborne. The ride along the ridges and over the valley can last anywhere from 10 minutes to more than an hour, depending on the weather.

Aspen Paragliding. Aspen Paragliding provides everything you need for a safe and memorable flight. ⊠ *414 E Cooper.* ☎ *970/925–6975, 970/379–6975* ⊕ *www.aspenparagliding.com.*

RAFTING

Aspen Kayak Academy. Long-time Aspen paddler Charlie MacArthur has set up the Aspen Kayak Academy, where you can learn to roll, drop in on a wave, and try stand-up kayaking, which is like surfboarding with a paddle. ⊠ *Box 5283 Snowmass* ☎ *970/925–4433* ⊕ *www. aspenkayakacademy.com.*

Aspen Seals. For the real adrenaline junkies, there's water sledging—kind of like cruising through rapids on a large kickboard. Aspen Seals provides the instruction, wet suits, helmets, and life jackets, and takes you out on the Roaring Fork and Arkansas rivers. ☎ *970/618–4569* ⊕ *www.aspenseals.com.*

Blazing Adventures. For the truly adventurous, Blazing Adventures runs mild to wild rafting excursions on the Shoshone, Upper Roaring Fork, Colorado, and Arkansas rivers. ⊠ *48 Upper Village Mall, Snowmass Village* ☎ *970/923–4544, 800/282–7238* ⊕ *www.blazingadventures. com.*

WHERE TO EAT

Use the coordinate (✛ B2) at the end of each listing to locate a site on the corresponding map.

$$$
AMERICAN
★

✕ **Ajax Tavern.** So close to the gondola you can keep your boots on, this pub-style restaurant is mountainside in the Little Nell. Most of the tavern has big glass windows, and there's also a nice patio with slopeside views. Wide plank floors and brick walls with dark wood paneling define this spot popular both for its location and hearty surf-n-turf dishes (they also have a raw bar). A popular dish to kick off with some brews is the Grand Plate: 18 oysters, 9 clams, 9 shrimp, and half a crab. Filling entrées include grilled lamb T-bones and pan-roasted arctic char. ⊠ *675 E. Durant St.* ☎ *970/920–4600* ⊕ *www.thelittlenell. com* ⌔ *Reservations essential* ✛ *C5.*

$
AMERICAN

✕ **Boogie's Diner.** This cheerful spot filled with diner memorabilia resounds with rock-and-roll faves from the 1950s and '60s. The menu has true range—from vegetarian specialties to pub comfort food. There are also excellent soups, a monster chef salad, meat loaf and mashed potatoes, and a turkey Reuben. Save room for a gigantic milk shake, malted, or float. ⊠ *534 E. Cooper Ave.* ☎ *970/925–6610* ✛ *C5.*

$$$$
MEDITERRANEAN

✕ **Cache Cache.** The sunny flavors of Provence are given pride of place here, thanks to chef Chris Lanter's savvy use of garlic, tomato, eggplant, fennel, and rosemary. The Black Angus rib eye, served with roasted mushrooms, is a perfect way to end a day spent on the slopes; salads and rotisserie items are sensational; desserts are worth leaving room for. The bar menu is a more budget-friendly way to sample this outstanding cuisine. ⊠ *205 S. Mill St.* ☎ *970/925–3835, 888/511–3835* ⊕ *www. cachecache.com* ☼ *No lunch* ✛ *B4.*

$
SOUTHERN

✕ **Hickory House Ribs.** Tie on your bib and dig in. No one will mind if your hands and face are covered in the secret sauce that tops the slow-cooked meats and chicken at this log cabin–style joint with a grizzly bear over the door. These hickory-smoked baby back ribs have won more than 40 national competitions. Feeling brave? Bring a buddy and try "The Feast," one-and-a-half racks of baby back ribs, barbecue chicken, smoked pork and beef, and a pint of baked beans ($50). The Hickory House is also home to Aspen's only Southern-style breakfast, grits and all. And after a late night on the town, nothing beats a breakfast of ribs and eggs. ⊠ *730 W. Main St.* ☎ *970/925–2313* ⊕ *www. hickoryhouseribs.com* ✛ *C2.*

$$$$
ASIAN

✕ **Kenichi.** This Asian restaurant's dark wood and stone walls play nicely against rice-paper panels. It also gets the nod for its delectable bamboo salmon and *char siu* duck, in a sweet barbecue sauce. Blackened sea scallops are popular, as is everything from the sushi bar. With a crowd? Book one of the private tatami rooms or a curtained-off "rock star"

6

Where to Eat and Stay in Aspen

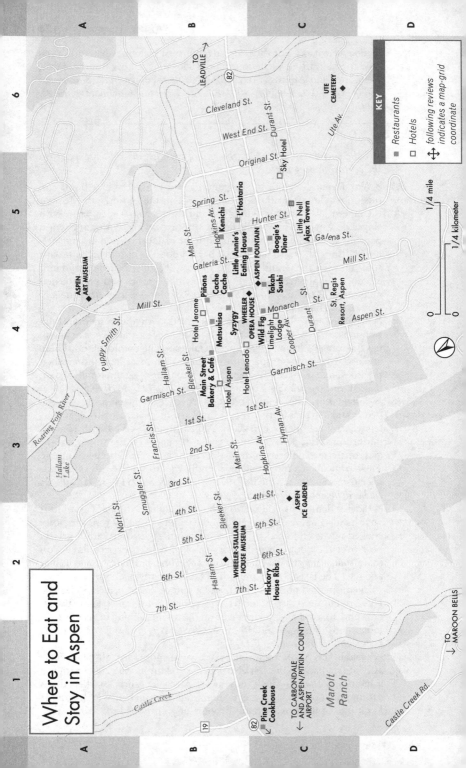

KEY

■ Restaurants

□ Hotels

⬧ following reviews indicates a map-grid coordinate

TO LEADVILLE

82

Cleveland St.

West End St.

Original St.

Spring St.

Hopkins Av.

Main St.

Galena St.

Hunter St.

Durant St.

Mill St.

Galena St.

Aspen St.

Cooper Av.

Durant St.

Garmisch St.

Hyman Av.

Hopkins Av.

Main St.

1st St.

2nd St.

3rd St.

4th St.

5th St.

6th St.

7th St.

Bleeker St.

Francis St.

Smuggler St.

North St.

Hallam St.

Garmisch St.

Hallam St.

Bleeker St.

Hotel Jerome

Hotel Aspen

Hotel Lenado

Mill St.

Puppy Smith St.

Roaring Fork River

Hallam Lake

Castle Creek

Marolt Ranch

Castle Creek Rd.

TO MAROON BELLS

TO CARBONDALE AND ASPEN/PITKIN COUNTY AIRPORT

19

82

UTE CEMETERY ⬧

ASPEN ART MUSEUM ⬧

Kenichi ■

L'Hostaria ■

Little Annie's Eating House ■

ASPEN FOUNTAIN ⬧

Boogie's Diner ■

Little Nell □

Ajax Tavern ■

Sky Hotel □

Piñons ■

Cache Cache ■

Matsuhisa ■

Syzygy ■

WHEELER OPERA HOUSE ⬧

Wild Fig ■

Main Street Bakery & Café ■

Takah Sushi ■

Monarch St.

Limelight Lodge □

St. Regis Resort, Aspen □

WHEELER-STALLARD HOUSE MUSEUM ⬧

Hickory House Ribs ■

ASPEN ICE GARDEN ⬧

Pine Creek Cookhouse ■

0   1/4 mile

0   1/4 kilometer

booth. ✉ *533 E. Hopkins Ave.* ☎ *970/920–2212* ⊕ *www.kenichiaspen. com* 🕙 *No lunch* ✛ *B5.*

$$$ ✕ **L'Hostaria.** This subterranean hot spot is sophisticated yet rustic, with
MODERN an open-beam farmhouse ceiling, sleek blond-wood chairs, contem-
AMERICAN porary art, and a floor-to-ceiling glass wine "cellar" in the center of
the main room. The menu relies on simple, subtle flavors in specialties
such as grilled beef tenderloin with a grain-mustard sauce and mashed
potatoes, and traditional dishes like house-made spaghetti topped with
Maine lobster, zucchini, fresh basil, and a lobster reduction sauce.
✉ *620 E. Hyman Ave.* ☎ *970/925–9022* ⊕ *www.hostaria.com* ✛ *B5.*

$$ ✕ **Little Annie's Eating House.** Everything at this casual red-trimmed house
AMERICAN is simple, from the wood paneling and red-and-white-checked table-
cloths to the fresh trout, barbecued ribs and chicken, and Colorado
lamb. Annie's is a big favorite with locals, who like the relaxed atmosphere, dependable food, and reasonable prices, not to mention the
Bundt cake and "shot and a beer" special at the noisy bar. ✉ *517 E.
Hyman Ave.* ☎ *970/925–1098* ⊕ *www.littleannies.com* ✛ *B5.*

$ ✕ **Main Street Bakery & Café.** Perfectly brewed coffee and hot breakfast
CAFÉ buns and pastries are served daily at this café, along with a full breakfast menu that includes homemade granola. On sunny days, head out
back to the deck for the mountain views. This is also a good spot
for lunch and dinner (it's a quiet respite during the heart of the season). Try the chicken potpie and homemade soups. ✉ *201 E. Main St.*
☎ *970/925–6446* ✛ *B4.*

$$$$ ✕ **Matsuhisa.** After restaurants in Los Angeles, New York, London,
JAPANESE and Tokyo, celebrity chef Nobu Matsuhisa brought his Nouveau Japa-
★ nese cuisine to Aspen in 1998, opening in a former miner's cottage
that's listed on the National Register of Historic Places. Although you
shouldn't expect to see Nobu in the kitchen, his recipes and techniques
are unmistakable. His shrimp with wasabi pepper sauce is scrumptious,
his king crab tempura is delicious, his new-style sashimi marvelous,
and his prices astronomical. Check out Matsuhisa Lounge upstairs (or
outdoors in warm weather) for cocktails and a limited but still superb
menu. ✉ *303 E. Main St.* ☎ *970/544–6628* ⊕ *www.matsuhisaaspen.
com* ⌕ *Reservations essential* 🕙 *No lunch* ✛ *B4.*

$$$$ ✕ **Pine Creek Cookhouse.** You can drive here, but it's more fun to strap on
MODERN cross-country skis or board a horse-drawn sleigh (or hike in summer) to
AMERICAN get to this homey log cabin. The emphasis is on game, including bison,
elk, and wild boar. Lunch offerings include hot smoked-salmon salad,
spinach crepes, and Hungarian goulash. In winter or summer, shoot for
a seat on the deck for breathtaking views of the Elk Mountains. ✉ *11399
Castle Creek Rd.* ☎ *970/925–1044* ⊕ *www.pinecreekcookhouse.com*
⌕ *Reservations essential* ✛ *C1.*

$$$$ ✕ **Piñons.** Romantic and sophisticated, Piñons attracts a primarily over-
MODERN forty crowd. Its second-story location removes you from the hustle
AMERICAN of downtown while also providing great views. The Southwestern
ranch–style dining room harks back to the monied saloon days, with
leather-wrapped railings, a faux-tin ceiling, and upholstered walls.
The contemporary American menu scores high on creativity. Try the
duck quesadilla appetizer, a Southwestern surprise from chef-owner

6

Rob Mobilian, or (as an entrée) the pan-seared buffalo tenderloin with huckleberry sauce. The service and wine list are impeccable. The interior tends to fill up fast, but you can always eat at the bar or on the cozy patio when it's nice outside. ✉ *105 S. Mill St.* ☎ *970/920–2021* ⊕ *www.pinons.net* ⌖ *Reservations essential* ⊘ *No lunch* ✦ *B4.*

$$$$
EUROPEAN

✕ **Syzygy.** Small tables and glass partitions make the interior of this pleasant restaurant quiet and romantic. Personable owner Walt Harris succeeds at providing equally harmonious cuisine (the name refers to the alignment of heavenly bodies) thanks to a sterling waitstaff and the assured creations of executive chef Thomas Fritz. The food is crisply flavored and sensuously textured, floating from French to Asian to Southwestern influences without skipping a beat. Standouts include roasted elk tenderloin and pistachio schnitzel. The patient and knowledgeable will find a few good buys on the extensive wine list; enjoy a glass while listening to some great live jazz. ✉ *520 E. Hyman Ave.* ☎ *970/925–3700* ⊕ *www.syzygyrestaurant.com* ⌖ *Reservations essential* ⊘ *No lunch* ✦ *B4.*

$$$$
JAPANESE
★

✕ **Takah Sushi.** In a town with several sushi haunts, locals will tell you that Takah Sushi has the best plates and prices (the Samurai Sashimi for two runs around $50). There's an outdoor patio right off the pedestrian mall for the see-and-be-seen crowd, and a rowdy basement for larger parties. The large and tasty appetizers include *gyoza* (pork and shrimp pot stickers) and Takah's terrific egg roll. Those who are sushied-out might like straight seafood plates such as lamb chops in garlic sauce and teriyaki-glazed salmon. ✉ *320 S. Mill St.* ☎ *970/925–8588, 888/925–8588* ⊕ *www.takahsushi.com* ✦ *C4.*

$$$$
MEDITERRANEAN
Fodor's Choice
★

✕ **Wild Fig.** For Mediterranean-meets-the-Middle East tastes, head to the Wild Fig, a friendly brasserie with an unbeatable location right off the pedestrian mall. The restaurant is small but cozy, with cheerful yellow walls trimmed in dark wood and a marble bar. In addition to favorites like house-made spinach tagliatelle, the Wild Fig also has one of Aspen's more unusual plates: "fish in a bag," in which the fish of the night is cooked and served in a brown paper bag. For dessert, try chocolate panna cotta and a cup of Amante coffee, roasted in the northern Italian tradition. ✉ *315 E. Hyman Ave.* ☎ *970/925–5160* ⊕ *www.thewildfig.com* ⌖ *Reservations essential* ✦ *C4.*

WHERE TO STAY

For expanded hotel reviews, visit Fodors.com.

Use the coordinate (✦ B2) at the end of each listing to locate a site on the corresponding map.

$$$$
HOTEL

🏨 **Hotel Aspen.** Just a few minutes from the mall and the mountain, this hotel on the town's main drag is a good, if sometimes noisy, find. **Pros:** great location; free parking; refurbished in 2011. **Cons:** traffic can be noisy; no restaurant. ✉ *110 W. Main St.* ☎ *970/920–1379, 800/527–7369* ⊕ *www.hotelaspen.com* ⇌ *32 rooms, 11 suites* ⌂ *In-room: a/c, kitchen, Wi-Fi. In-hotel: pool, business center, some pets allowed* �‖❘ *Breakfast* ✦ *B4.*

$$$$
HOTEL

Hotel Jerome. One of the state's truly grand hotels since it opened in 1889, Hotel Jerome is filled with romantic Victoriana. **Pros:** historic property with modern amenities; great location; great bar; summer music in the gardens. **Cons:** street-facing rooms can be noisy; very expensive, with rates that don't include resort fee. ✉ *330 E. Main St.* ☎ *970/920–1000, 800/367–7625* ⊕ *hoteljerome.aubergeresorts.com* ⇨ *92 rooms, 8 suites* ⊘ *In-room: a/c, safe, Internet. In-hotel: restaurant, bar, pool, gym, business center, parking, some pets allowed* ⫛ *No meals* ⊹ *B4.*

$$$$
B&B/INN

Hotel Lenado. The focal point of this dramatic inn, a favorite with couples, is a modern, 28-foot-tall stone-and-concrete fireplace. **Pros:** romantic; great breakfast cooked to order. **Cons:** no restaurant; rooms facing street can be noisy; management can be a little aloof. ✉ *200 S. Aspen St.* ☎ *970/925–6246, 800/321–3457* ⊕ *www.hotellenado.com* ⇨ *19 rooms* ⊘ *In-room: a/c, Wi-Fi. In-hotel: bar, business center, parking, some pets allowed* ⫛ *Breakfast* ⊹ *B4.*

$$$$
HOTEL
Fodor's Choice
★

Limelight Lodge. This classic is the place to stay for families who want to enjoy a taste of luxury without tip-heavy service (there are no bellhops or ski butlers). **Pros:** family- and pet-friendly; downtown location. **Cons:** no bellhops; busy; often fully booked. ✉ *55 S. Monarch St.* ☎ *970/925–3025, 800/433–0832* ⊕ *www.limelightlodge.com* ⇨ *126 rooms* ⊘ *In-room: a/c, Wi-Fi. In-hotel: pool, laundry facilities, parking, some pets allowed* ⫛ *Breakfast* ⊹ *C4.*

$$$$
HOTEL
Fodor's Choice
★

Little Nell. Right at the base of the gondola, this hotel is the only true ski-in ski-out property in town. **Pros:** best location in town; great people-watching; luxurious. **Cons:** extremely expensive; difficult to get a room in high season. ✉ *675 E. Durant Ave.* ☎ *970/920–4600, 888/843–6355* ⊕ *www.thelittlenell.com* ⇨ *78 rooms, 14 suites* ⊘ *In-room: a/c, safe, Wi-Fi. In-hotel: restaurant, bar, pool, gym, business center, parking, some pets allowed* ⫛ *No meals* ⊹ *C5.*

$$$$
HOTEL

Sky Hotel. Aspen's trendiest hotel, part of the boutique-loving Kimpton Group, attracts a young, show-offy crowd. **Pros:** dramatic style; great location for skiers. **Cons:** can be noisy; valet parking only. ✉ *709 E. Durant Ave.* ☎ *970/925–6760, 800/882–2582* ⊕ *www.theskyhotel.com* ⇨ *90 rooms* ⊘ *In-room: a/c, safe, Wi-Fi. In-hotel: restaurant, bar, pool, gym, business center, parking, some pets allowed* ⫛ *No meals* ⊹ *C5.*

$$$$
HOTEL
Fodor's Choice
★

St. Regis Resort, Aspen. Fresh from a $40-million renovation, the Gothic-Victorian St. Regis has been reinvented as a 19th-century mountain manor. **Pros:** one of Aspen's most luxurious properties; close to the slopes; ultraposh spa. **Cons:** very expensive; rooms are small; only valet parking. ✉ *315 E. Dean St.* ☎ *970/920–3300, 888/454–9005* ⊕ *www.stregisaspen.com* ⇨ *153 rooms, 26 suites* ⊘ *In-room: safe, Wi-Fi. In-hotel: restaurant, bar, pool, gym, spa, business center, parking, some pets allowed* ⊹ *C4.*

6

ASPEN LODGING ALTERNATIVES

Aspen Alps. Aspen Alps, right behind the Little Nell on the slope-side, has nicely appointed ski-in ski-out condos. ⊠ *700 Ute Ave.* ☎ *970/925–7820, 877/711–0526* ⊕ *www.aspenalps.com.*

Frias Properties. Frias Properties rents lavish townhomes, condos, and houses in the mountains. ⊠ *730 E. Durant Ave.* ☎ *970/920–2010,*

800/633–0336 ⊕ *www. friasproperties.com.*

The Gant. The Gant has impressive accommodations as well as two heated outdoor pools and a meeting space. ⊠ *610 W. End St.* ☎ *970/925–5000, 800/345–1471* ⊕ *www.gantaspen.com.*

NIGHTLIFE AND THE ARTS

THE ARTS

Aspen Writers' Foundation. The Aspen Writers' Foundation has a weekly writers' group that visitors are welcome to attend. Its Aspen Summer Words literary festival brings a week of readings, parties, and other events to town every June. ⊠ *110 East Hallam St., Suite 116* ☎ *970/ 925–3122* ⊕ *www.aspenwriters.org.*

Jazz Aspen Snowmass. Jazz Aspen Snowmass has festivals in June and September, and also sponsors free Thursday-night concerts in summer. ☎ *970/920–4996* ⊕ *www.jazzaspen.com.*

★ **Wheeler Opera House.** Wheeler Opera House presents big-name classical, jazz, pop, and opera performers, especially in summer. ⊠ *320 E. Hyman Ave.* ☎ *970/920–5770* ⊕ *www.wheeleroperahouse.com.*

NIGHTLIFE
BARS AND LOUNGES

East Hyman Avenue is the best place for barhopping—a cluster of night-spots share the same address and phone number.

Aspen Billiards. Aspen Billiards is the town's most upscale pool hall. Challenge the locals to a game of eight ball. ⊠ *315 E. Hyman Ave.* ☎ *970/920–6707.*

Cigar Bar. The Cigar Bar, the only place you can smoke indoors in Aspen, is a dimly lit joint straight from Humphrey Bogart movies. Overstuffed chairs, cherrywood wall panels, and sofas set the mood. ⊠ *315 E. Hyman Ave.* ☎ *970/920–6707.*

Eric's Bar. Whiskey—and lots of it—is the claim to fame of Eric's Bar, a hip little watering hole that attracts a rowdy crowd. There's a varied lineup of 14 microbrews and other beers on tap. Go Thursday nights for dancing. ⊠ *315 E. Hyman Ave.* ☎ *970/920–6707.*

J-Bar. Inside Hotel Jerome, the J-Bar is a fun, lively spot. You can't say you've seen Aspen until you've set foot in this place. ⊠ *330 E. Main St.* ☎ *970/920–1000.*

The Regal Watering Hole. Once a country-and-western saloon and now a swanky dance club with grooved, wavy walls and a warm wooden bar, the Regal Watering Hole is just about the only place in town to shake it up on the dance floor. ✉ *220 S. Galena St.* ☎ *970/925–4567.*

Su Casa. Su Casa is the place to get your fill of carefully crafted margaritas or sangria. ✉ *315 E. Hyman Ave.* ☎ *970/920–1488.*

Woody Creek Tavern. Woody Creek Tavern is a great place to grab a house margarita and play some games; gonzo journalist Hunter S. Thompson was a regular. Join the party by riding your bike here in summer via the Rio Grande Trail. ✉ *2 Woody Creek Plaza, Woody Creek* ☎ *970/923–4585* ⊕ *www.woodycreektavern.com.*

MUSIC AND DANCE CLUBS

Little Nell. Jazz is what draws the crowds to the cozy but crowded bar at Little Nell. ✉ *675 E. Durant Ave.* ☎ *970/920–4600.*

Syzygy. For late-night jazz of extremely high quality, head to Syzygy. ✉ *520 E. Hyman Ave.* ☎ *970/925–3700.*

SHOPPING

Downtown Aspen is an eye-popping display of conspicuous consumption. To get a mix of glitz and glamour, T-shirts, and trinkets, stroll past the shops lining Cooper Street.

★ **Aspen Saturday Market.** Show up on Hyman Avenue (between Galena and Hunter streets) any Saturday from mid-June to late October and you can enjoy the Aspen Saturday Market, a sort of farmers' market–meets–arts fair. You can buy ceramic plates, mugs, and serving dishes from a number of local potters. Hungry? Zephyros Farm and Garden from Colorado's Western Slope shows up with organic peaches, peppers and onions, and Louis' Swiss Pastry has artisan breads, meat pies, and potato knishes. Look for the international food market, hidden away in a small park off Hopkins Avenue, for gyro or falafel, then grab a sorbet at Jeffreeze Aspen Sorbetto. ⊕ *www.aspenpitkin.com.*

Brand Building. For chic boutiques, check out the Brand Building. This edifice is home to Gucci, Louis Vuitton, and Christian Dior, as well as local lions like Cashmere Aspen. ✉ *Hopkins Ave. between Mill and Galena Sts.*

Hyman Avenue Mall. For something silly for the folks back home, your best bet is the Hyman Avenue Mall. ✉ *Hyman Ave. between Mill and Galena Sts.*

SPECIALTY SHOPS

ART GALLERIES

Baldwin Gallery. Baldwin Gallery is the place to see and be seen at receptions for nationally known artists. ✉ *209 S. Galena St.* ☎ *970/920–9797* ⊕ *www.baldwingallery.com.*

David Floria Gallery. David Floria Gallery exhibits the hottest new artists. ✉ *525 E. Cooper Ave.* ☎ *970/544–5705* ⊕ *www.floriagallery.com.*

Galerie Maximillian. Galerie Maximillian is the place to find prints, sculpture, and paintings—including original Picassos and Chagalls. ✉ *602 E. Cooper Ave.* ☎ *970/925–6100, 877/339–6100* ⊕ *www.galeriemax.com.*

6

Joel Soroka Gallery. The Joel Soroka Gallery specializes in rare and fine-art photographs. ⊠ *400 E. Hyman Ave.* ☎ *970/920–3152* ⊕ *www. joelsorokagallery.com.*

BOOKS

Explore. Explore is an independent bookstore in a Victorian house. The store stocks more than 100,000 books and is especially strong in politics, travel, and literature. The upstairs bistro is a perfect place for a light meal or snack. ⊠ *221 E. Main St.* ☎ *970/925–5336 bookstore, 970/925–5338 bistro* ⊕ *www.explorebooksellers.com* ☽ *Bookstore, daily 10–9; bistro, early Sept.–Nov., daily 11:30–9; Dec.–Aug., daily 11:30–10.*

BOUTIQUES

Boogie's. Boogie's sells clothing and accessories, including jeans (they have thousands of pairs) and cowboy boots. ⊠ *534 E. Cooper Ave.* ☎ *970/925–6111.*

Pitkin County Dry Goods. Pitkin County Dry Goods has a good selection of men's and women's apparel as well as locally crafted jewelry. ⊠ *520 E. Cooper Ave.* ☎ *970/925–1681* ⊕ *www.pitkincountydrygoods.com.*

SPORTING GOODS

Aspen Sports. Aspen Sports is the biggest sporting-goods store in town, with clothing and equipment for just about any kind of athletic activity. ⊠ *408 E. Cooper Ave.* ☎ *970/925–6331* ⊕ *www.aspensports.com.*

Ute Mountaineer. Ute Mountaineer has mountaineering clothes and equipment for sale and rent. ⊠ *201 S. Galena St.* ☎ *970/925–2849* ⊕ *www.utemountaineer.com.*

THE ROARING FORK VALLEY

Moving down-valley from Aspen along the Roaring Fork River, down past the family resort of Snowmass, is a journey to a much less ritzy Colorado. The landscape changes, too, going from lush, aspen groves into the drier Western Slope steppe.

SNOWMASS

10 mi northwest of Aspen via Hwy. 82.

One of four ski mountains owned by Aspen Skiing Company and one of the best intermediate hills in the country, Snowmass has more ski-in ski-out lodgings and a slower pace than Aspen. Snowmass was built in 1967 as Aspen's answer to Vail—a ski-specific resort—and although it has never quite matched Vail's panache or popularity, it has gained stature with age, finding its identity as a resort destination rather than the village it once called itself. In general, Snowmass is better for families with young children, leaving the town of Aspen to a more up-at-the-crack-of-noon crowd.

The town at the mountain's base, also called Snowmass, has a handful of chic boutiques and restaurants, but it's less self-absorbed and more family-oriented and outdoorsy than Aspen.

GETTING HERE AND AROUND

Heading east along Highway 82 toward Aspen, you'll spot the turn-offs (Brush Creek and Owl Creek roads) to the Snowmass Ski Area. Snowmass is best navigated with your own car or the free Aspen Skiing Company Shuttle Bus, which runs roughly every 15 minutes. All parking in Snowmass is free during the summer, but there's usually a fee in the winter season.

WHEN TO GO

Snowmass Village is a year-round resort, though the peak times are June through September for hiking and November through April for skiing.

OFF THE BEATEN PATH

Basalt. As you drive down Highway 82 through the bedroom communities of Carbondale and El Jebel on the way to Aspen and Snowmass, a detour through this old railroad town is well worth the trouble. Basalt, at the confluence of the Fryingpan and Roaring Fork rivers, has the feeling of a ski town without the lift. Walking down its main drag, Midland Avenue, you get a hint of what Aspen must have been like years ago. Browse the town's small shops and upscale galleries, then dine at one of the intriguing restaurants here.

Ruedi Reservoir. At the gateway to Ruedi Reservoir, take to the water for a day of fishing, boating, or just relaxing away from the hustle and bustle of the town's noisy neighbors.

6

DOWNHILL SKIING AND SNOWBOARDING

Snowmass. Snowmass is a sprawling ski area, the biggest of the four Aspen–area mountains. Aspen Highlands, Aspen Mountain, Buttermilk, and Snowmass can all be skied with the same ticket. A free shuttle system connects all four. Snowmass now includes 64,000 square feet of shops and restaurants, the Elk Camp Gondola, and Elk Camp Meadows Activity Center. There are six distinct sectors: Elk Camp, High Alpine–Alpine Springs, Big Burn, Sam's Knob, Two Creeks, and Campground. Except for the last two, all these sectors funnel into the pedestrian mall at the base. Snowmass is probably best known for Big Burn, itself a great sprawl of wide-open, intermediate skiing. Experts head to such areas as Hanging Valley and the Cirque for the best turns.

At Snowmass 50% of the 3,132 skiable acres are designated for intermediate-level skiers. The route variations down Big Burn are essentially inexhaustible, and there are many other places on the mountain for intermediates to find entertainment. The novice and beginning-intermediate terrain on the lower part of the mountain makes Snowmass a terrific place for younger children.

But don't overlook the fact that Snowmass is four times the size of Aspen Mountain, and has triple the black- and double-black-diamond terrain of its famed sister, including several fearsomely precipitous gullies at Hanging Valley. Although only 32% of the terrain is rated advanced or expert, this huge mountain has enough difficult runs, including the consistently challenging Powderhorn and the more-relaxed Sneaky's Run, to satisfy all but the most demanding skiers.

This mountain has one of the most comprehensive snowboarding programs in the country, with the heart of the action in the Headwall Cirque. A special terrain map points out the numerous snowboard-friendly trails and terrain parks while steering riders away from flat spots. You'll want to visit Trenchtown in the Coney Glade area, which has two lift-accessed pipes, video evaluation, piped-in music, and a yurt hangout complete with couches and snacks. ✉ *West of Aspen via Brush Creek Rd. or Owl Creek Rd.* ☎ *970/925–1220, 800/525–6200* 🌐 *www.aspensnowmass.com* ⏲ *Late Nov.–mid-Apr., daily 9–4.*

FACILITIES 4,406-foot vertical drop; 3,132 skiable acres; 91 trails; 6% beginner, 50% intermediate, 12% advanced, 32% expert; 24 lifts, 1 8-passenger gondola, 1 high-speed 6-passenger chair, 1 6-passenger gondola, 6 high-speed quad chairs, 2 quads, 4 double lifts, 5 magic carpets, 2 school lifts, 2 platter pulls.

LESSONS AND PROGRAMS **Aspen Skiing Company.** Aspen Skiing Company gives lessons at Snowmass and Aspen's other mountains. ✉ *97 Lower Mall, Snowmass Village Mall* ☎ *970/925–1220, 800/525–6200.*

LIFT TICKETS Lift tickets are $87, but almost nobody pays full price, thanks to multi-day savings, early- and late-season specials, and other discounts.

RENTALS Snowmass has numerous ski shops offering rental packages (skis, boots, and poles).

Aspen Sports. Aspen Sports is one of the best-known outfitters in Snowmass. ✉ *70 Snowmass Village Mall* ☎ *970/923–6111* 🌐 *www.aspensports.com.*

Incline Ski Shop. Incline Ski Shop is just steps from the shuttle-bus stop. ✉ *1 Snowmass Village Mall* ☎ *970/923–4726* 🌐 *www.inclineski.com.*

NORDIC SKIING

TRACK SKIING

Aspen/Snowmass Nordic Council. Aspen/Snowmass Nordic Council has 48 mi of maintained trails in the Roaring Fork Valley. Probably the most varied, in terms of scenery and terrain, is the 18-mi Snowmass Club trail network. For a longer ski, try the Owl Creek Trail, connecting the Snowmass Club trail system and the Aspen Cross-Country Center trails. More than 10 mi long, the trail provides both a good workout and a heavy dose of woodsy beauty, with many ups and downs across meadows and aspen-gladed hillsides. Best of all, you can take the bus back to Snowmass Village when you're finished. ☎ *970/429–2039* 🌐 *www.aspennordic.com.*

OTHER SPORTS AND THE OUTDOORS

BALLOONING

Unicorn Balloon Company. Unicorn Balloon Company flies you over the slopes of Aspen. ☎ *970/925–5752* 🌐 *www.unicornballoon.com.*

DOGSLEDDING

★ **Krabloonik.** With about 200 dogs ready to go, Krabloonik can always put together a half-day ride. These trips, beginning at 8:30 am and 12:30 pm and costing about $300, include lunch at the Krabloonik restaurant, one of the best in the area. Twilight rides (with dinner) are also available. In summer, meet the dogs during daily kennel tours. ✉ *4250 Divide Rd.* ☎ *970/923–3953* 🌐 *krabloonikrestaurant.com.*

MOUNTAIN BIKING

Aspen Skiing Company. Aspen Skiing Company can give you a map of area trails, including the terrain park accessed by the Burlingame Lift. The company can also sell you a lift ticket so you won't have to ride uphill. ☒ *97 Lower Mall, Snowmass Village Mall* ☎ *970/925–1220.*

Aspen Sports. Aspen Sports has the widest selection of rental bikes in town, plus carriers for the kids. ☒ *70 Snowmass Village Mall* ☎ *970/ 923–6111* ⊕ *www.aspensports.com.*

Treehouse Kids' Adventure Center. Interactive age-appropriate playgrounds and a full menu of summer and winter activities for older children and teens make the Treehouse Kids' Adventure Center at the bottom of Snowmass Village a good headquarters for family fun. Summer activities include mountain biking, skateboarding, and paintball. When winter comes, kids can rent ski and board gear here and also take lessons. ☒ *120 Carriage Way, Snowmass Village* ☎ *970/923–8733.*

WHERE TO EAT

$$$
ITALIAN
✕ **Il Poggio.** In the cutthroat competition between resort-town restaurants, this unassuming Italian place (complete with bar) is smart enough to let the big boys duke it out. It wins in the end; it's quite possibly the best casual restaurant in the village. Its homemade pastas and breads and the rest of the classic Italian food served here is well received by the après-ski crowd. Try one of the hearth-baked pizzas or any beef or chicken entrée. ☒ *57 Elbert La.* ☎ *970/923–4292* ⊕ *www. snowmassvillage.com* ⊙ *No lunch.*

$$$$
AMERICAN
✕ **Krabloonik.** Owner Dan MacEachen has a penchant for dogsled racing, and Krabloonik (Eskimo for "big eyebrows," and the name of his first lead dog) helps subsidize his expensive hobby. This rustic yet elegant log cabin is on the slopes, which means you'll be treated to wonderful views on your way there. You'll dine sumptuously on some of the best game in Colorado, like caribou, elk, and wild boar, as well as house-smoked trout and its signature wild-mushroom soup. Wash it all down with a selection from Snowmass's most extensive wine list. ☒ *4250 Divide Rd.* ☎ *970/923–3953* ⊕ *www.krabloonikrestaurant. com* ⌂ *Reservations essential.*

WHERE TO STAY

For expanded hotel reviews, visit Fodors.com.

$$$$
HOTEL
Silvertree Hotel. This ski-in ski-out property, under the same management as the Wildwood Lodge next door, is built into Snowmass Mountain. **Pros:** very handy location; steam room. **Cons:** self-parking is a walk from hotel; rooms get hot in summer; rooms book fast in high season. ☒ *100 Elbert La.* ☎ *970/923–3520, 800/525–9402* ⊕ *www. silvertreehotel.com* ⇆ *262 rooms, 15 suites, 200 condos* ☾ *In-room: no a/c, safe, Wi-Fi. In-hotel: restaurant, bar, pool, gym, spa, laundry facilities, business center, parking, some pets allowed* ❙⊙❙ *No meals.*

$$$
B&B/INN
Snowmass Inn. This family-owned lodge is one of Snowmass's original digs; it commands a prime location in the middle of the Snowmass Village Mall, a short walk from the slopes. **Pros:** good location for skiers; big rooms; a good price for Snowmass. **Cons:** minimal customer service; few room or hotel amenities. ☒ *67 Daly La.* ☎ *800/843–1579* ⇆ *39*

rooms ⚹ *In-room: no a/c. In-hotel: laundry facilities, business center, parking* ⧮ *Breakfast.*

$$$
HOTEL
★
Stonebridge Inn. Slightly removed from the hustle and bustle of the Village Mall, this inn is the nicest lodging option in Snowmass. **Pros:** quiet location; good on-site restaurant. **Cons:** must catch a shuttle to lifts. ✉ *300 Carriage Way* ☎ *866/939–2471* ⊕ *www.stonebridgeinn.com* ⬎ *88 rooms, 5 suites, 28 condos* ⚹ *In-hotel: restaurant, bar, pool, gym, laundry facilities, business center, parking.*

$$$$
HOTEL
Fodor's Choice
★
Viceroy Snowmass. Perched like a Tibetan palace overlooking the Roaring Fork Valley, the brand-new Viceroy Snowmass is the undisputed king of the village. **Pros:** ski-in ski-out; attractive decor; ski valet. **Cons:** a short walk or gondola ride to the main village; some staff still inexperienced; small gym. ✉ *130 Wood Rd., Snowmass Village* ☎ *888/622–4567, 970/923–8001* ⊕ *www.viceroyhotelsandresorts.com/snowmass/* ⬎ *173 rooms* ⚹ *In-room: a/c, safe, kitchen, Internet, Wi-Fi. In-hotel: restaurant, pool, gym, spa, children's programs, laundry facilities, business center, parking* ⧮ *No meals.*

SNOWMASS LODGING ALTERNATIVES

Snowmass Lodging Company. Snowmass Lodging Company rents condos. ⌂ *425 Wood Rd. 81615* ☎ *970/923–3232, 800/365–0410.*

Stay Aspen Snowmass. Stay Aspen Snowmass is the central lodging service for the area. ☎ *888/649–5982* ⊕ *www.stayaspensnowmass.com.*

Village Property Management. Snowmass Hospitality can help you locate everything from studio apartments to three-bedroom condos. ⌂ *16 Kerns Rd. 81615* ☎ *970/923–4350, 877/734–7776.*

NIGHTLIFE

Conservatory. For a mellow experience, try the Conservatory. It has a heated deck and occasional live music. ✉ *100 Elbert La.* ☎ *970/923–3520.*

Zane's Tavern. Zane's Tavern is your classic mountain town bar with pool tables, $1.25 drafts, and an Internet jukebox. ✉ *10 Snowmass Village Sq.* ☎ *970/923–3515* ⊕ *www.zanestavern.com.*

SHOPPING

Anderson Ranch Arts Center. Anderson Ranch Arts Center exhibits the work of emerging artists. It also hosts lectures, summer workshops, and other events. ✉ *5263 Owl Creek Rd.* ☎ *970/923–3181* ⊕ *www.andersonranch.org.*

Aspen Sports. Aspen Sports is the biggest sporting-goods store in the area. ✉ *70 Snowmass Village Mall* ☎ *970/923–6111* ⊕ *www.aspensports.com.*

GLENWOOD SPRINGS

27 mi northwest of Aspen via Hwy. 82; 159 mi west of Denver via I–70.

Once upon a time, Glenwood Springs, the famed spa town that forms the western apex of a triangle with Vail and Aspen, was every bit as tony as those chic resorts are today, attracting a faithful legion of the pampered and privileged who came to enjoy the healing waters of the world's largest natural hot springs, said to cure everything from acne to rheumatism.

GETTING HERE AND AROUND

The easiest way to arrive is by car on I–70, the main east–west highway in Colorado. Public transport is more limited than in Aspen, so you'll need a vehicle to explore much beyond the main street.

WHEN TO GO

Glenwood Springs comes into its own in the early summer, when rafters, anglers, and spa goers arrive to sample the gifts of the Colorado River and its underground mineral springs.

ESSENTIALS

Visitor Information Glenwood Springs Chamber Resort Association
⊠ *1102 Grand Ave.* ☎ *970/945–6589* ⊕ *glenwoodchamber.com.*

EXPLORING

☙ **Fairy Caves and Glenwood Caverns.** Glenwood is home to many caves, including Fairy Caves and Glenwood Caverns, whose subterranean caverns, grottoes, and labyrinths are truly a marvel of nature (the area was touted as the "Eighth Wonder of the World" when it opened to the public in the 1890s). Now part of the Glenwood Caverns Adventure Park (think tourist trap), the still-amazing caves are easily accessible via the Iron Mountain Tramway, a seven-minute gondola ride with a bird's-eye view of Glenwood Springs and the surrounding landscape. You can take one of two cavern tours: a 70-minute, family-friendly "Wild Tour" walk; or a more extensive, crawl-on-your-belly spelunking adventure. For a second helping of adrenaline, try the gravity-powered alpine coaster that drops 3,400-feet, ride the 50-mph zip line, or sail out over 1,300 feet above the Colorado River cliffs on a giant swing. ⊠ *51000 Two Rivers Plaza Rd.* ☎ *800/530–1635, 970/945–4228* ⊕ *www.glenwoodcaverns.com* ⊠ *$12 and up* ⊙ *Times vary; call ahead.*

Glenwood Canyon. Along I–70 east of town is the 15-mi-long Glenwood Canyon. Nature began the work as the Colorado River carved deep granite, limestone, and quartzite gullies—buff-tint walls brilliantly streaked with lavender, rose, and ivory. This process took a half-billion years. Then man stepped in, seeking a more direct route west. In 1992 the work on I–70 through the canyon was completed, at a cost of almost $500 million. Much of the expense was attributable to the effort to preserve the natural landscape as much as possible. When contractors blasted cliff faces, for example, they stained the exposed rock to simulate nature's weathering. Riverside biking trails were also created, along with a hiking trail to the hauntingly beautiful **Hanging Lake Recreation Area.** Here Dead Horse Creek sprays delicate flumes from curling limestone tendrils into a turquoise pool, as jet-black swifts fly to and fro. It may be the most transcendent of several idyllic spots in the canyon reachable by bike or on foot. The intrepid can scale the limestone cliffs here, which are pocked with caverns and covered with pastel-hue gardens.

Hotel Colorado. Modern-day Glenwood Springs is where many of those who work in Aspen live. Its many strip malls, chain motels, and fast-food outlets may surprise visitors expecting a purely historical town that time forgot. That said, remnants of her glory days can still be seen in the grand old Hotel Colorado, regally commanding the vaporous pools from a patrician distance. Modeled after the Villa de Medici in Italy, the property opened its doors in 1893. Teddy Roosevelt even made it his unofficial "Little White House" in 1905. ⊠ *526 Pine St.*

○ **Hot Springs Pool.** Hot Springs Pool, formerly called Yampah Hot Springs, ★ was discovered by the Utes (yampah is Ute for "big medicine"). Even before the heyday of the hotel, Western notables that included Annie Oakley and Doc Holliday came to take the curative waters. In Doc's case, however, the cure didn't work, and six months after his arrival in 1887 he died from tuberculosis at age 36—broke and broken down. (He lies in Linwood Cemetery, 0.5 mi east of town.) The smaller pool is 100 feet long and maintained at 104°F. The larger is more than two city blocks long (405 feet), and contains more than a million gallons of constantly filtered water that is completely refilled every six hours and maintained at a soothing 90°F. ⊠ *401 N. River St.* ☎ *970/947–2955, 800/537–7946* ⊕ *www.hotspringspool.com* ▨ *$19* ♡ *Late May–early Sept., daily 7:30 am–10 pm; mid-Sept.–mid-May, daily 9 am–10 pm.*

Yampah Spa & Salon. Now part of a spa, the Hot Springs Vapor Caves are a series of three natural underground steam baths. The same 120°F-plus springs that supply the Hot Springs Pool flow under the floors of the only known natural vapor caves in North America, which were used by the Ute Indians for centuries. Each chamber is successively hotter than the last, and with 15 minerals in the waters, you can purify your body (and soul, according to Ute legend) in a matter of minutes. A variety of spa treatments is also available, whether you prefer a massage, body wrap, or private mineral bath. ⊠ *709 E. 6th St.* ☎ *970/945–0667* ⊕ *www.yampahspa.com* ▨ *$12 for caves, additional cost for treatments* ♡ *Daily 9–9.*

DOWNHILL SKIING AND SNOWBOARDING

Sunlight Mountain Resort. Sunlight Mountain Resort, 20 minutes south of Glenwood Springs, is affordable Colorado skiing at its best. Overshadowed by world-class neighbors, the resort sees far less traffic than typical Colorado slopes. Fresh powder, typically skied off at Aspen within an hour, can last as long as two days here on classic downhill runs like Sun King and steeps like Beaujolais; you won't stand in any lines at the four lifts. The resort has 67 trails, including the super-steep glades of Extreme Sunlight, with a drop of 2,010 vertical feet. The varied terrain, sensational views, and lack of pretension make this a local favorite. The lift tickets are also half as much as those at nearby Aspen. Snowboarders have a dedicated feature—the Peace Pipe. Families will appreciate that every child under 12 skis free with an adult, and that every slope meets at the bottom. For winter sports enthusiasts who don't want to ride a chairlift, there's a 20-mi network of cross-country ski and snowshoe trails just off the slopes. The cafeteria has cold sandwiches, burgers, and pizzas. ⊠ *10901 County Rd. 117* ☎ *970/945–7491, 800/445–7931* ⊕ *www.sunlightmtn.com* ♡ *Dec.–Apr., daily 9–4.*

FACILITIES   2,010-foot vertical drop; 470 skiable acres; 67 trails; 20% beginner, 55% intermediate, 20% advanced, 5% expert; 4 lifts, 1 triple chair, 2 double chairs, 1 surface lift.

CLOSE UP

Doc Holliday

 Born on August 14, 1851, in Griffin, Georgia, John Henry "Doc" Holliday would grow up to be a gunslinger with an attitude. Part scholar, part rebel, he was often only one step ahead of the law. In 1872, after earning a dental degree in Philadelphia, he moved to Atlanta, where he opened a practice. Soon after, a diagnosis of tuberculosis led him to move west in search of a drier climate.

While living in Texas, Holliday took up gambling, which became his sole means of support. His violent temper turned him into a killer. After shooting a prominent citizen and leaving him for dead, Holliday had to flee Texas. Carrying one gun in a shoulder holster, another on his hip, and a long-bladed knife (just in case), he blazed a trail of death across the Southwest. It's not known just how

many men died at his hands, but some have estimated the number to be as high as 25 or more. However, historians generally believe the true number is considerably less. Holliday's reasons for killing ranged from fights over cards to self-defense—or so he claimed. He will forever be known for his role in one of the most famous gunfights in the history of the Wild West: a 30-second gunfight at the O.K. Corral in Tombstone, Arizona.

In May 1887 Holliday moved to Glenwood Springs, hoping that the sulfur vapors of the hot springs there would help his failing lungs. He lived out his dying days at the Hotel Glenwood. On the last day of his life Holliday knocked back a glass of whiskey and remarked, "This is funny." A few minutes later he was dead. Holliday was just 36 years old.

6

LESSONS AND PROGRAMS
Two-hour ski lessons (including gear rental and lift ticket) cost $90; snowboarding is $95. Four-hour ski lessons are $140, $145 for snowboarding.

The resort, in conjunction with Glenwood Springs, also has a ski-stay-swim package. It includes one night's lodging, a big breakfast, a full-day ski pass, and a full day at the Glenwood Hot Springs Pool.

LIFT TICKETS
Lift tickets are the second-cheapest in the state, only $50 at the window. But, as at all Colorado ski resorts, no one ever needs to pay full price. Purchase a discounted pass at the Safeway or King Soopers grocery store in Glenwood Springs.

RENTALS
Sunlight Mountain Ski Resort. Sunlight Mountain Ski Resort has complete rental gear setups on shaped skis. Rentals of the latest snowboards are available for as little as $20. ✉ *10901 County Rd. 117* ☎ *970/945–7491, 800/445–7931* ⊕ *www.sunlightmtn.com.*

Sunlight Ski and Bike Shop. The resort's retail outlet, Sunlight Ski and Bike Shop, is in Glenwood Springs. ✉ *309 9th St.* ☎ *970/945–9425.*

OTHER SPORTS AND THE OUTDOORS
BICYCLING
Glenwood Canyon Bike Path. Though it's a shame that I–70 heads through the spectacular depths of Glenwood Canyon, the busy corridor has opened up this gorge to biking. The Glenwood Canyon Bike Path, a concrete path sandwiched between the Colorado River and the freeway

traffic, runs about 35 mi from Dotsero east to Glenwood Springs. The path generally runs below, and out of sight of the interstate, and the roar of the river drowns out the sound of traffic. Because of the mild climate on Colorado's Western Slope, the trail can be ridden almost year-round. The concrete path also has several dirt spurs that head up into White River National Forest for hikers and mountain bikers. A choice ride is the 18-mi round-trip from Glenwood Springs east up to the trailhead at Hanging Lake, where you can leave your bike and hike a steep mile (climbing 900 feet) to the beautiful lake. Horseshoe Bend, 2 mi from the Vapor Caves, is a perfect picnic spot, since the highway ducks out of sight into a series of tunnels. ✉ *Trailhead: enter path from either Hot Springs Vapor Caves in Glenwood Springs or farther west on I-70 at Grizzly Creek rest area.*

OUTFITTER **Sunlight Ski and Bike Shop.** Sunlight Ski and Bike Shop rents mountain
★ and comfort bikes; $7 per hour, $18 for four hours, or $22 for the day.
✉ *309 9th St.* ☎ *970/945–9425.*

FISHING

Roaring Fork Anglers. Roaring Fork Anglers leads wade and float trips throughout the area. ✉ *2205 Grand Ave.* ☎ *970/945–0180* ⊕ *www.roaringforkanglers.com.*

Roaring Fork Outfitters. Roaring Fork Outfitters has a huge selection of flies; their helpful guides will help you find the right ones. ✉ *2022 Grand Ave.* ☎ *970/945–5800* ⊕ *www.rfoutfitters.com.*

GOLF

River Valley Ranch Golf Club. Jay Moorish designed this course on the banks of the Crystal River. There is lots of water, a constant breeze, and superb—if not downright distracting—views of Mount Sopris. The course is about 15 mi from Glenwood Springs. ✉ *303 River Valley Ranch Dr., Carbondale* ☎ *970/963–3625* ⊕ *www.rvrgolf.com* ⚐ *18 holes. Yards: 7348/5168. Par: 72/72. Green fee: $85.*

RAFTING

Colorado River. When the ski season is over and Colorado's "white gold" starts to melt, many ski instructors swap their sticks for paddles and hit the mighty Colorado River for the spring and summer rafting seasons. Stomach-churning holes, chutes, and waves beckon adrenaline junkies, while calmer souls can revel in the shade of Glenwood Canyon's towering walls.

All the outfitters below run a basic half-day raft trip on the Colorado.

OUTFIT- **Blue Sky Adventures.** Blue Sky Adventures offers a "pedals and pad-
TER AND dles" deal that includes a half-day raft trip followed by a half-day
EXPEDITIONS bike tour. ✉ *319 Hwy. 6J* ☎ *970/945–6605, 877/945–6605* ⊕ *www.*
↻ *blueskyadventure.com.*
★ **Colorado Division of Wildlife.** If you're the independent type, lead your own white-water rafting adventure by putting in at the boat ramp operated by the Colorado Division of Wildlife. It's on the Roaring Fork River, just east of town. ✉ *County Rd. 106* ☎ *970/947–2920.*

Colorado Whitewater Rafting. Colorado Whitewater Rafting has tours that include the "Double Shoshone," a round-trip through the area's most hair-raising white-water rapids. ⊠ *2000 Devereux Rd.* ☎ *970/945–8477, 800/993–7238* ⊕ *www.coloradowhitewaterrafting.com.*

Rock Gardens Rafting. Rock Gardens Rafting runs trips down the Colorado and Roaring Fork rivers, and operates a full-service campground on the banks of the Colorado. ⊠ *1308 County Rd. 129* ☎ *970/945–6737, 800/958–6737* ⊕ *www.rockgardens.com.*

WHERE TO EAT

$$
ITALIAN
✕ **Florinda's.** The peach walls of this handsome space are give over to constantly changing art exhibits. The chef has a deft hand with northern and southern Italian dishes. Try the double-cut veal chops served with a shiitake mushroom sauce or the nightly specials, which are usually extensive and superb. And don't miss the tried-and-true Italian desserts, like tiramisu, zabaglione, and cannoli. ⊠ *721 Grand Ave.* ☎ *970/945–1245* ⊘ *Closed Sun. No lunch.*

$$
ASIAN
✕ **Narayan's Nepal Restaurant.** Finding good Asian fare in Glenwood Springs is no easy feat, but this little eatery, tucked into a strip mall beside the highway, has tasty Nepalese food. The chef, a former sherpa who now owns this restaurant and its twin in Aspen, serves dishes so authentic that you might think for a second that you're in the high Himalayas. Try fish *kawab* (marinated overnight and then baked in a tandoor) with a side of garlicky *naan* (chewy flat bread) if you're skeptical. ⊠ *6824 Hwy. 82* ☎ *970/945–8803* ⊘ *No lunch Sun.*

WHERE TO STAY

For expanded hotel reviews, visit Fodors.com.

$$$
HOTEL
♺
🏨 **Glenwood Hot Springs.** This lodge is perfectly located, just steps from the Hot Springs Pool (which is used to heat the property). **Pros:** right next to the hot springs; attractive rooms that were renovated in 2011. **Cons:** no bar; small rooms. ⊠ *415 E. 6th St., Glenwood Springs* ☎ *970/945–6571, 800/537–7946* ⊕ *www.hotspringspool.com* ⤶ *107 rooms* ♿ *In-room: a/c, safe, Wi-Fi. In-hotel: restaurant, pool, gym, laundry facilities, business center, parking* ❙❍❙ *Breakfast.*

$$
HOTEL
🏨 **Hotel Colorado.** When you catch sight of the graceful sandstone colonnades, and Italianate campaniles of this exquisite building, you won't be surprised that it's listed in the National Register of Historic Places. **Pros:** one of the most historic properties in the valley; across the street from the hot springs. **Cons:** not all rooms have air-conditioning; some rooms are small. ⊠ *526 Pine St.* ☎ *970/945–6511, 800/544–3998* ⊕ *www. hotelcolorado.com* ⤶ *130 rooms, 30 suites* ♿ *In-room: a/c, kitchen, Wi-Fi. In-hotel: restaurant, bar, gym, spa, parking, some pets allowed* ❙❍❙ *No meals.*

$$
HOTEL
🏨 **Hotel Denver.** Right across from Glenwood Springs's also-historic train station, this hotel was built in 1914. **Pros:** right downtown; romantic; on-site brewpub. **Cons:** no concierge; no room service. ⊠ *402 7th St.* ☎ *970/945–6565, 800/826–8820* ⊕ *www.thehoteldenver.com* ⤶ *72 rooms* ♿ *In-room: a/c, kitchen, Wi-Fi. In-hotel: restaurant, bar, gym, laundry facilities, parking, some pets allowed* ❙❍❙ *No meals.*

$
B&B/INN
♺
🏨 **Sunlight Mountain Inn.** This traditional ski lodge, perfect for couples and families, is a few hundred feet from the Sunlight Mountain Resort lifts. **Pros:** a wonderfully remote getaway; delicious meals; no

CLOSE UP

Rafting the Roaring Fork Valley

The key to understanding white-water rafting is the rating system. Rivers are rated from Class I, with small waves where you really don't need to paddle to avoid anything, to Class VI, which is almost impossible to run and where a mistake can be fatal. To confuse matters, rivers change classes depending on how fast they are flowing (measured in cubic feet of water per second). May and June are peak rafting seasons for those who want the adrenaline rush of fighting spring runoff. By mid-August many rivers are little more than lazy float trips.

The Roaring Fork, a free-flowing river (no dams), is usually considered a Class III. Because it runs away from major highways through the heart of ranch country, you're liable to see more wildlife than on the Colorado; in June your guides may point out a nest full of croaking bald eaglets. Cemetery Rapids, a half-mile churning stretch of white water, is the most exciting run.

The stretch of the mighty Colorado that runs through the steep, spectacular walls of Glenwood Canyon alongside I–70 is divided into two sections: the rough and tumble Shoshone below the dam, and the wider, mellower regions beyond. During the peak runoff season, the Shoshone is considered a Class IV river, with aptly named rapids like Maneater and Baptism. The lower Colorado still has some exciting stretches, including Maintenance Shack, a Class III rapid that can flip a large raft. By July and August you can hit the same rapid sideways or backward and barely get wet. The lower stretches of the Colorado pass by several hidden, and not-so-hidden shallow hot springs. If you'd like to warm up in them, ask your guides.

distractions. **Cons:** no cell-phone service; limited room and hotel amenities; restaurant open seasonally. ⊠ *10252 County Rd. 117* ☎ *970/945–5225, 800/733–4757* ⊕ *www.sunlightinn.com* ⇆ *20 rooms* ⚒ *In-room: no a/c, no TV. In-hotel: restaurant, bar, parking, some pets allowed* ⦿ *Breakfast.*

REDSTONE AND MARBLE

29 mi south of Glenwood Springs via Hwy. 82 and Hwy. 133.

Less than an hour from Aspen, Redstone has streets that are lined with galleries and boutiques. Its boundaries are ringed by the impressive sandstone cliffs from which the town draws its name. Since the 1930s, it's been known as an artists' colony. Summer brings streams of visitors strolling the main drag, Redstone Boulevard; in winter, horse-drawn carriages carry people along the snow-covered road.

GETTING HERE AND AROUND

The best way to reach Redstone and Marble is by car, both because the scenery demands plenty of stops and (more important) there isn't any public transportation available anyway.

WHEN TO GO

Redstone and Marble are popular June through August destinations for hiking in the nearby Elk Mountains and fly fishing. From September to October there is usually a brief autumn, which peaks with the blazing turning of the aspen trees. From October to May, the area offers downhill and cross-country skiing and ice climbing.

EXPLORING

Marble. A few miles up Highway 133 from Redstone lies Marble, a sleepy town that's changing as seekers of rural solitude make it their summer residence and winter retreat. Incorporated in 1899 to serve workers of the Colorado Yule Marble Quarry, the tiny hamlet includes many historic sites, including the old quarry (marble from this spot graces the Lincoln Memorial and Tomb of the Unknowns in Washington, D.C.), a one-room schoolhouse now used by the Marble Historical Society Museum, and the Marble Community Church. Marble is also the gateway to one of Colorado's most-photographed places: the **Crystal Mill.** Set on a craggy cliff overlooking the river, the 1917 mill harkens back to the area's mining past; it's also the perfect place to enjoy a picnic lunch in the solitude of the Colorado Rockies. A four-wheel-drive vehicle is needed to get you here in good weather (your feet will have to do on rainy days when the road isn't passable).

6

Redstone Castle. Redstone's history dates to the late 19th century, when J.C. Osgood, director of the Colorado Fuel and Iron Company, built Cleveholm Manor, now known as Redstone Castle. Here he entertained other titans of his day, including John D. Rockefeller, J.P. Morgan, and Teddy Roosevelt. Among the home's embellishments are gold-leaf ceilings, maroon velvet walls, silk brocade upholstery, marble and mahogany fireplaces, Persian rugs, and Tiffany chandeliers. Plans are afoot to open the Castle as a luxury hotel and spa, but in the meantime you can check out the extravagance during a 90-minute tour run by the Redstone Historical Society; call ahead or check the Castle's Web site to verify tour availability. ⊠ *58 Redstone Blvd.* ☎ *970/963–9656* ⊕ *www.redstonecastle.us* ⊠ *$15* ⊙ *Tours: Memorial Day–Labor Day, daily 1:30; Labor Day–Memorial Day generally Sat.–Mon., daily 1:30.*

SPORTS AND THE OUTDOORS

FISHING

Often overlooked by anglers anxious to cast their lines in the Roaring Fork, the Crystal River runs for more than 35 mi from its headwaters near the town of Marble to its junction with the Roaring Fork in Carbondale. In spring and fall this junction has excellent fishing for brown and rainbow trout as they attempt a run up the Crystal to spawn. Mountain whitefish can also be hooked. The upper reaches of the river traverse public land in the White River National Forest, but the last 6 mi are mostly private property. Be sure to check signage. Near the confluence, public fishing is possible at the Days Inn in Carbondale, Satank Road, and the Division of Wildlife Fish Hatchery on Highway 133, 1 mi south of Carbondale. The riverscape ranges from deep boulder pools and white-water rapids to slow, flat sections. Because of the steep shore terrain, storm runoff can sometimes cloud the river, making sight-casting difficult.

OUTFITTER **Roaring Fork Anglers.** Roaring Fork Anglers has everything you need to get fishing, including lessons as well as gear. ⊠ *2205 Grand Ave., Glenwood Springs* ☎ *970/945–0180* ⊕ *www.roaringforkanglers.com.*

See ⊕ *www.wildlife.state.co.us/fishing* for more fishing information.

WHERE TO EAT AND STAY
For expanded hotel reviews, visit Fodors.com.

$$$
ECLECTIC
Fodor'sChoice
★

✕ **SIX89.** Locals might argue that the best food in the valley is not served in the posh eateries of Aspen but in this Carbondale favorite. The irreverent menu and whimsical lexicon (a glossary is provided for your reference), superb service, and inventive preparations of excellent local produce, game, and fish create a downright delightful dining experience. Try the Palisade peach slow-roasted Berkshire pork shoulder or the seared striped bass with mustard pan sauce. There's an extensive wine list (and a knowledgeable sommelier) as well. If you're feeling adventurous, put yourself in chef Mark Fischer's capable hands with "Random Acts of Cooking," a family-style tasting menu. ⊠ *689 Main St., Carbondale* ☎ *970/963–6890* ⚠ *Reservations essential* ☉ *No lunch.*

$$
B&B/INN

⌂ **Crystal Dreams Bed & Breakfast and Spa.** Built in 1994 in the Redstone National Historic District, this three-story Victorian has all the charm along with the benefits of modern construction. **Pros:** beautiful views; romantic place for couples; impressive breakfast. **Cons:** no credit cards accepted; no children under 12. ⊠ *0475 Redstone Blvd., Redstone* ☎ *970/963–8240* ⊕ *www.crystaldreamsgetaway.com* ⤴ *3 rooms* ⌂ *In-room: no a/c, Wi-Fi. In-hotel: parking, some age restrictions* ☐ *No credit cards* ❏ *Breakfast.*

THE ARTS
Redstone Arts Center. The studio gallery and sculpture garden at the Redstone Arts Center display sculpture, painting, jewelry, and pottery. ⊠ *173 Redstone Blvd.* ☎ *970/963–3790* ⊕ *www.redstoneart.com.*

Boulder and North Central Colorado

WITH ESTES PARK AND GRAND COUNTY

WORD OF MOUTH

"Boulder [has] shops, restaurants and numerous hiking trails in the Flatirons as well as walking/biking along Boulder Creek up to Boulder Canyon. There is also the Shakespeare Festival and other cultural events."

—historytraveler

Updated by
Ricardo Baca

With spectacular scenery and an equally appealing climate, north central Colorado contains a string of sophisticated yet laid-back cities and the endless opportunities for outdoor adventure in Colorado's Front Range. Restaurants serving cuisines from around the world, celebrated universities, eclectic shopping, high-tech industries, ranching, Colorado's best-known breweries, bustling nightlife, and concerts are mere minutes from the wilderness, with hiking, rock climbing, bicycling, skiing, and kayaking.

North central Colorado encompasses three counties—Boulder, Grand, and Larimer—each with its own unique appeal. But despite their differences, these areas share a few common traits: natural beauty, rich history, and an eclectic cultural scene.

This part of Colorado also encompasses the Front Range, the easternmost edge of the Rocky Mountains—where the Rockies meet the Great Plains. The Front Range is Colorado's most populous area, and it's just west of what's known as the I–25 Corridor, a strip that includes the cities of Fort Collins, Denver, Colorado Springs, and Pueblo, which line up almost perfectly along the north–south interstate. The Range is known for its blend of historic cities and towns, verdant landscapes, and wealth of outdoor recreational opportunities.

North central Colorado became part of the United States in 1803 through the Louisiana Purchase—hence towns with names like La Porte, Platteville, and La Salle, as well as the river named Cache la Poudre. Coal and silver mines attracted settlers in the late 1800s and early 1900s, but the region grew mostly on agriculture and ranching. Out-of-state leisure travelers first came in the early 20th century to benefit from both the dry air and the curative waters of spas like Eldorado Springs and Hot Sulphur Springs. Reminders of a grand style of touring survive in resort towns such as Estes Park and Grand Lake, the gateways to Rocky Mountain National Park.

ORIENTATION AND PLANNING

GETTING ORIENTED

Outside of Denver, Boulder and Fort Collins are the second and third largest and most prominent cities of the region (after Denver). Between these two energetic university towns you'll find the sprawling cities of Loveland and Longmont and a few former coal-mining towns with homey, small-town character (like Marshall, Louisville, Lafayette, and Erie). To the west are the proud, independent mountain hamlets of

TOP REASONS TO GO

The Arts: Theater buffs have enjoyed the Colorado Shakespeare Festival every summer since 1958, and the Grammy-Award winning Takács Quartet is beloved for its stunning performances.

Boulder Dushanbe Teahouse: This traditional Central Asian teahouse was carved and painted by master artisans and given to Boulder by the city of Dushanbe, Tajikistan.

Chautauqua Park: You can still attend a lecture, a silent film, or a classical concert here much like visitors did 100 years ago. Enjoy a picnic on the green or eat in the hall before the event.

Hiking near Boulder and in the Indian Peaks Wilderness: On weekends year-round you'll find the trails packed. The views are spectacular, especially when the wildflowers bloom in midsummer.

The local breweries: It's basically the Napa Valley of beer here, and you could fill a whole vacation with the myriad ales, stouts, and lagers on offer. In late June the state's small brewers congregate in Fort Collins for the Colorado Brewers' Festival.

Lyons, Nederland, Ward, and Jamestown. Beyond the high peaks are broad valleys dotted with unpretentious ranching communities like Granby and Kremmling, and right in the middle of it all is the area's crown jewel, Rocky Mountain National Park, with its two gateways, Grand Lake and Estes Park.

Boulder. Even though every conceivable trend in food, alternative health care, education, and personal style has come through town, Boulder still feels wild. It's also very much a college town—home of the scenic University of Colorado at Boulder campus.

Boulder Side Trips. Nederland, Niwot, and Lyons are easy to explore from Boulder—all can be reached in less than an hour. Each is known for its natural beauty, historic character, and funky atmosphere.

Estes Park. The Eastern gateway to Rocky Mountain National Park, resort town Estes Park is nestled against Roosevelt National Forest on its other three sides.

Grand County. West of the Rocky Mountain National Park, guest ranches and golf courses dot the land. In Grand Lake, waterskiing, sailing, canoeing, ice fishing, and snowmobiling dominate the scene.

Fort Collins. Famous for its own university, as well as its open spaces and its beer, Fort Collins also has a rich history and vibrant cultural scene.

PLANNING

WHEN TO GO

Visiting the Front Range is pleasurable in any season. Wintertime in the urban corridor is generally mild, but the mountainous regions can be cold and snowy. Snowfall along the Front Range is highest in spring, particularly March, making for excellent skiing but unpredictable driving and potentially lengthy delays. Spring is unpredictable—75°F one day and a blizzard the next—and June can be hot or cool (or both). July typically ushers in high summer, which can last through September, although most 90-plus–degree days occur in July and early August and at lower elevations. In the higher mountains summer temperatures are generally 15–20 degrees cooler than in the urban corridor. Afternoon spring and summer thunderstorms can last 10 minutes or a few hours. Fall has crisp sunny days and cool nights, some cold enough for frost in the mountains.

Art and music festivals start up in May and continue through September. With them comes an increase in visitor traffic. Spring and summer are typically the best times to fish or watch for wildlife.

GETTING HERE AND AROUND

AIR TRAVEL

Denver International Airport, known to locals as DIA (although its airport code is DEN), 23 mi northeast of downtown Denver, is the primary commercial passenger airport serving north central Colorado. Allegiant Air connects Fort Collins and Las Vegas with scheduled service to the Fort Collins/Loveland Airport (FNL). Boulder and Granby have municipal airports but no commercial service.

TRANSFERS The Denver Airport's Ground Transportation Information Center assists visitors with car rentals, door-to-door shuttles, public transportation, wheelchair services, charter buses, and limousine services. Boulder is approximately 45 mi (45 minutes–1 hour) from Denver International Airport; Granby approximately 110 mi (a little more than 2 hours); Fort Collins approximately 80 mi (1¼–1½ hours); and Estes Park approximately 80 mi (about two hours).

Estes Park Shuttle (reservations essential) serves Estes Park and Rocky Mountain National Park from Denver, Denver International Airport, and Boulder. Super Shuttle serves Denver and Boulder, and Shamrock Airport Shuttle serves Fort Collins. Home James serves Granby, Grand Lake, and the guest ranches of Grand County.

Airports Denver International Airport (DEN) ⊠ *8500 Peña Blvd., Denver* ☎ *800/247-2336, 303/342-2000* ⊕ *www.flydenver.com.* **Fort Collins–Loveland Municipal Airport (FNL)** ⊠ *4900 Earhart Rd., Loveland* ☎ *970/962-2852* ⊕ *www.fortloveair.com.*

Airport Shuttles Estes Park Shuttle ☎ *970/586-5151* ⊕ *www. estesparkshuttle.com.* **Ground Transportation Information Center** ☎ *303/342-4059* ⊕ *www.flydenver.com/parkinggt.* **Home James** ☎ *970/726-5060, 800/359-7536* ⊕ *www.homejamestransportation.com.* **Super Shuttle** ☎ *970/482-0505* ⊕ *www.rideshamrock.com.*

BUS TRAVEL

The expansive network of the Regional Transportation District (RTD) includes service from Denver and Denver International Airport to and within Boulder, Lyons, Niwot, Nederland, and the Eldora Ski Resort. The Hop bus (part of the RTD network) is a circulator that makes for easy carless travel within Boulder between the university, the Hill, the Twenty-Ninth Street shopping area, and downtown. Transfort serves Fort Collins's main thoroughfares.

Bus Contacts Regional Transportation District (RTD) ☎ *303/299–6000, 800/366–7433* ⊕ *www.rtd-denver.com.* **Transfort** ☎ *970/221–6620* ⊕ *www. fcgov.com/transfort.*

CAR TRAVEL

Interstate 25, the most direct route from Denver to Fort Collins, is the north–south artery that connects the cities in the urban corridor along the Front Range. From Denver, U.S. 36 runs through Boulder, Lyons, and Estes Park to Rocky Mountain National Park. The direct route from Denver to Grand County is I–70 west to U.S. 40 (Empire exit) and to U.S. 34. If you're driving directly to Fort Collins or Estes Park and Rocky Mountain National Park from Denver International Airport, take the E–470 tollway to Interstate 25. U.S. 36 between Boulder and Estes Park is heavily traveled, but Highways 119, 72, and 7 have much less traffic.

Gasoline and service are available in all larger towns and cities in the region. Bicyclists are common except on arteries; state law gives them the same rights and holds them to the same obligations as those using any other vehicle. Expect extensive road construction along the northern Front Range; arterial routes, state highways, and city streets are being rebuilt to accommodate increasing traffic in the urban corridor. Although the state plows roads regularly, a winter snowstorm can slow traffic and create wet, slushy, or icy conditions. Note that you can't always count on getting cell-phone service in sparsely populated—or very mountainous—areas.

Car Travel Contacts AAA Colorado ☎ *303/753–8800* ⊕ *www.aaa.com.* **Colorado Department of Transportation CDOT Road Information** ☎ *303/639–1111* ⊕ *www.dot.state.co.us.* **Colorado State Patrol** ☎ *303/239–4501, *277 from cell phone.* **Rocky Mountain National Park Road Information** ☎ *970/586–1333.*

TRAIN TRAVEL

Amtrak provides passenger rail service to and within north central Colorado. The Chicago–San Francisco *California Zephyr* stops in downtown Denver, in Winter Park/Fraser, and in Granby, once each day in both directions.

Train Contact Amtrak ☎ *800/872–7245, 303/534–2812* ⊕ *www.amtrak.com.*

PARKS AND RECREATION AREAS

Rocky Mountain National Park is known for its scenery, hiking, wildlife-watching, camping, and snowshoeing. *See the Rocky Mountain National Park chapter in this book.*

Indian Peaks Wilderness. Spanning the Continental Divide between Grand Lake and Nederland just south of Rocky Mountain National Park is the Indian Peaks Wilderness, a 76,586-acre area that lies within the Arapaho and Roosevelt national forests and is a favorite destination for hiking and backcountry camping. Permits are required for camping, and popular spots regularly sell out in advance. ⊠ *Boulder Ranger District, 2140 Yarmouth Ave., Boulder* ☎ *303/541–2500* ⊕ *www.fs.fed. us/r2/arnf/recreation/wilderness/indianpeaks.*

7

Arapaho and Roosevelt National Forests and Pawnee National Grassland. The Arapaho and Roosevelt National Forests and Pawnee National Grassland, an enormous area that encompasses 1.5 million acres, has fishing, sailing, canoeing, and waterskiing, as well as hiking, mountain biking, birding, and camping. Contained within the Arapaho National Forest is the **Arapaho National Recreation Area (ANRA),** a 36,000-acre expanse that contains Lake Granby, Shadow Mountain Lake, Monarch Lake, and Willow Creek and Meadow Creek reservoirs, collectively known as Colorado's Great Lakes. ⊠ *USDA Forest Service Sulphur Ranger District, 9 Ten Mile Dr., Granby* ☎ *970/887–4100* ⊕ *www.fs.fed.us/r2/arnf.*

North central Colorado has six state parks. Eldorado Canyon, Barr Lake, and St. Vrain are all close to Boulder; Boyd Lake, State Forest, and Lory are close to Fort Collins. In Boulder and Fort Collins you can literally walk out your door, up the street, and into the mountains or foothills on a hiking trail. There are also plenty of riparian trails and open-space paths within the city limits that can take you for miles; they usually have plenty of access points.

The northern Front Range is home to a small downhill ski area. Eldora Mountain Resort is 21 mi west of Boulder.

RESTAURANTS

Thanks to the influx of people from around the world, you have plenty of options here. Restaurants in north central Colorado run the gamut—you'll find simple diners with tasty, homey basics and elegant establishments with exhaustive wine lists. Increasingly, eateries feature organic and sustainable ingredients, and several are given over exclusively to organic, locally produced dishes. Some restaurants take reservations, but many, particularly those in the middle price range, seat on a first-come, first-served basis.

HOTELS

The area's ever-popular guest ranches and spas are places to escape and be pampered after having fun outdoors. In the high-country resorts of Estes Park and Grand Lake and in towns nearby, the elevation keeps the climate cool, which means that there are very few air-conditioned accommodations. The region is also full of chain motels and hotels, often on the outskirts of cities.

WHAT IT COSTS					
	¢	$	$$	$$$	$$$$
Restaurants	under $8	$8–$12	$13–$18	$19–$25	over $25
Hotels	under $80	$80–$120	$121–$170	$171–$230	over $230

Restaurant prices are for a main course at dinner, excluding 5.75%–8.46% tax. Hotel prices are for two people in a standard double room in high season, excluding service charges and 5.75%–12.40% tax.

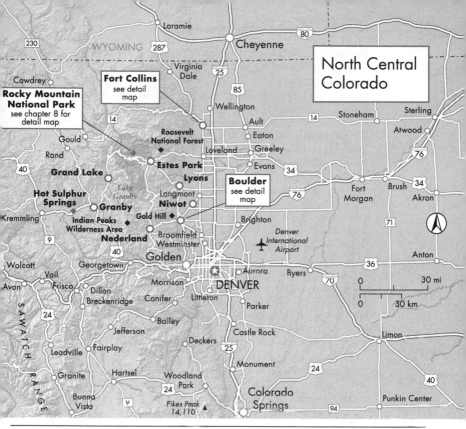

North Central Colorado

BOULDER

No place in Colorado better epitomizes the state's outdoor mania than Boulder, where sunny weather keeps locals busy through all seasons. There are nearly as many bicycles as cars in this uncommonly beautiful and beautifully uncommon city, and Boulder has more than 1,500 mi of trails for hiking, walking, jogging, and bicycling. One of Boulder's most uncommon features is its setting. In 1960 its citizens voted to buy the land surrounding the city to protect it from urban sprawl and preserve its historic and ecological resources. Boulder started taxing itself in 1967 in order to buy these greenbelts, and now can boast more than 43,000 acres of city-owned open space—there are more than 120,000 acres if you include lands owned by Boulder County. This means that there's three times as much protected land surrounding the city as developed land. Even in winter, residents bicycle to work and jog on the open-space paths. It's nearly a matter of civic pride to spend a lunch hour playing Frisbee, in-line skating, hiking with the family dog, and even rock climbing on the Flatirons.

Boulder is also a brainy place. The University of Colorado at Boulder and Naropa University are here. In addition, Boulder is home to a number of IT companies and more than a dozen national laboratories, including the National Center for Atmospheric Research (NCAR) and the National Oceanic and Atmospheric Administration (NOAA).

GETTING ORIENTED

One of the best places to take a first look at this beautiful town is from the scenic overlook on Davidson Mesa (it's on U.S. 36, about 6 mi south of town, on the westbound side of the highway). In the distance west of town are the craggy (and often snow-capped) peaks in the Roosevelt National Forest, Indian Peaks Wilderness Area, and Rocky Mountain National Park. Closer by, to the southwest, are Bear Peak and the Devil's Thumb on its left slope, marking the entrance to Eldorado Canyon. Just north of there are Green Mountain and its trademark red-sandstone Flatirons, which you can see from almost every vantage point in town. These massive rock upthrusts, named for their flat faces, are popular among rock climbers and hikers. To the east are flat plains, dotted with parks and reservoirs.

In town, the red-tile roofs of the University of Colorado dominate the landscape in the southern end of the city, where Boulder Creek courses along the south side of the downtown area at the bottom of University Hill (called "the Hill" by locals), on which both the university and its surrounding neighborhood are located. At the northern end of town you'll find Boulder Reservoir, a 700-acre park used for swimming, rowing, kayaking, sailing, windsurfing, and waterskiing.

GETTING HERE AND AROUND

Although a 10-minute walk separates downtown from the Hill, both areas have their own flavor. Downtown—particularly the Pearl Street pedestrian mall—bustles with families, street performers, upscale boutiques, and eateries, while the Hill pulsates with trendy shops, packed coffeehouses, bars and rock clubs, and restaurants geared more to students. Parking and driving in these sections of Boulder can be frustrating and time-consuming. Leave your car at the hotel and try the Hop, a bus that circulates in both directions through downtown, the Hill, and the university for about the cost of an hour at a parking meter. Buses run in both directions every 6–10 minutes weekdays and 15–20 minutes on weekends.

TOURS **Banjo Billy's Bus Tours.** Banjo Billy's Bus Tours offers a 90-minute tour of downtown Boulder, Chautauqua Park, the Hill, and part of the University of Colorado, aboard a bus that has been built to look like a log cabin. Everyone on the bus gets to vote on the topic of the tour: ghost stories, history, folklore, or crime stories. Your seat may be a saddle or a recliner, or you can opt to sit on the couch. ☎ *720/938–8885* ⊕ *www. banjobilly.com.*

Historic Boulder. Historic Boulder provides free brochures for seven self-guided walking tours, including the University of Colorado at Boulder, the Hill, Chautauqua Park, the Mapleton Historic District, and the Downtown Boulder Historic District. The handiest place to pick up the maps is the kiosk just east of 13th Street on the Pearl Street Mall. ☎ *303/444–5192* ⊕ *www.historicboulder.org.*

WHEN TO GO

Like the rest of the Front Range, Boulder has beautiful weather year-round. The city definitely feels livelier when school is in session, especially on big football weekends, and summer weekends often bring big crowds of tourists (including day-trippers from Denver).

FESTIVALS **Boulder Creek Festival.** The Boulder Creek Festival lasts all Memorial Day weekend: you can feast at the pancake breakfast, browse the bazaar, learn about alternative healing, and see regional artistic talent at the art show and the artists' marketplace. Children have fun with dance, theater, and hands-on activities at the Kids' Place. Live music is all over the map: Irish, Senegalese, John Philip Sousa, and jazz. Don't miss the **Great Rubber Duck Race** on Memorial Day afternoon. Get a rubber duck and compete against hundreds of others in Boulder Creek. The fest runs along Canyon Boulevard between 9th and 14th streets.

ESSENTIALS

Transportation Contacts Yellow Cab ☎ 303/777–7777 ⊕ www. boulderyellowcab.com. **Boulder Custom Rides** ☎ 303/442–4477 ⊕ www. bouldercustomrides.com.

Visitor and Tour Information Banjo Billy's Bus Tours ✉ Tour starts from Hotel Boulderado, 2115 13th St. ☎ 720/938–8885 ⊕ www.banjobilly.com ✉ $22–$23 ⚑ Reservations essential ☉ Closed Mon. **Boulder Convention & Visitors Bureau** ✉ 2440 Pearl St. ☎ 303/442–2911, 800/444–0447 ⊕ www. bouldercoloradousa.com. **Boulder Creek Festival** ☎ 303/449–3137 ⊕ www. bouldercreekevents.com. **Historic Boulder** ✉ 1123 Spruce St. ☎ 303/444–5192 ⊕ www.historicboulder.org.

EXPLORING

TOP ATTRACTIONS

Boulder Museum of Contemporary Art. The Boulder Museum of Contemporary Art hosts local and national contemporary art exhibits, performance art, dance, experimental film, and poetry readings. From May to September, when the farmers' market takes place in front of the museum, hours are extended. Admission is free on Saturday. ✉ 1750 13th St. ☎ 303/443–2122 ⊕ www.bmoca.org ✉ $5 ☉ Tues.–Fri. 11–5, weekends 11–4.

Downtown Boulder Historic District. The late-19th- and early-20th-century commercial structures of the Downtown Boulder Historic District once housed mercantile stores and saloons. The period architecture—including Queen Anne, Italianate, and Romanesque styles in stone or brick—has been preserved, but stores inside cater to modern tastes, with fair-trade coffees and Tibetan prayer flags. The area is bounded by the south side of Spruce Street between 10th and 16th streets, Pearl Street between 9th and 16th streets, and the north side of Walnut Street between Broadway and 9th Street.

The Hill. Across Broadway from the CU campus is the Hill, a favorite student hangout. The neighborhood is home to restaurants, music and dance venues, bars, coffeehouses, and boutiques. ✉ 13th St. between Pennsylvania St. and College Ave.

7

Pearl Street. Pearl Street, between 8th and 20th streets in the downtown area, is the city's hub, an eclectic collection of boutiques, consignment shops, bookstores, art galleries, cafés, bars, and restaurants. There's a four-block pedestrian mall between 11th and 15th streets.

University of Colorado at Boulder. South of downtown is the University of Colorado at Boulder. Red sandstone buildings with tile roofs (built in the "Rural Italian" architectural style that Charles Z. Klauder created in the early 1920s) complement the campus's green lawns and small ponds.

WORTH NOTING

Boulder Beer Company. The scent of hops fills the air during free one-hour tours and ale tastings at the Boulder Beer Company, Colorado's first microbrewery. The brew house's own pub is open weekdays 11 am–9 pm. ⊠ *2880 Wilderness Pl.* ☎ *303/444–8448* ⊕ *www.boulderbeer. com* ⊠ *Free* ☉ *Tours weekdays 2 pm; Sat. at 2 and 4 pm.*

Boulder History Museum. Housed in the 1889 Harbeck-Bergheim mansion, the Boulder History Museum documents the story of Boulder and the surrounding region from 1858 to the present. If you're interested in the sartorial styles of the 19th century—whether rugged cowboy and miner duds or high-society finery—this museum makes a great stop. It's home to one of Colorado's largest clothing collections, with pieces dating as far back as 1820. ⊠ *1206 Euclid Ave.* ☎ *303/449–3464* ⊕ *www.boulderhistorymuseum.org* ⊠ *$6* ☉ *Tues.–Fri. 10–5, weekends noon–4, closed Mon.*

CU campus. The CU campus began in 1875 with the construction of Old Main, which borders the **Norlin Quadrangle,** now on the National Register of Historic Places, a broad lawn where students sun themselves or play a quick round of Frisbee between classes. You can take a walking tour of the campus year-round.

CU Heritage Center. The CU Heritage Center preserves the history of the university—including notable alumni accomplishments and a lunar sample on long-term loan from NASA. Also displayed are the personal memorabilia of alumni such as Robert Redford and Glenn Miller. One room is devoted to CU's 20 astronauts, including Ellison Onizuka, who was killed aboard the *Challenger* space shuttle in 1986, and Kalpana Chawla, who died on the *Columbia* in 2003. ⊠ *Old Main Bldg. on Norlin Quadrangle* ☎ *303/492- 6329* ⊕ *cuheritage.org* ⊠ *Free* ☉ *Weekdays 10–6.*

University of Colorado Museum. The natural history collection at the University of Colorado Museum includes dinosaur relics and has permanent and changing exhibits. ⊠ *Henderson Bldg., 15th and Broadway* ☎ *303/492–6892* ⊕ *cumuseum.colorado.edu* ⊠ *$3 (suggested donation)* ☉ *Weekdays 9–5, Sat. 9–4, Sun. 10–4* ⊠ *University Memorial Center* ☎ *303/492–1411, 303/492–6301 to reserve tour* ⊕ *www.colorado. edu* ⊠ *Free* ☉ *Campus tours year-round weekdays 10:30 and 2:30; most Sat. at 10:30* ☞ *Reservations essential.*

Fiske Planetarium and Science Center. Star shows and laser shows set to classic compositions like *Peter and the Wolf* or the music of well-known rock bands entertain at the university's Fiske Planetarium and Science Center. During the academic year shows begin Friday at 9:30 and 10:45

pm. "Star Talks" are at 7:30 pm on Thursday and Friday during the school year and 8 during the summer. Matinees take place in summer on Tuesday, Wednesday, and Thursday at 2 pm and 3 pm. ⊠ *Regent Dr.* ☎ *303/492–5002* ⊕ *fiske.colorado.edu* ✉ *Laser shows and matinees $7; Star Talks $3.50–$7; observatory free* ☉ *Planetarium, year-round, days vary. Observatory: Fri. night open house late Aug.–early Dec..*

Mapleton Historic District. Three blocks north of Pearl Street and west of Broadway is the Mapleton Historic District. This neighborhood of turn-of-the-20th-century homes shaded by old maple and cottonwood trees is bounded roughly by Broadway, the alley between Pearl and Spruce streets, 4th Street, and the alley between Dewey Street and Concord Avenue.

QUICK BITES

The Sink. The actor Robert Redford worked at The Sink during his years as a student at the University of Colorado. The restaurant has served great pizza, burgers, beer, and other student staples since 1958. ⊠ *1165 13th St.* ☎ *303/444–7465* ⊕ *thesink.com.*

⟳ **National Center for Atmospheric Research.** Talking about the weather is *not* boring at the National Center for Atmospheric Research, where the hands-on exhibits, video presentation, and one-hour tour fires up kids' enthusiasm for what falls out of the sky. The architect I.M. Pei's distinctive buildings stand majestically on a mesa at the base of the mountains, where you can see mule deer and other wildlife. After browsing the field guides and science kits, follow the interpretive Walter Orr Roberts Nature and Weather Trail to learn about the mesa's weather, climate, plants, and wildlife. The 4-mi loop is wheelchair accessible. If you can't make the guided tour, self-guided and audio tours are available during regular hours. ⊠ *1850 Table Mesa Dr., from southbound Broadway, turn right onto Table Mesa Dr.* ☎ *303/497–1174* ⊕ *www. ncar.ucar.edu* ✉ *Free* ☉ *Weekdays 8–5, weekends and holidays 9–4. Tour weekdays at noon.*

PARKS AND GREENBELTS

★ **Chautauqua Park.** For the prettiest views of town, follow Baseline Road west from Broadway to Chautauqua Park, site of the Colorado Music Festival and a favorite hiking and picnic spot for locals on weekends. Continue farther up Flagstaff Mountain to Panorama and Realization points, where people jog, bike, and climb. ⊠ *900 Baseline Rd.*

★ **Eldorado Canyon State Park.** Eldorado Canyon State Park, with its steep walls and pine forests, offers outdoor activities for thrill-seekers and observers. Kayakers get adrenaline rushes on the rapids of South Boulder Creek, while rock climbers scale the canyon's granite walls. Picnickers can choose from 42 spots, and anglers' catches average 8 inches. Bird-watchers and artists find plenty of inspiration, and hikers have 12 mi of trails to wander. The **Streamside Trail** is a mostly level, 1-mi round-trip that parallels South Boulder Creek 0.5 mi to West Ridge; 300 feet of the trail is wheelchair accessible. Half of 1.5-mi round-trip **Fowler Trail** is wheelchair accessible. The trail has interpretive signs about the wildlife. For the best views of the canyon and the Front Range plains, head up **Rattlesnake Gulch Trail.** The round-trip 3-mi switchback trail ends at an overlook 800 feet higher in elevation than the trailhead, where you can see the high Rockies of the Continental Divide. Snowshoeing is popular here in winter. Mountain bikers crank on Rattlesnake Gulch Trail and Fowler Trail. **Eldorado Canyon Trail** is open to horseback riding. ⊠ *9 Kneale Rd.* ✛ *Drive south on Broadway (Hwy. 93) 3 mi to Eldorado Canyon Dr. (Rte. 170); paved road ends at the village of Eldorado Springs. Drive through town to park entrance* ☎ *303/494–3943* ⊕ *www.parks.state.co.us/Parks/ eldoradocanyon* 🎫 *$8 per vehicle.*

SPORTS AND THE OUTDOORS

RACES

Fodor'sChoice **Bolder Boulder.** Memorial Day brings the annual 10-km Bolder Boulder,
★ when more than 54,000 runners, including top international competitors, run the country's largest race in which all participants are timed. About 100,000 spectators line the route and fill CU's Folsom Stadium to cheer on the participants. Along the racecourse rock bands, jazz musicians, African drumming groups, Elvis impersonators, belly dancers, and classical quartets spur on the runners. The race ends in Folsom Stadium for a ceremony that includes a flyover by U.S. Air Force fighter jets and skydivers who parachute onto the stadium field. ☎ *303/444–7223* ⊕ *www.bolderboulder.com.*

BICYCLING

IN BOULDER **Boulder Creek Path.** The Boulder Creek Path winds through town for about 5.5 mi from Boulder Canyon in the west to the Stazio Ballfields (near the intersection of Arapahoe Avenue and Cherryvale Road) in the east, connecting to more than 100 mi of city and greenbelt trails and paths. You can access paths from nearly every cross street in town, but don't always count on parking nearby. ⊠ *Trailheads: From downtown, the best access points are behind public library parking lot on south side of Canyon Blvd. between 9th St. and Broadway or in Central Park on 13th St. between Canyon Blvd. and Arapahoe Ave.*

Marshall Mesa/Community Ditch Trails. The 8-mi round-trip Community Ditch portion of the Marshall Mesa/Community Ditch Trails takes you up through pine stands and over a plateau where you can look down on Boulder, with the Flatirons and the Rockies in full view. The trail continues across Highway 93 almost to Eldorado Springs. ⊠ *Trailhead: Just east of intersection of Hwy. 93 and Marshall Rd. Parking is on right.*

IN THE **Canyon Loop Trail.** For scenic cycling, try the 6-mi round-trip trek on the
MOUNTAINS Canyon Loop Trail in Betasso Preserve, about 6 mi west of Boulder. ⊠ *Trailhead: Take Broadway south to Hwy. 119 and go west to Sugarloaf Rd.; turn right onto Sugarloaf and then right again onto Betasso Rd. Look for the turnout on the left.*

Switzerland Trail. For a long journey, take the Switzerland Trail, a 9- to 13-mi ride one-way that follows the route of an old narrow-gauge railroad, taking you past the historic mining hamlet of Sunset. ⊠ *Trailhead: From Broadway, drive west 5 mi on Canyon Blvd./Hwy. 119 and turn* *right onto Sugarloaf Rd./Hwy. 72. After 5 mi, turn right onto Sugarloaf Mountain Rd. Parking area is 1 mi farther.*

Walker Ranch. For a strenuous mountain bike ride, head 8 mi west out of town to Walker Ranch; the 7.5-mi loop has great views of the Indian Peaks. ✉ *Trailhead: Look for trailhead on east side of Flagstaff Rd., about 7.5 mi west of Baseline Rd.*

OUTFITTERS **Full Cycle.** The conveniently located Full Cycle rents mountain bikes with helmets and locks for four-hour, one-day, and multiple-day biking adventures. There's a second location at 1211 13th Street. ✉ *1795 Pearl St.* ☎ *303/440–1002* ⊕ *www.fullcyclebikes.com.*

University Bicycles. University Bicycles rents mountain and town bikes with a helmet, lock, and map included for four hours to one week. ✉ *839 Pearl St.* ☎ *303/444–4196* ⊕ *ubikes.com.*

BIRD-WATCHING

Eldorado Canyon State Park. Ornithologists have spotted kestrels, falcons, and the occasional bald eagle in the steep cliffs of Eldorado Canyon State Park. Owls, chickadees, nuthatches, and woodpeckers are at home in the pine forests along South Boulder Creek in the park. ✉ *9 Kneale Rd., Eldorado Springs* ☎ *303/494–3943* ⊕ *www.parks.state. co.us/Parks/eldoradocanyon* 🚗 *$8 per vehicle.*

Walden Ponds Wildlife Habitat/Sawhill Ponds. Walden Ponds Wildlife Habitat/Sawhill Ponds, formerly a gravel quarry, now attracts songbirds, waterfowl, and raptors. Nearly 3 mi of groomed paths encircle and connect the area's ponds and lead into wooded areas along Boulder Creek, where owls roost. April to May is when most birds migrate through the Front Range, although the ponds have plenty of year-round residents. ✉ *Jay Rd. and N. 75th St.* ✛ *Drive north on 28th St. (U.S. 36) and turn right at Valmont Rd. Drive east 4 mi and turn left at 75th St. Sign marking ponds is about ½ mi farther* ☉ *Dawn–dusk.*

FISHING

Eldorado Canyon State Park offers excellent fly-fishing. Fish generally measure between 8 and 14 inches long, although anglers bring in a few specimens up to 24 inches long each year. See ⊕ *www.wildlife.state. co.us/fishing* for more information.

Front Range Anglers. Front Range Anglers specializes in half-day and full-day trips for individuals and groups. Fees include lunch, lessons, transportation, and gear. Private guides offer half-day and full-day trips for one to three people to premier public and private fishing spots. ✉ *2344 Pearl St.* ☎ *303/494–1375* ⊕ *frontrangeanglers.com.*

OUTFITTERS **Rocky Mountain Anglers.** Rocky Mountain Anglers can sell you a few flies or set up a guided tour. The guides have access to private ranches and know where to find secluded fishing holes on public lands. Fees include transportation, gear including flies, and lunch. ✉ *1904 Arapahoe Ave.* ☎ *303/447–2400* ⊕ *www.rockymtanglers.com.*

GOLF

Indian Peaks Golf Course. This local favorite has views of the Continental Divide, plus some "Fourteeners" (mountain peaks over 14,000 feet) not visible from Boulder. The well-tended course boasts low scores and has tee boxes for all skill levels. ✉ *2300 Indian Peaks Trail, Baseline Rd. to Indian Peaks Trail, 10 mi east of Boulder, Lafayette* ☎ *303/666–4706* 🛈 *18 holes. Yards: 7083/5468. Par: 72/72. Green fee: $40–$55, $47–$62 with cart.*

HIKING

City of Boulder Open Space & Mountain Parks. The City of Boulder Open Space & Mountain Parks administers most of the 150 mi of trails in and close to Boulder. Most trails are open to dogs, provided they are leashed or under voice control and registered with the city's Voice and Sight Dog Tag Program. There are 34 trailheads in and around Boulder. Most are free, but a few require a $3 parking permit for all non-resident vehicles. You can purchase a daily pass either at self-serve kiosks in the mountain parks or at the OSMP office. ✉ *66 S. Cherryvale Rd.* ☎ *303/441–3440* ⊕ *www.osmp.org* ☉ *Weekdays 8–5.*

IN BOULDER   **Boulder Creek Path.** For a relaxing amble, take the Boulder Creek Path *(see Bicycling, above),* which winds from west of Boulder through downtown and past the university to the eastern part of the city—there are multiple places to access the trail. Within the eastern city limits are ponds, gaggles of Canada geese, and prairie-dog colonies. People-watching is also great fun: you'll see cyclists, joggers, and rollerblading dads and moms with their babies in jogging strollers. You'll have great views of the mountains as you walk back toward downtown. Walk west along the path from Broadway to Boulder Canyon, and you'll see kayakers negotiating the boulders and inner-tubers cooling off in the summer heat.

Even a short walk up the grassy slope between **Chautauqua Park** and the base of the mountains brings out hikers and their dogs to take in some sun. On sunny summer mornings the dining hall at Chautauqua Park fills with hungry people ready for a hearty breakfast. Afternoon walkers relax on the park's gently sloping lawn with a picnic and gaze up at the foothills stretching along the Front Range. To reach the parking lot, take Baseline Road west from Broadway. The park is on the left just past the intersection with 9th Street.

★   **Chautauqua Trail.** Locals love the Chautauqua Trail, a 1.6-mi round-trip loop, for its great views of the city and the occasional peeks it provides of rock climbers on the Flatirons. From the trailhead, go up the Chautauqua Trail 0.6 mi to the Bluebell/Baird trail. Go left 0.4 mi and then left again onto the Mesa Trail, which takes you the 0.6 mi back to the parking area. The trail is a long slope at the beginning, but once you're in the trees you won't gain much more elevation. Allow a couple of hours for a leisurely walk on this easy hike. ✉ *Trailhead: 900 Baseline Rd., Main parking lot.*

Royal Arch Trail. The 4-mi round-trip Royal Arch Trail leads to Boulder's own rock arch. The Royal Arch is definitely worth the steep hike, as are the views of the foothills and cities of the Front Range. The trail spurs off the Chautauqua Trail loop and follows along the base of the Flatirons. You'll climb 1,270 feet in 2 mi. Go under the arch to the precipice for the views. If you turn around, the arch frames a couple of Flatirons for a good photo. ✉ *Trailhead: 900 Baseline Rd., main parking lot.*

IN THE
MOUNTAINS

Two popular trails on the edge of town get you into the mountains quickly. The parking areas are across the street from each other and fill fast, so it's best to go early in the morning or later in the afternoon.

Red Rocks Loop. Carry a picnic on the Red Rocks Loop and enjoy the mountain and city views. The Red Rocks Trail goes to the right from the parking lot and takes you through wildflowers and grassy meadows on the way up to the rock outcropping. The 0.5-mi round-trip trek takes about 20 minutes and gains 340 feet. If you have time for the full 2.3-mi loop, allow about an hour. You'll gain most of the 600 feet in elevation change on the way back. ⊠ *Trailhead: Mapleton Ave., 1 mi west of Broadway on left.*

Sanitas Valley Loop. The Sanitas Valley Loop, known locally as Mount Sanitas, is an easy 3.5-mi hike that provides constant mountain scenery in Sunshine Canyon as you climb 540 feet going up the west flank of Mount Sanitas. From the trailhead, head left onto the Mount Sanitas Trail, which becomes the East Ridge Trail as it wraps around the north side of the mountain. From here you can descend to the right on either the Sanitas Valley Trail back to the parking area or along the Dakota Ridge Trail if you want more city views. Be sure not to take the sharp left at the Dakota Ridge intersection, which leads straight downhill to town. Boulder will be on your left all the way back to the trailhead. Allow two hours. ⊠ *Trailhead: Mapleton Ave., 1 mi west of Broadway on left.*

★ **Flagstaff Mountain Open Space.** Flagstaff Mountain Open Space offers hikers several different hikes. An easy walk along the **Boy Scout Trail** to May's Point offers glorious views of the city and Boulder Valley along the way and exceptional views of the Indian Peaks once you reach May's Point. The 1.5-mi round-trip trail starts at Sunrise Amphitheater, where it goes to the left into the spruce forest. After about 0.75 mi and only 140 feet elevation gain, head to the right at the fork in the trail. It's a short distance to May's Point. ⊠ *Trailhead: Drive west on Baseline Rd. to sharp curve to right that is Flagstaff Rd., then turn right at Summit Rd. The trail starts from parking area about 0.5 mi in.*

Green Mountain Loop. Green Mountain Loop, which begins in Boulder Mountain Park, rewards ambitious hikers with beautiful vistas of the Front Range and the Indian Peaks. The Gregory Canyon, Ranger, E.M. Greenman, and Saddle Rock trails create a 5.5-mi loop that takes three to four hours to hike. It's a 2,344-foot gain in elevation to Green Mountain's summit at 8,144 feet. Follow the Gregory Canyon Trail to the Ranger Trail, and go left. Stay to the right at the E.M. Greenman Trail. At the intersection with Green Mountain West Ridge Trail, turn left. Go on to the summit and descend along the E.M. Greenman and Saddle Rock trails after taking in the view. ⊠ *Trailhead (Gregory Canyon Trail): Drive west on Baseline Rd. to Flagstaff Rd., and then turn left immediately after curve. Parking area is at end of short road where trail starts.*

7

INNER-TUBING

In July and August, when the daytime temperatures can reach the 90s, Boulderites take to tubing in **Boulder Creek**—especially near Eben G. Fine Park, at the mouth of Boulder Canyon near the junction of Arapahoe Avenue and Canyon Boulevard on the western end of town.

Conoco. Need a tube? The Conoco gas station, which is about a block away from the creek, sells inner tubes (about $15, tax included). The station is open from 7 am until 9 pm weekdays and Saturday, and 8 am–8 pm Sunday. ⊠ *1201 Arapahoe Ave., at Broadway* ☎ *303/442–6293.*

KAYAKING AND CANOEING

Serious kayakers run the slaloms in Clear Creek, Lefthand Canyon, and the South Platte, but Boulder Creek—from within Boulder Canyon midway into the city—is one of the locals' favorites. Water in the creek can create Class II–III rapids when summer conditions are right.

Boulder Outdoor Center. Boulder Outdoor Center organizes group rafting trips to rivers on the Front Range and also offers canoeing and kayaking instruction. ⊠ *2525 Arapahoe Ave., Suite E4–228* ☎ *303/444–8420, 800/364–9376* ⊕ *www.boc123.com.*

Boulder Reservoir. If calm waters are what you want, you can rent a canoe at the Boulder Reservoir. ⊠ *6 mi northeast of downtown. Drive northeast on Hwy. 119 and turn left at Jay Rd. Turn right immediately onto 51st St. and follow it to sign that marks entrance station, 5100 N. 51st St.* ☎ *303/441–3461* ⊕ *www.bouldercolorado.gov* ⊠ *$8.*

SNOWSHOEING

Winter sports in Colorado are not limited to skiing and snowboarding. You can strap on a pair of snowshoes and tramp along many trails you would walk in summer, taking in stunning views and getting a fair amount of exercise, too. Don't forget the sunscreen—at this altitude, you can sunburn quickly, even in winter. Dressing in layers is also imperative, as temperatures and weather conditions can fluctuate dramatically throughout the day.

The Brainard Lake Recreation Area. The Brainard Lake Recreation Area, in the Roosevelt National Forest, has well-marked trails and gorgeous views of the snow-covered Indian Peaks and the Continental Divide. There's a $9 fee for a five-day pass. ⊠ *5 mi west of Rte. 72 on Brainard Lake Rd. (Rte. 102) at Ward. Drive west on Hwy. 119 to Nederland and turn north at Rte. 72* ☎ *303/541–2500* ⊕ *www.fs.fed.us/r2/arnf/recreation/brainard/.*

Peaceful Valley Campground. Head to Peaceful Valley Campground for crisp, pine-scented air and plenty of terrain to explore—it's closed to campers during the winter. ✛ *Drive 15 mi west from Boulder on Hwy. 199 to Nederland (about 15 mi). Go north on Hwy. 72 for 17.6 mi, then take a left onto Peaceful Valley Rd. (near mile marker 50), then a quick right onto County Rd. 92. The campground is on your right.* ⊠ *Allenspark* ☎ *303/541–2500.*

OUTFITTER **REI.** REI's popular Boulder outpost, built in an eco-conscious manner, offers snowshoe rentals, as well as all the necessary accessories. ⊠ *1789 28th St* ☎ *303/583-9970* ⊕ *www.rei.com/stores/44.*

CLOSE UP

Quick Bites in Boulder

Not every meal requires a lengthy restaurant visit. Boulder has plenty of healthy, inexpensive, and prepared-to-order food, as well.

Abo's. The thin and crispy pizzas at Abo's will not disappoint. ✉ 1124 13th St. ☎ 303/443–3199 ⊕ www. abospizza.com.

Breadworks Cafe. For breakfast, try a crisp, light brioche or buttery croissant at Breadworks Cafe. Lunch is casseroles or mac and cheese, meat or vegetarian panini—made with one of their artisan breads—or pizza, a savory soup, and a saucer-size cookie. ✉ 2644 Broadway ☎ 303/444–5667 ⊕ www.breadworks.net.

Falafel King. Falafel King has excellent pita pockets of hot and crispy falafel, spicy gyros, and marinated grilled chicken breast. Get an order of tabouli, hummus, or dolmas (stuffed grape leaves) to round out lunch. ✉ 1314 Pearl St. ☎ 303/449–9321 ⊕ www.falafelkingboulder.com.

Illegal Pete's. Illegal Pete's serves hefty burritos made to order with fresh ingredients and a choice of three salsas. There's also another location at 1320 College Avenue. ✉ 1447 Pearl St. ☎ 303/440–3955 ⊕ www.illegalpetes.com.

Salvaggio's Italian Delicatessen. If you're hankering for a delicious Philly cheesesteak, a sub, or another classic sandwich, Salvaggio's Italian Delicatessen makes them to order. ✉ 2609 Pearl St. ☎ 303/938–1981 ⊕ www. salvaggiositaliandelicaties.lbu.com.

7

WHERE TO EAT

Use the coordinate (✛ B2) at the end of each listing to locate a site on the corresponding map.

The variety of the restaurants here would be enviable in a city several times Boulder's size. Enjoy a tangy pizza slice for lunch and tempura with sweet eel sauce or tandoori grilled meats and naan for dinner. The menus of the more than 300 restaurants in town Vietnamese, Nepalese, Ethiopian, and many other cuisines. Prices at the showier restaurants in town reflect their high quality and service, but because of the large student population many eateries also offer up some excellent fare at more reasonable prices. Smoking is banned in all workplaces, (including restaurants and bars) throughout the state.

$$$
LATIN AMERICAN

✕**Aji.** Enjoy a South American cocktail like a *caipirinha, mojito,* or pisco sour before dinner in this busy restaurant. The storefront windows let in plenty of light, the seating is spacious, and the service is great. Try *ceviche* (shrimp or fish marinated in lime juice and served with fun accompaniments like banana, pickled peppers, or mango) or empanadas (savory pastries) to start. The presentation of entrées such as pumpkin seed–crusted trout, grilled duck breast, or steak stuffed with caramelized onions and garlic, is innovative and stunning. A chocolate empanada and a cup of French-press coffee round out a meal here wonderfully. ✉ 1601 Pearl St. ☎ 303/442–3464 ⊕ www.ajirestaurant. com ✛ G5.

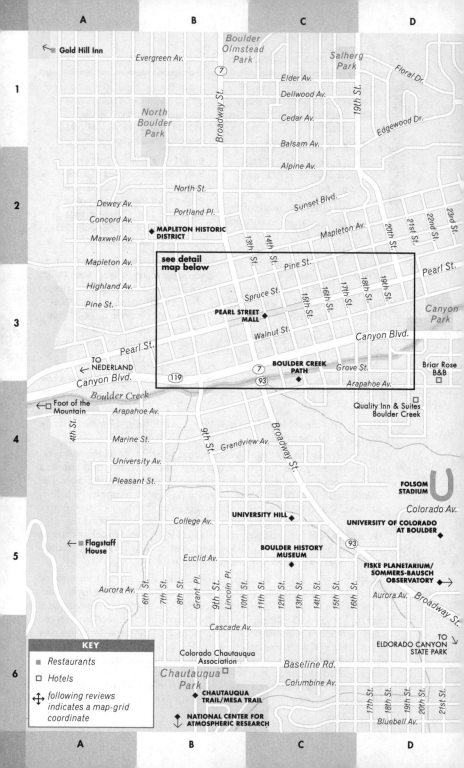

A

1

← ■ **Gold Hill Inn**

Evergreen Av.

North Boulder Park

2

Dewey Av.

Concord Av.

Maxwell Av. ◆ **MAPLETON HISTORIC DISTRICT**

Mapleton Av.

Highland Av.

Pine St.

3

Pearl St.

← TO NEDERLAND

Canyon Blvd.

Boulder Creek

← ■ **Foot of the Mountain**

4th St.

4

Arapahoe Av.

Marine St.

University Av.

Pleasant St.

5

← ■ **Flagstaff House**

Aurora Av.

6th St. *7th St.* *8th St.*

6

KEY

■ *Restaurants*

□ *Hotels*

✢ *following reviews indicates a map-grid coordinate*

B

Boulder Olmstead Park

⑦

North St.

Portland Pl.

13th St. *14th St.*

see detail map below

Spruce St.

◆ **PEARL STREET MALL**

Walnut St.

Pearl St.

⑪⑨ ⑦

⑨③ **BOULDER CREEK PATH** ◆

9th St. *Grandview Av.*

College Av.

◆ **UNIVERSITY HILL**

Euclid Av.

BOULDER HISTORY MUSEUM ◆

Grant Pl. *9th St.* *Lincoln Pl.* *10th St.* *11th St.* *12th St.* *13th St.* *14th St.* *15th St.* *16th St.*

Cascade Av.

Colorado Chautauqua Association □

Chautauqua Park

◆ **CHAUTAUQUA TRAIL/MESA TRAIL**

◆↓ **NATIONAL CENTER FOR ATMOSPHERIC RESEARCH**

C

Elder Av.

Dellwood Av.

Cedar Av.

Balsam Av.

Alpine Av.

Sunset Blvd.

Mapleton Av.

Pine St.

15th St. *16th St.* *17th St.* *18th St.* *19th St.*

Canyon Blvd.

Grove St.

Arapahoe Av.

Broadway St.

FOLSOM STADIUM U

Colorado Av.

UNIVERSITY OF COLORADO AT BOULDER ◆

⑨③

FISKE PLANETARIUM/ SOMMERS-BAUSCH OBSERVATORY ◆→

Aurora Av. *Broadway St.*

TO ELDORADO CANYON STATE PARK ↘

Baseline Rd.

Columbine Av.

17th St. *18th St.* *19th St.* *20th St.* *21st St.*

Bluebell Av.

D

Salherg Park

Floral Dr.

19th St.

Edgewood Dr.

23rd St. *22nd St.* *21st St.* *20th St.*

Pearl St.

Canyon Park

Briar Rose B&B □

Quality Inn & Suites Boulder Creek □

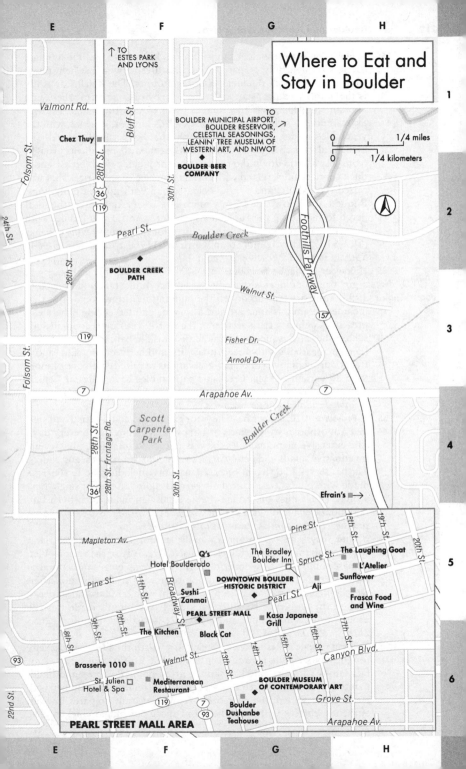

Where to Eat and Stay in Boulder

E   F   G   H

Valmont Rd.

↑ TO ESTES PARK AND LYONS

TO
BOULDER MUNICIPAL AIRPORT,
BOULDER RESERVOIR,
CELESTIAL SEASONINGS,
LEANIN' TREE MUSEUM OF
WESTERN ART, AND NIWOT →

Chez Thuy ■

Bluff St.

28th St.

30th St.

**BOULDER BEER
COMPANY**

36
119

24th St.

Folsom St.

26th St.

Pearl St.

Boulder Creek

Foothills Parkway

0   1/4 miles
0   1/4 kilometers

**BOULDER CREEK
PATH**

Walnut St.

157

119

Folsom St.

Fisher Dr.

Arnold Dr.

7

Arapahoe Av.

7

28th St.

28th St. Frontage Rd.

30th St.

**Scott
Carpenter
Park**

Boulder Creek

36

Efrain's ■→

Pine St.

Mapleton Av.

18th St.

19th St.

20th St.

Q's

The Bradley
Boulder Inn

Spruce St.

The Laughing Goat

Hotel Boulderado

**DOWNTOWN BOULDER
HISTORIC DISTRICT**

■ **L'Atelier**

Pine St.

11th St.

Broadway St.

Sushi
Zanmai

Aji

Sunflower

Pearl St.

**Frasca Food
and Wine**

PEARL STREET MALL

Kasa Japanese
Grill

9th St.

10th St.

The Kitchen

Black Cat

13th St.

14th St.

15th St.

16th St.

17th St.

Walnut St.

Canyon Blvd.

8th St.

93

Brasserie 1010 ■

St. Julien □
Hotel & Spa

Mediterranean
Restaurant

7

119

**BOULDER MUSEUM
OF CONTEMPORARY ART**

Grove St.

22nd St.

Boulder
Dushanbe
Teahouse

93

Arapahoe Av.

PEARL STREET MALL AREA

E   F   G   H

1

2

3

4

5

6

$$$ ✕ **Black Cat.** Is this Boulder's most famous bistro? No, but the intimate
BISTRO   eatery's thoughtfully prepared food and diverse wine list help put it
right up there with Boulder's elite restaurants. The Black Cat really
is the whole package, starting at the nearby organic farm where Eric
Skokan tends his crops and animals by day. After the sun goes down,
Skokan dons his chef hat in the Black Cat's kitchen, working with the
vegetables, meats, seasonings, and herbs that he specifically raised. The
menu is always changing, but it always begins with ingredients brought
from just a little down the road—it might include duck breast and a
duck confit strudel, served with currents braised in wine, pork that was
raised on walnuts and is now being served with nutmeg dumplings.
Request a window seat when you make a reservation to get the ideal
perch for admiring the Parisian atmosphere. And if you indulge with
the tasting menu ($62–$71), also splurge for the intuitive wine pairings
($99–$109). They're more than worth it. ⊠ *1964 13th St.* ☎ *303/444–
5500* ⊕ *www.blackcatboulder.com* ✛ *F6.*

$$ ✕ **Boulder Dushanbe Teahouse.** Unique to Colorado, this teahouse was
CAFÉ   a gift from Boulder's sister city Dushanbe, Tajikistan, and opened in
Fodor's Choice   1998. Tajik artisans decorated the building in a traditional style that
★   includes ceramic Islamic art and a carved, painted ceiling. The menu
presents a culinary cross section of the world; your meal could include
such dishes as Basque-style steak, Tajik shish kebab, or Tabrizi *kufteh*
(Persian meatballs with dried fruits, nuts, and herbs in a tomato sauce).
Relax during high tea at 3 pm (reservations required) with one of more
than 80 varieties of tea. Creekside patio tables have views of Central
Park. Brunch is served on weekends. ⊠ *1770 13th St.* ☎ *303/442–4993*
⊕ *www.boulderteahouse.com* ✛ *G6.*

$$ ✕ **Brasserie 1010.** Locals head here for great food and a casual and spir-
FRENCH   ited atmosphere, which starts at happy hour (from 3 to 6 every day).
The extensive menu includes the classic French offerings, plus several
imaginative salads and *petit plats* featuring burgers, crepes, and sliders.
The bar serves 23 different beers, 20 martinis (including the TenTenTini,
made with blue cheese-stuffed olives) and eight varieties of single-malt
scotch. Don't miss the grilled-cheese sandwich made with fresh buf-
falo mozzarella and figs. ⊠ *1011 Walnut St.* ☎ *303/998–1010* ⊕ *www.
brasserietenten.com* ⚇ *Reservations essential* ✛ *F6.*

$ ✕ **Chez Thuy.** This restaurant is popular among Boulder's vegetarians,
VIETNAMESE   who line up for the flavorful, inexpensive fare. Any of the various Viet-
★   namese soups make a wonderful starter before an entrée of seafood or
tofu pad thai, or a traditional hotpot made with seafood or pork. The
well-lighted dining room fills up every night with families and students,
though the ambience is a little lacking. Everything is made fresh to
order, portions are ample, and the service is fast and friendly. ⊠ *2655
28th St.* ☎ *303/442–1700* ⊕ *www.chezthuy.com* ✛ *E1.*

$ ✕ **Efrain's Mexican Restaurant & Cantina.** It's worth the drive to Lafayette
MEXICAN   for the savory *chile verde* (green chile) that Efrain cooks every day.
His family's homey café has simple, green-painted arbors and hand-
painted tables. The porch is a great place to relax before dinner with
a margarita served in a pint-size mason jar. Efrain prepares low-fat,
authentic entrées with fresh beef and succulent pulled chicken. The

large-grain rice is light, and refried beans are creamy but not greasy. Finish your meal with a crisp, hot *sopapilla* (a light, fried pastry served hot with honey). Expect to wait for a table on a Friday or Saturday night. ⊠ *101 E. Cleveland St., Lafayette ✛ Drive 11 mi east on Baseline Rd. to Lafayette and turn right onto Public Rd., then left onto Cleveland St.* ☎ *303/666–7544* ◷ *Closed Tues.* ✛ *F4.*

$$$$
AMERICAN
★ ✕ **Flagstaff House Restaurant.** Sit on the patio at one of Colorado's finest restaurants and drink in the sublime views of Boulder from the side of Flagstaff Mountain, about 5 minutes from downtown. Executive Chef Mark Monette has fresh fish flown in daily, grows some of his own herbs, and is noted for his exquisite combinations of ingredients and fanciful, playful presentations. The menu changes daily, but sample entrées include ruby red trout with salmon and scallops in caviar butter and watercress sauce; buffalo filet mignon and foie gras. The wine list is remarkably comprehensive. ⊠ *1138 Flagstaff Rd. ✛ Drive west on Baseline Rd. and turn right onto Flagstaff Rd. Follow it up the hill for about ¾ mi, then look for the restaurant on your right.* ☎ *303/442–4640* ⊕ *www.flagstaffhouse.com* ⌂ *Reservations essential* ◷ *No lunch ✛ A5.*

$$$$
ITALIAN
★ ✕ **Frasca Food and Wine.** In the Friuli region of Italy the *frasca* (tree branch) is a historic marker for a neighborhood eatery where you'll be warmly welcomed and well fed. At this Frasca, you can start with *salumi,* a platter of northern Italian cured meats such as prosciutto *daniele, speck,* and *salumeria biellese coppa,* then dig into sliced Québec veal loin salad, house-made tagliatelle, or butter-roasted Atlantic halibut. The menu is based on locally and naturally raised foods, while the extensive wine list focuses on Italian regional wines. A four-course meal will run you $75 per person, but indulge with a prosciutto sampler ($18) to start. ⊠ *1738 Pearl St.* ☎ *303/442–6966* ⊕ *www.frascafoodandwine. com* ⌂ *Reservations essential* ◷ *Closed Sun. No lunch ✛ H5.*

$$$$
AMERICAN ✕ **Gold Hill Inn.** About 10 mi from downtown Boulder, this humble log cabin, on the dirt road going through the former mining town of Gold Hill, hardly looks like a bastion of haute cuisine, but the six-course, $33 prix-fixe dinner is something to rave about. Entrées stick to a Western theme, and may include roast duck with raspberry sauce or leg of lamb marinated in buttermilk, juniper berries, and cloves. Portions are generous, but try to save room for dessert. Service is friendly, and the inn also hosts regular "murder mystery" nights with professional actors in the adjacent Bluebird Lodge. ⊠ *401 Main St., Gold Hill ✛ Take Mapleton Ave. west from Broadway. It becomes Sunshine Canyon Dr., then Main St.* ☎ *303/443–6461* ⊕ *www.goldhillinn.com* ⌂ *Reservations essential* ◷ *Closed Tues. June–Sept., and Mon. and Tues. in May and Oct. No lunch ✛ A1.*

$
JAPANESE
★ ✕ **Kasa Japanese Grill and Bar.** Architect Edward Suzuki designed this elegant and understated restaurant that features black-granite tables, wooden flooring, imported Japanese tiles, and inverted white umbrellas hanging from the ceiling (*kasa* means "umbrellas" in Japanese). The menu is filled with authentic Japanese *yakitori* (meat and vegetable skewers), sushi, and sashimi. Don't miss the yogurt ice cream

for dessert. ✉ *1468 Pearl St.* ☎ *303/938–8888* ⊕ *www.kasainboulder. com* ☾ *Closed Mon.* ⊹ *G5.*

$$$
AMERICAN
Fodor'sChoice
★

✕ **The Kitchen.** This unique bistro offers an elegant yet relaxed dinner with great service, and includes a casual wine and beer lounge on its second floor. Locals come in for "shared plates" during Community Hour (3 to 5:30 weekdays), a boardinghouse-like experience that provides the same great food and drinks at reduced prices. Exceptional entrées like the lamb sausage ravioli and the beef flank steak spotlight free-range meats and organic and seasonal local produce. Don't forget dessert: lemon tart with mascarpone and a glass of muscatel or the sticky toffee pudding with vanilla ice cream and a cup of robust coffee are both heavenly. This combination of chic bistro and big-city hot spot can be a bit loud. ✉ *1039 Pearl St.* ☎ *303/544–5973* ⊕ *www.thekitchencafe. com* ⚑ *Reservations essential* ⊹ *F6.*

$$$
FRENCH
★

✕ **L'Atelier.** Chef Radek Cerny, a native of Prague and master of nouvelle cuisine, creates delicious French meals with artistic flourish (and a slight Spanish influence). Seafood is his forte, and the tuna tartare salad with oranges is a wonderful starter before an entrée of lobster ravioli with beurre blanc or Maine lobster meunière. Be sure to save a crust of bread to use with the savory sauces before ending with a chocolate raspberry *miroir*, a glazed cake made with chocolate mousse and almond meringue. The extraordinary wine list covers a broad range of prices and vintages. ✉ *1739 Pearl St.* ☎ *303/442–7233* ⊕ *www.latelierboulder. com* ☾ *No lunch; closed on Sun.* ⊹ *H5.*

¢
CAFÉ

✕ **The Laughing Goat Coffeehouse.** This bohemian-style café two blocks west of the pedestrian mall serves bagels, muffins, cinnamon rolls, and granola for breakfast, and sandwiches and soups for lunch. The lattes, made with cow, goat, or soy milk, are excellent. Students like to take up table space with laptops and textbooks, but they'll happily make room for you. You can hear live music and poetry by locals Tuesday through Sunday. ✉ *1709 Pearl St.* ☎ *303/440–4628* ⊕ *www.thelaughinggoat. com* ⊹ *H5.*

$$
MEDITERRANEAN

✕ **Mediterranean Restaurant.** After work, when all of Boulder seems to show up to enjoy tapas, "the Med" becomes a real scene. If the crowd gets to be too much, try a table on the patio. The decor is Portofino meets Santa Fe, with abstract art, terra-cotta floors, and brightly colored tile. The open kitchen turns out Italian, Spanish, French, and Greek fare, including daily specials such as pork saltimbocca, halibut puttanesca, and horseradish-crusted tuna—all complemented by an extensive, well-priced wine list. ✉ *1002 Walnut St.* ☎ *303/444–5335* ⊕ *www.themedboulder.com* ⊹ *F6.*

$$$
AMERICAN

✕ **Q's.** Coffered ceilings, stained-glass windows, and mosaic tile floors create a classy feel at this quiet restaurant housed in the 100-year-old Hotel Boulderado. The menu features dishes using local, seasonal, organic, and sustainably produced ingredients, and the excellent international wine list features a few local vintages, as well. Sweet-corn soup or roast beef and arugula salad are delightful starters before entrées like roast Colorado rack of lamb. If you're in the mood to be surprised, try the five-course chef's tasting menu. End on a sweet note with a dish of homemade ice cream or a seasonal fruit tart. ⊠ *2115 13th St., in Hotel Boulderado* ☎ *303/442–4880* ⊕ *www.qsboulder.com* ✛ *F5.*

$$$
JAPANESE
✕ **Sushi Zanmai.** The delicious seafood is prepared fresh, and the wasabi is zesty at this perennially popular sushi restaurant, a bright, open place that fills early. Enjoy dinner at a table or sit at the sushi bar and watch the chefs' artful methods. The miso soup is salty and tangy, and the mochi-ice dessert (a truffle-size bite of ice cream wrapped in a fruit- or chocolate-flavored rice paste) is not to be missed. Happy hour for sushi and drinks is Monday–Saturday from 5 to 6:30 and all night on Sunday. The official karaoke night is Saturday (10 to midnight, with no food served after 11). ⊠ *1221 Spruce St.* ☎ *303/440–0733* ⊕ *www. sushizanmai.com* ☽ *No lunch weekends* ✛ *F5.*

WHERE TO STAY

For expanded hotel reviews, visit Fodors.com.

Use the coordinate (✛ B2) at the end of each listing to locate a site on the corresponding map.

$$$
B&B/INN
★
⊡ **The Bradley Boulder Inn.** Elegant and contemporary, this downtown inn has a spacious great room with warm tones and an inviting stone fireplace. **Pros:** quiet inn one block from Pearl Street shopping and dining; daily wine-and-cheese hour; privileges at nearby gym. **Cons:** books early; no young children. ⊠ *2040 16th St.* ☎ *303/545–5200, 800/858–5811* ⊕ *www.thebradleyboulder.com* ⇦ *12 rooms* ⟁ *In-room: a/c, Internet, Wi-Fi. In-hotel: business center, parking, some age restrictions* ❏ *Breakfast* ✛ *G5.*

$$
B&B/INN
⊡ **Briar Rose B&B.** Innkeeper Gary Hardin, a Zen monk, warmly welcomes guests to his ecologically sound B&B. **Pros:** the only B&B in central Boulder; close to downtown shopping and dining; delicious (and healthy) breakfast. **Cons:** on a busy and noisy street; small inn that books early. ⊠ *2151 Arapahoe Ave.* ☎ *303/442–3007* ⊕ *www. briarrosebb.com* ⇦ *10 rooms* ⟁ *In-room: a/c, no TV, Wi-Fi. In-hotel: parking* ❏ *Breakfast* ✛ *D3.*

$$
HOTEL
⊡ **Colorado Chautauqua Association.** Imagine: a hike through the Flatirons, a quick shower in your cottage, dinner at the dining hall, a Josh Ritter show at the auditorium, and a drink back on your front porch with friends—an entire day of natural beauty without ever having to get in the car. **Pros:** unique lodging; arts, dining, and recreation on property; well-kept cabins; amazing views of town and mountains. **Cons:** no maid service; park tends to fill with nonresidents there for various events and dining. ⊠ *900 Baseline Rd.* ☎ *303/952–1611* ⊕ *www.chautauqua.com* ⇦ *22 rooms, 60 cottages* ⟁ *In-room: no a/c, kitchen, no TV, Wi-Fi. In-hotel: restaurant, tennis court, some pets allowed* ❏ *No meals* ✛ *B6.*

$
HOTEL
⊡ **Foot of the Mountain Motel.** With its knotty-pine siding, bright red doors, and colorful flower boxes, this motel has a distinctive charm. **Pros:** excellent value for the area; quiet neighborhood; close to recreation. **Cons:** no-frills accommodations; no on-site restaurant. ⊠ *200 Arapahoe Ave.* ☎ *303/442–5688, 866/773–5489* ⊕ *www.footofthemountainmotel.com* ⇦ *18 rooms, 2 suites* ⟁ *In-room: no a/c. In-hotel: parking, some pets allowed* ❏ *No meals* ✛ *A4.*

7

$$$
HOTEL
Fodor's Choice
★

Hotel Boulderado. The gracious lobby of this elegant 1909 beauty has a soaring stained-glass ceiling, and the mezzanine beckons with romantic nooks galore. **Pros:** well-maintained historic building; downtown location; excellent restaurants. **Cons:** on busy and noisy streets; large, busy hotel. ⊠ *2115 13th St.* ☎ *303/442–4344, 800/433–4344* ⊕ *www.boulderado. com* ⤳ *160 rooms* ⟁ *In-room: Wi-Fi. In-hotel: restaurant, bar* ▮◎▮ *No meals* ✢ *F5.*

$$
HOTEL

Quality Inn & Suites Boulder Creek. Just a 10-minute walk from the Pearl Street Mall and 5 minutes from the University of Colorado, this hotel provides the personal attention and services of a B&B, including a free hot-breakfast buffet. **Pros:** friendly and personable staff; free off-street parking; close to sights and activities. **Cons:** on busy street; chain hotel has less personality than some local options. ⊠ *2020 Arapahoe Ave.* ☎ *303/449–7550* ⊕ *www.qualityinnboulder.com* ⤳ *47 rooms, 2 suites* ⟁ *In-room: a/c, Wi-Fi. In-hotel: pool, gym, business center, parking* ▮◎▮ *Breakfast* ✢ *D4.*

$$$$
HOTEL

St. Julien Hotel & Spa. Unwind in the indulgent luxury of this classy yet casual hotel. **Pros:** convenient downtown location; close to outdoor activities and mountains. **Cons:** large hotel; quite busy. ⊠ *900 Walnut St.* ☎ *720/406–9696, 877/303–0900* ⊕ *www.stjulien.com* ⤳ *201 rooms, 11 suites* ⟁ *In-room: a/c, safe, Wi-Fi. In-hotel: restaurant, bar, pool, gym, spa, parking* ▮◎▮ *No meals* ✢ *F6.*

> ## CHAUTAUQUA MOVEMENT
>
> The Colorado Chautauqua National Historic Landmark is on 26 acres in Boulder at the base of the foothills. It opened on July 4, 1898, and still has its original buildings. One of only three remaining in the United States today, it was once one of 12,000 venues on the national circuit where educational speeches and artistic performances took place. You can still have dinner and attend seasonal concerts, lectures, and a silent film series here.

NIGHTLIFE AND THE ARTS

THE ARTS

ARTS FESTIVALS

Colorado Music Festival. Between late June and early August, the Colorado Music Festival brings classical music to Chautauqua Auditorium. Since the festival began in 1976, visiting artists have included the Santa Fe Guitar Quartet and the Takács Quartet, as well as plenty of international talent such as William Barton, a didgeridoo performer from Australia, and Lynn Harrell, who plays a 1673 Stradivarius. Evening meals are available in the dining hall, or you can pack a picnic and settle in on the Green to take in views of the mountains before the concert. ⊠ *Chautauqua Park, 900 Baseline Rd.* ☎ *303/440–7666, 303/449–1397* ⊕ *www.comusic.org.*

Fodor's Choice
★

Colorado Shakespeare Festival. CU's stunning Mary Rippon Outdoor Theater is the venue for the annual Colorado Shakespeare Festival, presenting the bard's comedies and tragedies (along with select other plays, including *The Little Prince* and *The Inspector General*) from early July to mid-August. ☎ *303/492–0554* ⊕ *www.coloradoshakes.org.*

THEATER, MUSIC, AND DANCE

Boulder's Dinner Theatre. Dine while you catch a popular musical at Boulder's Dinner Theatre—with actors who double as your waitstaff. ⊠ *5501 Arapahoe Ave.* ☎ *303/449–6000* ⊕ *www.bouldersdinnertheatre.com.*

The Boulder Philharmonic. The Boulder Philharmonic presents its own concert season, as well as chamber music concerts, the Boulder Ballet Ensemble, and performances by visiting divas such as Kathleen Battle. ⊠ *University of Colorado, Macky Auditorium, 17th St. and University Ave.* ☎ *303/449–1343* ⊕ *www.boulderphil.org.*

Boulder Theater. The art deco Boulder Theater is a venue for top touring bands and movies, as well as for most installments of the weekly radio show *eTown* (⊕ *www.etown.org*), broadcast on NPR. The show's emcees, Helen and Nick Forster, host musical talent and discuss environmental and community issues. ⊠ *2032 14th St.* ☎ *303/786–7030* ⊕ *www.bouldertheater.com.*

★ **Chautauqua Community Hall.** Concerts take place throughout summer at Boulder's peaceful Chautauqua Community Hall. Performers have included Josh Ritter, Branford Marsalis, Lucinda Williams, Indigo Girls, Andrew Bird, and the Afro Celt Sound System. ⊠ *900 Baseline Rd.* ☎ *303/442–3282* ⊕ *www.chautauqua.com.*

College of Music. The University of Colorado's superb College of Music presents concerts year-round, including chamber music by the internationally renowned Takács String Quartet. ☎ *303/492–8008* ⊕ *www. cuconcerts.org.*

Dairy Center for the Arts. The Dairy Center for the Arts hosts art shows featuring local painters. It's also a venue for locally produced plays; music, ballet, and dance performances; and film. ☎ *303/440–7826* ⊕ *www.thedairy.org.*

Department of Theater and Dance. The Department of Theater and Dance stages excellent student productions year-round. ☎ *303/492–8181* ⊕ *www.colorado.edu/theatredance.*

NIGHTLIFE

BARS AND LOUNGES

Bitter Bar. Tucked inside the charming and moderately priced Happy Noodle House is what might be Boulder's greatest bar. The staff is passionate about cocktails, and they're not shy with advice, starting with a favorite base liquor and building from there. ⊠ *835 Walnut St.* ☎ *303/442–3050* ⊕ *www.happynoodlehouse.com.*

Corner Bar. Business lunches and after-work gatherings take place at the Corner Bar in the Hotel Boulderado. It's a contemporary American pub with both indoor and outdoor seating The happy hour, from 3 to 6, brings $3 beers and $6 martinis. ⊠ *2115 13th St.* ☎ *303/442–4344* ⊕ *www.boulderado.com/thecornerbar.html.*

Pearl Street Pub and Cellar. The cozy Pearl Street Pub and Cellar, with its laid-back atmosphere and impressive beer list, is a great place to chat

7

over a quiet drink. There's pool and darts downstairs if you're in the mood for a game. ⊠ *1108 Pearl St.* ☎ *303/939–9900.*

Rio Grande Mexican Restaurant. Bartenders at Rio Grande Mexican Restaurant make Boulder's best margaritas—so good, in fact, that there's a three-per-person limit. There's also a great rooftop patio here. ⊠ *1101 Walnut St.* ☎ *303/444–3690* ⊕ *www.riograndemexican.com.*

West End Tavern. The West End Tavern, with its rooftop deck, is a popular after-work hangout serving beers, cocktails, and good pub grub, including legendary burgers. ⊠ *926 Pearl St.* ☎ *303/444–3535* ⊕ *www. thewestendtavern.com.*

BREWPUBS AND BREWERIES

Mountain Sun Pub & Brewery. The casual Mountain Sun Pub & Brewery crafts more than 50 beers throughout the year, and there are always about 18 on tap. A favorite of Boulderites is the Colorado Kind, a nicely hopped amber. Tours are available upon request. Stay to have a burger or for the live music or comedy on Sunday nights. ⊠ *1535 Pearl St.* ☎ *303/546–0886* ⊕ *www.mountainsunpub.com.*

Walnut Brewery. The Walnut Brewery keeps several brews and cask-conditioned ales on tap. A new seasonal is tapped each month, and every season also has a new wheat beer. Try the Buffalo Gold ale (a local favorite) or the malty St. James Irish Red Ale. The excellent beer goes well with the upscale pub fare, which includes mahimahi tacos, smoked salmon fish-and-chips, and buffalo fajitas. Tours are available anytime. ⊠ *1123 Walnut St.* ☎ *303/447–1345* ⊕ *www.walnutbrewery.com.*

MUSIC AND DANCE CLUBS

Fox Theatre. The Fox Theatre, a former movie palace, hosts touring music and comedic talent. The intimate room on the Hill has been a pivotal space for underground hip-hop artists throughout the last few decades. ⊠ *1135 13th St.* ☎ *303/443–3399* ⊕ *www.foxtheatre.com.*

Rock 'n Soul Cafe. Rock 'n Soul Cafe serves up live music most nights, accompanied by espresso drinks and wine by the glass. The café also serves food: soups, teriyaki, and pastries. ⊠ *5290 Arapahoe Ave.* ☎ *303/ 443–5108* ⊕ *www.rocknsoulcafe.com* ⊙ *Mon.–Sat. 9 am–11 pm.*

Round Midnight. Whether DJs are spinning for '80s or hip-hop night, there's dancing every Wednesday through Saturday at this student favorite. ⊠ *1005 Pearl St.* ☎ *303/442–2176* ⊕ *www.roundmidnight. tv* ⊙ *Daily 5 pm–2 am.*

SHOPPING

SHOPPING NEIGHBORHOODS

Flatiron Crossing. One of the metropolitan area's most popular shopping centers is Flatiron Crossing, about 10 mi southwest of Boulder. Shoppers can hit stores such as Nordstrom, Coach, Borders, and Sharper Image; browse at a few locally owned jewelers and galleries; and take a break in the food court or in one of the full-service restaurants. ⊠ *U.S. 36 between Boulder and Denver, Broomfield* ☎ *720/887–9900* ⊕ *www. flatironcrossing.com.*

Pearl Street Mall. Boulder's Pearl Street Mall is a shopping extravaganza, with upscale boutiques, art galleries, bookstores, shoe shops, and stores with home and garden furnishings. Street musicians and magicians, caricaturists, and buskers with lovebirds entertain locals and visitors alike. ✉ *Pearl St. between 11th and 15th Sts.*

Twenty-Ninth Street. Stroll along Twenty-Ninth Street, one of Boulder's newest areas to shop, and pick up a pair of shoes, some outdoor gear, a funny greeting card, or a new yoga outfit. The outdoor mall has plenty of nationally known clothiers, a bookstore, a stationer, coffee shops, and eateries. ✉ *29th St. between Arapahoe Ave. and Pearl St.* ⊕ *www. twentyninthstreet.com.*

University Hill. University Hill (the Hill) is a great place for hip clothes, new and used CDs, and CU apparel. ✉ *13th St. between College Ave. and Pennsylvania St.*

SPECIALTY SHOPS

ANTIQUES

Amazing Garage Sale. Serendipitous discoveries and glorious antique furniture, jewelry, and silverware move fast at the Amazing Garage Sale, so it's worth a visit while you're in Boulder. ✉ *4919 N. Broadway* ☎ *303/447–0417* ⊕ *www.theamazinggaragesale.com.*

BOOKSTORES

Boulder has one of the largest concentrations of used-book sellers in the United States. Most shops are on Pearl Street between 8th and 20th streets.

★ **Boulder Bookstore.** Boulder Bookstore has thousands of new and used books in many genres, including a great selection of photography, history, and art books about Colorado. It also carries a few out-of-town and foreign newspapers and periodicals. The store also thoughtfully pays for your parking if you buy anything—or even if you're just dropping off used books. ✉ *1107 Pearl St.* ☎ *303/447–2074* ⊕ *www. boulderbookstore.com.*

Trident Booksellers and Cafe. Sip a robust latte at Trident Booksellers and Cafe while browsing the eclectic collection of mostly used books—including foreign-language, but also many new books at marked-down prices. ✉ *940 Pearl St.* ☎ *303/443–3133* ⊕ *www.tridentcafe.com.*

CHILDREN'S ITEMS

Grandrabbit's Toy Shoppe. Many Boulder kids' favorite store is Grandrabbit's Toy Shoppe. ✉ *2525 Arapahoe Ave.* ☎ *303/443–0780* ⊕ *www. grtoys.com.*

Into the Wind. The coolest kites can be found at Into the Wind, which sells traditional and out-of-the-ordinary kites, plus imaginative wind decorations, flags, and boomerangs. ✉ *1408 Pearl St.* ☎ *303/449–5356* ⊕ *www.intothewind.com.*

PlayFair Toys. PlayFair Toys sells all kinds of educational toys, including Lego and Brio brands, as well as books, puzzles, and fun items like robotic tarantulas and "brain kits." ✉ *2550 Arapahoe Ave.* ☎ *800/824–7255* ⊕ *www.playfairtoys.com.*

7

CLOTHING BOUTIQUES

Alpaca Connection. Alpaca Connection sells gorgeous alpaca garments, mostly made in Peru, for men and women. ⊠ *1326 Pearl St.* ☎ *303/447–2047* ⊕ *www.thealpacaconnection.com.*

Fresh Produce. Fresh Produce is a Boulder-based company that makes brightly colored and whimsically designed cotton clothing for women and children. ⊠ *1218 Pearl St.* ☎ *303/442–7507* ⊕ *www. freshproducesportswear.com.*

Jacque Michelle. Jacque Michelle has fashionably casual and unique women's clothing and accessories. The store also sells clever, appealing gifts. ⊠ *2670 Broadway* ☎ *303/786–7628* ⊕ *www.jacquemichelle.com.*

CRAFTS AND ART GALLERIES

Art Source International. Art Source International is Colorado's largest antique print and map dealer. ⊠ *1237 Pearl St.* ☎ *303/444–4079* ⊕ *www.rare-maps.com.*

Boulder Arts & Crafts Gallery. Boulder Arts & Crafts Gallery, owned and operated by 42 artists, is a popular place to find unique gifts and decorative items. The works from the 150-odd Colorado artists represented by the gallery include photographs, pottery, hand-painted silk scarves, leather handbags, furniture, and glass objets d'art. ⊠ *1421 Pearl St.* ☎ *303/443–3683* ⊕ *www.boulderartsandcrafts.com.*

SmithKlein Gallery. SmithKlein Gallery showcases classic modern art—glass and bronze sculpture, jewelry, and paintings. ⊠ *1116 Pearl St.* ☎ *303/444–7200* ⊕ *www.smithklein.com.*

FARMERS' MARKET

Boulder Farmers' Market. Each summer the Boulder Farmers' Market sells baked goods, plants, and seasonal produce. The market is open from 4 pm to 8 pm Wednesday from early May through early October, and Saturday from 8 am until 2 pm early April through early November. Later in summer and fall, watch for cherries and peaches brought in by growers from the state's famed orchards near Palisade. The bakers always have pastries and excellent loaves for a picnic. Locally made organic peanut butter mixed with honey or cinnamon makes a good gift to bring home. ⊠ *13th St. between Canyon Blvd. and Arapahoe Ave.* ☎ *303/910–2236* ⊕ *www.boulderfarmers.org.*

GIFT STORES

Two Hands Paperie. Two Hands Paperie carries elegant European stationery, handmade paper, and handcrafted, leather-bound journals. ⊠ *803 Pearl St.* ☎ *303/444–0124* ⊕ *www.twohandspaperie.com.*

Where the Buffalo Roam. Where the Buffalo Roam sells quirky T-shirts, CU and Colorado souvenirs, and a variety of trinkets. ⊠ *1320 Pearl St.* ☎ *303/938–1424.*

HOME AND GARDEN

Peppercorn. Peppercorn's the store to visit for the finest selection in crockery, cookware, table linen, and kitchen utensils, as well as upscale food items and cookbooks. ⊠ *1235 Pearl St.* ☎ *303/449–5847, 800/447–6905* ⊕ *www.peppercorn.com.*

West End Gardener. Gardeners will find treasures at the West End Gardener, purveyors of vintage and new garden tools and accessories. ⊠ *777 Pearl St.* ☎ *303/938–0607.*

SPORTING GOODS

Boulder Army Store. Boulder Army Store packs the racks and shelves tightly with name-brand outdoor clothing and camping gear from manufacturers like Columbia, Under Armour, and Carhartt marked a few dollars less than regular retail. ⊠ *1545 Pearl St.* ☎ *303/442–7616* ⊕ *www.boulderarmystore.com.*

McGuckin Hardware. McGuckin Hardware is a Boulder institution that stocks home appliances and gadgets, hardware, and a mind-boggling array of outdoor merchandise. The seemingly omniscient salespeople know where everything is. ⊠ *Village Shopping Center, 2525 Arapahoe Ave.* ☎ *303/443–1822* ⊕ *www.mcguckin.com.*

REI. The Boulder branch of REI carries outdoor equipment for all sports and has some rental camping gear. ⊠ *1789 28th St.* ☎ *303/583–9970* ⊕ *www.rei.com/stores/44.*

SIDE TRIPS FROM BOULDER

Boulder has a few neighboring towns that are interesting destinations in their own right, well worth a drive and a short stop if not a longer layover. Mountainous Nederland, rural Niwot, and stunning Lyons all have quirky, interesting (albeit small) downtown areas and gorgeous surroundings filled with mountains, forests, and streams.

7

NEDERLAND

16 mi west of Boulder.

A former mining and mill town at the top of Boulder Canyon and on the scenic Peak-to-Peak Highway, "Ned" embodies that small, mountain-town spirit in look and attitude: laid-back, independent, renegade, and friendly.

Nederland started out as a mill town, processing the silver mined in the now-deserted nearby town of Caribou. The town got its name from a Dutch company that owned several mines in the area: "Nederland" is Dutch for "Netherlands," or low lands, and Nederland was below Caribou. Nederland was also well known for its tungsten mining during World War I. Around town you'll see references to "wolf's tongue," a word play on wolframite, the ore from which tungsten is extracted. The downtown retains the character of its silver-milling days, and has several good bars, cafés, and restaurants. Shops sell used books, antiques, organic groceries, fabrics, and gemstones. Nederland is the gateway to skiing at Eldora Mountain Resort and high-altitude hiking in the Indian Peaks Wilderness.

GETTING HERE AND AROUND

Nederland is an easy drive from Boulder. Take Highway 119 (Canyon Boulevard) west.

WHEN TO GO

FESTIVALS **Frozen Dead Guy Days.** Every March, Nederland celebrates an annual event that's true to its oddball spirit. The three-day event includes a slow-motion parade, coffin races, and a charity polar plunge into (usually frozen) Chipeta Park Pond. ⊠ *Chipeta Park and Town Square* 🕾 *303/258–3936* ⊕ *www.nederlandchamber.org* ⊠ *Free* ☉ *First weekend in Mar.*

NedFest. The Nederland Music & Arts Festival, a weekend of bluegrass, world beat, and jazz music known as the NedFest, takes place in late August on the west shore of Barker Reservoir. A few thousand people come to relax in the sun, dance, or stroll by the art stands. Admission is steep ($30–$65 for a single day, $115–$160 for all three days), but children under 12 get in for free. ⊕ *www.nedfest.com.*

ESSENTIALS

Visitor Information Nederland Area Chamber of Commerce ⌂ *Box 85, 80466* 🕾 *303/258–3936* ⊕ *www.nederlandchamber.org.*

EXPLORING

Carousel of Happiness. No visit to Nederland is complete without a spin (it's $1) on the Carousel of Happiness, a restored 1910 carousel featuring 56 hand-carved, hand-painted animals running 'round to the tune of a 1913 Wurlitzer band organ. The complex also includes a gift shop and a puppet theater. ⊠ *20 Lakeview Dr.* 🕾 *303/258–3457* ⊕ *www. carouselofhappiness.org.*

★ **Peak-to-Peak Scenic and Historic Byway.** The Peak-to-Peak Scenic and Historic Byway (CO Hwys. 119, 72, and 7), a 55-mi stretch that winds from Central City through Nederland to Estes Park, is not the quickest route to the eastern gateway to Rocky Mountain National Park, but it's certainly the most scenic. You'll pass through the old mining towns of Ward and Allenspark and enjoy spectacular mountain vistas. Mount Meeker and Longs Peak rise magnificently behind every bend in the road. The descent into Estes Park provides grand vistas of snow-covered mountains and green valleys.

An afternoon drive along this route is especially memorable in fall, when the sky is deeper blue and stands of aspens contrast with the evergreen pine forests. ⊠ *From Nederland, drive north on Hwy. 72. Turn left at intersection with Hwy. 7 and continue to Estes Park.*

SPORTS AND THE OUTDOORS

HIKING

If you aren't used to it, high altitude can catch you off guard. Drink plenty of water to help stave off the effects of altitude sickness—dizziness, shortness of breath, headache, and nausea. You also should slather on the sunscreen, as it's easy to get sunburned up here. And in summer an early morning start is best, as afternoon thunderstorms are frequent and potentially dangerous above the tree line.

★ **Indian Peaks Wilderness.** The Indian Peaks Wilderness has some of the most popular hiking in the area, and you'll always have company in summer. The area encompasses more than 50 lakes, 133 mi of trails, and six mountain passes crossing the Continental Divide. Wildflowers are prolific, and peak in late July and early August. Cinquefoil, harebell, stonecrop, flax, wild geranium, yarrow, larkspur, lupine, and columbine (the state flower) all mix in a mosaic of colors on the slopes and in the meadows. Parking at trailheads in the wilderness area is limited, so plan to start out early in the day. "No Parking" signs are posted, and, if the designated parking lot is full, the etiquette is to park your car on the outbound side of the road at a spot where there's still room for vehicles to pass. There's no central access point to the area; contact the U.S. Forest Service or check its Web site for trail information and driving directions. Permits are not required for day visitors.

Lost Lake. The easy, 2.8-mi (round-trip) hike to Lost Lake has enough altitude to give you views of the high peaks under the brilliant blue sky. You'll gain a mere 800 feet on this two-hour walk. ☒ *Trailhead: From Nederland, drive south on Hwy. 119 to County Rd. 130. About 1 mi after the pavement ends, look for a road on the left that goes sharply downhill (marked Hessie Trail). Park there and hike ½ mi to the trailhead.*

Diamond Lake. The well-traveled trail to Diamond Lake starts out as the Arapaho Pass Trail at the Fourth of July trailhead. It's steep as you climb through the pines, but the elevation gain between the trailhead and the lake is only 800 feet. The trail delivers terrific views of Jasper Peak and the Arapaho Peaks. In late July, when the snowfields are gone, the wildflowers cover the slopes and meadows with bursts of color. At the junction with the Diamond Lake trailhead to the left, the trail passes a waterfall and crosses a stream (with a bridge) before it descends to Diamond Lake. Relax at the lake and enjoy the views before returning. Allow three hours to hike the 5-mi round-trip. ☒ *Trailhead: From Nederland, drive south on Hwy. 119 to County Rd. 130. About 5 mi after the pavement ends, look for signs for the Fourth of July trailhead.* ☒ *Boulder Ranger District Office, Arapaho National Forest, 2140 Yarmouth Ave.* ☎ *303/541-2500* ⊕ *www.fs.fed.us/arnf/recreation/wilderness/indianpeaks.*

DeLonde Trail/Blue Bird Loop. The DeLonde Trail/Blue Bird Loop at the Caribou Ranch Open Space is an easy 4.5-mi walk through forests and wildflower-filled meadows. An elk herd resides on the open space, so listen for the bulls bugling in fall. The 1.2-mi DeLonde Trail starts to the left of the trailhead information kiosk and connects to the Blue Bird Loop just above the former DeLonde homestead site. You can take a break at the picnic table overlooking the pond near the ranch house before continuing on the loop to the former Blue Bird Mine complex. Allow about one to two hours to complete the hike. ☒ *Trailhead: From Nederland, drive north on Hwy. 72 to County Rd. 126, turn left, and go 1 mi* ☎ *303/678-6200* ⊕ *www.bouldercounty.org.*

SUPPLIES **B&F Mountain Market.** You can get water and food for your hike plus deli sandwiches and other groceries at the B&F Mountain Market. ☒ *60 Lakeview Dr.* ☎ *303/258-9470.*

Indian Peaks Ace Hardware. Indian Peaks Ace Hardware is a good (and super-friendly) place to get information, maps, and gear. ☒ *74 Hwy. 119* ☎ *303/258-3132.*

SKIING AND SNOWBOARDING

Eldora Mountain Resort. With a 1,600-foot vertical drop (the longest run is 3 mi), Eldora Mountain Resort has 53 trails, 12 lifts, and 680 acres; 25 mi (40 km) of groomed Nordic track; and four terrain parks accommodating different ability levels for snowboarders and skiers. Tucked away in the mountains at 9,200 feet (summit elevation is 10,800 feet), Eldora's annual snowfall is more than 300 inches. Daily lift tickets are $69. The Indian Peaks Lodge rents skis, runs a ski school, and has a cafeteria-style restaurant. ✉ *2861 Eldora Ski Rd., 5 mi west of Nederland off Hwy. 119 and Eldora Rd., Nederland* ☎ *303/440–8700* ⊕ *www.eldora.com* 🎫 *$69* ⊙ *Mid-Nov.–mid-Apr., weekdays 9–4; weekends and holidays 8:30–4.*

WHERE TO EAT AND STAY

For expanded hotel reviews, visit Fodors.com.

$ | ✕ **Kathmandu Restaurant.** Given its modest size, Ned has a good selec-
INDIAN | tion of delicious Asian food. This large Indian/Nepali restaurant is busy at all hours. Plenty of vegetarian offerings are available, as are lamb, chicken and seafood entrées. Try one of the *saags*, creamy spinach dishes, to fill your body with warmth on a cold day. When things are warmer, opt for a *lassi*, a refreshing yogurt drink. ✉ *110 N. Jefferson St.* ☎ *303/258–1169* ⊕ *www.nepalidining.com.*

$$ | ✕ **Sundance Café and Lodge.** Locals love this place for its low-key atmo-
CAFÉ | sphere and great, diner-style breakfasts, lunches, and dinners. Try the Robbie Burger, which is topped with bacon and Brie. From both the deck and the inside, you can enjoy the great views of the Indian Peaks to the west, Boulder to the east, and Roosevelt National Forest on all sides. ✉ *23492 Hwy. 119* ☎ *303/258–0804* ⊕ *www.sundance-lodge. com* ⊙ *Daily 8 am–9 pm (close at 2:30 on Tues., early Nov.–early Apr.).*

$$ | ✕ **Wild Mountain Smokehouse and Brewery.** This brewpub has it all: hand-
AMERICAN | crafted beer, delicious food, and a truly spectacular deck. Stop in for some seriously smoky BBQ (like the Ned-E-Que Platter) or a salad topped with maple-glazed salmon. Add a pint of the home brew and soak in the atmosphere, whether you're sitting out on the deck or inside the lodge-style dining room, where there's a fireplace and cathedral ceilings. ✉ *70 E. 1st St.* ☎ *303/258–9453* ⊕ *www.wildmountainsb.com* ⊙ *Mon.–Thurs. 11:30 am–8:30 pm, Fri. and Sat. 11 am–9 pm, Sun. 11 am–8:30 pm.*

$$ | ▣ **Best Western Lodge at Nederland.** Built in 1994 with rough-hewn tim-
HOTEL | ber, this lodge is all modern inside. **Pros:** property has mountain style; quiet; good value for location. **Cons:** Nederland can feel remote unless you're spending a lot of time hiking and skiing; hotel is on a heavily traveled road. ✉ *55 Lakeview Dr., Nederland* ☎ *303/258–9463, 800/279–9463* ⊕ *www.bestwesterncolorado.com* ⇥ *23 rooms, 8 suites* ⌂ *In-room: no a/c, Wi-Fi. In-hotel: parking* ⦿ *Breakfast.*

NIWOT

10 mi northeast of downtown Boulder via CO Hwy. 119.

Niwot is the Arapaho Indian word for "left hand," and this is where Chief Niwot (born circa 1820) and his tribe lived along the banks of

Left Hand Creek until the early 1860s. European settlers arrived in the latter half of the 1800s to take up farming, after gold mining in the mountains became less lucrative. The town's importance grew once the railroad came in the 1870s. These days its most famous business is Crocs footwear, which was started in Niwot in 2004. Antiques aficionados have made Niwot a prime destination in Boulder County. The historic district, full of brick buildings decorated with flower boxes, runs along 2nd Avenue between the cross streets Franklin and Murray.

EN ROUTE

On the way to or from Niwot from Boulder on Highway 119 you pass by the Celestial Seasonings tea factory and the Leanin' Tree Museum of Western Art. Both are worth a visit; plan an extra hour or two if you stop.

Celestial Seasonings. Celestial Seasonings, North America's largest herbal-tea producer (sealing 8 million tea bags every 24 hours), offers free tours of its factory. Before the tour you can sample from more than 60 varieties of tea. The famous "Mint Room" will clear your sinuses. You can also grab a bite to eat at the on-site café. ⊠ *4600 Sleepytime Dr., 8 mi northeast of downtown Boulder. Take Hwy. 119 to Jay Rd., turn right and follow for about 1 mi., then turn left onto Spine Rd. After about ½ mi, turn left onto Sleepytime Dr., Boulder* ☎ *303/581–1202* ⊕ *www.celestialseasonings.com* ⊠ Free ⊗ *Tours hourly; weekdays 10–4, Sat. 10–3, Sun. 11–3.*

Leanin' Tree Museum of Western Art. The Leanin' Tree Museum of Western Art is one of the country's largest privately owned collections of post-1950 cowboy and Western art. More than 250 paintings of Western landscapes, wildlife, and the pioneers' ranch life, and 150 bronze sculptures by renowned, contemporary artists, including Bill Hughes and Frank McCarthy, recall an era in the Boulder Valley before lattes and snowboards. ⊠ *6055 Longbow Dr., about 8 mi northeast of downtown Boulder. From Hwy. 119, take 63rd St. south, then Longbow Dr. west, Boulder* ☎ *303/530–1442* ⊕ *www.leanintreemuseum.com* ⊠ Free ⊗ *Weekdays 8–5, weekends 10–5; closed on major holidays.*

QUICK BITES

The Eye Opener Coffee House. The Eye Opener Coffee House serves delicious coffee drinks, breakfast burritos, and bagels, plus gourmet sandwiches and fresh pastries, muffins, and Danishes. ⊠ *136 2nd Ave.* ☎ *303/652–8137.*

Sachi Sushi. This modest sushi stall, tucked away in the Niwot Market, is known for fresh ingredients and friendly service. But the real treasure here comes on Sunday, when the chef-owner makes a gigantic batch of steaming, flavorful, authentic ramen. Plans may be afoot for an expansion or two, in Boulder and possibly Denver. ⊠ *7980 Niwot Rd.* ☎ *303/652–0919.*

WHERE TO EAT AND STAY
For expanded hotel reviews, visit Fodors.com.

$$$
ITALIAN

✕ **Treppeda's Italian Restaurant.** For lunch, try one of the tasty panini made from authentic ingredients and fresh focaccia at this casual but elegant Italian café. There's shaded outdoor seating, and the cozy terra-cotta-painted dining room has pleasant paintings on the walls. Enjoy a crunchy house-made cannoli and an espresso for dessert at the bar. Dinner features traditional dishes like primavera gnocchi, lemon and garlic shrimp bucatini, and lamb Siciliana, along with some delicious daily specials like roasted white sea bass. Desserts include *tres leches* cake, berry napoleon, and chocolate truffles with fresh strawberries. ✉ *300 2nd Ave.* ☎ *303/652–1606* ⊕ *www.treppedas.com* ☽ *Closed Sun.*

$$ **Niwot Inn and Spa.** This small inn has a cozy, Southwestern feel, right **B&B/INN** down to the hardwood floors and handwoven wool rugs. **Pros:** great Continental breakfast buffet; close to excellent restaurants. **Cons:** somewhat noisy neighborhood; drive to Boulder can be horribly congested. ✉ *342 2nd Ave.* ⊕ *Box 1044, 80544* ☎ *303/652–8452* ⊕ *www. niwotinn.com* ⟿ *14 rooms* ⚲ *In-room: a/c, Wi-Fi. In-hotel: parking* ⫿ *Breakfast.*

SHOPPING

Antiques dealers and a few shops selling vintage women's clothing and quilts are in the Niwot historic district along 2nd Avenue. Just ¼ mi east of old-town Niwot is Cottonwood Square, with a grocer, a gas station, a handful of gift shops, and a few eateries.

Elysian Fields. Elysian Fields is an antiques auction house that holds a country estate auction the second Sunday of most months. ✉ *6924 79th St.* ☎ *303/652–2587.*

Wise Buys Antiques. Wise Buys Antiques sells and repairs antique furniture, including fireplace mantels—some with mirrors. It usually has more than a hundred in stock. ✉ *190 2nd Ave.* ☎ *303/652–2888.*

LYONS

14 mi north of Boulder.

Lyons is a peaceful, down-to-earth community of 1,600 residents that's just inside the red-sandstone foothills at the confluence of the North St. Vrain and South St. Vrain creeks. Founded in 1881, it's crammed with historic buildings—there are 15 structures listed in the National Register of Historic Places—and the whole downtown area feels like a turn-of-the-century frontier outpost. The cafés, restaurants, art galleries, and antiques stores attract lots of visitors, who also come for the recreation opportunities and top-notch music festivals.

GETTING HERE AND AROUND

To drive to Lyons from Boulder, travel north on U.S. 36.

WHEN TO GO

FESTIVALS The summer outdoor music season kicks off with **Lyons Good Old Days** at the end of June, and goes into September with midweek concerts in Sandstone Park (at 4th and Railroad avenues). Cafés and restaurants host bands regularly. Check the Chamber of Commerce Web site for event schedules.

Planet Bluegrass. Planet Bluegrass presents artists such as Jackson Browne, Susan Tedeschi, Patty Griffin, and Warren Haynes at the three bluegrass festivals it holds in Lyons: RockyGrass, at the end of July; the Folks Festival in August; and the Festival of the Mabon (autumnal equinox) in September. (Its biggest and most prestigious festival is the Telluride Bluegrass Festival, held each June in southwestern Colorado, an eight-hour drive from Lyons.) ☎ *303/823–0848, 800/624–2422* ⊕ *www.bluegrass.com.*

ESSENTIALS

Visitor Information Lyons Chamber of Commerce ✉ *Box 426, 80540* ☎ *303/823–5215, 877/596–6726* ⊕ *www.lyons-colorado.com.*

EXPLORING

Lyons Classic Pinball. You wouldn't expect such a pinball extravaganza in tiny Lyons, but there it is, behind the Oskar brewpub, with more than 40 classic pinball games. Elvira, the Rolling Stones, Elvis, and the Simpsons—they're all there. And the change machines (and fellow gamers) make it a simple and fun stop. ✉ *339-A Main St.* ☎ *303/823–6100* ⊕ *www.lyonspinball.com.*

SPORTS AND THE OUTDOORS
BIRD-WATCHING

Bohn Park. Ornithologists gather at Bohn Park at sunrise and sunset to spot some of the many species of songbirds that reside along St. Vrain Creek. Golden eagles have been sighted in the red cliffs on the southwest side of town. Lazuli buntings inhabit the foliage along both the Old St. Vrain Road southwest of town and Apple Valley Road northwest of town. ✉ *From northbound U.S. 36, turn left onto Park St. and then left onto 2nd St.*

HIKING AND MOUNTAIN BIKING

★ **Hall Ranch.** More than 12 mi of trails at Hall Ranch are open to hikers, mountain bikers, and equestrians. The **Bitterbrush Trail/Nelson Loop** follows the Bitterbrush Trail for 3.7 mi and has a 680-foot elevation gain, crossing meadows and ascending and descending through stands of pine trees and rock outcroppings. It connects to the 2.2-mi Nelson Loop, which leads to the original Nelson Ranch House. The slight 400-foot elevation gain of the Nelson Loop brings you up onto a plateau that provides great views of the mountains to the north. Allow five to six hours to hike the trail, less for biking it. ✉ *0.75 mi west of Lyons on Hwy. 7* ⊕ *www.co.boulder.co.us/openspace.*

Rabbit Mountain. Rabbit Mountain has several lengthy but easy trails that afford views of the High Rockies and the plains. Be sure to pick up the interpretive pamphlet at the trailhead that explains the history of the area, including the dramatic metamorphosis of Rabbit Mountain from a lush, tropical swamp inhabited by dinosaurs to the present-day, mile-high desert that's home to raptors, prairie dogs, coyotes, and the occasional rattlesnake. The 2-mi round-trip **Little Thompson Overlook Trail** forks off to the left before you come to the gravel road and climbs a mere 500 feet to the point where you can see Longs Peak, the plains to the east, and Boulder Valley to the south. The 5-mi **Eagle Wind Trail** loop has short spurs to viewpoints. From the parking area, head out on the trail to the gravel road and then right onto the single-track loop. ✉ *2 mi east of Lyons* ⊕ *www.co.boulder.co.us/openspace.*

WHERE TO EAT

$$$
AMERICAN

✕**Lyons Fork.** Locals call it "the Fork," and this upscale-for-Lyons spot is known for its beer-friendly menu and delicate cooking. If the weather permits, sit on the cozy back patio, decorated with mismatched furniture and twinkle lights, though don't expect snappy service. Sit back, relax, and take in the view. Perhaps most noteworthy: the restaurant makes its own sour mix, and as a result the margaritas are nothing short of spectacular. ✉ *450 Main St.* ☎ *303/823–5014* ⊕ *www.lyonsfork.com.*

$
AMERICAN

✕**Oskar Blues Cajun Grill & Brewery.** The first U.S. microbrewery to put its beer into cans, and now the largest-producing brewpub in America, Oskar Blues has become Lyons's hot spot for beer as well as music and pub grub. Try Dale's Pale Ale—it's not as hoppy as most American ales—or any of the other robust beers brewed in small (20-barrel) batches. The burgers are consistently awesome, and come in interesting varieties, including a spicy Creole number, plus three named in honor of music legends—Elvis, B.B. King, and Satchmo. Blues instruments and covers of blues CDs decorate the restaurant. In the basement, a "juke joint" frequently hosts live music, and there's a bluegrass jam every Tuesday night. Free tours of the brewery are offered Monday–Thursday at 4 pm and Friday–Sunday at 2, 3, 4, and 5 pm. ✉ *303 Main St.* ☎ *303/823–6685* ⊕ *www.oskarblues.com.*

ESTES PARK

40 mi northwest of Boulder via U.S. 36 (28th St. in Boulder).

The scenery on the U.S. 36 approach to Estes Park gives little hint of the grandeur to come, but if ever there was a classic picture-postcard Rockies view, Estes Park has it. The town sits at an altitude of more than 7,500 feet, in front of a stunning backdrop of 14,255-foot Longs Peak and surrounding mountains. The town itself is family-oriented and a little kitschy, with lots of stores selling Western-theme trinkets, sweets, and regional toys for the kids. Many of the small businesses and hotels lining the roads are mom-and-pop outfits that have been passed down through several generations. Estes Park is also the most popular gateway to Rocky Mountain National Park (RMNP), which is a few miles down the road.

GETTING HERE AND AROUND

To get to Estes Park from Boulder, take U.S. 36 north through Lyons and the town of Pinewood Springs (about 38 mi). You also can reach Estes Park via the incredibly scenic Peak-to-Peak Scenic and Historic Byway. To reach the byway from Boulder, take Highway 119 west to Nederland and turn right (north) onto Highway 72, or follow Sunshine Canyon Drive/Gold Hill Road into Ward, and pick up Highway 72 there.

Estes Park's main downtown area is walkable, which is good news on summer weekends, when traffic can be heavy (and parking can be challenging). Keep an eye out for parking signs throughout town, as they're your best chance at a close-in spot.

The National Park Service operates a free bus service in and around Estes Park and between Estes Park and Rocky Mountain National Park.

Buses operate daily from early June to Labor Day, then on weekends until the end of September.

ESSENTIALS

Transportation Contacts NPS Shuttle Buses ⊕ *www.nps.gov/romo/ planyourvisit/shuttle_bus_route.htm.*

Visitor Information Estes Park Convention and Visitors Bureau ✉ *500 Big Thompson Ave.* ⬠ *Box 1200, 80517* ☎ *970/577–9900, 800/443–7837* ⊕ *www. estesparkcvb.com.*

EXPLORING

On its road to be becoming a resort town, Estes attracted the attention of genius entrepreneur F.O. Stanley, inventor of the Stanley Steamer automobile and several photographic processes. In 1905, having been told by his doctors he would soon die of tuberculosis, he constructed the regal **Stanley Hotel** on a promontory overlooking the town. Stanley went on to live another 30-odd years, an extension that he attributed to the area's fresh air. The hotel soon became one of the most glamorous resorts in the Rockies, a reputation it holds to this day. The hotel was the inspiration for Stephen King's horror novel *The Shining*, part of which he wrote while staying here. (No scenes in the 1980 Stanley Kubrick movie, however, were filmed here.)

Estes Park Area Historical Museum. Archaeological evidence displayed at the Estes Park Area Historical Museum makes an eloquent case that Native Americans used the area as a summer resort. The museum also has an assortment of pioneer artifacts, displays on the founding of Rocky Mountain National Park, and changing exhibits. The museum publishes a self-guided walking tour of historic sites, mostly along Elkhorn Avenue downtown. ✉ *200 4th St.* ☎ *970/586–6256* ⊕ *www. estesnet.com/Museum* 🎟 *Free* ⊙ *May–Oct., Mon.–Sat. 10–5, Sun. 1–5; Nov.–Apr., Fri. and Sat. 10–5, Sun. 1–5.*

MacGregor Ranch Museum. The MacGregor Ranch Museum, on the National Register of Historic Places and a working ranch, offers views of the Twin Owls and Longs Peak (towering more than 14,000 feet). Although the ranch was homesteaded in 1873, the present house was built in 1896; it provides a well-preserved record of typical ranch life. ✉ *MacGregor Ave. off U.S. 34* ☎ *970/586–3749* ⊕ *www.macgregorranch.org* 🎟 *$3* ⊙ *June–Aug., Tues.–Sat. 10–4.*

SPORTS AND THE OUTDOORS

Rocky Mountain National Park, 4 mi from Estes Park, is ideal for hiking, fishing, wildlife-viewing, rock climbing, snowshoeing, and cross-country skiing. *See the Rocky Mountain National Park section in this book.*

FISHING

The Big Thompson River, which runs east of Estes Park along U.S. 34, is popular for its good stock of rainbow and brown trout. See ⊕ *www. wildlife.state.co.us/fishing* for more information on fishing licenses.

Rocky Mountain Adventures. Rocky Mountain Adventures offers guided fly-fishing trips on the Big Thompson and in Rocky Mountain National Park from its Estes Park office. ✉ *358 E. Elkhorn Ave.* ☎ *970/586–6191, 800/858–6808* ⊕ *www.shoprma.com.*

HORSEBACK RIDING

Sombrero Ranches. Sombrero Ranches has several stables in the Estes Park region, including Rocky Mountain National Park. They offer both guided and unguided trail rides (from one to eight hours long), plus overnight camping trips, breakfast rides, and steak dinner rides. ☎ *970/586–4577* ⊕ *www.sombrero.com.*

RAFTING AND KAYAKING

White-water rafting trips fill up fast, so it's a good idea to book with an outfitter a couple of weeks in advance. Early-season trips in May catch the biggest runoff and the wilder rides, while late-season excursions (in August) will be tamer.

OUTFITTERS **Rapid Transit Rafting.** Rapid Transit Rafting arranges guided rafting trips on the Colorado and Cache la Poudre rivers. ☎ *970/577–7238, 800/367–8523* ⊕ *www.rapidtransitrafting.com.*

Rocky Mountain Adventures. Rocky Mountain Adventures provides half- and full-day kayaking-instruction trips for all levels. All gear is included. ☎ *970/493–4005, 800/858–6808* ⊕ *www.shoprma.com.*

WHERE TO EAT

$$ ✕ **Bighorn Restaurant.** An Estes Park staple since 1972, this family-run
AMERICAN outfit is where the locals go for breakfast. Since it opens as early as 6 am,
★ you can get a double-cheese omelet, huevos rancheros, or grits before heading into the park. Owners Laura and Sid Brown are happy to pack up a lunch for you—just place your order along with breakfast, and your sandwich, chips, homemade cookie, and drink will be ready to go when you leave. This homey spot also serves lunch and dinner. ✉ *401 W. Elkhorn Ave.* ☎ *970/586–2792* ⊕ *www.estesparkbighorn.com.*

$$ ✕ **Ed's Cantina and Grill.** The fajitas and well-stocked bar make this lively
MEXICAN Mexican restaurant popular with locals and visitors alike. The decor is bright, with light woods and large windows. Try to get patio seating by the river. If you're hungry, try one of the enchilada platters (including mahimahi, chicken *mole,* and vegetarian); the authentic pork tamales, smothered in green or red chile sauce; or the *carne asada.* Breakfast is also good here (it's served until 11 am on weekends), with both Mexican and all-American options. ✉ *390 E. Elkhorn Ave.* ☎ *970/586–2919* ⊕ *www.edscantina.com.*

$$ ✕ **Estes Park Brewery.** If you're not sure which beer suits you or would go
AMERICAN with your meal, head downstairs to the tasting area to sample a couple of brews. There are eight beers and four seasonals on tap. The Staggering Elk, a crisp lager, and the Estes Park Gold ale come highly recommended. The food is no-frills (beer chili is the specialty here), and the menu includes pizza, burgers, sandwiches, and chicken or steak dinners. ✉ *470 Prospect Village Dr.* ☎ *970/586–5421* ⊕ *www.epbrewery.com.*

$$$ ✕ **Hunter's Chophouse.** This popular steak house fills quickly in the eve-
STEAKHOUSE ning, and for good reason. The locals head here for the savory and spicy

barbecue: steaks, venison, buffalo, chicken, and seafood. If you're not hungry enough for 12 ounces of beef (or buffalo), Hunter's has special burgers, like the avocado bacon burger, and a long list of sandwiches, including a traditional French dip and a grilled salmon fillet on focaccia. There's a good kids' menu, too, with fish-and-chips, a junior sirloin, and a mini burger. ⊠ *1690 Big Thompson Ave.* ☎ *970/586–6962* ⊕ *www. hunterschophouse.com* ⌂ *Reservations essential.*

$$ ✕**Mama Rose's.** An Estes institution, Mama Rose's serves consistently
ITALIAN good family-style Italian meals. The lasagna with sliced meatballs and sausage and the tricolor baked pasta are popular entrées, and the wine cellar has a good selection. The spacious Victorian dining room with plenty of fine art harks back to earlier eras in Estes Park, minus the formal dress code. In warm weather there's a patio along the Big Thompson River. ⊠ *338 E. Elkhorn Ave.* ☎ *970/586–3330* ⊕ *www. mamarosesrestaurant.com* ⊘ *No lunch.*

$ ✕**Poppy's Pizza & Grill.** This casual riverside eatery serves the classics,
PIZZA plus creative signature pizzas. Try the spinach, artichoke, and feta pie made with sun-dried tomato pesto or one made with smoked trout, capers, and cream cheese. You can also create your own pie from the five sauces and 40 toppings on the menu. They also sell sandwiches, wraps, salads, and burgers. Poppy's has patio seating at the river and an extensive selection of wine and beer. ⊠ *342 E. Elkhorn Ave.* ☎ *970/586– 8282* ⊕ *www.poppyspizzaandgrill.com* ⊘ *Closed Jan., plus Thanksgiving, Christmas, and Easter.*

WHERE TO STAY

For expanded hotel reviews, visit Fodors.com.

$$$ ⊞ **Boulder Brook.** Luxury suites at this secluded spot on the river are
HOTEL tucked into the pines, yet close to town and 1½ mi from Rocky Mountain National Park. **Pros:** scenic location; quiet area; attractive grounds. **Cons:** not within walking distance of attractions; no nearby dining. ⊠ *1900 Fall River Rd.* ☎ *970/586–0910, 800/238–0910* ⊕ *www. boulderbrook.com* ⇔ *19 suites* ⌂ *In-room: no a/c, kitchen. In-hotel: parking* ▮◯▮ *No meals.*

$ ⊞ **Estes Park Center/YMCA of the Rockies.** This 890-acre family-friendly
RESORT property has a wealth of attractive and clean lodging options among
⟲ its five lodges and 11 cabins. **Pros:** good value for large groups and for longer stays; lots of family-oriented activities and amenities; stunningly scenic setting. **Cons:** very large, busy, and crowded property; fills fast; location requires vehicle to visit town or the national park. ⊠ *2515 Tunnel Rd.* ☎ *970/586–3341, 303/448–1616, 800/777–9622* ⊕ *www. ymcarockies.org* ⇔ *688 rooms, 220 cabins* ⌂ *In-room: no a/c, no TV. In-hotel: restaurant, pool, tennis court, children's programs, parking* ▮◯▮ *Some meals.*

$ ⊞ **Glacier Lodge.** Families are the specialty at this secluded, 19-acre guest
RESORT resort on the banks of the Big Thompson River. **Pros:** great place for
⟲ families; attractive grounds on the river; on free bus route. **Cons:** not within walking distance of attractions; along rather busy road. ⊠ *2166 Hwy. 66* ⌂ *Box 2656, 80517* ☎ *970/586–4401, 800/523–3920* ⊕ *www.*

7

glacierlodge.com ⇙ 24 *single-family cabins, 4 cabins for 12–30* ⚭ *In-room: no a/c, kitchen. In-hotel: pool, children's programs, parking.*

$$$ ⊡ **Mary's Lake Lodge and Resort.** This 1913 chalet-style lodge overlooks
HOTEL   peaceful Mary's Lake, a couple of miles south of town. **Pros:** two excellent on-site restaurants; beautiful views. **Cons:** not within walking distance of attractions or other dining; large, older hotel. ✉ *2625 Mary's Lake Rd.* ☎ *970/586–5958, 877/442–6279* ⊕ *www.maryslakelodge. com* ⇙ *16 rooms, 54 condos* ⚭ *In-room: a/c, Wi-Fi. In-hotel: restaurant, pool, spa, parking* ¶⊙¶ *Breakfast.*

$ ⊡ **Riverview Pines.** Do some fishing or just sit and read on the expansive
HOTEL   lawn at this peaceful hotel, the least expensive along the beautiful Fall River Road between Estes and Rocky Mountain National Park. **Pros:** friendly and helpful owner-managers; quiet and scenic location on river; low rates for the area. **Cons:** very basic rooms without much decoration; on a busy road. ✉ *1150 W. Elkhorn Ave.* ⌖ *Box 690, 80517* ☎ *970/586–3627, 800/340–5764* ⊕ *www.riverviewpines.com* ⇙ *18 rooms, 8 cabins* ⚭ *In-room: no a/c, kitchen. In-hotel: laundry facilities, parking* ☾ *Closed mid-Oct.–May* ¶⊙¶ *No meals.*

$ ⊡ **Saddle & Surrey Motel.** Friendly owners manage this comfortable and
HOTEL   quiet 1950s-style motel that is close to town and outdoor activities. **Pros:** good value; on shuttle-bus route; quiet area at night. **Cons:** not within walking distance of attractions or downtown dining. ✉ *1341 S. St. Vrain Ave.* ⌖ *Box 591, 80517* ☎ *970/586–3326, 800/204–6226* ⊕ *www.saddleandsurrey.com* ⇙ *26 rooms* ⚭ *In-room: Wi-Fi. In-hotel: pool, parking* ¶⊙¶ *Breakfast.*

$$ ⊡ **Stanley Hotel.** Perched regally on a hill, with a commanding view of
HOTEL   the town, the Stanley is one of Colorado's great old hotels, impeccably
★   maintained in its historic state, yet with all the modern conveniences. **Pros:** historic hotel; many rooms have been updated recently; good restaurant. **Cons:** some rooms are small and tight; building is old; no air-conditioning. ✉ *333 Wonderview Ave.* ☎ *970/577–4000, 800/976–1377* ⊕ *www.stanleyhotel.com* ⇙ *127 rooms, 13 suites* ⚭ *In-room: no a/c, no TV, Wi-Fi. In-hotel: restaurant, bar, pool, spa, parking* ¶⊙¶ *No meals.*

$$ ⊡ **Taharaa Mountain Lodge.** Every room at this luxury B&B has access to
B&B/INN   the wraparound deck and its views of the High Rockies and Estes Valley. **Pros:** beautiful mountain views; friendly hosts. **Cons:** not within walking distance of attractions; not on bus route; no young children allowed; two-day minimum stay (three-day minimum for summer and holidays). ✉ *3110 S. St. Vrain Ave.* ⌖ *Box 2586, 80517* ⊹ *4 mi south of downtown Estes Park* ☎ *970/577–0098, 800/597–0098* ⊕ *www.taharaa.com* ⇙ *9 rooms, 9 suites* ⚭ *In-room: a/c, Wi-Fi. In-hotel: gym, spa, parking, some age restrictions* ¶⊙¶ *Breakfast.*

NIGHTLIFE AND THE ARTS

THE ARTS

Cultural Arts Council of Estes Park. Visit up to 20 galleries and artists' studios on the self-guided **Summer Art Walk** daily from mid-June through Labor Day—or take the same route in the **Autumn Art Walk,** which goes from mid-September to late November. Maps and information are available at Cultural Arts Council of Estes Park. The Council also operates a fine art gallery and hosts other art walks, studio tours, art shows, concerts, and film events throughout the year. ☒ *423 W. Elkhorn Ave.* ☎ *970/586–9203* ⊕ *www.estesarts.com.*

Estes Park Music Festival. The Estes Park Music Festival stages concerts at 2 pm on Sunday afternoons from November through April at the Stanley Hotel. ☎ *970/586–9519* ⊕ *www.estesparkmusicalfestival.org.*

ESTES PARK LODGING ALTERNATIVES

Range Property Management. Range Property Management rents fully equipped houses, condos, and cabins in the Estes Park area. Pets are not allowed. ☋ *342 W. Riverside Dr., Box 316, 80517* ☎ *970/586-7626, 888/433–5211* ⊕ www.rangeprop.com ⮌ 25 condos, 45 homes ▭ No credit cards.

Rocky Ridge Music Center. Relax with some chamber music while taking in views of the mountains at the Rocky Ridge Music Center. The faculty hold their own classical chamber music concerts June through August. ☒ *465 Longs Peak Rd., 9 mi south of Estes Park off Hwy. 7 at the turnoff to Longs Peak Campground* ☎ *970/586–4031* ⊕ *www. rockyridge.org.*

NIGHTLIFE

Lonigans Saloon. Blues and rock bands play regularly at Lonigans Saloon, and there are open mike nights on Tuesday and karaoke on Monday, Wednesday, Friday, and Saturday. ☒ *110 W. Elkhorn Ave.* ☎ *970/586–4346* ⊕ *www.lonigans.com.*

The Tavern. The Tavern has live music, ranging from bluegrass to funk, every night. ☒ *Mary's Lake Lodge, 2625 Mary's Lake Rd.* ☎ *970/586–5958* ⊕ *www.maryslakelodge.com.*

Wheel Bar. The venerable Wheel Bar is one of the better watering holes in town. ☒ *132 E. Elkhorn Ave.* ☎ *970/586–9381* ⊕ *www.thewheelbar. com.*

SHOPPING

Shopping in Estes Park includes several T-shirt and souvenir shops, plus a number of more upscale gift shops and galleries.

CRAFTS AND ART GALLERIES

Earthwood Artisans. The cooperative Earthwood Artisans features the work of jewelers, sculptors, wood-carvers, and potters. ☒ *360 E. Elkhorn Ave.* ☎ *970/586–2151* ⊕ *www.earthwoodartisans.com.*

Earthwood Collections. Earthwood Collections is a cooperative that sells a wide assortment of art, including ceramics and photography. ☒ *141 E. Elkhorn Ave.* ☎ *970/577–8100* ⊕ *www.earthwoodartisans.com.*

Estes Park Glassworks. Estes Park Glassworks offers glassblowing demonstrations and sells a rainbow of glass creations. ☒ *323 Elkhorn Ave.* ☎ *970/586–8619* ⊕ *www.epglassworks.com.*

Images of Rocky Mountain National Park. Images of Rocky Mountain National Park showcases photographer Erik Stensland's stunning images of the park. This is a must-see collection of local photography. ⊠ *203 Park La.* ☎ *970/372–5212* ⊕ *www.imagesofrmnp.com.*

Wild Spirits Gallery, Ltd. Wild Spirits Gallery, Ltd. carries open and limited-edition prints, both photographs and paintings or drawings, of the Southwest and Rocky Mountain National Park. ⊠ *148 W. Elkhorn Ave.* ☎ *970/586–4392* ⊕ *www.wildspiritsgallery.com.*

GIFTS

Thirty Below Leather. Head to Thirty Below Leather for leather travel gear, handbags, wallets, and accessories, all priced under $30. ⊠ *356 E. Elkhorn Ave.* ☎ *970/586–2211* ⊕ *www.thirtybelowleather.com* ⊙ *Closed Sun.*

Rocky Mountain Chocolate Factory and Malt Shop. Rocky Mountain Chocolate Factory and Malt Shop sells fudge, truffles, and fantastic caramel apples, plus traditional malts and shakes. Estes in general is a paradise for sweets and candies, but this storefront stands out for its way with caramel, chocolate, and nuts. ⊠ *517 Big Thompson Ave.* ☎ *970/586–6601* ⊕ *www.rmcf.com.*

WESTERN PARAPHERNALIA

Rustic Mountain Charm. Rustic Mountain Charm sells clothing, local foodstuffs, and home accessories with the lodge look, including furniture, quilts, baskets, and throws. ⊠ *135 E. Elkhorn Ave.* ☎ *970/586–4344* ⊕ *www.rusticmountaincharm.net.*

The Twisted Pine Fur and Leather Company. The Twisted Pine Fur and Leather Company carries certified Native American–made weavings and traditional leather or fur Western clothing, as well as housewares, rugs, and jewelry. ⊠ *450 Moraine Ave.* ☎ *970/586–4539, 800/896–8086* ⊕ *www.thetwistedpine.com.*

GRAND COUNTY

Grand County combines high country and rolling ranchlands. Vistas of the Rockies to the east and south and of the Gore Range to the west frame these grasslands, which the early French explorers named Middle Park. By the time the Moffat Railroad came to Grand County in 1905, ranchers were already living on the flat, open meadows.

Although Grand County is ranching country, the word "range" today evokes more the excellent golf courses instead of the plains where cowboys herd cattle. The town of Granby has two golf courses, and Grand County hosts several annual tournaments. Golfers aren't the only sportspeople in town: summer brings droves of anglers and bicyclists, and large-game hunters replace them in the late fall. The area west of Granby along U.S. 40 is marked by a number of small towns with resorts and guest ranches.

Base Camp: Estes Park or Grand Lake?

Many more people stay in **Estes Park** rather than Grand Lake because it's closer to the cities of the Front Range—but the traffic, particularly on summer weekends, reflects that. Expect parking in downtown Estes Park to be difficult, and count on delays while driving through town. There are also more options for lodging and meals here than in Grand Lake. A hotel room averages $150 per night, and a burger will run you about $8. The Safeway in Stanley Village at the intersection of U.S. 34 (Big Thompson Avenue) and U.S. 36 (St. Vrain Avenue) is the best place to pick up insect repellent, sunscreen, and water and snacks (including deli sandwiches) for hiking.

Grand Lake is a smaller resort than Estes Park. Getting around in a car is easier, and parking is rarely a problem. It's also a bit closer—only 2 mi—from Grand Lake village to the RMNP entrance. The outdoor activities here are more diverse than in Estes Park; the list includes water sports on Grand Lake, mountain biking, and snowmobiling. Grand Lake village is also close to skiing and ice-fishing, and hiking in the Indian Peaks Wilderness and the Arapaho National Recreation Area. A hotel room averages about $110 per night, and a burger costs around $8. The Mountain Food Market at 400 Grand Avenue is a handy spot to stock up on supplies before entering the park.

GRAND LAKE

1½ mi west of Rocky Mountain National Park via U.S. 34.

The tiny town of Grand Lake, known to locals as Grand Lake Village, is doubly blessed by its surroundings. It's the western gateway to Rocky Mountain National Park and also sits on the shores of its namesake, the state's largest natural lake and the highest-altitude yacht anchorage in America. With views of snowy peaks and verdant mountains from any vantage point, Grand Lake Village is favored by Coloradans for sailing, canoeing, waterskiing, and fishing. In winter it's *the* snowmobiling and ice-fishing destination. Even with its wooden boardwalks, Old West–style storefronts, and usual assortment of souvenir shops and motels, Grand Lake seems less spoiled than many other resort towns.

GETTING HERE AND AROUND

Grand Lake is about 60 mi from Boulder or 96 mi from Denver, as the crow flies, but to get there by car you've got to circle around the mountains and travel more than 100 mi from Boulder and 171 mi from Denver. You've got two options: Take the highway the whole way (U.S. 36, CO Highway 93, I–70, U.S. 40, and U.S. 34) or take the scenic route (U.S 36 north to Estes Park, then U.S. 34 across Rocky Mountain National Park). The section of U.S. 34 that passes through RMNP, known as Trail Ridge Road, is the highest paved road in America. Trail Ridge Road closes every winter, typically between mid-October and late May.

When you get there, you can explore most of the town on foot, including the historic boardwalk on Grand Avenue, with more than 60

7

shops and restaurants. Happily, Grand Lake doesn't get the hordes of tourists that can descend on Estes Park, meaning traffic and parking aren't a problem.

ESSENTIALS

Visitor Information **Grand Lake Chamber of Commerce Visitor Center** ⊠ *West Portal Rd. and U.S. 34, at the western entrance of Rocky Mountain National Park* ☎ *970/627–3402, 800/531–1019* ⊕ *www.grandlakechamber.com.*

EXPLORING

★ **Grand Lake.** According to Ute legend, the fine mists that shroud Grand Lake at dawn are the risen spirits of the women and children whose raft capsized as they were fleeing a marauding party of Cheyennes and Arapahoes. Grand Lake feeds into two much larger man-made reservoirs, Lake Granby and Shadow Mountain Lake, which together form the "Great Lakes of Colorado."

SPORTS AND THE OUTDOORS

Rocky Mountain National Park, 2 mi from Grand Lake Village, is ideal for hiking, fishing, wildlife-viewing, rock climbing, snowshoeing, and cross-country skiing. *See the Rocky Mountain National Park section in this book.*

BICYCLING

One of the best bike rides in the state starts just down the road from Grand Lake, in Granby.

Willow Creek Pass. The Willow Creek Pass route covers about 25 mi (round-trip) of rolling terrain and climbs 1,770 feet to the summit of one of the gentler passes on the Continental Divide. This ride takes you through quiet aspen and pine forests where you'll encounter little traffic (but perhaps some moose and deer, which are often spotted just off the road). ⊠ *The route starts on U.S. 40 in Granby and goes north to Hwy. 125 to County Rd. 21, then turns around and goes back the same way.*

BIRD-WATCHING

The islands in Shadow Mountain Reservoir and Lake Granby are wildlife refuges that attract osprey and many other migrating birds. The best way to get close to them is by canoe or foot trail. Be sure to take binoculars, because you're not permitted to land on the islands.

East Shore Trail. East Shore Trail and Knight Ridge Trail will take you along the shores of Shadow Mountain Reservoir and Lake Granby for good bird-spotting opportunities. Shadow Mountain Lake lies within the Arapaho National Recreation Area, and is maintained through the Sulphur Ranger District in Granby; contact them for more information: 970/887–4100. ⊠ *Access trails either from Grand Lake Village between Grand Lake and Shadow Mountain Reservoir, or from Green Ridge Campground at south end of Shadow Mountain Reservoir.*

BOATING AND FISHING

There's plenty of water to share here. Anglers enjoy plentiful catches of rainbow trout, mackinaw (lake trout), and kokanee salmon; recreational sailors and water-skiers ply acres of water; and paddlers still get to canoe in peace. Ice fishers will not want to miss the big contest held the first weekend in January on Lake Granby. Contestants must catch five different species of fish, and winners collect from the booty of $20,000 in cash and prizes. See ⊕ *www.wildlife.state.co.us/fishing* for information on fishing licenses.

OUTFITTERS **Beacon Landing Marina.** Beacon Landing Marina rents 20-, 24-, and 25-foot pontoon boats and fishing equipment, including ice augers and ice rods. ✉ *1026 County Rd 64, drive south 5 mi on U.S. 34 to County Rd. 64, turn left and go 1 mi* ☎ *970/627–3671* ⊕ *www.beaconlanding.us.*

Trail Ridge Marina. Visit the Trail Ridge Marina on the western shore of Shadow Mountain Lake to rent a Sea-Doo or motor boat for two to six hours. ✉ *12634 U.S. 34, 2 mi south of Grand Lake on U.S. 34* ☎ *970/627–3586* ⊕ *www.trailridgemarina.com.*

HIKING

A hike here can be a destination in itself: generally speaking, the trails on this side of the Continental Divide are longer than those on the Western Slope, meaning you'll trek farther and higher than you might have expected to your destination. Many trails take you 5 mi one-way before you reach a lake or peak. If you hike in the backcountry, be sure you're outfitted for adverse weather. The *National Geographic Trails Illustrated Map No. 503* (Winter Park/Grand Lake) has excellent coverage of hiking and bicycling trails in the area, with information about regulations.

For those who'd rather not venture quite so far, there are many shorter hikes in and around Grand Lake, all of which offer gorgeous scenery and wonderful relaxation, as the trails here tend to have fewer hikers on them than those near Estes Park.

Indian Peaks Wilderness Area. At the southeast end of Lake Granby, the Indian Peaks Wilderness Area, located within the Arapaho National Recreation Area, is great for hiking. The area around Monarch Lake is popular with families for the selection of trails and the views of the Indian Peaks and the Continental Divide. Trails range in distance from 1.5 to 10.8 mi one-way. The easy **Monarch Lake Loop** is 3.8 mi and a mere 110 feet in elevation gain. You can get a day pass ($5) from the staff or at the self-serve pay station. ✉ *Take U.S. 34 south to County Rd. 6. Follow the lakeshore road about 10 mi* ☎ *970/887–4100* ⊕ *www.fs.fed.us/r2/arnf/recreation/trails/srd/monarchlake/shtml.*

HORSEBACK RIDING

Sombrero Ranches. Sombrero's Grand Lake stables offers guided rides into the wilderness and national park, including scenic and relaxing early-morning breakfast rides, evening rides (including cowboy-style steak and beans for dinner), and "drop camps," in which they'll bring you and your gear into the backcountry via horseback, then bring the horses back and get you a day or two later. Guided horseback-riding trips last two hours, four hours, or all day. ✉ *304 W. Portal Rd.* ☎ *970/627–3514* ⊕ *www.sombrero.com* 🖃 *$50–$120 for guided rides, $200 per horse for drop camps* ☉ *Mid-May–mid-Sept.*

7

NORDIC SKIING AND SNOWSHOEING

Grand Lake Metropolitan Recreation District. When snow glitters under the clear blue sky, it's time to strap on skis or snowshoes and hit the trails in Rocky Mountain National Park, the Arapaho National Recreation Area, and the Indian Peaks Wilderness Area. You also can stay in town: the Grand Lake Metropolitan Recreation District has nearly 22 mi (35 km) of cross-country ski trails with views of the Never Summer Range and the Continental Divide. Come springtime, 15 mi of hiking and biking trails open up. ⊠ *1415 County Rd. 48* ⌂ *Box 590, 80447* ☎ *970/627–8872* ⊕ *www.grandlakerecreation.com.*

Never Summer Mountain Products. Never Summer Mountain Products rents cross-country skis, backcountry skis and snowshoes, plus packs and camping equipment. ⊠ *919 Grand Ave.* ☎ *970/627–3642.*

SNOWMOBILING

Many consider Grand Lake to be Colorado's snowmobiling capital, with more than 300 mi of trails (150 mi groomed), many winding through virgin forest. There are several rental and guide companies in the area. If you're visiting during the winter holidays, it's wise to make reservations about three weeks ahead.

Grand Adventures LLC. Grand Adventures LLC offers guided tours and arranges unguided rentals. The cost ranges from $75 for one hour to $195 for four hours. ⊠ *304 W. Portal Rd.* ☎ *970/726–9247, 800/726–9247* ⊕ *www.grandadventures.com.*

On The Trail Rentals. On The Trail Rentals rents snowmobiles and organizes unguided trips into Arapaho National Forest. Prices range from $90 for two hours on a smaller machine to $220 for eight hours on a larger model. ⊠ *1447 County Rd. 491* ☎ *970/627–0171, 888/627–2429* ⊕ *www.onthetrailrentals.com.*

WHERE TO EAT

$
CAFÉ
Fodor's Choice
★
✕ **Fat Cat Cafe.** Located right on the boardwalk, this small one-room breakfast and lunch spot serves delicious food at very reasonable prices. The $12 weekend breakfast buffet is downright amazing, with close to 50 items at a time—everything from biscuits and gravy to scones and Scotch eggs to Mexican-style omelets with beans and green chile. If you have to wait for a table (which you might on a summer Sunday), they offer coffee and cinnamon rolls to tide you over. ⊠ *916 Grand Ave.* ☎ *970/627–0900* ☉ *Open Mon. and Wed.–Fri. 7–2, weekends 7–1, closed Tues.*

$
AMERICAN
✕ **Grand Lake Brewing Company.** A handcrafted beer and a bratwurst with the works or a pulled chicken sandwich will hit the spot at this rustic brewpub outfitted with a tin ceiling and wooden bar with brass rails. Eat at the bar or at a table in the small but sunny dining area; the food is standard pub fare, inexpensive if uninspired. The beer's the real draw here. For example, the crisp and light White Cap Wheat is an unfiltered brew that tastes best with a slice of orange or lemon, while the Plaid Bastard, a rich Scotch ale served in a brandy snifter to highlight its deep aromas and flavors, really packs a punch (it's 8% alcohol). Can't decide? Try a flight—4 oz of each of the nine available beers—then take home a 64-oz growler as a memento of your visit. There's

also a second location, at 9921 U.S. Highway 34. ✉*915 Grand Ave.* ☎*970/627–1711* ⊕*www. grandlakebrewing.com.*

$$ ✕**Sagebrush BBQ & Grill.** Falling-off-
SOUTHERN the-bone, melt-in-your-mouth barbecue pork, chicken, and beef draw local and out-of-town attention to this homey café, where you can munch on old-fashioned peanuts (and toss the shells on the floor) while waiting for your table. Comforting sides such as baked beans, corn bread, coleslaw, and potatoes top off the large plates. The breakfast menu includes omelets, pancakes, and biscuits as well as chicken-fried steak and huevos rancheros platters for heartier appetites. ✉*1101 Grand Ave.* ☎*970/627–1404, 866/900–1404* ⊕*www.sagebrushbbq.com.*

> **GRAND LAKE LODGING ALTERNATIVES**
>
> **Grand Mountain Rentals.** Grand Mountain Rentals arranges rentals—some pet-friendly—around Grand Lake for from three days to six months. ✉ *1028 Grand Ave.* ⌂ *Box 808, 80447* ☎ *970/627–1131, 877/982–2155* ⊕ *www. grandmountainrentals.com* ⇦ *42* ¶❘ *No meals.*

WHERE TO STAY

For expanded hotel reviews, visit Fodors.com.

$ ▦**Historic Rapids Lodge & Restaurant.** This handsome lodgepole-pine struc-
HOTEL ture on the Tonahutu River dates to 1915. **Pros:** in-house restaurant;
Fodor's Choice condos are great for longer stays; quiet area of town. **Cons:** unpaved
★ parking area; lodge rooms are above restaurant; all lodge rooms are on second floor and there's no elevator. ✉*209 Rapids La.* ⌂ *Box 1400* ☎*970/627–3707* ⊕*www.rapidslodge.com* ⇦*7 rooms, 8 suites, 6 cabins, 12 condos* ⌂ *In-room: no a/c, kitchen. In-hotel: restaurant, bar, parking, some pets allowed* ⊘ *Closed Apr. and Nov.* ¶❘*No meals.*

$ ▦**Mountain Lakes Lodge.** The scent of the pine forest welcomes you to
HOTEL these charming and comfortable log cabins whimsically decorated with animal and sports themes—down to the curtains and drawer pulls. **Pros:** dog-friendly; close to fishing; good value. **Cons:** 4 mi from town (and services); two-day minimum stay (three-day minimum for holidays and special events). ✉*10480 U.S. 34* ⌂ *Box 2062, 80447* ☎*970/627–8448, 877/627–3220* ⊕*www.mountainlakeslodge.com* ⇦*10 cabins, 1 house* ⌂ *In-room: no a/c, kitchen, Wi-Fi. In-hotel: parking, some pets allowed* ¶❘*No meals.*

$ ▦**Western Riviera Motel and Cabins.** All rooms in this friendly motel face
HOTEL the lake. **Pros:** helpful and friendly staff; views of the lake; clean rooms. **Cons:** rooms and bathrooms can be a little cramped; lobby is a bit small. ✉*419 Garfield Ave.* ☎*970/627–3580* ⊕*www.westernriv.com* ⇦*16 rooms, 22 cabins* ⌂ *In-room: no a/c, Wi-Fi* ¶❘*No meals.*

NIGHTLIFE AND THE ARTS
THE ARTS
Rocky Mountain Repertory Theatre. The professional Rocky Mountain Repertory Theatre stages performances of popular Broadway shows like *Brigadoon* and musicals such as *Footloose* and *Seussical* in a cabin-style theater. ✉ *Community Centre, 1025 Grand Ave.* ⌂ *Box 1682, 80447* ☎*970/627–3421* ⊕*www.rockymountainrep.com.*

7

NIGHTLIFE

Lariat Saloon. The Lariat Saloon is the local hot spot, with live rock music almost every night. Look for the talking buffalo amid the eclectic Western decor. The bar also has pinball, pool, and darts. ✉ *1121 Grand Ave., on Boardwalk* ☎ *970/627–9965.*

SHOPPING

Shopping in Grand Lake tends toward the usual resort-town souvenir shops, although a handful of stores stand out.

Grand Lake Art Gallery. Grand Lake Art Gallery sells excellent photographs, original oil paintings, wood carvings, weavings, pottery, stained glass, and works done by more than 180 Colorado artists. ✉ *1117 Grand Ave.* ☎ *970/627–3104* ⊕ *www.grandlakeartgallery.com.*

Humphrey's Cabin Fever. Humphrey's Cabin Fever, housed in a 130-year-old log building, sells upscale cabin collectibles, rustic home furnishings, clothes, bedding, and ceramics—and lots of moose-themed stuff. ✉ *1100 Grand Ave.* ☎ *970/627–8939.*

Never Summer Mountain Products. For outdoor gear and clothing, head for Never Summer Mountain Products. ✉ *919 Grand Ave.* ☎ *970/627–3642.*

GRANBY

20 mi south of Grand Lake via U.S. 34.

The small, no-nonsense town of Granby (elevation 7,935 feet) serves the working ranches in Grand County, and you'll see plenty of cowboys, especially if you go to one of the weekly rodeos in summer. What the town lacks in attractions it makes up for with its views of Middle Park and the surrounding mountains of the Front and Gore ranges and with its proximity to outdoor activities, particularly its top-class golf courses just south of town.

GETTING HERE AND AROUND

Granby is 20 minutes from Rocky Mountain National Park and 15 minutes from the ski resorts Winter Park and Mary Jane and the mountain-biking trails of the Fraser Valley.

To get here from Grand Lake, take U.S. 34 south for 20 mi. From Boulder, you'll drive about 18 mi south on CO 93, 28 mi west on I–70, then take U.S. 40 north about 46 mi. From Denver, take I–70 west (about 30 mi) to U.S. 40, then drive north about 45 mi. The town is pretty small, and you can easily find a parking spot and walk from one end to the other.

ESSENTIALS

Visitor Information Greater Granby Area Chamber of Commerce ✉ *365 E. Agate, Suite B* ⌂ *Box 35, 80446* ☎ *970/887–2311, 800/325–1661* ⊕ *www. granbychamber.com.*

EXPLORING

Flying Heels Rodeo Arena. Watch cowboys demonstrate their rodeo skills at the Flying Heels Rodeo Arena, held every weekend beginning Memorial Day weekend. The rodeo finale and fireworks show is on the

Saturday nearest the July 4 holiday. ✉ *63032 U.S. 40, 1½ mi east of Granby* ☏ *970/887–2311* ⊕ *www.granbyrodeo.com.*

SPORTS AND THE OUTDOORS

Greater Granby Area Chamber of Commerce. The Greater Granby Area Chamber of Commerce branch has a free *Grand County Trail Map*, published by the Headwaters Trails Alliance (⊕ *www.headwaterstrails. org*), that shows trails for hiking, biking, horseback riding, snowmobiling, and snowshoeing as well as information about regulations. You can also find the map online and at local sporting goods and outdoor stores. ☏ *970/887–2311* ⊕ *www.granbychamber.com.*

BIRD-WATCHING

Windy Gap Wildlife Viewing Area. The reservoir at Windy Gap Wildlife Viewing Area is on the waterfowl migration route for geese, pelicans, swans, eagles, and osprey. The park has information kiosks, viewing scopes, viewing blinds, a picnic area, and a nature trail that's also wheelchair accessible. ✉ *2 mi west of Granby on U.S. 40 where it meets Rte. 125* ☏ *970/725–6200* ⊗ *May–Sept., daily dawn–dusk.*

FISHING

Serious fly fishers head to the rivers and streams of Grand County. Angling on the **Fraser River** begins downstream from Tabernash, and is not appropriate for families or dogs. At **Willow Creek** you'll bag plenty of rainbow trout and brookies. The **Colorado River** between Shadow Mountain Dam and Lake Granby and downstream from Hot Sulphur Springs is also popular with anglers. See ⊕ *www.wildlife.state.co.us/ fishing* for more information on fishing licenses.

GOLF

The scenery and wildlife-viewing opportunities at Grand County's four golf courses make good excuses for being distracted during a critical putt or drive. You can expect secluded greens, expansive vistas, and an occasional interruption from deer, foxes, elk, or even a moose.

★ **Grand Elk Ranch & Club.** Designed by PGA great Craig Stadler, the challenging course is reminiscent of traditional heathland greens in Britain. ✉ *1300 Tenmile Dr.* ☏ *970/887–9122, 877/389–9333* ⊕ *www. grandelk.com* ⌒ *Reservations essential* ⚑ *18 holes. Yards: 7144/5095. Par: 71/71. Green fee: $75/$95.*

Headwaters Golf Course at Granby Ranch. Tucked back in a valley at the end of a gravel road, entirely within the mountains and meadows, this club has roomy practice facilities as well as a large deck at the clubhouse. ✉ *2579 County Rd. 894* ✛ *Drive 2 mi south on U.S. 40 from Granby to the Inn at Silver Creek. Turn left and drive past the lodge to the gravel road marked by the sign. Follow the road about 3 mi into the valley* ☏ *970/887–2709, 888/850–4615* ⊕ *www.granbyranch.com* ⌒ *Reservations essential* ⚑ *18 holes. Yards: 7206/5095. Par: 72/72. Green fee: $75–$90.*

MOUNTAIN BIKING

Indian Peaks Wilderness Area is not open to mountain biking, but there are moderate and difficult trails in the **Arapaho National Forest** (☏ *970/887–4100* ⊕ *www.fs.fed.us/r2/arnf*). In addition, Grand County has several hundred miles of easy to expert-level bike trails, many of which are former railroad rights-of-way and logging roads.

Doe Creek Trail. The Doe Creek Trail, 3.2-mi one-way, is a good workout of uphill climbs (and descents) with plenty of forest scenery. ⊠ *From Granby, take U.S. 34 to County Rd. 6 (Arapaho Bay Rd.) and follow it for about 3 mi. The trailhead is on your right.*

DOWNHILL SKIING

SolVista Basin at Granby Ranch. You can get in some skiing at SolVista Basin at Granby Ranch, a small, family-friendly ski area 2 mi south of Granby. ⊠ *999 Village Rd.* ☎ *888/850–4615* ⊕ *www.solvista.com* ☒ *$56.*

WHERE TO EAT AND STAY

For expanded hotel reviews, visit Fodors.com.

$$ ✕ **Longbranch Restaurant and Schatzi's Pizza & Pasta.** This smoke-free
ECLECTIC Western-style family restaurant has a warming fireplace, rustic wood interior, and wagon-wheel chandeliers and is popular for its delicious German food (bratwurst, goulash, schnitzel, sauerbraten, and heavenly homemade spaetzle)—plus some decidedly non-German food (pizza and spaghetti). The traditional German desserts are authentic, and the strudel gets particularly high marks. The bar serves many domestic and foreign beers as well as a few microbrews. ⊠ *185 E. Agate Ave. (U.S. 40)* ☎ *970/887–2209* ⊙ *Closed Sun. No lunch Oct.–May.*

$$$$ ▦ **C Lazy U Guest Ranch.** Secluded in a broad, verdant valley, this deluxe
RESORT dude ranch attracts an international clientele, including both Holly-
ↄ wood royalty and the real thing. The healthy all-inclusive rates (starting
Fodor's Choice at $2,590/week) include your own personal horse, luxurious Western-
★ style accommodations (with humidifiers), fine meals, live entertainment, and just about any outdoor activity you can dream up—it's the ultimate in hedonism without ostentation. **Pros:** kid- and family-friendly; helpful staff; deluxe in every respect. **Cons:** distant from other area attractions; no pets; very expensive. ⊡ *Box 379, 80446* ✦ *3½ mi north on Hwy. 125 from U.S. 40 junction* ☎ *970/887–3344* ⊕ *www.clazyu.com* ⇔ *19 rooms, 20 cabins* ☒ *In-room: no a/c, no TV. In-hotel: restaurant, bar, pool, tennis court, gym, children's programs, parking* ⊙ *Closed mid-Sept.–mid-Dec. and mid-Jan.–mid-May* ♨ *All-inclusive.*

HOT SULPHUR SPRINGS

10 mi west of Granby via U.S. 40.

The county seat, Hot Sulphur Springs (population 512), is a faded resort town whose hot springs were once the destination for trains packed with people, including plenty of Hollywood types in the 1950s.

GETTING HERE AND AROUND

From Boulder, take U.S. 36 about 43 mi north to Estes Park. Take U.S. 34 west to Granby (53½ mi), then take U.S. 40 west for another 9 mi. From Fort Collins, take U.S. 287 south to Loveland (about 10 mi), then head west on U.S. 34 into Estes Park and then across Rocky Mountain National Park and into Granby (about 54 mi). Turn onto U.S. 40 and drive about 9 mi west.

You'll need a car to explore this area, as attractions, dining, and lodging are spread out.

EXPLORING

Grand County Museum. The old Hot Sulphur School is now the Grand County Museum. Artifacts depict Grand County history, including the original settlers 9,000 years ago, the role of pioneer women, and the archaeology of Windy Gap. Photographs show life in the early European settlements, and the original county courthouse and jail are on the site. ⊠ *110 E. Byers Ave.* ☎ *970/725–3939* ⊕ *www.grandcountymuseum. com* ⌦ *$5* ⊘ *Oct.–May, Wed.–Sat. 10–4; May–Oct., Tues.–Sat. 10–5.*

Hot Sulphur Springs Resort & Spa. Soak or pamper yourself with a massage, wrap, facial, or salt glow at the Hot Sulphur Springs Resort & Spa. Temperatures range from 85° to 112°F in 20 open-air pools and four private, indoor pools. For views at 102°F, head for the slate pools uphill from the others. The seasonal swimming pool is just right for recreation, at a comparatively frigid 80°F. Bring sandals if you have them with you. ⊠ *5609 County Rd. 20, From U.S. 40, head north onto Park St., then go left onto Spring Rd./County Rd. 20. The resort is 0.7 mi ahead, on your right* ☎ *970/725–3306, 800/510–6235* ⊕ *www.hotsulphursprings. com* ⌦ *$17.50* ⊘ *Daily 8 am–10 pm.*

WHERE TO STAY

For expanded hotel reviews, visit Fodors.com.

$ 🏨 **Hot Sulphur Springs Resort & Spa.** The basic, no-nonsense rooms here
HOTEL have comfortable lodgepole beds, desks, and en-suite showers; rates include unlimited use of the pools during your stay. **Pros:** quick access to hot pools and spa; close enough that a visit can be tacked onto an outdoor activity. **Cons:** trains passing through during the night are noisy; most restaurants are at least 15 minutes away. ⊠ *5609 County Rd. 20* ☎ *970/725–3306, 800/510–6235* ⊕ *www.hotsulphursprings. com* ⇆ *17 rooms, 1 cabin* ⌂ *In-room: no a/c, no TV. In-hotel: pool, parking* ⍢ *No meals.*

$$$$ 🏨 **Latigo Ranch.** Considerably more down-to-earth than other Colorado
RESORT guest ranches, Latigo has a caring staff that helps create an authentic
☼ ranch experience. **Pros:** stunning scenery; quiet and secluded area. **Cons:** no nearby restaurants or other attractions. ⊠ *County Rd. 1911* ☎ *Box 237, Kremmling 80459* ☎ *970/724–9008, 800/227–9655* ⊕ *www. latigotrails.com* ⇆ *10 cabins* ⌂ *In-room: no a/c, no TV. In-hotel: restaurant, pool, children's programs, laundry facilities, parking* ⊘ *Closed Apr., May, and mid-Oct.–mid-Dec.* ⍢ *All-inclusive.*

FORT COLLINS

The city sits on the cusp of the high plains of eastern Colorado, but is sheltered on the west by the lower foothills of the Rockies, giving residents plenty of nearby hiking and mountain-biking opportunities. By plugging a couple of gaps in the foothills with dams, the city created Horsetooth Reservoir, which you won't be able to see from town. To view the high mountains, you'll need to head up into Lory State Park or Horsetooth Mountain Park, which are just west of town. A walk through Old Town Square and the neighborhoods to its south and west demonstrates Fort Collins's focus on historic preservation.

The city was established in 1868 to protect traders from the natives, while the former negotiated the treacherous Overland Trail. After the flood of 1864 swept away Camp Collins—a cavalry post near today's town of LaPorte—Colonel Will Collins established a new camp on 6,000 acres where Fort Collins stands today. The town grew on two industries: education (CSU was founded here in 1879) and agriculture (rich crops of alfalfa and sugar beets). Today there are plenty of shops and art galleries worth visiting in this relaxed university city. With nearly 10 microbreweries—the most microbreweries per capita in the state—crafting ales, lagers, and stouts, as well as a Budweiser brewery, it's the perfect location for the two-day Colorado Brewers' Festival every June.

GETTING HERE AND AROUND

From Boulder, take U.S. 36 east to Interlocken Loop/Storage Tek Drive, follow for about ½ mi, then get onto Northwest Highway for about 8½ mi. Take Interstate 25 North for about 41 mi, get off at the Prospect Road exit. Head west on East Prospect Road for about 4 mi.

You can also get to Fort Collins via Allegiant Air, which flies into Fort Collins/Loveland Airport (FNL), about 15 mi south of town. They offer a direct flight to and from Las Vegas. There's a local taxi service, and the city's bus system, Transfort, operates more than a dozen routes throughout the city, which run primarily Monday to Saturday.

Downtown is walkable, but you can also borrow wheels—for free— from the city's Bike Library for as little as an hour or as long as a week. There are two locations: the Café Bicyclette, at the corner of Walnut and Linden streets in Old Town Square, and at the Lory Student Center on the CSU campus.

WHEN TO GO

Fort Collins's outdoor recreation and cultural pursuits attract visitors year-round, but it is definitely a college town, so you can expect a decidedly different atmosphere depending on whether CSU is in session.

FESTIVALS   **Bohemian Nights at NewWestFest.** Called "Fort Collins largest community festival," this music-centered event is a proud showing-off of the bustling Colorado music community, which has produced the Fray, Tennis, 3OH!3, OneRepublic, Candy Claws, and others in the last decade. Sure, there are national headliners—including G. Love & Special Sauce and Asleep at the Wheel in previous years—but the real stars here are the locals who fill the outdoor stages during this three-day August fest. ✉ *Old Town Square* ☎ *970/407–7867* ⊕ *www.bohemiannights.org.*

Colorado Brewers' Festival. During the last full weekend of June, more than 40 Colorado brewers show off their finest with 300 kegs of beer in Civic Center Park at the Colorado Brewers' Festival. There's live music by regional talent for the two-day, Colorado-brews-only festival, which Fort Collins brewers started in 1989. ✉ *Old Town Sq.* ☎ *970/484–6500* ⊕ *www.downtownfortcollins.com.*

ESSENTIALS

Transportation Contacts Allegiant Air ☎ 702/505–8888 ⊕ www.allegiantair. com. **Bike Library** ☎ 970/419–1050 ⊕ www.fcbikelibrary.org. **Ft. Collins/Love-land Airport (FNL)** ✉ 4900 Earhart Rd., about 3½ mi west of I–25, off Mulberry St., Loveland ☎ 970/962–2850 ⊕ www.fortloveair.com. **Ft. Collins Yellow Cab.** ☎ 970/224–2222. **Transfort** ⊕ www.fcgov.com/transfort.

Visitor Information Fort Collins Convention & Visitors Bureau ✉ 19 Old Town Square, Suite 137 ☎ 970/232–3840, 800/274–3678 ⊕ www.ftcollins.com.

EXPLORING

TOP ATTRACTIONS

Avery House. The Fort Collins Convention & Visitors Bureau has desig-nated a historic walking tour of more than 20 buildings, including the original university structures and the stately sandstone Avery House, named for Franklin Avery, who planned the old town's broad streets when he surveyed the city in 1873. ✉ 328 W. Mountain Ave. ☎ 970/221–0533 ⊕ www.poudrelandmarks.com ☑ Free ☉ Weekends 1–4.

Fort Collins Museum and Discovery Science Center. The Fort Collins Museum and Discovery Science Center has historical and scientific exhibits designed to draw visitors of all ages. An 1860s-era cabin from the town's original military camp and a 1905 vintage schoolhouse are right on the museum grounds, and there are interactive exhibits geared to younger kids at the science center. ✉ 200 Matthews St. ☎ 970/221–6738 ⊕ www. fcmdsc.com ☑ $4 ☉ Tues.–Sat. 10–5, Sun. noon–5. Closed Mon.

★ **New Belgium Brewing Company.** Famous for its **Fat Tire** brand, the New Belgium Brewing Company also crafts a few brews available only on-site at the "mother ship" (the employees' term of endearment for their brewery). Tours of what happens to be the first 100% wind-powered brewery in the United States are first-come, first-served, or can be reserved online. The brewery is north of Old Town, near Heritage Center Park. ✉ 500 Linden St. ☎ 970/221–0524 ⊕ www.newbelgium. com ☑ Free ☉ Tours Tues.–Sat. 10–6.

Old Town Square. Old Town Square, a National Historic District, is a pedestrian zone with sculptures, fountains, and 24 historic buildings, which now house shops, galleries, jewelers, boutiques, and bars. The square's several restaurants and cafés have plenty of shaded outdoor seating. In summer, musicians and theater groups entertain Thursday and Friday evenings and Sunday afternoon at 3 pm. ✉ Mountain and College Aves. ☎ 970/484–6500 ⊕ www.downtownfortcollins.com.

WORTH NOTING

Anheuser-Busch. Learn lots of facts about the large-scale brewing process at Anheuser-Busch during a free tour. Free tours start every 30 minutes and last one hour and 15 minutes. If you're really interested in the goings on, sign up for a lengthier Brewmaster Tour ($25 per person, reservations required), which will take you through the starting cellar, packaging facility, quality assurance department, and the Clydesdales stables. ✉ 2351 Busch Dr. ☎ 970/490–4691 ⊕ www.budweisertours. com ☑ Free ☉ June–Sept., daily 10–4; Oct.–May, Thurs.–Mon. 10–4.

7

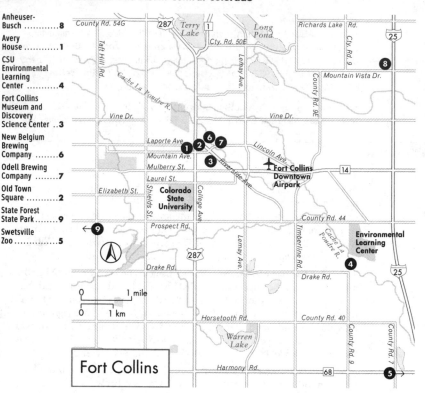

Fort Collins

☺ **Environmental Learning Center.** CSU's Warner College of Natural Resources' Environmental Learning Center conducts educational tours for families and other groups on a 1.2-mi trail loop within a 200-acre nature preserve. The raptor cages and the walk-through wetland animal habitat are an excellent educational family activity, and fun for anyone curious about animal habitats. Staff conduct special walks like the full-moon hike. ⊠ *2400 S. County Rd. 9* ☎ *970/491–1661* ⊕ *www. cnr.colostate.edu/elc* ⊠ *$3.50* ⬥ *Reservations essential* ⊙ *Information center mid-May–Aug., daily 9–3; Sept.–Apr., weekends 10–5. Learning Center year-round, daily dawn–dusk.*

Odell Brewing Company. Take in the brewing process up close and personally in a tour at the Odell Brewing Company, one of the first microbreweries to open shop in town in 1989—out of a pickup-truck bed. Favorites like 90 Shilling, Easy Street Wheat, and 5 Barrel Pale Ale are not to be missed. In winter, try the seasonal Isolation Ale. ⊠ *800 E. Lincoln Ave.* ☎ *970/498–9070, 888/887–2797* ⊕ *www.odellbrewing. com* ⊠ *Free* ⊙ *Tap Room Mon.–Sat. 11–6; tours Mon.–Sat. 1, 2, and 3.*

☺ **Swetsville Zoo.** Swetsville Zoo is the unique creation of an insomniac dairy farmer who stayed up nights fashioning more than 150 dinosaurs, birds, insects, and other fantastic creatures from scrap metal, car parts, and old farm equipment. ⊠ *4801 E. Harmony Rd., ¼ mi east of I–25*

☎ *970/484–9509* ✉ *Free* ☉ *Daily dawn–dusk (call for details).*

OFF THE BEATEN PATH

State Forest State Park. Rugged peaks, thick forests, and burbling streams make up this 70,768-acre park. Here you can fish for trout, boat the azure alpine lakes, ride horseback, hike or mountain bike, and explore a few four-wheel-drive roads with views of the 12,000-foot Medicine Bow and Never Summer mountain ranges. Yurts and camping are available in winter, so you can explore the 70 mi of groomed snowmobiling trails or the 50 mi of groomed and signed cross-country skiing and snowshoeing trails.

NORTHERN FRONT RANGE BREWERIES

The Front Range boasts several brewing firsts. In 1959 Coors, located in Golden, introduced the first beer in an aluminum can. Boulder Beer is Colorado's first microbrewery, founded in 1979. The Great American Beer Festival, which started in 1981 in Boulder (now held in Denver), was the nation's first beer festival. A tour of northern Front Range breweries could take you through Boulder, Nederland, Lyons, Longmont, Loveland, Greeley, and finally Fort Collins, where you can visit the legendary Clydesdales at Anheuser-Busch.

Red Feather Guides and Outfitters. Red Feather Guides and Outfitters arranges guided fly-fishing and horseback-riding trips. It's in Walden, a few miles west of the park. ✉ *49794 Hwy. 14, Walden* ☎ *970/723–4204, 970/524–5054* ⊕ *www.redfeatherguides.com*

Never Summer Nordic. Never Summer Nordic rents the yurts in the state park to hikers and mountain bikers (as well as snowshoers and backcountry or cross-country skiers) for hut-to-hut trips year-round. They also offer half-day, full-day, and overnight guided trips into the park. ✉ *247 County Rd. 41, Walden* ☎ *970/723–4070* ⊕ *www.neversummernordic.com* ✉ *56750 Hwy. 14, Walden* ✦ *From Ft. Collins, drive 75 mi west on Rte. 14 to County Rd. 41. From Granby, take U.S. 125 north to Walden (about 53 mi), then Hwy. 14 south for about 32 mi to County Rd. 41* ☎ *970/723–8366* ⊕ *www.parks.state.co.us/Parks/StateForest* ✉ *$7 a day per vehicle.*

SPORTS AND THE OUTDOORS

BICYCLING

Both paved-trail cycling and single-track mountain biking are within easy access of town.

Poudre River Trail. The Poudre River Trail (about 20 mi round-trip) is an easy jaunt within Fort Collins. ✉ *Trailheads: Lions Park on North Overland Trail or Environmental Learning Center on East Drake Rd.*

For short, single-track rides, Pineridge and Maxwell trails do not disappoint, and they connect to other trails for longer adventures. Head west on Drake Road to where it bends right and becomes South Overland Trail; turn left on County Road 42C and drive almost 1 mi to the posted fence opening.

Horsetooth Mountain Park. Serious gearheads crank at Horsetooth Mountain Park on the southwest side of Horsetooth Reservoir. Several single-tracks and jeep trails provide any level of challenge. ⊕ *www.co.larimer. co.us/parks/htmp.htm.*

OUTFITTER   **Recycled Cycles.** Recycled Cycles rents city bikes, mountain bikes, road bikes, kid trailers, and tandems for $25–$40 per day. ⊠ *4031-A S. Mason St.* ☎ *970/223–1969, 877/214–1811* ⊕ *www.recycled-cycles.com.*

FISHING

The North Platte, Laramie, and Cache la Poudre rivers are renowned for excellent fishing. See ⊕ *www.wildlife.state.co.us/fishing* for more information on fishing licenses.

OUTFITTER   **St. Peter's Fly Shop.** The knowledgeable chaps at St. Peter's Fly Shop
★   arrange half-day to full-day guided or instructional wade and float trips in northern Colorado and southern Wyoming that can include permits for waters not open to the public. The store also sells gear, and the staff gladly provides information on conditions to independent fishermen. ⊠ *202 Remington St.* ☎ *970/498–8968* ⊕ *www.stpetes.com.*

GOLF

Mariana Butte Golf Course. This hilly course in Loveland has 30-mi views of the mountains. The course, designed by Dick Phelps, is along the Big Thompson River and skirts rock outcroppings and plenty of ponds. Don't forget your camera. ⊠ *701 Clubhouse Dr., Loveland* ✛ *Go west on 1st St., take a right onto Rossum Dr. and another quick right onto Clubhouse Dr.* ☎ *970/667–8308* ⊕ *www.golfloveland.com* ⌂ *Reservations essential* 🏌 *18 holes. Yards: 6572/5420. Par: 36/72. Green fee: $42/$58.*

HIKING

Horsetooth Mountain Park. Twenty-nine miles of trails in Horsetooth Mountain Park offer easy to difficult hikes, some with views of the mountains to the west and the plains to the east. An easy 2.25-mi round-trip walk to **Horsetooth Falls** is a good hike that takes you into the foothills for a couple of hours. From the parking area, head up the Horsetooth Falls Trail and keep right at the junction with the Soderberg Trail. Go left at the next junction to get to the falls. ⊠ *Drive west on Harmony Rd., which becomes County Rd. 38E. Follow for about 5 mi to park entrance* ☎ *970/679–4570* ⊕ *www.larimer.org/parks/htmp.htm* 💲 *$6 per vehicle.*

Lory State Park. Wildlife, songbirds, and springtime wildflowers abound along the trails in Lory State Park, about 15 minutes west of downtown.

   Arthur's Rock Trail. For unbelievable views of the Front Range and the city from 7,000-foot Arthur's Rock, take Arthur's Rock Trail. You climb fast on the switchbacks in the sparse woods before the trail levels off to cross the meadow, a breather before the final steep approach to the summit. Allow about two to three hours to hike the trail (3.4 mi round-trip and about 1,300 feet gain in elevation). Watch for poison ivy and be mindful of the occasional rattlesnake. ⊠ *Trailhead: Parking area at end of service road* ⊠ *708 Lodgepole Dr., Bellvue* ✛ *Drive north on Overland Trail and turn left on Bingham Hill Rd. Turn left* *at County Rd. 23 north and go 1.3 mi to County. Rd. 25G and turn right. It's 1½ mi to park entrance* ☎ *970/493–1623* ⊕ *parks.state.co.us/ Parks/lory* ▭ *$7 per vehicle.*

RAFTING AND KAYAKING

The Cache la Poudre River is famous for its rapids, and river trips fill fast. It's wise to book with an outfitter at least two weeks in advance.

A-1 Wildwater Rafting. The state-certified guides of A-1 Wildwater Rafting arrange guided tours as well as daylong and half-day trips for groups. A-1 also rents inflatable rafts for one to two people called "duckies." ✉ *2801 N. Shields St.* ☎ *970/224–3379, 800/369–4165* ⊕ *www.a1wildwater.com.*

WHERE TO EAT

$$ ✕ **Canino's.** Hearty Italian specialties are served in this historic four-square house that still has a few stained-glass windows. Tables are set in wood-trim rooms that have hardwood floors with carpets. Appetizers like bruschetta and entrées such as *pollo alla cacciatora* and veal marsala are made in classic Italian style. Homemade cheese-cake, tiramisu, or gelato—paired with a robust espresso—finish dinner on a sweet note. ✉ *613 S. College Ave.* ☎ *970/493–7205* ⊕ *www. caninositalianrestaurant.com.*
ITALIAN ★

$$ ✕ **Cozzola's.** Base your pizza on thin "New York"–style crust or a thick herb or whole-wheat and poppy-seed crust, and then select a sauce: basil-tomato, fresh garlic, pesto, or spinach ricotta. Finally, select from the seemingly endless list of toppings that includes everything from artichoke hearts to feta cheese to applewood-smoked bacon. The roomy restaurant is done in rough-hewn wood and is bright and airy. You can also get a couple of slices as a snack—made to order with your choices of toppings. There's a second location at 1112 Oakridge Drive. ✉ *241 Linden St.* ☎ *970/482–3557* ⊕ *www.cozzolaspizza.com.*
PIZZA

$$ ✕ **Rio Grande Mexican Restaurant.** Like its other Front Range brethren, the Fort Collins branch of this six-location chain always satisfies, with old favorites such as tacos, quesadillas, burritos, flame-broiled Yucatan shrimp, and fajita steak dishes, as well as spicier Tex-Mex fare such as *camarones diabla* (shrimp with chile de árbol). This spacious restaurant with old storefront windows draws mostly casual diners out for a wonderful, relaxed dinner. ✉ *143 W. Mountain Ave.* ☎ *970/224–5428* ⊕ *www.riograndemexican.com.*
MEXICAN

$ ✕ **Silver Grill Cafe.** This cool spot, sleek with hardwood floors, red soda-fountain stools, and boxy booths, is the oldest café in northern Colorado, operating since 1933. The cinnamon rolls are legendary, and the cinnamon-roll French toast is also popular. The café's coffee is custom roasted, and the Café Royal, a house special that mixes cappuccino with brown sugar, vanilla, and a twist of lemon, is particularly tasty. The breakfast menu includes omelets, biscuits and gravy, hotcakes, breakfast burritos, and grilled trout with eggs, plus a few vegetarian options. Lunch is sandwiches or salads, burgers, or platters of chicken-fried steak and a few other traditional, homey comfort foods. Doors open
AMERICAN

at 6:30 for breakfast, and lunch is served until 2 pm. ⊠ *218 Walnut St.* 📞 *970/484–4656* ⊕ *www.silvergrill.com* ◷ *No dinner.*

¢   ✕ **Starry Night Coffee Company.** Espresso drinkers sip their sustenance,
CAFÉ including espresso smoothies, on leather couches or at tables under the night-blue ceiling while reading, chatting, or mulling over the sunflowers and the mural *Starry Night over Fort Collins* (inspired by van Gogh's original). Beyond breakfast, there are soups, salads, and sandwiches at lunch and dinnertime. For dessert, there are pastries, scones, and tiramisu. ⊠ *112 S. College Ave.* 📞 *970/493–3039.*

$ ✕ **Suehiro.** Sit at the high bar overlooking Linden Street in this light and
JAPANESE open restaurant or, for more intimacy, ask for a table in the tearoom. The well-priced sushi is made fresh at the bar, and seafood entrées like salmon teriyaki or tempura are satisfying. Choose from more than 10 hot and cold sakes and specialty drinks. The green-tea ice cream makes a refreshing dessert. ⊠ *223 Linden St., Suite 103* 📞 *970/482–3734* ⊕ *www.suehirofc.com.*

WHERE TO STAY

For expanded hotel reviews, visit Fodors.com.

$$ ▦ **Armstrong Hotel.** Walk into this downtown hotel's art deco lobby, with
HOTEL an original terrazzo floor and pressed-tin ceiling, and go back in time to the 1920s, when the hotel was built. **Pros:** helpful staff; downtown location; low rates for a classy, historic lodging. **Cons:** on a rather noisy street, particularly on weekend nights. ⊠ *259 S. College Ave.* 📞 *970/484–3883, 866/384–3883* ⊕ *www.thearmstronghotel.com* ⇆ *24 rooms, 2 apartment suites, 2 studios, 15 suites* ⟁ *In-room: kitchen, Wi-Fi. In-hotel: parking* ⊯ *No meals.*

$$$$ ▦ **Colorado Cattle Company & Guest Ranch.** A real-deal working ranch,
RESORT the adults-only cattle company has 750 head of cattle and 10,000 acres of land in the canyons and plains of northeast Colorado. **Pros:** truly authentic experience; ability to mix cattle work with relaxation. **Cons:** no kids allowed; authentic experience includes chores. ⊠ *70008 Weld County Rd. 132, New Raymer* 📞 *970/437–5345* ⊕ *www. coloradocattlecompany.com* ⇆ *14 cabins* ⟁ *In-hotel: bar, pool, gym, parking, some pets allowed, some age restrictions* ◷ *Closed Nov.–mid-Apr.* ⊯ *All-inclusive.*

$ ▦ **Edwards House B&B.** This quiet Victorian inn with hardwood floors
B&B/INN and light birchwood trim is four blocks from downtown. **Pros:** on a
★ busy but quiet street near downtown; helpful and professional staff; pleasant grounds. **Cons:** small inn; fills up quickly. ⊠ *402 W. Mountain Ave.* 📞 *970/493–9191, 800/281–9190* ⊕ *www.edwardshouse.com* ⇆ *8 rooms* ⟁ *In-room: Wi-Fi. In-hotel: gym, parking, some age restrictions* ⊯ *Breakfast.*

¢   ▦ **LaQuinta Inn Fort Collins.** This chain hotel is bright, well maintained,
HOTEL and a better buy than many of its competitors. **Pros:** good value, near interstate for easy access; pets welcome. **Cons:** rather distant from dining and attractions; along busy and noisy thoroughfare. ⊠ *3709 E. Mulberry St.* 📞 *970/493–7800, 800/753–3757* ⊕ *www.lq.com* ⇆ *132*

rooms, 1 suite ⬧ *In-room: Wi-Fi. In-hotel: pool, gym, parking, some pets allowed* ⦿ *Breakfast.*

NIGHTLIFE

BARS AND CLUBS

Lucky Joe's Sidewalk Saloon. College students line the bar at Lucky Joe's Sidewalk Saloon for live music Wednesday to Sunday nights. ✉ *25 Old Town Sq.* ☎ *970/493–2213* ⊕ *www.luckyjoes.com.*

Mishawaka Amphitheater. Mishawaka Amphitheater, an outdoor venue on the banks of the Poudre River about 25 mi outside of Fort Collins, corrals an eclectic mix of bands on weekends, including national acts like the Subdudes and the reggae stars Steel Pulse. Most shows are evenings, and some are afternoons. ✉ *13714 Poudre Canyon Hwy., 25 mi north of Fort Collins on Rte. 14, Bellvue* ☎ *970/482–4420* ⊕ *www. themishawaka.com.*

BREWPUBS AND MICROBREWERIES

C.B. & Potts Restaurant and Brewery. The sports bar C.B. & Potts Restaurant and Brewery is known for its burgers, barbecue, and beers. The establishment has a game room and a pool hall with a full bar. The brewery always has six house beers and two seasonals on tap. All brews are crafted and bottled on-site in a 15-barrel, direct-fire brewing system. Tours are available by appointment. ✉ *1415 W. Elizabeth St.* ☎ *970/221–1139* ⊕ *www.cbpotts.com.*

Coopersmith's Pub & Brewery. After taking a tour of the brewery at Coopersmith's Pub & Brewery, you can enjoy lunch on the patio with a crisp Punjabi Pale Ale or one of the other seven house-made beers on tap. The brewery always has three to five seasonal specialties to offer. Coopersmith's own pool hall, just outside the front door at 7 Old Town Square, has 12 tournament-style tables and serves pizza. ✉ *5 Old Town Sq.* ☎ *970/498–0183* ⊕ *www.coopersmithspub.com.*

SHOPPING

Alpine Arts. The family-owned Alpine Arts has some real standouts, particularly the photography and watercolors, among the more usual pottery, carved wooden boxes, and jewelry. Everything is made by Colorado artists. ✉ *112 N. College Ave.* ☎ *970/493–1941.*

Art On Mountain. Peruse the sculptures and the Colorado landscapes rendered in paintings and photography at Art On Mountain. ✉ *102 W. Mountain Ave.* ☎ *970/223–6450* ⊕ *www.artonmountain.com.*

Clothes Pony and Dandelion Toys. The shopkeepers at the Clothes Pony and Dandelion Toys enjoy playing with the toys as much as their young customers do. The shop carries books, CDs, imported toys, and classics like marbles, dolls, and stuffed animals. ✉ *111 N. College Ave.* ☎ *970/224–2866* ⊕ *www.clothespony.com.*

Green Logic. Green Logic purveys boxes made from books, notepads with old floppy disks as covers, clocks made from 45-rpm vinyl records, and dishes made from recycled glass. Clothing made from organic cotton is also available. ✉ *261 Linden St.* ☎ *970/484–1740* ⊕ *www.green-logic.net.*

Repeat Boutique. Repeat Boutique carries classy castoffs: silverware, antique furniture, paintings, and suits, vintage wedding dresses, casual outfits, and furs—mostly for women. ✉ *1502 S. College Ave.* ☎ *970/493–1039.*

The Right Card. The Right Card carries a huge selection of greeting cards—everything from tasteful to tacky—plus quirky, hip handbags, gorgeous handmade leather journals, and other memorable gifts. ✉ *17 Old Town Sq., #135* ☎ *970/221–3030.*

Trimble Court Artisans. Trimble Court Artisans, a co-op with more than 40 members, sells paintings, jewelry, clothing, weavings, stained glass, and pottery. ✉ *118 Trimble Ct.* ☎ *970/221–0051* ⊕ *www.trimblecourt.com.*

Wagz. Wagz has just the perfect treat or toy to take home to your favorite pooch. ✉ *132 N. College Ave.* ☎ *970/482–9249* ⊕ *www.wagzcolorado.com.*

Rocky Mountain National Park

WORD OF MOUTH

"[For a hike,] I recommend starting at Bear Lake, simply because the flexibility is unmatched. If the hike you plan is too difficult (or too easy) for you, then you can easily alter your plans, and make a hike more to your preferences."

—PaulRabe

WELCOME TO ROCKY MOUNTAIN NATIONAL PARK

TOP REASONS TO GO

★ **Awesome ascents:** Seasoned climbers can trek to the summit of 14,259-foot Longs Peak or attack the rounded granite domes of Lumpy Ridge. Novices can summit Twin Sisters Peaks or Mount Ida, both reaching more than 11,000 feet.

★ **Continental Divide:** Straddle this great divide, which cuts through the western part of the park, separating water's flow to either the Pacific or Atlantic Ocean.

★ **Gorgeous scenery:** Peer out over more than 100 lakes, gaze up at majestic mountain peaks (more than 60 that tower over 12,000 feet), and soak in the splendor of lush wetlands, pine-scented woods, forests of spruce and fir, and alpine tundra in the park's four distinct ecosystems.

★ **More than 355 mi of trails:** Hike to your heart's content on dozens of marked trails, which range from easy lakeside strolls to strenuous mountain climbs.

★ **Wildlife viewing:** Spot elk and bighorn sheep, along with moose, otters, and more than 280 species of birds (including woodpeckers, owls, and ptarmigan).

Long Draw Reservoir

Flatiron Mountain 12,335 ft

Mummy Ra

Ypsilon Mountai 13,514

Skeleton Gulch

Cache la Poudre River

Visitor Center

Mount Chiquita 13,069 ft

Old Fall River Road

34

Continental Divide

Big Thompson River

3

Trail Ridge

Alluvi Fa

34

4 Timber Creek

🏕 **Holzwarth** ◆ **Lodge**

🏔 **Forest Canyon**

Mount Julian 12,928 ft

Colorado River

Long Meadows

Spruce Canyon

Bighorn Flats

Kawuneeche

Snowdrift Peak 12,274 ft

1 Bear Lak

Valley

34

Visitor Center

Grand Lake

Ptarmigan Mountain 12,324 ft

Shadow Mountain Lake

Grand Lake

Isolation Peak 13,118 ft

Paradise Park

Mount Adams 12,121 ft

0   3 mi
0   3 km

1 **Bear Lake.** One of the most photographed (and crowded) places in the park, Bear Lake is the hub for many trailheads and a major stop on the park's shuttle service.

2 **Longs Peak.** The highest peak in the park and the toughest to climb, this Fourteener pops up in many park vistas. A round-trip trek to the top takes 10 to 15 hours, so most visitors forego summit fever and opt for a (still spectacular) partial journey.

3 **Trail Ridge Road.** The alpine tundra of the park is the highlight here, as the road—the highest continuous highway in the U.S.— climbs to more than 12,000 feet (almost 700 feet above timberline).

4 **Timber Creek Campground.** The park's far-western area is much less crowded than most other sections, though it has its share of amenities and attractions, including evening programs, 98 camping sites, and a visitor center.

5 **Wild Basin Area.** Far from the crowds, the park's southeast quadrant consists of lovely expanses of subalpine forest punctuated by streams and lakes.

COLORADO

GETTING ORIENTED

Rocky Mountain National Park's 416-square-mi wilderness of meadows, mountains, and mirrorlike lakes lies about 70 mi from Denver. The park is roughly an eighth of the size of Yellowstone, yet it receives almost as many visitors—3 million a year.

8

ighorn Mountain
11,463 ft

Black Canyon

Visitor Center

34

Estes Park

34

36

oraine ark

36

Visitor Center and Park Headquarters

66

7

agua ke

Glacier Basin

Visitor Center

Longs Peak

2

Longs Peak 14,255 ft

Meeker Park

7

North St. Vrain Creek

5

Allenspark

KEY	
🏚	*Ranger Station*
🅰	*Campground*
🎋	*Picnic Area*
🍴	*Restaurant*
🏨	*Lodge*
🏃	*Trailhead*
🚻	*Restrooms*
⚜	*Scenic Viewpoint*
⋯⋯	*Walking/Hiking Trails*
⋯⋯	*Bicycle Path*

Updated
by Martha
Connors

Anyone who delights in alpine lakes, dense forests, and abundant wildlife—not to mention dizzying heights—should consider Rocky Mountain National Park. Here, a single hour's drive leads from a 7,800-foot elevation at park headquarters to the 12,183-foot apex of the twisting and turning Trail Ridge Road. More than 355 mi of hiking trails take you to the park's many treasures: meadows flush with wildflowers, cool dense forests of lodgepole pine and Engelmann spruce, and the noticeable presence of wildlife, including elk and bighorn sheep.

PLANNER

WHEN TO GO

More than 80 percent of the park's annual 3 million visitors come in summer and fall. **For thinner high-season crowds, come in early June or September.** But there is a good reason to put up with summer crowds: only from Memorial Day to mid-October will you get the chance to make the unforgettable drive over Trail Ridge Road (note that the road may still be closed during those months if the weather turns bad).

Spring is capricious—75°F one day and a blizzard the next (March sees the most snow). June can range from hot and sunny to cool and rainy. July typically ushers in high summer, which can last through September. Up on Trail Ridge Road, it can be 15°–20° cooler than at the park's lower elevations. Wildlife viewing and fishing is best in any season but winter. In early fall, the trees blaze with brilliant foliage. Winter, when backcountry snow can be 4 feet deep, is the time for cross-country skiing, snowshoeing, and ice fishing.

AVG. HIGH/LOW TEMPS.

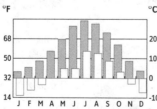

FESTIVALS AND EVENTS

MID-MAY **Jazz Fest.** Pack a picnic and bring the kids for a weekend afternoon of free jazz performances and an art walk at the outdoor theater in downtown Estes Park. ⊠ *Performance Park Amphitheater, 417 W. Elkhorn Ave., Estes Park* ⌂ *Box 1967, Estes Park 80517* ☎ *970/586–6104* ⊕ *www.estesnet.com/events/.*

JUNE **The Wool Market.** Watch shearing, spinning, and sheepdog herding contests, plus angora goats, sheep, llamas, and alpacas being judged for their wool. Shop for knitting and weaving supplies as well as finished woolen items, such as hats, coats, and mittens. ⊠ *Fairgrounds at Stanley Park, Intersection of U.S. 36 and Community Dr., Estes Park* ⌂ *Box 1967, Estes Park 80517* ☎ *970/586–6104* ⊕ *www.estesnet.com/events/ woolmarket.htm.*

JULY-AUGUST **Estes Park Music Festival.** In July and August, the Colorado Music Festival Chamber Orchestra teams with the Estes Park Music Festival for a series of concerts at the historic Stanley Hotel Concert Hall ($30 for adults; children are free). Come winter, concerts featuring a variety of performances are held at 2 pm on Sunday afternoon from November through April (admission is $5). ⊠ *Stanley Hotel, 333 E. Wonderview Ave., Estes Park* ⌂ *Box 4290, Estes Park 80517* ☎ *970/586–9519, 800/443–7837* ⊕ *www.estesparkmusicalfestival.org.*

Rooftop Rodeo. Consistently ranked one of the top small rodeos in the country (and a tradition since 1908), this six-day event features a parade and nightly rodeo events, such as barrel racing and saddle bronc riding. ⊠ *Fairgrounds at Stanley Park, Intersection of U.S 36 and Community Dr., Estes Park* ⌂ *Box 1967, Estes Park 80517* ☎ *970/586–6104* ⊕ *www.rooftoprodeo.com* ▭ *$10–$15.*

SEPTEMBER ★ **Longs Peak Scottish/Irish Highland Festival.** A traditional tattoo (drum- and bugle-filled parade) kicks off this four-day fair of ancient Scottish athletic competitions, including full-armor jousting and throwing contests involving hammers and 20-foot-long, 140-pound wooden poles (called cabers). The festival also features Celtic music, Irish dancing, and events for dogs of the British Isles (such as terrier racing and sheepdog demonstrations). ⊠ *Fairgrounds at Stanley Park, Intersection of U.S. 36 and Community Dr., Estes Park* ⌂ *Box 1820, Estes Park 80517* ☎ *970/586–6308, 800/903–7837* ⊕ *www.scotfest.com.*

PLANNING YOUR TIME

ROCKY MOUNTAIN IN ONE DAY

Starting out in Estes Park, begin your day at the **Bighorn Restaurant,** a classic breakfast spot and a local favorite. While you're enjoying your short stack with apple-cinnamon-raisin topping, you can put in an order for a packed lunch (it's a good idea to bring your food with you, as dining options in the park consist of a single, seasonal snack bar at the top of Trail Ridge Road).

Drive west on U.S. 34 into the park, and stop at the **Beaver Meadows Visitor Center** to watch the orientation film and pick up a park map. Also inquire about road conditions on Trail Ridge Road, which you should plan to drive either in the morning or afternoon, depending on the weather. If possible, save the drive for the afternoon, and use the morning to get out on the trails, before the chance of an afternoon lightning storm.

For a beautiful and invigorating hike, head to Bear Lake and follow the route that takes you to **Nymph Lake** (an easy ½-mi hike), then onto **Dream Lake** (an additional 0.6 mi with a steeper ascent), and finally to **Emerald Lake** (an additional 0.7 mi of moderate terrain). You can stop at several places along the way. The trek down is much easier, and quicker, than the climb up. ■TIP→ **If you prefer a shorter, simpler (yet still scenic) walk, consider the Bear Lake Nature Trail, a 0.6-mi loop that is wheelchair- and stroller-accessible.**

You'll need the better part of your afternoon to drive the scenic **Trail Ridge Road.** Start by heading west toward Grand Lake, stop at the look-out at the Alluvial Fan, and consider taking Old Fall River Road the rest of the way across the park. This single-lane dirt road delivers unbeatable views of waterfalls and mountain vistas. You'll take it westbound from Horseshoe Park (the cutoff is near the Endovalley Campground), then rejoin Trail Ridge Road at its summit, near the Alpine Visitor Center. If you're traveling on to Grand Lake or other points west, stay on Trail Ridge Road. If you're heading back to Estes Park, turn around and take Trail Ridge Road back (for a different set of awesome scenery). End your day with a ranger-led talk or evening campfire program.

GETTING HERE AND AROUND

AIR TRAVEL

The closest commercial airport is **Denver International Airport** (DEN). Its **Ground Transportation Information Center** (☎ *800/247–2336 or 303/342–4059 ⊕ www.flydenver.com*) assists visitors with car rentals, door-to-door shuttles, and limousine services. From the airport, the eastern entrance of the park is 80 mi (about two hours). **Estes Park Shuttle** (☎ *970/586–5151 ⊕ www.estesparkshuttle.com; reservations essential*) serves Estes Park and Rocky Mountain from both Denver International Airport and Longmont/Boulder.

CAR TRAVEL

Estes Park and Grand Lake are the Rocky Mountain's gateway communities; from these you can enter the park via U.S. 34 or 36 (Estes Park) or U.S. 34 (Grand Lake). U.S. 36 runs from Denver through Boulder, Lyons, and Estes Park to the park; the portion between Boulder and Estes Park is heavily traveled—especially on summer weekends. Though less direct, Colorado Routes 119, 72, and 7 have much less traffic (and better scenery). If you're driving directly to Rocky Mountain from the airport, take the E–470 tollway from Peña Boulevard to Interstate 25.

The **Colorado Department of Transportation** (for road conditions ☎ *303/639–1111 ⊕ www.cotrip.org*) plows roads efficiently, but winter snowstorms can slow traffic and create wet or icy conditions. In summer, the roads into both Grand Lake and Estes Park can see heavy traffic, especially on weekends.

CAR TRAVEL
WITHIN
THE PARK
The main thoroughfare in the park is Trail Ridge Road (U.S. 34); in winter, it's closed from the first storm in the fall (typically in October) through the spring (depending on snowpack, this could be at any time between April and June). During that time, it's plowed only up to Many Parks

CLOSE UP

Plants and Wildlife in Rocky Mountain

Volcanic uplifts and the savage clawing of receding glaciers created Rocky Mountain's majestic landscape. You'll find four distinct ecosystems here—a riparian (wetland) environment with 150 lakes and 450 mi of streams; verdant montane valleys teeming with proud ponderosa pines lush grasses; higher and colder subalpine mountains with wind-whipped trees (krummholz) that grow at right angles; and harsh, unforgiving alpine tundra with dollhouse-size versions of familiar plants and wildflowers. Alpine tundra is seldom found outside the Arctic, yet it makes up one-third of the park's terrain. Few plants can survive at this elevation of 11,000–11,500 feet, but many beautiful wildflowers—including alpine forget-me-nots—bloom here briefly in late June or early July.

The park has so much wildlife that you can often enjoy prime viewing from the seat of your car. Fall, when many animals begin moving down from higher elevations, is an excellent time to spot some of the park's animal residents. This is also when you'll hear the male elk bugle mating calls (popular spots to see and hear bugling elk are Kawuneeche Valley, Horseshoe Park, Moraine Park, and Upper Beaver Meadows).

May through mid-October is the best time to see the bighorn sheep that congregate in the Horseshoe Park/ Sheep Lakes area, just past the Fall River entrance. If you want to glimpse a moose, try Kawuneeche Valley. Other animals in the park include mule deer, squirrels, chipmunks, pikas, beavers, and marmot. Common birds include broad-tailed and rufous hummingbirds, peregrine falcons, woodpeckers, mountain bluebirds, and Clark's nutcracker, as well as the white-tailed ptarmigan, which live year-round on the alpine tundra.

Mountain lions, black bears, and bobcats also inhabit the park but are rarely seen by visitors. Altogether, the park is home to roughly 60 species of mammals and 280 bird species.

8

Curve on the east side and the Colorado River trailhead on the west side. (For current road information: ☎ 970/586–1222 ⊕ *www.coloradodot. info*). The spectacular Old Fall River Road runs one-way between the Endovalley Picnic Area on the eastern edge of the park and the Alpine Visitor Center at the summit of Trail Ridge Road, on the western side. It is typically open from July to September, depending on snowfall. It's a steep, narrow road (no wider than 14 feet), and trailers and vehicles longer than 25 feet are prohibited, but a trip on this 90-year-old thoroughfare is well worth the effort. For information on road closures, contact the park: ☎ 970/586–1206 ⊕ *www.nps.gov/romo*.

To see Trail Ridge Road the easy way—in a bus, with an expert tour guide pointing out items of interest along the way—then $27 ($13 for kids) will get you a ticket with Trail Ridge Road Tours, jointly operated by Rocky Mountain Transit and the park. Tours depart Beaver Meadows Visitor Center at 10 am and return at 3 pm (there's an hour-long break for lunch at the Alpine Visitor Center) (☎ 970/577–7477; *reservations essential*).

SHUTTLES　The park has limited parking, but offers two free shuttle buses, which operate daily from 7 am to 7 pm, mid-June to mid-October (there's weekend-only service from Memorial Day through mid-June). The Moraine Park bus runs every 30 minutes from the Fern Lake Trailhead to the Park & Ride (on Bear Lake Road, by Glacier Basin). The Bear Lake bus runs every 10 to 15 minutes from the Park & Ride to the Bear Lake Trailhead. In addition, the town of Estes Park offers two shuttle bus services, which run from the Estes Park Visitor Center to the park during the peak summer season (☎ 800/443–7823 or 970/577–9900 ⊕ www.estesparkcvb. com). The first, called the Hiker Shuttle, stops at the park's Beaver Meadows Visitor Center and the Park & Ride. The second, called the Visitor Shuttle, has three separate routes, two of which enter the park. The town also shuttles passengers between the Visitor Center and the Fairgrounds at Stanley Park, about 1 mi away. The town shuttle buses are free, but you must have a park pass to ride the buses that enter the national park.

TRAIN TRAVEL
Amtrak trains stop in downtown Denver, Winter Park/Fraser (80 mi away) and Granby (66 mi) (☎ 800/872–7245 ⊕ www.amtrak.com).

PARK ESSENTIALS
PARK FEES AND PERMITS
Entrance fees are $20 for a weekly pass, or $10 if you enter on bicycle, motorcycle, or foot. An annual pass costs $40.

Backcountry camping requires a permit that's $20 per party from May through October, and free the rest of the year. Visit ⊕ www.nps.gov/ romo/planyourvisit/backcntry_guide.htm before you go for a planning guide to backcountry camping. You can get your permit by mail, by phone, or in person. To get it by mail or in person, you can apply any time after May 1 for a permit for that calendar year (✉ Backcountry/Wilderness Permits, Rocky Mountain National Park, 1000 Hwy. 36, Estes Park, CO 80517). By phone, you can reserve a permit for that calendar year between March 1 and May 15 and after October 1 (☎ 970/586–1242). In person, you can get a day-of-trip permit year-round at one of the park's two backcountry offices, located next to the Beaver Meadows Visitor Center and in the Kawuneeche Visitor Center.

PARK HOURS
The park is open 24/7, year-round; some roads close in winter. It is in the Mountain Time zone.

CELL-PHONE RECEPTION
Cell phones work in some sections of the park. Pay phones can be found at the Glacier Basin and Moraine Park Campgrounds.

RESTAURANTS
In the park itself, there are no real dining establishments, though you can get snacks and light fare at the Trail Ridge Store, adjacent to the Alpine Visitor Center at the top of the Trail Ridge Road. The park also has a handful of scenic picnic areas, all with tables and pit or flush toilets.

HOTELS

In Estes Park, Grand Lake, and other nearby towns, the elevation keeps the climate cool, and you'll scarcely need (and you'll have a tough time finding) air-conditioned lodging. For a historic spot, try the Stanley Hotel in Estes Park, which dates to 1909 and features 138 guestrooms. The park has no hotels or lodges.

WHAT IT COSTS				
	$	$$	$$$	$$$$
Restaurants	under $8	$8–$12	$13–$20	$21–$30

Restaurant prices are per person for a main course at dinner.

VISITOR INFORMATION

PARK CONTACT INFORMATION

Rocky Mountain National Park. ⊠ *1000 U.S. 36, Estes Park* ☎ *970/586–1206* ⊕ *www.nps.gov/romo.*

VISITOR CENTERS

Alpine Visitor Center. At the top of Trail Ridge Road, this visitor center is open only when that road is navigable. There's also a small store and snack bar here. ⊠ *Fall River Pass, at junction of Trail Ridge and Old Fall River Rds., 22 mi from Beaver Meadows entrance* ☎ *970/586–1206* ⊙ *Late May–mid-June and Labor Day–Columbus Day, daily 10:30– 4:30; mid-June–Labor Day, daily 9–5.*

★ **Beaver Meadows Visitor Center.** Housing the park headquarters, this visitor center was designed by students of the Frank Lloyd Wright School of Architecture at Taliesen West using the park's popular rustic style, which integrates buildings into their natural surroundings. Completed in 1966, it was named a National Historic Landmark in 2001. The surrounding utility buildings are also on the National Register and are noteworthy examples of the rustic-style buildings that the Civilian Conservation Corps constructed during the Depression. The center has a terrific orientation film and a large relief map of the park. ⊠ *U.S. 36, 3 mi west of Estes Park and 1 mi east of Beaver Meadows Entrance Station* ☎ *970/586–1206* ⊙ *Mid-June–late Aug., 8 am–9 pm; late Aug.– Labor Day, 8–7; Labor Day–late Oct. and late Apr.–mid-June, 8–5; late Oct.–late Apr., 8–4:30.*

☼ **Fall River Visitor Center.** The Discovery Room, which houses everything from old ranger outfits to elk antlers, coyote pelts, and bighorn sheep skulls for hands-on exploration, is a favorite with kids at this visitor center. ⊠ *U.S. 34, at the Fall River Entrance Station* ☎ *970/586–1206* ⊙ *late Mar.–late Oct., daily 9 am–5 pm; winter hours vary.*

Kawuneeche Visitor Center. The only visitor center on the park's far west side, Kawuneeche has exhibits on the plant and animal life of the area, as well as a large three-dimensional map of the park and an orientation film. ⊠ *U.S. 34, 1 mi north of Grand Lake and ½ mi south of Grand Lake Entrance Station* ☎ *970/586–1206* ⊙ *Mid-June–Labor Day, 8–6; Labor Day–Sept. and May–mid-June, 8–5; Oct.–Apr., 8–4:30.*

8

EXPLORING

SCENIC DRIVES

Bear Lake Road. This 9-mi drive offers superlative views of Longs Peak (14,259-foot summit) and the glaciers surrounding Bear Lake, winding past shimmering waterfalls perpetually shrouded with rainbows. You can either drive it yourself or hop on one of the park's free shuttle buses. ⊠ *Runs from the Beaver Meadow Entrance Station to Bear Lake.*

Old Fall River Road. Nearly 100 years old and never more than 14 feet wide, this road stretches for 9 mi, from the park's east side to the Fall River Pass on the west. The drive provides spectacular views and a few white-knuckle moments, as the road is steep, serpentine, and completely lacking in guard rails. Start at West Horseshoe Park, which has the park's largest concentrations of sheep and elk, and head up the gravel road, passing Chasm Falls (there are a few places to park for a quick hike). The road is generally open from July through mid-October. ⊠ *Runs north of and roughly parallel to Trail Ridge Road, starting near Endovalley Campground (on east) and ending at Fall River Pass/Alpine Visitor Center (on west)* ⊙ *July–Oct.*

Fodor's Choice
★

Trail Ridge Road. This is the park's star attraction and the world's highest continuous paved highway, topping out at 12,183 feet. The 48-mi road connects the park's gateways of Estes Park and Grand Lake. The views around each bend—of moraines and glaciers, and craggy hills framing emerald meadows carpeted with columbine and Indian paintbrush—are truly awesome. As it passes through three ecosystems—montane, subalpine, and arctic tundra—the road climbs 4,300 feet in elevation. As you drive the road, take your time at the numerous turnouts to gaze over the verdant valleys, brushed with yellowing aspen in fall, that slope between the glacier-etched granite peaks. **Rainbow Curve** affords views of nine separate mountain peaks, each more than 10,000 feet high, and of the **Alluvial Fan**, a 42-acre swath of rocks and boulders (some the size of cars) left behind after an earthen dam broke in 1982. ∎**TIP→ You can complete a one-way trip across the park on Trail Ridge Road in two hours, but it's best to give yourself three or four hours to allow for leisurely breaks at the overlooks.** Note that the middle part of the road closes with the first big snow (typically by mid-October) and most often reopens around Memorial Day, though you can still drive up about 10 mi from the west and 8 mi from the east. ⊠ *Trail Ridge Rd. (U.S. 34), Runs between Estes Park and Grand Lake* ⊙ *June–mid-Oct.*

HISTORIC SITES

Rocky Mountain has more than 1,000 archaeological sites and 150 buildings of historic significance; 47 of the buildings are listed in the National Register of Historic Places, which is reserved for structures that tie in strongly to the park's history in terms of architecture, archaeology, engineering, or culture. Most buildings at Rocky Mountain are done in the rustic style, a design preferred by the National Park Service's first director, Stephen Mather, that works to incorporate nature into these man-made structures.

☾ **Holzwarth Historic Site.** A scenic ½-mi interpretive trail leads you over the Colorado River to the original dude ranch that the Holzwarth family ran between the 1920s and 1950s. Allow about an hour to view the buildings—including a dozen small guest cabins—and chat with a ranger. It's a great place for families to learn about homesteading. ⊠ *Off U.S. 34, about 7 mi north of Grand Lake Entrance Station, Estes Park.*

Lulu City. The remains of a few cabins are all that's left of this onetime silver mining town, established around 1880. Reach it by hiking the 3.6-mi Colorado River Trail. Look for wagon ruts from the old Stewart Toll Road and mine tailings in nearby Shipler Park (this is also a good place to spot moose). The Colorado River is a mere stream at this point, flowing south from its headwaters at nearby La Poudre Pass. ⊠ *Off Trail Ridge Rd., 9½ mi north of Grand Lake Entrance Station.*

Moraine Park Museum. Lectures, slide shows, and displays explain the park's geology, botany, and history. ⊠ *Bear Lake Rd., off U.S. 36* ▣ *Free* ☉ *Late Apr.–mid-June and Labor Day–Columbus Day, daily 9–4:30; mid-June–Labor Day, daily 9–5.*

SCENIC STOPS

Alluvial Fan. In 1982, the 79-year-old dam at Lawn Lake burst, and 220 million gallons of water roared into Estes Park, killing three people and causing millions of dollars in damage to the town. Within the park, the flood created the alluvial fan, a pile of glacial and streambed debris up to 44 feet deep on the north side of Horseshoe Park. A ½-mi trail gets you close enough to explore the area. You also can view it from the Rainbow Curve lookout on Trail Ridge Road. ⊠ *Fall River Rd., 3 mi from the Fall River Visitor Center.*

★ **Bear Lake.** Thanks to its picturesque location, easy accessibility, and the good hiking trails nearby, this small alpine lake below Flattop Mountain and Hallett Peak is one of the most popular destinations in the park. Free park shuttle buses can take you there. ⊠ *Bear Lake Rd., 7 mi southwest of Moraine Park Visitor Center, off U.S. 36.*

Forest Canyon Overlook. Beyond the classic U-shaped glacial valley lies a high-alpine circle of ice-blue pools (the Gorge Lakes) framed by ragged peaks. ⊠ *Trail Ridge Rd., 6 mi east of Alpine Visitor Center.*

EDUCATIONAL OFFERINGS

ART PROGRAM

Artist-in-Residence. Professional writers, sculptors, composers, and visual and performing artists can stay in a rustic cabin for two weeks in summer while working on their art. During their stay, they must make two presentations and donate a piece of original work to Rocky Mountain that relates to their stay. Applications must be received by December for requests for the following summer. ☏ *970/586–1206.*

CLASSES AND SEMINARS

★ **Rocky Mountain Field Seminars.** Each year, the Rocky Mountain Nature Association (RMNA) sponsors up to 100 hands-on seminars for adults and children on such topics as natural history, fishing, geology, bird-watching, wildflower identification, wildlife biology, photography, and sketching. Classes range from lectures of a few hours to overnight and multiday camping trips. Most are fairly rigorous, incorporating hiking and other outdoor activities as well as instruction. All are taught by expert instructors. ⊠ *1895 Fall River Rd., Estes Park* ☎ *970/586–3262* ⊕ *www.rmna.org* ⊠ *$10–$175 per day* ⊙ *Jan.–Nov.*

RANGER PROGRAMS

☾ **Junior Ranger Program.** Pick up a Junior Ranger activity book (in English or Spanish) at any visitor center. Program content has been developed for children ages 12 and under; the material focuses on environmental education, identifying birds and wildlife, and outdoor safety skills. Once a child has completed all of the activities in the book, a ranger will look over his or her work and award a Junior Ranger badge. Kids can also become Junior Rangers online. ☎ *970/586–1206* ⊕ *www.nps. gov/webrangers* ⊠ *Free.*

☾ **Ranger-Led Programs.** With hundreds of programs available each summer,
★ there are many opportunities to join in on free hikes, talks, and activities conducted by those who know the park best. Topics may include the wildlife, geology, vegetation, or park history. At night, storytelling, slide shows, and talks may be part of the evening campfire program, held in summer at park campgrounds and at Beaver Meadows Visitor Center. There are also evening hikes and stargazing sessions. Special programs for kids include "Skins and Skulls," a popular hands-on learning experience. Look for the extensive program schedule in the park's newspaper. ☎ *970/586–1206* ⊠ *Free.*

SPORTS AND THE OUTDOORS

BIRD-WATCHING

Spring and summer, early in the morning, are the best times for bird-watching in the park. **Lumpy Ridge** is a nesting ground for several kinds of birds of prey. Migratory songbirds from South America have summer breeding grounds near the **Endovalley Picnic Area.** The **alpine tundra** is habitat for white-tailed ptarmigan. The **Alluvial Fan** is the place for viewing broad-tailed hummingbirds, hairy woodpeckers, ouzels, and the occasional raptor.

FISHING

Rocky Mountain is a wonderful place to fish, especially for trout—German brown, brook, rainbow, cutthroat, and greenback cutthroat—but check at a visitor center about regulations and information on specific closures, catch-and-release areas, and limits on size and possession. No fishing is allowed at Bear Lake. To avoid the crowds, rangers

SPOTTING WILDLIFE

If you see a group of cars pulled over at a seemingly random section of road, with passengers staring intently at something in the distance, it's a good bet that an animal is within sight. May through mid-October is the best time to see the bighorn sheep that congregate in the Horseshoe Park/Sheep Lakes area, just past the Fall River entrance. Elk can be seen year-round throughout the park and the surrounding area (downtown Estes Park can get serious "traffic jams" when elk decide to congregate on the streets). Kawuneeche Valley, on the park's western side, is the most likely location to glimpse a moose. In the early mornings and evenings, listen for the eerie howling of coyotes throughout the park.

Fall is an excellent time to spot many types of wildlife, when certain animals begin moving down from the higher elevations. This is also when you'll hear the male elk bugle mating calls to their female counterparts. The sound also serves to draw large crowds to popular "listening" spots—Horseshoe Park, Moraine Park, and Upper Beaver Meadows—in the early evening.

Spring and summer are the best times for bird-watching. Go early in the morning, before the crowds arrive. Lumpy Ridge is the nesting ground of raptors such as golden eagles, red-tailed hawks, and peregrine. You can see migratory songbirds from South America in their summer breeding grounds near the Endovalley Picnic Area. The alpine tundra is habitat for white-tailed ptarmigan. The Alluvial Fan, along the Roaring River, is an excellent place for viewing broad-tailed hummingbirds, hairy woodpeckers, robins, ouzels, and the occasional raptor.

Keep a camera with a good telephoto lens handy for those close-ups of animals. Approaching, chasing, or feeding any wildlife in the park is forbidden, and it also unduly stresses the animals and can create real problems for both humans and the animals themselves.

recommend angling in the more-remote backcountry. To fish in the park, anyone 16 and older must have a valid Colorado fishing license, which you can obtain at local sporting-goods stores. See ⊕ *www. wildlife.state.co.us/fishing* for details.

TOURS AND OUTFITTERS

Estes Angler. This popular fishing guide arranges four-, six-, and eight-hour fly-fishing trips—as well as full-day horseback excursions—into the park's quieter regions, year-round, with a maximum of three people per guide. The best times for fishing are generally from April to mid-November. Equipment is also available for rent. ⊠ *338 W. Riverside Dr., Estes Park* ☎ *970/586–2110, 800/586–2110* ⊕ *www.estesangler. com* ⊗ *Daily 9–5.*

Kirks Fly Shop. This Estes Park outfitter offers various guided fly-fishing trips, as well as backpacking, horseback, and llama pack trips. The store also carries fishing and backpacking gear. ⊠ *230 E. Elkhorn Ave., Estes Park* ☎ *970/577–0790, 877/669–1859* ⊕ *www.kirksflyshop.com* ⊗ *In summer, daily 7 am–8 pm; winter hrs vary.*

Scot's Sporting Goods. This shop rents and sells fishing gear, and provides four-, six-, and eight-hour instruction trips daily from May through September. Clinics, geared toward first-timers, focus on casting, reading the water, identifying insects for flies, and properly presenting natural and artificial flies to the fish. Half-day excursions into the park are available for three or more people. A range of camping and hiking equipment is also for sale. ⊠ *870 Moraine Ave., Estes Park* ☎ *970/586–2877 May–Sept., 970/443–4932 Oct.–Apr.* ⊕ *www.scotssportinggoods.com* ☉ *June–Aug., daily 8–8; May and Sept–mid-Oct., daily 9–5* ⊠ *870 Moraine Ave., Estes Park* ☎ *970/586–2877* ⊕ *www.scotssportinggoods.com.*

HIKING

Fodor's Choice
★

Rocky Mountain National Park contains more than 355 mi of hiking trails, so you could theoretically wander the park for weeks. Most visitors explore just a small portion of these trails—those that are closest to the roads and visitor centers—which means that some of the park's most accessible and scenic paths can resemble a backcountry highway on busy summer days. The high-alpine terrain around Bear Lake is the park's most popular hiking area, and although it's well worth exploring, you'll get a more frontierlike experience by hiking one of the trails in the less-explored sections of the park, such as the far northern end or in the Wild Basin area to the south. Keep in mind that trails at higher elevations may have some snow on them, even in late summer. And because of afternoon thunderstorms on most summer afternoons, an early morning start is highly recommended: the last place you want to be when a storm approaches is on a peak or anywhere above the tree line. All trail mileages are round-trip unless stated otherwise.

EASY

★ **Bear Lake Trail.** The virtually flat nature trail around Bear Lake is an easy, 1-mi walk that's wheelchair and stroller accessible. Sharing the route with you will likely be plenty of other hikers as well as songbirds and chipmunks. *Easy.* ⊠ *Trailhead at Bear Lake, Bear Lake Rd.*

☉ **Copeland Falls.** The 0.6-mi hike to these Wild Basin Area falls is a good option for families, as the terrain is relatively flat (there's only a 15-foot elevation gain). *Easy.* ⊠ *Trailhead at Wild Basin Ranger Station.*

Cub Lake. This 4.6-mi, three-hour (round-trip) hike takes you through meadows and stands of aspen trees and up 540 feet in elevation to a lake with water lilies. *Easy.* ⊠ *Trailhead at Cub Lake, 1.7 mi from Moraine Park Campground.*

East Inlet Trail. An easy hike of 0.3 mi from East Inlet trailhead, just outside the park in Grand Lake, will get you to **Adams Falls** in about 15 minutes. The area around the falls is often packed with visitors, so if you have time, continue east to enjoy more solitude, see wildlife, and catch views of **Mount Craig** from near the East Meadow campground. Note, however, that the trail beyond the falls has an elevation gain of between 1,500 and 1,900 feet, making it a more challenging hike. *Easy.* ⊠ *Trailhead at East Inlet, end of W. Portal Road (CO 278) in Grand Lake, Grand Lake.*

Glacier Gorge Trail. The 4.5-mi hike to **Mills Lake** can be crowded, but the reward is one the park's prettiest lakes, set against the breathtaking backdrop of Longs Peak, Pagoda Mountain, and the Keyboard of the Winds. There's a modest elevation gain of 700 feet. On the way, about 1 mi in, you pass **Alberta Falls,** a popular destination in and of itself. The hike travels along Glacier Creek, under the shade of a subalpine forest. Give yourself at least four hours for hiking and lingering. *Easy.* ✉ *Trailhead off Bear Lake Rd., about 1 mi southeast of Bear Lake.*

★ **Sprague Lake.** With virtually no elevation gain, this 1-mi, pine-lined path near a popular backcountry campground is wheelchair accessible and provides views of Hallet Peak and Flattop Mountain. *Easy.* ✉ *Trailhead at Sprague Lake, Bear Lake Rd., 4.4 mi southwest of Moraine Park Visitor Center.*

HIKERS SHUTTLE

The many trails in the Bear Lake area of the park are so popular that parking areas at the trailheads usually cannot accommodate all of the hikers' cars. Shuttle buses connect a large park-and-ride facility at the Glacier Basin Campground with the Cub Lake, Fern Lake, Glacier Gorge Junction, Sprague Lake, and Bear Lake trailheads. Buses run daily between mid-June and mid-September (and on weekends between Memorial Day and mid-June), 7 am to 7 pm. The Bear Lake shuttle runs approximately every 10 to 15 minutes; the Moraine Park shuttle runs approximately every 30 minutes.

MODERATE

Fodor's Choice **Bear Lake to Emerald Lake.** This scenic, caloric-burning hike begins with
★ a moderately level, ½ mi journey to **Nymph Lake.** From here, the trail gets steeper, with a 425-foot elevation gain, as it winds around for 0.6 mi to **Dream Lake.** The last stretch is the most arduous part of the hike, an almost all-uphill 0.7-mi trek to lovely **Emerald Lake,** where you can perch on a boulder and enjoy the view. All told, the hike is 3.6 mi, with an elevation gain of 605 feet. Allow two hours or more, depending on stops. *Moderate.* ✉ *Trailhead at Bear Lake, off Bear Lake Rd., 7.9 mi southwest of the Moraine Park Visitor Center.*

Colorado River Trail. This walk to the ghost town of Lulu City on the west side of the park is excellent for looking for the bighorn sheep, elk, and moose that reside in the area. Part of the former stagecoach route that went from Granby to Walden, the 3.1-mi trail parallels the infant Colorado River to the meadow where Lulu City once stood. The elevation gain is 300 feet. *Moderate.* ✉ *Trailhead at Colorado River, off Trail Ridge Rd., 1.7 mi north of the Timber Creek Campground.*

Fern Lake Trail. Heading to Odessa Lake from the north involves a steep hike, but on most days you'll encounter fewer other hikers than if you had begun the trip at Bear Lake. Along the way, you'll come to the Arch Rocks; the Pool, an eroded formation in the Big Thompson River; two waterfalls; and Fern Lake (4.9 mi from your starting point). Odessa Lake itself lies at the foot of Tourmaline Gorge, below the craggy summits of Gabletop Mountain, Little Matterhorn, Knobtop Mountain,

8

Bear Lake Region

0 _____ 1 mi

0 _____ 1 km

Bierstadt Lake

0.7mi

Bierstadt

0.5mi

Bear Lake

🏕️ 🚻 **Bear Lake**

Nymph Lake

Emerald Lake 0.7mi 0.6mi

Dream Lake 0.5mi

Glacier Gorge

0.9mi

Lake Haiyaha 1.7mi

0.2mi

1.9mi 2.3mi

0.5mi

0.9mi 0.6mi 3.0mi

0.6mi The Loc Mills Lake

Jewel Lake

and Notchtop Mountain. For a full day of spectacular scenery, continue past Odessa to Bear Lake (9 mi total), where you can pick up the shuttle back to the Fern Lake Trailhead. *Moderate.* ⊠ *Trailhead off Bear Lake Rd., about 2.5 mi south of Moraine Park Visitor Center.*

Sun Valley Trail System. This 3,100-mi corridor, which extends from Montana's Canadian border to the southern edge of New Mexico, enters Rocky Mountain National Park in two places, at trailheads only about 4 mi apart and located on either side of the Kawuneeche Visitor Center on Trail Ridge Road, at the park's southwestern end. Within the park, it covers about 30 mi of spectacular montane and subalpine terrain and follows the existing Green Mountain, Tonahutu Creek, North Inlet, and East Shore Trails. *Moderate.* ⊠ *Trailheads at Harbison Meadows Picnic Area, off Trail Ridge Rd., about 1 mi inside park from Grand Lake Entrance, and at East Shore Trailhead, just south of Grand Lake.*

DIFFICULT

Chasm Lake Trail. Nestled in the shadow of Longs Peak and Mount Meeker, Chasm Lake offers one of Colorado's most impressive backdrops, which also means you can expect to encounter plenty of other hikers on the way. The 4.2-mi Chasm Lake Trail, reached via the Longs Peak Trail, has a 2,360-foot elevation gain. Just before the lake, you'll need to climb a small rock ledge, which can be a bit of a challenge for

CLOSE UP

Longs Peak: The Northernmost Fourteener

At 14,259 feet above sea level, **Longs Peak** has long fascinated explorers to the region. Explorer and author Isabella L. Bird wrote of it, "It is one of the noblest of mountains, but in one's imagination it grows to be much more than a mountain. It becomes invested with a personality."

It was named after Major Stephen H. Long, who led an expedition in 1820 up the Platte River to the base of the Rockies. Long never ascended the mountain—in fact, he didn't even get within 40 mi of it—but a few decades later, in 1868, the one-armed Civil War veteran John Wesley Powell climbed to its summit.

Longs Peak is the northernmost of the Fourteeners—the 54 mountains in Colorado that reach above the 14,000-foot mark—and one of more than 114 named mountains in the park that are higher than 10,000 feet. The peak, in the park's southeast quadrant, has a distinctive flat-topped, rectangular summit that is visible from many spots on the park's east side and on Trail Ridge Road.

The ambitious climb to Longs summit is only recommended for those who are strong climbers and well acclimated to the altitude. If you're up for it, be sure to begin before dawn so that you're down from the summit when the typical afternoon thunderstorm hits.

the less surefooted; follow the cairns for the most straightforward route. Once atop the ledge, you'll catch your first memorable view of the lake. *Difficult. ⊠ Trailhead at Longs Peak Ranger Station, off Rte. 7, 10 mi from the Beaver Meadows Visitor Center.*

★ **Longs Peak Trail.** Climbing this 14,259-foot mountain (one of 54 "Fourteeners" in Colorado) is an ambitious goal for almost anyone—but only those who are very fit and acclimated to the altitude should attempt it. The 16-mi round-trip climb requires a predawn start (3 am is ideal), so that you're off the summit before the typical summer afternoon thunderstorm hits. Also, the last 2 mi or so of the trail are very exposed—you have to traverse narrow ledges with vertigo-inducing drop-offs. That said, summiting Longs can be one of the most rewarding experiences you'll ever have. The Keyhole route is the most popular means of ascent, and the number of people going up it on a summer day can be astounding, given the rigors of the climb. Though just as scenic, the Loft route, between Longs and Mount Meeker from Chasm Lake, is less crowded but not as clearly marked and therefore more difficult to navigate. *Difficult. ⊠ Trailhead at Longs Peak Ranger Station, off Rte. 7, 10 mi from Beaver Meadows Visitor Center.*

HORSEBACK RIDING

Horses and riders can access 260 mi of trails in Rocky Mountain.

TOURS AND OUTFITTERS

Sombrero Ranches, Inc. Part of the Sombrero Ranches operation, which runs five several stables in the Rocky Mountain area, Estes Park Stables offers guided rides into the Roosevelt National Wilderness and Rocky Mountain National Park, including scenic and relaxing early-morning breakfast rides and pack trips. ✉ *1895 Big Thompson Ave., Estes Park* ⌖ *Sombrero Ranches, Inc., 911 Kimbark St. 80501* ☎ *970/586–4577* ⊕ *www.sombrero.com* ◔ *Open year-round* ✉ *Glacier Creek Campground, off Bear Lake Rd. near Sprague Lake80517* ☎ *970/586–3244 stables, 970/586–4577 off-season reservations* ◔ *Open May–mid-Sept.* ✉ *Moraine Park Campground, off Bear Lake Rd.80517* ☎ *970/586–2327 stables, 970/586–4577 off-season reservations* ◔ *Open May–mid-Sept..*

ROCK CLIMBING

Expert rock climbers as well as novices can try hundreds of classic and big wall climbs here (there's also ample opportunity for bouldering and mountaineering). The burgeoning sport of ice climbing also thrives in the park. The Diamond, Lumpy Ridge, and Petit Grepon are the places for serious rock climbing, while well-known ice-climbing spots include Hidden Falls, Loch Vale, and Emerald and Black lakes.

OUTFITTERS

★ **Colorado Mountain School.** Colorado Mountain School has been guiding climbers since 1877 and is an invaluable resource for climbers in the Rocky Mountain area (they're also the park's only official provider of technical climbing services). They can teach you rock climbing, mountaineering, ice climbing, avalanche survival, and many other skills. Take introductory half-day and one- to seven-day courses on climbing and rappelling technique, or sign up for guided introductory trips, full-day climbs, and longer expeditions. Make reservations as far as six weeks in advance for summer climbs. The school also runs a 16-bed hostel ($25 a night). ✉ *341 Moraine Ave., Estes Park* ☎ *800/836–4008, 303/447–2804* ⊕ *www.totalclimbing.com.*

WINTER SPORTS

Each winter, the popularity of snowshoeing in the park increases. It's a wonderful way to experience Rocky Mountain's majestic winter side, when the jagged peaks are softened with a blanket of snow and the summer hordes are nonexistent. You can snowshoe any of the summer hiking trails that are accessible by road; many of them also become well-traveled cross-country ski trails. Two trails to try are Tonahutu Creek Trail (near Kawuneeche Visitor Center) and the Colorado River Trail to Lulu City (start at the Timber Creek Campground).

Backcountry skiing within the park ranges from gentle cross-country outings to full-on, experts-only adventures down steep chutes and open bowls. Ask a ranger about conditions, and gear up as if you were spending the night. If you plan on venturing off trail, take a shovel, probe pole, and avalanche transceiver. Only on the west side of the park are you permitted to snowmobile, and you must register at Kawuneeche Visitor Center before traveling the unplowed section of Trail Ridge Road up to Milner Pass. Check the park newspaper, *High Country Headlines,* for ranger-guided tours.

TOURS AND OUTFITTERS

Estes Park Mountain Shop. You can rent or buy snowshoes and skis here, as well as fishing, hiking, and climbing equipment. The store is open year-round and gives four-, six-, and eight-hour guided snowshoeing, fly-fishing, and climbing trips to areas in and around Rocky Mountain National Park. ⊠ *2050 Big Thompson Ave., Estes Park* ☎ *970/586–6548, 866/303–6548* ⊕ *www.estesparkmountainshop.com* ⊗ *Daily 8 am–9 pm.*

Never Summer Mountain Products. This well-stocked shop sells and rents all sorts of outdoor equipment, including cross-country skis, hiking gear, kayaks, and camping supplies. ⊠ *919 Grand Ave., Grand Lake* ☎ *970/627–3642.*

Trail Ridge Store. This is the park's only official store (though you'll find a small selection of park souvenirs and books at the visitor centers). Trail Ridge stocks sweatshirts and jackets, postcards, and assorted craft items. ⊠ *Trail Ridge Rd., adjacent to Alpine Visitor Center* ⊗ *Closed mid-Oct.–late May (when Trail Ridge Rd. is closed).*

NEARBY TOWNS

Estes Park, 5 mi east of Rocky Mountain, is the park's most popular gateway. The town sits at an altitude of more than 7,500 feet, with 14,259-foot Longs Peak and a legion of surrounding mountains as its stunning backdrop. Many of the small hotels lining the roads are mom-and-pop outfits that have been passed down through several generations. Estes Park's quieter cousin, **Grand Lake,** 1½ mi outside the park's west entrance, gets busy in summer, but has a low-key, quintessentially Western graciousness. In winter, it's *the* snowmobiling and ice-fishing destination for Front Range Coloradans. At the park's southwestern entrance are the Arapaho and Roosevelt National Forests, Arapaho National Recreational Area, and the small town of **Granby,** the place to go for big-game hunting and mountain biking. There are also skiing and other mountain activities (both summer and winter varieties) at nearby SolVista Basin and the Winter Park/Mary Jane ski areas. ⇨ *For more information on Estes Park, Grand Lake, and Granby, see the Boulder and North Central Colorado section.*

WHERE TO EAT

IN THE PARK

¢ ✕ **Cafe at Trail Ridge and Trail Ridge Coffee Bar.** The park's only source for
AMERICAN food, Cafe offers snacks and sandwiches, burgers, and soups. At the Coffee Bar, you'll find fair trade coffee, espresso drinks, and tea, plus water, juice, and salads. The Cafe and Coffee Bar are in the same building as

CLOSE UP

Best Campgrounds in Rocky Mountain

Five top-notch campgrounds and one group camping area accommodate campers looking to stay in a tent, trailer, or RV (only three campgrounds accept reservations; the others fill up on a first-come, first-served basis).

Aspenglen Campground. This quiet, east-side spot near the north entrance is set in open pine woodland along Fall River. It doesn't have the views of Moraine Park or Glacier Basin, but it is small and peaceful. There are a few excellent walk-in sites for those who want to pitch a tent away from the crowds but still close to the car. Reservations are not accepted. ✉ *Drive past Fall River Visitor Center on U.S. 34 and turn left at the campground road.*

Glacier Basin Campground. Rest near the banks of Glacier Creek and take in views of the Continental Divide. There's easy access to a network of many popular trails,

and rangers come here for campfire programs. ✉ *Drive 5 mi south from U.S. 36 along Bear Lake Rd.* ☎ *877/444–6777.*

Longs Peak Campground. Hikers going up Longs Peak can stay at this year-round campground. Sites are first-come, first-served. ✉ *9 mi south of Estes Park on Rte. 7.*

Moraine Park Campground. This popular campground hosts ranger-led campfire programs and is near hiking trails. You'll hear elk bugling if you camp here in September or October. ✉ *Drive south on Bear Lake Rd. from U.S. 36, ¾ mi to campground entrance* ☎ *877/444–6777*

Timber Creek Campground. Anglers love this spot on the Colorado River, 10 mi from Grand Lake village. In the evening you can sit in on ranger-led campfire programs. Reservations are not accepted. ✉ *Trail Ridge Rd. 1, 2 mi west of Alpine Visitor Center.*

---

the Trail Ridge Store, adjacent to the Alpine Visitor Center, and are open seasonally, whenever Trail Ridge Road is open. ✉ *Trail Ridge Rd., at Alpine Visitor Center* ☎ *970/586–3097* ☽ *Late May–mid-June and late Aug.–mid-Oct., daily 10–4:30; mid-June–late Aug., daily 8–5.*

PICNIC AREAS

Endovalley. With 32 tables and 30 fire grates, this is the largest picnic area in the park. Here, you'll find aspen groves, nice views of Fall River Pass—and lovely Fan Lake a short hike away. ✉ *Off U.S. 34, at beginning of Old Fall River Rd., 4.4 mi from Fall River Visitor Center.*

Hollowell Park. In a meadow near Mill Creek, this lovely spot for a picnic has nine tables and is open year-round. It's also close to the Hollowell Park and Mill Creek Basin Trailheads. ✉ *Off Bear Lake Rd., 2.4 mi from Moraine Park Visitor Center.*

☽ **Sprague Lake.** With 27 tables and 16 fire grates, there's plenty of room for the whole gang at this alfresco dining spot. It's open year-round, with flush toilets in the summer and vault toilets the rest of the year. ✉ *0.6 mi from intersection of Bear Lake Rd. and U.S. 36, 3.9 mi from Bear Lake.*

Northwest Colorado and Steamboat Springs

WORD OF MOUTH

"Steamboat is a great choice for the summer, especially if you're bringing your family! [It's] surrounded by world-class mountain biking and hiking, or if you want to just hang out you can take a relaxing tube ride down the river, play a round of golf or disc golf, or hang out by the pool at one of the great resorts."

—RQSteamboat

Updated by
Kyle Wagner

Varied terrain attracts bold outdoors enthusiasts, and gen-teel towns are tucked among the craggy cliffs for those seeking quieter pursuits. Whatever your choice, the northwest region's more remote location and mountain-dominated landscape give it a largely undiscovered feel, and many of the activities lack the crowds and frenzy attached to those in more heavily populated areas.

Adventures in these far-western and northern regions of the state might range from a bone-jarring mountain-bike ride on the Kokopelli Trail—a 142-mi route through remote desert sandstone and shale canyon from Grand Junction to Moab—to a heart-pounding raft trip down the Green River, where Major John Wesley Powell made his epic exploration of this continent's last uncharted wilderness in 1869. Colorado National Monument and Dinosaur National Monument have endless opportunities for hiking. For the less adventurous, a visit to the wine country makes for a relaxing afternoon, or try your hand at excavating prehistoric bones from a dinosaur quarry. Rich in more recent history as well, the area is home to the Museum of Western Colorado and Escalante Canyon, named after Spanish missionary explorer Francisco Silvestre Velez de Escalante, who with father Francisco Atanasio Dominguez led an expedition through the area in 1776.

Farther east, flanked by mountains with some of the softest snow in the world, even the cowboys don skis. Steamboat Springs is Colorado at its most authentic, where hay bales and cattle crowd pastures, McMansions are regarded with disdain, high-schoolers compete in local rodeos, deer hang from front porches during hunting season, and high fashion means clean jeans. Steamboat Ski Resort has none of the pretensions of the glitzier Colorado resorts.

Even the less-visited corners of the region have plenty of cultural opportunities for those willing to seek them out. Dotting the area are art galleries, antiques shops, and many small eateries with alfresco seating. People are friendly and share plenty of tourist tips just for the asking. As for quirky festivals, you might have a hard time choosing between the Olathe Sweet Corn Festival, Country Jam, or the Mike the Headless Chicken Festival. The laid-back lifestyle here is the perfect example to follow—chill out and explore the region at your own pace.

ORIENTATION AND PLANNING

GETTING ORIENTED

A little planning goes a long way when visiting this region. Grand Junction, the largest city between Denver and Salt Lake City, makes an ideal hub for exploring. Many of the sights, except for Steamboat

TOP REASONS TO GO

Colorado National Monument: Gaze out over Grand Junction toward the Bookcliffs along the 23-mi Rim Rock Drive or hike one of the many trails through sandstone canyons.

Dinosaur National Monument: Wander among thousands of fossilized skeletons that remain embedded in the rugged hillsides or take a raft trip down the Green or Yampa rivers.

Grand Junction and Palisade Wine tasting: More than two-dozen local wineries have garnered attention for their grapes grown in the unique high-altitude soil.

Steamboat Springs Horseback riding: Choose from an authentic dude ranch experience, a pack trip into the wilderness, or a gentle alpine trail ride.

Strawberry Park Hot Springs: Though it takes some work to get here, it's well worth the effort to soak away what ails you in the rustic, rock-lined setting.

Springs, are less than two hours from Grand Junction. You can make the loop from Delta to Cedaredge and Grand Mesa to Palisade easily in a day. If you want to break up the trip, stop in Cedaredge. The loop in the opposite direction—including Meeker, Craig, Dinosaur National Monument, and Rangely—is longer, but there's decent lodging along the way, with the exception of Dinosaur National Monument, where there's only camping.

If you're headed to Steamboat Springs from Denver in winter, exercise caution on Highway 40. It sees less traffic than I–70, but it can be treacherous in the Berthoud Pass stretch during snowstorms.

Grand Junction and Around. This narrow city is a quiet, gracious locale that easily balances raucous outdoor adventures and a thriving cultural scene. The Colorado National Monument and Bookcliffs dominate the landscape, but Palisade, with its peaches and wines, and Fruita, a burgeoning mountain-biking mecca, command ever-increasing attention.

Steamboat Springs. Unlike some of the other ski towns, Steamboat has always been a "real" town. With its touch of the Old West and plenty of cowboys still hanging around, visitors are usually torn—hot springs, horseback riding, or skiing?

Northwest Corner. The world's largest flat-topped mountain, the Grand Mesa, has a 55-mile Scenic Byway that feels a little like Land of the Lost. Meanwhile, Dinosaur National Monument offers thousands of fossils and hiking trails. Stop in nearby Craig or Rangely to refuel yourself and your vehicle.

PLANNING

WHEN TO GO

The region has four distinct seasons. The heaviest concentration of tourists is in summer, when school is out and families hit the road for a little together time. Temperatures in summer frequently reach into the high 80s and 90s, although the mercury has been known to top triple digits on occasion. You might have a hard time finding a hotel room during late May and late June thanks to the National Junior College World Series (baseball) and Country Jam music festival, both in Grand Junction. Hotels fill quickly in fall, which brings an explosion of colors. Days are warm, but nights are crisp and cool. There's still time to enjoy activities like fishing, hiking, and backpacking before the snow flies. Grand Mesa is a winter favorite among locals looking for a quick fix for cabin fever. Powder hounds can't wait to strap on their newly waxed skis and hit the slopes at Steamboat and Powderhorn ski resorts.

GETTING HERE AND AROUND

AIR TRAVEL

Grand Junction Regional Airport (GJT) is served by America West Express, Sky West, Great Lakes (Frontier), and United Express.

Yampa Valley Regional Airport (HDN) is in Hayden, 22 mi from Steamboat Springs. American, Continental, Delta, Northwest, and United fly nonstop from various gateways during ski season.

Taxis and shuttle services are available in Grand Junction and Steamboat Springs.

Airport Contacts Grand Junction Regional Airport (GJT) ✉ *2828 Walker Field Dr., Grand Junction* ☎ *970/244–9100* ⊕ *www.gjairport.com.* **Yampa Valley Regional Airport (HDN)** ✉ *Hayden* ☎ *970/276–3669.*

CAR TRAVEL

In northwestern Colorado I–70 (U.S. 6) is the major thoroughfare, accessing Grand Junction and Grand Mesa (via Route 65, which runs to Delta). Meeker is reached via Route 13 and Rangely and Dinosaur via Route 64. U.S. 40 east from Utah is the best way to reach Dinosaur National Monument and Craig.

From Denver, Steamboat Springs is about a three-hour drive northwest via I–70 and U.S. 40. The route traverses some high-mountain passes, so it's a good idea to check road conditions before you travel.

Grand Junction has gas stations that are open 24 hours. Most gas stations in the smaller towns are open until 10 pm in summer, and even some automated credit-card pumps shut down at that hour.

Most roads are paved and in fairly good condition. Summer is peak road-construction season, so expect some delays. Be prepared for winter driving conditions at all times. Enterprise car rental is in downtown Grand Junction, with free pickup. Avis and Hertz are in the Walker Field Airport terminal. Depending on where you're traveling, you might want a four-wheel drive. Avis has car rentals in Steamboat Springs.

Car Travel Contacts AAA Colorado ☎ *970/245–2236* ⊕ *www.aaa.com.* **Colorado State Patrol** ☎ *970/249–4392* ⊕ *www.csp.state.co.us.* **Road Report** ☎ *877/315–7623* ⊕ *www.cotrip.org.*

TRAIN TRAVEL

Amtrak provides daily service to the East and West coasts through downtown Grand Junction.

Train Contacts Amtrak ☎ *800/872–7245* ⊕ *www.amtrak.com.*

PARKS AND RECREATION AREAS

The blushing red-rock cliffs of the **Colorado National Monument** are easily accessible by winding roads that open to miles of hiking trails. **Dinosaur National Monument** holds a stunning cache of fossils as well as spectacular scenery aboveground for family-friendly hiking.

Browns Park Wildlife Refuge. A bird-watcher's destination with species from ducks to bald eagles, the remote Browns Park Wildlife Refuge northwest of Maybell can be navigated by car or horseback, or on foot. ⊕ *www.fws.gov/brownspark.*

Flat Tops Wilderness. The Flat Tops Wilderness is an alpine mesa with good stream and lake fishing and excellent deer and elk hunting. It's southwest of Steamboat Springs. ⊕ *www.fs.fed.us/r2/whiteriver.*

Grand Mesa National Forest. Grand Mesa National Forest shimmers with peaceful alpine lakes and great fishing and hiking in summer, along with trails for snowmobiling in winter. ⊕ *www.fs.fed.us/r2/gmug.*

Medicine Bow/Routt National Forests. Steamboat Springs is surrounded by the Medicine Bow/Routt National Forests, which stretch across northern Colorado and into southern Wyoming, embracing more than half a dozen mountain ranges, including the Gore, Flat Tops, Park, Medicine Bow, Sierra Madre, and Laramie. ⊕ *www.fs.fed.us/r2/mbr.*

RESTAURANTS

The usual chain restaurants ring Grand Junction, but they're joined by eclectic gourmet pizza joints and authentic Mexican restaurants. Look for made-from-scratch delicacies at mom-and-pop bakeries—especially worth seeking out during summer fruit harvests. In season, Palisade peaches, Olathe sweet corn, and Cedaredge apples find their way onto menus, and they're sometimes paired with a multitude of local wines. For something traditional, it's hard to beat a great hand-battered chicken-fried steak smothered in creamy gravy—which is available in just about any town in the area.

The town of Steamboat Springs, in the heart of cattle country, has far more carnivorous delights—including elk, deer, and bison—than you're likely to find in the trendier resorts of Aspen, Telluride, and Vail. The Steamboat ski resort, separated geographically from town, is more eclectic, with small sushi bars and Mediterranean cafés hidden among the boutiques.

HOTELS

In Grand Junction Horizon Drive has the largest concentration of hotels and motels, conveniently near the airport and within walking distance of a handful of restaurants. For the budget conscious, there are many no-frills motels as well as hotel branches of the well-known chains. History buffs might enjoy a stay at a dude ranch, one of the many rustic cabin rentals, or the famed Meeker Hotel, once frequented by Teddy Roosevelt. For those looking for the comforts of home, the area has a nice selection of bed-and-breakfasts, including one that has a llama herd and others set in fruit orchards and vineyards. Be sure to ask for off-season lodging rates, which could save you a bundle.

Steamboat Springs is unique in the state because it has high-end dude ranches and ranch resorts, which are less abundant in resort areas like Aspen, Summit County, and Vail.

WHAT IT COSTS					
	¢	$	$$	$$$	$$$$
Restaurants	under $8	$8–$12	$13–$18	$19–$25	over $25
Hotels	under $80	$80–$120	$121–$170	$171–$230	over $230

Restaurant prices are for a main course at dinner, excluding 6.5%–8.4% tax. Hotel prices are for two people in a standard double room in high season, excluding service charges and 9.4%–10.65% tax.

GRAND JUNCTION AND AROUND

With its mild climate and healthy economy, Grand Junction and the surrounding area make northwestern Colorado an inviting destination. A thriving retirement community and mountain-biking headquarters, the Grand Valley also counts superior soil and top-notch ranching among its assets. The contrast between the sandstone of the Bookcliffs and the canyons of the Colorado National Monument with the greenery of the lush orchards below, particularly in nearby Palisade, makes for a pleasant road trip.

GRAND JUNCTION

255 mi west of Denver via I–70.

Grand Junction is where the mountains and desert meet at the confluence of the mighty Colorado and Gunnison rivers—a grand junction indeed. No matter which direction you look, there's an adventure waiting to happen. The city, with a population of approximately 58,000, is nestled between the picturesque Grand Mesa to the south and the towering Bookcliffs to the north. It's a great base camp for a vacation—whether you're into art galleries, boutiques, hiking, horseback riding, rafting, mountain biking, or winery tours.

The Art on the Corner exhibit showcases leading regional sculptors, whose latest works are installed on the Main Street Mall. Passersby may find their faces reflected in an enormous chrome buffalo (titled *Chrome on the Range II*) or, a few streets down, encounter an enormous cactus made entirely of rusted (but still prickly) chainsaw chains.

GETTING HERE AND AROUND

A Touch With Class has regular limo service into Grand Junction and outlying communities. Sunshine Taxi serves Grand Junction. Amtrak runs the California Zephyr round-trip from San Francisco to Chicago, which stops in Grand Junction, Glenwood Springs, Winter Park, and Denver. Grand Valley Transit operates 11 public bus routes that are geared to commuters between Grand Junction, Palisade, Clifton, Orchard Mesa, and Fruita.

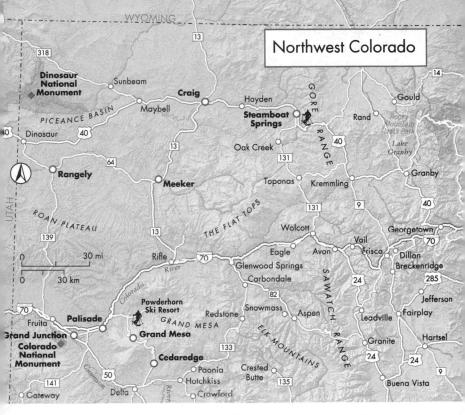

Northwest Colorado

TOURS American Spirit Shuttle runs custom tours of Colorado National Monument and the Grand Junction area, and will also run shuttles for biking and hiking in the area. Dinosaur Journey leads one- and three-day paleontological treks that include work in a dinosaur quarry.

WHEN TO GO

FESTIVALS **Country Jam** is held every June and draws the biggest names in country music, such as Lady Antebellum and Alan Jackson, while **Rock Jam** is held in September with headliners such as Def Leppard and Godsmack.

ESSENTIALS

Festivals Country Jam and Rock Jam. ⊠ *Country Jam USA Ranch, Mack* ☎ *800/780–0526* ⊕ *countryjam.com.*

Tour Information Dinosaur Journey ⊠ *550 Jurassic Ct., Fruita* ☎ *970/858–7282* ⊕ *www.dinosaurjourney.org.* **Eagle Tree Tours** ⊠ *339 S. 1st St.* ☎ *970/523–7662* ⊕ *www.americanspiritshuttle.com.*

Transportation Contacts A Touch With Class ☎ *970/245–5466.* **Amtrak** ☎ *800/872–7245* ⊕ *www.amtrak.com.* **Grand Valley Transit** ☎ *970/256–7433* ⊕ *www.gvt.mesacounty.us.* **Sunshine Taxi** ☎ *970/245–8294.*

Visitor Information Grand Junction Visitor & Convention Bureau ⊠ *740 Horizon Dr.* ☎ *800/962–2547, 970/244–1480* ⊕ *www.visitgrandjunction.com.*

EXPLORING

Art Center. The Art Center rotates a fine permanent collection of Native American tapestries and Western contemporary art, including the only complete series of lithographs by noted printmaker Paul Pletka. The fantastically carved doors—done by a WPA artist in the 1930s—alone are worth the visit. Take time to view the elegant historic homes along North 7th Street afterward. Admission is free on Tuesdays and always for children under 12. ✉ *1803 N. 7th St.* ☎ *970/243-7337* ⊕ *www.gjartcenter.org* ✑ *$3* ⊙ *Tues.–Sat. 9–4.*

Museum of Western Colorado/Museum of the West. The Museum of Western Colorado/Museum of the West relates the history of the area since the 1880s, with a time line, a firearms display, and a Southwest pottery collection. The area's rich mining heritage is perfectly captured in the uranium mine that educates with interactive sound and exhibit stations. The museum also runs the Cross Orchards Living History Farm and the Dinosaur Journey Museum, and oversees paleontological excavations. ✉ *462 Ute Ave.* ☎ *970/242-0971* ⊕ *www.museumofwesternco.com* ✑ *$6.50* ⊙ *May–Sept., Tues.–Sat. 10–5, Oct.–Apr., Tues.–Sat. 10–3.*

EXPERIENCE A DINOSAUR DIG

Dino Digs. Ever wonder what it's like to be on a dinosaur expedition? Here's your chance. The Museum of Western Colorado sponsors one- to five-day Dino Digs all over northwestern Colorado, and folks find fresh fossils all the time. The area includes some rich Late Jurassic soil, Morrison Formation sites, and other well-preserved zones that make for impressive discoveries, and you never know what might be unearthed. ☎ *888/488-3466* ⊕ *www.dinodigs.org.*

OFF THE BEATEN PATH

Little Bookcliffs Wild Horse Range. One of just three ranges in the United States set aside for wild horses, this range encompasses 36,113 acres of rugged canyons and plateaus in the Bookcliffs. Ninety to 150 wild horses roam the sagebrush-covered hills. Most years new foals can be spotted with their mothers in spring and early summer on the hillsides just off the main trails. Local favorites for riding include the Coal Canyon Trail and Main Canyon Trail, where the herd often goes in winter. Vehicles are permitted on designated trails. ✉ *2815 H Rd., about 8 mi northeast of Grand Junction* ☎ *970/244-3000, 800/417-9647* ⊕ *www.co.blm.gov* ✑ *Free* ⊙ *Daily dawn–dusk.*

SPORTS AND OUTDOOR ACTIVITIES

For information about hiking, horseback riding, and rafting, see Colorado National Monument.

GOLF

★ **The Golf Club at Redlands Mesa.** The 18-hole championship course is set at an elevation of 4,600 feet in the shadows of the Colorado National Monument, just minutes from downtown. ✉ *2299 W. Ridges Blvd.* ☎ *970/263-9270, 866/863-9270* ⊕ *www.redlandsgolf.com* ⚐ *Reservations essential* ⚑ *18 holes. Yards: 7007/4890. Par: 72/72. Green fee: $61/$89.*

MOUNTAIN BIKING

Several routes through Grand Junction are well suited to bicycle use. The city also has designated bike lanes in some areas. You can bike along the Colorado Riverfront Trails, a network that winds along the Colorado River, stretching from the Redlands Parkway to Palisade.

Colorado Plateau Mountain Bike Trail Association. Those interested in bike tours should contact the Colorado Plateau Mountain Bike Trail Association. ☎ *970/244–8877* ⊕ *www.copmoba.org.*

Kokopelli Trail. Kokopelli Trail links Grand Junction with the famed Slickrock Trail outside Moab, Utah. The 142-mi stretch winds through high desert and the Colorado River valley before climbing the La Sal Mountains.

OUTFITTERS **Brown Cycles.** Brown Cycles rents road, mountain, and hybrid bikes that start around $40 a day. It also sells and fixes bikes, and offers a full line of tandems for families with expanded kid options for rent and sale, as well. Aficionados should allow some extra time to check out the interesting bike museum, with models from as early as the 1860s. ⊠ *549 Main St., Grand Junction* ☎ *970/245–7939* ⊕ *www.browncycles.com.*

Over the Edge Sports. Over the Edge Sports offers mountain-biking lessons and half- or full-day customized bike tours. ⊠ *202 E. Aspen Ave., Fruita* ☎ *970/858–7220* ⊕ *www.otesports.com.*

Ruby Canyon Cycles. Ruby Canyon Cycles rents high-end, full-suspension mountain bikes for $60 the first day and $50 on consecutive days. The cycle shop also sponsors weekly evening rides around the area. ⊠ *301 Main St.* ☎ *970/241–0141* ⊕ *www.rubycanyoncycles.com.*

WHERE TO EAT

$ **✕ Dos Hombres.** Casual and colorful, Dos Hombres serves the usual
MEXICAN variety of combination platters and Mexican specialties, and loads up
☾ the plates for low prices. The fajitas and enchiladas are particularly well made, with quality meats and a noticeable lack of grease, and they have an unusually large menu of interesting salads (check out the Cancun version, with pineapple and fried tortilla strips). Service is snappy and friendly, and the staff is accommodating to kids. The margaritas and cervezas are inexpensive, too—and half-price during the weekday 3-hour happy hour. ⊠ *421 Brach Dr.* ☎ *970/242–8861* ⊕ *www.go2dos.com.*

$$ **✕ Il Bistro Italiano.** With a chef hailing from the birthplace of Parmigiano-
ITALIAN Reggiano, this restaurant's authenticity is assured, down to that per-
★ fectly delivered final shredded topping. Diners are greeted by a case of pasta made fresh daily and assisted by a staff that knows the origins of each home-style dish. Entrées include seafood lasagna and wood-fired pizzas along with meat dishes finished with innovative sauces such as artichokes and capers in a white-wine cream sauce. The standout, though, is the Rosetta, a dish of house-made noodles wrapped around rosemary ham and provolone in a spicy tomato sauce. ⊠ *400 Main St.* ☎ *970/243–8622* ⊕ *www.ilbistroitaliano.com.*

$ **✕ Pablo's Pizza.** Drawing inspiration from Pablo Picasso's artwork, the
PIZZA pizzas at this funky joint make for a diverse palette of flavors and fun.
☾ Specialties include creations such as Popeye's Passion (featuring spinach

9

and "olive oyl") or Dracula's Nemesis (studded with roasted garlic). For kids, they even serve (we're not making this up) a peanut-butter-and-jelly pizza. With brick walls covered only by eclectic local paintings, Pablo's can get loud when busy. They pour local wines by the glass and Palisade Brewery beer and root beer by the bottle. ⊠ *319 Main St.* ☎ *970/255–8879* ⊕ *www.pablospizza.com.*

$$$$
AMERICAN

✕ **The Winery.** This is *the* place for that big night out and other special occasions. It's awash in stained glass, wood beams, exposed brick, and hanging plants, with dark nooks and crannies and ends of aging barrels as art, all of which combines for an intimate atmosphere. The menu isn't terribly adventuresome, but the kitchen does turn out fresh-fish specials and top-notch steak, chicken, prime rib, and shrimp in simple, flavorful sauces. The real draw is for wine fans who want to try a more obscure bottle from the extensive, domestic-heavy roster. ⊠ *642 Main St.* ☎ *970/242–4100* ⊕ *www.winery-restaurant.com* ⚑ *Reservations essential* ☉ *No lunch.*

WHERE TO STAY

For expanded hotel reviews, visit Fodors.com.

$$
HOTEL
☼

Doubletree Hotel. At this sprawling full-service property service begins with a hot cookie at check-in, and the attention to detail continues from there. **Pros:** outdoor heated pool and hot tub welcome on cool evenings; kid-friendly; friendly staff. **Cons:** restaurant and room service food is so-so. ⊠ *743 Horizon Dr.* ☎ *970/241–8888, 800/222–8733* ⊕ *www. doubletree.com* ⤶ *259 rooms, 14 suites* ⚐ *In-room: a/c, Wi-Fi. In-hotel: restaurant, bar, pool, tennis court, gym* ❙◯❙ *No meals.*

¢
HOTEL
☼

Grand Vista Hotel. Plush high-back chairs invite visitors to relax in the spacious lobby of this hotel that lives up to its name. **Pros:** you can't beat the views; they will store your bike for you; the price is right. **Cons:** the breakfast buffet is mediocre; service is hit or miss. ⊠ *2790 Cross-roads Blvd.* ☎ *970/241–8411, 800/800–7796* ⊕ *www.grandvistahotel. com* ⤶ *158 rooms* ⚐ *In-room: a/c, Wi-Fi. In-hotel: restaurant, bar, pool, gym, business center, some pets allowed* ❙◯❙ *No meals.*

$$
B&B/INN

Los Altos Bed & Breakfast. This luxurious, panoramic hilltop is a peaceful, centralized home base for exploring the area. **Pros:** close to downtown but quiet; stunning views; private baths. **Cons:** thin walls mean that sometimes you can hear your neighbors. ⊠ *375 Hillview Dr.* ☎ *970/256–0964, 888/774–0982* ⊕ *www.losaltosgrandjunction. com* ⤶ *5 rooms, 2 suites* ⚐ *In-room: Wi-Fi. In-hotel: business center* ❙◯❙ *Breakfast.*

$$
B&B/INN
★

Two Rivers Winery & Chateau. Open a bottle of wine inside the vineyard where it was created at this country French–styled inn set among acres of vines. **Pros:** idyllic locale for weddings or other special occasions; tasty wines always at hand; expansive continental breakfast. **Cons:** winery and functions make this noisier than the usual B&B; rooms are chilly in winter; owners can be hard to find and staff is not overly helpful. ⊠ *2087 Broadway* ☎ *970/255–1471, 866/312–9463* ⊕ *www. tworiverswinery.com* ⤶ *10 rooms* ⚐ *In-room: a/c, Wi-Fi. In-hotel: some pets allowed* ❙◯❙ *Breakfast.*

NIGHTLIFE AND THE ARTS

THE ARTS

Avalon Theatre. The Avalon Theatre is one of the largest performing arts complexes in western Colorado, offering traveling lectures, dance, theater, and other cultural performances. The popular monthly "Dinner and a Movie" Tuesday nights bring classic and popular old blockbusters to the big screen, with receipts from a meal in town garnering free admission. ✉ *645 Main St.* ☎ *970/263–5700* ⊕ *www. tworiversconvention.com.*

Grand Junction Symphony. The highly regarded, 95-piece Grand Junction Symphony performs in venues throughout the city. ☎ *970/243–6787* ⊕ *www.gjsymphony.org.*

NIGHTLIFE

Bistro 743 Lounge. Bistro 743 Lounge inside the Doubletree Hotel serves beverages, appetizers, and light snacks. Occasionally entertainers perform outside on the beer-garden stage. ✉ *743 Horizon Dr.* ☎ *970/ 241–8888.*

Blue Moon. The Blue Moon is a favorite local bar where patrons nurse their favorite brew while catching up with colleagues and friends. ✉ *120 N. 7th St.* ☎ *970/242–4506.*

Rockslide Brewery. The Rockslide Brewery has won awards for its ales, porters, and stouts, and the menu of burgers and other sandwiches, steaks, and pastas has something for just about everyone. The patio is open in summer. ✉ *401 Main St.* ☎ *970/245–2111.*

SHOPPING

Champion Boots & Saddlery. The best place in the area for Tony Lama boots and Minnetonka moccasins is Champion Boots & Saddlery, in business since 1936. ✉ *545 Main St.* ☎ *970/242–2465.*

Enstrom's. The sweetest deal in town, Enstrom's is known for its scrumptious candy and world-renowned toffee. ✉ *701 Colorado Ave.* ☎ *970/ 683–1000.*

Girlfriends. The Main Street boutique Girlfriends sells a line of comfy clothes, pottery, benches, candles, and one-of-a-kind gifts. ✉ *316 Main St.* ☎ *970/242–3234.*

Heirlooms for Hospice. The cute but upscale boutique Heirlooms for Hospice has great secondhand designer clothing and shabby-chic furniture. ✉ *635 Main St.* ☎ *970/254–8556, 866/310–8900.*

Working Artists Studio and Gallery. Working Artists Studio and Gallery carries prints, pottery, stained glass, and unique gifts. ✉ *520 Main St.* ☎ *970/256–9952.*

PALISADE

12 mi east of Grand Junction via I–70.

Palisade is Colorado's version of Napa Valley, with the highest concentration of wineries in the state. It's an easy day trip from Grand Junction; meander through the vineyards and stop for lunch in the tiny, slow-paced town framed by stately Victorian homes and sweetened by homespun festivals. The orchards also are a big draw; the long, frost-free growing season intensifies the fruit sugars, resulting in intensely flavorful peaches, cherries, apricots, and nectarines. At harvest time the area sees a steady flow of visitors stopping by the orchards themselves, many of which have on-site sales, as well as the roadside stands that pop up seasonally to sell preserves, salsas, pies, and other fruit-based products.

GETTING HERE AND AROUND

A car is the best way to get to and around Palisade. Public transportation options are limited.

WHEN TO GO

A variety of produce is available through the summer months, but the peaches and other fruits famous in the Palisade area are at the height of their season from late June to early October.

FESTIVALS **Colorado Mountain Winefest.** September brings the annual Colorado Mountain Winefest. ☎ 800/704–3667 ⊕ *www.coloradowinefest.com.*

Grande River Vineyards. In summer Grande River Vineyards hosts a concert series featuring classical, country, blues, and rock music. The natural landscape contributes to the good acoustics, not to mention the spectacular sunsets. Concertgoers lounge in lawn chairs, enjoying picnics and dancing barefoot on the grass, and sometimes the concerts are held in the cellars. ✉ *787 Elberta Ave.* ☎ *970/464–5867* ⊕ *www. granderiverwines.com.*

Palisade Peach Festival. Palisade celebrates the harvest for four days every August during the Palisade Peach Festival. ☎ *970/464–7458* ⊕ *www. palisadepeachfest.com.*

ESSENTIALS

Visitor Information Palisade Chamber of Commerce ✉ *319 Main St.* ☎ *970/464–7458* ⊕ *www.palisadecoc.com.*

EXPLORING

American Spirit Shuttle. American Spirit Shuttle operates scheduled tours in 14-passenger vans on Saturdays. The tours visit at least four wineries and last approximately four hours. Wine lovers get to sample a variety of Colorado wines in the tasting rooms, with the added benefit of having someone else do the driving. ✉ *204 4th St., Clifton* ☎ *970/523–7662* ⊕ *www.americanspiritshuttle.net* ✉ *$40* ⊘ *May–Oct., Sat. 1–5.*

Fodor's Choice **Winery Tours.** One of Colorado's best-kept secrets is its winery tours. It's
★ a great way to see how your favorite wine goes from vineyard to glass. You can learn about the grape-growing process and what varieties of grapes grow best in western Colorado's mild climate. Depending on the time of the year, you may also see the grape harvesting and crushing process. For a self-guided tour, visit Grand Junction's Web site for maps and directions to the wineries. If you're taking the self-guided route, call to reserve tours that take you beyond the tasting room and into the winemaking process. Of course the best part of the tour is sampling the wines. ⊕ *www.visitgrandjunction.com.*

QUICK
BITES

Palisade Café. Changing artwork decorates the light and airy Palisade Café, which offers a nice selection of breakfast, lunch, and dinner choices, including soups, salads, burgers, French dips, Reuben sandwiches, and vegetarian dishes. ✉ *113 W. 3rd St.* ☎ *970/464–0657.*

WHERE TO EAT AND STAY

For expanded hotel reviews, visit Fodors.com.

¢
CAFÉ
Fodor'sChoice
★

✗**Slice O' Life Bakery.** Aromatic goodies are baked with whole grains and fresh local fruits at this down-home–style bakery known around the region for its melt-in-your-mouth pastries, sweet rolls, "jamocha" brownies, and fresh-fruit cobblers. Owners Tim and Mary Lincoln have made their fruitcakes craveable commodities, studding them with fresh Palisade peaches and mailing them around the country (in fact, they do lots of great things with peaches, including pie). Cold sandwiches and fresh-baked bread are also available. ✉ *105 W. 3rd St.* ☎ *970/464–0577* 💳 *No credit cards* ☺ *Closed Sun. and Mon. No dinner.*

$$
B&B/INN

⊞ **Wine Country Inn.** The richly colored fabrics and spacious design of the rooms in a well-established vineyard give an upscale feel to what's an appealingly casual and welcoming farmhouse-style lodging. **Pros:** convenient location off the interstate; vineyard property evokes surrounding locale; convenient to rest of wine properties. **Cons:** nearby truck traffic can be noisy; service spotty, especially when the place is full. ✉ *777 Grande River Dr.* ☎ *888/855–8330* ⊕ *www.coloradowinecountryinn. com* 🛏 *80 rooms, 6 suites* ⚐ *In-room: a/c, Wi-Fi. In-hotel: bar, pool, gym, spa, business center, parking* ⌾ *Breakfast.*

9

SHOPPING

Alida's Fruits. Alida's Fruits sells a wide range of fresh and dried fruits, including cherries, pears, apricots, and peaches, as well as chocolate-dipped fruits, nuts and locally produced jams, jellies, and syrups. ✉ *3402 C 1/2 Rd.* ☎ *970/434–8769.*

Talbott Farms Mountain Gold Market. Talbott Farms Mountain Gold Market puts out nearly two-dozen kinds of peaches, as well as apples and pears and the juices of all three. The huge, fourth generation–run operation sells local products and will take you on a tour of the place if you ask. ✉ *3782 F½ Rd.* ☎ *877/834–6686, 970/464–5943.*

FARM STAND PICNIC

Considering the plethora of produce in the Grand Junction and Palisade area, you would think that great restaurants would be easy to come by, but not so. Better to eat the ingredients in their most unadulterated form straight from the source; spend some time stopping by the dozens of farm stands that dot the landscape. A favorite is Talbott Farms and its store, the Mountain Gold Market, where two-dozen kinds of peaches can be had, as well as other local products. Look for local jams, honey, fruits and vegetables, cider, and freshly baked items, all perfect for an impromptu picnic.

COLORADO NATIONAL MONUMENT

23 mi west of Grand Junction via Rte. 340.

GETTING HERE AND AROUND

From I–70 westbound, take Exit 31 (Horizon Drive) and follow signs through Grand Junction; eastbound take Exit 19 (Fruita) and drive south 3 mi on Highway 340 to the west entrance.

TOURS American Spirit Shuttle offers scheduled and customized tours of Colorado National Monument.

WHEN TO GO

FESTIVALS **Fruita Fat Tire Festival.** The town's Fat Tire Festival brings mountain bikers from all over together to take on the area's trails every April. ☎ 970/858–7220 ⊕ *www.fruitamountainbike.com.*

Mike the Headless Chicken Days. Fruita celebrates Mike the Headless Chicken Days every May with the Chicken Dance and the Run Like A Headless Chicken 5K Race. ☎ 970/858–0360 ⊕ *www. miketheheadlesschicken.org.*

ESSENTIALS

Tour Contacts American Spirit Shuttle ✉ *204 4th St., Clifton* ☎ *970/523–7662* ⊕ *www.americanspiritshuttle.net.*

EXPLORING

Colorado National Monument. Sheer red-rock cliffs open to 23 mi of steep canyons and thin monoliths that sprout as high as 450 feet from the floor of Colorado National Monument. This vast tract of rugged, ragged terrain was declared a national monument in 1911 at the urging of an eccentric visionary named John Otto. Now it's popular for rock climbing, horseback riding, cross-country skiing, biking, and camping. Cold Shivers Point is just one of the many dramatic overlooks along **Rim Rock Drive,** a 23-mi scenic route with breathtaking views. The town of Fruita, at the base of Colorado National Monument, is a haven for mountain bikers and hikers. It makes a great center for exploring the area's canyons—whether from the seat of a bike or the middle of a raft, heading for a leisurely float trip.

Visitor Center. Scheduled programs, such as guided walks and campfire talks, are posted at the Visitor Center. Maps and trail information are also available. ☎ 970/858–3617 ⊗ *Feb.–Apr., daily 9–5; May–Sept., daily 8–6; Oct.–Nov., daily 8–5; Dec.–Jan., daily 9–4* ✉ *Fruita* ☎ 970/858–3617 ⊕ *www.nps.gov/colm* 🔒 *$10 per wk per vehicle. Visitors entering on bicycle, motorcycle, or foot pay $5 for weekly pass* ⊗ *Daily.*

☾ **Dinosaur Journey.** Roaring robotic stegosaurus and meat-shredding ani-
★ matronic allosaurus prowl Dinosaur Journey, a fun, informative attraction just off I–70 a few minutes from the western entrance to Colorado National Monument. Unlike many museums, this one encourages kids to touch everything—friendly paleontologists may even allow kids to hold a chunk of fossilized dino dung. In addition to the amazing lifelike replicas, there are more than 20 interactive displays. Children can stand in an earthquake simulator; dig up "fossils" in a mock quarry; or make

dino prints in dirt, along with reptile and bird tracks for comparison. The museum also sponsors daily digs nearby, where many of the fossils were found. Local volunteers are at work cleaning and preparing fossils for study. ✉ *550 Jurassic Ct., Fruita* ☎ *970/858–7282, 888/488–3466* ⊕ *www.dinosaurjourney.org* ✍ *$8.50* ◷ *Daily 9–5.*

Fodor's Choice ★ **McInnis Canyons National Conservation Area.** Ten miles west of Grand Junction, stretching from Fruita to just across the Utah border, the McInnis Canyons National Conservation Area (formerly Colorado Canyons National Conservation Area) is rife with natural arches, along with numerous rock canyons, caves, coves, and spires. **Rattlesnake Canyon** has nine arches, making it the second-largest concentration of natural arches in the country. The canyon can be reached in summer from the upper end of Rim Rock Drive with four-wheel-drive vehicles or via a 7-mi hike by the intrepid.

Though much of the territory complements the red-dirt canyons of Colorado National Monument, McInnis Canyons is more accessible to horseback riding, mountain biking, all-terrain vehicle and motorcycle trails, and for trips with dogs (most of these activities aren't allowed at the monument). Designated in 2000 by act of Congress, the conservation area was created from a desire of nearby communities to preserve the area's unique scenery while allowing multiple-use recreation. Be prepared for biting gnats from late May to late July. Contact the Bureau of Land Management for a map before venturing out. ✉ *2815 H Rd.* ☎ *970/244–3000* ⊕ *www.blm.gov/co/st/en/nca/mcnca.html* ✍ *Free* ◷ *Year-round.*

SPORTS AND THE OUTDOORS
HIKING
Colorado National Monument. A good way to explore Colorado National Monument is by trail. There are more than a dozen short and backcountry trails ranging from 0.25 mi to 8.5 mi.

Otto's Trail. An easy 30-minute stroll with sweeping canyon views, Otto's Trail greets hikers with breezes scented by sagebrush and juniper, which stand out from the dull red rock and sand. The trail leads to stunning sheer drop-offs and endless views. At the end of the half-mile trail at Otto's Overlook you can hear the wind in the feathers of birds as they soar out of the canyon. ✉ *Trailhead: Rim Rock Dr., 1 mi from western gate visitor center, Fruita.*

Serpents Trail. Serpents Trail has been called the "Crookedest Road in the World" because of its more than 50 switchbacks. The fairly steep but rewarding trail, which ascends several hundred feet, takes about two hours to complete, depending on your ability (and the heat). ✉ *Trailhead: Serpents Trail parking lot, 0.25 mi from east gate* ☎ *970/858–3617* ⊕ *www.nps.gov/colm.*

HORSEBACK RIDING
Rimrock Adventures. Rimrock Adventures runs horseback rides near Colorado National Monument as well as through Little Bookcliffs Wild Horse Preserve. ✉ *927 Hwy. 340, Fruita* ☎ *970/858–9555, 888/712–9555* ⊕ *www.rradventures.com.*

9

The Legacy of Mike the Headless Chicken

Mike the Headless Chicken was a freak bound for fame. It all started with a run-in with a Fruita farmer who had bad aim, or so the tale goes. The year was 1945. Mike, a young Wyandotte rooster, was minding his own business in the barnyard when farmer Lloyd Olsen snatched him from the chicken coop. It seems that Clara, the farmer's wife, wanted chicken for dinner that night. Mike was put on death row. Well, faster than you can say pinfeathers, farmer Olsen stretched Mike's neck across the chopping block and whacked off his head. Apparently undaunted by the ordeal, Mike promptly got up, dusted off his feathers and went about his daily business pecking for food, fluffing his feathers, and crowing, except Mike's crow was now reduced to a gurgle. Scientists surmised that Mike's brain stem was largely untouched, leaving his reflex actions intact. A blood clot prevented him from bleeding to death. The headless chicken dubbed "Miracle Mike" toured the freak-show circuit, where the morbidly curious could sneak a peek at his nogginless nub for a quarter. Mike's incredible story of survival (he lived for 18 months without a head!) soon hit the pages of two national magazines, *Time* and *Life*. The headless wonder, who was fed with an eyedropper, eventually met his demise in an Arizona motel room, where he choked to death. His legacy lives on in Fruita, where the tiny town throws a gigantic party every May to celebrate Mike's life. Even in death, Mike is still making headlines.

RAFTING

Adventure Bound River Expeditions. Adventure Bound River Expeditions runs trips on the Colorado, Green, and Yampa rivers—the latter through the canyons of Dinosaur National Monument. ✉ *2392 H Rd., Grand Junction* ☎ *970/245–5428, 800/423–4668* ⊕ *www.adventureboundusa.com.*

Rimrock Adventures. Rimrock Adventures runs a variety of rafting excursions and easygoing float trips. ✉ *927 Hwy. 340, Fruita* ☎ *970/858–9555, 888/712–9555* ⊕ *www.rradventures.com.*

ROCK CLIMBING

The stunning stark sandstone and shale formations of Colorado National Monument are a rock climber's paradise. Independence Monument is a favorite climb.

Desert Crags & Cracks. Experienced desert-rock guide Kris Hjelle owns and operates Desert Crags & Cracks, specializing in guiding and instruction on the desert rocks of western Colorado and eastern Utah. ✉ *Box 2803, Grand Junction 81502* ☎ *970/245–8513* ⊕ *www.desertcrags.com.*

WHERE TO EAT

$
BURGER

✕ **The End Zone Sports Pub.** A quintessential sports bar with plenty of TVs and pool tables for playing your own games when there's nothing to watch. The menu is pub grub done well and for a fair price: burgers, hefty sandwiches, fish-and-chips, and steaks, as well as huge wedges of cake for dessert and a kids' menu priced according to age—$4.75 for

10 and under, $6.95 11 and over. The "holy moley" Buffalo-style wings will blow your ears off, but locals swear by them. The atmosphere is noisy but never overly raucous, and it's popular with mountain bikers, who stop in for a post-ride beer. ⊠ *152 S. Mesa St., Fruita* ☎ *970/858–0701* ✆ *Closed Mon.*

$ ✕ **Fiesta Guadalajara Restaurant.** Authentic and family-friendly, this
MEXICAN Mexican restaurant serves up good food. Try the chiles rellenos, super
ꙮ nachos, and especially the chili Colorado: fork-tender beef simmered in a savory red-pepper sauce. The appetizer combo plate is a meal in itself, and to feed an army, order Fiesta Fajitas. ⊠ *103 Hwy. 6 and 50, Fruita* ☎ *970/858–1228.*

$ ▦ **Comfort Inn.** Some rooms in this Southwestern-style budget motel have
HOTEL views of the Colorado National Monument. ⊠ *400 Jurassic Ave., Fruita* ☎ *970/858–1333* ⊕ *www.comfortinn.com* ⤳ *53 rooms, 13 suites* ⛄ *In-room: a/c, Wi-Fi. In-hotel: pool, laundry facilities, some pets allowed* ❢⃝ *Breakfast.*

GRAND MESA

47 mi southeast of Grand Junction via I–70 and Hwy. 65.

Small, quiet towns along the 63-mi Grand Mesa Scenic and Historic Byway (Highway 65) provide just enough support for the plethora of outdoor opportunities available in the diverse range of ecosystems on the world's largest flat-topped mountain.

GETTING HERE AND AROUND

A car is needed to explore Grand Mesa. In northwestern Colorado I–70 (U.S. 6) is the major thoroughfare, accessing Grand Junction and Grand Mesa (via Route 65, which runs to Delta).

ESSENTIALS

Transportation Contacts Amtrak ☎ *800/872–7245* ⊕ *www.amtrak.com.*
Walker Field Airport (GJT) ⊠ *Grand Junction* ☎ *970/244–9100* ⊕ *www. gjairport.com.*

Visitor Information Battlement Mesa Chamber of Commerce ⎙ *Box 93, Parachute 81635* ☎ *970/285–7934* ⊕ *www.parachutechamber.org.*

EXPLORING

Grand Mesa National Forest. The world's largest flattop mountain tow-ers nearly 11,000 feet above the surrounding terrain and sprawls an astounding 53 square mi. Grand Mesa National Forest attracts the outdoor enthusiast who craves the simple life: fresh air, biting fish, spectacular sunsets, a roaring campfire under the stars, and a little elbow room to take it all in. The landscape is filled with more than 300 sparkling lakes—a fisherman's paradise in summer. The mesa, as it's referred to by locals, offers excellent hiking and camping (try Island Lake Campground) opportunities. There are also a handful of lodges that rent modern cabins. You can also downhill ski at Powderhorn Resort, cross-country ski, snowshoe, snowmobile, or ice fish. ⊠ *2250 Hwy. 50, Delta* ☎ *970/874–6600* ⊕ *www.fs.fed.us/r2/gmug.*

9

SPORTS AND THE OUTDOORS

DOWNHILL SKIING

Powderhorn Resort. Powderhorn Resort has 42 trails, 4 lifts, 1,600 acres, and a 1,650-foot vertical drop. The slopes intriguingly follow the fall line of the mesa, carving out natural bowls. Those bowls on the western side are steeper than they first appear. Lift tickets are reasonable, the skiing is surprisingly good, and the addition of a half-pipe and an improved terrain park have gone a long way toward modernizing the resort. Powderhorn averages 250 inches of snowfall per year. ✉ *Rte. 65, Mesa* ☎ *970/268–5700* 🌐 *www.powderhorn.com* 🎫 *Lift ticket $56* 🕙 *Dec.–Apr., daily 9–4.*

FISHING

The lakes and reservoirs provide some of the best angling opportunities in Colorado for rainbow, cutthroat, and brook trout.

HIKING

Grand Mesa Discovery Trail. Grand Mesa Discovery Trail is a great beginning hike for kids and adults attempting to acclimate themselves to the altitude—and the slow-paced attitude—of the mesa. Pick up a brochure at the visitor center for information on the landscape. The gently sloping 20-minute trail offers a taste of what to expect on longer hikes. ✉ *Trailhead: Grand Mesa visitor center, near intersection of Hwy. 65 and Trickel Park Rd.*

WHERE TO STAY

For expanded hotel reviews, visit Fodors.com.

$$ HOTEL **Alexander Lake Cabins.** The mirror-calm Alexander Lake reflects towering pine trees that also overlook the vast majority of this resort's cozy cabins, which are designed for tranquillity. **Pros:** pay cash and save $20–$30; fishing and snowmobiling right on the property; quiet and peaceful. **Cons:** rather remote. ✉ *21221 Baron Lake Dr., 17 mi north of Cedaredge, 2 mi from Grand Mesa visitor center on Forest Rd. 121* ☎ *970/856–2539, 800/850–7221* 🌐 *www.alexanderlakelodge.com* *7 cabins* *In-room: kitchen, no TV. In-hotel: some pets allowed* *No meals.*

EN ROUTE **Grand Mesa Scenic Byway.** The Grand Mesa Scenic Byway is 63 mi long and winds its way along Highway 65 through meadows sprinkled with wildflowers, shimmering aspen groves, aromatic pine forests, and endless lakes. Scenic overlooks (Land-O-Lakes is a standout), rest areas, and picnic areas are clearly marked. There are two visitor centers on the Byway, which has endpoints at I–70 near Palisade and in Cedaredge. ☎ *970/856–3100.*

CEDAREDGE

15 mi south of Grand Mesa via Hwy. 65.

Cedaredge is called the gateway to the Grand Mesa, the world's largest flat-topped mountain. An elevation of 6,100 feet makes for a mild climate that is perfect for ranching, as well as for growing apples, peaches, and cherries. It's also abundant in galleries, gift shops, antiques stores, and wineries.

GETTING HERE AND AROUND

Driving is the best way to get around the area; this small town is best explored on foot.

ESSENTIALS

Visitor Information Cedaredge Chamber of Commerce ✆ *245 W. Main St. 81413* ☎ *970/856–6961* ⊕ *www.cedaredgechamber.com.*

EXPLORING

Pioneer Town. The town site was originally the headquarters of a cattle spread, the Bar-I Ranch. Pioneer Town, a cluster of 23 authentic buildings that re-create turn-of-the-20th-century life, includes a country chapel, the Lizard Head Saloon, original silos from the Bar-I Ranch, and a working blacksmith shop. ✉ *315 S.W. 3rd Ave.* ☎ *970/856–7554* 🎫 *$3* ☺ *Memorial Day weekend–late Sept., Mon.–Sat. 10–4, Sun. 1–4.*

WHERE TO EAT AND STAY

For expanded hotel reviews, visit Fodors.com.

$$$
ECLECTIC

✕ **Grill at Deer Creek Village.** With dishes ranging from crab-and-artichoke dip to Thai chicken satay, this casual but elegant restaurant satisfies golfers from the adjoining Deer Creek Golf Club, as well as tourists looking to fill up after a long day on the mesa or antiques shopping. Simply prepared steaks and seafood dishes are the mainstays, accompanied by an extensive local wine list. Call for directions. ✉ *500 S. E. Jay Ave.* ☎ *970/856–7782* ⊕ *deercreekvillage-golf.com.*

$
AMERICAN
☺

✕ **Pizza to the Limit.** This locals' pizza joint has many tables jammed into a tiny space. The old-fashioned letterboard menu is hard to read behind the counter, but whatever pie you order—maybe the Taco, with its beef, onions, lettuce, tomato and tortilla chips, or the Cheezzy that lives up to its name—it's sure to be a crunchy-crusted pie with plenty of sauce and toppings. ✉ *105 S.E. Frontier Ave.* ☎ *970/856–7229* ▭ *No credit cards.*

$
B&B/INN
☺

▦ **Cedars' Edge Llamas B&B.** A herd of curious—and hungry—llamas greets you at this modern cedar house and guest cottage and its four neatly furnished rooms, each with its own theme, overlooking 100-mi views of the Grand Valley. **Pros:** breakfast on your private deck is a nice option; close proximity to national forest; who doesn't love a llama? **Cons:** dated decor; maybe everyone doesn't love a llama; some of the rooms require stairs or walking a graded gravel path to the back of the property. ✉ *2169 Hwy. 65* ☎ *970/856–6836* ⊕ *www.llamabandb.com* 🛏 *4 rooms, 1 cottage* ☒ *In-room: a/c, no TV* ⦿ *Breakfast.*

SHOPPING

Apple Shed. Once an apple-packing shed, the Apple Shed has been restored and remodeled into a series of unusual gift shops and arts and crafts galleries. The attached Loading Dock Deli ($) serves fresh peach milk shakes in season and top-notch sandwiches, sure to fuel your drive up the next pass. ✉ *250 S. Grand Mesa Dr.* ☎ *970/856–7007.*

9

STEAMBOAT SPRINGS

42 mi east of Craig via U.S. 40; 160 mi west of Denver via I–70, Rte. 9, and U.S. 40.

Steamboat got its name from French trappers who, after hearing the bubbling and churning hot springs, mistakenly thought a steamboat was chugging up the Yampa River. Here Stetson hats are sold for shade and not for souvenirs, and the Victorian-era buildings, most of them fronting the main drag of Lincoln Avenue, were built to be functional, not ornamental.

Steamboat Springs is aptly nicknamed Ski Town, U.S.A., because it has sent more athletes to the Winter Olympics than any other ski town in the nation. When sizing up the mountain, keep in mind that the part that's visible from below is only the tip of the iceberg—much more terrain lies concealed in back. Steamboat is famed for its eiderdown-soft snow; in fact, the term "champagne powder" was coined (and amusingly enough registered as a trademark—still pending) here to describe the area's unique feathery drifts, the result of Steamboat's fortuitous position between the arid desert to the west and the moisture-magnet of the Continental Divide to the east, where storm fronts duke it out.

The mountain village, with its maze of upscale condos, boutiques, and nightclubs, is certainly attractive, but spread out and a little lacking in character. To its credit, though, this increasingly trendy destination has retained much of its down-home friendliness.

GETTING HERE AND AROUND

Yampa Valley Regional Airport (HDN) is in Hayden, 22 mi from Steamboat Springs. American, Continental, Delta, Northwest, and United fly nonstop from various gateways during ski season. Alpine Taxi and Storm Mountain Express provide door-to-door service to Steamboat Springs from Yampa Valley Regional Airport. A one-way trip with either costs $35.

Steamboat Springs Transit (SST) provides free shuttle service between the ski area and downtown Steamboat year-round. Most of the major properties also provide shuttles between the two areas for their guests.

From Denver, Steamboat Springs is about a three-hour drive northwest via I–70 and U.S. 40. The route traverses some high-mountain passes, so it's a good idea to check road conditions before you travel.

TOURS   Steamboat's Sweet Pea Tours visits nearby hot springs.

WHEN TO GO

A popular year-round destination, Steamboat becomes most dramatic in mid-September, when the leaves turn brilliant gold in the forests along the highways and the air cools considerably. By the first week of November, the ski season has begun, and it doesn't end until mid-April.

FESTIVALS   **Hot Air Balloon Rodeo and Annual Art in the Park.** Every year since 1980, mid-July in Steamboat has meant hot-air balloons and fine art, a combination that draws folks from miles around to watch more than 40 balloons float out over the valley from Bald Eagle Lake each morning of the free event. The rest of the weekend is devoted to the display and sale of hundreds of works of art from all over the world at West Lincoln Park. ✉ *35565 S. U.S. 40* ☎ *877/754–2269* ⊕ *www. steamboat-chamber.com.*

Strings in the Mountains Music Festival. The focus is on chamber music and chamber-orchestra music presented by more than 150 musicians, including Grammy winners and other internationally renowned talents, throughout summer, primarily in the tent on the weekends. But Strings also offers big names in jazz, country, big band, bluegrass, and world music, as well as free concerts during its "Music on the Green" lunchtime series at Yampa River Botanic Park on Thursday in summer. ✉ *Steamboat Springs Music Festival Tent at the corner of Mt. Werner and Pine Grove Rds.* ☎ *970/879–5056* ⊕ *www.stringsmusicfestival.com.*

> ## WHERE IS STEAMBOAT SPRING?
>
> Don't waste time looking for Steamboat Springs, the hot springs for which the town was named—they are dry now. The springs once sat next to the Yampa River, where the 13th Street Bridge now stands, and once were so feisty that people miles away thought the 15-foot-high spewer sounded like a steamboat churning down the river. When the railroad came to Steamboat in 1909, the springs mysteriously became nothing but a burble; some believe the railroad company somehow had something to do with that.

ESSENTIALS

Tour Contacts Sweet Pea Tours ☎ 970/879–5820 ⊕ www.sweetpeatours.com.

Transportation Contacts Alpine Taxi ☎ 800/343-7433 ⊕ www.alpinetaxi. com. **Steamboat Springs Transit** ☎ 970/879-3717. **Storm Mountain Express** ☎ 877/844-8787 ⊕ www.stormmountainexpress.com. **Sunshine Taxi** ✉ Grand Junction ☎ 970/245-8294. **Yampa Valley Regional Airport (HDN)** ☎ 970/276-3669.

Visitor Information Steamboat Ski & Resort Corporation ✉ 2305 Mount Werner Circle ☎ 970/879-6111 ⊕ www.steamboat.com. **Steamboat Springs Chamber Resort Association** ✉ 125 Anglers Dr. ☎ 970/879-0880, 800/922-2722 ⊕ www.steamboat-chamber.com. **Steamboat Springs Snow Report** ☎ 970/879-7300 ⊕ www.steamboat.com/snowreport.

EXPLORING

Medicine Bow/Routt National Forests. In summer Steamboat serves as the gateway to the magnificent Medicine Bow/Routt National Forests, with a wealth of activities from hiking to mountain biking to fishing. Among the nearby attractions are the 283-foot **Fish Creek Falls** and the splendidly rugged **Mount Zirkel Wilderness Area.** To the north, two sparkling man-made lakes, **Steamboat** and **Pearl,** each in its own state park, are a draw for those into fishing and sailing. In winter the area is just as popular. Snowshoers and backcountry skiers are permitted to use the west side of Rabbit Ears Pass, whereas snowmobilers are confined to the east side. ✉ *Hahns Peak-Bears Ears Ranger District Office* ☎ *970/870–2187* ⊕ *www.fs.fed.us/r2/mbr.*

9

Old Town Hot Springs. There are more than 150 mineral springs of varying temperatures in the Steamboat Springs area, including this one, in the middle of town. Old Town Hot Springs gets its waters from the all-natural Heart Spring. The modern facility has a lap pool, relaxation pool, climbing wall, and health club. Two waterslides are open noon to 6 pm in summer and 4 to 8 pm in winter; they require an additional fee. ⊠ *136 Lincoln Ave.* ☎ *970/879–1828* ⊕ *www.steamboathotsprings. org* ⊠ *$15* ⊙ *Weekdays 5:30 am–9:45 pm, Sat. 7 am–8:45 pm, Sun. 8 am–8:45 pm.*

Fodor's Choice ★ **Strawberry Park Hot Springs.** About 7 mi west of town, the Strawberry Park Hot Springs is a bit remote and rustic, although only the winter drive on the gravel portion of the road is challenging. The way the pool is set up to offer semi-privacy at this extremely popular spot makes for an intimate setting and relaxation. It's family-oriented during the day, but after dark clothing is optional, and no one under 18 is admitted. ⊠ *Strawberry Park Rd.* ☎ *970/879–0342* ⊕ *www.strawberryhotsprings. com* ⊠ *$10* ▤ *No credit cards* ⊙ *Sun.–Thurs. 10 am–10:30 pm; Fri. and Sat. 10 am–midnight.*

Tread of Pioneers Museum. The Tread of Pioneers Museum, in a restored Queen Anne–style house, is an excellent spot to bone up on local history. It includes ski memorabilia dating to the turn of the 20th century, when Carl Howelsen opened Howelsen Hill, still the country's preeminent ski-jumping facility. ⊠ *8th and Oak Sts.* ☎ *970/879–2214* ⊕ *www. treadofpioneers.org* ⊠ *$5* ⊙ *Tues.–Sat. 11–5.*

DOWNHILL SKIING AND SNOWBOARDING

Howelsen Hill Ski Area. The tiny Howelsen Hill Ski Area, in the heart of Steamboat Springs, is the oldest ski area still open in Colorado. Howelsen, with 4 lifts, 15 trails, 1 terrain park, and a 440-foot vertical drop, is home of the Steamboat Springs Winter Sports Club, which has more than 800 members. The ski area not only has an awesome terrain park, but has night skiing as well. It's the largest ski-jumping complex in America, and a major Olympic training ground. ⊠ *845 Howelsen Pkwy.* ☎ *970/879–8499* ⊙ *Nov.–Mar., Tues.–Fri. 1–8; weekends 10–4.*

Steamboat Springs Ski Area. The Steamboat Springs Ski Area is perhaps best known for its tree skiing and "cruising" terrain—the latter term referring to wide, groomed runs perfect for intermediate-level skiers. The abundance of cruising terrain has made Steamboat immensely popular with those who ski once or twice a year and who aren't looking to tax their abilities. On a predominantly western exposure—most ski areas sit on north-facing exposures—the resort benefits from intense sun, which contributes to the mellow atmosphere. In addition, one of the most extensive lift systems in the region allows skiers to get in lots of runs without having to spend much time waiting in line. The Storm Peak and Sundown high-speed quads, for example, each send you about 2,000 vertical feet in less than seven minutes. Do the math: A day of more than 60,000 vertical feet is entirely within the realm of possibility.

All this is not to suggest, however, that Steamboat is a piece of cake for more experienced skiers. Pioneer Ridge encompasses advanced and intermediate terrain. Steamboat is renowned as a breeding ground for top mogul skiers, and for good reason. There are numerous mogul runs, but most are not particularly steep. The few with a vertical challenge, such as Chute One, are not especially long. If you're looking for challenging skiing at Steamboat, take on the trees. The ski area has done an admirable job of clearing many gladed areas of such nuisances as saplings, underbrush, and fallen timber, making Steamboat tree skiing much less hazardous than at other areas. The trees are also where advanced skiers—as well as, in some places, confident intermediates—can find the best of Steamboat's much-ballyhooed powder. Statistically, Steamboat doesn't report significantly more snowfall than other Colorado resorts, but somehow snow piles up here better than at the others. Ask well-traveled Colorado skiers, and they'll confirm that when it comes to consistently good, deep snow, Steamboat is hard to beat. ✉ *2305 Mount Werner Circle* ☎ *970/879–6111* ⊕ *www.steamboat.com* ⊙ *Late-Nov.–mid-Apr., daily 8:30–3:30.*

FACILITIES 3,668-foot vertical drop; 2,965 skiable acres; 14% beginner, 42% intermediate, 44% advanced; 1 8-passenger gondola, 5 high-speed quad chairs, 1 high-speed 6-person, 1 quad chair, 6 triple chairs, 2 double chairs, and 2 surface lifts.

LESSONS AND PROGRAMS Half-day group lessons begin at $89; all-day lessons are $102. Clinics in moguls, powder, snowboarding, and "hyper-carving"—made possible by the design of shaped skis—are available.

Billy Kidd Center for Performance Skiing. Intensive one- and three-day training camps in racing and advanced skiing are available through the Billy Kidd Center for Performance Skiing. ☎ *800/299–5017.*

Kids' Vacation Center. Programs for children from 6 months to 15 years of age are given through the Kids' Vacation Center. Day care is also available. ☎ *970/879–0740.*

Steamboat Ski and Resort Corporation. General information about the ski areas is available through the Steamboat Ski and Resort Corporation. ☎ *970/879–6111, 877/783–2628 reservations* ⊕ *www.steamboat.com.*

Snow-cat skiing—where a vehicle delivers you to hard-to-reach slopes—has been called the poor man's version of helicopter skiing, although at $375 to $450 a day that's probably a misnomer. It's true that snow-cat users don't have to worry about landing, and can get to places that would be inaccessible by helicopter.

Steamboat Powder Cats. Buffalo Pass, northeast of Steamboat, is one of the snowiest spots in Colorado, and that's why it's the base for Steamboat Powder Cats. There's a maximum of 24 skiers per group, so the open-meadow skiing is never crowded. ☎ *970/879–5188, 800/288–0543* ⊕ *www.steamboatpowdercats.com.*

LIFT TICKETS $99. Savings of 5% or less on multiday tickets. Children 12 and under ski free when adults purchase a five-day ski ticket.

RENTALS **Steamboat Central Reservations.** Equipment packages are available at the gondola base as well as at ski shops in town. Packages (skis, boots, and poles) average about $55 a day, less for multiday rentals. Call Steamboat Central Reservations for rental information. ☎ *970/879–0740, 800/922–2722* ⊕ *www.steamboat.com.*

9

NORDIC SKIING
BACKCOUNTRY SKIING

The most popular area for backcountry skiing around Steamboat Springs is Rabbit Ears Pass, southeast of town. It's the last pass you cross if you're driving from Denver to Steamboat. Much of the appeal is its easy access to high-country trails from U.S. 40. There are plenty of routes you can take.

Hahns Peak Ranger Office. A popular backcountry spot is Seedhouse Road, about 25 mi north of Steamboat, near the town of Clark. A marked network of trails across the rolling hills has good views of distant peaks. For maps and information on snow conditions, contact the Hahns Peak Ranger Office. ⊠ *925 Weiss Dr.* ☎ *970/879–1870.*

Ski Haus. Touring and telemarking rentals are available at ski shops in the Steamboat area. One of the best is the Ski Haus. ⊠ *1457 Pine Grove Rd.* ☎ *970/879–0385* ⊕ *www.skihaussteamboat.com.*

Steamboat Ski Touring Center. Arrangements for backcountry tours can be made through Steamboat Ski Touring Center. ☎ *970/879–8180* ⊕ *www. steamboatnordiccenter.com.*

TRACK SKIING

Steamboat Ski Touring Center. Laid out on and along the Sheraton Steamboat Golf Club, Steamboat Ski Touring Center has a relatively gentle 18.5-mi trail network. A good option for a relaxed afternoon of skiing is to pick up some vittles at the Picnic Basket in the main building and enjoy a picnic along Fish Creek Trail, a 3-mi-long loop that winds through pine and aspen groves. Rental packages (skis, boots, and poles) are available. ☎ *970/879–8180* ⊕ *www.steamboatnordiccenter. com* ☞ *Trail fee $18.*

★ **Vista Verde Guest Ranch.** Vista Verde Guest Ranch has a well-groomed network of tracks, as well as access to the adjacent national forest. ☐ *Box 465, Steamboat Springs 80477* ☎ *970/879–3858, 800/526–7433* ⊕ *www.vistaverde.com.*

OTHER SPORTS AND THE OUTDOORS

Steamboat Central Reservations. Dogsledding, hot-air ballooning, and snowmobiling can be arranged by calling the activities department at Steamboat Central Reservations. ☎ *970/879–4070, 800/922–2722.*

GOLF

Haymaker Golf Course. Three miles south of Steamboat Springs, this public-access 18-hole Keith Foster course has a pro shop and café. The challenging, rolling course has hills, streams, and native grasses, as well as exceptional views. The course is noted for being well maintained, with large greens and a 10,000-square-foot putting green. ⊠ *34855 U.S. 40* ☎ *970/870–1846* ⊕ *www.haymakergolf.com* ☜ *Reservations essential* ⚑ *18 holes. Yards: 7308/5059. Par: 72/72. Green fee: $58/$69.*

Rollingstone Ranch Golf Club at the Sheraton Steamboat Resort. Expect to see plenty of wildlife; bear and elk have been spotted on the 18-hole championship course, which was designed by the legendary Robert Trent Jones Jr. The extensive practice facilities include a driving range, a bunker, and a putting green. The Fish Creek Grille ($) serves lunch and a well-rounded happy hour and appetizer menu after 3 pm. ✉ *1230 Steamboat Blvd.* ☎ *970/879–1391* ⊕ *www.rollingstoneranchgolf.com* ⚒ *Reservations essential* ⛳ *18 holes. Yards: 6902/5462. Par: 72/72. Green fee: $75/$140.*

HIKING

Medicine Bow/Routt National Forests. In the Medicine Bow/Routt National Forests. You can extend your hike another 2 mi to the Upper Falls and then another 5 mi to 9,850-foot-high Long Lake.

Fish Creek Falls. A mellow half-mile trail leads to a 280-foot waterfall at Fish Creek Falls. ✉ *Hahns Peak-Bears Ears Ranger District Office* ☎ *970/879–1870* ⊕ *www.fs.fed.us/r2/mbr.*

HORSEBACK RIDING

Because of the ranches surrounding the Yampa and Elk rivers, Steamboat is full of real cowboys as well as visitors trying to act the part. Horseback riding is popular here for good reason: seeing the area on horseback is not only easier on the legs, but it also allows riders to get deeper into the backcountry—which is crisscrossed by a web of deer and elk trails—and sometimes closer to wildlife than is possible on foot. Riding, however, isn't for everyone. There's usually a personal weight limit of 250 pounds, and children need to be able to handle their own mount. If you've never ridden a horse before, book a short test ride first. Allergies and sore muscles can turn a dream ride into an epic journey. Riding, instruction, and extended pack trips are offered at a number of ranches in the area, although some may require a minimum stay of a week.

OUTFITTERS ★ **Del's Triangle 3 Ranch.** One facility that can organize rides from hour-long tours to journeys lasting several days is Del's Triangle 3 Ranch. It's about 20 mi north of Steamboat via Highway 129. ✉ *Box 893, Clark 80428* ☎ *970/879–3495* ⊕ *www.steamboathorses.com.*

Howelsen Rodeo Grounds. Every Friday and Saturday evening in summer, rodeos are held at the Howelsen Rodeo Grounds. ✉ *5th St. and Howelsen Pkwy.* ☎ *970/879–1818.*

Sombrero Ranch. Sombrero Ranch is right in town and has one-hour guided tours perfect for novices. ✉ *835 River Rd.* ☎ *970/879–2306* ⊕ *www.sombrero.com/steamboatsprings.*

MOUNTAIN BIKING

Fodor's Choice ★ Steamboat Springs' rolling mountains, endless aspen glades, mellow valleys, and miles and miles of jeep trails and single-track make for great mountain biking. In summer, when Front Range trails are baking in the harsh summer sun and cluttered with mountain bikers, horse riders, and hikers, you can pedal some of the cool backcountry trails in Steamboat without passing a single cyclist.

Gore Pass Loop. The 27½-mi Gore Pass Loop takes you through aspen and pine forests, with gradual hill climbs and long, sweet descents. ✉ *Trailhead: Follow Hwy. 134 to Gore Pass Park, Hwy. 134 and Forest Rd. 185.*

Orange Peel Bikes. Orange Peel Bikes offers a sweet line of demos that cost $15–$20 more than the regular rental rates, which start at $30.

It's a good deal if you're in the market for a new bike. ✉ *1136 Yampa St.* ☎ *970/879–2957* ⊕ *www.orangepeelbikes.com.*

RAFTING

High Adventures/Bucking Rainbow Outfitters. High Adventures/Bucking Rainbow Outfitters runs rafting excursions to the Yampa, Elk, and Eagle rivers. Half-day to two-day trips are available for all levels. ✉ *730 Lincoln Ave.* ☎ *970/879–8747, 888/810–8747* ⊕ *www. buckingrainbow.com.*

SNOWMOBILING

Steamboat Snowmobile Tours. Steamboat Snowmobile Tours has guided tours. A shuttle serves most hotels. ☎ *970/879–6500, 877/879–6500* ⊕ *www.steamboatsnowmobile.com.*

WHERE TO EAT

$$
AMERICAN
✕ **Carl's Tavern.** Named after Karl Hovelsen, the Norwegian ski jumper who brought the sport to Colorado in the early 1900s and who also lent his name to Steamboat's Howelsen Hill, this modern tavern serves updated takes on comfort food, with an emphasis on locally sourced ingredients and as many items produced in-house as possible. Local favorites include chicken-fried steak, three-cheese mac and a lemon icebox pie, but it's also tough to pass up the pot roast made from Angus beef or the banana-chocolate bread pudding. ✉ *700 Yampa Ave.* ☎ *970/761–2060* ⊕ *www.carlstavern.com.*

$
AMERICAN
☺
✕ **Creekside Café & Grill.** This café's hearty breakfasts and lunches, which are crafted to get folks through a day of skiing or biking, are served in a casual atmosphere that's family—and group—friendly. The most popular item on the menu, and for good reason, is the roster of a dozen eggs Benedicts, including "the Arnold," with smoked bacon, ham, and chorizo. On nice days, ask to sit on the patio next to pretty Soda Creek. In season the place is usually jam-packed. Everything on the great kids' menu is about $4. ✉ *131 11th St.* ☎ *970/879–4925* ⊕ *www.creekside-cafe.com* ⚑ *Reservations essential* ☽ *No dinner.*

$
ITALIAN
. ☺
✕ **Cugino's Pizzeria & Italian Restaurant.** The South Philly sensibility of this pizzeria lends authenticity to its filling strombolis, stuffed pizzas that may have originated just outside Philadelphia. The casual dining room offers a lot of breathing room, with the wooden tables that allow plenty of space for big groups to maneuver, a spacious patio deck, and a small bar area with a TV and an attached deck. Food comes in big portions, there are two patios for people-watching and views of the Yampa River, and the staff here will take good care of you. Try the crispy New York–style pizza and the authentic-tasting spaghetti. ✉ *41 8th St.* ☎ *970/879–5805* ⊕ *www.cuginosrestaurant.com.*

$$$$
FRENCH
★
✕ **Harwigs/L'Apogee.** Steamboat's most intimate restaurant is in a building that once housed Harwig's Saddlery and Western Wear. There are two dining rooms, one that is more formal, the other casual. The classic French cuisine, with subtle Asian influences, is well crafted. Especially fine are the innovative duck dishes, the Alaskan king crab cakes, and rotating foie gras appetizers. Still, the menu takes a backseat to the admirable wine list: owner Jamie Jenny is a collector whose wine cellar contains more than 10,000 bottles, and you can order

more than 40 wines by the glass. From May to December there's a popular and reasonably priced Thai menu on Monday nights. ⊠ *911 Lincoln Ave.* ☎ *970/879–1919* ⊕ *www.lapogee.com* ⚊ *Reservations essential* ⊘ *No lunch.*

$ ✕ **Johnny B. Good's Diner.** Between the appealing kids' menu and the
AMERICAN memorabilia that suggests Elvis has not left the building, Johnny's is
☺ all about fun and family. Breakfast (until 2 pm), lunch, and dinner are served daily, and they are all budget minded and large portioned. The menu is mostly what you'd expect—comfort food like meat loaf and mashed potatoes, burgers, milk shakes, and biscuits and gravy—but they also do an above-average rib eye and some tasty Mexican, as well as a popular list of hot "dawgs." ⊠ *738 Lincoln Ave.* ☎ *970/870–8400* ⊕ *www.johnnybgoodsdiner.com.*

$$$ ✕ **La Montaña.** This Southwestern and Tex-Mex establishment is among
MEXICAN Steamboat's most popular restaurants, and with good reason. The kitchen incorporates indigenous specialties into the traditional menu. Among the standouts are sunflower seed–crusted tuna with a margarita beurre blanc, enchiladas layered with Monterey Jack and goat cheese and roasted peppers, and buffalo loin crusted with pecan nuts and bourbon cream sauce. ⊠ *2500 Village Dr., at Après Ski Way* ☎ *970/879–5800* ⊘ *Closed Sun. and Mon. June–Nov. No lunch.*

$$ ✕ **Riggio's.** In a dramatic industrial space, this Italian eatery evokes the
ITALIAN Old Country with tapestries, murals, and landscape photos. The menu includes tasty pizzas (with toppings such as goat cheese and clams) and pasta dishes (*sciocca,* with rock shrimp, eggplant, tomatoes, and basil, is superb). Standards such as manicotti, chicken cacciatore, and saltimbocca are also well prepared. Try the house salad with Gorgonzola vinaigrette. ⊠ *1106 Lincoln Ave.* ☎ *970/879–9010* ⊕ *www. riggiosfineitalian.com* ⊘ *No lunch.*

WHERE TO STAY
For expanded hotel reviews, visit Fodors.com.

$$ 🏨 **Alpine Rose Bed and Breakfast.** Views of Strawberry Park and an easy
B&B/INN walk into town make the Alpine Rose a wonderful alternative to pricey hotels, especially during ski season. **Pros:** close to town; relatively close to ski area (five-minute drive); reasonably priced. **Cons:** not right next to ski area; two-night minimum can be an issue. ⊠ *724 Grand St.* ☎ *970/879–1528, 888/879–1525* ⊕ *www.alpinerosesteamboat.com* ☞ *4 rooms, 1 suite* ⚹ *In-room: no a/c, Wi-Fi. In-hotel: business center, some age restrictions* ⦿ *Breakfast.*

$$$$ 🏨 **Home Ranch.** You won't be roughing it at this all-inclusive retreat,
RESORT a high-end property that's among towering stands of aspen north of
☺ Steamboat, near Clark. **Pros:** luxury experience; excellent food; family-friendly. **Cons:** pricey; seven-day stay can be prohibitive in summer; less authentic. ⊠ *54880 County Rd. 129, Clark* ☎ *970/879–1780, 800/688–1780* ⊕ *www.homeranch.com* ☞ *6 rooms, 8 cabins* ⚹ *In-hotel: bar, pool* ⊘ *Closed late Mar.–May and early Oct.–late Dec.* ⦿ *All meals.*

$ 🏨 **Hotel Bristol.** A delightful small hotel nestled in a 1948 building, the
HOTEL Bristol not only has location working for it, but also old-fashioned per-
☺ sonalized service. **Pros:** families and groups can stay comfortably for a little bit extra; convenient location; ski lockers; computer in lobby.

9

Cons: rooms may seem uncomfortably small, bathrooms even more so. ✉ *917 Lincoln Ave.* ☎ *970/879–3083, 800/851–0872* ⊕ *www. steamboathotelbristol.com* ➲ *24 rooms* ♿ *In-room: Wi-Fi. In-hotel: restaurant* ⦿ *No meals.*

$$
B&B/INN
▦ **Inn at Steamboat.** Rustic knotty pine, leather furniture, comfortable linens, and panoramic views of the Yampa Valley make the inn a good choice for folks looking to stay somewhere that feels like a mountain lodge at lower-than-ski-resort prices. **Pros:** magnificent views, even from the heated pool and particularly in fall; reasonable rates. **Cons:** not ski-in ski-out. ✉ *3070 Columbine Dr.* ☎ *800/872–2601, 970/879–2600* ⊕ *www.innatsteamboat.com* ➲ *31 rooms, 3 suites* ♿ *In-room: a/c, Wi-Fi. In-hotel: pool, laundry facilities, business center* ⦿ *Breakfast.*

$$$
HOTEL
▦ **Ptarmigan Inn.** Situated on the slopes, this laid-back lodging couldn't have a more convenient location. **Pros:** great location; ski-in ski-out; mountain views. **Cons:** feels a bit like a chain hotel. ✉ *2304 Après Ski Way* ⌂ *Box 773240, Steamboat Springs 80477* ☎ *970/879–1730, 800/538–7519* ⊕ *www.steamboat-lodging.com* ➲ *77 rooms* ♿ *In-room: a/c, Internet, Wi-Fi. In-hotel: restaurant, bar, pool* ⦿ *No meals.*

$
HOTEL
☺
▦ **Rabbit Ears Motel.** The playful, pink-neon bunny sign outside this motel has been a local landmark since 1952, making it an unofficial gateway to Steamboat Springs. **Pros:** great location; family- and pet-friendly. **Cons:** kitschy; nothing fancy; it can be noisy along the main drag. ✉ *201 Lincoln Ave.* ☎ *970/879–1150, 800/828–7702* ⊕ *www. rabbitearsmotel.com* ➲ *65 rooms* ♿ *In-room: a/c, Wi-Fi. In-hotel: laundry facilities, some pets allowed* ⦿ *Breakfast.*

$$$$
HOTEL
▦ **Sheraton Steamboat Resort & Conference Center.** This bustling high-rise is one of Steamboat's few ski-in ski-out properties. **Pros:** convenient location, with the slopes, restaurants, and town right there; large size means lots of amenities. **Cons:** rooms somewhat cramped; lobby areas noisy; prices now on par with major ski areas. ✉ *2200 Village End Ct.* ☎ *970/879–2220, 800/848–8877* ⊕ *www.starwoodhotels.com* ➲ *315 rooms* ♿ *In-room: a/c, safe, Wi-Fi. In-hotel: restaurant, bar, golf course, pool, gym, some pets allowed.*

$
HOTEL
☺
▦ **Steamboat Mountain Lodge.** River or mountain views await you at this budget-minded spot, which has changed nothing but its name from the former Bunkhouse. **Pros:** great views; spacious rooms; bargain prices. **Cons:** very simple decor; linens are not exactly luxury. ✉ *3155 S. Lincoln St.* ☎ *877/245–6343, 970/871–9121* ⊕ *www.thebunkhouselodge. com* ➲ *38 rooms* ♿ *In-room: a/c. In-hotel: pool, laundry facilities* ⦿ *Breakfast.*

$$$$
RESORT
Fodor's Choice
★
▦ **Vista Verde Guest Ranch.** On a working ranch, the luxurious Vista Verde provides city slickers with an authentic Western experience. **Pros:** authentic experience; variable stays; family-friendly. **Cons:** pricey; remote. ✉ *3100 County Rd. 64, Clark* ☎ *970/879–3858, 800/526–7433* ⊕ *www.vistaverde.com* ➲ *3 rooms, 9 cabins* ♿ *In-room: no a/c, no TV. In-hotel: gym* ⊘ *Closed mid-Mar.–early June and Oct.–mid-Dec.* ⦿ *All meals.*

STEAMBOAT SPRINGS LODGING ALTERNATIVES

Mountain Resorts. This vacation rental company manages condominiums at more than 15 locations. ⊠ *2145 Resort Dr., Suite 100* ☎ *888/686–8075* ⊕ *www.mtnresorts.com* ⦿ *No meals.*

Resort Quest Steamboat. Torian Plum, one of the properties managed by Wyndham Worldwide/ Resort Quest Steamboat, has elegant one- to six-bedroom units in a ski-in ski-out location. Hot tubs are available. Note that rental prices can vary a great deal among the units and from one week to the next here. ⊠ *1855 Ski Time Sq.* ☎ *970/879–8811, 866/634–9616* ⊕ *www. resortqueststeamboat.com* ⦿ *64 condos* ⦿ *No meals.*

Steamboat Resorts. Steamboat Resorts rents plenty of properties near the slopes. ⦿ *Box 772995, Steamboat Springs 80477* ☎ *800/276–6719* ⊕ *www. steamboatresorts.com* ⦿ *100s of condos* ⦿ *No meals.*

NIGHTLIFE

Mahogany Ridge Brewery & Grill. Mahogany Ridge Brewery & Grill serves superior pub grub and pours an assortment of its own ales, lagers, porters, and stouts. Live music is a nice bonus on weekends. ⊠ *435 Lincoln Ave.* ☎ *970/879–3773.*

Old Town Pub. The Old Town Pub serves juicy burgers accompanied by music from some great bands. ⊠ *600 Lincoln Ave.* ☎ *970/879–2101.*

Tugboat. On the mountain, the Tugboat is the place for loud rock and roll. You can also challenge locals to a game of pool. ⊠ *1860 Ski Time Sq.* ☎ *970/879–7070.*

SHOPPING

At the base of the ski area are three expansive shopping centers—Ski Time Square, Torian Plum Plaza, and Gondola Square.

Old Town Square. Downtown Steamboat's Old Town Square is a collection of upscale boutiques and retailers. There are also plenty of places to get a good cup of coffee. ⊠ *7th St. and Lincoln Ave.*

BOOKSTORES

Off the Beaten Path. Off the Beaten Path is a throwback to the Beat Generation, with poetry readings, lectures, and concerts. It has an excellent selection of New Age works, in addition to the usual best sellers and travel guides. ⊠ *68 9th St.* ☎ *970/879–6830* ⊕ *www. steamboatbooks.com.*

BOUTIQUES AND GALLERIES

Silver Lining. The Silver Lining displays art, crafts, and clothing from around the world, including Balinese cradle watchers, which are carved wooden figures believed to keep evil spirits away from sleeping children. You can make your own earrings at the bead counter. ⊠ *Torian Plum Plaza, 1855 Ski Time Sq. Dr.* ☎ *970/879–7474* ⊕ *www. silverliningsteamboat.com.*

White Hart Gallery. White Hart Gallery is a magnificent clutter of Western-theme paintings and objets d'art. ⊠ *843 Lincoln Ave.* ☎ *970/879–1015.*

9

Wild Horse Gallery. Native American images adorn the walls of the Wild Horse Gallery. This shop across from the Steamboat Art Museum is the place to buy artwork, jewelry, and blown glass. ✉ *802 Lincoln Ave.* ☎ *970/879–7660* ⊕ *www.wildhorsegallery.com.*

SPORTING GOODS

Ski Haus. Ski Haus can outfit you for the slopes. ✉ *1457 Pine Grove Rd.* ☎ *970/879–0385, 800/932–3019* ⊕ *www.skihaussteamboat.com.*

Straightline Sports. Straightline Sports is a good bet for downhill necessities. ✉ *744 Lincoln Ave.* ☎ *970/879–7568* ⊕ *www.straightlinesports.com.*

WESTERN WEAR

F.M. Light and Sons. Owned by the same family for four generations, F.M. Light and Sons caters to the cowpoke in all of us. If you're lucky you'll find a bargain on the Western wear here. ✉ *830 Lincoln Ave.* ☎ *800/530–8908* ⊕ *www.fmlight.com.*

Into the West. Into the West is owned by Jace Romick, a former member of the U.S. Ski Team and a veteran of the rodeo circuit. He crafts splendid textured lodgepole furniture. There are also antiques (including ornate potbellied stoves), cowhide mirrors, and handicrafts such as Native American–drum tables and fanciful candleholders fashioned from branding irons. A recent move into a new building, more than five times as large as the old, means a lot more is on display. ✉ *402 Lincoln Ave.* ☎ *970/879–8377.*

Soda Creek Western Outfitters. Soda Creek Western Outfitters is about 30 mi west of Steamboat and worth the drive if authentic attire, including boots and hats, is on your shopping list. They also sell all manner of cowboy collectibles; home-decor items; gear; kitschy stuff for your dog, horse, and truck; and locally crafted jewelry. ✉ *224 Arthur Ave., Oak Creek* ☎ *800/824–8426* ⊕ *www.soda-creek.com.*

NORTHWEST CORNER

Between the Flat Tops Scenic Byway and Dinosaur National Monument, the northwest corner of the state, which feels remote and desolate in parts, overflows with history. Dinosaur fans will delight in exploring the monument, and folks looking for evidence of early Indian habitation will delight in the petroglyphs and pictographs. The towns are small and sleepy, but their inhabitants, many devoted to fishing, hunting, and other area outdoor pursuits, could not be more welcoming.

MEEKER

43 mi north of Rifle via Rte. 13.

Once an outpost of the U.S. Army, Meeker is still a place where anyone in camouflage is in fashion. Famous for its annual sheepdog championships—a sheepdog statue keeps watch over the sleepy town—it remains a favorite spot for hunting, fishing, and snowmobiling. Interesting historical buildings include the Meeker Hotel on Main Street, where Teddy Roosevelt stayed.

GETTING HERE AND AROUND

Meeker is fairly isolated, and nearly equidistant between Grand Junction and Steamboat Springs. There is no public transportation in town, and a car is needed.

WHEN TO GO

FESTIVALS **Meeker Classic Sheepdog Trials.** You can watch professional sheepdogs in action at the annual Meeker Classic Sheepdog Trials, a prestigious five-day international competition and one of the town's biggest draws. Sheepdogs and their handlers perform sheepherding maneuvers on a closed course while competing for a $25,000 purse. The event takes place the weekend after Labor Day. ☎ 970/878–5510, 970/878–0111 ⊕ *www.meekersheepdog.com* 🖃 *$10.*

ESSENTIALS

Visitor Information Meeker Chamber of Commerce 🗁 *Box 869, 81641* ☎ *970/878-5510* ⊕ *www.meekerchamber.com.*

EXPLORING

White River Museum. The White River Museum is housed in a long building that served as a barracks for U.S. Army officers. Inside are exhibits such as a collection of guns dating to the Civil War and the plow used by Nathan Meeker to dig up the Ute's pony racetrack. ⊠ *565 Park St.* ☎ *970/878–9982* ⊕ *www.meekercolorado.com/museum.htm* 🖃 *Free* ◷ *Mid-Apr.–Nov., daily 9–5; Dec.–mid-Apr., daily 10–4.*

SPORTS AND THE OUTDOORS

FISHING

JML Outfitters. The White River valley is home to some of the best fishing holes in Colorado, including Meeker Town Park, Sleepy Cat Access, and Trappers Lake. Some of the best fishing is on private land, so you need to ask permission, and you might have to pay. Your best bet—if you don't want to go it alone—is to hire a guide familiar with the area, such as JML Outfitters, which has been in the outfitting business for three generations, offering photography and wildlife-viewing trips, kids' camps, and trail rides. ⊠ *300 Country Rd. 75* ☎ *970/878–4749* ⊕ *www.jmloutfitters.com.*

SNOWMOBILING

Welder Outfitting Services. One of Meeker's best-kept secrets is the fantastic snowmobiling through pristine powder in the backcountry, which some say rivals Yellowstone—without the crowds. Trail maps for self-guided rides are available through the Chamber of Commerce or the U.S. Forest Service, or from Welder Outfitting Services, which organizes snowmobile trips in the White River National Forest and Flat Tops Wilderness. ☎ *970/878–9869* ⊕ *www.welderoutfitters.com.*

WHERE TO STAY

For expanded hotel reviews, visit Fodors.com.

$ 🏨 **Meeker Hotel and Cafe.** The Old West–style restaurant ($$–$$$) in this
HOTEL hotel is filled with a veritable forest of rustic furniture, and dozens of massive trophy elk and deer peer down from every wall. **Pros:** delightful decor; delicious food in the café; bargain-hunters can go the communal-bathroom route. **Cons:** the café can get crowded and noisy; the walls are

9

paper-thin. ⊠ *560 Main St.* ☎ *970/878–5062, 970/878–5255* ⊕ *www. themeekerhotel.com* ⤳ *19 rooms, 5 suites* ⚿ *In-room: a/c. In-hotel: restaurant, bar* |◯| *No meals.*

SHOPPING

Fawn Creek Gallery. Featuring original watercolor paintings and limited-edition prints by Colorado artist John T. Myers, Fawn Creek Gallery also sells Fremont and Ute rock-art replicas and duck carvings made from 100-year-old cedar fence posts. ⊠ *315 6th St.* ☎ *970/878–0955* ⊕ *www.fawncreekgallery.com.*

Wendll's Wondrous Things. An old-fashioned mercantile building with original display cases, tin ceilings, and wood floors, Wendll's Wondrous Things sells an eclectic mix of clothing, housewares, body-care products, greeting cards, Brighton jewelry, and Native American turquoise and sterling silver from Arizona. The attached coffee shop, Cuppa Joe, makes a welcoming stop. ⊠ *594 Main St.* ☎ *970/878–3688.*

CRAIG

48 mi north of Meeker via Rte. 13; 42 mi west of Steamboat Springs via U.S. 40.

Craig is home to some of the best fishing in the area. Guided trips to some of the hottest fishing spots are available, as are horseback pack trips into the wilderness. Depending on the season, you might spot bighorn sheep, antelope, or nesting waterfowl, including the Great Basin Canada goose.

GETTING HERE AND AROUND

U.S. 40 west from Denver or east from Utah is the best way to reach Craig. All Around Taxi provides service in town.

ESSENTIALS

Transportation Contacts All Around Taxi ☎ *970/824–1177.*

Visitor Information Greater Craig Chamber of Commerce ⊠ *360 E. Victory Way* ☎ *970/824–5689* ⊕ *www.craig-chamber.com.*

EXPLORING

Marcia Car. One of Craig's most prized historical possessions, the Marcia Car in City Park was the private Pullman car of Colorado magnate David Moffat, who at one time was full or partial owner of more than 100 gold and silver mines. Moffat was also instrumental in bringing railroad transportation to northwest Colorado. He used his private car to inspect construction work on the Moffat Railroad line. Named after his only child, the car has been restored and makes for an interesting tour. ⊠ *U.S. 40* ☎ *970/824–5689* ▭ *Free* ◔ *Late May–mid-Oct., weekdays 8–5.*

Museum of Northwest Colorado. The Museum of Northwest Colorado elegantly displays an eclectic collection of everything from arrowheads to a fire truck. The upstairs of this restored county courthouse holds the largest privately owned collection of working cowboy artifacts in the world. Bill Mackin, one of the leading traders in cowboy collectibles, has spent a lifetime gathering guns, bits, saddles, bootjacks, holsters, and spurs of all descriptions. ✉ *590 Yampa Ave.* ☎ *970/824–6360* ⊕ *www.museumnwco.org* 🎫 *Free, donations accepted* 🕐 *Weekdays 9–5, Sat. 10–4.*

SPORTS AND THE OUTDOORS

FISHING

Craig Sports. Get the scoop on hot fishing spots from Craig Sports while loading up on tackle and other supplies. ✉ *124 W. Victory Way* ☎ *970/824–4044* ⊕ *www.craigsports.net.*

Sportsman's Center at the Craig Chamber of Commerce. The Yampa and Green rivers, Trappers Lake, Lake Avery, and Elkhead Reservoir are known for pike and trout. Contact the Sportsman's Center at the Craig Chamber of Commerce for information. ✉ *360 E. Victory Way* ☎ *970/824–3046* ⊕ *www.craig-chamber.com/hunting.html.*

WHERE TO EAT

$ ✕ **Cugino's Pizzeria & Italian Restaurant.** The same South Philly sensibil-
ITALIAN ity found at Cugino's Steamboat Springs location is here, too. Filling
🧒 strombolis and stuffed pizzas are authentic Philadelphia-style. Food
comes in big portions, and the staff is friendly and accommodating.
The dining areas are inviting, with plenty of space between tables and
a great foliage-lined patio, which looks like someone's backyard. ✉ *572
Breeze St.* ☎ *970/824–6323* ⊕ *www.cuginosrestaurant.com.*

$$ ✕ **Golden Cavvy.** A cavvy is the pick of a team of horses, and this res-
AMERICAN taurant is a town favorite. Its coffee-shop atmosphere is enlivened by
mirrors, hanging plants, faux-antique chandeliers, and masonry of the
1900s fireplace of the Baker Hotel, which burned down on this spot.
Homemade pies and ice cream, burgers, pork chops, and anything deep-
fried—try the mesquite-fried chicken—are your best bets. They also
serve decent, hearty breakfasts. ✉ *538 Yampa Ave.* ☎ *970/824–6038.*

DINOSAUR NATIONAL MONUMENT

90 mi west of Craig via U.S. 40.

GETTING HERE AND AROUND

U.S. 40 west from Denver or east from Utah is the best way to reach Dinosaur National Monument. You also can take Highway 139 and Route 64 from Grand Junction. The town of Dinosaur, with a few somewhat dilapidated concrete dinosaur statues watching over their namesake town, merits only a brief stop on the way to the real thing: the bones at Dinosaur National Monument.

EXPLORING

🧒 **Dinosaur National Monument.** Straddling the Colorado–Utah border,
Fodor'sChoice Dinosaur National Monument is a must for any dinosaur enthusiast.
★ A two-story hill teeming with fossils—many still in the complete skel-
etal shapes of the dinosaurs—greets visitors at one of the few places
in the world where you can touch a dinosaur bone still embedded in
the earth. The Colorado side of the park offers some of the best hik-
ing in the West, along the Harpers Corner and Echo Park Drive routes
and the ominous-sounding Canyon of Lodore (where the Green River
rapids buffet rafts). The drive is only accessible in summer—even then,

four-wheel drive is preferable—and some of the most breathtaking over-looks are well off the beaten path.

Dinosaur Quarry. After its predecessor was closed for five years because of structural damage, the much-anticipated new Dinosaur Quarry Exhibit Hall opened in 2011, showcasing an estimated 1,500 dinosaur bones that date to the late Jurassic Period still embedded in the clay. A half-mile away is a massive and new 7,595-square-foot visi-tor center. ⊠ *Visitor center: 7 mi north of Jensen, Utah, on Rte. 139* ☎ *970/374–3000* ⊠ *4545 E. Hwy. 40* ☎ *435/781–7700* ⊕ *www.nps. gov/dino* ☜ *$10 per vehicle; $5 per individual* ☉ *Daily.*

SPORTS AND THE OUTDOORS

HIKING

☾ **Desert Voices Nature Trail.** The Desert Voices Nature Trail is near the Dinosaur Quarry. The 1½-mi loop is moderate in difficulty and has a series of trail signs produced for kids by kids. ⊠ *Split Mountain area, across from boat ramp.*

RAFTING

Adventure Bound River Expeditions. One of the best ways to experience the rugged beauty of the park is on a white-water raft trip. Adven-ture Bound River Expeditions runs two- to five-day excursions on the Colorado, Yampa, and Green rivers. ⊠ *2392 H Rd., Grand Junction* ☎ *800/423–4668* ⊕ *www.adventureboundusa.com.*

WHERE TO EAT

¢ ✕ **BedRock Depot.** Co-owners and longtime residents Leona Hemmerich
AMERICAN and Bill Mitchem understand both the cravings of the area's visitors and
☾ the spectacular vistas they come to see. New batches of homemade ice
★ cream show up almost every day at their roadside shop, where the walls are a gallery for their photography and artwork. The shop sells fresh sandwiches—including a terrific roast beef on house-baked rolls—and specialty coffees (with names like "Mochasaurus") and bottled root beer, cream soda, and ginger ale. The Depot's immaculate restroom makes for one of the most pleasant pit stops on the long drive ahead. ⊠ *214 Brontosaurus W. Blvd.* ☎ *970/374–2336* ⊕ *www.bedrockdepot. com* ☉ *Closed Wed. Call for hrs Nov.–Mar.*

$$ ✕ **Massadona Tavern & Steakhouse.** A restaurant and bar, Massadona
AMERICAN is small, homey, and rustic, with a smattering of Western decor items and a mixture of tables and booths. It's also a casual, inviting, and relaxing place—kind of in the middle of nowhere, even though it's about 20-minutes east of Dinosaur and a half-hour drive from the monument—to stop after a day of digging around in dinosaur dirt, and the inexpensive steaks go down well with a cocktail (also reason-ably priced). They also do excellent breaded shrimp, good burgers (try the bacon cheeseburger), fish-and-chips, and classic Reubens. ⊠ *22927 Hwy. 40* ☎ *970/374–2324* ☉ *Closed Mon., no lunch weekdays.*

RANGELY

20 mi southeast of Dinosaur National Monument; 96 mi northwest of Grand Junction via Rte. 139 and 1–70.

The center of one of the last areas in the state to be explored by European settlers, Rangely was dubbed an "isolated empire" by early pioneers. You can search out the petroglyphs left by Native American civilizations or just stroll the farmers' market in Town Square. If you enjoy back-road mountain biking, the Raven Rims have an abundance of trails. You may even spot elk, mules, deer, coyotes, and other wildlife as you spin your wheels through the multihued sandstone rims and mesas north of town. Kenney Reservoir 5 mi north of town offers fishing and swimming, and a trip on the Cathedral Bluffs trail gives new definition to "isolated empire."

GETTING HERE AND AROUND

U.S. 40 west from Denver or east from Utah and then Route 64 south is the best way to get to Rangely. You can also take Highway 139 from Grand Junction. There are no transportation services in town.

ESSENTIALS

Visitor Infomation Rangely Chamber of Commerce ⊠ *209 E. Main St.* ☎ *970/675–5290* ⊕ *www.rangelychamber.com.*

EXPLORING

★ **Canyon Pintado National Historic District.** One of Rangely's most compelling sights is the superb Fremont petroglyphs—carved between AD 600 and 1300—in Douglas Creek canyon, south of town along Route 139. This stretch is known as the Canyon Pintado National Historic District, and the examples of rock art are among the best-preserved in the West; half the fun is clambering up the rocks to find them. A brochure listing the sights is available at the Rangely Chamber of Commerce. ⊠ *209 E. Main St.* ☎ *970/675–5290* ⊕ *www.blm.gov/co* ⊠ *Free* ⊙ *Daily.*

SPORTS AND THE OUTDOORS

FISHING

Kenney Reservoir. Just below Taylor Draw Dam, Kenney Reservoir draws anglers in search of black crappie, channel catfish, and rainbow trout. The best fishing is right below the dam. If you hook one of Colorado's endangered pikeminnow, you'll have to throw it back. You can also go camping, boating, waterskiing, wildlife-watching, and picnicking. Locals come to the reservoir to watch the sun's last rays color the bluffs behind the lake. ⊕ *www.rangely.com/fishing.htm.*

MOUNTAIN BIKING

Town of Rangely. The best mountain-biking trails north of town are in the Raven Rims, named in honor of the abundant population of the large, noisy birds that live in the area. Contact the Town of Rangely for trail information. ⊠ *209 E. Main St.* ☎ *970/675–8476* ⊕ *www.rangely.com.*

9

WHERE TO EAT AND STAY

For expanded hotel reviews, visit Fodors.com.

$ ╳ **Giovanni's Italian Grill.** Between the thick, hearty pizzas, big-as-your-
ITALIAN head strombolis, and overflowing plates of pasta served at this incred-
☺ ibly friendly, casual eatery, it's hard to walk out of here without feeling
stuffed. The sauces are homemade, and the red sauce in particular is
flavorful and authentic. The reasonably priced kids' menu, with nothing over $5, helps families feel welcome, and so does the staff, which is
sometimes made up of the owners' family members. ⊠ *855 E. Main St.*
☎ *970/675–2670* ⊕ *www.giovannisrangely.com* ☉ *Closed Sun.*

$ ╳ **Los Tres Potrillos.** This casual Mexican restaurant has the usual selec-
MEXICAN tion of burritos and tacos, along with the only patio in town. Try the
fajitas, enchiladas, and carne asada. Mexican pottery, serapes, and
sombreros in green, orange, and black make up the colorful backdrop. The service staff is accommodating, and the inexpensive beers
and so-so margaritas come fast. ⊠ *302 W. Main St.* ☎ *970/675–8870*
☉ *Closed Sun.*

$ ▦ **Blue Mountain Inn & Suites.** Rooms are simple but spacious at this
HOTEL reliable hotel, which is next to the grocery store. **Pros:** inviting heated
indoor pool and hot tub; pleasant lobby with soft, cozy chairs; centrally
located. **Cons:** has a chain feel; rooms are sparsely decorated. ⊠ *37
Park St.* ☎ *970/675–8888* ⊕ *www.bluemountaininnrangely.com* ⇌ *47
rooms, 3 suites* ☖ *In-room: a/c, Wi-Fi. In-hotel: pool, water sports,
laundry facilities, business center* ❖ *Breakfast.*

SHOPPING

Main Street Farmers' Market. Fresh produce, baked goods, and live entertainment can be found at the Main Street Farmers' Market, held Saturday from 8:30 to 12:30. One of the more popular items is the elk jerky.
⊠ *Town Square* ☎ *970/675–5290.*

Sweetbriar. A wood-burning stove graces the front of charming Sweetbriar, a little store that sells a variety of gifts and home decor. ⊠ *781
W. Hwy. 64* ☎ *970/675–5353.*

Southwest Colorado

THE SAN JUAN MOUNTAINS AND BLACK CANYON OF THE GUNNISON

WORD OF MOUTH

"Unlike the Grand Canyon, Black Canyon is very narrow and the walls are nearly vertical, so hiking into the canyon is very difficult and the routes are not good. There are no maintained trails into the canyon itself. So that leaves just a few trails on the rim, most of which are pretty short and just lead to a couple viewpoints. If you're in the area, absolutely stop in because the views are amazing."

—WhereAreWe

Updated
by Martha
Connors

The reddish rocks found in much of the state, particularly in the southwest, give Colorado its name. The region's terrain varies widely—from yawning black canyons and desolate moonscapes to pastel deserts and mesas, glistening sapphire lakes, and wide expanses of those stunning red rocks. It's so rugged in the southwest that a four-wheel-drive vehicle or a pair of sturdy hiker's legs is necessary to explore much of the wild and beautiful backcountry.

The region's history and people are as colorful as the landscape. Southwestern Colorado, as well as the "Four Corners" neighbors of northwestern New Mexico, northeastern Arizona, and southeastern Utah, was home to the Ancestral Puebloans formerly known as Anasazi, meaning "ancient ones." These people, ancestors of today's Puebloan peoples (including the Zuni and Hopi tribes) constructed impressive cliff dwellings in what are now Mesa Verde National Park, Ute Mountain Tribal Park, and other nearby sites. This wild and woolly region, dotted with rowdy mining camps and boomtowns, also witnessed the antics of such notorious outlaws as Butch Cassidy, who embarked on his storied career by robbing the San Miguel Valley Bank in Telluride in 1889, and Robert "Bob" Ford, who hid out in Creede after famously shooting Jesse James in 1882.

Southwest Colorado has such diversity that, depending on where you go, you can have radically different vacations. You can spiral from the towering peaks of the San Juan range to the plunging Black Canyon of the Gunnison, taking in alpine scenery along the way, as well as the eerie remains of old mining camps, before winding through striking desert landscapes, and Old West railroad town. Even if you're not here to ski or golf in the resorts of Crested Butte, Durango, or Telluride, you'll still find plenty to experience in this part of the state.

ORIENTATION AND PLANNING

GETTING ORIENTED

Southwest Colorado is the land beyond the interstates. Old mining roads, legacies of the late 19th and early 20th centuries, when gold and silver mining was ascendant, lead through drop-dead gorgeous mountain valleys and rugged high country. Much of this part of the state is designated as wilderness area, which means that no roads may be built and no wheeled or motorized vehicles are permitted. Even some state highways are unpaved, and a federal highway known as U.S. 550 corkscrews over a high mountain pass best known for its cliff-hugging turns and lack of guardrails. While backcountry roads demand

TOP REASONS TO GO

Downhill skiing and snowboarding in Telluride: There's never much of a wait to take a lift up to the sweeping, groomed trails and challenging tree and mogul runs at this world-famous ski area, tucked among the highest concentration of 14,000-foot peaks in North America.

Hiking the Colorado Trail: Bike, hike, or photograph along the nearly 500 mi of volunteer-maintained trail traversing eight major mountain ranges, seven national forests, and six wilderness areas from Durango to Denver.

Mountain biking in Crested Butte: There's a reason the Mountain Biking Hall of Fame resides here—the town is one of the birthplaces of fat-tire biking, and it's completely surrounded by up-close mountain scenery.

Riding the Durango & Silverton Narrow Gauge Railroad: This 3½-hour journey along the Animas River will take you back in time in trains mostly powered by coal-fired locomotives. The views include dramatic canyons and the sweeping panoramas of the San Juan National Forest.

four-wheel-drive vehicles in summer and snowmobiles in winter, regular roads are no problem for passenger cars.

Black Canyon of the Gunnison National Park and Montrose. The western town of Montrose makes a great base for exploring the majestic canyon, which plunges 2,000 feet down sheer vertical cliffs to the roaring Gunnison River.

Crested Butte and Gunnison. Explore this mountain paradise on single-track in summer and Nordic track in winter. The Taylor and Gunnison rivers round out the adventure possibilities, with white-water rafting, kayaking, and great fly-fishing.

Durango and Mesa Country. Durango makes an ideal base for exploring nearby Mesa Country and its star attraction, Mesa Verde National Park. This college town is known for its eclectic eateries and historic hotels, as well as its many hiking and mountain biking options.

Lake City and Creede. Route 149 meanders south from the Black Canyon of the Gunnison through a scattering of cozy, laid-back communities with deep mining roots.

Telluride and the San Juan Mountains. Old mining camps including Silverton, Ouray, and Telluride now welcome adventurers seeking other riches—wilderness trekking, rugged four-wheeling, mountain biking, skiing, and horseback riding.

PLANNING

WHEN TO GO

Like the rest of the state, southwestern Colorado is intensely seasonal. Snow typically begins falling in the high country in late September or early October, and by Halloween seasonal closures turn some unpaved alpine roads into routes for snowmobiles. The San Juan Mountains see average annual snowfalls approaching 400 inches in the highest spots. Winter lingers well into the season that is called spring on the calendar—the greatest snowfalls generally occur in March and April.

Skiing winds down in early- to mid-April, as the snow in the higher elevations begins to melt. Cresting streams provide thrilling, if chilling, white-water rafting and kayaking. Hiking and biking trails become accessible, and wildflowers begin their short, intense season of show. Summer is glorious in the mountains, with brilliant sunshine and cobalt-blue skies. Late summer brings brief and often intense showers on many an afternoon, sometimes accompanied by dramatic thunder and lightning. Summer tourism winds down after Labor Day and, in some areas, shuts down completely in October. The mountains are popular year-round, but spring and fall are the best times to visit the hot, dry climate of the Mesa Country around the Four Corners.

GETTING HERE AND AROUND
AIR TRAVEL

The Gunnison–Crested Butte Regional Airport (GUC) serves the nearby resort area. GUC is served by American Airlines, United, and United Express.

The closest regional airport to the Black Canyon of the Gunnison National Park is Montrose Regional Airport (MTJ). It's served by American, Continental, United, and Delta.

Telluride is one of the hardest ski resorts in the country to fly into, mainly because the elevation of Telluride Regional Airport (TEX) is well above 9,000 feet. A little turbulence, a few clouds, and the next thing you know you're landing at Montrose Airport, 68 mi away, and taking a shuttle. Telluride Airport welcomes flights from Frontier, Great Lakes, US Airways, and United.

The Durango–La Plata Airport (DRO) is your closest option for Silverton, Durango, Pagosa Springs, Mesa Verde National Park, and the Four Corners region. It's served by American Eagle, Frontier, US Airways, and United Express.

Something to consider for travel to the Four Corners region, given your location and airline schedules, is to check into flying to Albuquerque instead of Denver. The Albuquerque International Sunport (ABQ) is host to many of the major airlines and is closer than Denver.

TRANSFERS   Several companies run transportation options between the airports and the resort towns of Telluride and Crested Butte. Shuttle fares vary; it's about $48 per person from Montrose Regional Airport to Telluride, and $34 per person from Gunnison–Crested Butte Regional Airport to Crested Butte. To get to Crested Butte from Gunnison or Montrose, try Alpine Express. Telluride Express offers service to Telluride from Durango, Montrose, Cortez, Gunnison, and Grand Junction.

In addition, the towns of Crested Butte and Durango operate shuttles to and from the ski areas.

Airports Albuquerque International Sunport (ABQ) ☎ 505/244–7700 ⊕ www.cabq.gov/airport. **Durango–La Plata County Airport (DRO)** ☎ 970/247–8143 ⊕ www.flydurango.com. **Gunnison–Crested Butte Regional**

Airport (GUC) ☎ *970/641–2304* ⊕ *www.gunnisoncounty.org/airport.html.*
Montrose Regional Airport (MTJ) ☎ *970/249–3203* ⊕ *www.montroseairport.*
com. **Telluride Regional Airport (TEX)** ☎ *970/728–8600* ⊕ *www.*
tellurideairport.com.

Airport Transfers Alpine Express ☎ *970/641–5074, 800/822–4844* ⊕ *www.*
alpineexpressshuttle.com. **Telluride Express** ☎ *970/728–6000, 888/212–8294*
⊕ *www.tellurideexpress.com.*

CAR TRAVEL

Alamo, Avis, Budget, Enterprise, and Hertz have car-rental counters at
the Montrose Regional Airport. Avis, Budget, Enterprise, Hertz, and
National all have counters at Durango–La Plata Airport. Gunnison–
Crested Butte Regional Airport has Avis, Budget, and Hertz. National
and Hertz have counters at Telluride Regional Airport.

The main roads in the region are Route 135 between Crested Butte and
Gunnison; U.S. 50 linking Poncha Springs, Gunnison, Montrose, and
Delta; Route 149 between Gunnison, Lake City, and Creede; U.S. 550
from Montrose to Ridgway, Ouray, Silverton, and Durango; Route 62
and Route 145 linking Ridgway with Telluride, Dolores, and Cortez;
and U.S. 160, which passes from Cortez to Durango to Pagosa Springs
via Mesa Verde National Park. With the exception of Kebler Pass, none
of these roads officially closes for winter, but be prepared at any time
during snowy months for portions of the roads to be closed or down to
one lane for avalanche control or to clear ice or snowdrifts.

TAXI TRAVEL

In the resort towns, you'll probably never need to call for a cab. You're
most likely to use one to get to or from the airport.

PARKS AND RECREATION AREAS

Southwest Colorado includes a wealth of national and state parks and
recreation areas. Three of the 13 rivers designated as "gold medal"
waters by the Colorado Wildlife Commission—the Animas, Gunnison,
and Rio Grande—are here. Blue Mesa and McPhee reservoirs, the state's
largest bodies of water, are destinations for boaters, waterskiers, wind-
surfers, and anglers (including the ice-fishing kind). Up in rustic Almont,
a small community near the Gunnison headwaters, they *live* fly-fishing.
Anglers also love Ridgway State Park, with access to rainbow trout and
other prize fish. ■TIP→ **Anyone older than 16 needs a Colorado fishing
license, which you can obtain at local sporting-goods stores.**

The precipitous Black Canyon of the Gunnison National Park is a
mysterious and powerful attraction. Some of the most intact remains
of the ancient, little-known Ancestral Puebloan culture are inside Mesa
Verde National Park and Canyons of the Ancients National Monument.

The San Juan Mountains stretch through 12,000 square mi of southwest
Colorado, encompassing three national forests and seven wilderness
areas. The enormous San Juan National Forest is a virtual paradise for
all kinds of adventuring. Directly north, the Uncompahgre National
Forest encompasses nearly a million acres of alpine wilderness and the
picturesque peaks of Mount Sneffels and Lizard Head. To the east, the

Rio Grande National Forest stretches from the magisterial Sangre de Cristo Mountains across the San Luis Valley.

RESTAURANTS

With dining options ranging from creative international cuisine in the resort towns of Telluride, Crested Butte, and Durango to no-frills American fare in down-home communities like Delta and Creede, no one has any excuse to visit a chain restaurant here. The leading chefs are tapping into the region's local bounty, so you can find innovative recipes for ranch-raised game, lamb, and trout. Many serve only locally raised, grass-fed meats. Olathe sweet corn is a delicacy enjoyed across the state (and found in grocery stores and roadside stands as well as restaurants). Seasonal produce is always highlighted on the best menus.

HOTELS

No matter what you're looking for in vacation lodging—luxurious slope-side condominium, landmark inn in a historic town, riverside cabin, guest ranch, country inn, budget motel, or chock-full-of-RVs campground—southwest Colorado has it in abundance. Rates vary season to season, particularly in the resort towns. Some properties close in fall once the aspens have shed their golden leaves, open in winter when the lifts begin running, close in spring after the snow melts, and open again in mid-June.

WHAT IT COSTS				
	¢	$	$$	$$$	$$$$
Restaurants	under $8	$8–$12	$13–$18	$19–$25	over $25
Hotels	under $80	$80–$120	$121–$170	$171–$230	over $230

Restaurant prices are for a main course at dinner, excluding 5.9%–8.1% tax. Hotel prices are for two people in a standard double room in high season, excluding service charges and 7.6%–9.9% tax.

VISITOR INFORMATION
Contact Southwest Colorado Travel Region ☎ 800/933–4340 ⊕ www. swcolotravel.org.

CRESTED BUTTE AND GUNNISON

This area is dominated and shaped by the Gunnison River, which gathers water from the Taylor and East rivers at Almont, meets the Uncompahgre River near Delta, and finally hooks up with the Colorado River near Grand Junction. West of Gunnison, the river has cut the Black Canyon of the Gunnison, a forbidding, 48-mi-long abyss often deeper than it is wide. The Elk Mountains stretch from the northern edge of the Black Canyon through Crested Butte. Almont, off Highway 135 between Crested Butte and Gunnison, is a still-rustic fly-fishing hideaway.

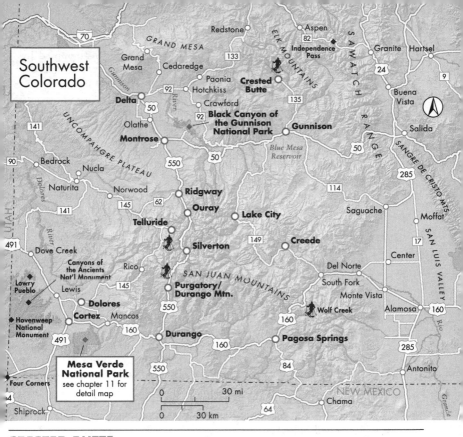

CRESTED BUTTE

28 mi north of Gunnison via Rte. 135; 92 mi northeast of Montrose via Rte. 135 and U.S. 50.

Like Aspen, the town of Crested Butte was once a small mining village (albeit for coal, not silver). The Victorian gingerbread-trim houses remain, many of them now painted in whimsical shades of hot pink, magenta, and chartreuse. Unlike Aspen, however, Crested Butte has retained much of its small-town charm despite its development as a ski area.

A lovelier setting could not be imagined. The town sits at the top of a long, broad valley that stretches 17 mi south toward Gunnison. Mount Crested Butte, which looms over the town, is the most visible landmark. It's surrounded by the Gunnison National Forest and the Elk Mountain Range.

Crested Butte has always been cutting-edge when it comes to embracing new ways to take advantage of the powdery snow. It was an early hotbed of telemark skiing, and was popular with snowboarders back when few people had heard of the sport. But it's as an extreme-skiing mecca that Crested Butte earned its reputation with some of the best skiers in the land. Over the years, Crested Butte has steadily increased its extreme-skiing terrain to 550 ungroomed acres. But although this area, known as the Extreme Limits, should only be attempted by experts, there are plenty of cruise-worthy trails for skiers of all levels. The groomed trails are rarely crowded, which allows for plenty of long, fast, sweeping turns.

Crested Butte is just as popular in summer. Blanketed with columbine and Indian paintbrush, the landscape is mesmerizing. Crested Butte is also one of the country's major mountain-biking centers. Once the snow melts, mountain bikers challenge the hundreds of miles of trails surrounding the town.

GETTING HERE AND AROUND

Crested Butte is just over the mountain from Aspen, but there are no paved roads—just unpaved routes over the challenging Pearl, Taylor, and Schofield passes and hiking trails through White River National Forest. If you're coming from the north or west, the most direct route is over Kebler Pass. The drive is one of the state's prettiest, passing through one of the state's largest stands of aspens. If you're coming from the east, the beautiful Cottonwood Pass will deposit you on Route 135, just south of town. Both graded gravel roads are closed in winter, making it necessary to take a circuitous route on U.S. 24 and U.S. 50 through Poncha Springs and Gunnison, then up Route 135 to Crested Butte.

Alpine Express will transport you between the Gunnison-Crested Butte Regional Airport and the resort. Mountain Express is a reliable free shuttle-bus that travels the 3 mi between the town and the resort throughout the year.

WHEN TO GO

Ski season—mid-December to mid-April—is definitely the busiest time in Crested Butte. The weeks between Memorial Day and Labor Day are hopping, as well. Things slow down dramatically in the in-between times, with some businesses closing completely.

FESTIVALS
★
Crested Butte Music Festival. From early July to mid-August, the Crested Butte Music Festival presents a six-week concert series featuring bluegrass, opera, gypsy jazz, and classical music in various venues in town and at the ski area. ⊠ *326 Elk Ave.* ☎ *970/349–0619* ⊕ *www. crestedbuttemusicfestival.com.*

Crested Butte Wildflower Festival. The surrounding mountains are carpeted with such abundant foliage that Crested Butte has been nicknamed the "Wildflower Capital of Colorado." For one glorious week in mid-July, the town celebrates this bounty with an imaginative lineup of events: guided walks, wildflower identification workshops, classes on medicinal plants, and four-wheel-drive tours. ⊠ *Box 216* ☎ *970/349–2571* ⊕ *www.crestedbuttewildflowerfestival.com.*

ESSENTIALS

Transportation Contacts Alpine Express ☎ *970/641–5074, 800/822–4844* ⊕ *alpineexpressshuttle.com.* **Mountain Express** ☎ *970/349–5616* ⊕ *www. mtnexp.org.*

Visitor Information Crested Butte–Mount Crested Butte Chamber of Commerce ⊠ *601 Elk Ave.* ☎ *970/349–6438, 800/545–4505* ⊕ *www.cbchamber.*

com. **Crested Butte Snow Report**
☎ *800/810-7669* ⊕ *www.skicb.com.*
Crested Butte Vacations ⌂ *12
Snowmass Rd. 81224* ☎ *970/349-2222,
800/810-7669* ⊕ *www.skicb.com.*

EXPLORING

Crested Butte Mountain Heritage Museum. Housed in a turn-of-the-20th-century hardware store, this museum showcases the essentials for life in an 1880s mining town, such as clothing, furniture, and household items. There's an exquisite diorama of the town in the 1920s, complete with a moving train, plus exhibits on skiing, sledding, and Flauschink, a quirky local ceremony that welcomes the return of spring. The **Mountain Bike Hall of Fame and Museum** is also here, with a collection of vintage bikes, classic photos, and other memorabilia. ⊠ *331 Elk Ave.* ☎ *970/349-1880* ⊕ *www.crestedbutteheritagemuseum.com* ⌂ *$3* ⊙ *Mid-June–early Oct., daily 10–8; mid-Oct.–mid-Nov., daily 8–6; late Nov.–early Apr., daily 11–6.*

> ### CRESTED BUTTE WILDFLOWERS
>
> Take a four-wheel-drive tour almost any time in summer and picnic in a galaxy of wildflowers. Look for the blue-and-white columbine, Colorado's state flower. But remember to bring your friend to the flower, not the flower to your friend—it is illegal to pick a blue columbine within state borders.

DOWNHILL SKIING AND SNOWBOARDING

Crested Butte Mountain Resort. Crested Butte skiing has a split personality, which is plain to see when you check out the skiers who descend on the place year after year. Its mellow half is the network of trails on the front side of the mountain, characterized by long intermediate runs. Families flock to Crested Butte for these trails, as well as the children's ski school facilities and the laid-back and friendly vibe.

The wilder side of Crested Butte's personality is the Extreme Limits, more than 500 acres of backcountry-like terrain (all double black diamond), with steep bowls, gnarly chutes, and tight tree skiing. It's some of the toughest in-bounds skiing in North America. Sign up for one of the guided programs for expert instruction (and insider info on the best powder stashes on the mountain).

The best expert skiing on the front side of the mountain is off the Silver Queen high-speed quad, which shoots you up 2,000 vertical feet in one quick ride. For beginners there's a wonderful expanse of easy terrain from the Red Lady Express lift. ⊠ *12 Snowmass Rd.* ☎ *970/349-2222, 800/810-7699* ⊕ *www.skicb.com* ⊙ *Late Nov.–early Apr., daily 9–4.*

FACILITIES 2,775-foot vertical drop; 1,167 skiable acres; 121 trails, of which 23% are beginner, 57% intermediate, and 20% advanced; 4 detachable high-speed quad chairs, 2 fixed-grip quad chairs, 2 triple chairs, 3 double chairs, 3 surface lifts, and 2 magic carpets (beginners' lifts).

LESSONS AND PROGRAMS **CB Mountain School.** The Full Day Beginner Adventure, an adult group lesson with a lift ticket, costs $130 and practically guarantees you'll be tackling green runs by the end of the day. For kids ages 3 through 16, Camp CB offers single all-day lessons starting at $160. Intermediate, advanced, and private lessons are also available. ⊠ *12 Snowmass Rd.* ☎ *800/444-9236* ⊕ *www.skicb.com.*

10

LIFT TICKETS   The walk-up rates for high-season lift tickets range from $92 for one day to $609 for a week; prices are lower in early and late season.

RENTALS   **Crested Butte Sports.** Full rental packages (including skis, boots, and poles), as well as telemark, snowshoe, and snowboard equipment, are available at this outfitter. Rates start at $19 per day. There's also a retail store and full repair shop. ⊠ *35 Emmons Loop Rd.* ☎ *970/349–7516, 800/970–9704* ⊕ *www.crestedbuttesports.com.*

> ### ICE BAR
>
> **Ice Bar.** Mount Crested Butte's cool Ice Bar relies on temperatures in the freezing range. Made partly of ice, the bar is set up in November near Twister Lift, midway up Mount Crested Butte, next to Uley's Cabin. When the sun starts to warm things up, the Ice Bar goes away, as do the fur-clad servers and bartenders who wait on the 20 stools set up around this chilly, but very hot, après-ski and lunch spot. ⊠ *At base of Twister Lift.*

NORDIC SKIING
BACKCOUNTRY SKIING
Crested Butte Nordic Center. Crested Butte abounds with backcountry possibilities. You can rent cross-country skis or snowshoes, then head out on one of the old mining roads that radiate from town—particularly Washington Gulch, Slate River Road, and Gothic Road. You can also head into the backcountry on a guided tour. You can hike up the slopes for above-tree-line trips, but this requires strong legs and lungs, the right equipment, and lots of experience. This is the high country—the town itself is around 9,000 feet, and things go up from there—and weather and snow conditions can change with little or no warning.

The Crested Butte Nordic Center offers half- and full-day packages that include transportation, guides, and equipment. If you're traveling with a group you can rent one of two ski huts in the old town site of Gothic. The center also hosts the Annual Alley Loop Nordic Marathon, held in early February. This is an American Birkebeiner qualifying race, but local amateurs and visitors can join the experts in their cross-country race through the town's snow-covered streets and alleys, past snow-corniced homes, and down the scenic trails along the edge of town. ⊠ *620 2nd St.* ☎ *970/349–1707* ⊕ *www.cbnordic.org.*

RENTALS   **The Alpineer.** This iconic Crested Butte shop rents top-notch backcountry and telemark equipment, as well as classic nordic and skate skis. The staff offers expert advice on routes and snow conditions. ⊠ *419 6th St.* ☎ *970/349–5210* ⊕ *www.alpineer.com.*

TRACK SKIING
Crested Butte Nordic Center. The Crested Butte Nordic Center maintains an extensive network of cross-country ski and snowshoe trails. There are 34 mi of trails radiating out to the northwest, south, and east of Crested Butte. The trails cover flat and moderately rolling terrain across meadows and through aspen groves near the valley floor. The views of some of the distant peaks are stunning. The Moonlight Dinner—on full-moon nights from December to March—includes a trek to a cozy yurt for a full dinner prepared by local chefs; the cost is $45 per person. ⊠ *620 2nd St.* ☎ *970/349–1707* ⊕ *www.cbnordic.org.*

LESSONS AND **Crested Butte Nordic Center.** You can take lessons in skate and track skiing,
PROGRAMS as well as snowshoeing, at the Crested Butte Nordic Center. Packages
start at $45 for a 60-minute group lesson. An annual **Thanksgiving
Training Camp** is held every November. Former Olympians and collegiate coaches present clinics for expert, advanced, intermediate, and
beginning skate and classic skiers. Clinics are $40 for beginners, $50 for
intermediate and advanced students. ⊠ *620 2nd St.* ☎ *970/349–1707*
⊕ *www.cbnordic.org.*

TRAIL PASSES An adult day pass costs $15. The center also has a variety of season
passes, ranging from $165 for one adult and $390 for a family of four.

RENTALS **Crested Butte Nordic Center.** The Crested Butte Nordic Center rents classic
track skis, skate skis, backcountry touring skis, snowshoes, ice skates,
and sleds. ⊠ *620 2nd St.* ☎ *970/349–1707* ⊕ *www.cbnordic.org.*

OTHER SPORTS AND THE OUTDOORS

TOURS AND **Alpine Express.** Take an open-top four-wheel-drive tour on the old
OUTFITTERS mining roads that crisscross the Elk Mountain range, heading past
meadows of wildflowers and pristine mountain streams. Half-day jeep
tours are $50 for adults. ☎ *970/641–5074, 800/822–4844* ⊕ *www.
alpineexpressshuttle.com.*

FISHING

Almont. Located where the East and Taylor rivers join to form the Gunnison River, this tiny angler-oriented hamlet is one of Colorado's top
fly-fishing centers. It's also one of the most crowded. Local fishing outfitters rent equipment, teach fly-fishing, and lead guided wading or float
trips to both public and private waters. ⊠ *Almont.*

TOURS AND **Almont Anglers.** This outfitter and guide has a solid fly and tackle shop
OUTFITTERS with an enormous selection. There are clinics for beginners as well as
guided wading and float-fishing excursions on the East, Taylor, and
Gunnison rivers. ⊠ *10209 Hwy. 135, Almont* ☎ *970/641–7404* ⊕ *www.
almontanglers.com.*

Dragonfly Anglers. Crested Butte's oldest year-round guide service and
fly-fishing outfitter, Dragonfly Anglers offers guided half-day, full-day,
and multiday trips to choice fly-fishing spots, including the famed Gunnison Gorge in the Black Canyon. The shop concentrates on high-tech
rods and has a solid selection of reels, flies, and outdoor gear. ⊠ *307 Elk
Ave.* ☎ *970/349–1228, 800/491–3079* ⊕ *www.dragonflyanglers.com.*

Willowfly Anglers. Sharing space with Three Rivers Resort and Outfitting,
Willowfly Anglers offers half- and full-day trips for all skill levels and
has a full-service fly shop. ⊠ *130 County Rd. 742, Almont* ☎ *970/641–
1303, 888/761–3474* ⊕ *www.willowflyanglers.com.*

GOLF

The Club at Crested Butte. Golf legend Robert Trent Jones Jr. designed
this ravishing 18-hole course surrounded by gorgeous mountain peaks.
The first nine holes follow a traditional format, but the back nine offer
a Highlands-style surprise with a Scottish-links design. Water hazards
are present on 14 of the 18 holes, so be sure to bring extra balls. The
semi-private course belongs to the country club, but it's open to the
public. The dress code bars denim and mandates stand-up collars for

10

all. ✉ *385 Country Club Dr.* ☎ *970/349–6127, 800/628–5496* ⊕ *www. theclubatcrestedbutte.com* ⌔ *Reservations essential* ⅃ *18 holes. Yards: 7208/5702. Par: 72/72. Green fee: $135/$95.*

HIKING

Judd Falls. Nestled among three designated wilderness areas (Maroon Bells–Snowmass to the north, Raggeds to the west, and Collegiate Peaks to the east), Crested Butte is close to an extensive system of trails. One of the easiest hiking trails is the 2-mi round-trip to Judd Falls, located within the Gunnison National Forest near the ghost town of Gothic. The path slices through groves of aspen and, in spring, a crop of more than 70 local wildflower varieties. At the end, look over Judd Falls from a bench named after Garwood Judd, "the man who stayed" in the now-deserted mining town. In the wilderness areas you can find splendid trails far off the beaten path. ✉ *Gunnison National Forest, off Gothic Rd., Delta* ☎ *970/874–6600* ⊕ *www.fs.usda.gov/gmug.*

HORSEBACK RIDING

Fantasy Ranch. One of the best ways to see the Crested Butte area is from atop a horse. Fantasy Ranch gives guided horseback tours into the Elk Mountains, Maroon Bells, and Gunnison National Forest. Ninety-minute trail rides are $55, half-day trips start at $85, and full-day wilderness adventures are $120. The company also offers multiday pack trips. ✉ *Box 236 81224* ☎ *970/349–5425, 888/688–3488* ⊕ *www. fantasyranchoutfitters.com.*

HOT-AIR BALLOONING

Big Horn Balloon Company. On a clear, windless morning, Crested Butte must surely be one of the country's best places to be aloft in a balloon. Trips are $325 per person. ✉ *14522 Mustang La., Montrose* ☎ *970/ 596–1008* ⊕ *www.balloon-adventures.com.*

ICE-SKATING

Crested Butte Nordic Center. If you're eager to practice a figure eight, the Crested Butte Nordic Center operates an outdoor skating rink. The lodge rents skates for $9. ✉ *620 2nd St.* ☎ *970/349–1707* ⊕ *www. cbnordic.org.*

KAYAKING AND RAFTING

Three Rivers Resort and Outfitting. The rivers around Crested Butte are at their best from May through September. Three Rivers offers rafting trips and kayaking lessons on the Taylor and Gunnison rivers. ✉ *130 Country Rd. 742, Almont* ☎ *970/641–1303, 888/761–3474* ⊕ *www.3riversresort.com.*

MOUNTAIN BIKING

★ **Mountain Biking.** Crested Butte is the mountain biking center of Colorado. This is a place where there are more bikes than cars, and probably more bikes than residents. Many locals own two: a cruiser (or "townie") for hacking around and a mountain bike for *serious* hacking around. Nearby Pearl Pass is known as the route that got the fat-tire craze started. After a group of motorcyclists rode the rough old road from Aspen to Crested Butte, a few of the town's cyclists decided to do the same ride in reverse. They hopped onto their clunky two-wheelers— a far cry from today's sophisticated machinery—and with that, the sport had arrived. The 40-mi trip over Pearl Pass can be done in a day, but it's tough, and you must be in excellent condition and acclimatized to the elevation.

Lower Loop. Great for beginners, the Lower Loop is a popular 8- to 9-mi ride that will help orient you to the area. The views up the Slate River valley to the peaks of Paradise Divide are wonderful. **Tony's Trail** consists of a short, moderate climb leading to an intersection with the Upper Loop Trail. Here you can take in the view of the town below and the mountains above, then enjoy a fun descent back down or venture further in either direction on the Upper Loop.

Strand Hill. Starting southeast of town along Brush Creek Road, Strand Hill Trail is about 6 mi out and back. It includes a 900-ft climb on a double-track road followed by a twisting, roller-coaster-like single-track descent that will leave you feeling exhilarated. ⊠ *Brush Creek Rd.*

TOURS AND OUTFITTERS **The Alpineer.** This shop prides itself on having the latest gear and a staff knowledgeable enough to get you on the right bike and trail as quickly as possible. ⊠ *419 6th St.* ☎ *970/349–5210* ⊕ *www.alpineer.com.*

Big Al's Bicycle Heaven. This downtown shop, a favorite with locals, sells and rents all manner of two-wheelers, from knock-around "townies" to state-of-the-art mountain bikes. The shop also carries road and cross-country bikes and a full line of clothing, helmets, and other necessities. ⊠ *207 Elk Ave.* ☎ *970/349–0515* ⊕ *www.bigalsbicycleheaven.com.*

Crested Butte Mountain Guides. Experienced riders can take overnight tours (with meals, lodging, and transportation) starting at $175 per person, per day. ⊠ *218 Maroon Ave.* ☎ *970/349–5430* ⊕ *www. crestedbutteguides.com.*

FESTIVALS **Crested Butte Bike Week.** Each summer, mountain-biking enthusiasts roll in for Crested Butte Bike Week, the country's longest-running mountain-bike festival. The event, held in late June, is a solid week of racing, touring, silly competitions, and mountain-biker bonding. ☎ *800/545–4505, 970/349–6438.*

RENTALS **Crested Butte Sports.** Come here to rent Cannondale mountain bikes, plus helmets and other gear. It also has a full repair shop. ⊠ *35 Emmons Loop Rd.* ☎ *970/349–7516, 800/301–9169* ⊕ *www.crestedbuttesports. com.*

WHERE TO EAT

$$ ✗ **Donita's Cantina.** This down-home, adobe-washed Mexican restaurant
MEXICAN is housed in an 1880s hotel with the original pressed tin ceilings. The food is simply good, with solid standards such as fajitas and enchiladas served with homemade red and green chile. The specialty at the bar is predictably the margarita—concocted in all flavors and colors with agave tequila. The cantina is popular with local families as well as with skiers. ⊠ *330 Elk Ave.* ☎ *970/349–6674* ⊕ *www.donitascantina.com* ⌲ *Reservations not accepted* ⊗ *No lunch.*

$$ ✗ **Ginger Cafe.** The small, sunny dining room provides a cheerful back-
ASIAN drop for the superb East–West fusion and pan-Asian food, with a good selection of vegetarian options. There is also a full bar with an inven-

10

tive cocktail menu including ginger-infused martinis and mango ginger mojitos. ⊠ *425 Elk Ave.* ☎ *970/349–7291.*

$
PIZZA
✕ **Secret Stash.** Aptly named, this place in a 100-year-old miner's cabin serves absolutely amazing pizza, in a mind-bending array of formulations—from the "Notorious F.I.G." (prosciutto, dried figs, and truffle oil) to the "Philly Pete's Zaa" (with grilled steak, sautéed onions, and bell peppers). There's a full bar with an impressive list of specialty drinks, and a daily special—a slice of pizza, a shot of tequila, and a beer—for $6. Join the locals upstairs, where you sit on the floor around a low table. The wait can be long, so order an appetizer. ⊠ *21 Elk Ave.* ☎ *970/349-6245.*

$$$
AMERICAN
✕ **Slogar.** In a lovingly renovated Victorian tavern awash in handmade lace and stained glass, this restaurant is just plain cozy. A fixed-price menu spotlights skillet-fried chicken or steak paired with flaky biscuits fresh from the oven, creamy mashed potatoes swimming in chicken gravy, or sweet-and-sour coleslaw from a Pennsylvania Dutch recipe. Served family style, dinner is only $16 (or $28 for steak). Reservations are recommended. ⊠ *517 2nd St., at Whiterock Ave.* ☎ *970/349–5765* ⊙ *Closed mid-Oct.–Nov. and mid-Apr.–mid-May. No lunch.*

$$$$
FRENCH
★
✕ **Soupçon.** "Soup's on" (get it?) occupies two intimate rooms in this historic cabin and dishes up Nouveau American cuisine with a strong French accent. Local produce is accented with organic herbs grown on the premises. Try the seared Hudson Valley foie gras to start, followed by the Colorado elk tenderloin complemented by a glass of wine from the comprehensive wine cellar. Call ahead for your seating time: 6 or 8:15. ⊠ *127 Elk Ave.* ☎ *970/349–5448* ⊕ *www.soupconcrestedbutte. com* ⌁ *Reservations essential* ⊙ *Closed Sun. and Apr.–May. No lunch.*

$
MEXICAN
✕ **Teocalli Tamale.** Known locally as "Teo's," this Mexican restaurant is housed in a small, historic building and is a local favorite venue for tasty, inexpensive takeout (or a claustrophobic eat-in experience). You can get a generous (even gigantic) portion of tacos, tamales, or fish for less than $13. The place also serves margaritas and a good selection of bottled beers. ⊠ *311 Elk Ave.* ☎ *970/349–2005* ⊕ *www. teocallitamale.com.*

WHERE TO STAY
For expanded hotel reviews, visit Fodors.com.

$
B&B/INN
▦ **Cristiana Guesthaus.** With a huge stone fireplace in a wood-beamed lobby, this alpine-style ski lodge provides a cozy, unpretentious haven. **Pros:** comfortable lodge; knowledgeable hosts; great value. **Cons:** TV only in common area. ⊠ *621 Maroon Ave.* ☎ *970/349–1962, 800/824–7899* ⊕ *www.cristianaguesthaus.com* ⌁ *21 rooms* ⌁ *In-room: no a/c, no TV, Wi-Fi. In-hotel: business center, some age restrictions* ⊙ *Closed mid-Apr.–early April* ℗ *Breakfast.*

$$
HOTEL
▦ **Elk Mountain Lodge.** Step into the lobby of the Elk Mountain Lodge and encounter a slower pace of life and unsurpassed attention to detail. **Pros:** historic building; intimate feel; in the middle of Crested Butte. **Cons:** 3 mi from ski area; stairs are a bit steep and there's no elevator. ⊠ *129 Gothic Ave.* ☎ *970/349–7533, 800/374–6521* ⊕ *www. elkmountainlodge.com* ⌁ *19 rooms* ⌁ *In-room: no a/c, Internet, Wi-Fi.*

In-hotel: bar, business center, some pets allowed, some age restrictions IOI *Breakfast.*

$$$$ **Grand Lodge Crested Butte.** This luxurious ski-in ski-out lodge, part
HOTEL of Crested Butte Mountain Resort, features a warm and welcoming
stone-and-log lobby with a huge fireplace. **Pros:** close to ski lift; luxurious rooms with many amenities; terrific restaurant. **Cons:** basic rooms
are small; 3 mi from town; can feel impersonal. ⊠ *6 Emmons Loop,
Mt. Crested Butte* ☎ *866/539–0036, 970/349–8000* ⊕ *www.skicb.
com* 🛏 *245 rooms* ♿ *In-room: no a/c, safe, Internet, Wi-Fi. In-hotel:
restaurant, bar, pool, gym, spa, business center, some pets allowed*
IOI *No meals.*

$$ **Nordic Inn.** This slope-side inn is one of the last old-style ski lodges
HOTEL in a sea of cookie-cutter condominiums. **Pros:** a block from ski lifts;
informal setting; breakfast included. **Cons:** old and starting to fray; 3 mi
from town. ⊠ *14 Treasury Rd., Mt. Crested Butte* ☎ *970/349–5542,
800/542–7669* ⊕ *www.nordicinncb.com* 🛏 *24 rooms, 2 cabins* ♿ *In-
room: no a/c, kitchen, no TV, Wi-Fi* IOI *Breakfast.*

$ **Pioneer Guest Cabins.** On a riverside meadow in the Gunnison
HOTEL National Forest, this getaway is about 8 mi from town. **Pros:** secluded
setting; close to trails and fishing. **Cons:** 8 mi from town; no restaurant;
minimum stay required. ⊠ *2094 Cement Creek Rd.* ☎ *970/349–5517*
⊕ *www.pioneerguestcabins.com* 🛏 *8 cabins* ♿ *In-room: a/c, no a/c,
kitchen, no TV. In-hotel: some pets allowed* IOI *No meals.*

NIGHTLIFE

Kochevar's Saloon and Gaming Hall. An 1896 cabin built from hand-hewn
logs, Kochevar's is a classic saloon where locals play pool. ⊠ *127 Elk
Ave.* ☎ *970/349–6745.*

Wooden Nickel. The popular Wooden Nickel is packed for happy hour
each day from 4 to 6. Stay for dinner, as the steaks are terrific. ⊠ *222
Elk Ave.* ☎ *970/349–6350* ⊕ *www.woodennickelcb.com.*

GUNNISON

*64 mi east of Montrose via U.S. 50; 28 mi south of Crested Butte via
Rte. 135.*

10

At the confluence of the Gunnison River and Tomichi Creek, Gunnison
is an old mining and ranching community and college town. It's been
adopted by nature lovers because of the excellent outdoor activities,
including hiking, climbing, fishing, and hunting. In fact, long before
any settlers arrived, the Ute Indians used the area as summer hunting
grounds. Gunnison provides economical lodging and easy access to
Crested Butte and Blue Mesa Reservoir. Gunnison's other claim to fame
is that it has recorded some of the coldest temperatures ever reported
in the continental United States.

GETTING HERE AND AROUND

Getting in and out of Gunnison is a breeze. U.S. 50 travels right through
town, heading east to I–25 in Pueblo and northwest to I–70 in Grand
Junction. U.S. 50 goes by the name Tomichi Avenue as it travels 18
blocks through town. Western State College and the Pioneer Museum

are on the east side of town, and the rodeo grounds and airport are to the south.

WHEN TO GO

FESTIVALS **Cattlemen's Days.** Don't miss Gunnison's Cattlemen's Days, the state's oldest rodeo, held every July at the Fred R. Field Western Heritage Center. Check out traditional 4-H horse and livestock exhibits, then thrill to the sight of professional bull riding, barrel racing and calf roping. You can also listen to country music and the dulcet strains of cowboy poetry. ⊠ *275 S. Spruce St.* ⊕ *www.cattlemensdays.com.*

Gunsmoke-n-Gunnison. For an amazing display of marksmanship and horsemanship, attend Gunsmoke-n-Gunison, held at the Fred R. Field Western Heritage Center during the last weekend in June and again in July. ☎ *970/641–8561.*

ESSENTIALS

Visitor Information Gunnison County Chamber of Commerce ⊠ *500 E. Tomichi Ave.* ☎ *970/641–1501, 800/274–7580* ⊕ *www.gunnisonchamber.com.*

EXPLORING

★ **Curecanti National Recreation Area.** This nature preserve, named in honor of a Ute Indian chief, encompasses 40 mi of striking eroded volcanic landscape along U.S. 50, between Gunnison and Montrose. Three reservoirs were created by dams built on the Gunnison River in the 1960s: Morrow Point, Crystal Dam, and Blue Mesa, Colorado's largest lake at almost 20 mi long. You can go boating, windsurfing, fishing, and swimming in all three. Camping, horseback riding, and hiking are also available. The Elk Creek Visitor Center on U.S. 50 provides more information.

Cimarron Visitor Center. At the western entrance to the recreation area, near Morrow Point Dam, the Cimarron Visitor Center displays relics from the narrow-gauge Cimarron Canyon Railroad, including cars and livestock chutes. ⊠ *Off U.S. 50, 20 mi west of Montrose, Cimarron* ☎ *970/249–4074* ⊠ *Free* ⊙ *Mid-May–Labor Day, hours vary* 🄳 *Elk Creek Visitor Center, 102 Elk Creek, Gunnison 81230* ☎ *970/641–2337* ⊕ *www.nps.gov/cure* ⊠ *$15 at east entrance only* ⊙ *Park, daily; visitor centers, hrs. vary.*

🄲 **Pioneer Museum.** Anyone interested in the region's history shouldn't miss the Pioneer Museum. The complex spreads out over 6 acres, and includes an extensive collection of vehicles from Model Ts to 1960s sedans. There's also a great train, complete with coal tender, caboose, and boxcar; a red barn with wagons and displays of ranch life; and an old schoolhouse. ⊠ *803 E. Tomichi Ave.* ☎ *970/641–4530* ⊠ *$7* ⊙ *June–Sept., Mon.–Sat. 9–5, Sun. 11–5.*

SPORTS AND THE OUTDOORS

FISHING

Gene Taylor's. This outfitter conducts half- and full-day fly-fishing tours on the Taylor, East, and Gunnison rivers, as well as the Blue Mesa and Taylor reservoirs. Guides also have access to private waters on the East River and Tomichi and Cochtopa creeks. ⊠ *201 W. Tomichi Ave.* ☎ *970/641–1845* ⊕ *www.highmtndrifters.com.*

Gunnison Sports Outfitters. This outfitter offers guided fishing trips on Blue Mesa Reservoir for anglers of all abilities. ⊠ *201 W. Tomichi Ave.* ☎ *970/641–1845* ⊕ *www.gunnisonsportsoutfitters.com.*

HORSEBACK RIDING

Lazy F Bar Outfitters. The stables at Lazy F Bar Ranch offer everything from hour-long rides to overnight pack trips into the high country from June to early September. There are also breakfast and dinner rides. Come winter, you can take a three-hour sleigh ride and dinner. ⊠ *2991 County Rd. 738* ☎ *970/641–3313* ⊕ *www.lazyfbarranch.com.*

Tenderfoot Outfitters. With a variety of guided backcountry trail rides ranging from 90 minutes to a full day, Tenderfoot Outfitters also offers two-day camping trips with comfortable tents and real beds. The booking desk is inside Gunnison Outdoors. ⊠ *Scheduling desk located in Gunnison Outdoors shop, 501 Tomichi Ave.* ⊕ *www.tenderfoot-outfitters.com.*

WATER SPORTS

At 26 mi long, Blue Mesa Reservoir ranks as Colorado's largest body of water. Located within the Curecanti National Recreation Area, the reservoir was created in the mid-1960s when the state dammed the Gunnison River. It has become a mecca for water-sports enthusiasts. Anglers are drawn by the 3 million stocked kokanee salmon and rainbow, lake, brown, and brook trout.

If you have your own boat, you can use the ramps at Elk Creek (northern end at Soap Creek Arm), Stevens Creek (eastern end of the north shore), and Lake Fork (eastern end on the south shore). A two-day boat permit is $4, and a two-week permit is $10. Annual boat permits run $30.

Elk Creek Marina. About 15 mi west of Gunnison, this marina offers a range of services: boat and slip rentals, gas and ice, bait and supplies. It's open from May to September. It runs guided fishing trips to Blue Mesa and Morrow Point reservoirs. A small restaurant, Pappy's, is located above the dock, where you can enjoy a light meal while watching anglers try their luck. ⊠ *24830 U.S. 50 W* ☎ *970/641–0707, 877/258–6372* ⊕ *www.bluemesares.com.*

WHERE TO EAT

¢
CAFÉ
✕ **The Bean.** This brightly hued coffee shop is a great place to grab and go (or stay and hang out). The walls are decorated with frequently changing art exhibits, and for light reading there are plenty of newspapers and magazines (as well as free Wi-Fi). There's an impressive selection of espresso drinks, plus fresh-baked pastries and savory sandwiches, many made with organic ingredients. Get here early, as it closes at 8 pm. ⊠ *120 N. Main St.* ☎ *970/641–2408* ⊕ *www.thebeancoffeehouseandeatery.com.*

$$
ITALIAN
✕ **Garlic Mike's.** The menu at this unpretentious Italian spot is surprisingly rich and complex. Don't miss the fried calamari, thin-crust pizza, and eggplant parmigiana. The marinated steak carbonara is a hands-down house favorite. The heated outdoor patio overlooking the Gunnison River is a divine place to relax in summer. Be prepared for a leisurely dinner, as the service can be slow. ⊠ *2674 Hwy. 135* ☎ *970/641–2493* ⊕ *www.garlicmikes.com* ☼ *No lunch.*

10

$ ✕ **Gunnison Brewery.** A revolving selection of hand-crafted beers is on tap
AMERICAN   at this busy bar in downtown Gunnison. It's known for the fine Dun-
kel Weizen, a strong-flavored wheat beer. The menu has the usual pub
fare, with burgers and fried food, plus a selection of salads and wraps.
There's live music on Wednesday and Friday night. ✉ *138 N. Main
St.* ☎ *970/641–2739* ⊕ *www.gunnisonbrewery.com* ✆ *No lunch Sun.*

$$ ✕ **Ol' Miner Steakhouse.** A meat lover's dream—choose T-bone, strip, rib
STEAKHOUSE   eye, or prime rib cooked the way you like it—in a rustic, down-home
setting, complete with elk and deer mounts, tin ceilings, and scarred
wood furniture. Rocky Mountain oysters (bull testicles) are available
for culinary risk-takers. There's also an unlimited soup-and-salad bar,
a respectable array of sandwiches, and traditional breakfasts. ✉ *139 N.
Main St.* ☎ *970/641–5153.*

WHERE TO STAY

For expanded hotel reviews, visit Fodors.com.

$ ⊞ **Holiday Inn Express.** This chain hotel's lobby has a large gray stone
HOTEL   fireplace and leather couches, making it a great place for relaxing with
friends and family. **Pros:** numerous amenities; business facilities; reason-
ably priced. **Cons:** 1 mi from town; no restaurant; large and impersonal
feel. ✉ *910 E. Tomichi Ave.* ☎ *970/641–1288, 800/315–2621* ⊕ *www.
hiexpress.com* ⇨ *107 rooms, 23 suites* ⚅ *In-room: Wi-Fi. In-hotel:
pool, gym, laundry facilities, business center* ⦿❘ *Breakfast.*

¢   ⊞ **Rockey River Resort.** A tetherball on the turf, sheets hung on the line,
RESORT   and the smell of cowboy coffee: these are just a few of the touches that
make this old homestead a uniquely pleasant place to stay. **Pros:** close
to fishing; historic setting; very pet-friendly. **Cons:** 6 mi from Gunnison;
TV only in common areas. ✉ *4359 Rte. 10* ☎ *970/641–0174* ⇨ *15 cab-
ins* ⚅ *In-room: no a/c, kitchen, no TV. In-hotel: business center, some
pets allowed* ✆ *Open early May–late Nov.* ⦿❘ *No meals.*

SHOPPING

Rocky Mountain Gear. Stop by for a good selection of supplies for sum-
mer (climbing, running, mountain- and road biking) and winter (down-
hill and backcountry skiing). ✉ *608 W. Tomichi Ave.* ☎ *970/641–9150*
⊕ *www.rockandrollsports.com.*

Western World. This authentic tack shop—with saddles, bridles, and
other horse equipment—outfits Gunnison's real-life cowboys. Western
World is also one-stop shopping for anyone who'd just like to dress the
part, with a huge selection of hats, boots, and belts for adults and kids.
✉ *200 W. Tomichi Ave.* ☎ *970/641–6566.*

BLACK CANYON OF THE GUNNISON NATIONAL PARK

*South Rim: 15 mi east of Montrose, via U.S. 50 and Rte. 347. North
Rim: 11 mi south of Crawford, via Rte. 92 and North Rim Rd.*

The Black Canyon of the Gunnison River is one of Colorado's, and
indeed the West's, most awe-inspiring places. A vivid testament to
the powers of erosion, the canyon is roughly 2,000 feet deep. At its

narrowest point, it spans 1,000 feet at the rim and only 40 feet at the bottom. The steep angles of the cliffs make it difficult for sunlight to fully break through during much of the day, and ever-present shadows blanket the canyon walls, leaving some places in almost perpetual darkness. No wonder it's called the "Black Canyon."

The primary gateway to Black Canyon is **Montrose**, 15 mi west of the park. The legendary Ute chief, Ouray, and his wife, Chipeta, lived near here in the late 1800s. Today, Montrose straddles the important agricultural and mining regions along the Uncompahgre River, and is the area's main shopping hub.

BLACK CANYON OF THE GUNNISON PLANNER

GETTING ORIENTED

Black Canyon of the Gunnison is a park of extremes—great depths, narrow widths, tall cliffs, and steep descents. It is not a large park, but it offers incredible scenery and unforgettable experiences, whether you're hiking, fishing, camping, or just taking it all in from the overlooks.

East Portal. The only way you can get down to the river via automobile in Black Canyon is on the steep East Portal Road.

North Rim. The area's remoteness and difficult location mean the North Rim is never crowded; the road is unpaved and closes in the winter. There's also a small ranger station here.

South Rim. This is the main area of the park. The park's only visitor center is here, along with a campground and a few picnic areas.

WHEN TO GO

Summer is the busiest season, with July experiencing the greatest crowds. However, a spring or fall visit gives you two advantages: fewer people and cooler temperatures—in summer, especially in years with little rainfall, daytime temperatures can reach into the 90s. A winter visit to the park brings even more solitude, as all but one section of campsites are shut down and only about 2 mi of South Rim Road, the park main road, are plowed.

November through March is when the snow hits, with an average of about 3 to 8 inches of it monthly. April through May and September and October are the rainiest, with about an inch of precipitation each month. June is generally the driest month. Temperatures at the bottom of the canyon are about 8 degrees warmer than at the rim.

PLANNING YOUR TIME

BLACK CANYON OF THE GUNNISON NATIONAL PARK IN ONE DAY

Pack a lunch and head to the canyon's South Rim, beginning with a stop at the **South Rim Visitor Center.** Before getting back into the car, take in your first view of Black Canyon from **Gunnison Point**, adjacent to the visitor center. Then set out on a driving tour of the 7-mi **South Rim Road,** allowing the rest of the morning to stop at the various viewpoints that overlook the canyon. Don't miss **Chasm View** and **Painted Wall View,** and be sure to stretch your legs along the short (0.7-mi round-trip) **Cedar Point Nature Trail.** If your timing is good, you'll reach **High Point,** the end of the road, around lunchtime.

10

After lunch, head out on **Warner Point Nature Trail** for an hour hike (1½ mi round-trip). Then retrace your drive along South Rim Road back to the visitor center.

GETTING HERE AND AROUND

AIR TRAVEL

The Black Canyon of the Gunnison lies between the cities of Gunnison and Montrose, both of which have small regional airports.

CAR TRAVEL

The park has three roads. South Rim Road, reached by Route 347, is the primary thoroughfare and winds along the canyon's South Rim. From about late November to early April, the road is not plowed past the visitor center at Gunnison Point. North Rim Road, reached by Route 92, is usually open from May through Thanksgiving; in winter, the road is unplowed. On the park's south side, the serpentine East Portal Road descends abruptly to the Gunnison River below. The road is usually open from the beginning of May through the end of November. Because of the grade, vehicles or vehicle-trailer combinations longer than 22 feet are not permitted. The park has no public transportation.

PARK ESSENTIALS

PARK FEES AND PERMITS

Entrance fees are $15 per week per vehicle. Visitors entering on bicycle, motorcycle, or on foot pay $7 for a weekly pass. To access the inner canyon, you must pick up a backcountry permit (no fee).

PARK HOURS

The park is open 24/7 year-round. It's in the mountain time zone.

CELL-PHONE RECEPTION

Cell-phone reception in the park is unreliable and sporadic. There are public telephones at South Rim Visitor Center and South Rim Campground.

VISITOR INFORMATION

Black Canyon of the Gunnison National Park ⊠ *102 Elk Creek* ☎ *970/641–2337* ⊕ *www.nps.gov/blca.*

VISITOR CENTERS

North Rim Ranger Station. This small facility on the park's North Rim is open only in summer. Rangers can provide information and assistance and can issue permits for backcountry use and rock climbing. ⊠ *North Rim Rd., 11 mi from Rte. 92 turnoff* ☎ *970/641–2337* ☉ *Late May–Labor Day, daily 8–6.*

South Rim Visitor Center. The park's only visitor center offers interactive exhibits and introductory films detailing the park's geology and wildlife. ⊠ *1½ mi from the entrance station on South Rim Rd.* ☎ *970/249–1914* ☉ *Late May–early Sept., daily 8–6; early Sept.–late May, daily 8:30–4.*

EXPLORING

SCENIC DRIVES

The scenic South and North Rim roads offer deep and distant views into the canyon. Both also offer several lookout points and short hiking trails along the rim. The trails that go down into the canyon are steep and strenuous, and essentially unmarked, and so are reserved for experienced (and very fit) hikers.

East Portal Road. The only way to access the Gunnison River from the park by car is via this paved route, which drops approximately 2,000 feet down to the water in only 5 mi, giving it an extremely steep grade. Vehicles longer than 22 feet are not allowed on the road. If you're towing a trailer, you can unhitch it near the entrance to South Rim campground. The bottom of the road is actually in the adjacent Curecanti National Recreation Area. A tour of East Portal Road, with a brief stop at the bottom, takes about 45 minutes.

North Rim Road. Black Canyon's North Rim is much less frequented, but no less spectacular—the walls here are near vertical—than the South Rim. To reach the 15½-mi-long North Rim Road, take the signed turn-off from Route 92 about 3 mi south of Crawford. The road is paved for about the first 4 mi; the rest is gravel. After 11 mi, turn left at the intersection (the North Rim Campground is to the right). There are six overlooks along the road as it snakes along the rim's edge. Kneeling Camel, at the road's east end, provides the broadest view of the canyon. Set aside about two hours for a tour of the North Rim.

South Rim Road. This paved 7-mi stretch from Tomichi Point to High Point is the park's main road. The drive follows the canyon's level South Rim; 12 overlooks are accessible from the road, most via short gravel trails. Several short hikes along the rim also begin roadside. Allow between two and three hours round-trip.

SCENIC STOPS

The vast depths that draw thousands of visitors each year to Black Canyon have also historically prevented any extensive human habitation from taking root, so cultural attractions are largely absent here. But what the park lacks in historic sites it more than makes up for in scenery.

★ **Chasm and Painted Wall Views.** At the heart-in-your-throat Chasm viewpoint, the canyon walls plummet 1,820 feet to the river, but are only 1,100 feet apart at the top. As you peer down into the depths, keep in mind that this section is where the Gunnison River descends at its steepest rate, dropping 240 feet within the span of a mile. A few hundred yards farther, you'll find the best place to see Painted Wall, Colorado's tallest cliff. Pinkish swaths of pegmatite (a crystalline, granitelike rock) give the wall its colorful, marbled appearance. ⊠ *Approximately 3½ mi from the Visitor Center on South Rim Rd.*

Narrows View. Look upriver from this North Rim viewing spot and you'll be able to see into the canyon's narrowest section, just a slot really, with only 40 feet between the walls at the bottom. The canyon is also taller (1,725 feet) here than it is wide at the rim (1,150 feet). ⊠ *North Rim Rd., first overlook past the ranger station.*

10

★ **Warner Point.** This viewpoint, at the end of the Warner Point Nature Trail, delivers awesome views of the canyon's deepest point (2,722 feet), plus the nearby San Juan and West Elk mountain ranges. ⊠ *End of Warner Point Nature Trail, westernmost end of South Rim Rd.*

EDUCATIONAL OFFERINGS
RANGER PROGRAMS

Ⓒ **Junior Ranger Program.** Kids ages 5 to 12 can participate in this program, which includes an activities booklet to fill in while exploring the park.

SPORTS AND THE OUTDOORS

Recreational activities in Black Canyon run the gamut from short and easy nature trails to world-class (and experts-only) rock climbing and kayaking. The cold waters of the Gunnison River are well known to trout anglers.

BIRD-WATCHING

The sheer cliffs of Black Canyon, though not suited for human habitation, provide a great habitat for birds. Peregrine falcons, white-throated swifts and other cliff-dwelling birds revel in the dizzying heights, while at river level you'll find American dippers foraging for food in the rushing waters. Canyon wrens, which nest in the cliffs, are more often heard than seen, but their hauntingly beautiful songs are unforgettable. Blue grouse are common in the sagebrush areas above the canyon, and red-tailed and Cooper's hawks and turkey vultures frequent the canyon rims. Best times for birding: spring and early summer.

BOATING AND KAYAKING

★ With Class V rapids, the Gunnison River is one of the premier kayak challenges in North America. The spectacular 14-mi stretch of the river that passes through the park is so narrow in some sections that the rim seems to be closing up above your head. Once you're downstream from the rapids (and out of the park), the canyon opens up into what is called the Gunnison Gorge. The rapids ease considerably, and the trip becomes more of a quiet float on Class I to Class IV water.

Kayaking the river through the park requires a wilderness use permit (and lots of expertise), and rafting is not allowed. Access to the Gunnison Gorge is only by foot or horseback. However, several outfitters offer guided raft and kayak trips in the Gunnison Gorge and other sections of the Gunnison River.

TOURS

Morrow Point Boat Tours. Starting in neighboring Curecanti National Recreation Area, these guided tours run twice daily (except Tuesday) in the summer, at 10 am and 12:30 pm. Morrow Point Boat Tours take passengers on a 90-minute tour via pontoon boat. The cost is $16, and reservations are required. ⊠ *Pine Creek Trail and Boat Dock, U.S. 50, milepost 130, 25 mi west of Gunnison* ☎ *970/641–2337.*

FISHING

★ The three dams built upriver from the park in Curecanti National Recreation Area have created prime trout fishing in the waters below. Certain restrictions apply: Only artificial flies and lures are permitted, and a Colorado fishing license is required for people age 16 and older. Rainbow trout are catch-and-release only, and there are size and possession limits on brown trout (check at the visitor center). Most anglers access the river from the bottom of East Portal Road; an undeveloped trail goes along the riverbank for about ¾ mi.

HIKING

All trails can be hot in summer and most don't receive much shade, so bring water, a hat, and plenty of sunscreen. Dogs are permitted, on leash, on Rim Rock, Cedar Point Nature, and Chasm View Nature trails. Hiking into the inner canyon, while doable, is not for the faint of heart—or step. Six named routes lead down to the river, but they are not maintained or marked. In fact, the park staff won't even call them trails; they refer to them as "controlled slides." These super-steep, rocky routes vary in one-way distance from 1 to 2.75 mi, and the descent can be anywhere from 1,800 to 2,702 feet. Your reward, of course, is a rare look at the bottom of the canyon and the fast-flowing Gunnison. ■TIP➔ **Don't attempt an inner-canyon hike without plenty of water (the park's recommendation is one gallon per person, per day).** For descriptions of the routes and the necessary permit to hike them, stop at the visitor center at the South Rim or North Rim ranger station. Dogs are not permitted in the inner canyon.

EASY

Cedar Point Nature Trail. This 0.7-mi round-trip interpretive trail leads out from South Rim Road to two overlooks. It's an easy stroll, and signs along the way detail the surrounding plants. *Easy.* ⊠ *Trailhead off South Rim Rd., 4.2 mi from South Rim Visitor Center.*

Deadhorse Trail. Despite its name, the 5-mi Deadhorse Trail is actually a pleasant hike, starting on an old service road from the Kneeling Camel View on the North Rim Road. The trail's farthest point provides the park's easternmost viewpoint. From this overlook, the canyon is much more open, with pinnacles and spires rising along its sides. *Easy.* ⊠ *Trailhead at the southernmost end of North Rim Rd.*

MODERATE

Chasm View Nature Trail. The park's shortest trail (0.3 mi round-trip) starts at North Rim Campground and offers an impressive 50-yard walk right along the canyon rim as well as an eye-popping view of Painted Wall and Serpent Point. This also an excellent place to spot raptors, swifts, and other birds. *Moderate.* ⊠ *Trailhead at North Rim Campground, 11¼ mi from Rte. 92.*

North Vista Trail. The round-trip hike to Exclamation Point is 3 mi; a more difficult foray to the top of 8,563-foot Green Mountain (a mesa, really) is 7 mi. You'll hike along the North Rim; keep an eye out for especially gnarled pinyon pines—the North Rim is the site of some of the oldest groves of pinyons in North America, between 400 and 700 years old. *Moderate.* ⊠ *Trailhead at North Rim ranger station, off North Rim Rd., 11 mi from Rte. 92 turnoff.*

Fodor's Choice ★ **Warner Point Nature Trail.** The 1½-mi round-trip hike starts from High Point. You'll enjoy fabulous vistas of the San Juan and West Elk Mountains and Uncompahgre Valley. Warner Point, at trail's end, has the

10

steepest drop-off from rim to river: a dizzying 2,722 feet. *Moderate.*
⊠ *Trailhead at the end of South Rim Rd.*

DIFFICULT

Oak Flat Loop Trail. This 2-mi loop is the most demanding of the South
Rim hikes, as it brings you about 300 feet below the canyon rim. In
places, the trail is narrow and crosses some steep slopes, but you won't
have to navigate any steep drop-offs. Oak Flat is the shadiest of all the
South Rim trails; small groves of aspen and thick stands of Douglas fir
along the loop offer some respite from the sun. *Difficult.* ⊠ *Trailhead
just west of the South Rim Visitor Center.*

HORSEBACK RIDING

TOURS AND OUTFITTERS

Elk Ridge Ranch and Trail Rides. You can take 90-minute and two-hour
rides at this ranch. Elk Ridge also offers a half-day ride to the rim of
the Black Canyon. ⊠ *10203 Bostwick Park Rd., Montrose* ☎ *970/240–
6007* ⊕ *www.elkridgeranchinc.com* ☉ *May–Sept., daily.*

ROCK CLIMBING

Fodor's Choice For expert rock climbers, the sheer cliffs of the Black Canyon represent
★ one of Colorado's premier big-wall challenges. Some routes can take
several days to complete, with climbers sleeping on narrow ledges, or
"portaledges." Though there's no official guide to climbing in the park,
reports from individual climbers are kept on file at the South Rim Visitor Center. Nesting birds of prey may lead to wall closure at certain
times of year.

Rock climbing in the park is for experts only, but you can do some
bouldering at the Marmot Rocks area, about 100 feet south of South
Rim Road between Painted Wall and Cedar Point overlooks (park at
Painted Wall). Four boulder groupings offer a variety of routes rated
from easy to very difficult; a pamphlet with a diagrammed map of the
area is available at the South Rim Visitor Center.

TOURS AND OUTFITTERS

Crested Butte Mountain Guides. Intermediate and expert climbers can take
a full-day guided tour for $395. ⊠ *218 Maroon Ave., Crested Butte*
☎ *970/349–5430* ⊕ *www.crestedbutteguides.com.*

Skyward Mountaineering. Intermediate and advanced climbers can take
lessons and guided tours on the Black Canyon's fabled climbs with this
internationally certified guide and outfitter. ⊡ *Box 323, Ridgway 81432*
☎ *970/209–2985* ⊕ *www.skywardmountaineering.com* ☉ *Mar.–Nov.*

WINTER SPORTS

From late November to early April, South Rim Road is not plowed past
the visitor center, offering park guests a unique opportunity to cross-
country ski or snowshoe on the road. It's possible to ski or snowshoe
on the unplowed North Rim Road, too, but it's about 4 mi from where
the road closes, through sagebrush flats, to the canyon rim.

CLOSE UP

Best Campgrounds in Black Canyon

There are two campgrounds in the national park. The smaller North Rim Campground is first-come, first-served, and is closed in winter. South Rim Campground is considerably larger, and has one section that's open year-round. Vehicles more than 35 feet long are discouraged from either campground.

South Rim Campground. Stay on the canyon rim at this main campground right inside the park entrance. Loops A and C have tent sites only; RV hookups are in Loop B. ⊠ *South Rim Rd., 1 mi from the visitor center, Black Canyon of the Gunnison National Park, CO.*

North Rim Campground. This small campground, nestled amid pine trees, offers the basics along the quiet North Rim. ⊠ *North Rim Rd., 11¼ mi from Rte. 92, Black Canyon of the Gunnison National Park, CO.*

MONTROSE

15 mi west of Black Canyon of the Gunnison; 65 mi west of Gunnison; 22 mi south of Delta via U.S. 50.

The self-described "Home of the Black Canyon" sits amid glorious surroundings, but it's otherwise a sleepy little town with a small historic center and a collection of truck stops, strip malls, and big-box stores along its outskirts. Montrose also has a small airport that's a major gateway for skiers heading to Telluride and Crested Butte. Montrose is perfectly placed for exploring the Black Canyon of the Gunnison and Curecanti National Recreation Area to the east; the San Juan Mountains to the south; Grand Mesa to the north; and the spectacular Uncompahgre National Forest to the southwest.

GETTING HERE AND AROUND

U.S. 550 enters Montrose from the south; it's known as Townsend Avenue as it passes through town. At Main Street, U.S. 550 merges with U.S. 50, which continues north to Delta and east to Black Canyon National Park and Gunnison.

10

ESSENTIALS

Visitor Information Montrose Visitors and Convention Bureau ⊠ *1519 E. Main St.* ☎ *970/249–5000, 800/873–0244* ⊕ *www.visitmontrose.com.*

EXPLORING

Ute Indian Museum. If you're interested in the lives of the region's original residents, stop by the excellent Ute Indian Museum, 3 mi south of town. The museum contains several dioramas and the most comprehensive collection of Ute materials and artifacts in Colorado. It's housed in the 1956 homestead of Ute Chief Ouray and his wife, Chipeta. Today, the complex includes the Chief Ouray Memorial Park, Chipeta's Crypt, a native plants garden, picnic areas, and shaded paths linked to the citywide walking trail. ⊠ *17253 Chipeta Rd.* ☎ *970/249–3098* ⊕ *www. historycolorado.org* ⊠ *$4.50* ☉ *July–Sept., Mon.–Sat. 9–4:30, Sun. 11–4:30; Oct.–Dec., Mon.–Sat. 9–4.*

SPORTS AND THE OUTDOORS

BOATING

Lake Fork Marina. Located on the western end of Blue Mesa Reservoir off U.S. 92, the Lake Fork Marina rents all types of boats. If you have your own, there's a ramp at the marina and slips for rent. ⊠ *Off U.S. 92, near Lake Fork Campground, Gunnison* ☎ *970/641–3048* ⊕ *www. bluemesares.com.*

HIKING

Grand Mesa, Uncompahgre, and Gunnison national forests. With some of the most spectacular scenery in the Colorado Rockies, this trio of national forests has a total of more than 3 million acres. The area contains many historic mining sites, 3,600 mi of streams, 3,500 mi of trails, and 30 lakes. ⊠ *2250 U.S. 50, Delta* ☎ *970/874–6600* ⊕ *www. fs.fusda.gov/gmug.*

WHERE TO EAT AND STAY

For expanded hotel reviews, visit Fodors.com.

$ ✕ **Amelia's Hacienda.** This is a local favorite, for good reason: authentic
MEXICAN   south-of-the-border food, expertly mixed margaritas, and a lively yet family-friendly atmosphere. There's seating in the dining room and on the patio. ⊠ *44 S. Grand Ave., Montrose* ☎ *970/249–1881* ⊕ *www. ameliashacienda.com* ☻ *Closed Sun.*

$ ✕ **Camp Robber.** This chic restaurant serves Montrose's most creative
SOUTHWESTERN   cuisine. Try entrées such as basil-crusted salmon, Southwest chicken linguine, or the house specialty: pork medallions covered with green chili pistachios. At lunch, salads, hearty sandwiches, and blue-corn enchiladas fuel hungry hikers. The Sunday brunch will leave you happily stuffed. When the weather permits, you can sit in the enclosed patio. ⊠ *1515 Ogden Rd., Montrose* ☎ *970/240–1590* ⊕ *www.camprobber. com* ☻ *No dinner Sun.*

¢   🛏 **Best Western Red Arrow Motor Inn.** This low-key establishment is one
HOTEL   of the nicest lodgings in the area, mainly because of the large, pretty rooms filled with handsome wood furnishings. **Pros:** spacious and comfortable rooms; good breakfast. **Cons:** pets add an extra $10 per day. ⊠ *1702 E. Main St., Montrose* ☎ *970/249–9641, 800/780–7234* ⊕ *www.bestwesterncolorado.com* ⇖ *57 rooms, 2 suites* ☙ *In-room: Wi-Fi. In-hotel: pool, gym, laundry facilities, some pets allowed.*

¢   🛏 **Black Canyon Motel.** One of Montrose's better values, this motel has
HOTEL   rooms that are large and clean and a good selection of amenities. **Pros:** inexpensive; central location; hot tub. **Cons:** showing its age; common areas are a little gloomy. ⊠ *1605 E. Main St., Montrose* ☎ *970/249–3495, 800/348–3495* ⊕ *www.blackcanyonmotel.com* ⇖ *46 rooms, 3 suites* ☙ *In-room: Wi-Fi. In-hotel: pool, laundry facilities, some pets allowed.*

SHOPPING

Russell Stover Factory Outlet. The Russell Stover Factory Outlet, south of downtown Montrose, sells fresh chocolates and ice cream made right across the street. ⊠ *2200 Stover Ave., Montrose* ☎ *970/249–6681* ⊕ *www.russellstover.com.*

Montrose Farmers' Market. Pack a picnic lunch for the Black Canyon from the Montrose Farmers' Market, held every Saturday from May through October. It's also open Wednesday between July and September. ⊠ *Centennial Plaza, S. 1st St. and S. Uncompahgre Ave., Montrose* ☎ *970/209–8463* ⊕ *www.montrosefarmersmarket.com* ⊙ *May–Oct., Sat. 8:30–1; mid-July–late Sept., Wed. 8:30–1.*

DELTA

46 mi south of Grand Junction via U.S. 50; 22 mi north of Montrose via U.S. 50.

Colorful murals painted by local artists line the streets of Delta. The town is a good jumping-off point for visiting Black Canyon of the Gunnison National Park and the nearby farming and ranching communities of Crawford, Hotchkiss, and Paonia—the last known for its many vineyards and orchards.

GETTING HERE AND AROUND

From Delta, Highway 65 heads north to Cedaredge, which is the starting point for the Grand Mesa Scenic and Historic Byway. Highway 92 heads east to Hotchkiss and south through the tiny town of Crawford, where you can access Black Canyon of the Gunnison National Park. From Hotchkiss, a short 9-mi jaunt on Highway 133 leads to Paonia.

WHEN TO GO

The abundance of ripening fruits and vegetables paired with a delightful array of local wines make summer the best time to visit this remote area.

ESSENTIALS

Visitor Information Crawford Area Chamber of Commerce ⊘ *P.O. Box 22, Crawford 81415* ☎ *970/921–4000* ⊕ *www.crawfordcountry.org.* **Delta Area Chamber of Commerce** ⊠ *301 Main St.81416* ☎ *970/874–8616* ⊕ *www. deltacolorado.org.* **Hotchkiss Community Chamber of Commerce** ⊘ *P.O. Box 158, Hotchkiss 81419* ☎ *970/872–3226* ⊕ *www.hotchkisschamber.com.* **Paonia Chamber of Commerce** ⊘ *P.O. Box 366, Paonia 81428* ☎ *970/527–3886* ⊕ *www.paoniachamber.com.* **Cedaredge Area Chamber of Commerce** ⊠ *245 W. Main St., Cedaredge 81413* ☎ *970/856-6961* ⊕ *www.cedaredgecolorado.com.*

EXPLORING

Creamery Arts Center. In a renovated milk processing plant, the two-story Creamery Arts Center showcases the work of more than 100 regional artists. ⊠ *165 W. Bridge St.* ☎ *970/872–4848* ⊕ *www.creameryartscenter. org* ⊙ *Mon.–Sat. 11–6.*

Delta County Historical Museum. One of the more interesting artifacts at the Delta County Museum is a collection of guns used in a failed bank robbery in 1893. Other attractions include dinosaur bones, pioneer-era housewares, and an impressive collection of antique bells. ⊠ *251 Meeker St.* ☎ *970/874–8721* 🎟 *$2* ⊙ *May–Sept., Tues.–Sat. 10–4; Oct.–Apr., Wed. and Sat. 10–4.*

Fort Uncompahgre. Learn about the area's rich history with a visit to Fort Uncompahgre, which has a self-guided tour that takes you through the 1826 fur-trading post. ⊠ *Confluence Park, 230 Gunnison River Dr.* ☎ *970/874–1718* 🎟 *$3.50* ⊙ *Apr.–Sept., weekdays 9–3.*

10

⟳ **Tru-Vu Drive-in Theater.** A blast from the past, the Tru-Vu Drive-in Theater is one of the country's 370 remaining drive-in movie theaters. ✉ *1001 Hwy. 92* ☎ *970/874–9556* ⌧ *$7* ⊘ *May–Sept.*

OFF THE BEATEN PATH

Escalante Canyon. Named after Spanish missionary Francisco Silvestre Velez de Escalante, who helped lead an expedition through the area in 1776, Escalante Canyon is home to some of the best rock climbing in Colorado. It also shelters homesteader cabins, Native American rock art, and hiking trails. One of the pioneer homes was built by Captain H.A. Smith. His stone cabin, built into the side of a boulder, has a hollowed-out slab for a bed and a smaller niche carved out of the stone wall to hold a bedside pistol. Escalante Canyon is part of the Dominguez-Escalante National Conservation Area, which encompasses 210,000 acres in Mesa, Delta, and Montrose counties. ✉ *Escalante Canyon Rd., 12 mi west of Delta on U.S. 50* ☎ *970/244–3000* ⊕ *www.blm.gov* ⌧ *Free.*

TOP EXPERIENCE: FARMS, ORCHARDS, AND WINERIES
FARMS AND ORCHARDS

Vineyards, orchards, and farms add a green sheen to this high mountain valley. If you're visiting in summer, be sure to check out the selection of fresh fruits and vegetables at the many roadside stands.

Delicious Orchards Organic Farm Market. This lovely orchard markets its own organic apples, apricots, cherries, nectarines, peaches, pears, and plums all summer long. The gift shop also showcases local wines, produce, and other products. ✉ *39126 Hwy. 133, Hotchkiss* ☎ *970/527–1110* ⊕ *www.deliciousorchardstore.com* ⊘ *Mar.–Jan., daily 8–6.*

Orchard Valley Farms & Market. Family fun takes an organic approach at this friendly farm. Take a stroll through the gardens and orchards and pick your own fruits and vegetables or choose from a nice selection at the farm market. The on-site Black Bridge Winery offers free tastings of its chardonnay, Riesling, merlot, and pinot noir. ✉ *15836 Black Bridge Rd., Paonia* ☎ *970/527–6838* ⊕ *www.orchardvalleyfarms.com* ⊘ *Late May–Oct., daily 9–6.*

WINERIES

Located in eastern Delta County, the West Elks American Viticultural Area contains the highest-altitude vineyards in the northern hemisphere and produces an array of Central European varietals, including merlot and chardonnay. **Check out** ⊕ **www.coloradowine.com for a wine trail map,** then hit a few of the highlights while enjoying the fresh mountain air and scenery.

Alfred Eames Cellars. Located at the Puesta del Sol Vineyards, 3 mi south of Paonia, this casual winery offers a nice selection of top-notch reds. For a great pairing of wines and local foods, check out the annual wine festival held here in August. ✉ *11931 4050 Rd., Paonia* ☎ *970/527–3269* ⊕ *www.alfredeamescellars.com* ⊘ *Call ahead for hrs.*

Black Bridge Winery. This winery, part of Orchard Valley Farms, has made great strides with its nice selection of cabernet, merlot, pinot noir, and chardonnay wines. ✉ *15836 Black Bridge Rd., Paonia* ☎ *970/527–6838* ⊕ *www.blackbridgewinery.com* ⊘ *June–Oct., daily 9–6.*

Peak Spirits Distillery. Spice things up a bit with the spirited selections at this organic distillery. Organic fruit products combine to create Cap-Rock Organic Gin, CapRock Organic Vodka, Peak Organic Eaux de Vie, and Peak Biodynamic Grappas. ⊠ *26567 North Rd., Hotchkiss* ☏ *970/872–3677* ⊕ *www.peakspirits.com* ☉ *Call ahead for hrs.*

Stone Cottage Cellars. This North Fork Valley Winery specializes in chardonnay, merlot, and Syrah varietals. Stop by for a vineyard tour and wine tasting. ⊠ *41716 Reds Rd., Paonia* ☏ *970/527–3444* ⊕ *www. stonecottagecellars.com* ☉ *June–Oct., daily 11–6.*

WHERE TO EAT AND STAY
For expanded hotel reviews, visit Fodors.com.

$$ ✕ **Flying Fork Café & Bakery.** This charming café serves tasty Italian fare
ECLECTIC in a comfortable dining room and, in the summer, a shady outdoor garden. An assortment of artisan breads and pastries is sold in the small bakery at the front of the building (where you can also order a meal to go). Local ingredients are used whenever possible to create dishes like braised Colorado lamb shank or farfalle in a sauce of smoked chicken, pear, and Gorgonzola. The individual pizzas, made with whole-wheat flour and fresh basil and mozzarella, are good for smaller appetites. ⊠ *101 3rd St., Paonia* ☏ *970/527–3203* ⊕ *www.flyingforkcafe.com* ☉ *Closed Mon.*

$ ✕ **Miller's Deitch Haus.** Braced by thick wooden beams, this well-known
AMERICAN diner serves a wide selection of chicken, steaks, and fish. Specialties include prime rib on weekends and *Jäger Schnitzel* (breaded veal in a hearty mushroom sauce). The all-you-can-eat buffet includes plates for the popular soup and salad bar. This bustling eatery is light on atmosphere and on your wallet. For a bit extra you can try one of the homemade pies for dessert. ⊠ *820 Hwy. 92* ☏ *970/874–4413* ☉ *Closed Sun. No dinner Wed.*

$ ▦ **Best Western Sundance.** Within walking distance of Delta's downtown,
HOTEL this motel has up-to-date rooms, a full-service restaurant and lounge, a heated seasonal pool, and a spa and fitness room. **Pros:** reasonably good restaurant; full hot breakfast. **Cons:** chain-hotel feel. ⊠ *903 Main St.* ☏ *970/874–9781, 800/626–1994* ⊕ *www.bestwesternsundance.com* ◄ *41 rooms* ⚿ *In-room: a/c, Wi-Fi. In-hotel: restaurant, pool, gym, spa, laundry facilities, some pets allowed* ⎀ *Breakfast.*

¢ ▦ **Fresh & Wyld Farmhouse Inn and Gardens.** This rambling Paonia farm-
B&B/INN house has three suites on the main floor and four smaller rooms with shared bathrooms on the second floor. **Pros:** comfortable rooms; delicious food; farmhouse setting. **Cons:** the four rooms upstairs are basic and have shared bathrooms. ⊠ *1978 Harding Rd., Paonia* ☏ *970/527–4374* ⊕ *www.freshandwyld.com* ◄ *7 rooms* ⚿ *In-room: no a/c. In-hotel: some pets allowed* ⎀ *Breakfast.*

$$$$ ▦ **Smith Fork Ranch.** Rustic charm and warm hospitality are the key
RESORT to this historic ranch's success. **Pros:** fabulous staff; luxurious accom-
☉ modations; variety of ranch activities. **Cons:** very expensive; din-
★ ing options are limited; no refund for cancellations 90 days prior to arrival date. ⊠ *45362 Needle Rock Rd., Crawford* ☏ *970/921–3454* ⊕ *www.smithforkranch.com* ◄ *5 rooms, 4 cabins* ⚿ *In-room: no a/c.*

10

In-hotel: restaurant, bar, gym, spa, children's programs, business center ⑩ All-inclusive.

OFF THE
BEATEN
PATH

Grand Mesa, Uncompahgre, and Gunnison national forests. For information on backcountry hiking in the Uncompahgre Plateau and other nearby wilderness areas, contact the district office of the Grand Mesa, Uncompahgre, and Gunnison national forests. ✉ 2250 U.S. 50 ☎ 970/641–6600 ⊕ www.fs.fed.us/r2/gmug.

Grand Mesa Scenic and Historic Byway. For spectacular views of wildflower meadows, evergreen mesa forests, and high-mountain lakes, take a drive through Grand Mesa, Uncompahgre, and Gunnison national forests on the 63-mi-long Grand Mesa Scenic and Historic Byway. Dubbed the "Playground in the Sky," it follows Highway 64 from Cedaredge at the southern end to I–70 on the northern end (a spur road takes you to the Lands End Overlook). This route travels along the rim of the world's largest flat-top mountain, offering breathtaking views of Grand Valley more than a mile below. Plan on at least an hour and a half. ⊕ www.grandmesabyway.org.

LAKE CITY AND CREEDE

Lake City and Creede are in one of the most beautiful areas of Colorado. Both have colorful histories and excellent access to the many hiking and mountain-biking trails in the Gunnison National Forest and the Rio Grande National Forest. If you're driving through here, especially on the Silver Thread Scenic Byway or the Alpine Loop Scenic Byway, allow plenty of time, because you'll want to keep stopping to take pictures of the surrounding mountains.

LAKE CITY

45 mi from Ouray via Alpine Loop Scenic Byway (summer only); 55 mi southwest of Gunnison via U.S. 50 and Rte. 149; 49 mi northwest of Creede via Rte. 149.

Lake City—with its collection of lacy gingerbread-trim houses and other Victorian buildings—has one of the largest National Historic Districts in Colorado. But the town is perhaps best known for the lurid story of Alfred Packer, who led a party of five prospectors into the mountains during the winter of 1874. That spring, only Packer emerged from the wilderness, claiming that the miners had all perished from the cold. But Packer looked fit and well fed, and was spending money freely (from several different wallets, according to some accounts). Soon after, a grisly pile of human remains was discovered a few miles away. Packer protested his innocence and fled, but was eventually caught and sentenced to life in prison.

Its grisly history notwithstanding, Lake City is a quaint little town and a point of departure for superb hiking and fishing in the Gunnison National Forest. A geological phenomenon known as the Slumgullion Earthflow occurred some 800 years ago, when a mountainside sloughed off into the valley, blocking the Lake Fork of the Gunnison River and creating Lake San Cristobal, the state's second-largest natural lake.

There's a scenic overlook along Highway 149, just south of town, with a sign explaining how this happened.

GETTING HERE AND AROUND

Highway 149 turns into Gunnison Avenue as it passes through the seven blocks of Lake City. The majority of the town's shops are on this road. Running parallel to Gunnison Avenue, Silver Street and Bluffs Street are lined with historic homes.

ESSENTIALS

Visitor Information Lake City/Hinsdale County Chamber of Commerce
⊠ *800 N. Gunnison Ave.* ☎ *970/944–2527, 800/569–1874* ⊕ *www.lakecity.com.*

EXPLORING

Alpine Loop Scenic Byway. The inspiring 65-mi Alpine Loop Scenic Byway joins Lake City with Ouray and Silverton. The road, typically open late May or early June through October, has unpaved sections that require a high-clearance, four-wheel-drive vehicle. Dizzily spiraling from 12,800-foot-high passes to gaping valleys, the trip is well worth the effort.

Silver Thread Scenic Byway. Lake City is at the northern tip of the Silver Thread Scenic Byway, which ends 75 mi south in Southfork. The paved route, also called Highway 149, climbs over Slumgullion Pass from Lake City, overlooks the headwaters of the Rio Grande, and then drops down into the lush Rio Grande Valley. Along the way, you'll see plenty of old gold and silver mining camps and spectacular North Clear Creek Falls.

SPORTS AND THE OUTDOORS

FISHING

Numerous high-alpine lakes and mountain streams make the area around Lake City an angler's heaven. Lake San Cristobal is known around the region for its rainbow and brown trout, while the Lake Fork of the Gunnison attracts anglers for rainbow and brook trout.

Dan's Fly Shop. Stop here to rent gear, book a guided trip, or arrange for a fishing license. ⊠ *723 N. Gunnison Ave.* ☎ *970/944–2281* ⊕ *www. dansflyshop.com.*

HIKING

There are lots of trails in this region, with choices for all abilities. Many follow logging roads, so it's best to get the latest scoop on conditions before heading out. Ambitious hikers often overnight in Lake City before attempting three of Colorado's Fourteeners—Handies, Sunshine, and Red Cloud Peaks—all within about 15 mi of town. Sunshine and Redcloud are generally climbed together, which makes it fairly easy for fit hikers to bag three Fourteeners in just two days.

WHERE TO STAY

For expanded hotel reviews, visit Fodors.com.

$$$
B&B/INN
🏠 **Old Carson Inn.** This peaceful A-frame log cabin is nestled among stands of towering aspen and spruce. **Pros:** beautiful setting; comfortable rooms. **Cons:** not centrally located; three-night minimum stay. ⊠ *8401 County Rd. 30* ☎ *970/944–2511, 800/294–0608* ⊕ *www. oldcarsoncabin.com* 🛏 *7 rooms* ⚿ *In-room: no a/c, Wi-Fi. In-hotel: some pets allowed* ⊙ *No meals.*

10

CREEDE

105 mi south of Gunnison via U.S. 50 and Rte. 149; 52 mi southeast of Lake City via Rte. 149.

Creede, a flash-in-the-pan silver town, was known in its heyday as Colorado's rowdiest mining camp. When silver was discovered here in 1889, hotels, saloons, banks, and brothels opened virtually overnight, often in tents and other makeshift structures. By 1892, Creede had become a collection of wood-framed buildings, at least 30 of which were saloons and dance halls. That year, Creede was immortalized in a poem written by the local newspaper editor Cy Warman: "It's day all day in daytime," he wrote, "and there is no night in Creede."

True, every other building back in the silver-boom days seems to have been a bar or bordello. Bob Ford, who killed Jesse James, was himself gunned down here; other notorious residents included Calamity Jane and Bat Masterson.

As delightful as the town's history may be, its location is even more glorious. Mineral County is almost all public land, including the nearby Weminuche Wilderness to the south and west and the Wheeler Geological Area to the west, where the unusual rock formations resemble playful abstract sculptures or M.C. Escher creations. The Colorado Trail and the Continental Divide Trail, two of the country's most significant long-distance recreational paths, pass through Mineral County.

GETTING HERE AND AROUND
Highway 149 turns into Main Street as it passes through the 15 blocks of Creede.

ESSENTIALS
Visitor Information Creede–Mineral County Chamber of Commerce ⊠ *904 S. Main St.* ☎ *719/658–2374, 800/327–2102* ⊕ *www.creede.com.*

EXPLORING
Creede Historic Museum. Occupying the original Denver & Rio Grande Railroad Depot, the Creede Historic Museum paints a vivid portrait of the town's rough-and-tumble early days. ⊠ *17 Main St.* ☎ *719/658–2004* ▱ *$2* ☉ *June–Aug., daily 10–4.*

Underground Mining Museum. The Underground Mining Museum is housed in rooms that modern miners blasted out of solid rock to commemorate the lives of 1880s-era miners. Exhibits tracing the history of mining reveal the difference between a *winze* (reinforced shaft leading straight down) and a *windlass* (hand-operated hoist). There are guided tours at 10 and 3 daily, but you can also poke about on your own. After you've toured the mine, ask if you can look into the world's only underground firehouse, directly next door. If a volunteer firefighter is around, he'll gladly show you. ⊠ *503 Forest Service Rd. #9* ☎ *719/658–0811* ▱ *$7 self-guided tour, $15 guided tour* ☉ *June–Sept., daily 10–4; Oct.–May, weekdays 9:30–3.*

WHERE TO EAT AND STAY
For expanded hotel reviews, visit Fodors.com.

$ ✕ **The Old Firehouse.** The decor in this casual café and ice-cream par-
CAFÉ lor reflects the building's 120-year-long history, with plenty of old-
fashioned fire equipment and other antiques on display. There's an
equally charming bed-and-breakfast upstairs with three rooms and one
suite. ⊠ *123 N. Main St.* ☎ *719/658–0212* ⊕ *www.theoldfirehouse.com*
⊗ *Closed Oct.–mid-Apr.*

$$ ⊡ **Antler's Rio Grande Lodge.** Dating back to the late 1800s, this cozy
HOTEL lodge has rooms in the main building as well as rustic, secluded cabins
with their own kitchens. **Pros:** mountain setting; solid restaurant. **Cons:**
off the beaten path. ⊠ *26222 Hwy. 149* ☎ *719/658–2423* ⊕ *www.
antlerslodge.com* ⊅ *9 rooms, 15 cabins* ⚇ *In-room: no a/c, kitchen,
no TV, Wi-Fi. In-hotel: restaurant, bar, laundry facilities* ⊗ *Closed Oct.–
Apr.* ⑩ *No meals.*

$$$$ ⊡ **Wason Ranch.** This historic ranch house, dating from the early 1870s,
RENTAL is a local landmark. **Pros:** beautiful setting; great option for families.
Cons: off the beaten path; three-night minimum. ⊠ *19082 Hwy. 149*
☎ *719/658–2413, 877/927–6626* ⊕ *www.wasonranch.com* ⊅ *9 cot-
tages, 1 ranch house* ⚇ *In-room: no a/c, kitchen* ⑩ *No meals.*

THE ARTS

★ **Creede Repertory Theatre.** Housed in the beautifully restored 1892 Creede
Opera House, this theater stages at least seven plays, plus concerts and
other events, every year between May and September. ⊠ *124 N. Main
St.* ☎ *866/658–2540, 719/657–2540* ⊕ *www.creederep.org.*

SHOPPING

San Juan Sports. San Juan Sports specializes in sales and rentals of out-
door gear for hiking, biking, camping, and winter backcountry expedi-
tions. There are also good selections of maps, books, and the ubiquitous
Colorado T-shirts. ⊠ *102 S. Main St.* ☎ *719/658–2359.*

**EN
ROUTE** From Lake City, follow Route 149—the Silver Thread National Scenic
Byway—on its journey southeast to South Fork. Between Lake City and
Creede you'll pass the beautiful Clear Creek Falls. The road flirts with
the Rio Grande, now just a small river formed at nearby Stony Pass.

Wheeler Geologic Area. You need a four-wheel-drive vehicle to navi-
gate the roads in the Wheeler Geologic Area, a 640-acre area distin-
guished by dramatically eroded pinnacles of volcanic tuff, but it's worth
the effort. A drive through subalpine terrain takes you to a series of
magical-looking spires, pinnacles, and domes. Once there, exploring is
on foot or horseback. It's about 7 mi southeast of Creede. ⊠ *La Garita
Wilderness Area, Off Hwy. 149.*

10

TELLURIDE AND THE SAN JUAN MOUNTAINS

The San Juan Mountains cover more than 12,000 square mi of south-
western Colorado. This striking mountain range ranks as one of the
most rugged in the country, and is defined by the hundreds of peaks ris-
ing to an elevation of 13,000 feet or more. This high mountain country
is the perfect playground for laid-back camping and hiking, and extreme
sports like ice climbing and heli-skiing.

TELLURIDE

66 mi south of Montrose via U.S. 550 and Rte. 62; 111 mi north of Durango via U.S. 160 and Rtes. 184 and 145.

Tucked away between the azure sky and the gunmetal mountains is Telluride, the colorful mining-town-turned-ski resort famous for its celebrity visitors (Oprah Winfrey, Tom Cruise, and Oliver Stone spend time here).

Telluride's first mines were established in the 1870s, and by the early 1890s the town was booming. The allure of the place was such that Butch Cassidy robbed his first bank here in 1889. These days the savage but beautiful San Juan range attracts mountain people of a different sort—skiers, snowboarders, mountain bikers, and four-wheelers—who attack any incline, up or down, with abandon.

GETTING HERE AND AROUND

Although Telluride and the ski resort town of Mountain Village are two distinct areas, you can travel between them via a 2½-mi, over-the-mountain gondola ride, arguably one of the most beautiful commutes in Colorado. The gondola makes a car unnecessary, as both the village and the town are pedestrian friendly.

The free Galloping Goose shuttle loops around Telluride every 15 minutes in summer and winter, less often in the off-season. The Dial-a-Ride shuttle, also free, serves the Mountain Village area during high season. Telluride Express, a private taxi company, serves Telluride Regional Airport and the rest of the surrounding area.

Telluride magazine prints an excellent historic walking tour in its "Visitors' Guide" section. The town is made up of one pastel Victorian residence or frontier trading post after another. It's hard to believe that the lovingly restored shops and restaurants once housed gaming parlors and saloons known for the quality of their "waitressing." That party-hearty spirit lives on, evidenced by numerous annual summer celebrations.

WHEN TO GO

Telluride has two off seasons, when most restaurants and many lodgings take a breather. The town closes up from late September or early October until ski season gets going in late November. Many people also flee town during "mud season," leaving after the ski area shuts down in mid-April and returning in early or mid-June. But with the growing popularity of Mountainfilm, a film festival held over Memorial Day weekend, more places are staying open. Off-season rates offer you a chance to enjoy the town's charm for less. However, when the summer festivals are in full swing, prices skyrocket and rooms book up fast. The biggies are the Telluride Bluegrass Festival in June, the Telluride Jazz Celebration in July, the Telluride Film Festival in August, and the Telluride Blues and Brews Festival in September. Whenever you decide to go, you should check for upcoming events at least three months in advance.

FESTIVALS

Highly regarded wine and wild-mushroom festivals alternate with musical performances celebrating everything from bluegrass to jazz to chamber music.

CLOSE UP

The Spirit of Telluride

Telluride's independent spirit is nothing new. The town was established by a handful of very independent types—men who'd hauled themselves and their equipment (and in some cases, their families) over high mountain passes. Gold was discovered in 1858, but because of its remote location the town remained isolated until the railroad arrived in 1891, bringing prosperity with it. By the turn of the century, Telluride had close to 5,000 inhabitants—and more millionaires per capita than New York City. Soon afterward the boom went bust as the minerals market crashed, and Telluride's population dropped to a few hundred people.

Everything changed again in the 1970s, when the first chair lift went in (and the last of the mines were shut down). Skiing seemed to fit with Telluride's wild-and-woolly character—local legend holds that the miners of old, often of Norwegian descent, would ski down the mountain after a day in the mines, as this was the quickest way to get to the town's bordellos. Nowadays, Telluride's independent types are busy designing bigger and better ski terrain (and organizing music and film festivals), all the while working to preserve what makes Telluride unique.

Telluride Bluegrass Festival. The Telluride Bluegrass Festival in June has gone far beyond its bluegrass roots and is now one of the country's premier acoustic folk–rock gatherings. ☎ *800/624–2422* ⊕ *www.bluegrass. com/telluride.*

★ **Telluride Film Festival.** Held each year in early September, the Telluride Film Festival is up there with Sundance as one of the world's leading showcases for foreign and domestic films. ☎ *510/665–9494* ⊕ *www. telluridefilmfestival.org.*

ESSENTIALS

Transportation Contacts Dial-a-Ride ☎ *970/728-8888.* **Galloping Goose** ☎ *970/728-5700.* **Telluride Express** ☎ *970/728-6000, 888/212-8294* ⊕ *www. tellurideexpress.com.*

Visitor Information Mountain Village Visitor Information Center ⊠ *450 Mountain Village Blvd.* ☎ *970/728-3014, 888/605-2578.* **Telluride and Mountain Village Visitor Services** ⊠ *700 W. Colorado Ave.* ☎ *970/728-3041, 888/605-2578* ⊕ *www.visittelluride.com.* **Telluride Ski Resort** ⊠ *565 Mountain Village Blvd.* ☎ *970/728-6900, 800/778-8581* ⊕ *www.tellurideskiresort.com.* **Telluride Snow Report** ☎ *970/728-7425.*

10

EXPLORING

Historic Tours of Telluride. Operated by local thespian Ashley Boling, Historic Tours of Telluride provides humorous walking tours around the downtown streets, adding anecdotes about infamous figures such as Butch Cassidy and Jack Dempsey. ☎ *970/728–6639.*

New Sheridan Hotel & Opera House. Built by miners in 1913 as a venue for vaudeville acts and other entertainments, this landmark has since hosted performances by Jackson Browne and Jimmy Buffett. The Sheridan presents a variety of shows, featuring musicians, comedians, and other performers. ✉ *231 W. Colorado Ave.* ☎ *970/728–6363* ⊕ *www.sheridanoperahouse.com.*

Telluride Historical Museum. Housed in the 1888 Miner's Hospital, the Telluride Historical Museum hosts exhibits on the town's past, including work in the nearby mines, techniques used by local doctors, and skiing on the mountain before the resort was built. ✉ *201 W. Gregory Ave.* ☎ *970/728–3344* ⊕ *www.telluridemuseum.org* ✉ *$5* ⊙ *May–Oct., Mon.–Sat. 11–5; Nov.–Apr., Tues.–Sat. 11–5.*

EN ROUTE

★ **San Juan Skyway.** One of the country's most stupendously scenic drives, the 236-mi San Juan Skyway weaves through an impressive series of Fourteeners (peaks reaching more than 14,000 feet). From Telluride, it heads north on Route 145 to Placerville, where it turns east on Route 62. On U.S. 550 it continues south to historic Ouray and over Red Mountain Pass to Silverton and then on to Durango, Mancos, and Cortez via U.S. 160. From Cortez, Route 145 heads north, passing through Rico and over lovely Lizard Head Pass before heading back into Telluride. In late September and early October, this route has some of the state's most spectacular aspen viewing.

Fodor's Choice
★ **DOWNHILL SKIING AND SNOWBOARDING**

Telluride Ski Resort. Dubbed "the most beautiful place you'll ever ski," the Telluride Ski Resort once was known as an experts-only ski area. Indeed, the north-facing trails are impressively steep and long, and the moguls can be massive. The terrain accessed by Chairlift 9, including the famed Spiral Staircase and the Plunge, is for experts only. Hikes to Gold Hill, Bald Mountain, Black Iron Bowl, and Palmyra Peak deliver seriously steep chutes and plenty of natural terrain.

But then there is the other side—literally—of the ski area, the gently sloping valley called the Gorrono Basin, with long groomed runs excellent for intermediates and beginners. On the ridge that wraps around the ski area's core is the aptly named See Forever, a long cruiser that starts at 12,255 feet and seems to go on and on. The best areas for beginners are the Meadows, off Lift 1, and Galloping Goose, a long winding trail off Lifts 12 or 10. Near Gorrono Basin, off Lift 4, is another section that includes super-steep, double-diamond tree runs on one side and glorious cruisers on the other.

Slide through a Western-style gate and you come to Prospect Bowl, a 733-acre area with a network of runs cut around islands of trees. One cluster of intermediate runs is served by a swift high-speed quad (Lift 12). The terrain here runs the gamut from nearly flat beginner terrain to double-diamond chutes, cliff bands, and open glades.

Telluride also has four terrain parks, one open at night, for skiers and snowboarders of all levels. ✉ *565 Mountain Village Blvd.* ☎ *970/728–6900, 800/778–8581* ⊕ *www.tellurideskiresort.com* ⊙ *Late Nov.–early Apr., daily 9–4.*

FACILITIES 4,425-foot vertical drop; 2,000 skiable acres; 23% beginner, 36% intermediate, 41% advanced and expert; 2 high-speed gondolas, 7 high-speed quad chairs, 1 fixed quad lift, 2 triple chairs, 2 double chairs, 2 surface lifts, 2 magic carpets.

CLOSE UP

Telluride Bluegrass Festival

Bluegrass may have evolved from country's "Appalachian mountain music," but Telluride's Bluegrass Festival has added a distinctive Rocky Mountain note to the mix.

Since its inception in 1973, the festival has featured traditional bluegrass bands from across the nation, but when contemporary Colorado bands started adding the quintessential bluegrass instruments—mandolin, fiddle, guitar, upright bass, and banjo—to their lineups, their version of the "high lonesome sound" garnered national attention. It forced bluegrass to undergo several transformations, sometimes right before the Telluride audience's eyes, as the crowd's enthusiasm prompted more and more on-stage experimentation.

As the festival gained in popularity, it brought more bluegrass artists to Colorado, and crossover between bluegrass and other musical styles became more common. The festival earned the moniker "Woodstock of the West." Colorado bands such as String Cheese Incident, Leftover Salmon, and Yonder Mountain String Band performed regularly at the event, appealing to a younger audience and encouraging more experimentation.

Now the Telluride Bluegrass Festival draws such popular acts as Emmylou Harris, Alison Krauss, Los Lobos, and Counting Crows—not exactly bluegrass purists. It has also spawned other popular and successful gatherings, including a sister festival held each July at Planet Bluegrass Ranch in Lyons, Colorado, a town of about 1,600 that has become a bluegrass artists' colony. The towns of Greeley and Pagosa Springs have gotten in on the act, too, both hosting bluegrass festivals of their own in August.

LESSONS AND PROGRAMS

Telluride Ski & Snowboard School. At this well-regarded school, adult half-day group clinics are $85, and full-day adventure classes are $140. Lessons are available for alpine and telemark skiers as well as snowboarders. Children's programs are $160 per day and include a lift ticket, lesson, and lunch. The Women's Week programs include three or five days of skills-building classes with female instructors that cost $675 to $1,075, including lift tickets. Sessions are scheduled for January, February, and March. ✉ *565 Mountain Village Blvd.* ☎ *970/728–7540* ⊕ *www.tellurideskiresort.com.*

LIFT TICKETS

The one-day walk-up rate is $92. On multiday, advance-purchase tickets the daily rate can drop as low as $59.

RENTALS

Paragon Ski and Sport. Telluride's oldest and best-known ski shop rents all manner of skis, boots, and snowboards, along with backcountry gear and snowshoes. It also offers ski tuning, boot fitting, and repairs. ✉ *213 W. Colorado Ave.* ☎ *970/728–4525* ⊕ *www.paragontelluride.com.*

Telluride Sports. All manner of ski and snowboard rentals are available from the ubiquitous Telluride Sports, with several locations in Telluride and Mountain Village. The shop will deliver everything to your hotel for no extra charge. ✉ *150 W. Colorado Ave.* ☎ *970/728–4477, 877/754–7991* ⊕ *www.telluridesports.com.*

10

NORDIC SKIING
TRACK SKIING
Telluride Nordic Center. Operated by the Telluride Nordic Association, the center offers ski and snowshoe tours and cross-country ski lessons. It also rents ski equipment and ice skates for adults and children. ✉ *500 W. Colorado Ave.* ☎ *970/728–1144* ⊕ *www.telluridetrails.org.*

TopAten Snowshoe and Nordic Area. Located near the unloading area for Chair 10, TopAten has 10 mi of rolling trails groomed for cross-country skiing and snowshoeing. There's a warming teepee, a picnic deck and restroom facilities here. To access TopAten, you'll need to buy a "foot passenger" lift ticket for $20. ☎ *970/728–7517.*

OTHER SPORTS AND THE OUTDOORS
Telluride Outside. Telluride Outside organizes a variety of summer and winter activities in the Telluride area, including 4WD tours, whitewater rafting, snowmobile tours, mountain-biking trips, and even winter fly-fishing excursions. ✉ *121 W. Colorado Ave.* ☎ *970/728–3895, 800/831–6230* ⊕ *www.tellurideoutside.com.*

FISHING
For an afternoon in some of the finest fishing spots around, with abundant rainbow, cutthroat, brown, and brook trout, head for the beautiful San Miguel and Dolores rivers.

Telluride Outside. This service runs guided fly-fishing trips from its store, the Telluride Angler. It also organizes a variety of summer and winter activities in the Telluride area, including four-wheel drive, white-water rafting, mountain biking, and photography excursions. ✉ *Telluride Angler, 121 W. Colorado Ave.* ☎ *970/728–3895, 800/831–6230* ⊕ *www.tellurideoutside.com.*

FOUR-WHEELING
The Tomboy Road, also known as Imogene Pass Road, which can be accessed directly from Oak Street at the northern edge of town, leads to one of the country's most interesting mining districts. The area went down in history in 1901, when the Western Federation of Miners organized a strike to protest the horrific working conditions. The state militia was eventually called in, but the miners won a wage increase. The ruins of the Smuggler-Union and Tomboy mines are all that remain of those turbulent times. The road has fabulous views of Bridal Veil Falls and Ingram Falls. After about 7 mi, it crests over 13,114-foot-high Imogene Pass, the highest pass road in the San Juans. If you continue down the other side, you end up in Yankee Boy Basin, near Ouray.

Dave's Mountain Tours. In summer, this outfit conducts tours to the Tomboy Mine site, Imogene Pass, and other historic and scenic areas. It also runs snowmobile tours in winter. ⌂ *Box 2736 81435* ☎ *970/728–9749* ⊕ *www.telluridetours.com.*

GLIDER RIDES

Telluride Soaring. Offering a rare bird's-eye view of the town, the ski area, and the San Juans, Glider Bob operates out of the Telluride Regional Airport. Rates are $180 per hour; rides are conducted daily, weather permitting. ✉ *1500 Last Dollar Rd.* ☎ *970/708–0862* ⊕ *www. glidetelluride.com.*

HIKING

The peaks of the rugged San Juan Mountains around Telluride require some scrambling, occasionally bordering on real climbing, to get to the top. A local favorite is Wilson Peak, which is one of the easier Four-teeners to climb. July and August are the most popular months on this 8-mi round-trip hike.

Sound a bit too grueling?

Bear Creek Falls. An immensely popular trail leads to Bear Creek Falls, 2½ mi from the trailhead. The route is also used by mountain bikers. ✉ *Trailhead at end of S. Pine St.*

Jud Wiebe Trail. The Jud Wiebe Trail, a 3-mi loop, is an excellent hike that is generally passable from spring until late fall. The Jud Wiebe Trail links with the Sneffels Highline Trail, a 14-mi loop that leads through wildflower-covered meadows. ✉ *Trailhead at north end of Aspen St.*

Bridal Veil Falls. A 1.8-mi trail from the old Pandora Mill leads to spectacular Bridal Veil Falls. At 365 feet, it tumbles lavishly from the top of the box canyon. A beautifully restored powerhouse sits beside the falls. ✉ *Trailhead near Pandora Mill, at the east end of Colorado Ave.*

HORSEBACK RIDING

Ride with Roudy. Roudy Roudebush is a cowboy straight out of central casting (he starred in a television commercial and in Disney's 2004 film *America's Heart and Soul*). His company, Ride with Roudy, offers trail rides through aspen groves and across open meadows with views of the Wilson Range. You can book rides lasting from an hour to a week, plus sleigh rides in the winter. ✉ *242 Hawn La.* ⌂ *Box 2091 81435* ☎ *970/728–9611* ⊕ *www.ridewithroudy.com.*

MOUNTAIN BIKING

San Juan Hut System. Having a fully equipped hut waiting at the end of a tough day of riding makes the San Juan Hut System a backcountry biker's dream come true. The company, which started out as a hut-to-hut service for backcountry skiers, operates a 215-mi route from Telluride to Moab, Utah, suitable for intermediate and advanced riders. Trips run from June to October and last five or seven days, covering alpine meadows, desert slick rock, and canyon country. Along the way, the six one-room huts are supplied with beds, blankets, heating and cooking stoves, food, and water. ⌂ *Box 773, Ridgway 81432* ☎ *970/626–3033* ⊕ *www.sanjuanhuts.com.*

10

RAFTING

Telluride Outside. There's plenty of whitewater around Telluride, and this outfitter explores the rapids in the Dolores and San Miguel rivers. ⊠ *121 W. Colorado Ave.* ☎ *970/728–3895, 800/831–6230* ⊕ *www. tellurideoutside.com.*

WHERE TO EAT

$$$$
EUROPEAN

✕ **221 South Oak.** Housed in a beautifully restored Victorian, this elegant bistro entices you to linger with its cozy ambiance and scrumptious meals. Sunday brunch in summer only draws locals and visitors alike with a fabulous menu including several varieties of frittatas, French toast, and eggs Benedict. The dinner menu changes frequently, but always includes dishes made with locally sourced fish (like Rocky Mountain trout or Colorado striped bass), meat (elk, lamb, and bison), and vegetables. ⊠ *221 S. Oak St.* ☎ *970/728–9507* ⊕ *www.221southoak.com* ⊙ *Closed early Apr.–May, and mid-Oct.–mid-Dec. No lunch.*

$$$$
MODERN
AMERICAN

✕ **Allred's.** Unless you're planning some serious hiking, the only way to reach this sky-high eatery is via the gondola that connects Telluride with the Mountain Village. The view is understandably awesome, as are the meals. Choose from a selection of steak, chicken, and seafood, then add a mouth-watering sauce—a fondue made with goat cheese and leeks, for example, or an Argentinean-style chimichurri. Other menu offerings include roasted Colorado lamb chops and pan-seared elk loin. The drink menu is simple but elegant, with a nice selection of wines and champagnes, as well as vintage cocktails and modern martinis. ⊠ *Top of San Sophia gondola station* ☎ *970/728–7474* ⊕ *www.allredsrestaurant. com* ⊙ *No lunch.*

$
CAFÉ

✕ **Baked in Telluride.** This Telluride institution has expanded enormously over the years, as you can tell from the racks of fresh-baked breads, rolls, bagels, and other pastries that are on display. The kitchen turns out heavenly sandwiches, pizzas, and pastas (check out the Alfredo), as well as huge, inexpensive salads. Order your meal to go or grab one of the tables in the back. The front porch is especially busy as locals meet and greet. ⊠ *127 S. Fir St.* ☎ *970/728–4775.*

$
PIZZA
★

✕ **Brown Dog Pizza.** This local hangout serves a mean pizza—not too doughy, not too cheesy. The thin-crust pie is the big draw, and slices are served until midnight. Specialty toppings include artichoke hearts, broccoli, eggplant, pickles, jalapeño peppers, and sun-dried tomatoes. However, the most popular choices are also the meatiest. The barbecued chicken with bacon is a favorite, as is the Boone's Meaty, loaded with pepperoni, sausage, meatballs, bacon, and Canadian bacon. There's also a good selection of pastas, burgers, and subs. Brown Dog is one of the few places in town that will feed you for less than the cost a lift ticket. ⊠ *110 E. Colorado Ave.* ☎ *970/728–8046* ⊕ *www.browndogpizza.net.*

$$$$
AMERICAN
★

✕ **Cosmopolitan.** Located in the Hotel Columbia, right at the base of the gondola, the Cosmopolitan specializes in elegant dishes like barbecued wild salmon with spinach and leek polenta, crab-stuffed chicken breast with Gruyère fondue, and teriyaki-smoked short ribs. Try the New Orleans–style beignets with a cappuccino for dessert, cheekily listed as "coffee and donuts" on the menu. There's an exhaustive wine list with more than 200 bottles. The restaurant's contemporary style includes copper metallic accents and historic photos. ⊠ *Hotel Columbia, 300 W. San Juan Ave.* ☎ *970/728–1292* ⊕ *www.cosmotelluride.com* ⚍ *Reservations essential* ⊗ *No lunch.*

$$
SOUTHERN

✗ **Fat Alley BBQ.** In the Camel's Garden Hotel, this place serves messy, mouthwatering ribs and Carolina-style pulled-pork sandwiches. You'll find the famous sides—fried okra, red beans and rice, and sweet potato fries—and artery-clogging desserts, plus the Southern-style beverages. There are a dozen or so beers (including Schlitz), 30 bourbons, and homemade sweet tea. Some lighter options have joined the menu, which is good news to anyone concerned with cholesterol. There's outdoor seating, with a huge patio that's hopping every afternoon throughout the year. ⊠ *Camel's Garden Hotel, 250 San Juan Ave.* ☎ *970/728–3985* ⊕ *www.oakstelluride.com* ⚍ *Reservations not accepted.*

$$$
ASIAN

✗ **Honga's Lotus Petal.** A local favorite, this chic eatery serves Japanese, Thai, and Balinese fare in an elegant dining room. The sushi bar is the best in town, with fish flown in from Hawaii four times a week. Many dishes are vegetarian, but meat-eaters can find free-range chicken and organic beef on the ever-changing menu, as well. Blackened tofu is the signature dish, and the crowds also go wild for the coconut curry and the crunchy shrimp inside-out roll. Don't leave without sampling the addictive pot stickers. Honga's specialty drinks, such as the potent and imaginative mojitos and martinis, keep them coming to the patio bar. ⊠ *135 E. Colorado Ave.* ☎ *970/728–5134* ⊕ *www.hongaslotuspetal. com* ⊗ *Closed early Apr.–late May and mid-Oct.–late Nov. No lunch.*

$$$$
FRENCH
Fodor'sChoice
★

✗ **La Marmotte.** With its rough brick and timber walls, lacy curtains, and baskets overflowing with flowers, this romantic bistro would be right at home in Provence. It's a veteran on the often-changing roster of restaurants in Telluride, having been in business for more than 20 years in one of the town's oldest buildings. It's known for its French country charm, consistently great food, stellar wine pairings, and homey dining experience. The menu changes nightly depending on the availability of fresh, local ingredients. ⊠ *150 W. San Juan Ave.* ☎ *970/728–6232* ⊕ *www.lamarmotte.com* ⚍ *Reservations essential* ⊗ *Closed Wed. No lunch.*

$
CAFÉ

✗ **Maggie's Bakery & Cafe.** A little spot with a blue awning and a couple of tables set up outside, Maggie's often has the front door propped open and the smell of fresh-baked breads and oatmeal cookies lures customers in. You can grab breakfast and lunch here as well as a sweet treat (the sticky buns are the best), including piled-high sandwiches, Mexican food, and soup. ⊠ *300 W. Colorado Ave.* ☎ *970/728–3334* ⊕ *www. maggiestelluride.com* ▭ *No credit cards* ⊗ *No dinner.*

$$$$
STEAKHOUSE
★

✗ **New Sheridan Chop House.** New meets old at the Chop House, arguably the best steak house in town. Here you can choose your meat (sirloin, filet mignon, and succulent bison rib eye are among the choices), then your topping (think caramelized onions, blue cheese, or glazed wild mushrooms), then your sauce (anything from béarnaise to chimichurri). Other options include elk loin and pork chops. The extensive wine list includes many by the glass. Mirrors aged with gold patina, dark wood,

10

and oil lamps complement the red-leather booths and brightly colored murals. ⊠ *New Sheridan Hotel, 231 W. Colorado Ave.* ☎ *970/728–9100, 800/200–1891* ⊕ *www.newsheridan.com* ☾ *Closed mid-Apr.–mid-May and mid-Oct.–mid-Nov.*

WHERE TO STAY

For expanded hotel reviews, visit Fodors.com.

$$$$ ▦ **Camel's Garden.** An ultramodern lodge that's all gleaming glass and
HOTEL sleek surfaces bears the name of one of the town's oldest mines. **Pros:** convenient to lifts; intimate and romantic. **Cons:** very modern; not especially kid-friendly. ⊠ *250 W. San Juan Ave.* ☎ *970/728–9300, 888/772–2635* ⊕ *www.camelsgarden.com* ⇛ *31 rooms, 8 condos* ⚹ *In-room: Wi-Fi. In-hotel: restaurant, spa* ¶⊙¶ *Breakfast.*

$$$$ ▦ **Hotel Columbia Telluride.** It's hard to go wrong with views of the moun-
HOTEL tains, the gondola, and the San Miguel River. **Pros:** stunning views;
★ spacious rooms; convenient to gondola and lift. **Cons:** expensive; can be noisy. ⊠ *301 W. San Juan Ave.* ☎ *970/728–0660, 800/201–9505* ⊕ *www.columbiatelluride.com* ⇛ *21 rooms* ⚹ *In-room: Wi-Fi. In-hotel: restaurant, parking, some pets allowed.*

$$$$ ▦ **Hotel Telluride.** This hotel looks like an old stone mansion nes-
HOTEL tled against the mountain. **Pros:** terrific value; abundant breakfast; free shuttle to the gondola. **Cons:** hot tubs often taken; small hotel fills up quickly. ⊠ *199 N. Cornet St.* ☎ *970/369–1188* ⊕ *www.thehoteltelluride.com* ⇛ *59 rooms, 2 suites* ⚹ *In-room: Wi-Fi. In-hotel: restaurant, bar, gym, spa, laundry facilities, business center, some pets allowed* ¶⊙¶ *Breakfast.*

$$$$ ▦ **Inn at Lost Creek.** A grand stone-and-wood structure, this rambling
HOTEL five-story luxury hotel in the Mountain Village resembles an alpine lodge. **Pros:** ski-in ski-out convenience; romantic feeling; top-notch amenities. **Cons:** minimum stay during holidays; fee for parking. ⊠ *119 Lost Creek La., Mountain Village* ☎ *970/728–5678, 888/601–5678* ⊕ *www.innatlostcreek.com* ⇛ *32 suites* ⚹ *In-room: kitchen, Wi-Fi. In-hotel: restaurant, bar, gym, spa, laundry facilities, business center, parking* ¶⊙¶ *No meals.*

$$$$ ▦ **Lumière.** "Lumière" means "light" in French, and this luxury lodge
HOTEL lives up to its name. **Pros:** ski-in ski-out property; sumptuous rooms; friendly and attentive staff. **Cons:** incredibly pricey; minimum stay during holidays; layout can be confusing. ⊠ *118 Lost Creek La.* ☎ *970/369–0400, 866/530–9466* ⊕ *www.lumierehotels.com* ⇛ *29 suites, 1 house* ⚹ *In-room: safe, kitchen, Wi-Fi. In-hotel: bar, gym, spa, laundry facilities, parking* ¶⊙¶ *Breakfast.*

$$$ ▦ **New Sheridan Hotel.** This century-old Telluride landmark has updated
HOTEL its look with historic black-and-white photos and contemporary furnishings. **Pros:** rooftop hot tubs; accommodating staff; secure ski storage with boot warmers. **Cons:** narrow hallways; noise from the bar can drift upstairs at night. ⊠ *231 W. Colorado Ave.* ☎ *970/728–4351, 800/200–1891* ⊕ *www.newsheridan.com* ⇛ *24 rooms, 2 suites* ⚹ *In-room: safe, Wi-Fi. In-hotel: restaurant, bar, business center* ☾ *Closed mid-Apr.–mid-May and mid-Oct.–mid-Nov.* ¶⊙¶ *No meals.*

NIGHTLIFE AND THE ARTS
THE ARTS

Sheridan Arts Foundation. The Sheridan Arts Foundation is a mentoring program that brings top actors and singers to town to perform alongside budding young artists in the Sheridan Opera House. ⊠ *110 N. Oak St.* ☏ *970/728–6363* ⊕ *www. sheridanoperahouse.com.*

Telluride Repertory Theatre Company. This not-for-profit group performs year-round in various venues. In summer it stages productions in the park. ☏ *970/728–4539* ⊕ *www. telluridetheatre.org.*

NIGHTLIFE

Fly Me to the Moon Saloon. Telluride's favorite spot to catch a band, this saloon has live music—jazz, blues, funk, ska, rock, you name it—most nights. The action gets wild on the spring-loaded dance floor. ⊠ *132 E. Colorado Ave.* ☏ *970/728–6666.*

Last Dollar Saloon. A favorite après-ski and after-hours destination, the Last Dollar (locals know it as the "Buck") has scads of beers, great margaritas, and a jukebox filled with old favorites. It's housed in an authentic Victorian building with original brick walls and high tin ceilings. ⊠ *100 E. Colorado Ave.* ☏ *970/728–4800* ⊕ *www. lastdollarsaloon.com.*

New Sheridan Bar. The century-old bar at the New Sheridan Hotel is a favorite hangout for skiers returning from the slopes and, in summer, for everybody else. There's occasionally live music. ⊠ *New Sheridan Hotel, 231 W. Colorado Ave.* ☏ *970/728–9100* ⊕ *www.newsheridan.com.*

SHOPPING
BOOKS

Between the Covers Bookstore and Cafe. This place is perfect for browsing through the latest releases while sipping a foam-capped cappuccino from the coffee bar at the back of the shop. ⊠ *224 W. Colorado Ave.* ☏ *970/728–4504* ⊕ *www.between-the-covers.com.*

BOUTIQUES

Bounty Hunter. This is the place for leather items, especially boots and vests. It has an astonishing selection of hats, some of them just plain outrageous. ⊠ *226 W. Colorado Ave.* ☏ *970/728–0256* ⊕ *www. shopbountyhunter.com.*

CRAFTS

Hell Bent Leather & Silver. This shop is a fine source for leather goods and sterling silver jewelry, plus Native American objects. ⊠ *215 E. Colorado Ave.* ☏ *970/728–6246.*

TELLURIDE LODGING ALTERNATIVES

Telluride Central Reservations. This branch of the Telluride Tourism Board handles all the properties at Telluride Mountain Village and several more in town. ☏ *970/728–3041, 800/605–2578* ⊕ *www.visittelluride.com.*

Telluride Rentals. This agency handles 60 luxury properties, including private homes and condos. ⊠ *315 Adams Ranch Rd., Mountain Village* ☏ *800/970–7541* ⊕ *www.telluride-rentals.com.*

10

SPORTING GOODS

Further Adventures. Further Adventures will set you up with gear and guides for your whitewater-rafting, mountain-biking, and fly-fishing trip. They also operate as Boot Doctors for winter sports needs. ⊠ *650 Mountain Village Blvd.* ☎ *970/728–8954* ⊕ *www.bootdoctors.com/ further.*

Telluride Sports. Telluride Sports has equipment and clothing for all seasons. ⊠ *150 W. Colorado Ave.* ☎ *970/728–4477, 800/828–7547* ⊕ *www.telluridesports.com.*

RIDGWAY

40 mi from Telluride via Rtes. 62 and 145; 26 mi south of Montrose via U.S. 550.

The 19th-century railroad town of Ridgway has been the setting for some classic Westerns, including *True Grit* (the original John Wayne version) and *How the West Was Won.* Though you'd never know it from the rustic town center, the area is also home to many swank ranches, including one belonging to fashion designer Ralph Lauren.

GETTING HERE AND AROUND

U.S. 550 runs along the eastern side of town, heading north to Montrose and south to Ouray. Route 62 heads right through the middle of town on its way to Telluride. The rest of the main part of town encompasses all of seven blocks, making side travel a breeze.

EXPLORING

Ridgway Railroad Museum. Ridgway is the birthplace of the Rio Grande Southern, the narrow-gauge railroad that connected Durango to Ridgway between 1893 and 1951. The Ridgway Railroad Museum exhibits artifacts from railroading in Ouray County and the surrounding area. ⊠ *U.S. 550 and Hwy. 62* ☎ *970/626–5458* ⊕ *www. ridgwayrailroadmuseum.org* ⊡ *Free* ☉ *June–Sept., daily 9–4; Oct.– May, weekdays 10–3.*

SPORTS AND THE OUTDOORS

BACKCOUNTRY SKIING

San Juan Hut System. Among the better backcountry skiing routes is the San Juan Hut System. It leads toward Telluride along the Sneffels Range. The five huts in the system are about 7 mi apart, and are well equipped with beds, blankets, wood-burning stoves, and cooking stoves. Previous backcountry experience is highly recommended. Reservations are recommended at least two weeks in advance. ⊲ *Box 773, Ridgway 81432* ☎ *970/626–3033* ⊕ *www.sanjuanhuts.com.*

GOLF

Divide Ranch and Club. This semi-private 18-hole, Byron Coker–designed course twists through a maze of high-mesa forest, complete with mountain views and wildlife. It's long and often demanding, but at 8,000 feet your drives might go a little farther and higher than they do at sea level. Course and driving range are open from May to October. Cart rental is $20. ⊠ *151 Divide Ranch Circle* ☎ *970/626–5284* ⊕ *www.eqresorts. com/divide* ⚑ *18 holes. Yards: 7039. Par: 72. Green fee: $69/$89.*

WATER SPORTS

Ridgway State Park. At this peaceful state park, 4 mi north of Ridgway, the 5-mi-long reservoir is stocked with plenty of rainbow trout, as well as the larger and tougher brown trout. Anglers also pull up kokanee salmon and yellow perch. There's a boat ramp, swimming beach, picnic areas, playgrounds, and a campground. ⌖ 28555 U.S. 550 81432 ☎ 970/626–5822 ⊕ www.parks.state.co.us/ridgway ✉ $7.

WHERE TO EAT AND STAY

For expanded hotel reviews, visit Fodors.com.

$$ ✕ **True Grit Cafè.** This local hangout is a shrine to the original 1968
AMERICAN film, portions of which were filmed nearby. The Grit serves standard cowboy cuisine—chili, burgers, and delicious chicken-fried steak—along with Tex-Mex offerings like burritos and tacos. The huge stone fireplace, two-story balcony, and cozy interior would make even the Duke feel at home. ✉ 123 N. Lena Ave. ☎ 970/626–5739 ⊕ www.truegritcafe.com.

$$ ◫ **Chipeta Sun Lodge & Spa.** The dramatic Southwestern-style adobe
HOTEL rooms and suites at Chipeta Sun have rough-hewn log beds, hand-painted Mexican tiles, and stunning views from the decks. **Pros:** unique rooms; on-site restaurant; ideal for outdoor activities. **Cons:** fills up on weekends; limited parking. ✉ 304 S. Lena St. ☎ 970/626–3737, 800/633–5868 ⊕ www.chipeta.com ↪ 25 rooms ⌂ In-room: no a/c, kitchen, no TV, Wi-Fi. In-hotel: restaurant, gym, spa, laundry facilities, some pets allowed ◫ No meals.

OURAY

10 mi south of Ridgway; 23 mi north of Silverton via U.S. 550.

The town of Ouray (pronounced *you-ray*) is nestled in a narrow, steep-walled canyon in the shadow of the San Juan Mountains. It was named for the great Southern Ute chief Ouray, labeled a visionary by the U.S. Army and branded a traitor by his people because he attempted to assimilate the Utes into white society. The former mining town is filled with lavish old hotels, commercial buildings, and residences. More than 25 classic edifices are included in the walking-tour brochure issued by the Ouray County Historical Society. Among the points of interest are the grandiose Wright's Opera House, the Western Hotel, and the St. Elmo Hotel. The town's ultimate glory lies in its surroundings, and it has become an increasingly popular destination for climbers (both the mountain and ice varieties), mountain-bike fanatics, and hikers.

10

GETTING HERE AND AROUND

U.S. 550 runs straight through town and turns into Main Street for the six blocks from 3rd Avenue to 9th Avenue. The Visitors' Information Center and the Hot Springs Park are on the north end of town, and the historic landmark hotel, the Beaumont, is smack in the middle of town between 5th and 6th avenues. The Uncompahgre River runs parallel to Main Street just a couple blocks west of town, and Box Canyon Park is just southwest of Main Street, at the confluence of Canyon Creek and the Uncompahgre River.

ESSENTIALS

Visitor Information Ouray Visitors Center ✉ *1230 Main St.* ☎ *970/325–4746, 800/228–1876* ⊕ *www.ouraycolorado.com.*

EXPLORING

TOP ATTRACTIONS

Box Cañon Falls. One particularly gorgeous jaunt is to Box Cañon Falls, where the turbulent waters of Clear Creek thunder 285 feet down a narrow gorge. A steel suspension bridge and well-marked trails afford breathtaking views. Birders flock to the park, and a visitor center has interpretive displays. ✉ *West end of 3rd Ave. off U.S. 550* ☎ *970/325–7080* ⌨ *$4* ☉ *Daily 8–8.*

Historic Wiesbaden Hot Springs Spa & Lodge. At the source of several of Ouray's famed springs, this European-style spa has a series of subterranean chambers where you can soak in the steamy pools and inhale the pungent vapors. In addition, there's an outdoor pool, also fed by continuously flowing spring water, and a private pool big enough for two to four people. Massages, mud wraps, and other treatments are offered at the spa. This is a strictly no-smoking facility, and they request that anyone who has smoked in the last three months not use the facilities because of potential allergy issues. ✉ *625 5th St.* ☎ *970/325–4347* ⊕ *www.wiesbadenhotsprings.com* ⌨ *$15 for 3 hrs* ☉ *Daily 8 am–9:45 pm.*

Fodor'sChoice ★ **Red Mountain Pass.** Ouray is also the northern end of the Million Dollar Highway, the awesome stretch of U.S. 550 that climbs over Red Mountain Pass (arguably the most spectacular part of the 236-mi San Juan Skyway). As it ascends steeply from Ouray, the road clings to the cliffs hanging over the Uncompahgre River. Guardrails are few, hairpin turns are many, and behemoth RVs seem to take more than their share of road. This priceless road is kept open all winter by heroic plow crews. The road on the Ouray side of the Pass is more dramatic (and intimidating) than on the Silverton side.

WORTH NOTING

Ouray County Museum. This small museum highlights the history of mining, ranching, and railroading in the San Juan Mountains. Mining equipment, railroad paraphernalia, and commercial artifacts are carefully arranged in the former St. Joseph's Hospital, built in 1887. ✉ *420 6th Ave.* ☎ *970/325–4576* ⊕ *www.ouraycountyhistoricalsociety.org* ⌨ *$5* ☉ *Call for hrs.*

Ouray Hot Springs Pool. After a day of hiking, biking, or skiing, hit one of the area's hot springs. The Ouray Hot Springs Pool is brimming with a million gallons of naturally heated water kept between 96°F and 106°F. There's also a fitness center in the bathhouse. ✉ *1220 Main St.* ☎ *970/325–7073* ⊕ *www.ourayhotsprings.com* ⌨ *$12* ☉ *Weekdays noon–9, weekends 11–9.*

SPORTS AND THE OUTDOORS

FOUR-WHEELING

Off-roaders delight in the more than 500 mi of four-wheel-drive roads around Ouray. Popular routes include the Alpine Loop Scenic Byway to the Silverton and Lake City areas, and Imogene Pass to Telluride.

Switzerland of America Tours. If you have the skill and confidence but not the four-wheel-drive vehicle, you can rent one from Switzerland of America Tours. The company also operates guided tours in open-air six-passenger jeeps. Full-day tours cost $60 to $130. ⊠ *226 7th Ave.* ☎ *970/325–4484, 866/990–5337* ⊕ *www.soajeep.com.*

Yankee Boy Basin. About the first 7 mi of the road to Yankee Boy Basin are accessible by regular cars, but it takes a four-wheel drive to reach the heart of this awesome alpine landscape. After leaving Ouray, the route climbs west into a vast basin ringed with soaring summits and carpeted with lavish displays of wildflowers. At 17 mi round-trip, this is one of the region's premier day-trip destinations.

Ouray Ranger District. For information, contact the Ouray Ranger District. ⊠ *2505 S. Townsend Rd.* ☎ *970/240–5300* ⊕ *www.fs.fed.us/ r2/gmug* ⊠ *County Rd. 361.*

ICE CLIMBING

★ **Ouray Ice Park.** Ouray is known in ice-climbing circles for its abundance of frozen waterfalls. The Ouray Ice Festival, held each January, helped to cement the town's reputation as America's ice-climbing mecca. The Ouray Ice Park is the world's first facility dedicated to the sport. In the Uncompahgre Gorge, just south of town, the Ice Park has three climbing areas with more than 40 routes. ⊠ *306 6th Ave.* ☎ *970/325–4288* ⊕ *www.ourayicepark.com.*

Ouray Mountain Sports. This outfitter sells and rents all sorts of alpine equipment, including ice-climbing gear. The staff will also sharpen your ice screws, generally within a day or two. ⊠ *732 Main St.* ☎ *970/325– 4284* ⊕ *www.ouraysports.com.*

NORDIC SKIING

Ouray County Nordic Council. Managed by the Ouray County Nordic Association, Ironton Park is a marked trail system for Nordic skiers and snowshoers. About 9 mi south of town, it has several interconnecting loops that let you spend a day on the trails. Local merchants stock trail maps. ⋔ *Rte. 550 81427* ☎ *970/325–0480* ⊕ *www.ouraytrails.org/nordic.*

WHERE TO EAT

$$ ╳ **Buen Tiempo.** Brick walls and sage-green wainscoting are paired with
MEXICAN   Southwestern-styled cactus-carved benches and brightly painted chairs at this popular cantina. Menu selections include traditional Sonoran entrées (tacos, chiles rellenos, and burritos) along with souped-up options like blue corn and spinach enchiladas and chili-rubbed sirloin. A comprehensive margarita menu adds to the experience. ⊠ *515 Main St.* ☎ *970/325–4544.*

$ ╳ **Ouray Brewery.** This brewpub boasts the town's only rooftop deck,
AMERICAN   and it has great views of the surrounding canyon as well as the goings-on below on Main Street. There are actually three levels, the first two offering a choice between an "intimate pub" or "lively restaurant" experience. The beers—five standards plus a few seasonal offerings—cover the gamut, from so-red-it's-almost-black Katie's Stout to blonde San Juan IPA. A favorite with locals is the Camp Bird Kolsch, a German-style ale named for one of the area's now-deserted mining

10

camps. There's typical pub fare for lunch and dinner. ⊠ *607 Main St.* ☎ *970/325–7388.*

WHERE TO STAY

For expanded hotel reviews, visit Fodors.com.

$$$
HOTEL
Fodor's Choice
★

📷 **Beaumont Hotel and Spa.** No detail has been overlooked at this restored 1887 hotel, a gold-rush-era landmark that has hosted such VIPs as Theodore Roosevelt and Oprah Winfrey. **Pros:** soundproofed rooms mean a quiet stay; good value. **Cons:** rooms aren't overly large; no children under 16. ⊠ *505 Main St.* ☎ *970/325–7000, 888/447–3255* ⊕ *www.beaumonthotel.com* ☞ *5 rooms, 5 junior suites, 2 grand suites* ♿ *In-room: Wi-Fi. In-hotel: restaurant, bar, spa, business center, parking, some age restrictions* ⏸ *No meals.*

$
B&B/INN

📷 **Black Bear Manor Bed & Breakfast.** Tucked away on a quiet side street, this tidy B&B has terrific views of the surrounding San Juan Mountains from its outdoor decks. **Pros:** welcoming hosts; plenty of privacy; generous amenities. **Cons:** not a typical antique-filled B&B; no children under 16. ⊠ *118 6th Ave.* ☎ *970/325–4219, 800/845–7512* ⊕ *www.blackbearmanor.com* ☞ *9 rooms* ♿ *In-room: no a/c, Wi-Fi. In-hotel: some age restrictions* ⏸ *Breakfast.*

$
HOTEL

📷 **Box Canyon Lodge & Hot Springs.** If bathing with the masses at the local hot springs is not your cup of tea, opt for a semi-private plunge at this friendly lodge. **Pros:** proximity to hot springs; welcoming staff; off-the-beaten-path feel. **Cons:** looks dated; no-frills rooms. ⊠ *45 3rd Ave.* ☎ *970/325–4981, 800/327–5080* ⊕ *www.boxcanyonouray.com* ☞ *33 rooms, 6 suites* ♿ *In-room: Wi-Fi* ⏸ *Breakfast.*

$$
B&B/INN

📷 **China Clipper Inn.** Although it was built in the early 1990s, this stately inn fits in perfectly with its Victorian neighbors. **Pros:** beautiful property; small and romantic. **Cons:** minimum stay on some holidays and weekends; can be noisy between rooms. ⊠ *525 2nd St.* ☎ *970/325–0565, 800/315–0565* ⊕ *www.chinaclipperinn.com* ☞ *13 rooms* ♿ *In-room: Wi-Fi. In-hotel: business center, some age restrictions* ⏸ *Breakfast.*

$$
HOTEL

📷 **St. Elmo Hotel.** This 1898 hostelry was originally a haven for "miners down on their luck," or so the story goes. **Pros:** central location; reasonable rates. **Cons:** street side can be noisy; can feel a bit cramped. ⊠ *426 Main St.* ☎ *970/325–4951, 866/243–1502* ⊕ *www.stelmohotel.com* ☞ *7 rooms, 2 suites* ♿ *In-room: no a/c, no TV. In-hotel: restaurant, some age restrictions* ⏸ *Breakfast.*

SHOPPING

Buckskin Booksellers. In the Beaumont Hotel, Buckskin Booksellers has maps and books on local-interest topics like Colorado history, mining, railroading, and ranching, as well as collectibles and Native American items. ⊠ *505 Main St.* ☎ *970/325–4044* ⊕ *www.buckskinbooksellers.com.*

North Moon Gallery. This funky gallery carries irresistible, one-of-a-kind pieces of jewelry, plus paintings and others artworks. ⊠ *505 Main St.* ☏ *970/325–4885.*

Ouray Glassworks & Pottery. This shop sells exquisite handblown glass objects—ornaments, vases, and hummingbird feeders, for example—and pottery mugs, bowls, platters made with a distinctive matte finish, all created by local artists. ⊠ *619 Main St.* ☏ *800/748–9421* ⊕ *www.ourayglassworks.com.*

SILVERTON

23 mi south of Ouray; 48 mi north of Durango via U.S. 550.

Glorious peaks surround Silverton, an old mining community. The town reputedly got its name when a miner exclaimed, "We ain't got much gold but we got a ton of silver!" Silverton is the county seat, as well as the only remaining town, in San Juan County. The last mine here went bust in 1991 (which is recent as such things go), leaving Silverton to boom only in summer, when the Durango & Silverton Narrow Gauge Railroad deposits four trainloads of tourists a day. But the Silverton Mountain ski area has also helped the town to shake off its long slumber, and more businesses are finding it worthwhile to stay open year-round.

Silverton's hardy and spirited populace still commemorates its rowdy past. At 5:30 on certain summer evenings, a gunfight erupts at the corner of Blair and 12th streets. Unsurprisingly, the good guys always win.

The downtown area has been designated a National Historic Landmark District. Be sure to pick up the walking tour brochure that describes—among other things—the most impressive buildings lining Greene Street: Miners' Union Hall, Teller House, the Town Hall, the San Juan County Courthouse (home of the county historical museum), and the Grand Imperial Hotel. These structures have historical significance, but more history was probably made in the raucous red-light district along Blair Street.

GETTING HERE AND AROUND

U.S. 550 N and U.S. 550 S meet at a junction in front of the Silverton Chamber of Commerce and Visitor Center. At the intersection, Greene Street—with the main stores, restaurants, hotels, and the only paved street in town—heads northeast from 6th Street to 15th Street before splitting into Country Road 110 heading to the Silverton Mountain Ski Area to the north and Country Road 2 heading to the Old Hundred Gold Mine and the Mayflower Mill to the east.

DISCOUNTS AND DEALS

Ask at the Silverton Chamber of Commerce about a Heritage Pass, good for savings on admission to the Silverton Jail and Museum, Old Hundred Gold Mine, and Mayflower Mill.

ESSENTIALS

Visitor Information Silverton Chamber of Commerce ⊠ *414 Greene St.* ☏ *970/387–5654, 800/752–4494* ⊕ *www.silvertoncolorado.com.*

10

EXPLORING

Christ of the Mines Shrine. If you look north toward Anvil Mountain, you'll see the Christ of the Mines Shrine, the centerpiece of which is a 12-ton statue of Jesus carved of Italian marble. The shrine was erected in 1959, and has been credited with a handful of miracles over the subsequent years. A moderately strenuous 1-mi hike leads to the shrine, which has memorable views of the surrounding San Juan Mountains. ⊠ *Trailhead at end of 10th St.*

Mayflower Mill. Just a few miles outside of town, the Mayflower Mill (also known as the Shenandoah-Dives Mill) is a beautifully restored landmark with tours that explain how precious gold, silver and other metals were extracted and processed. It's 2 mi northeast of Silverton. ⊠ *135 County Rd. 2* ☎ *970/387–0294* ⊕ *www.silvertonhistoricsociety. org* ✉ *$8* ⊙ *Memorial Day–late Sept.*

Old Hundred Gold Mine. A tram takes you 1,500 feet into the Old Hundred Gold Mine for a tour of one of the area's oldest mining facilities. Old Hundred operated for about a century, from the first strike in 1872 until the last haul in the early 1970s. Temperatures remain at a steady 48°F, so be sure to bring a sweater or a jacket. Guided tours leave every hour on the hour. Your ticket price also covers panning for gold (and silver and semiprecious stones) in the sluice boxes outside the mine. The facility is 5 mi north of Silverton. ⊠ *721 County Rd. 4A* ☎ *970/387–5444, 800/872–3009* ⊕ *www.minetour.com* ✉ *$18* ⊙ *Mid-May–mid-Oct. 5, daily 10–4.*

San Juan County Historical Society Museum. In the old San Juan County Jail, built in 1902 to house criminals as well as the sheriff and his family, this small but impressive museum houses an assortment of mining memorabilia, minerals, and local artifacts. ⊠ *1559 Greene St.* ☎ *970/387–5838* ⊕ *www.silvertonhistoricsociety.org* ✉ *$5* ⊙ *June–mid-Oct., daily 9–5.*

SPORTS AND THE OUTDOORS

DOWNHILL SKIING AND SNOWBOARDING

Kendall Mountain Recreation Area. Run by the town, Kendall Mountain Recreation Area is a single-tow ski center open weekends during ski season, weather permitting. It's not a challenging slope, so it's perfect for beginners. You can also skate, sled, and cross-country ski here. Rentals are available. ⊠ *1 Kendall Mountain Pl.* ☎ *970/387–0182* ⊕ *www. skikendall.com* ✉ *$15.*

Silverton Mountain. About 6 mi north of town, Silverton Mountain is one of the country's simplest yet most innovative ski areas. Open to advanced and expert skiers and boarders only, Silverton Mountain operates one double lift that accesses more than 1,800 acres of never-groomed backcountry steeps. It's the highest ski area in North America, as well as the steepest. The mountain sets a limit of 475 people per day, and most of the time you feel like you have the mountain to yourself. There's no fancy lodge, either—in fact, there's no running water, but you can buy bottled water, along with simple lunches, at the base area. You can rent equipment, including a mandatory avalanche beacon, and other gear. Guided and unguided excursions are available. ⊠ *Off Hwy.*

110 ☎ *970/387–5706* ⊕ *www.silvertonmountain.com* 🖃 *$49–$99*
⊙ *Dec.–Apr., Thurs.–Sun., 9–4.*

FOUR-WHEELING

Silverton provides easy access to such popular four-wheel-drive routes as Ophir Pass to the Telluride side of the San Juans, Stony Pass to the Rio Grande Valley, and Engineer and Cinnamon passes, components of the Alpine Loop. With an all-terrain vehicle you can see some of Colorado's most famous ghost towns, remnants of mining communities, and jaw-dropping scenery. The four-wheeling season is May to mid-October, weather permitting. In winter these unplowed trails are transformed into fabulous snowmobile routes.

Silver Summit RV Park and Jeep Rentals. You can rent a four-wheel-drive vehicle here for about $150 per day. ✉ *640 Mineral St.* ☎ *970/387–0240* ⊕ *www.silversummitrvpark.com.*

ICE-SKATING

Silverton Town Rink. At the Kendall Mountain Recreation Area, the Silverton Town Rink lets you skate for free, weather permitting. Rentals are available. ✉ *Kendall Mountain Recreation Area, 1 Kendall Mountain Pl.* ☎ *970/387–5522.*

NORDIC SKIING

The local snowmobile club grooms nearly 170 mi of cross-country skiing and snowshoeing trails around Silverton, so the route is flat, easy, and safe. Molas Pass, 6 mi south of Silverton on U.S. 550, has a variety of Nordic routes, from easy half-milers in broad valleys to longer, more demanding ascents.

St. Paul Lodge and Hut. This place is an incredible find for anyone enchanted by remote high country. Above 11,000 feet and about a half-hour ski-in from the summit of Red Mountain Pass (between Ouray and Silverton), the St. Paul Lodge (a converted mining camp) and backcountry Hut provide access to above–tree line exploring via telemark or cross-country skis, snowboard, snowshoes, or any combination thereof. The Hut is also available in the summer, when you can reach the property via four-wheel-drive vehicle (or by hiking in). Reservations are essential. ✉ *511 Butte Cir., Durango* ☎ *970/799–0785* ⊕ *www.skistpaul.com* 🖃 *$110* ⊙ *Lodge closed June–Nov.*

10

WHERE TO EAT AND STAY

For expanded hotel reviews, visit Fodors.com.

$$
SOUTHERN

✕ **Handlebars.** As much a museum as an eatery, the restaurant is crammed with mining artifacts, odd antiques, and stuffed animals—including a full-grown elk. Don't pass up the huge platter of baby back ribs basted with the restaurant's own barbecue sauce (bottles of it are also for sale). The hearty menu also includes steaks, hamburgers, chicken, pasta, prime rib, and chicken-fried steak. ✉ *117 E. 13th St.* ☎ *970/387–5395* ⊕ *www.handlebarssilverton.com* ⊙ *Closed Nov.–Apr.*

$
B&B/INN

🖼 **Animas B&B at the Wingate House.** Owner Judy Graham, a landscape artist, adorns the walls of this 1886 inn with her own work and family photos from the Civil War. **Pros:** terrific views; comfortable rooms. **Cons:** lots of stairs; two rooms have a shared bath. ✉ *1045 Snowden St.*

☎ *970/387–5520* ⊕ *www.wingatehouse.com* ➡ *5 rooms, 3 with bath* ☾ *In-room: no a/c, no TV. In-hotel: some pets allowed* ¡◯¡ *Breakfast.*

$ 🖵 **The Wyman Hotel and Inn.** On the National Register of Historic Places,
HOTEL this wonderful red-sandstone building dates from 1902. **Pros:** quiet;
centrally located; updated amenities. **Cons:** stairs are steep; rooms can
feel cramped. ✉ *1371 Greene St.* ☎ *970/387–5372, 800/609–7845*
⊕ *www.thewyman.com* ➡ *17 rooms, 5 suites* ☾ *In-room: no a/c, Wi-Fi*
¡◯¡ *Breakfast.*

NIGHTLIFE AND THE ARTS
THE ARTS
A Theatre Group. Housed in the historic Miners Union Theatre, this
nonprofit group stages productions throughout the year in various
venues around town. ✉ *1069 Greene St.* ☎ *970/387–5337* ⊕ *www.*
atheatregroup.org.

NIGHTLIFE
Silverton Brewery. Check out Silverton Brewery, which serves a nice selection of handcrafted microbrews and a casual menu of brats, hot dogs,
and chili. ✉ *1333 Greene St.* ☎ *970/387–5033.*

SHOPPING
Remember that many of Silverton's retail establishments only operate
in the months when the Durango & Silverton Narrow Gauge Railroad
is operating, May to October.

Blair Street Emporium. This little shop in Silverton's historic Old Town
Square sells carved bears, holiday decorations, and other gifts. ✉ *1147*
Blair St. ☎ *970/387–5323* ⊙ *Closed Nov.–Apr.*

My Favorite Things. This gift shop specializes in all things Victorian,
including home decor, porcelain dolls, antique jewelry, and romantic, lacy wearables. ✉ *1145 Greene St.* ☎ *970/387–5643* ⊕ *www.4my-*
favorite-things.com.

**EN
ROUTE** The section of U.S. 550 between Silverton and Purgatory includes a diz-
zying series of switchbacks as it climbs over Coal Bank Pass and Molas
Pass and past splendid views of the Grand Turks, the Needles Range, and
Crater Lake. This is prime mountain-biking and four-wheeling territory.

MESA COUNTRY

Discover the southern reaches of the San Juan Mountains and Mesa
Verde National Park in the high country of southwestern Colorado,
known as Mesa Country. You can ride the rails on the Durango & Silverton Narrow Gauge Railroad, raft the Animas River, explore 2,000
mi of hiking and biking trails, and ski at the Durango Mountain Resort.

DURANGO

28 mi south of Silverton via U.S. 550; 45 mi east of Cortez; 60 mi west
of Pagosa Springs via U.S. 160.

Wisecracking Will Rogers had this to say about Durango: "It's out of
the way and glad of it." His statement is a bit unfair, considering that

as a railroad town Durango has always been a cultural crossroads and melting pot (as well as a place to raise hell). Laid out at 6,500 feet along the winding Animas River, with the San Juan Mountains as backdrop, the town was founded in 1879 by General William Palmer, president of the all-powerful Denver & Rio Grande Railroad, at a time when nearby Animas City haughtily refused to donate land for a depot. Within a decade, Durango had completely absorbed its rival. The booming town quickly became the region's main metropolis and a gateway to the Southwest.

A walking tour of the historic downtown offers ample proof of Durango's prosperity during the late 19th century, although the northern end of Main Avenue has the usual assortment of cheap motels and fast-food outlets.

North of the U.S. 160 and U.S. 550 junction are two well-known recreational playgrounds: the ravishing golf course and development at the Lodge at Tamarron and Purgatory at Durango Mountain Resort. Purgatory (as everyone still calls this ski area, despite its name change in 2001) is about as down-home as a ski resort can get. The clientele includes cowboys, families, and college students.

GETTING HERE AND AROUND

Durango Transit has regular bus service up and down Main Avenue, as well as to Purgatory during ski season. Durango Transportation will transport you between the airports and the resorts.

Purgatory isn't a proper town, but simply a collection of resorts, restaurants, and ski shops clustered around the ski area on U.S. 550, some 25 mi north of Durango. The mountain is named for the nearby Purgatory Creek, a tributary of the River of Lost Souls.

ESSENTIALS

Transportation Contacts Durango Transit ☎ 970/259-5438 ⊕ www.durangotransit.com. **Durango Transportation** ☎ 970/259–4818 ⊕ www.durangotransportation.net.

Visitor Information Durango Area Tourism Office and Visitor Center ✉ 111 S. Camino del Rio ☎ 970/247–3500, 800/525–8855 ⊕ www.durango.org.

10

EXPLORING

3rd Avenue National Historic District. This prestigious residential area (known simply as "The Boulevard") lies two blocks east of Main Avenue and contains 98 buildings built between 1875 and 1949. It's best known for its Victorian residences, ranging from the imposing mansions built by railroad barons to more modest homes of well-to-do merchants. ✉ *E. 3rd Ave. between 5th St. and 15th St.*

🕐 **Durango & Silverton Narrow Gauge Railroad.** The most entertaining way to
Fodor'sChoice relive the halcyon days of the Old West is to take a ride on the Durango
★ & Silverton Narrow Gauge Railroad, a nine-hour round-trip journey along the 45-mi railway to Silverton. You'll travel in comfort in lovingly restored coaches or in the open-air cars called gondolas as you listen to the train's shrill whistle as it chugs along. On the way, you get a good look at the Animas Valley, which in some parts is broad and green and in others narrow and rimmed with rock. The train runs daily from early-May to

mid-October. A shorter excursion—to Cascade Canyon, 26 mi away—in heated coaches is available in winter.

Durango Depot. This lovingly restored building, originally constructed in 1882, sits adjacent to the Durango & Silverton Narrow Gauge Railroad Museum. ⊠ *479 Main Ave.* ⊠ *479 Main Ave.* ☎ *970/ 247–2733, 888/872–4607* ⊕ *www. durangotrain.com* ✆ *$83–$179.*

National Historic District. The intersection of 13th Avenue and Main Avenue (locals also refer to it as Main Street) marks the northern edge of Durango's Main Avenue National Historic District. Old-fashioned streetlamps line the streets, casting

WORD OF MOUTH

"We booked the Alamosa Parlor Car for our train journey. To us, it was a real upgrade from the regular bus-style small seats in the other compartments. The best part was being able to get up and walk around and also being able to go out the back door of the train (since this was like the caboose), where we'd stand, taking pictures from side to side, unobstructed by other people's heads or thru a window."
—swisshiker

a warm glow on the elegant Victorians filled with upscale galleries, restaurants, and the occasional factory outlet store. Dating from 1887, the Strater Hotel is a reminder of the time when this town was a stop for many people headed west. ⊠ *Main Ave. between 13th St. and 12th St.*

Trimble Spa and Natural Hot Springs. About 5 mi north of Durango, this is a great place to soak your aching bones after some hiking or skiing. The complex includes an Olympic-size swimming pool (open May through October) and two natural mineral pools ranging from 83°F to 107°F (open year-round). Massage and spa treatments are also available. ⊠ *6475 County Rd. 205* ☎ *970/247–0212* ⊕ *www. trimblehotsprings.com* ✆ *$15* ⊗ *Mid-May–mid-Sept., Sun.–Wed. 8–10, Thurs. 8–9, Fri. and Sat. 8–1; late Sept.–early May, Sun.–Thurs. 10–9, Fri. and Sat. 10–10.*

DOWNHILL SKIING AND SNOWBOARDING

★ **Purgatory at Durango Mountain Resort.** Formerly known simply as Purgatory, this ski resort 27 mi north of Durango has plenty of intermediate runs and glade and tree skiing, but what's unique about it is its stepped terrain: lots of humps and dips and steep pitches followed by virtual flats. A great powder day on the mountain's back side will convince anyone that Purgatory isn't just "Pleasant Ridge," as it's sometimes known in the bigger resorts of Crested Butte and Telluride. The truth is that Purgatory is just plain fun, and return visitors like it that way. The ski area is perfect for families and those who are open to other diversions, such as snowshoeing, cross-country skiing, and snowmobiling. ⊠ *1 Skier Pl.* ☎ *970/247–9000, 800/982–6103* ⊕ *www. durangomountainresort.com* ⊗ *Late Nov.–early Apr., daily 9–4.*

FACILITIES 2,029-foot vertical drop; 1,360 skiable acres; 20% beginner, 45% intermediate, 35% advanced or expert; 1 high-speed 6-passenger chair, 1 high-speed quad chair, 4 triple chairs, 3 double chairs, and 1 magic carpet.

LESSONS AND
PROGRAMS

Adult Adventure School. On the second level of the Village Center, the Adult Ski and Ride School runs full-day and half-day group lessons during the season ranging from $100 to $120. A "First-Timer" package (lesson, equipment rental, and lift ticket) is $105. The school also offers private lessons and specialty clinics for telemark and bump skiers of all levels. ✉ *Village Center* ☎ *970/385–2149.*

Kids Mountain Adventure. Getting kids onto the slopes is a cinch at the Kids Ski and Ride School, which offers programs for skiers ages 4 to 12 and snowboarders ages 5 to 12. A full-day package, which includes lunch, a lesson, equipment rental, and a lift ticket, costs $115. A half-day package is $90. Classes are on the second floors of the Village Center. ✉ *Village Center* ☎ *970/385–2149.*

San Juan Ski Company. Out-of-bounds types can explore 35,000 acres of untamed wilderness with the San Juan Ski Company. One day of guided skiing or riding, including safety gear, is $250. The company will rent you some fat powder skis for $28 a day. Full- and half-day clinics on backcountry skiing, powder skiing, steep skiing, and avalanche safety are available. ☎ *800/208–1780* ⊕ *www.sanjuanski.com.*

LIFT TICKETS

The at-the-window rates are $69 to $75 for a one-day lift ticket. A First Timer package is a good deal for beginner skiers, as it combines a full-day lesson with a lift ticket and equipment rental. The cost is $105 to $115.

RENTALS

Bubba's Boards. This is Durango Mountain Resort's full-service snowboard shop, with top-name rentals from Never Summer, Burton, and Gnu. It also offers expert tuning and sells clothing and other essentials. ✉ *1 Skier Pl.* ☎ *970/259–7377* ☼ *Daily 8–6.*

Expert Edge. This shop at the base village rents top-of-the-line skis and boots from K2, Salomon, Dynastar, Volkl, Nordica, Dolomite, and Rossignol. Expert Edge also does custom boot fitting, ski tuning, and equipment repair, and has Atlas snowshoes for sale and rent. ✉ *Village Center* ☎ *970/385–2181* ☼ *Daily 8–5.*

Purgatory Rentals. This base-area shop has skis, boots, and poles, plus snowboards, helmets, and other equipment for kids and adults. You should make reservations at least four days in advance if you'll be renting during the busy holiday periods. ✉ *1 Skier Pl.* ☎ *970/385–2182.*

OTHER SPORTS AND THE OUTDOORS

San Juan Public Lands Center. Stop at this office for information on hiking, fishing, and camping, as well as cross-country skiing, snowshoeing, and snowmobiling in the San Juan Public Lands. The 2½ million acres of land includes three designated wilderness areas and other federal lands in southwestern Colorado. ✉ *15 Burnett Ct.* ☎ *970/247–4874* ☼ *Apr.–mid-Dec., weekdays 8–5; late-Dec.–Mar., weekdays 8–4:40.*

BICYCLING

With a healthy college population and a generally mild climate, Durango is extremely bike friendly and a popular destination for single-track enthusiasts. Many locals consider bikes to be their main form of transportation. The bike lobby is active, the trail system is well developed, and mountain biking is a particularly popular recreational activity.

10

Animas River Trail. This 7-mi trail parallels the river from Animas City Park south to Dallabretta Park. It's the main artery, linking up with several of the town's other trail systems.

Hermosa Creek Trail. This singletrack trail travels roughly 19 mi from Purgatory at Durango Mountain Resort to the town of Hermosa. It's an intermediate-to-difficult ride with a couple of steep spots and switchbacks along with mellow rolls through open meadows and towering aspen and pine forests. The trail hugs the steep riverbank at a few places and there are a few creek crossings, so you shouldn't try it too early in the season, while the snow is still melting (the water can be waist-high in the spring and early summer). ⊠ *Trailhead 2 mi from Purgatory's upper parking lots.*

Iron Horse Bicycle Classic. Every Memorial Day weekend, the Iron Horse Bicycle Classic pits cyclists against the steam engine of the Durango and Silverton Narrow Gauge Railroad. The 47-mi course roughly parallels the tracks from Durango to Silverton (although the train actually follows a shorter, easier route). The event, one of the biggest bike races in the U.S., draws more than 2,000 competitors. ⊠ *College Ave. and Camino del Rio* ☎ *970/259–4621* ⊕ *www.ironhorsebicycleclassic.com.*

TOURS AND EXPEDITIONS

Mountain Bike Specialists. Although everybody in town seems to be an expert, the staff at this shop can rent you a bike, help arrange a tour, or just give you directions to the trail of your dreams. It also does expert repairs. ⊠ *949 Main Ave.* ☎ *970/247–4066* ⊕ *www.mountainbikespecialists.com* ⊘ *Mon.–Sat. 9–5:30.*

NEED A BREAK?

Jean-Pierre Bakery and Café. For a little taste of France, stop by this cheery café in a 19th-century brick building in the historic downtown district. Try the fresh-baked breads, pastries, croissants, or the specialty, butter galettes impressed with the image of the Silverton and Durango Railroad. The Jean-Pierre also has a wine bar in the back. ⊠ *601 Main Ave.* ☎ *970/247–7700* ⊕ *www.jeanpierrebakery.com.*

FISHING

Duranglers. In business since 1983, Duranglers sells rods, reels, flies, and other equipment, gives fly-fishing lessons, and runs guided trips to top trout-fishing spots in the area, including the San Juan, Animas, Dolores, Piedras, and Los Pinos rivers. ⊠ *923 Main Ave.* ☎ *970/385–4081* ⊕ *www.duranglers.com.*

GOLF

Dalton Ranch Golf Club. About 6 mi north of Durango, Dalton Ranch is an 18-hole championship course with inspiring views of the Animas River Valley and surrounding San Juans. Carts cost $14 per person for 18 holes. The Swing, the clubhouse's full-service restaurant and bar, is a popular hangout for golfers and locals who like watching the resident elk herd take its afternoon stroll. The golf season is early April to late October, weather permitting. ⊠ *589 County Rd. 252, off U.S. 550* ☎ *970/247–8774* ⊕ *www.daltonranch.com* ⚐ *Reservations essential* ⛳ *18 holes. Yards: 6934/5539. Par: 72/72. Green fee: $59/$89.*

Hillcrest Golf Course. Hillcrest is an 18-hole public course perched on a mesa near the campus of Fort Lewis College. Carts are $13 for 18 holes. The course is open from February to December, weather permitting. ⊠ *2300 Rim Dr.* ☎ *970/247–1499* ⊕ *www.golfhillcrest.com* ⤳ *Reservations essential* ⅄ *18 holes. Yards: 6838/5252. Par: 71/71. Green fee: $36.*

HIKING

Hiking trails are everywhere in and around Durango. Many trailheads at the edges of town lead to backcountry settings, and the San Juan Forest has plenty of mind-boggling walks and trails for those with the urge to explore.

Animas View Overlook Trail. If you're pressed for time (but still want spectacular views), try the 0.7-mi Animas View Overlook Trail. It takes you past signs explaining local geology, flora, and fauna before bringing you to a precipice with an unparalled view of the valley and the surrounding Needle Mountains. It's the only wheelchair-accessible trail in the area. ⊠ *Trailhead at Forest Rd. 171, milepost 8.*

The **Lion's Den Trail** hooks up with the **Chapman Hill Trail** west of Fort Lewis College for a nice moderate hike, climbing switchbacks that take you away from town and hook up with the **Rim Trail.**

Fodor's Choice
★

Colorado Trail. Starting a few miles northwest of Durango, the Colorado Trail covers about 500 mi on its way to Denver. You're not obliged to go that far, of course. Just a few miles in and out will give you a taste of this epic trail, which winds through mountain ranges and high passes and some of the most amazing mountain scenery around. ⊠ *Trailhead off County Rd. 204* ⊕ *www.coloradotrail.org.*

Trails2000. Before you go, check the local organization Trails2000 for directions, information, and news about hiking in and around Durango. ⊕ *www.trails2000.org.*

HORSEBACK RIDING

Rapp Corral. At the entrance to Haviland Lake, about 20 mi north of town, Rapp Corrall offers a variety of trail rides into San Juan National Forest. Trips range from one-, two-, or three-hour jaunts to daylong adventures to Hermosa Cliffs or the above-timberline trails on Engineer Mountain. In the winter, you can take a sleigh ride. ⊠ *51 Haviland Lake Rd.* ☎ *970/247–8454.*

RAFTING

Durango Rivertrippers. This outfitter runs two- and four-hour trips down the Animas River, as well as one- to six-day wilderness expeditions on the Dolores River. You can up your adrenaline output by swapping the raft for an inflatable kayak on any of the Animas River trips. ⊠ *720 Main Ave.* ☎ *970/259–0289* ⊕ *www.durangorivertrippers.com.*

ROCK-CLIMBING

East Animas. You'll find some of the best crack and face climbing at East Animas, just a few miles east of town. Don't miss the "Watch Crystal" route, a favorite with the locals. East Animas is off County Road 250, about 2 mi east of U.S. 550. The parking area is on the east side of the road. ⊠ *Off County Rd. 250, 2 mi east of U.S. 550.*

10

San Juan National Forest. There are plenty of opportunities for climbing in the Columbine Ranger District of the San Juan National Forest, just outside of Durango. Some of the more popular spots are Julia's Spire, Golf Wall, and Fume Wall. ⊠ *15 Burnett Ct.* ☎ *970/247–4874* ⊕ *www. fs.usda.gov/sanjuan.*

X-Rock. Just north of town, X-Rock offers a little bit of everything—slag, crack climbs, bouldering—for novice and intermediate climbers. It's also a great place to learn (or just brush up on) basic climbing skills. One look at the distinctive natural cracks that cross its face will tell you how it got its name. ⊠ *Off U.S. 550, just north of 32nd St.*

TOURS AND EXPEDITIONS

SouthWest Adventure Guides. For classes and guided trips in some of the area's most beautiful and challenging crags, talk to Southwest Adventure Guides. Courses run from March through November and cover the basics (beginning climbing techniques, belaying, and rappelling) as well as specifics such as rock rescue and desert crack climbing. Trips run from one to five days. ⊠ *1111 Camino del Rio, Suite 105* ☎ *970/259–0370* ⊕ *www.mtnguide.net.*

SNOWMOBILING

Snowmobile Adventures. With access to more than 75 mi of trails traversing mountain passes, old stagecoach roads, and mining sites, Snowmobile Adventures leads one- to four-hour tours from base area of Purgatory at Durango Mountain Resort. Rides are available daily during ski season between 9 and 5. ⊠ *Village Center* ☎ *970/385–2141.*

WHERE TO EAT

$
AMERICAN

✕ **Brickhouse Cafe and Coffee Bar.** This popular little place looks like a bed-and-breakfast—it's a nicely restored Victorian house with a picture-perfect lawn and a small patio outside—but it's really a restaurant that takes breakfast seriously. You can't miss with the malted buttermilk waffles, pigs in a blanket, or huevos rancheros—or the big burgers at lunch. ⊠ *1849 Main Ave.* ☎ *970/247–3760* ⊕ *www.brickhousecafe.com* ⊗ *No dinner. Closed Mon.*

$$
AMERICAN

✕ **Carver Brewing Company.** The "Brews Brothers," Bill and Jim Carver, have about eight beers on tap at any given time, including such flavors as Raspberry Wheat Ale, Jackrabbit Pale Ale, and Colorado Trail Nut Brown Ale. If you're hungry, try one of the signature bread bowls filled with chili, soup, or chicken stew. There's a patio out back where you can soak up the sun. From breakfast to the wee hours, the place is always hopping. ⊠ *1022 Main Ave.* ☎ *970/259–2545* ⊕ *www.carverbrewing. com* ♣ *Reservations not accepted.*

$$$
MEDITERRANEAN

✕ **Cyprus Cafe.** In warm weather you can sit on the patio to enjoy the fresh mountain air, and the rest of the year you'll have to cozy up to your fellow diners in the tiny Cyprus Cafe, housed in a quaint Victorian just off Main Avenue. Mediterranean food receives the upscale treatment: try the salmon baked with goat cheese and olive-caper tapenade, or the risotto with walnuts and shaved manchego. The wine list is small, eclectic, and reasonably priced. Lunch is also interesting, with curried lamb and mushroom empanadas or phyllo chicken pot pie. ⊠ *725 E. 2nd Ave.* ☎ *970/385–6884* ⊕ *www.cypruscafe.com.*

$$$
JAPANESE
✕ **East by Southwest.** Asian food gets a bit of a Latin treatment in this snazzy but comfortable space. The menu has a strong Japanese bent, with sushi and sashimi, tempura, and other traditional dishes elegantly presented and layered with complementary flavors. Also among the favorites are the steaks, including free-range Black Angus beef. The sake, beer, and wine selections are well varied, and the tea and tonic bar is fun, too. ✉ *160 E. College Dr.* ☎ *970/247–5533* ⊕ *eastbysouthwest. com* ⊙ *No lunch Sun.*

$$
MODERN
AMERICAN
✕ **Ken & Sue's.** Plates are big and the prices are reasonable at Ken & Sue's, one of Durango's favorite restaurants. Locals are wild for the artfully prepared contemporary cuisine, served in an open and airy space. Try the pistachio–crusted grouper with vanilla-rum butter, or Aunt Lydia's meatloaf with red-wine gravy and mashed potatoes. ✉ *636 Main Ave.* ☎ *970/385–1810* ⊕ *www.kenandsues.com* ⊙ *No lunch weekends.*

$$
PIZZA
✕ **Olde Schoolhouse Cafe & Saloon.** The pizza and calzones are made with homemade dough and fresh ingredients, and the local brew is on tap in this funky building near the ski area (and worlds away from its scholarly roots). All that, plus the dart board, pool table, and old shuffleboard, make this a favorite local hangout. ✉ *46778 Hwy. 550* ☎ *970/259–2257* ⊙ *No lunch weekdays.*

$
AMERICAN
✕ **Olde Tymer's Cafe.** If you're looking for the locals, look no farther than Olde Tymer's Cafe—known in these parts as OTC—a bustling café and bar in a beautiful old building on Main Avenue with an inviting patio in the back. The hamburger is a huge specimen on a fat, fresh bun, and the salads and sandwiches are piled high. There's a different special every night—burgers, enchiladas, and the like—and a respectable roster of beers on tap, including local Durango brews. ✉ *1000 Main Ave.* ☎ *970/259–2990* ⊕ *www.otcdgo.com.*

$$$$
STEAKHOUSE
✕ **Ore House.** Durango is a meat-and-potatoes kind of town, and the Ore House is Durango's idea of a steak house. The aroma of beef smacks you in the face as you walk past, but there are also chicken and seafood dishes available. This local favorite serves enormous slabs of aged Angus that are hand cut daily. For a special occasion try the chateaubriand for two ($64). ✉ *147 E. College Dr.* ☎ *970/247–5707* ⊕ *www.orehouserestaurant.com.*

$$$$
SEAFOOD
✕ **Red Snapper.** If you're in the mood for fresh fish head to Red Snapper, Durango's best seafood spot. There are three different versions of the signature dish, as well as other fish, shellfish, and "landfood" dishes (try the one-pound prime rib or, for smaller appetites and budgets, the creamy chicken diablo). The salad bar is enormous, and a good value at $11. It features a few main-course options and comes with potatoes, wild rice, or soup. Reservations are recommended. ✉ *144 E. 9th St.* ☎ *970/259–3417* ⊕ *www.redsnapperdurango.com* ⊙ *No lunch weekends.*

$$$$
STEAKHOUSE
★
✕ **Sow's Ear.** This airy eatery in Silverpick Lodge is known for providing "the best steaks on the mountain," which it does with aplomb. There are no pedestrian porterhouse or strip steaks here, just buttery rib eye (with a rub of smoked sea salt or blackened with a lime-coriander butter) and filet (served with peppercorns or grilled with mushrooms and wine). There are several delicious seafood options, and those with

10

smaller appetites will appreciate the assortment of equally imaginative "small plates." Reservations are recommended. ⊠ *48475 U.S. 550* ☎ *970/247–3527* ⊕ *www.sowseardurango.com* ☾ *No lunch.*

WHERE TO STAY

For expanded hotel reviews, visit Fodors.com.

$$
B&B/INN
Apple Orchard Inn. About 8 mi from downtown Durango, this little B&B sits on five acres in the lush Animas Valley. **Pros:** inspiring views; peaceful and quiet setting; cottages are intimate and romantic. **Cons:** no dinner on-site; several miles from town; rooms are all upstairs (no elevator). ⊠ *7758 County Rd. 203* ☎ *970/247–0751, 800/426–0751* ⊕ *www.appleorchardinn.com* ⇄ *4 rooms, 6 cottages* ⟳ *In-room: no a/c* ⦿*Breakfast.*

¢
HOTEL
Durango Quality Inn. This is one of the better budget properties along Durango's strip: it's reliable, comfortable, and has sizable rooms. **Pros:** spacious rooms; reasonable rates. **Cons:** on busy street; away from historic downtown area. ⊠ *2930 N. Main Ave.* ☎ *970/259–5373, 888/424–6423* ⊕ *www.qualityinn.com* ⇄ *48 rooms* ⟳ *In-room: Wi-Fi. In-hotel: pool, some pets allowed* ⦿*Breakfast.*

$$
HOTEL
General Palmer Hotel. Named after William Jackson Palmer, owner of the Denver & Rio Grande Railroad, the General Palmer Hotel is a faithfully restored historic property with a clean, bright look. **Pros:** nicely restored lodging; rooms are quiet; free off-street parking. **Cons:** no restaurant or bar; elevator is claustrophobic; pricey in season. ⊠ *567 Main Ave.* ☎ *970/247–4747, 800/523–3358* ⊕ *generalpalmer.com* ⇄ *39 rooms, 4 suites* ⟳ *In-room: Wi-Fi* ⦿*Breakfast.*

$$
HOTEL
Purgatory Village Hotel at Durango Mountain Resort. This comfortable slope-side hotel and condo complex has generously proportioned rooms and suites decorated with contemporary furnishings. **Pros:** slope-side location; good restaurants; reasonable price considering location. **Cons:** can be chaotic during ski season; unless you're skiing, it's far from the attractions. ⊠ *Durango Mountain Resort, 24 Sheol St.* ☎ *970/385–2100, 800/982–6103* ⊕ *www.durangomountainresort.com* ⇄ *133 rooms* ⟳ *In-room: no a/c, kitchen. In-hotel: restaurant, bar, pool, business center* ⦿ *No meals.*

$$
HOTEL
★
Rochester Hotel. The recently renovated Rochester Hotel is funky yet chic, with marquee-lighted movie posters from Hollywood Westerns lining the airy hallways. **Pros:** free guest parking; large rooms; free use of cruiser bikes in town. **Cons:** can be noisy. ⊠ *726 E. 2nd Ave.* ☎ *970/385–1920* ⊕ *www.rochesterhotel.com* ⇄ *25 rooms* ⟳ *In-room: Wi-Fi. In-hotel: some pets allowed* ⦿*Breakfast.*

$$$
HOTEL
Fodor's Choice
★
Strater Hotel. Still the hottest spot in town, this grande dame opened for business in 1887. **Pros:** right in the thick of things; genuine Old West feel. **Cons:** no off-street parking; when the bar gets going, rooms above it get no peace. ⊠ *699 Main Ave.* ☎ *970/247–4431, 800/247–4431* ⊕ *www.strater.com* ⇄ *93 rooms* ⟳ *In-room: Internet, Wi-Fi. In-hotel: restaurant, bar* ⦿*Breakfast.*

$$$
RESORT
☾
Wilderness Trails Ranch. It's only an hour drive from Durango, but this family-owned and -operated guest ranch in the Upper Pine River Valley might as well be a lifetime away. **Pros:** friendly owners; diverse activities; gorgeous setting. **Cons:** all-inclusive packages are pricey;

minimum stay required. ✉ 23486 County Rd. 501, Bayfield ☎ 970/ 247–0722, 800/527–2624 ⊕ www. wildernesstrails.com ➷ 10 cabins ♿ In-room: no TV. In-hotel: bar, pool, children's programs ⊘ Closed Oct.–late May ❑ All meals.

NIGHTLIFE AND THE ARTS
THE ARTS
Diamond Circle Melodrama. This group stages rip-roaring productions, staged in the classic Victorian music-hall style, all summer long in the historic Henry Slater Theater. ✉ 699 Main Ave. ☎ 970/375-7160 ⊕ www.durangomelodrama.com ⊘ Closed late Sept.–early June.

> **PURGATORY LODGING ALTERNATIVES**
>
> **Cascade Village.** There's a range of rental units at Cascade Village, about 1½ mi north of the ski area. All have one to three bedrooms. ✉ 50827 U.S. 550, Purgatory ☎ 970/259-3500, 800/648-9677 ⊕ www.cascadevillage.com ➷ 19 units.

Durango Lively Arts Co. You can see stage productions as well as visual arts exhibits, concerts, and films at the Durango Arts Center. Its resident performing groups include Durango Dot Comedy, the Durango Performing Arts Company, the San Juan Symphony, and the Durango Independent Film Festival. ✉ 802 2nd Ave. ☎ 970/259–2606 ⊕ www.durangoarts.org ⊘ The gallery and gallery shop are open Tues.–Sat., 10–5.

Fort Lewis College Community Concert Hall. This 600-seat auditorium on the campus of Fort Lewis College hosts a variety of local, regional, and touring performers. The theater operates an in-town ticketing office at 707½ Main Ave.

Durango Shakespeare Festival. The college's outdoor amphitheater is the setting for the Durango Shakespeare Festival, held each summer. ☎ 970/247–7089 ⊕ www.theatre.fortlewis.edu ✉ Fort Lewis College, 100 Rim Dr. ☎ 970/247–7657 ⊕ www.durangoconcerts.com.

BARS AND CLUBS
Diamond Belle Saloon. Awash in flocked wallpaper and lace, the Diamond Belle Saloon is dominated by a gilt-and-mahogany bar. With its primo location—on the ground floor of the historic Strater Hotel—and a staff of ragtime piano players and waitresses dressed as saloon girls, the Diamond Belle can really pack them in. ✉ 699 Main Ave. ☎ 970/247–4431 ⊕ www.diamondbelle.com.

Lady Falconburgh's Barley Exchange. A popular spot with locals and tourists alike, Lady Falconburgh's Barley Exchange has 100 different beers, 38 of them on tap. The restaurant serves burgers and sandwiches along with ribs and steak. ✉ 640 Main Ave. ☎ 970/382–9664 ⊕ www. ladyfalconburgh.biz.

Ska Brewery & Tasting Room. Beer fans shouldn't miss Ska Brewing, a home-grown business that boasts a two-floor "tasting room" with 12 taps. Although Ska is known for its many fine craft brews, including True Blonde Ale, Mexican Logger, and Pinstripe Red Ale, there's still a laid-back, garage-band feel to the place. ✉ 255 Girard St. ☎ 970/247–5792 ⊕ www.skabrewing.com ⊘ Closed Sun.

10

CASINOS

Sky Ute Casino & Lodge. About 23 mi southeast of Durango, the Southern Ute tribe operates this 45,000-square-foot facility, with hundreds of slot machines and tables for blackjack, poker, roulette, and craps. ⊠ *14824 Hwy. 172 N, Ignacio* ☎ *970/563–7777, 888/842–4180* ⊕ *www.skyutecasino.com.*

DINNER SHOWS

☾ **Bar D Chuckwagon.** This old-style-cowboy venue, about 10 mi from Durango, serves steaks, barbecued beef and chicken, and biscuits under the stars every evening. After supper, the Bar D Wranglers entertain the crowd with guitar music, singing, and corny comedy. Reservations are required. ⊠ *8080 County Rd. 250* ☎ *970/247–5753, 888/800–5753* ⊕ *www.bardchuckwagon.com* ⊘ *Closed Labor Day–Memorial Day.*

SHOPPING

FOOD

Honeyville. Honeyville, about 10 mi north of Durango, sells honey, jams, jellies (try the wild chokecherry), syrups, sauces, and other goodies. You can watch the bees go about their work in glass hives and listen to a lecture by a fully garbed beekeeper. ⊠ *33633 U.S. 550* ☎ *800/676–7690* ⊕ *www.honeyvillecolorado.com.*

BOOKS

Maria's Bookshop. This well-stocked general-interest shop specializes in regional literature and nonfiction. ⊠ *960 Main Ave.* ☎ *970/247–1438* ⊕ *www.mariasbookshop.com.*

BOUTIQUES

Appaloosa Trading Co. Your best source for all things leather, Appaloosa Trading Co. stocks everything from jackets and purses to boots and canteens. The dog collars, fitted with silver coins, are especially nice, and the leather home decor items are charming. ⊠ *750 Main Ave.* ☎ *970/385–1722* ⊕ *www.appaloosadurango.com.*

GIFTS

Artesanos Design Collection. The selection of furniture, rugs, and other handcrafted goods from Mexico and elsewhere is remarkable. Look for tables and beds made from hand-carved wood, copper and iron lighting fixtures, pottery and ceramics, and glassware. ⊠ *700 E. 2nd Ave.* ☎ *970/259–5755* ⊕ *www.artesanosdesign.com.*

Dietz Market. This gift shop carries specialty foods (like local tortilla chips, honey, and coffee), plus ceramics, candles, and other items celebrating the region. ⊠ *26345 U.S. 160* ☎ *970/259–5811* ⊕ *www.dietzmarket.com.*

Toh-Atin Gallery. Recognized as one of the region's best Native American galleries, Toh-Atin specializes in Navajo rugs and weavings. There's also a wide range of paintings and prints, pottery, baskets, and jewelry made by the artisans of many Southwestern tribes. ⊠ *145 W. 9th St.* ☎ *970/247–8277* ⊕ *www.toh-atin.com.*

PAGOSA SPRINGS

60 mi east of Durango via U.S. 160; 165 mi south of Gunnison via Hwy. 114, U.S. 285, and U.S. 160.

Although not a large town, Pagosa Springs has become a major center for outdoor sports. Hiking, biking, and cross-country skiing opportunities abound here, and there's excellent downhill skiing and snowboarding at the nearby Wolf Creek ski area.

GETTING HERE AND AROUND

Highway 160 turns into Pagosa Street when it enters the town limits and serves as the main drag, with the majority of restaurants, shops, and hotels. The town is 10 blocks long, and the other main thoroughfare, Lewis Avenue, runs parallel to Pagosa Street from 1st Street to 5th Street.

ESSENTIALS

Visitor Information Pagosa Springs Area Visitor Center ✉ *402 San Juan St.* ☎ *970/264–2360, 800/252–2204* ⊕ *www.visitpagosasprings.com.* **Wolf Creek Snow Report** ☎ *800/754–9653.*

EXPLORING

The Springs Resort. With 21 soaking tubs filled with warm, mineral-rich water, the Springs Resort is a great place to relax. There are 23 outdoor pools (including a large, cool-water swimming pool and a fresh-water whirlpool), plus a Mediterranean-style bathhouse and a full-service spa. ✉ *165 Hot Springs Blvd.* ☎ *800/225–0934, 970/264–4168* ⊕ *pagosahotsprings.com* ⊠ *$20* ⊙ *June–early Sept., daily 7 am–1 am; mid-Sept.– May, Sun.–Thurs. 7 am–11 pm, Fri. and Sat. 7 am–1 am.*

DOWNHILL SKIING AND SNOWBOARDING

Wolf Creek Ski Area. With more than 450 average inches of snow annually, Wolf Creek Ski Area is Colorado's best-kept secret. The trails accommodate all ability levels and traverse every kind of terrain, from wide-open bowls to steep glades, with commanding views of remote valleys and towering peaks. Because there are no slopeside accommodations, Wolf Creek has a reputation as a laid-back place for those with an aversion to the long lift lines and the other hassles of faster-paced, better-known ski areas.

At 2 mi, the longest run at Wolf Creek is Navajo Trail. Beginners can start on the Raven chairlift to the Snow Shoe or the Kelly Boyce Trail; both hook up with the Bunny Hop back down the hill.

The best area for advanced skiers stretches back to Horseshoe Bowl from the Waterfall area, serviced by the Alberta lift. The more intrepid will want to climb the Knife Ridge Staircase to the more-demanding Knife Ridge Chutes. Just below is the groomed Sympatico, which runs down a gentler ridge and through dense forest below the Alberta lift. ✉ *U.S. 160* ☎ *970/264–5639* ⊕ *www.wolfcreekski.com* ⊙ *Early Nov.– mid-Apr., daily 8:30–4.*

FACILITIES 1,604-foot vertical drop; 1,600 skiable acres; 20% beginner, 35% intermediate, 25% advanced, 20% expert; 1 detachable quad, 1 fixed quad, 2 triples, 1 double, 1 surface lift, 1 magic carpet.

LESSONS AND PROGRAMS **Wolf Creek Ski School.** Group lessons are a good bet here—they're $40 for two hours and $60 for four hours. Beginner packages are $54, and

10

private one-hour lessons are $67. Children over 4 can join the Wolf Pups program, which includes lift tickets and lunch. Kids ages 9 to 12 can join the Hot Shots program, which takes both skiers and boarders. ⊠ *Wolf Creek Ski Area* ✆ *P.O. Box 2800 81147* ☎ *970/264–5639.*

LIFT TICKETS   The walk-up rate is $54 for a full day, $42 for a half day, $159 for three consecutive days.

RENTALS   **Wolf Creek Ski Rental,** in the Sports Center Building across from the ticket office, rents skis and boards. Adult sets (skis, boots, poles) are $15 a day. Snowboards are $27 with or without boots; boot rentals are $11.

OTHER SPORTS AND THE OUTDOORS

GOLF

Pagosa Springs Golf Club. The 27 championship holes here can be played in three combinations, essentially creating three different 18-hole courses. A bonus is the gorgeous mountain scenery. The regular season runs from June to mid-September. Cart rental is $15 and club rental is $30 for 18 holes. Reservations are recommended during the regular season. ⊠ *1 Pine Club Pl.* ☎ *970/731–4755* ⊕ *www.golfpagosa.com* ⅃. *27 holes. Yards: 5074/7228. Par: 71/72. Green fee: $35/$79.*

HIKING

Pagosa Springs sits in a wondrous landscape, and there's no better way to enjoy its isolated natural beauty than to experience it from a trail. Around here, trails pass through green forests and along cold mountain streams.

Continental Divide Trail. Serious hikers in the Pagosa Springs area head to the Continental Divide Trail, which has a major access points near Wolf Creek Pass. The trail can be a fairly easy out-and-back day hike or the starting point for a longer backcountry trip. ⊠ *Trailhead at end of short gravel road that starts on east side of Wolf Creek Pass* ⊕ *www.cdtrail.org.*

☾ **Piedra Falls Trail.** This popular trail delivers an easy 1.2-mi (round trip) hike through conifer and aspen forest to the falls, which tumble in two big steps down a narrow wedge cut through volcanic rocks. ⊠ *Trailhead at end of Forest Rd. 637* ☎ *970/264–2268* ⊕ *www.fs.fed.us/r2/sanjuan.*

WHERE TO STAY

For expanded hotel reviews, visit Fodors.com.

$$$ ☷ **The Springs Resort and Spa.** Wrap yourself in a big white spa robe
HOTEL and head directly for the pools. **Pros:** proximity to hot springs; feels
★ very posh. **Cons:** service can be indifferent. ⊠ *165 Hot Springs Blvd.* ☎ *970/264–4168* ⊕ *www.pagosahotsprings.com* ⇱ *46 rooms, 33 suites* ⚘ *In-room: kitchen, Wi-Fi. In-hotel: bar, pool, spa, laundry facilities, some pets allowed.*

CORTEZ

45 mi west of Durango via U.S. 160; 76 mi southwest of Telluride via Hwy. 145.

The northern escarpment of Mesa Verde to the south and the volcanic blisters of La Plata Mountains to the west dominate the views around sprawling Cortez. A series of Days Inns, Dairy Queens, and Best Westerns, the town has a layout that seems to have been determined by neon-sign and aluminum-siding salesmen of the 1950s. Hidden among these eyesores, however, are fine galleries, shops showcasing Indian art, and a host of secondhand shops that can yield surprising finds.

GETTING HERE AND AROUND

Cortez sits at the junction of Highway 160 and Highway 491, making it a busy town for people heading north to Dolores and Telluride, south into New Mexico and Arizona, and east to Durango. Highway 491 turns into Broadway heading north, and Highway 160 splits off due east, turning into Main Street as it passes through the center of town on its way to Durango.

ESSENTIALS

Visitor Information Colorado Welcome Center ⊠ *Cortez City Park, 928 E. Main St.* ☎ *970/565–4048, 800/253–1616* ⊕ *www.mesaverdecountry.com.* **Cortez Area Chamber of Commerce** ⊠ *928 E. Main St.* ☎ *970/565–3414* ⊕ *www. cortezchamber.com.* **Mesa Verde Country** ⌂ *Box HH, Cortez 81321* ☎ *800/253–1616* ⊕ *www.mesaverdecountry.com.*

EXPLORING

★ **Cortez Cultural Center.** The Cortez Cultural Center has exhibits on regional artists and Ancestral Puebloan culture, as well as events and fairs. Summer evening programs include Native American dances, sand painting, rug weaving, pottery-making demonstrations, theater, and storytelling. ⊠ *25 N. Market St., Cortez* ☎ *970/565–1151* ⊕ *www. cortezculturalcenter.org* ⊠ *Free* ⊙ *June–Aug., Mon.–Sat. 10–9; Sept.– May, Mon.–Sat. 10–5.*

Crow Canyon Archaeological Center. The Crow Canyon Archaeological Center offers a variety of educational programs for professionals and students (or any would-be Indiana Jones with an interest in ancient relics). Among the more popular offerings are weeklong "Archaeology Adventures," which allow visitors to work alongside professional archaeologists as they search for pottery, stone tools, and other artifacts at excavation sites throughout the area, then clean and catalog their finds in the lab. The program includes a special guided tour of Mesa Verde National Park. ⊠ *23390 County Rd. K* ☎ *970/565–8975, 800/422–8975* ⊕ *www.crowcanyon.org.*

Ute Mountain Tribal Park. The only way to see this spectacular 125,000-acre park, located inside the Ute reservation, is by taking a guided tour. Expert tribal guides lead strenuous day-long hikes into this dazzling repository of Ancestral Puebloan ruins, including beautifully preserved cliff dwellings, pictographs, and petroglyphs. There are also less-demanding half-day tours, as well as private and custom tour options. Tours start at the park's visitor center, off Highway 160. ⌂ *P.O. Box 109 Towaoc 81334* ⊠ *Hwy. 160, 20 mi south of Cortez* ☎ *970/565– 3751, 800/847–5485* ⊕ *www.utemountainute.com.*

OFF THE BEATEN PATH

Mud Creek Hogan. This endearing bit of classic American kitsch has more than a dozen enormous arrows (made from telephone poles) stuck into the ground as if shot from gigantic bows. There are also a few faux teepees and a big plastic horse. The main attraction here is the trading post, which sells an assortment of Native American arts and crafts. Out back, there's a frontier town, complete with saloon, hotel, bank, jail,

10

and livery station. Don't breathe too hard, or you'll blow the town over: the paper-thin buildings are only facades. ⊠ *38651 U.S 160, Mancos* ☎ *970/533–7117.*

WHERE TO EAT AND STAY
For expanded hotel reviews, visit Fodors.com.

$$
ITALIAN
✗ **Nero's.** The menu at this unpretentious Italian eatery is fairly basic, with classic pasta dishes as well as steak, veal, and seafood, but the food is terrific. It has a full bar and a respectable wine list. The atmosphere is casual and the decor is Southwestern, with plenty of regional art. Reservations are a good idea in the busy summer months. ⊠ *303 W. Main St.* ☎ *970/565–7366* ⊕ *www.neroscortez.com.*

¢
HOTEL
🛏 **Cortez Mesa Verde Inn.** This is arguably the nicest motel on the strip, mostly because its air-conditioned rooms are spacious and pleasantly decorated. **Pros:** reasonably priced; near the national park. **Cons:** can get noisy; nothing fancy. ⊠ *640 S. Broadway* ☎ *970/565–3773* ⊕ *www.cortezmesaverdeinn.com* 🛏 *90 rooms* ♿ *In-room: Wi-Fi. In-hotel: bar, pool, laundry facilities, some pets allowed* ⏹*No meals.*

NIGHTLIFE
Ute Mountain Casino. At the base of Sleeping Ute Mountain, the state's first tribal casino rings with the sound of more than 700 slot machines. Ute Mountain Casino also draws the crowds for bingo, blackjack, and poker (both the live and the video versions). The resort is 11 mi south of Cortez on U.S. 160. ⊠ *3 Weeminuche Dr., Towaoc* ☎ *970/565–8800, 800/258–8007* ⊕ *www.utemountaincasino.com.*

SHOPPING
Mesa Indian Trading Company and Gallery. This gallery sells high-quality pottery made by the Ute and other Southwestern tribes. Look for traditional double-handled wedding vases, lustrous black and red pueblo jugs and bowls, and a variety of pieces painted in the distinctive geometric styles of the tribes of the Four Corners. ⊠ *27601 U.S. Hwy. 160* ☎ *970/565–4492, 800/441–9908* ⊕ *www.mesaverdepottery.com.*

Notah Dineh Trading Company and Museum. This store specializing in Navajo rugs has the largest collection in the area. There are also handmade baskets, beadwork, pottery, and jewelry. Be sure to stop in the free museum to see relics of the Old West. ⊠ *345 W. Main St.* ☎ *800/444–2024* ⊕ *www.notahdineh.com.*

Ute Mountain Pottery Plant. Stop by this factory store, about 15 mi south of Cortez, to watch the traditional and painstaking processes of molding, trimming, cleaning, painting, and glazing pottery. In the showroom you can buy pieces straight from the source. ⊠ *156 U.S. 160, Towaoc* ☎ *970/565–8548, 800/896–8548* ⊕ *www.utemountainute.com.*

DOLORES

10 mi northeast of Cortez via U.S. 160 and Rte. 145.

On the bank of the Dolores River, just downstream from the McPhee Reservoir, the tiny town of Dolores is midway between Durango and Telluride on State Highway 145. It attracts visitors with its spectacular scenery, fabulous fly-fishing, water sports, mountain hiking, and other outdoor adventures.

The gently rising hump to the southwest of town is Sleeping Ute Mountain, which resembles the reclining silhouette of a Native American, complete with headdress. This site is sacred to the Ute Mountain tribe, as it represents a great warrior god who, after being mortally wounded in a titanic battle with evil gods, lapsed into eternal sleep, his flowing blood turning into the life-giving Dolores and Animas rivers.

EXPLORING

Anasazi Heritage Center. Operated by the Federal Bureau of Land Management, this museum houses artifacts culled from more than 1,500 excavations in the region. The Anasazi Heritage Center has permanent exhibits showcasing the archaeology, history, and culture of the Ancestral Puebloans and other indigenous peoples. There are also two 12th-century pueblos, named after the Spanish friars Dominguez and Escalante, within walking distance. A full-scale replica of an ancient pit-house dwelling illustrates how the people lived around AD 850. ✉ *27501 State Hwy. 184, 3 mi west of Dolores* ☎ *970/882–5600* ⊕ *www.co.blm.gov/ahc* ✉ *$3* ⊙ *Mar.–Oct., daily 9–5; Nov.–Feb., daily 9–4.*

Canyons of the Ancients National Monument. Spread across 171,000 acres of arid mesa and canyon country, the Canyons of the Ancients National Monument holds more than 20,000 archaeological sites, the greatest concentration anywhere in the United States. Some sites, like apartment-style cliff dwellings and hewn-rock towers, are impossible to miss. Others are as subtle as evidence of agricultural fields, springs, and water systems. They are powerful evidence of the complex civilization of the Ancestral Puebloan people.

The monument includes several interesting sites: **Hovenweep National Monument**, straddling the Colorado–Utah border, is known for distinctive square, oval, round, and D-shape towers that were engineering marvels when they were built around AD 1200. **Lowry Pueblo,** in the northern part of the monument, is a 40-room pueblo with eight kivas (round chambers used for sacred rituals). Its Great Kiva is one of the largest known in the Southwest.

In the vast and rugged backcountry area west of Mesa Verde National Park, the monument is a must if you're fascinated by the culture of the Ancestral Puebloans. The going may be rough, however. Roads are few, hiking trails are sparse, and visitor services are all but nonexistent. The Anasazi Heritage Center, 3 mi west of Dolores on Highway 184, serves as the visitor center. A brochure, which details the self-guided tour, is available at the entrance to the site. ✉ *From Dolores, take Hwy. 184 west to U.S. 491, then head west onto County Rd. CC for 9 mi* ☎ *970/562–5600* ⊕ *www.co.blm.gov/canm* ✉ *$6* ⊙ *Daily 8–5.*

Galloping Goose Historical Society Museum. In Dolores, the Rio Grande Southern Railroad Museum is housed in a replica of the town's 1880s-era train station. The museum displays Galloping Goose No. 5, one of only seven specially designed engines built in the 1930s. The "Geese" were motored vehicles built from truck bodies that could operate for

10

much less than steam-powered engines. ⊠ *5th St. at Railroad Ave.* ☎ *970/882–7082* ⊕ *www.gallopinggoose5.com/pages/museum.html.*

McPhee Reservoir. In 1968, state officials approved the construction of an irrigation dam across the Dolores River, forming the McPhee Reservoir, the second largest in the state. It draws anglers looking to bag a variety of warm- and cold-water fish along its 50 mi of shoreline, which is surrounded by spectacular specimens of juniper and sage as well as large stands of pinyon pine. There's a boat ramp and a generous fish-cleaning station. The area also has camping, hiking, and a relatively easy mountain-bike trail, and the mesa offers panoramic views of the surrounding San Juan National Forest. ⊠ *Forest Service Rd. 271, off State Hwy. 184, about 9 mi northwest of Dolores.*

SPORTS AND THE OUTDOORS

FISHING AND BOATING

McPhee Reservoir, constructed in1985, is popular with boaters and anglers. The Colorado Division of Wildlife stocks it with plenty of trout. Other species found here include bass, bluegills, crappies, and kokanee salmon. The most easily reached fishing access spot is at the end of Highway 145, west of downtown Dolores.

RAFTING

★ Beginning in the mountains outside the town of Dolores, the Dolores River travels more than 150 mi before joining the Colorado River near Moab, Utah. This is one of those rivers that tend to flow madly in spring and diminish considerably by midsummer, meaning that most rafting trips run between May and June. Sandstone canyons, Ancestral Puebloan ruins, and the spring bloom of wildflowers and cacti are trip highlights. The current's strength depends mostly on how much water is released from McPhee Reservoir, but for the most part a Dolores River trip is a float interrupted by rapids that, depending on the flow level, can rate a Class IV.

Bill Dvořák's Kayak & River Rafting Expeditions. This outfitter offers rafting trips on the Dolores River that cover Class II to Class IV rapids and last up to 10 days. Or you can book a "Build-Your-Own-Adventure" trip that pairs rafting with other adventurous options, including zip lining, mountain biking, horseback riding, and rock climbing. ⊠ *17921 U.S. Hwy 285, Nathrop* ☎ *719/539–6851, 800/824–3795* ⊕ *www. dvorakexpeditions.com.*

WHERE TO EAT

$ ✕ **Dolores River Brewery.** This brewpub playfully advertises itself as
AMERICAN   "Dolores' Oldest Operating Brewery." (It's also the only one in town.) Order an ale or a stout to wash down good pub grub. Don't miss the amazing wood-fired pizzas. ⊠ *100 S. 4th St.* ☎ *970/882–4677* ⊕ *www. doloresriverbrewery.com* ⊘ *Closed Mon. No lunch.*

Mesa Verde National Park

WORD OF MOUTH

"No one knows when this ancient people lived and flourished, but if these silent canyons could speak, what a weird and wonderful story might be revealed."

—Author Edward Frank Allen, 1918

WELCOME TO MESA VERDE

TOP REASONS TO GO

★ **Ancient artifacts:** Mesa Verde is a time capsule for the Ancestral Puebloan culture, which flourished here between 700 and 1,400 years ago; more than 4,000 archaeological sites and 3 million objects have been unearthed at Mesa Verde.

★ **Bright nights:** Mesa Verde's lack of light and air pollution, along with its high elevation (between 6,000 and 8,500 feet) make for spectacular views of the heavens, punctuated by shooting stars, passing satellites, and—if the conditions are right—the Milky Way. Some nights you might also see eerie lightning flashes from distant thunderheads.

★ **Cliff dwellings:** Built atop the pinyon-covered mesa tops and hidden in the park's valleys is a wondrous collection of 600 ancient dwellings, some carved directly into the sandstone cliff faces.

★ **Geological marvels:** View the unique geology that drew the ancient Pueblo people to the area: protected desert canyons, massive alcoves in the cliff walls, thick bands of sandstone, continuous seep springs, and soils that could be used for both agriculture and architecture.

 **Morefield Campground.** Near the park entrance, this large campground (the only one in Mesa Verde) includes a village area with a gas station and grocery store. The best-known sites are farther in, but this one is close to some of the best hiking trails in the park.

2 Far View Visitor Center. Almost an hour's drive (but just 18 mi) from Mesa Verde's entrance, Far View is the park's epicenter, with a visitor center, restaurants, and the park's only overnight lodge. The fork in the road here takes you west toward the sites at Wetherill Mesa or south toward Chapin Mesa. You can also buy tickets for the popular ranger-led tours here.

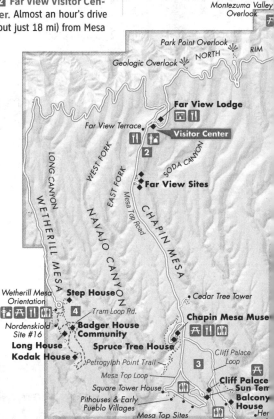

Montezuma Valley Overlook

Park Point Overlook

NORTH RIM

Geologic Overlook

Far View Lodge

Far View Terrace

Visitor Center

2

SODA CANYON

WEST FORK

EAST FORK

Far View Sites

LONG CANYON

WETHERILL MESA

NAVAJO CANYON

Mesa Top Road

CHAPIN MESA

Cedar Tree Tower

Step House

Wetherill Mesa Orientation

4   *Tram Loop Rd.*

Nordenskiold Site #16   **Badger House Community**

Long House   **Spruce Tree House**

Kodak House

Petroglyph Point Trail

Mesa Top Loop

Square Tower House

Pithouses & Early Pueblo Villages   *Mesa Top Sites*

Chapin Mesa Muse

Cliff Palace Loop

3

Cliff Palace
Sun Tem
Balcony
House

Her

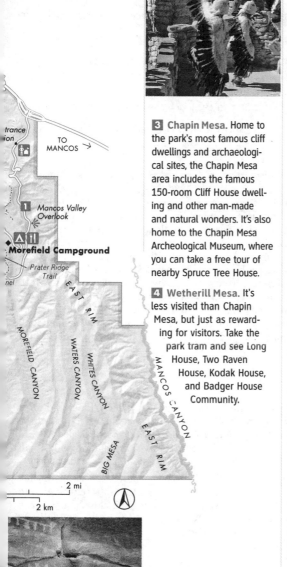

COLORADO
●

3 **Chapin Mesa.** Home to the park's most famous cliff dwellings and archaeological sites, the Chapin Mesa area includes the famous 150-room Cliff House dwelling and other man-made and natural wonders. It's also home to the Chapin Mesa Archeological Museum, where you can take a free tour of nearby Spruce Tree House.

4 **Wetherill Mesa.** It's less visited than Chapin Mesa, but just as rewarding for visitors. Take the park tram and see Long House, Two Raven House, Kodak House, and Badger House Community.

GETTING ORIENTED

Perhaps no other area offers as much evidence into the Ancestral Puebloan culture as Mesa Verde National Park. Several thousand archaeological sites have been found, and research is ongoing to discover more. The carved-out homes and assorted artifacts, many of which are displayed at the park's Chapin Mesa Archeological Museum, belonged to ancestors of today's Hopi, Zuni, and Pueblo tribes, among others. Due to the sensitive nature of these sites, hiking in the park is restricted to designated trails, and certain cliff dwellings may be accessed only on ranger-led tours during the peak summer season.

2 mi

2 km

KEY	
👫	Ranger Station
⛺	Campground
🌲	Picnic Area
🍴	Restaurant
🏨	Lodge
🚶	Trailhead
🚻	Restrooms
☀	Scenic Viewpoint
⋯⋯	Walking/Hiking Trails
⋯⋯	Bicycle Path

Updated
by Martha
Connors

Unlike the other national parks, Mesa Verde earned its status from its ancient cultural history rather than its geological treasures. President Theodore Roosevelt established it in 1906 as the first national park to "preserve the works of man," in this case that of the Ancestral Puebloans, also known as the Anasazi. They lived in the region from roughly 550 to 1300; they left behind more than 4,000 archaeological sites spread out over 80 square mi. Their ancient dwellings, set high into the sandstone cliffs, are the heart of the park.

Mesa Verde (which in Spanish means, literally, "Green Table," but translates more accurately to something like "green flat-topped plateau") is much more than an archaeologist's dreamland, however. It's one of those windswept places where man's footprints and nature's paintbrush—some would say chisel—meet. Rising dramatically from the San Juan Basin, the jutting cliffs are cut by a series of complex canyons and covered in several shades of green, from pines in the higher elevations down to sage and other mountain brush on the desert floor. From the tops of the smaller mesas, you can look across to the cliff dwellings in the opposite rock faces. Dwarfed by the towering cliffs, the sand-color dwellings look almost like a natural occurrence in the midst of the desert's harsh beauty.

MESA VERDE PLANNER

WHEN TO GO

The best times to visit the park are late May, early June, and most of September, when the weather is fine but the summer crowds have thinned. **Mid-June through August is Mesa Verde's most crowded time.** In July and August, lines at the museum and visitor center may last half an hour. Afternoon thunderstorms are common in July and August.

The park gets as much as 100 inches of snow in winter. Snow may fall as late as May and as early as October, but there's rarely enough to hamper travel. In winter, the Wetherill Mesa Road is closed, but you can still get a glimpse of some of the Wetherill Mesa sandstone dwellings, sheltered from the snow in their cliff coves, from the Chapin Mesa area.

AVG. HIGH/LOW TEMPS.

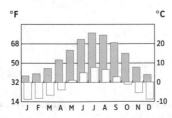

11

FESTIVALS AND EVENTS

JUNE **Mountain Ute Bear Dance.** This traditional dance, the local version of a Sadie Hawkins (in which the women choose their dance partners—and the selected men can't refuse), is held in June on the Tawaoc Ute reservation south of Cortez. The event celebrates spring and the legacy of a mythical bear who taught the Ute people her secrets. It's part of a multiday festival that includes an art fair, music, and storytelling, and culminates with an hour-long dance that's over when only one couple remains. ☎ 970/565–3751 ⊕ www.utemountainute.com.

JULY **Durango Fiesta Days.** A parade, rodeo, barbecue, street dance, and pie auction come to the La Plata County Fair Grounds in Durango on the last weekend of the month. ☎ 970/247–8835 ⊕ www.durangofiestadays.com.

OCTOBER **Durango Cowboy Poetry Gathering.** A parade and dance accompany art exhibitions, poetry readings, music, and storytelling in this four-day event sponsored by the Durango Cowboy Gathering, a nonprofit set up to preserve the traditions of the American West. It's held the first weekend in October. ☎ 970/749–2995 ⊕ www.durangocowboygathering.org.

PLANNING YOUR TIME
MESA VERDE IN ONE DAY

For a full experience, take at least one ranger-led tour of a major cliff dwelling site, as well as a few self-guided walks. Arrive early; it's 15 mi (about a 45-minute drive from the park entrance) to your first stop, the **Far View Visitor Center,** where you can purchase tickets for Cliff Palace and Balcony House tours on Chapin Mesa. If it's going to be a hot day, you might want to take an early morning or late-afternoon tour. Drive to the **Chapin Mesa Museum** to watch a 25-minute film introducing you to the area and its history. Just behind the museum is the trailhead for the ½-mi-long **Spruce Tree House trail,** which leads to the best-preserved cliff dwelling in the park. Then drive to Balcony House for an hour-long, ranger-led tour.

Have lunch at the Spruce Tree House cafeteria or the Cliff Palace picnic area. Afterward take the ranger-led tour of **Cliff Palace** (one hour). Use the rest of the day to explore the overlooks and trails off the 6-mi loop of **Mesa Top Loop Road.** Or head back to the museum and take **Petroglyph Point Trail** to see a great example of Ancestral Puebloan rock carvings. A leisurely walk along the Mesa Top's **Soda Canyon Overlook Trail** (off Cliff Palace Loop Road) gives you a beautiful bird's-eye view of the canyon below. On the drive back toward the park entrance, be sure to check out the view from **Park Point.**

GETTING HERE AND AROUND
AIR TRAVEL

The cities of Durango (35 mi east of the park entrance) and Cortez (30 mi to the west) have airports. There's also an airport in Farmington, Utah, about 94 mi away.

CAR TRAVEL

The park has just one entrance, off U.S. 160, between Cortez and Durango in what's known as the Four Corners area (which spans the intersection of Colorado, New Mexico, Arizona, and Utah). Most of the roads at Mesa Verde involve steep grades and hairpin turns, particularly on Wetherill Mesa. Vehicles over 8,000 pounds or 25 feet are prohibited on this road. Trailers and towed vehicles are prohibited past Morefield Campground. Check the condition of your vehicle's brakes before driving the road to Wetherill Mesa. For the latest road information, tune to 1610 AM, or call 970/529–4461. Off-road vehicles are prohibited in the park. At less-visited Wetherill Mesa, you must leave you car behind and hike or ride the tram to Long House, Kodak House, and Badger House Community.

PARK ESSENTIALS
PARK FEES AND PERMITS
Admission is $15 per vehicle for a seven-day permit. An annual pass is $30. Ranger-led tours of Cliff Palace, Long House, and Balcony House are $3 per person. You can also take ranger-guided bus tours from the Far View Lodge, which last between 3½ and 4 hours and cost $35–$45 ($17.50–$34 for kids 11 and under). Backcountry hiking and fishing are not permitted at Mesa Verde.

PARK HOURS
Mesa Verde's facilities each operate on their own schedule, but most are open daily, from Memorial Day through Labor Day, between about 8 am and sunset. The rest of the year, they open at 9 am. In winter, Spruce Tree House and Balcony House are open only to offer a few scheduled tours each day. Wetherill Mesa (and all of the sites it services) is open only from Memorial Day through Labor Day. Far View Visitor Center, Far View Terrace, and Far View Lodge are open between April and October. Morefield Campground and the sites nearby are open from mid-May through mid-October.

AUTOMOBILE SERVICE STATIONS
Morefield Service Station. The only place to find gas in the park is at the Morefield Service Station, in the Morefield Campground Village. The station offers the basics—gas and oil changes—and is open from mid-May through early October. ✉ *Morefield Campground, 4 mi south of park entrance* ☎ *970/565–2407.*

Shell Station. About 10 mi from the park entrance, this 24-hour station also has an ATM and convenience store. ✉ *2021 E. Main St., Cortez* ☎ *970/565–4999.*

CELL-PHONE RECEPTION AND INTERNET
Officially, there is no cell service in the park, although you might get a signal at the Morefield Campground area, which is the closest to the neighboring towns of Cortez and Mancos. Public telephones can be found at all the major visitor areas (Morefield, Far View, and Spruce Tree). You can get free Wi-Fi in the lobby of Far View Lodge and at the Morefield Campground store.

SHOPS AND GROCERS
Morefield Campground has a nicely stocked store that carries groceries as well as camping basics and last-minute supplies. It's open 7 am to 9 pm, mid-May to early October. The gift shops at Far View Terrace, Far View Lodge, and Spruce Tree Terrace have a small collection of essentials for sale as well.

RESTAURANTS

Dining options in Mesa Verde are limited inside the park, but comparatively plentiful and varied if you're staying in Cortez or Durango. In surrounding communities, southwestern restaurants and steak houses are the most common options.

HOTELS

All 150 rooms of the park's Far View Lodge, open April through October, fill up quickly—so reservations are recommended, especially if you plan to visit on a weekend in summer. Options in the surrounding area include chain hotels as well as bed-and-breakfast inns. Durango in particular has a number of hotels in fine old buildings reminiscent of the Old West.

WHAT IT COSTS					
	¢	$	$$	$$$	$$$$
Restaurants	under $8	$8–$12	$13–$20	$21–$30	over $30
Hotels	under $70	$70–$100	$101–$150	$151–$200	over $200

Restaurant prices are per person for a main course at dinner. Hotel prices are per night for two people in a standard double room in high season, excluding taxes and services charges.

VISITOR INFORMATION

PARK CONTACT INFORMATION

Mesa Verde National Park. Mesa Verde National Park ✆ P.O. Box 8 81330–0008 ☎ 970/529–4465 ⊕ www.nps.gov/meve.

VISITOR CENTERS

The official visitor center, at Far View, is open from May to October. The Chapin Mesa Archeological Museum, which also serves as a visitor center, is open year-round.

★ **Chapin Mesa Archeological Museum.** This is an excellent first stop for an introduction to Ancestral Puebloan culture as well as the area's development into a national park. Exhibits showcase original textiles and other artifacts, and a theater plays a well-done movie every 30 minutes. Rangers are available to answer your questions, and there's also a sign-in sheet for hiking trails. The museum sits at the south end of the park entrance road and overlooks Spruce Tree House. Nearby, you'll find park headquarters, a gift shop, snack bar, and bathrooms. ⊠ *Park entrance road, 5 mi south of Far View Visitor Center* ☎ 970/529–4465 ☞ *Free* ⊙ *Early Apr.–mid-Oct., daily 8–6:30; mid-Oct.–early Apr., daily 8–5.*

★ **Far View Visitor Center.** You can't miss this cylindrical brick building on the east side of the road in the Far View complex, but you actually must park across the street and walk through the tunnel under the road to reach it. ■ TIP→ **Stop here first and buy tickets for the Cliff Palace, Balcony House, and Long House ranger-led tours.** When deciding which tour to take, you can pick the less-crowded ones; computer screens show the number of available spaces left for each. This center also has a gift shop, viewing platform, and museum. An extensive selection of books, maps,

CLOSE UP

Plants and Wildlife in Mesa Verde

Mesa Verde is home to 640 species of plants, including a number of native plants found nowhere else. Its lower elevations feature many varieties of shrubs, including rabbitbrush and sagebrush. Higher up, you'll find mountain mahogany, yucca, pinyon, juniper, and Douglas fir. During warmer months, brightly colored blossoms, like the yellow perky Sue, blue lupines, and bright-red Indian paintbrushes, are scattered throughout the park.

The park is also home to a variety of migratory and resident animals, including 74 species of mammals. Drive slowly along the park's roads; mule deer are everywhere. You may spot wild turkeys, and black bear encounters are not unheard of on the hiking trails. Bobcats, coyotes, and mountain lions are also around, but they are seen less frequently. About 200 species of birds, including threatened Mexican spotted owls, red-tailed hawks, golden eagles, and noisy ravens, also live here. On the ground, you should keep your eyes and ears open for lizards and snakes, including the poisonous—but shy—prairie rattlesnake. As a general rule, animals are most active in the early morning and at dusk.

Many areas of the park have had extensive fire damage over the years. In fact, wildfires here have been so destructive they are given names, just like hurricanes. For example, the Bircher Fire in 2000 consumed nearly 20,000 acres of brush and forest, much of it covering the eastern half of the park. It will take several centuries for the woodland there to look as verdant as the area atop Chapin Mesa, which escaped the fire. But in the meantime, you'll have a chance to glimpse nature's powerful rejuvenating processes in action; the landscape in the fire-ravaged sections of the park is already filling in with vegetation.

and videos on the history of the park are available, and rangers are on-hand to answer questions and explain the history of the Ancestral Puebloans. ⊠ *Park entrance road, 15 mi south of entrance* ⊙ *Memorial Day–Labor Day, daily 8–7; Labor Day–mid-Oct., daily 8–5.*

EXPLORING

SCENIC DRIVES

Mesa Top Loop Road. This 6-mi drive skirts the scenic rim of Chapin Mesa and takes you to several overlooks and short, paved trails. You'll get great views of Sun Temple and Square Tower, as well as Cliff Palace, Sunset House, and several other cliff dwellings visible from the Sun Point Overlook. ⊙ *Daily 8 am–sunset.*

Park Entrance Road. The main park road, also known as SH 10, leads you from the entrance off U.S. 160 to the Far View complex, 15 mi from the park entrance. As a break from the switchbacks, you can stop at a couple of pretty overlooks along the way, but hold out for Park Point, which, at the mesa's highest elevation (8,572 feet), gives you unobstructed 360-degree views. Note that trailers and towed vehicles are not permitted beyond Morefield Campground.

Wetherill Mesa Road. This 12-mi mountain road, stretching from the Far View Visitor Center to the Wetherill Mesa, has sharp curves and steep grades (and is restricted to vehicles less than 25 feet long and 8,000 lbs). It's open from Memorial Day to Labor Day. Roadside pullouts offer unobstructed views of the Four Corners region. At the end of the road, you can access Step House and Long House, plus the parks' free tram service (which takes you to the Badger House Community). ⊗ *June–Aug., daily 8–4:30.*

HISTORIC SITES

Badger House Community. A self-guided walk takes you through a group of four mesa-top dwellings. The community, which covers nearly 7 acres, dates back to the year 650, the Basketmaker Period, and includes a primitive, semi-subterranean pit house and what's left of a multistoried stone pueblo. Allow about an hour to see all the sites. The trail is 2.4 mi round-trip; if you take the tram from the Wetherill kiosk, you'll save a mile of walking. ⊠ *Wetherill Mesa Rd., 12 mi from Far View Visitor Center* 🎫 *Free* ⊗ *Memorial Day–Labor Day, daily 9:30–4:30.*

🔄 **Balcony House.** The stonework of this 40-room cliff dwelling, which ★ housed about 40 or 50 people, is impressive, but you're likely to be even more awed by the skill it must have taken to reach this place. Perched in a sandstone cove 600 feet above the floor of Soda Canyon, Balcony House seems almost suspended in space. Even with the aid of modern passageways and a partially paved trail, today's visitors must climb two wooden ladders (the first one 32 feet high) to enter. Surrounding the house is a courtyard with a parapet wall and the intact balcony for which the house is named. A favorite with kids, the dwelling is accessible only on a ranger-led tour. Purchase your ticket at the Far View Visitor Center, Morefield Ranger Station, or the Chapin Mesa Archaeological Museum (mid-October through early November only). You can also get tickets at the Colorado Welcome Center in Cortez. ⊠ *Cliff Palace/Balcony House Rd., 10 mi south of Far View Visitor Center* 🎫 *$3* ⊗ *Late-April–mid-Oct., daily 9–5.*

Fodor's Choice **Cliff Palace.** This was the first major Mesa Verde dwelling seen by ★ cowboys Charlie Mason and Richard Wetherill in 1888. It is also the largest, containing about 150 rooms and 23 kivas on three levels. Getting there involves a steep downhill hike and five ladders. Purchase tickets at the Far View Visitor Center, Morefield Ranger Station,

Chapin Mesa Archaeological Museum (mid-October through early November only), and at the Colorado Welcome Center in Cortez. From Memorial Day through Labor Day, rangers lead a 90-minute Twilight Tour of the site (tours run daily at 7 pm; tickets available only at the Far View Visitor Center). ⊠ *Cliff Palace Overlook, about 2½ mi south of Chapin Mesa Archeological Museum* 🎫 *Basic tour $3; Twilight tour $10* ☉ *Late May–early Sept., daily 9–6; early Sept. to mid-Oct., daily 9–5.*

Far View Sites Complex. This was probably one of the most densely populated areas in Mesa Verde, comprising as many as 50 villages in a ½-square-mi area at the top of Chapin Mesa. Most of the sites here were built between 900 and 1300. Begin the self-guided tour at the interpretive panels in the parking lot, then proceed down a ½-mi, level trail. ⊠ *Park entrance road, 1½ mi south of Far View Visitor Center* 🎫 *Free* ☉ *Year-round, daily 8 am–sunset.*

Long House. This Wetherill Mesa cliff dwelling is the second largest in Mesa Verde. It is believed that about 150 people lived in Long House, so named because of the size of its cliff alcove. The spring at the back of the cave is still active today. The ranger-led tour begins a short distance from the parking lot and takes about 90 minutes. Buy your ticket at the Far View Visitor Center, Morefield Ranger Station, Chapin Mesa Archaeological Museum (mid-October through early November only), or at the Colorado Welcome Center in Cortez. ⊠ *Wetherill Mesa kiosk, 12 mi from Far View Visitor Center* 🎫 *Tours $3* ☉ *Memorial Day– Labor Day, daily 10–4.*

Spruce Tree House. This 138-room complex is the best-preserved site in the park, and the rooms and ceremonial chambers are more accessible to visitors than those in other sites. Here you can actually enter a kiva, via a short ladder, just as the original inhabitants did. It's a great place for kids to explore, but because of its location in the heart of the Chapin Mesa area, Spruce Tree House can resemble a crowded playground during busy periods. Tours are self-guided (allow 45 minutes to an hour), but a park ranger is on site to answer questions. The trail leading to Spruce Tree House starts behind the museum and leads you 100 feet down into the canyon. You may find yourself breathing hard by the time you make it back up to the parking lot. ⊠ *At the Chapin Mesa Archeological Museum, 5 mi south of Far View Visitor Center* 🎫 *Free* ☉ *Memorial Day–Labor Day, daily 8:30–6:30; early Sept.– mid-Oct., daily 9–6:30; mid-Oct.–early Nov., daily 9–5; early Nov.– Memorial day, open only during free guided tours at 10, 1, and 3:30.*

Step House. So named because of a crumbling prehistoric stairway leading up from the dwelling, Step House is reached via a paved (but steep) trail that's ¾ mi long. The house is unique in that it shows clear evidence of two separate occupations: the first around 626, the second a full 600 years later. The self-guided tour takes about 45 minutes. ⊠ *Wetherill Mesa Rd., 12 mi from Far View Visitor Center* 🎫 *Free* ☉ *Memorial Day–Labor Day, daily 9:30–4:30.*

Sun Temple. Although researchers assume it was probably a ceremonial structure, they're unsure of the exact purpose of this complex, which has no doors or windows in most of its chambers. Because the building was not quite half-finished when it was left in 1276, some researchers surmise it might have been constructed to stave off whatever disaster caused its builders—and the other inhabitants of Mesa Verde—to leave. ⊠ *Mesa Top Loop Rd., about 2 mi south of Chapin Mesa Archeological Museum* ⌸ *Free* ⊗ *Daily 8–sunset.*

Triple Village Pueblo Sites. Three dwellings, built on top of each other from 700 to 950, at first look like a mass of jumbled walls, but an interpretive panel helps identify the dwellings. The 325-foot trail from the walking area is paved and wheelchair accessible. ⊠ *Mesa Top Loop Rd., about 2½ mi south of Chapin Mesa Archeological Museum* ⌸ *Free* ⊗ *Daily 8 am–sunset.*

SCENIC STOPS

Cedar Tree Tower. A self-guided tour takes you to, but not through, a tower and kiva built between 1100 and 1300 and connected by a tunnel. The tower-and-kiva combinations in the park are thought to have been either religious structures or signal towers. ⊠ *Park entrance road, 1½ mi north of Chapin Mesa Archeological Museum.*

Kodak House Overlook. Get an impressive view into the 60-room Kodak House and its several small kivas from here. The house, closed to the public, was named for a Swedish researcher who absentmindedly left his Kodak camera behind here in 1891. ⊠ *Wetherill Mesa Rd., about 0.2 mi south of kiosk (tram stop)* ⊗ *Memorial Day–Labor Day, daily 9–4:15.*

Soda Canyon Overlook. Get your best view of Balcony House here. You can also read interpretive panels about the site and the surrounding canyon geology. ⊠ *Cliff Palace Loop Rd., about 1 mi north of Balcony House parking area.*

EDUCATIONAL OFFERINGS

BUS TOURS

ARAMARK Tours. If you want a well-rounded visit to the park's most popular sites, consider a group tour. The park concessionaire provides all-day and half-day guided tours of the Chapin Mesa and Far View sites, departing in air-conditioned buses from either Morefield Campground or Far View Lodge. Tour guides trade off with park rangers in educating you on history, geology, and excavation processes in Mesa Verde. ⌂ *Box 277, Mancos 81328* ☎ *970/529–4422, 800/449–2288* ⊕ *www.visitmesaverde.com* ⌸ *$25–$45* ⊗ *Mid-Apr.–mid-Oct., daily, departure times vary.*

RANGER PROGRAMS

⟳ **Evening Ranger Campfire Program.** Every night in summer, a park ranger presents a different 45- to 60-minute program on topics such as stargazing, history, wildlife, and archaeology. ⊠ *Morefield Campground Amphitheater, 4 mi south of park entrance* ☎ *970/529–4465* ⌸ *Free* ⊗ *Memorial Day–Labor Day, daily 9 pm.*

Far View Sites Walk. A one-hour, ranger-led walk through the mesa top sites in the Far View area takes place every weekday afternoon during the summer (and once a week from Labor Day through mid-October). ⊠ *Far View House, 1 mi south of Far View Visitor Center* ☎ *970/529–4465* ⊠ *Free* ⊙ *Memorial Day–Labor Day, weekdays 4 pm; Labor Day–mid-Oct., Mon. 4 pm.*

☺ **Junior Ranger Program.** Children ages 4 through 12 can earn a certificate and badge for successfully completing four activities in the park's Junior Ranger booklet (available at the park or online). ⊠ *Far View Visitor Center or Chapin Mesa Archeological Museum* ☎ *970/529–4465* ⊕ *www.nps.gov/meve/forkids/beajuniorranger.htm.*

Mesa Verde Institute Tours and Hikes. From May through October the park joins with its nonprofit partner, the Mesa Verde Institute, in offering a series of ranger-led hikes to some of the park's most significant sites. In summer you can take a 90-minute Twilight in Cliff Palace tour (every evening at 7; tickets available at the Far View Visitor Center only) or a two-hour backcountry hike to Oak Tree House and Fire Temple (Tuesday, Thursday, and Saturday, at 8 am; tickets available at the Far View Visitor Center or online at ⊕ *www.mesaverdeinstitute.org*). From September through mid-October, there are two different backcountry hikes, both of which start at 8 am. Tickets for both are sold online and through the visitor center. The two-hour hike to Square Tower House departs on Tuesday, Thursday, and Saturday; the eight-hour hike to Spring House leaves Wednesday, Friday, and Sunday. Note that all tour participants are required to have sturdy footwear and carry at least two quarts of water per person; anyone who's not prepared will be turned away, with no refund given. ☎ ⊕ *www.mesaverdeinstitute. org* ⊠ *$10–$40* ⊙ *Summer tours Memorial Day–Labor Day; fall tours Sept.–mid-Oct.*

★ **Ranger-Led Tours.** The cliff dwellings known as Balcony House, Cliff Palace, and Long House can be explored only on ranger-led tours; the first two last about an hour, the third is 90 minutes. Buy tickets at Far View Visitor Center, the Morefield Campground Ranger Station, Chapin Mesa Archeological Museum (mid-October through early November only), or in Cortez at the Colorado Welcome Center. These are active tours; each requires climbing ladders without handrails and squeezing through tight spaces. Be sure to bring water and sunscreen. ☎ *970/529–4465* ⊠ *$3* ⊙ *Memorial Day–early Nov. (Balcony House tours end mid-Oct.; Long House tours end on Labor Day).*

SPORTS AND THE OUTDOORS

At Mesa Verde, outdoor activities are restricted, due to the fragile nature of the archaeological treasures here. Hiking (allowed on marked trails only) is the best option, especially as a way to view some of the Ancestral Puebloan dwellings.

BIRD-WATCHING

Turkey vultures soar between April and October, and large flocks of ravens hang around all summer. Among the park's other large birds are red-tailed hawks, great horned owls, and a few golden eagles. The Steller's jay (the male looks like a blue jay with a dark hat on) frequently pierces the pinyon-juniper forest with its cries, and hummingbirds dart from flower to flower in the summer and fall. Any visit to cliff dwellings late in the day will include frolicking white-throated swifts, which make their home in rock crevices overhead. Pick up a copy of the park's "Checklist of the Birds" brochure or visit the National Park Service's Web site (⊕ *www.nps.gov/meve/planyourvisit/birdwatching.htm*) for a detailed listing of the feathered inhabitants here.

HIKING

A handful of trails lead beyond Mesa Verde's most visited sites and offer more solitude than the often-crowded cliff dwellings. The best canyon vistas can be reached if you're willing to huff and puff your way through elevation changes and switchbacks. Carry more water than you think you'll need, wear sunscreen, and bring rain gear—cloudbursts can come seemingly out of nowhere. Certain trails are open seasonally, so check with a ranger before heading out. No backcountry hiking is permitted in Mesa Verde, and pets are prohibited.

EASY

Farming Terrace Trail. This 30-minute, ½-mi loop begins and ends on the spur road to Cedar Tree Tower, about 1 mi north of the Chapin Mesa area. It meanders through a series of check dams, which the Ancestral Puebloans built to create farming terraces. *Easy.* ⊠ *Park entrance road, 4 mi south of Far View Visitor Center.*

Knife Edge Trail. Perfect for a sunset stroll, this easy 2-mi (round-trip) walk around the north rim of the park leads to an overlook of the Montezuma Valley. If you stop at all the flora identification points that the trail guide pamphlet suggests, the hike should take about 1½ to 2 hours. The patches of asphalt you're likely to spot along the way are leftovers from old Knife Edge Road, built in 1914 as the main entryway into the park. *Easy.* ⊠ *Morefield Campground, 4 mi from park entrance.*

☺ **Soda Canyon Overlook Trail.** One of the easiest and most rewarding hikes in the park, this little trail travels 1.5-mi round-trip through the forest on almost completely level ground. The overlook is an excellent point from which to photograph the Chapin Mesa-area cliff dwellings. *Easy.* ⊠ *Cliff Palace Loop Rd., about 1 mi north of Balcony House parking area.*

MODERATE

Fodor's Choice
★ **Petroglyph Point Trail.** Scramble along a narrow canyon wall to reach the largest and best-known petroglyphs in Mesa Verde. Older literature occasionally refers to the destination of this 2.4-mi loop hike as "Pictograph Point," but that's a misnomer. Pictographs are painted onto the rock, and petroglyphs are carved into it. If you pose for a photo just right, you can just manage to block out the gigantic "don't touch" sign

next to the rock art. A map—available at any ranger station—points out three dozen points of interest along the trail. The trail is open only when Spruce Tree House is open; check with a ranger to verify times. *Moderate.* ⊠ *Spruce Tree House, next to Chapin Mesa Archeological Museum* ☉ *May–early Nov., daily 9–5.*

Spruce Canyon Trail. While Petroglyph Point Trail takes you along the side of the canyon, this trail ventures down into its depths. It's only 2.4 mi long, but you descend about 600 feet in elevation. Remember to save your strength; what goes down must come up again. Access to the trail is limited to times when Spruce Tree House is open; check with a ranger beforehand. *Moderate.* ⊠ *Spruce Tree House, next to Chapin Mesa Archeological Museum* ☉ *Mar.–Nov., daily 9–5.*

DIFFICULT

Prater Ridge Trail. This 7.8-mi round-trip loop, which starts and finishes at Morefield Campground, is the longest hike you can take inside the park. It provides fine views of Morefield Canyon to the south and the San Juan Mountains to the north. About halfway through the hike, you'll see a cut-off trail that you can take, which shortens the trip to 5 mi. *Difficult.* ⊠ *West end of Morefield Campground, 4 mi from park entrance.*

STARGAZING

There are no large cities in the Four Corners area, so there is little artificial light to detract from the stars in the night sky. Far View Lodge and Morefield Campground are great for sky watching.

SHOPPING

Chapin Mesa Archeological Museum Shop. Books and videos are the primary offering here, with more than 400 titles on Ancestral Puebloan and southwestern topics. ⊠ *Spruce Tree Terrace, near Chapin Mesa Archeological Museum, 5 mi from Far View Visitor Center* ☎ *970/529–4465.*

Far View Terrace Shop. Adjacent to the Far View Lodge and Cafe, this is the largest gift shop in the park, with gifts, souvenirs, American Indian art, a Christmas section, and T-shirts galore. ⊠ *Mesa Top Loop Rd., 15 mi south of park entrance* ☎ *970/529–4421, 800/449–2288.*

NEARBY TOWNS

A onetime market center for cattle and crops, **Cortez, 30 mi west of the park,** is now the largest gateway town to Mesa Verde and a base for tourists visiting the Four Corners region. You can still see a rodeo here at least once a year. **Dolores,** steeped in a rich railroad history, is on the Dolores River, 20 mi north of Mesa Verde. Near both the San Juan National Forest and McPhee Reservoir, Dolores is a favorite of outdoor enthusiasts. East of Mesa Verde by 36 mi, **Durango,** the region's main hub, comes complete with a variety of restaurants and hotels, shopping, and outdoor equipment shops. Durango became a town in 1881 when the Denver and Rio Grande Railroad pushed its tracks across the neighboring San Juan Mountains.

WHERE TO EAT

$

AMERICAN

✕ **Far View Terrace Cafe.** This full-service cafeteria offers great views, plentiful choices, and reasonable prices. A coffee counter provides the requisite caffeine for the day's activities, and you can get your omelet and pancakes cooked to order as you watch. You can also get a Grab & Go breakfast (or lunch) if you're in a hurry to hit the park trails. Dinner options might include a Navajo taco piled high with all the fixings. Don't miss the creamy malts and homemade fudge. ✉ *Across from Far View Visitor Center* ☎ *970/529–4444* ⊘ *Closed late Oct.–early Apr.*

¢

CAFÉ

✕ **Knife's Edge Cafe.** Located in the Morefield Campground, this simple restaurant serves an all-you-can-eat pancake breakfast every morning from 7:30 to 10, and at night there's an all-you-can-eat barbecue dinner from 5 to 8. ✉ *4 mi south of park entrance* ☎ *970/565–2133* ⊘ *Closed late Oct.–mid-May. No lunch.*

$$$

AMERICAN

★

✕ **Metate Room.** The park's rugged high-desert terrain contrasts with this relaxing space just off the lobby of the Far View Lodge. Tables in this southwestern-style dining room are candlelighted and cloth covered, but the atmosphere remains casual. A wall of windows affords wonderful Mesa Verde vistas. The menu is based on regional heritage foods, including corn, beans, and squash (all staples for the Ancestral Puebloans). Entrées include American classics like steak and seafood, or you can try one of the dishes centered on regional game such as elk and quail. Every table gets mesa bread and black bean hummus for starters. There's a solid array of wines (many from Colorado) and cocktails with kitschy names, like the "mesa-tini." ✉ *Far View Lodge, across from Far View Visitor Center, 15 mi southwest of park entrance* ☎ *970/529–4421* ⊘ *Closed late Oct.–late Apr. No lunch.*

¢

AMERICAN

✕ **Spruce Tree Terrace Cafe.** This small cafeteria has a limited selection of hot food and sandwiches. The patio is pleasant, and it's conveniently located across the street from the museum. The Spruce Tree Terrace is also the only food concession in the park that's open year-round for lunch. ✉ *Near Chapin Mesa Archeological Museum, 5 mi south of the Far View Visitor Center* ☎ *970/529–4521* ⊘ *No dinner Dec.–Feb.*

PICNIC AREAS

Park Headquarters Loop Picnic Area. This is the nicest and largest picnic area in the park. It has about 40 tables under shade trees and a great view into Spruce Canyon, as well as flush toilets and running water. ✉ *Near Chapin Mesa Archeological Museum, 5 mi south of Far View Visitor Center.*

Wetherill Mesa Picnic Area. Ten tables placed under lush shade trees, along with drinking water and restrooms, make this a pleasant spot for lunch. ✉ *12 mi southwest of Far View Visitor Center.*

CLOSE UP

Best Campgrounds in Mesa Verde

Morefield Campground is the only option within the park, and it's an excellent one. Reservations are accepted; it's open May through October. In nearby Mancos, just across the highway from the park entrance, there's a campground with full amenities, while the San Juan National Forest offers backcountry camping.

Morefield Campground. With more than 400 shaded campsites, access to trailheads, and plenty of amenities, the only campground in the park is an appealing mini-city for campers. It's a 40-minute drive to reach the park's most popular sites. Reservations are accepted only for tent and group sites. ⊠ *4 mi south of park entrance, P.O. Box 8, Mesa Verde, CO* ☎ *970/564–4300 or 800/449–2288* ⊕ *www.visitmesaverde.com.*

WHERE TO STAY

For expanded hotel reviews, visit Fodors.com.

$
HOTEL
★

⊡ **Far View Lodge.** Talk about a view—all rooms have a private balcony, from which you can admire views of the neighboring states of Arizona, Utah, and New Mexico up to 100 mi in the distance. **Pros:** close to the key sites; views are spectacular. **Cons:** simple rooms and amenities, with no TV; walls are thin and less than soundproof. ⊠ *Across from Far View Visitor Center, 15 mi southwest of park entrance* ⊕ *Box 277, Mancos 81328* ☎ *602/331–5210, 800/449–2288* ⊕ *www.visitmesaverde.com* ⤳ *150 rooms* ⚱ *In-room: no a/c, no TV. In-hotel: restaurant, bar, laundry facilities, some pets allowed* ⊙ *Closed Nov.–Mar.*

South Central Colorado

COLORADO SPRINGS, ROYAL GORGE, AND GREAT SAND DUNES

WORD OF MOUTH

"One of the popular day trips from Colorado Springs is Pike's Peak. There is a cog railway. You would have to check the weather conditions, of course. Florissant Fossil Beds National Monument is farther West on Rte 24 and is very interesting. I was fascinating to learn that this area once had huge redwoods. In the town of Manitou Springs we walked around town, sampled some of the mineral water springs and had a good dinner at the Adams Mountain Café in the historic spa building."

—Vttraveler

Updated by
Ricardo Baca

Stretching from majestic mountains into rugged, high desert plains, south central Colorado has plenty of 14,000-foot peaks, striking red-rock outcroppings, rivers that boil with white-water rapids in spring, and even the incongruous sight of towering sand dunes dwarfed by a mountain range at their back. It's worth a few days for white-water rafting, hiking in the backcountry, and exploring historic gold-mining towns. Colorado Springs is bustling, but other parts of the area have a barely discovered feel. If it's peace and quiet you're after, staying put in a cabin in the woods can make for an utterly relaxed week.

South central Colorado was first explored by the United States in 1806, three years after it made the Louisiana Purchase. Zebulon Pike took up the assignment of scout, but he never did climb the peak that is now named for him. Weaving through the southeastern section of the state are the haunting remains of the Santa Fe Trail, which guided pioneers westward beginning in the 1820s.

Framed by Pikes Peak, Colorado Springs is the region's population center and a hub for the military and the high-tech industry. The city has been a destination for out-of-towners since its founding in 1870, due to the alleged healing power of the local spring water and clean air. The gold rush fueled the city's boom through the early 20th century, as the military boom did following World War II. With more than 550,000 residents in the metro area, Colorado Springs offers a mix of history and modernity, as well as incredible access to the trails and red-rock scenery in this section of the Rockies.

Surrounding Colorado Springs is a ring of smaller cities and alluring natural attractions. To the west, between alpine and desert scenery, are the Florissant Fossil Beds, the Royal Gorge, and Cripple Creek, which offers gambling in casinos housed in historic buildings. You can go rafting near Cañon City, while Pueblo has a dash of public art and history museums. Outdoorsy types love the entire area: camping and hiking are especially superb in the San Isabel and Pike national forests. Climbers head to the Collegiate Peaks around Buena Vista and Salida (west of Colorado Springs) and the Cañon City area for a variety of ascents from moderate to difficult. Farther south, you can take the Highway of Legends Scenic Byway, which travels through the San Isabel National Forest and over high mountain passes. You can even take a day trip on the Rio Grande Scenic Railroad or the Cumbres & Toltec Scenic Railroad, which travels through a region not reachable by car.

TOP REASONS TO GO

Hike a Fourteener: Coloradans collect hikes to the summit of Fourteeners—mountains that top 14,000 feet above sea level—like trophies.

Play on the Sand Dunes: At Great Sand Dunes, one of nature's most spectacular sandboxes, you'll feel like a kid again as you hike up a 750-foot dune then roll down the other side.

Raft on the Arkansas: The Arkansas River is one of the most popular rivers for rafting and kayaking—from

gentle floats to Class V rapids—in the United States.

Ride Up Pikes Peak: Katharine Bates wrote "America the Beautiful" after riding to the top of Pikes Peak. Today you can drive or ride the cog railway to the top for the same see-forever views.

Visit the U.S. Air Force Academy: Here you can learn more about the academy that trains future Air Force leaders and visit the stunning, nondenominational Cadet Chapel.

12

ORIENTATION AND PLANNING

GETTING ORIENTED

This region, which encompasses the south-central section of Colorado, stretches from a collection of the state's 14,000-foot-high mountains in the heart of the Rockies eastward to Kansas, and from Colorado Springs south to the New Mexico state line. Pikes Peak, one of the most famous of Colorado's Fourteeners, forms the backdrop for Colorado Springs. Farther west, the Arkansas River towns of Buena Vista and Salida are within view of the Fourteeners of the Collegiate Peaks. Farther south, the Rio Grande runs through the flat San Luis Valley, which is lined by the Sangre de Cristo range. Cuchara Valley, just north of New Mexico, is framed by the Spanish Peaks.

Colorado Springs. About 70 mi south of Denver, Colorado Springs is a comfortable base camp for travelers headed for high altitude and high adventure. Colorado's second-largest city has natural attractions like Pikes Peak and Garden of the Gods, and more recent additions like the Broadmoor luxury hotel and the U.S. Air Force Academy.

Colorado Springs Side Trips. You could gamble or visit a gold mine and learn more about the gold rush in Cripple Creek. If you prefer outdoor adventures, take a walk among petrified tree trunks in Florissant Fossil Beds or go river rafting near Cañon City.

Collegiate Peaks. Buena Vista and Salida provide easy access to the largest collection of 14,000-foot-or-higher peaks in Colorado, perfect for hiking, boating, river rafting, horseback riding, and mountain biking in wilderness areas.

Southeast Colorado. If you're looking for a mountain drive with spectacular and diverse scenery, take the Highway of Legends Scenic Byway. Tiny towns along the way are in Cuchara Valley; Pueblo and Trinidad are larger hubs.

The San Luis Valley. You can play like a child rolling around the dunes at the Great Sand Dunes National Park and Preserve. Leave time for a drive through the tiny nearby towns or a ride on one of the two scenic railroads.

PLANNING

WHEN TO GO

Colorado Springs is a good year-round choice, because winters are relatively mild. Late spring or early summer is best if you want adrenaline-rush rafting, because the snowmelt is feeding the rivers. Summer is tourist season everywhere in south central Colorado. Early fall is another good time to visit, especially when the aspen leaves are turning gold. Some of the lodging properties in the smaller towns are closed in winter, although there are always some open for the cross-country skiers who enjoy staying in the small high-mountain towns.

GETTING HERE AND AROUND

AIR TRAVEL

Colorado Springs Airport (COS) is the major airport in the region, with a dozen nonstop destinations. Most south-central residents south of Colorado Springs drive to this city to fly out.

Alternatively, you can choose to fly to Denver International Airport (DEN), which has a lot more nonstop flights from other major cities to Colorado. It's a 70-mi drive from Denver to the Springs, but during rush hour it might take a solid two hours, whether you're in your own car or in one of the Denver–Colorado Springs shuttles. If you take the E–470 toll road for part of the drive, the ride will be faster.

Airports Colorado Springs Airport (COS) ☎ 719/550–1972 ⊕ www.flycos.com. **Denver International Airport (DEN)** ☎ 303/342–2000 ⊕ www.flydenver.com. **Pueblo Memorial Airport (PUB)** ☎ 719/553–2760 ⊕ www.pueblo.us/airport.

CAR TRAVEL

In Colorado Springs (whose airport has the typical lineup of car-rental agencies), the main north–south roads are Interstate 25, Academy Boulevard, Nevada Avenue, and Powers Boulevard, and each will get you where you want to go in good time; east–west routes along Woodmen Road (far north), Austin Bluffs Parkway (north central), and Platte Boulevard (south central) can get backed up.

Running north–south from Wyoming to New Mexico, Interstate 25 bisects Colorado and is the major artery into the area. Colorado Springs and Pueblo (which also has a pair of car-rental counters at the airport) are on Interstate 25. Florissant and Buena Vista are reached via U.S. 24 off Interstate 25; Cañon City and the Royal Gorge via U.S. 50. Salida can be reached via Highway 291 from either U.S. 24 or U.S. 50. Palmer Lake and Larkspur are accessible via Interstate 25 and Highway 105. Aside from Colorado Springs and Pueblo, most cities in south central Colorado lack car-rental service.

Car Contacts AAA Colorado ☎ 719/591–2222. **Colorado Department of Transportation Road Condition Hotline** ☎ 303/639–1111. **Colorado State Patrol** ☎ 719/635–0385 ⊕ www.cotrip.org.

TRAIN TRAVEL

Amtrak's Southwest Chief stops daily in Trinidad and La Junta.

Train Contacts Amtrak ☎ *800/872–7245* ⊕ *www.amtrak.com.*

PARKS AND RECREATION AREAS

South central Colorado is chock-full of parks and recreational areas. Almost every chamber of commerce will have a list of trails in the near vicinity, so when you're asking for general information about the city, ask for a list of trails, too. The Arkansas River flows through this region, so every spring and summer people come here to raft through a mix of challenging white-water rapids interspersed with smoothly flowing sections. Pike, bass, and trout are plentiful in this region: popular fishing spots include Spinney Mountain Reservoir (between Florissant and Buena Vista), the Arkansas and South Platte rivers, and Trinidad Lake. Great Sand Dunes National Park and Preserve in the San Luis Valley is perfect for walking up (and sliding down) the dunes, hiking on mountain trails, kite flying, and wildlife viewing. Monarch, west of Salida, is the nearest ski area.

Arkansas Headwaters Recreation Area. Arkansas Headwaters Recreation Area is unique because it follows a linear 150-mi stretch of the Arkansas River, from the mountains near Leadville to Lake Pueblo. The Arkansas River is popular for rafting and kayaking, and fisherman love it for its brown trout. (Anglers near Salida reported good luck with 'hoppers.) There are six campgrounds along the river. ⊠ *307 W. Sackett Ave., Salida* ☎ *719/539–7289.*

Collegiate Peaks Wilderness Area. The Collegiate Peaks Wilderness Area, northwest of Buena Vista, includes 14 mountains above 14,000 feet and is known for superb hiking, mountain biking, and climbing—not to mention ghost towns. ⊠ *Leadville Ranger District, San Isabel National Forest, 810 Front St., Leadville* ☎ *719/486–0749.*

Pike National Forest. Pike National Forest encompasses millions of acres of public land that stretch along the Front Range and go deep into the Rockies. Pikes Peak is the best-known 14,000-footer in Pike—and one of the most famous in the state. ⊠ *Forest Service Office, 601 S. Weber, Colorado Springs* ☎ *719/553–1400.*

Ring of the Peak. Ring of the Peak is a collection of trails, four-wheel-drive roads, and a few roads that circle Pikes Peak. Altitudes range between 6,400 and 11,400 feet. Check the Web site for trail access. ⊕ *www.ringthepeak.com.*

RESTAURANTS

Many restaurants serve regional trout and game, as well as locally grown fruits and vegetables. In summer, look for cantaloupe from the town of Rocky Ford, dubbed the "Melon Capital of the World." Colorado Springs offers unique Colorado cuisine that zings taste buds without zapping budgets (plus the ubiquitous chain restaurants).

HOTELS

The lodging star is the Broadmoor resort in Colorado Springs, built from the booty of the late-19th-century gold-rush days, but there are also predictable boxy-bed motel rooms awaiting travelers at the junctions of major highways throughout the region. Interspersed are quaint mom-and-pop motels, as well as bed-and-breakfasts and small luxury hotels in tourist districts.

WHAT IT COSTS					
	¢	$	$$	$$$	$$$$
Restaurants	under $8	$8–$12	$13–$18	$19–$25	over $25
Hotels	under $80	$80–$120	$121–$170	$171–$230	over $230

Restaurant prices are for a main course at dinner, excluding 7.4% tax. Hotel prices are for two people in a standard double room in high season, excluding service charges and 9.4%–11.7% tax.

COLORADO SPRINGS

The contented residents of the Colorado Springs area believe they live in an ideal location, and it's hard to argue with them. To the west the Rockies form a majestic backdrop. To the east the plains stretch for miles. Taken together, the setting ensures a mild, sunny climate year-round, and makes skiing and golfing on the same day feasible with no more than a two- or three-hour drive. You don't have to choose between adventures here: you can climb the Collegiate Peaks one day and go white-water rafting on the Arkansas River the next.

The state's second-largest city, it is a politically and socially conservative bastion (the evangelical group Focus on the Family has its headquarters here). The cultural scene is strong here, too, between the outstanding Colorado Springs Fine Arts Center, the Colorado Springs Philharmonic, and the variety of plays and musicals offered at several theaters.

The region abounds in natural and man-made wonders, from the red sandstone monoliths of the Garden of the Gods to the space-age architecture of the U.S. Air Force Academy's Cadet Chapel. The most indelible landmark is unquestionably Pikes Peak (14,115 feet); after seeing the view from the peak, Katharine Lee Bates penned "America the Beautiful." Pikes Peak is a constant reminder that this contemporary city is still close to nature. Purple in the early morning, snow-packed after winter storms, capped with clouds on windy days, the mountain is a landmark for directions and, when needed, a focus of contemplation.

GETTING HERE AND AROUND

It's easiest to explore this region in a private car, because the attractions are spread out. If you're staying in the heart of town and don't intend to head out to Pikes Peak, the Air Force Academy or other attractions farther away, you could use the Mountain Metropolitan Transit bus system or grab a taxi. Gray Line offers tours of the Colorado Springs area, including Pikes Peak and Manitou Springs.

South Central Colorado

Aspen · Leadville · Jefferson · Deckers · 25 · 86 · Limon · 70
9 · Fairplay · Palmer Lake · Monument
82 · Granite · Hartsel · 24 · Woodland Park
285 · Florissant Fossil Beds · Pikes Peak 14,110 ft. · 94 · Colorado Springs see detail map · Punkin Center
Buena Vista · 9 · 24
St. Elmo · Cripple Creek · 115 · 71
Salida · Cañon City · Royal Gorge
50 · Florence · 67 · 50 · Pueblo · Ordway · 96
285 · 96 · 50 · Fowler · Rocky Ford
114 · Saguache · Westcliffe · 165 · La Junta
Moffat · 69 · Colorado City · Simpson · 109
285 · 17 · Great Sand Dunes National Park and Preserve · 10 · 350
Del Norte · Center · Walsenburg · Kim
South Fork · Monte Vista · Manassa, San Luis, and Fort Garland loop · 160
Alamosa · Ft. Garland · Cuchara Valley · 25
285 · 12 · Trinidad
Antonito · 159 · NEW MEXICO

30 mi
30 km

ESSENTIALS

Transportation Contacts City Cab ☎ 719/543–2525. **Colorado Springs Shuttle** ☎ 719/687–3456 ⊕ www.coloradoshuttle.com. **Mountain Metropolitan Transit** ☎ 719/385-7433 ⊕ www.mmtransit.com. **Yellow Cab** ☎ 719/634-5000.

Tour Contacts Gray Line ☎ 719/633-1181 ⊕ grayline.com.

Visitor Information Colorado Springs Convention and Visitors Bureau ✉ 515 S. Cascade Ave. ☎ 719/635-7506, 800/888-4748 ⊕ www. experiencecoloradosprings.com. **Colorado Springs Parks, Recreation and Cultural Services Department** ☎ 719/385-5940 ⊕ www.springsgov.com. **Manitou Springs Chamber of Commerce** ✉ 354 Manitou Ave. ☎ 719/685-5089, 800/642-2567 ⊕ www.manitousprings.org. **Tri-Lakes Chamber of Commerce (Palmer Lake)** ✉ 300 Hwy. 105, Monument ☎ 719/481-3282 ⊕ www. trilakes.net.

EXPLORING COLORADO SPRINGS

Pikes Peak is a must-do and pairs nicely with an afternoon of poking around in the shops of Manitou Springs. The red rocks of Garden of the Gods and Cheyenne Cañon Park are the other natural showstoppers—mix and match them with exploring the surrounding neighborhoods and tourist attractions. And don't forget the U.S. Air Force Academy, just north of town.

PIKES PEAK AND MANITOU SPRINGS

Access points for scaling the mighty Pikes Peak are in the Manitou Springs area, a quaint National Historic Landmark District that exudes an informal charm. Stop at the chamber for a free map of the 11 mineral-springs drinking fountains and historic sites. On your self-guided tour, stop by Soda Springs or Twin Springs during the day, or for an after-dinner spritz (it tastes and acts just like Alka-Seltzer).

TIMING It takes a full day to visit Pikes Peak, explore Manitou Springs, and visit some of the attractions along Highway 24, if you want to enjoy each without doing a marathon sprint. Whether you head up Pikes Peak in a car and stop for lunch at the top or take the train (which includes a stop at the summit), plan at least four hours. Visiting the variety of shops, which sell souvenirs to antiques, along historic Manitou Springs' main street is a good way to stretch your legs after the journey to the peak. Heading underground into Cave of the Winds or visiting the Cliff Dwellings Museum will easily fill up the rest of the day.

TOP ATTRACTIONS

Ⓒ **Pikes Peak.** If you want to see the view from the top of Pikes Peak, the
Fodor's Choice view that Katharine Bates described in "America the Beautiful," head
★ up this 14,115-foot-high mountain on a train, in a car, or in a pair of hiking boots if you've got the stamina. Summit House is a casual café and trading post at the very top of the mountain. Whichever route you choose to take up the prominent peak, you'll understand why the pioneers heading West via wagon train used to say: "Pikes Peak or Bust."

Pikes Peak Highway. You can drive the 19-mi Pikes Peak Highway, which rises nearly 7,000 feet in its precipitous, dizzying climb; stop at the top for lunch and to enjoy the view; then be at the base again in approximately three hours. This is the same route that leading race-car drivers follow every year in the famed Pikes Peak Hill Climb, at speeds that have reached 123 mi per hour. ✉ *$10–$12 per person; $35–$40 per carload.*

Barr Trail. The 12.6-mi hike up Barr Trail gains 7,510 feet in elevation before you reach the summit. Halfway up the steep trail is Barr Camp, where many hikers spend the night. ✉ *U.S. 24 west to Cascade, 5 mi from Manitou Springs* ☎ *719/684–9383* ☉ *Barr Camp: daily 7–7.*

Pikes Peak Cog Railway. The world's highest cog train departs from Manitou and follows a frolicking stream up a steep canyon, through stands of quaking aspen and towering lodgepole pines, before reaching the timberline, where you can see far into the plains until arriving at the 14,115-foot summit. Advance reservations are recommended in summer and on weekends, as this popular attraction sells out trips regularly. ✉ *515 Ruxton Ave.* ☎ *719/685–5401* ⊕ *www.cograilway.com* ✉ *$34* ⚓ *Reservations essential* ☉ *Open year-round; call for schedule.*

WORTH NOTING

Cave of the Winds. Discovered by two boys in 1880, the cave has been exploited as a tourist sensation ever since. The entrance is through the requisite "trading post," but once inside the cave you'll forget the hype

12

and commercialism. The cave contains examples of every major sort of limestone formation, from stalactites and stalagmites to delicate cave flowers, rare anthracite crystals, flowstone (rather like candle wax), and cave coral. Enthusiastic guides for the 45-minute tour also run more adventurous cave expeditions. A special lantern tour lasts 1½ hours. ⊠ *100 Cave of the Winds Rd. off Hwy. 24* ☎ *719/685–5444* ⊕ *www.caveofthewinds.com* ⊠ *$18–$22* ⊙ *June–Aug., daily 9–9; Sept.–May, daily 10–5.*

Manitou Cliff Dwellings Museum. Some Ancestral Puebloan cliff dwellings that date from the 1100s have been moved from other sites in southern Colorado to the museum. Two rooms of artifacts in the museum offer information on the history of the dwellings. Native American dance demonstrations take place several times a day in summer. ⊠ *U.S. 24* ☎ *719/685–5242, 800/359–9971* ⊕ *www.cliffdwellingsmuseum.com* ⊠ *$9.50* ⊙ *May–Sept., daily 9–6; Oct. and Nov., Mar. and Apr., daily 9–5; Dec.–Feb. 1, daily 9–4.*

Manitou Springs. The town grew around the springs, so all 11 of them are in or near downtown. Competitions to design the fountains that bring the spring water to the public ensured that each fountain design is unique. It's a bring-your-own-cup affair; the water (frequently tested) is potable and free. The chamber of commerce publishes a free guide to the springs. ☎ *719/685–5089* ⊠ *Free.*

Miramont Castle Museum. Commissioned in 1895 as the private home of French priest Jean-Baptiste Francolon, this museum in Manitou Springs is still decorated, in part, as if a family lived here. More than 40 rooms offer a wide variety of displays and furnishings primarily from the Victorian era. Have lunch or high tea in the Queens Parlour Tea Room. ⊠ *9 Capitol Hill Ave., Manitou Springs* ☎ *719/685–1011* ⊕ *www.miramontcastle.org* ⊠ *$8* ⊙ *June–Aug. Daily. 9–5; Sept.–May, Tues.–Sat. 10–4, Sun. noon–4.*

THE BROADMOOR AND CHEYENNE CAÑON

Up in the Cheyenne Cañon section of town there are some terrific natural sites. Along the way you can view some of the city's exclusive neighborhoods and stop for lunch at the Broadmoor.

TIMING This is a good drive if there are kids in your group, because you can include stops at the Cheyenne Mountain Zoo and the Will Rogers Shrine of the Sun. Young ones can also blow off any extra energy racing up and down the paths at Seven Falls. Depending upon where you decide to stop, this could take a half to a full day.

TOP ATTRACTIONS

Fodor's Choice **The Broadmoor.** This pink-stucco Italianate complex, built in 1918, is
★ truly one of the world's finest luxury resorts. Even if you don't stay here, stop by for lunch on one of the many restaurant patios in summer and to take a paddleboat ride on Lake Cheyenne, which anchors several of the resort's buildings. The Sunday brunch here is legendary, and reservations are almost mandatory. ⊠ *1 Lake Circle* ☎ *719/634–7711, 800/634–7711* ⊕ *www.broadmoor.com.*

Cheyenne Mountain Zoo. America's highest zoo, at 6,800 feet, has more
★ than 500 animals housed amid mossy boulders and ponderosa pines.

You can hand-feed the giraffe herd in the zoo's African Rift Valley and check out the animals living in Primate World, Wolves Alley, or the Asian Highlands. ⊠ *4250 Cheyenne Mountain Zoo Rd.* ☎ *719/633–9925* ⊕ *www.cmzoo.org* ⊒ *$14.25, includes admission to Will Rogers Shrine* ⊘ *June–Aug., daily 9–6; Sept.–May, daily 9–5.*

♻ **North Cheyenne Cañon Park.** This is Colorado Springs at its best. Nearby Seven Falls has the hand of man all over its natural wonders, but the 1,600 acres of this city park, which is open year-round, manifest nature and natural history without a hint of commercialism—or charge. The canyon's moderate hikes include the Lower Columbine and Mount Cutler trails, each less than a 3-mi round-trip. Both afford a view of the city and a sense of accomplishment.

   Starsmore Discovery Center. At the mouth of the canyon off Cheyenne Boulevard, this center is chock-full of nature exhibits and has a climbing wall where kids can try their hands and feet against gravity. ⊠ *2120 S. Cheyenne Canyon Rd* ⊘ *Apr.–Oct., daily. Call for hrs* ⊠ *2120 S. Cheyenne Cañon Rd.* ☎ *719/385–6086* ⊕ *www.springsgov. com* ⊒ *Free* ⊘ *June–Aug., daily 9–5; Sept.–Oct. and Apr.–May, Wed.–Sun. 9–5.*

★ **Seven Falls.** The road up to this transcendent series of cascades is touted as the "grandest mile of scenery in Colorado." That's an exaggeration, but the red-rock canyon *is* stunning—though no more so than the falls themselves, which plummet into a tiny emerald pool. A set of 224 steep steps leads to the top, but there's an elevator, too. Hours vary seasonally, so it may be wise to call ahead. ⊠ *2850 Cheyenne Cañon Rd.* ☎ *719/632–0765* ⊕ *www.sevenfalls.com* ⊒ *$9.25 before 5 pm; $10.50 after 5 pm* ⊘ *May–Sept., daily 8:30 am–10:30 pm; Oct.–Apr., daily 9–4.*

WORTH NOTING

Will Rogers Shrine of the Sun. This five-story tower was dedicated in 1937, after the tragic plane crash that claimed Rogers's life. Its interior is painted with all manner of Western murals in which Rogers and Colorado Springs benefactor Spencer Penrose figure prominently, and is plastered with photos and homespun sayings of America's favorite cowboy. In the chapel are 15th- and 16th-century European artworks. ⊠ *4250 Cheyenne Mountain Zoo Rd.* ☎ *719/578–5367* ⊒ *$14.25, includes admission to Cheyenne Mountain Zoo* ⊘ *June–Aug., daily 9–5; Sept.–May, daily 9–5. Last entrance one hour before closing.*

GARDEN OF THE GODS AND URBAN COLORADO SPRINGS

Depending on which museums you decide to visit, a tour of Garden of the Gods and urban Colorado Springs could take from two-thirds of a day to a full day to take everything in, from learning how the pioneers struggled to survive and thrive to strolling through the stunning red-rock cliffs and visiting the Trading Post at Garden of the Gods.

QUICK BITES

Café 36. Amuzé is simply decorated and built to give diners a spectacular view of trees and the mountains beyond. Lunch choices range from Maryland blue crab Caesar salad to six-cheese ravioli. The museum's Art Deco Lounge, with its tapas menu, is a popular gathering place. There's live jazz

Colorado Springs Vicinity

PIKE NATIONAL FOREST

Convent of St. Francis

Woodmen Rd.

S. Gate Blvd.

Research Pkwy.

83

25

Academy Blvd.

Union Blvd.

Centennial Blvd.

Rockrimmon Blvd.

Dublin Blvd.

Vickers Dr.

Ute Valley Park

Garden of the Gods Rd.

University of Colorado at Colorado Springs

Austin

Palmer Park

Bear Creek Rd.

Range Rd.

30th St.

Fillmore St.

Mesa Rd.

Nevada Av.

Cascade Av.

Templeton Gap Rd.

COLORADO SPRINGS

Garden of the Gods

Uintah St.

Colorado College

24

TO PIKES PEAK

MANITOU SPRINGS

Colorado Av.

8th St.

Wahsatch Av.

Hancock Av.

Circle Dr.

Pikes Peak Av.

Prospect Lake

Bear Creek Park

Gold Camp Rd.

26th St.

21st St.

Pikes Peak Av.

Fountain Blvd.

TO MUNICIPAL AIRPORT

Cheyenne Blvd.

112

Cheyenne Mt. Zoo Rd.

Nevada Av.

25

Hancock Expwy.

Academy Blvd.

Bear Creek

PIKE NATIONAL FOREST

115

Venetucci Blvd.

B St.

0   3 miles

0   2 km

on Friday. ⊠ *Colorado Springs Fine Arts Center, 30 W. Dale St.* ☎ *719/477–4377* ⊕ *www.csfineartscenter.org* ⊘ *No lunch Mon. No dinner Sun.–Wed.*

TOP ATTRACTIONS

★ **Colorado Springs Fine Arts Center.** This regional museum has a fine permanent collection of modern art and excellent rotating exhibits. Some highlight the cultural contributions of regional artists; others focus on famous artists such as the glassmaker Dale Chihuly. Enjoy the view of Pikes Peak and the mountains from the patio in the summer. ⊠ *30 W. Dale St.* ☎ *719/634–5581* ⊕ *www.csfineartscenter.org* ⊡ *$10* ⊘ *Tues.–Sun. 10–5.*

Fodor'sChoice **Garden of the Gods.** These magnificent, eroded red-sandstone forma-
★ tions—from gnarled jutting spires to sensuously abstract monoliths—were sculpted more than 300 million years ago. Follow the road as it loops past such oddities as the Three Graces, the Siamese Twins, and the Kissing Camels. High Point, near the south entrance, provides camera hounds with the ultimate photo op: a formation known as Balanced Rock and jagged formations that frame Pikes Peak. The visitor center has maps of the trails and several geological, historical, and hands-on displays, as well as a café. It's a short, paved hike into the park from the parking lot. ⊠ *Visitor and Nature Center, 1805 N. 30th St., at Gateway Rd.* ☎ *719/634–6666* ⊕ *www.gardenofgods.com* ⊡ *Free* ⊘ *May–Oct., daily 8–8; Nov.–May, daily 9–5.*

Pioneers Museum. Once the Old El Paso County Courthouse, this repository has artifacts relating to the entire Pikes Peak area. The historic courtroom is absolutely elegant, and so perfectly appointed that it looks as if a judge will walk in any minute to start a trial. It's most notable for the special exhibits the museum puts together or receives on loan from institutions like the Smithsonian, such as the quilt competition that commemorated the 100th anniversary of the song "America the Beautiful." ⊠ *215 S. Tejon St.* ☎ *719/385–5990* ⊕ *www.cspm.org* ⊡ *Free* ⊘ *June–Aug., Tues.–Sat. 10–4; call for Sept.–May hrs.*

Fodor'sChoice **U.S. Air Force Academy.** The academy, which set up camp in 1954, is one
★ of the most popular attractions in Colorado. Highlights include the futuristic design, 18,000 beautiful acres of land, and antique and historic aircraft displays. At the visitor center you'll find photo exhibits, a model of a cadet's room, a gift shop, a snack bar, and a 14-minute film designed to make you want to enlist on the spot. Other stops on the tour include a B-52 display, sports facilities, a parade ground, and the chapel. ■TIP→ **The impressive cadet lunch formation usually takes place on Monday, Wednesday, and Friday at noon.** The Air Force chapel, which can accommodate simultaneous Catholic, Jewish, and Protestant services, is easily recognized by its unconventional design, which features 17 spires that resemble sharks' teeth or billowing sails. Don't miss the smaller chapels, including the downstairs Buddhist room. Visitors can enter through North Gate or South Gate, both off Interstate 25. ⊠ *I–25* ☎ *719/333–2025* ⊕ *www.usafa.af.mil* ⊡ *Free* ⊘ *Daily 9–5.*

★ **U.S. Olympic Training Center.** America's hopefuls come to train and be tested here, and depending on which teams are in residence at the time, you might catch a glimpse of some future Wheaties-box material.

The hourly guided tours begin with a 12-minute video, followed by about a 30-minute walk around the facilities. ✉ *1750 E. Boulder St.* ☎ *719/866–4618* ⊕ *www.teamusa.org* ✆ *Free* ☉ *June–Aug.,Mon.–Sat. 9–4:30; Sept.–May, Mon.–Sat. 9–4.*

WORTH NOTING

☾ **ANA Money Museum.** The American Numismatic Association's fascinating Money Museum has a collection of old gold coins, mistakes made at the U.S. Mint, and currency from around the world. Tours are available Tuesday to Friday. ✉ *818 N. Cascade Ave.* ☎ *800/367–9723* ⊕ *www. money.org* ✆ *$5* ☉ *Tues.–Sat. 10:30–5.*

FAC Modern. This satellite venue of the Colorado Springs Fine Arts Center in the downtown area focuses on contemporary art. ✉ *Plaza of the Rockies, South Tower, 121 S. Tejon St.* ☎ *719/477–4308* ⊕ *www. csfineartscenter.org* ✆ *Free* ☉ *Mon.–Fri. 10–4.*

☾ **Ghost Town.** You can play a real player piano and a nickelodeon at this Western town with a sheriff's office, general store, saloon, and smithy. There's also gold panning in the summer. ✉ *400 S. 21st St.* ☎ *719/634–0696* ⊕ *www.ghosttownmuseum.com* ✆ *$6.50* ☉ *June–Aug., Mon.–Sat. 9–6, Sun. 11–6; Sept.–May, Mon.–Sat. 10–5, Sun. 11–5.*

Glen Eyrie. General William Jackson Palmer, the founder of Colorado Springs, was greatly influenced by European architecture and lifestyle, and lived in this evolving mansion-turned-castle from its beginnings in the 1870s until his death in 1909. Original gas lamps and sandstone structures remain. Many of its rocks were hewn with the moss still clinging, to give them an aged look. The grandiose estate is maintained by a fundamentalist Christian ministry called the Navigators, which runs programs and seminars. An afternoon English tea is offered daily in summer. ✉ *3820 30th St.* ☎ *719/634–0808* ⊕ *www.gleneyrie.org* ✆ *$6* ☉ *Tours: June–Aug., Tues.–Fri. at 11; Sept.–May, Fri.–Sun. at 1.*

Old Colorado City. Once a separate, rowdier town where miners caroused, today the stretch of Colorado Avenue between 24th Street and 28th Street, west of downtown, is a kitschy National Historic Landmark District whose restored buildings house galleries and boutiques as well as shops with inexpensive souvenirs and restaurants. ✉ *Colorado Ave., between 24th and 28th St.* ⊕ *www.shopoldcoloradocity.com.*

☾ **Pro Rodeo Hall of Fame and Museum of the American Cowboy.** Even a tenderfoot would get a kick out of this museum, which includes changing displays of Western art; permanent photo exhibits that capture the excitement of bronco-bustin' and the lonely life of the cowpoke; gorgeous saddles and belt buckles; and multimedia tributes to rodeo's greatest competitors. ✉ *101 Pro Rodeo Dr., off I-25* ☎ *719/528–4764* ⊕ *www.prorodeo.com* ✆ *$6* ☉ *Summer, daily 9–5; Nov.–Apr., Wed.–Sat. 9–5.*

Western Museum of Mining and Industry. The region's rich history of mining is represented through comprehensive exhibits of equipment and techniques and hands-on demonstrations, including gold panning. The 27-acre mountain site has several outdoor exhibits, and is a great spot for a picnic. ✉ *225 North Gate Blvd., off I-25* ☎ *719/488–0880* ⊕ *www.wmmi.org* ✆ *$8* ☉ *Mon.–Sat. 9–4.*

12

SPORTS AND THE OUTDOORS

A number of activities are available within an hour or two of Colorado Springs, including hot-air ballooning, white-water rafting, and access jeep tours. Riding in a jeep is one way to view the backcountry; a horseback ride on trails through meadows and along mountainsides is another.

Some of the best choices for hiking in this region are the Barr Trail, which heads up Pikes Peak (and is for hardy, well-conditioned hikers), and the array of trails in North Cheyenne Cañon Park.

ADVENTURE TOURS

Adventures Out West. Adventures Out West offers high-adventure trips through the Royal Gorge and gentler trips through Bighorn Sheep Canyon. It can also arrange other activities, such as ballooning, horseback riding, and jeep tours. ✉ *1680 S. 21st St.* ☎ *719/578–0935, 800/755–0935* ⊕ *www.adventuresoutwest.com.*

Echo Canyon River Expeditions. Rafting on the Arkansas and Colorado rivers is offered by Echo Canyon River Expeditions. A Raft and Rail trip includes a morning on the Arkansas River and a ride on the Royal Gorge Railroad in the afternoon. The company will also customize trips. ✉ *45000 U.S. Hwy. 50, Cañon City* ☎ *719/755–3246* ⊕ *www.raftecho.com.*

GOLF

★ **The Broadmoor Golf Club.** The three courses here offer distinctly diverse challenges, in part because they travel over a variety of terrain on the resort's 3,000 acres in the Rocky Mountain foothills. Donald Ross designed the original resort course in 1918, but today the East Course is a mix including nine of the original holes and nine more designed by Robert Trent Jones Sr. in 1965. The West Course is also a combination of holes designed by each golf-course architect, but it's at a higher elevation (6,800 feet above sea level), and has more-vicious doglegs, rolling fairways, and multilevel greens. The Mountain Course has some wide forgiving fairways and large greens, but there are major elevation changes that add special challenges while providing outstanding mountain views. ✉ *The Broadmoor, 1 Lake Circle* ☎ *719/577–5790* ⊕ *www.broadmoor.com* ⚓ *Reservations essential* ⛳ *East Course: 18 holes. Yards: 7310. Par: 72. Mountain Course: 18 holes. Yards: 7637. Par: 72. West Course: 18 holes. Yards: 7016. Par: 72. Green fee: $100–$235, depending on season and course.*

HIKING

Pikes Peak Greenway Trail. This trail combines with the New Santa Fe Regional Trail for 34 mi of multi-surface trails for hiking and biking. The trails run from Tejon Street through Colorado Springs and north to Palmer Lake. A 6.9-mi section goes through the Air Force Academy, but you are expected to stay on the 6-foot-wide trail. Helmets and ID are required on the academy grounds, which may be closed at times. Past the academy, the trail then flows over gently rolling hills and finally follows a straight line and level course over an abandoned railroad track for the last 6.5 mi into Palmer. ⊠ *Trail begins on Tejon St.* ☎ *719/520–6375* ⊕ *www.elpasocountyparks.com.*

Red Rock Canyon. Red Rock Canyon is a Colorado Springs city park. You can ramble on trails among the red sandstone monoliths and spires, balanced by white limestone and yellow-brown sandstone hogbacks. ⊠ *Trailhead south of U.S. 24, near 31st St.*

Red Rock Loop Trail. Red Rock Loop Trail, on Manitou Section 16, is a 5.5-mi, moderately difficult loop with an elevation gain of up to 1,100 feet. The topography varies from steep, mountainous terrain to moderate slopes, mesas, and canyons. There are views of sandstone formations and old quarries, as well as a terrific perspective of Colorado Springs and Pikes Peak. ⊠ *Trailhead on Trail Ridge Rd., off U.S. 24.*

HORSEBACK RIDING

Academy Riding Stables. Trail rides, most notably through the Garden of the Gods, are offered by Academy Riding Stables. ⊠ *4 El Paso Blvd.* ☎ *719/633–5667* ⊕ *www.arsriding.com.*

MOUNTAIN BIKING

Challenge Unlimited. Challenge Unlimited offers bike tours throughout Colorado, including the daily 20-mi bike tour down Pikes Peak May through mid-October. The tours include helmets and bikes. ☎ *800/798–5954* ⊕ *www.bikithikit.com.*

Pikes Peak Mountain Bike Tours. Pikes Peak Mountain Bike Tours will take you to the top of Pikes Peak, then let you ride all the way down on one of their lightweight mountain bikes. An alternative tour is the 20-mi tour on Upper Gold Camp Road, which is a self-paced downhill ride along an old railroad tract converted to a hiking–bicycling trail that cuts through the mountains. ☎ *888/593–3062* ⊕ *www.bikepikespeak.com.*

WHERE TO EAT

$$
AMERICAN

✕ **Adam's Mountain Café.** Join the locals sitting at mismatched tables, viewing drawings by regional artists, and mingling at the community table. The long dining room has tall windows overlooking the patio. The food has an organic bent, with many vegetarian options. Smashing breakfasts include orange-almond French toast and huevos rancheros; dinners such as Senegalese vegetables or Laoation lettuce wraps are hits as well. ⊠ *934 Manitou Ave.* ☎ *719/685–1430* ⊕ *www.adamsmountain.com* ⊗ *No dinner Sun. and Mon.*

$$$$
MODERN
AMERICAN
★

✕ **Blue Star.** Perch on a high stool in the bar while enjoying tapas like flash-fried squid with sweet chili sauce or spanakopita primavera, or head to the simple and elegant dining room for a leisurely dinner. Influences drift around the globe, from Asia to the Mediterranean. It's a place frequented by everyone from blue-haired ladies to college students, so it's best to make a reservation. Blue Star offers half-price wine on Sunday, half-price martinis on Monday, and half-price imperial beers on Thursday. ⊠ *1645 S. Tejon St.* ☎ *719/632–1086* ⊕ *www.thebluestar.net.*

$$$$
EUROPEAN

✕ **Briarhurst Manor.** One of the most exquisitely romantic restaurants in Colorado, Briarhurst Manor has several dining rooms, each with its own look and mood. The rich decor includes cherrywood wainscoting, balustrades, and furnishings, Van Briggle wood-and-ceramic fireplaces, tapestries, chinoiserie, and hand-painted glass. Dine in the Garden Room, which has massive bow windows, or in the book-lined Library. In the Drawing Room, with its ornate chandelier and fireplace, the tables are nicely spaced for conversation. Choose from classic European entrées such as trout almondine and Chateaubriand to more modern dishes like bison short ribs. ⊠ *404 Manitou Ave.* ☎ *719/685–1864* ⊕ *www.briarhurst.com.*

$$$$ ✕ **Carlos Bistro.** Although this chic spot with copper-and-black decor
MODERN is a ways from downtown, it's a local favorite thanks to its great
AMERICAN food and casual ambience. Here you'll find patrons—some wearing jeans, others in suits—dining in the dim light on what appear to be pieces of art framed by triangular white plates. Start with fresh oysters or a blue-lump crab cake, then move on to seared filet mignon with a black-peppercorn brandy sauce or lump blue-crab meat on filet mignon, topped with béarnaise sauce. If you're not full, try the New Orleans chocolate bread pudding, or the white-chocolate bread pudding with macadamia nuts. ⊠ *1025 S. 21st St.* ☎ *719/471–2905* ☉ *Closed Sun. No lunch Sat.*

$$$$ ✕ **Charles Court at the Broadmoor.** Charles Court's contemporary country-
MODERN manor decor lends warmth to a fine-dining setting in this large resort.
AMERICAN Many of the tables in the large open space have a wonderful view of Cheyenne Lake. Tabletop items such as napkin rings and centerpieces made from handblown glass add a lovely touch. The menu is American-oriented, with a Rocky Mountain flair. Try the Colorado rack of lamb, the tenderloin of buffalo, or the rainbow trout during a leisurely dinner. The wine cellar has more than 3,000 bottles. ⊠ *The Broadmoor West, 1 Lake Circle* ☎ *719/577–5733* ⊕ *www.broadmoor.com* ☉ *Closed Tues. and Wed.*

$$$$ ✕ **Craftwood Inn.** This intimate restaurant is a favorite with locals cel-
AMERICAN ebrating special occasions. A delightful Old English feel is achieved through wrought-iron chandeliers, stained-glass partitions, heavy wood beams, and a majestic stone-and-copper fireplace. Craftwood focuses on game, so try the Wild Grill, a combination of elk, antelope, and venison dishes. Wild Blue Russian boar is another favorite. Accompany your dinner with a selection from the well-considered wine list. ⊠ *404 El Paso Blvd., Manitou Springs* ☎ *719/685–9000* ⊕ *www.craftwood. com* ♨ *Reservations essential* ☉ *No lunch.*

$$$$ ✕ **Nosh 121.** Small plates are the focus at this popular restaurant next to
ECLECTIC the FAC Modern. People often share the more than 25 "noshers," ranging from lentil hummus to house-made potato chips. The koi murals represent the restaurant's flow of energy and good service. Specials include "nosh" deals Saturday to Monday and wine flights on Sunday and Monday nights. ⊠ *121 S. Tejon St.* ☎ *719/635–6674* ⊕ *www. nosh121.com* ☉ *No lunch weekends.*

$$$$ ✕ **Penrose Room at the Broadmoor.** Whatever number of courses you
MODERN choose from the prix-fixe menu, you're guaranteed a memorable culi-
AMERICAN nary experience. Executive chef Bertrand Bouquin varies the dishes
★ seasonally, offering fine dining without the constraints of French,

12

American, or any other single cuisine. Appetizers such as sautéed fois gras with caramelized apple butter, and entrées such as monkfish and lobster tail wrapped in country bacon with black-truffle risotto and baby fennel, are plated to look like edible works of art. Indulge yourself with the seven-course meal with wine pairings ($175). Request a table in the small glassed-in area, and you can watch the sun set behind Cheyenne Mountain, or ask about sitting at the 16-seat chef's table. Jackets are required for men. ⊠ *The Broadmoor South, 1 Lake Circle* ☎ *719/577–5733* ⊕ *www.broadmoor.com* ⌲ *Reservations essential* ☉ *Closed Sun. and Mon.*

$ ✕**Poor Richards.** This is a six-in-one store loved by locals of all ages.
AMERICAN On one side there's a pizza parlor, where you stand in line to order
⟳ hand-tossed pies, salads, and sandwiches. Step through a doorway and you're in a toy store. Step through another and you'll find yourself in Rico's Coffee, Chocolate, and Wine Bar, where the ambience is more upscale and the menu veers toward organic. Order a sandwich or a cheese plate, or try a wine and chocolate pairing. Step though another doorway and you've entered a used-book store. You can also enter each store from outside. ⊠ *320–324½ N. Tejon St.* ☎ *719/578–5549* ⊕ *www. poorrichardsdowntown.com.*

$$$ ✕**Summit at the Broadmoor.** The ambience at this "American brasserie"
MODERN is a successful blend of big-city elegance and Western casualness. The
AMERICAN 14-foot wine tower revolving slowly behind the bar is impossible to
Fodor's Choice miss. The menu includes year-round favorites and a seasonal section;
★ you may enjoy the subtle blending in the roasted potato soup with Hungarian paprika cream, the pan-seared Maine diver scallops with cumin, or the hanger steak with fries and red-wine shallot sauce. Thirty wines are served by the glass, and half the fun of dining here is the conversation with the sommelier or the knowledgeable waitstaff about pairing the wine to food. You can get a chef's tasting dinner paired with wine, beer, or cocktails. ⊠ *The Broadmoor, 19 Lake Circle* ☎ *719/577–5775* ⊕ *www.broadmoor.com* ⌲ *Reservations essential* ☉ *Closed Mon.*

WHERE TO STAY

For expanded hotel reviews, visit Fodors.com.

$$ ☷**Antlers Hilton Colorado Springs.** The marble-and-granite lobby strikes
HOTEL an immediate note of class at this downtown hotel, whose location provides easy access to restaurants and shops. **Pros:** good service; convenient location. **Cons:** little ambience; few amenities. ⊠ *4 S. Cascade Ave.* ☎ *719/955–5600, 866/299–4602* ⊕ *www.antlers.com* ⌐ *292 rooms, 8 suites* ⌖ *In-room: Internet. In-hotel: restaurant, bar, pool, gym, parking.*

$$$$ ☷**The Broadmoor.** The Broadmoor continues to redefine itself with
RESORT settings where guests can unwind and be pampered. **Pros:** you'll
Fodor's Choice feel thoroughly pampered; choosing where to eat may be difficult,
★ because there are so many good options. **Cons:** very expensive; rooms in the original West building are the least desirable. ⊠ *1 Lake Circle* ☎ *719/634–7711, 800/634–7711* ⊕ *www.broadmoor.com* ⌐ *593*

rooms, 107 suites, 44 cottages ⚭ In-room: safe, Internet. In-hotel: restaurant, bar, golf course, pool, tennis court, gym, spa, children's programs, parking, some pets allowed.

$$
RESORT
★
Cheyenne Mountain Resort. At this 217-acre resort on the slopes of Cheyenne Mountain, superb swimming facilities (including an Olympic-size pool), a variety of tennis courts, and a Pete Dye championship golf course tempt you to remain on-property, despite the easy access to the high country. **Pros:** resort ambience; outstanding views. **Cons:** you must walk outside to get to the main building; can get crowded for conferences. ⊠ 3225 Broadmoor Valley Rd. ☎ 719/538–4000, 800/428–8886 ⊕ www.cheyennemountain.com ⌂ 316 rooms, 5 suites ⚭ In-room: Wi-Fi. In-hotel: restaurant, bar, golf course, pool, tennis court, gym, children's programs, business center, parking.

$$$
HOTEL
Cliff House. This Victorian-era jewel was built in 1874 as a stage-coach stop between Colorado Springs and Leadville. **Pros:** convenient location; old-fashioned charm. **Cons:** not a good choice for those who prefer contemporary ambience, or those who want nightlife nearby. ⊠ 306 Cañon Ave., Manitou Springs ☎ 719/685–3000, 888/212–7000 ⊕ www.thecliffhouse.com ⌂ 37 rooms, 17 suites ⚭ In-room: safe, Internet, Wi-Fi. In-hotel: restaurant, bar, gym, parking.

$$$$
HOTEL
Garden of the Gods Club. The views are spectacular from this long-time private club overlooking the red rocks in the Garden of the Gods. **Pros:** great views; access to great golf on the Kissing Camels course. **Cons:** you'll have to drive to downtown; only one restaurant on-site. ⊠ 3320 Mesa Rd. ☎ 719/632–5541, 800/923–8838 ⊕ www.gardenofthegodsclub.com ⌂ 69 rooms, 18 golf cottages ⚭ In-room: safe. In-hotel: restaurant, bar, golf course, gym.

$$
B&B/INN
Fodor's Choice
★
Holden House. Innkeepers Sallie and Welling Clark realized their dream when they restored this 1902 home and transformed it into a B&B. **Pros:** good choice for travelers who want something homey; excellent breakfasts. **Cons:** in a residential neighborhood; must drive to attractions and restaurants. ⊠ 1102 W. Pikes Peak Ave. ☎ 719/471–3980 ⊕ www.holdenhouse.com ⌂ 5 rooms ⚭ In-room: Wi-Fi. In-hotel: some age restrictions ⏐⚭⏐ Breakfast.

NIGHTLIFE AND THE ARTS

THE ARTS

Pikes Peak Center. Colorado Springs' Pikes Peak Center presents a wide range of musical events as well as touring theater and dance companies. ⊠ 190 S. Cascade Ave. ☎ 719/520–7469 ⊕ www.pikespeakcenter.com.

NIGHTLIFE

BARS AND CLUBS

Cowboys. Cowboys is for country music lovers and two-steppers. ⊠ 25 N. Tejon St. ☎ 719/596–1212 ⊕ www.cowboyscs.com.

Golden Bee. The gloriously old-fashioned bar, with pressed-tin ceilings and magnificent woodwork, features a piano player leading sing-alongs. Watch out for the bees—as part of a long-standing tradition, they flick bee stickers into the audience during the show. ⊠ International

Center at the Broadmoor, 1 Lake Circle ☎ *719/634–7711* ⊕ *www. broadmoordining.com.*

Ritz. Located downtown, the Ritz fills up at cocktail hour and has a bistro-style menu for dining. The real action is on Wednesday, Friday, and Saturday, when the live music starts. Locals say to get there before 7 pm if you want to eat. ✉ *15 S. Tejon* ☎ *719/635–8484* ⊕ *www.ritzgrill.com.*

BREWPUBS

Bristol Brewing. At Bristol Brewing you can get fresh brews like Laughing Lab, Red Rocket, and Beehive in the tasting bar. ✉ *1647 S. Tejon St.* ☎ *719/633–2555* ⊕ *www.bristolbrewing.com.*

Judge Baldwin's. In the Antlers Hilton Colorado Springs, Judge Baldwin's is a popular local brewpub. ✉ *Antlers Hilton, 4 S. Cascade Ave.* ☎ *719/473–5600.*

Phantom Canyon Brewing Co. In a century-old warehouse, the Phantom Canyon Brewing Co. has billiards in an upstairs hall. There's great pub grub, plus sinful black-and-tan brownies. ✉ *2 E. Pikes Peak Ave.* ☎ *719/635–2800* ⊕ *www.phantomcanyon.com.*

COMEDY AND SHOWS

☺ ★ **Flying W Ranch.** The Flying W Ranch, open mid-May to September, ropes them in for the sensational Western stage show and a chuck-wagon dinner. The Winter Steakhouse indoors opens during the colder months. ✉ *3330 Chuckwagon Rd.* ☎ *719/598–4000* ⊕ *www.flyingw.com.*

Iron Springs Chateau. The Iron Springs Chateau offers comedy melodramas along with dinner mid-April through October and December. It's across from Pikes Peak Cog Railway. ✉ *444 Ruxton Ave.* ☎ *719/685–5104.*

Loonees Comedy Corner. Loonees Comedy Corner showcases live stand-up comedy Thursday to Saturday evening. Some of the performers are nationally known. ✉ *1305 N. Academy Blvd.* ☎ *719/591–0707* ⊕ *www. loonees.com.*

SHOPPING

Colorado Springs has a mix of upscale shopping in boutiques and major chain stores. Many boutiques and galleries cluster in Old Colorado City and the posh Broadmoor One Lake Avenue Shopping Arcade.

Manitou Springs, a small town between Garden of the Gods and Pikes Peak, has a historic district, and the Chamber of Commerce has free maps with a tasting guide that tells you what is in each of the 11 naturally effervescent springs around town. There's a large artists' population; walk along Manitou Avenue and Ruxton Avenue, where you'll find a mix of galleries, quaint shops, and stores selling souvenirs.

SHOPPING DISTRICTS AND MALLS

Chapel Hills Mall. Chapel Hills Mall, at the north end of town, has a Macy's and a Dick's Sporting Goods, plus many other stores. ✉ *1710 Briargate Blvd.* ⊕ *www.chapelhillsmall.com.*

Citadel. The Citadel counts Dillard's, Express, Foot Locker, and American Eagle Outfitters among its 100-plus stores. ✉ *750 Citadel Dr. E* ⊕ *www.shopthecitadel.com.*

Promenade Shops at Briargate. Among the tenants at the Promenade Shops at Briargate are clothiers Ann Taylor and Coldwater Creek, plus other retailers such as Pottery Barn and Williams-Sonoma. ✉ *1885 Briargate Pkwy.* ☎ *719/265–6264* ⊕ *www.thepromenadeshopsatbriargate.com.*

SPECIALTY SHOPS

ANTIQUES AND COLLECTIBLES

Ruxton's Trading Post. Ruxton's Trading Post has cowboy-and-Indian antiques and collectibles, Native American art, and nostalgia items from old TV programs and movies. ✉ *22 Ruxton Ave., Manitou Springs* ☎ *719/685–9024* ⊕ *www.oldwestantiques.com.*

CRAFT AND ART GALLERIES

Commonwheel Artists Co-Op. Commonwheel Artists Co-Op exhibits wall art in various mediums, jewelry, and fiber, clay, and glass art. ✉ *102 Cañon Ave., Manitou Springs* ☎ *719/685–1008* ⊕ *www.commonwheel. com.*

Dulcimer Shop. Like the sweet sounds of a dulcimer? At the Dulcimer Shop you can buy one, buy a kit to make one, or even get some lessons to start you off. ✉ *740 Manitou Ave., Manitou Springs* ☎ *719/685–9655* ⊕ *www.dulcimer.net/store.*

Flute Player Gallery. The Flute Player Gallery carries southwest Native American art, jewelry, and pottery. ✉ *2511 W. Colorado Ave.* ☎ *719/632–7702.*

Michael Garman Museum. The Michael Garman Museum offers Western-style paintings and contemporary sculpture. ✉ *2418 W. Colorado Ave.* ☎ *719/471–9391* ⊕ *www.michaelgarman.com.*

FOOD

Patsy's Candies. Renowned for its saltwater taffy and chocolate, Patsy's Candies offers tours weekdays mid-May to mid-September. ✉ *1540 S. 21st St.* ☎ *719/633–7215* ⊕ *www.patsyscandies.com.*

SPORTING GOODS

Kinfolks Mountain Outfitters. Kinfolks Mountain Outfitters is a unique operation. It's chock-full of gear and information for hikers, bikers, and climbers, but in the back it serves beer, wine, and coffee, so you can relax and swap stories while sitting creek-side. There's live music on Friday and Saturday evening. ✉ *950 Manitou Ave., Manitou Springs* ☎ *719/685–4433* ⊕ *www.kinfolksmanitou.com.*

COLORADO SPRINGS SIDE TRIPS

Easy day trips from Colorado Springs can lead you to the gambling or mining heritage in Cripple Creek. Florissant Fossil Beds attracts geology buffs. If you like heights, head to Cañon City and walk over the Royal Gorge Bridge, or take a lunchtime ride on the train that runs on a track through the most dramatic part of the canyon.

> **WORD OF MOUTH**
>
> "You'll probably find you can 'do' Cripple Creek in less than a day. It's very small and basically revolves around the casinos. If gambling's your main focus, you'll enjoy the town." —Virgogirl

CRIPPLE CREEK

46 mi west of Colorado Springs via U.S. 24 and Rte. 67.

Colorado's third legalized gambling town, Cripple Creek once had the most lucrative mines in the state—and 10,000 boozing, brawling, bawdy citizens. Today the main street is lined with casinos housed in Victorian buildings. Outside of the central area, old mining structures and the stupendous curtain of the Collegiate Peaks are marred by slag heaps and parking lots. Take a side trip to nearby Victor, walk down streets where hundreds of miners once took streetcars to the mines, and learn about their lives.

GETTING HERE AND AROUND

The town is tiny, though a bit hilly off the main drag, so it's easy to walk around and explore. Drive here in a private car, or hitch a ride on one of the Ramblin' Express casino shuttles from Colorado Springs to Cripple Creek. Ramblin' Express also runs between Cripple Creek and nearby Victor.

ESSENTIALS

Transportation Contacts Ramblin' Express ☎ 719/590–8687 ⊕ www.ramblinexpress.com.

Visitor Information Pikes Peak Heritage Center ✉ 9283 S. Hwy. 16 ☎ 877/858–4653 ⊕ www.visitcripplecreek.com.

TOP EXPERIENCE: CASINOS

Miners gathered around card games in most of the 100 saloons in Cripple Creek, which opened during the wild years after Bob Womack discovered gold in 1890. Today there's a lineup of casinos set into storefronts and buildings with exteriors meticulously maintained to retain the aura they had a century ago. But inside the 18 casinos and gambling parlors here today there's no question that these are gambling halls, chock-full of slot machines, video and live poker tables, and blackjack tables. Today there are even a few casinos in modern buildings, too. Since 2009 the maximum bet limit was raised to $100. You can play craps and roulette at many of the casinos, some of which stay open 24 hours a day.

Most of the casinos on East Bennett Avenue house predictable (albeit inexpensive) restaurants. Beef is the common denominator across all of the menus. The price goes up, along with the quality, at restaurants like the Steakhouse at Bronco Billy's Casino. Some casinos also have hotel rooms.

Gold Rush Hotel & Casino. The Rocky Mountain Victorian look of the Gold Rush Hotel & Casino is fairly typical of the establishments that line historic East Bennett Avenue. The casino offers craps and roulette, as well as blackjack, poker, and slot machines, and stays open 24/7. ⊠ *209 E. Bennett Ave.* ☎ *719/689–2646, 800/235–8239* ⊕ *grush.com.*

Imperial Hotel and Casino. Peek into the mining era's high life at the Imperial Hotel and Casino, where you'll see antiques, chandeliers, and hand-painted wallpaper from France as you play the latest slot machines. There's no craps or roulette here. ⊠ *123 N. 3rd St.* ☎ *719/689–2561* ⊕ *www.imperialhotelrestaurant.com.*

EXPLORING

Cripple Creek District Museum. The Cripple Creek District Museum provides a glimpse into mining life at the turn of the 20th century. ⊠ *500 Bennett Ave.* ☎ *719/689–2634* ⊕ *www.cripple-creek.org* ⊠ *$5* ☉ *June 1–Sept. 30, daily 10–5; Oct. 17–May 17, Sat.–Sun. 10–4.*

Cripple Creek and Victor Narrow Gauge Railroad. A favorite with kids, the Cripple Creek and Victor Narrow Gauge Railroad weaves over reconstructed trestles and past abandoned mines to the Anaconda ghost town, then returns to Cripple Creek during the 4-mi, 45-minute ride. In the boom days of the 1870s through the silver crash of 1893, more than 50 ore-laden trains made this run daily. For years Victor has been a sad town, virtually a ghost of its former self. Walking the streets—past abandoned or partially restored buildings—has been an eerie experience. But there's a partial renewal of the town, because Victor is again home to a gold mine, the Cripple Creek and Victor Mining Company. From mid-June to early October, trains depart every 40 minutes. ⊠ *520 E. Carr St., at Bennett Ave.* ☎ *719/689–2640* ⊕ *www.cripplecreekrailroad.com* ⊠ *$13* ☉ *Mid-June–early Oct., daily 10–5.*

Mollie Kathleen Gold Mine Tour. Descending 1,000 feet, the Mollie Kathleen Gold Mine Tour tours a mine that operated continuously from 1892 to 1961. The tours are wonderful, usually led by a former miner, but definitely not for the claustrophobic. Tours depart every 15 to 30 minutes. ⊠ *9388 Rte. 67, north of town* ☎ *719/689–2466* ⊕ *www.goldminetours.com* ⊠ *$18* ☉ *Mid-May–Mid-Sept., daily 10–5; late Apr.–mid-May and late Sept.–Oct., daily 10–4.*

FLORISSANT FOSSIL BEDS

35 mi west of Colorado Springs via U.S. 24.

GETTING HERE AND AROUND

From Cripple Creek, take Teller County Road 1, which goes right through the monument. It's about 17 mi from town.

EXPLORING

Florissant Fossil Beds National Monument. A temperate rain forest, Florissant Fossil Beds National Monument was perfectly preserved by volcanic ash 34 million years ago. This little-known site is a heaven for paleontologists. The visitor center offers a daily guided walk and ranger talks in the amphitheater in summer, or you can follow the well-marked hiking trails and lose yourself in the Eocene epoch among the remnants of petrified redwoods. ✉ *15807 Teller County 1* ☎ *719/748–3253* ⊕ *www.nps.gov/flfo* 🖼 *$3* ☉ *Summer daily 8–6; rest of year daily 9–5.*

12

PALMER LAKE

25 mi north of Colorado Springs via Interstate 25 and Hwy. 105.

Artsy, and very sleepy, Palmer Lake is a magnet for hikers who set out for the evergreen-clad peaks at several in-town trailheads. There are more good restaurants and working artists than one would expect from a population of about 1,700. The town developed around the railroad tracks that were laid here in 1871—the lake itself was used as a refueling point for steam engines.

EXPLORING

☺ **Colorado Renaissance Festival.** Larkspur is home to just a few hundred
★ residents, but it knows how to throw a heck of a party—and a medieval one at that. The Colorado Renaissance Festival annually throws open its gates to throngs of families, chain mail–clad fantasy enthusiasts, tattooed bikers, and fun lovers of every other kind. Within the wooded 350-acre "kingdom" there are performers who deliver everything from juggling stunts and fire-eating to hypnotism and comedy. The big event happens three times a day, when knights square off in the arena for a theatrical joust. There are also more than 200 artisans selling their wares, games, rides, and myriad food and drink booths. It's a great way to while away a summer day, though it can be a bit much to handle in the hottest weather. Larkspur is 9 mi north of Palmer Lake via Route 18. ✉ *Off Larkspur Rd.* ☎ *303/688 6010* ⊕ *www.coloradorenaissance. com* 🖼 *$17.95* ☉ *Early June–early Aug., weekends 10–6:30.*

Tri-Lakes Center for the Arts. In a landmark Kaiser-Frazer building on the north fringe of town, the Tri-Lakes Center for the Arts hangs rotating exhibits in its auditorium-gallery that also serves as a venue for music and theater. Classes and workshops are offered, and several resident artists work from studios on-site. ✉ *304 Hwy. 105* ☎ *719/481–0475* ⊕ *www.trilakesarts.org* 🖼 *Free* ☉ *Tues.–Sat. noon–4.*

QUICK BITES

Rock House Ice Cream. Rock House Ice Cream is a popular stop for hikers on their way home. Choose from among 24 different types, including cake batter, black raspberry, cookie dough, or rainbow sherbet, for your cone or milk shake. ✉ *24 Hwy. 105* ☎ *719/488–6917* ⊕ *www. rockhouseicecream.com.*

SPORTS AND THE OUTDOORS
FISHING

Upper Palmer Lake Reservoir. Palmer Lake is stocked with trout, but a more secluded angling spot, the Upper Palmer Lake Reservoir, has a mix of trout and bottom-feeders in a peaceful mountain setting. ☎ *719/481–3282.*

HIKING

New Santa Fe Regional Trail. The New Santa Fe Regional Trail goes from Palmer Lake along an abandoned railroad right-of-way, through the US Air Force Academy—where you must stay on the six-foot-wide trail—and links up with the Pikes Peak Greenway Trail in Colorado Springs. The trail is also popular with equestrians and bikers, as well as cross-country skiers and snowshoers. ☎ 719/520–6375.

Palmer Lake Reservoirs Trail. One of the most popular hiking trails between Denver and Colorado Springs, the Palmer Lake Reservoirs Trail begins near Glen Park. After a fairly steep incline, the 3-mi trail levels out and follows the shoreline of Upper and Lower Palmer Lake reservoirs between forested mountains. Bikes and leashed dogs are permitted. ✉ *Trailhead starts at bottom of Old Palmer Rd.* ☎ 719/481–3282.

WHERE TO EAT

$$$ ✕ **Folie à Deux.** Though it doesn't look like much from outside, casually
ECLECTIC   elegant dining is the name of the game at Folie à Deux, whose name means "a madness shared by two." Splurge on the elk medallions in a red wine reduction or chicken breast with blue crab covered in a wasabi cream sauce. The crisp dining room is set in a rustic adobe house from 1948. ✉ *25 Hwy. 105* ☎ *719/481–4780* ⊕ *www.folieadeuxdining.com* 🍴 *Reservations essential.*

NIGHTLIFE

O'Malley's. A roadhouse eatery, O'Malley's offers the most reliable nightlife in the area, with an upstairs poolroom, occasional bands, and plenty of local color. You can play chef here—cooking steaks to your liking on a communal grill. The outdoor deck has a great view of the nearby mountainside. ✉ *104 Hwy. 105* ☎ *719/488–0321* ⊕ *www.omalleys.biz.*

SHOPPING

Finders Keepers. The fun and eclectic Finders Keepers sells jewelry, antiques, homemade jams and jellies, and local arts and crafts. ✉ *91 Hwy. 105* ☎ *719/487–8020.*

CAÑON CITY AND ROYAL GORGE

59 mi east of Salida via U.S. 50; 45 mi southwest of Colorado Springs.

Cañon City is an undeniably quirky town. From its easy access to the nearby Royal Gorge, a dramatic slash in the earth, to its aggressive strip-mall veneer (softened, fortunately, by some handsome old buildings), you'd think Cañon City existed solely for tourism. Nothing could be further from the truth: Cañon City is in Fremont County, called "Colorado's Prison Capital" by some. In Cañon City and nearby Florence there are 13 prisons, including Supermax. While this may seem like a perverse source of income to court, the prisons have pumped more than $200 million into the local economy.

GETTING HERE AND AROUND

The route from Colorado Springs to Cañon City goes through Red Rock Canyon, with lovely views. You'll need a car to get to Cañon City, where there is no public transportation other than cab service.

ESSENTIALS

Visitor Information Cañon City Chamber of Commerce ✉ *403 Royal Gorge Blvd.* ☎ *719/275–2331, 800/876–7922* ⊕ *www.canoncitycolorado.com.*

EXPLORING

Museum of Colorado Prisons. Introduce yourself and your kids to what life is like behind bars at the Museum of Colorado Prisons, which formerly housed the Women's State Correctional Facility and where many of the exhibits are housed in cells. The museum exhaustively documents prison life in Colorado through old photos and newspaper accounts, as well as with inmates' confiscated weapons and contraband. The gas chamber sits in the courtyard. Many parents bring their children to this museum, but it might be disturbing for young kids. ✉ *201 N. 1st St.* ☎ *719/269–3015* ⊕ *www.prisonmuseum.org* ✉ *$7* ⊙ *June–Aug., daily 8:30–6; May, Sept.–mid-Oct., daily 10–5; mid-Oct.–Apr., Wed.–Sun. 10–5.*

FLORENCE PRISONS

The tiny, main-street town of Florence chalks up just a few antiques shops, galleries, and coffee shops. But when it comes to prisons, they have more than their share, with four correctional facilities, including the infamous ADX Supermax, where an unruly population passes time in 23-hour lockdown. The ADX is home to plenty of men with sinister claims to fame. Among the current and former residents are Ted Kaczynski, Timothy McVeigh, Ramsey Yusef, the alleged architect of the 1993 bombing of the World Trade Center, and Richard Reid, aka "The Shoebomber."

ⓒ **Royal Gorge.** Cañon City is the gateway to the 1,053-foot-deep Royal Fodors Choice Gorge, carved by the Arkansas River more than 3 million years ago. The ★ famed Royal Gorge War between the Denver & Rio Grande and Santa Fe railroads occurred here in 1877. The battle was over the right-of-way through the canyon, which could only accommodate one rail line. Rival crews would lay tracks during the day and dynamite each other's work at night. The dispute was finally settled in court—the Denver & Rio Grande won. Today there's a commercially run site, the Royal Gorge Bridge and Park, along one part of the gorge. ✉ *Hwy. 50, 12 mi west of Cañon City* ⊕ *www.royalgorgebridge.com.*

Royal Gorge Bridge and Park. The Royal Gorge Bridge and Park has the world's highest **suspension bridge.** Never intended for traffic, it was constructed in 1929 as a tourist attraction. The 1,053-foot-high bridge sways on gusty afternoons, adding to the thrill of a crossing. You can also ride the astonishing **aerial tram** (2,200 feet long and 1,178 feet above the canyon floor) or descend the steepest **incline rail line** in the world to stare at the bridge from 1,000 feet below. A ride on the **Royal Rush Skycoaster** ensures an adrenaline rush—you'll swing from a free-fall tower and momentarily hang over the gorge. Also on hand are a theater that presents a 25-minute multimedia show, outdoor musical entertainment in summer, and the usual assortment of food and gift shops. Visiting this attraction can prove to be expensive for a family—and some Fodors.com readers suggest that it is not worth the money.

✉ 4218 Fremont County Rd. 3A ☎ 719/275–7507, 888/333–5597 ⊕ www.royalgorgebridge.com 🎫 $18.75 ⏲ Hrs vary seasonally.

Royal Gorge Route Railroad. A ride on the Royal Gorge Route Railroad takes you under the bridge and through one of the most dramatic parts of the canyon. From the Santa Fe depot in Cañon City, the train leaves several times a day for the two-hour ride. The lunch ride is pleasant, and the food is good, although not exactly "gourmet" as advertised. For an extra fee you can ride in the cab with the engineer. *✉ 401 Water St. ☎ 888/724–5748 ⊕ www.royalgorgeroute.com 🎫 $33–$58.*

OFF THE BEATEN PATH

Winery at Holy Cross Abbey. The Benedictine monks once cloistered at Holy Cross Abbey came to Cañon City for spiritual repose. But for the faithful who frequent the winery on the eastern edge of the property, redemption is more easily found in a nice bottle of merlot reserve. Tours of the winery's production facility are by advance reservation in spring and summer. The Tasting Room, in a historic building, is open year-round. *✉ 3011 E. Hwy. 50 ☎ 719/276–5191, 877/422–9463 ⊕ www.abbeywinery.com 🎫 Free ⏲ Spring and summer, Mon.–Sat. 10–6, Sun. noon–5; Jan.–Mar., Mon.–Sat. 10–5, Sun. noon–5.*

SPORTS AND THE OUTDOORS

HIKING

Arkansas River Walk. For a pleasant stroll, try the Arkansas River Walk. The 4-mi trail is virtually flat, and the elevation is only 5,320 feet. It follows the Arkansas River for 3 mi through woods, wetlands, and the riparian river environment. *✉ Trailhead: Heading south on 9th St., turn east immediately past the bridge.*

Red Canyon Park. Cañon City–owned Red Canyon Park, 12 mi north of town, offers splendid easy to moderate hiking among the rose-color sandstone spires. The easy-to-find park is seven miles north of town on U.S. Highway 50, right at Reynolds Avenue.

RAFTING

TOURS AND OUTFITTERS

Colorado River Outfitters Association. With dozens of outfitters working from Salida, Buena Vista, and Cañon City, south-central Colorado is one of the top places in the country to go rafting. The Colorado River Outfitters Association is an organization of more than 50 licensed outfitters who run rafting trips on Colorado's 13 river systems. *☎ 303/280–2554 ⊕ www.croa.org.*

Echo Canyon River Expeditions. Echo Canyon River Expeditions offers float trips with gentle rapids for first-time rafters in Bighorn Sheep Canyon, family trips through Brown Canyon, and adrenaline-inducing rides through the Royal Gorge. Rafting through the Royal Gorge is not an experience for the faint of heart; you'll pass between narrow canyon walls through rolling Class IV and V waves, with hordes of tourists watching from the suspension bridge above. This company also runs combo trips including rafting-train ride, and paddle-saddle tours. *☎ 719/275–3154, 800/748–2953 ⊕ www.raftecho.com.*

WHERE TO EAT AND STAY

For expanded hotel reviews, visit Fodors.com.

$$$
ITALIAN

✕ **Merlino's Belvedere.** This Italian standby has ritzy coffee-shop decor, with floral banquettes and a rock grotto. Locals swear by the top-notch steaks, seafood, and pasta choices, which range from penne *vegetali* (with grilled vegetables) to Angela's Combo, which has cavatelli and spaghetti with garlic and Romano cheese. There is live music some weekend nights. ✉ *1330 Elm Ave.* ☎ *719/275–5558* ⊕ *www. belvedererestaurant.com.*

¢
HOTEL

⌸ **Quality Inn and Suites.** Some of the famous people who have stayed here—John Belushi, Jane Fonda, John Wayne, and Goldie Hawn among them—now have their names emblazoned on the door of a room. **Pros:** close to Royal Gorge. **Cons:** Wi-Fi only in business section. ✉ *U.S. 50 and Dozier St.* ☎ *719/275–8676, 800/525–7727* ⊕ *www.choicehotels. com* ⇨ *150 rooms* ⚁ *In-room: Internet, Wi-Fi. In-hotel: restaurant, bar, pool.*

THE COLLEGIATE PEAKS

Buena Vista and Salida are comfortable base towns for vacationers who love hiking and mountain biking the trails that zigzag up and down the 14,000 footers called the Collegiate Peaks. These towns are also favorites for folks who want to stay in rustic cabins or small mom-and-pop motels, perhaps take a rafting trip on the Arkansas River, and come home with a wallet still intact.

BUENA VISTA

94 mi west of Colorado Springs on U.S. 24 and U.S. 285.

Skyscraping mountains, the most impressive being the Collegiate Peaks, ring Buena Vista (pronounced *byoo*-na *vis*-ta by locals). The 14,000-foot, often snowcapped peaks were first summited by alumni from Yale, Princeton, Harvard, and Columbia, who named them for their respective alma maters. A small mining town–turned–casual resort community, Buena Vista's main street is lined with Wild West–style historic buildings. On U.S. 24, which bisects the town, there are inexpensive roadside motels. The town is also a hub for the white-water rafting industry that plies its trade on the popular Arkansas River, and a great central location for hiking, fishing, rafting, and horseback riding.

GETTING HERE AND AROUND

You'll need your own car to explore this region. Everything outdoors from hiking and mountain biking to rafting on the Arkansas is an easy drive from Buena Vista.

ESSENTIALS

Visitor Information Buena Vista Chamber of Commerce ✉ *343 Hwy. 24* ☎ *719/395–6612* ⊕ *www.buenavistacolorado.org.*

EXPLORING

Buena Vista Heritage Museum. Before leaving downtown, meander through the Buena Vista Heritage Museum. The falling-down miner's cabin and pretty carriage outside give a hint of what's inside. Each room is devoted to a different aspect of regional history: one to mining equipment, another to fashions, and another to household utensils. There are working models of the three railroads that serviced the area in its heyday, a schoolroom, and historical photos in the archives. ⊠ *506 E. Main St.* ☎ *719/395–8458* ⊕ *www.buenavistaheritage.org* ⊠ *$5* ⊙ *June–Sept., Mon.–Sat. 10–5, Sun. noon–5.*

Fodor's Choice
★
Collegiate Peaks Wilderness Area. Taking its own name from the many peaks named after famous universities, the 168,000-acre Collegiate Peaks Wilderness Area includes more 14,000-foot-high mountains than any other wilderness area in the lower 48 states. Forty miles of the Continental Divide snake through the area as well. The most compelling reason to visit Buena Vista is for the almost unequaled variety of hikes, climbs, biking trails, and fishing streams here. Two ranger offices, one in Leadville and one in Salida, handle inquiries about this region. ⊠ *Leadville Ranger District, 810 Front St., Leadville* ☎ *719/486–0749* ⊕ *www.fs.fed.us/r2/whiteriver/recreation/wilderness/collegiatepeaks/ index.shtml* ⊠ *Salida Ranger District, 325 W. Rainbow Blvd., Salida* ☎ *719/539–3591.*

★
Mount Princeton Hot Springs Resort. To relax sore muscles after your outdoor adventure, visit Mount Princeton Hot Springs Resort, 8 mi from Buena Vista. The resort has four pools plus several "hot spots in the creek"—the water temperature ranges between 85°F and 105°F. The restaurant has a large stone fireplace and a dramatic view of the Chalk Cliffs. The resort is 12 mi south of Buena Vista. ⊠ *15870 County Rd. 162, 4½ mi west of Hwy. 285, Nathrop* ☎ *719/395–2447* ⊕ *www. mtprinceton.com* ⊠ *$10 weekdays; $15 weekends* ⊙ *Lower pools: daily 9–9; upper pool: June–Sept., daily 11–6.*

SPORTS AND THE OUTDOORS
HIKING
Trailhead. The Trailhead is an outdoor specialty shop where you can get maps, guidebooks, gear, and clothing for hiking or climbing in the region. ⊠ *707 Hwy. 24* ☎ *719/395–8001* ⊕ *www.thetrailheadco.com.*

RAFTING
Arkansas River. The rafting and kayaking on the Arkansas River can be the most challenging in the state, ranging from Class II to Class V, depending on the season, water flow and section.

TOURS AND
OUTFITTERS
Independent Whitewater. A family-owned company, Independent Whitewater has been running the Arkansas River for nearly 20 years. Groups are small, and the take-out is at a private area after running Seidel's Suckhole and Twin Falls on regular half-day trips. ☎ *800/428–1479, 719/539–7737* ⊕ *www.independentrafting.com.*

Fodor's Choice
★
River Runners. River Runners has been offering rafting trips on the Arkansas for more than 30 years. This group also runs the Royal Gorge stretch, which is classed expert, but there are choices on the river for families who want a gentler experience. ☎ *800/723–8987* ⊕ *www. whitewater.net.*

12

WHERE TO EAT

$$ **✕ Casa del Sol.** Housed in an 1890

MEXICAN   blacksmith's shop, this stucco-clad restaurant has a quasi–tiki-hut feel inside and a nice outdoor seating area. The smothered burritos are tasty and hearty, the homemade salsa is spicy, and the service is quick and friendly. Among the most popular entrées are the Santa Fe, which has stacked corn enchiladas with meat sauce and cheddar cheese, and the Pechuga Suiza, a chicken breast rolled in a tortilla with Monterey Jack cheese and sour cream. The full-service bar specializes in tart but potent margaritas. ✉ *303 U.S. 24* ☎ *719/395–8810.*

RAFTING THE ARKANSAS

Adrenaline-charging rapids range from Class II to Class V on Colorado's Arkansas River, one of the most commercially rafted rivers in the world. Among the most fabled stretches of the Arkansas are the Narrows, the Numbers, and Browns Canyon, but extreme paddlers tend to jump on trips through the Royal Gorge, which the river has carved out over eons. Plan your trip for the early summer snowmelt for the biggest thrills.

$$ **✕ Eddyline Restaurant & Brewery.** The steel tables at this casual brewpub

AMERICAN   give the dining area and tiny bar a sophisticated vibe. The pub is by South Main River Park, so after dining on wood-fired pizzas, steaks, or seafood, washed down with ales brewed on-site, you can tackle the nearby miles of hiking and biking trails. Or you can just watch people from the patio. ✉ *926 S. Main St.* ☎ *719/966–6000* ⊕ *www.eddylinepub.com.*

$ **✕ Mothers Bistro.** Set in a historic hotel, the tiny restaurant focuses on

AMERICAN   organic and regional foods. Look for lunchtime favorites such as whole-

Fodor's Choice   wheat wraps stuffed with smoked turkey, cucumbers, and mango, or

★   fig and Brie panini on fresh ciabatta. Small plates in the evening range from meat loaf to mac and cheese (made with tortiglioni, sun-dried tomatoes, and Romano cheese). There's always freshly baked bread. A lovely outdoor patio and a full bar round out the attractions. ✉ *414 E. Main St.* ☎ *719/395–4443* ⊕ *www.mothersbistrobv.com* ☉ *June–Aug., daily; call for Sept.–May hrs.*

WHERE TO STAY

For expanded hotel reviews, visit Fodors.com.

$$ ▦ **Ghost Town Guest House.** Although it looks like one of the old build-

B&B/INN   ings in this authentic ghost town, this guesthouse is actually a modern structure built by a couple who decided to get away from urban living. **Pros:** unique setting; friendly hosts. **Cons:** 30-minute drive to civilization (Buena Vista), part of which is on a dirt road; some rooms up many stairs. ✉ *25850 County Rd. 162* ☎ *719/395–2120* ⊕ *www.ghosttownguesthouse.com* ⏎ *3 rooms* ⚒ *In-room: no a/c, no TV, Wi-Fi. In-hotel: parking* ▭ *No credit cards* ⏏ *Some meals.*

$$ ▦ **Liars' Lodge.** On the banks of the Arkansas River, this rugged B&B

B&B/INN   is surrounded by 23 acres of woodland. **Pros:** gorgeous setting; river

★   views (and sounds). **Cons:** you'll have to go into Buena Vista for dinner; good choice for romantic getaways. ✉ *30000 County Rd. 371* ☎ *719/395–3444, 888/542–7756* ⊕ *www.liarslodge.com* ⏎ *5 rooms,*

1 house ♿ *In-room: no a/c, Wi-Fi. In-hotel: parking* ✏️ *Breakfast.*

$$
RENTAL

📺 **Thunder Lodge.** On Cottonwood Creek, this place is a great spot for families and is among the nicest cabin resorts in the area. ✉️ *207 Brookdale Ave.* ☎ *719/395–2245, 800/330–9194* ⊕ *www.thunderlodge.com* 🛏 *7 cabins* ♿ *In-room: no a/c, kitchen. In-hotel: some pets allowed.*

NIGHTLIFE

Green Parrot. Head to the Green Parrot, a long-standing Buena Vista watering hole with live music some weekends. Friendly locals abound, and the dive bar is also popular with the river rats for pre- and post-river nights out. ✉️ *304 E. Main St.* ☎ *719/395–9046.*

Lariat. Pool, darts, and video games are the main diversions at this local favorite. There are live DJs on some Friday nights. As the sign says: "Selling and servicing hangovers since 1885." ✉️ *206 E. Main* ☎ *719/395–9494.*

SHOPPING

Rustic Woods. There are a few antiques shops right across the highway from the Buena Vista Visitors Center. Rustic Woods has attractive decorative items to heavy furniture, all centered around various types of wood, of course. ✉️ *310 U.S. 24* ☎ *719/395–2561.*

OFF THE BEATEN PATH

St. Elmo. If you want to see an authentic ghost town, head 15 mi west on County Road 162. Once the supply center for the Mary Murphy Mine and dozens of smaller mines, St. Elmo is the best-preserved ghost town in Colorado. It doesn't take long to walk along the main street and peer into some of the rickety old buildings. There is a B&B, as well as a general store that's open in the summer. Don't forget to feed the chipmunks! ✉️ *Western end of Rte.162.*

> **BUENA VISTA LODGING ALTERNATIVES**
>
> **Buena Vista Chamber of Commerce.** There are many cabins and some B&Bs in this region. For information about rental units in the Buena Vista area, contact the Buena Vista Chamber of Commerce. ☎ *719/395–6612* ⊕ *www.buenavistacolorado.org.*

SALIDA

25 mi south of Buena Vista via U.S. 24 and 285 and Rte. 291; 102 mi southwest of Colorado Springs.

Imposing peaks, including 14,000-plus-foot Mount Shavano, dominate the town of Salida, which is on the Arkansas River. Salida draws some of the musicians who appear at the Aspen Music Festival—classical pianists, brass ensembles, and the like—for its Salida–Aspen Concerts in July and August. The town's other big event is the annual **Kayak and Rafting White-Water Rodeo** in June, on a section of river that cuts right through downtown. It's been taking place since 1949.

GETTING HERE AND AROUND

You need a private car to explore this area. There's a compact, walkable downtown area, but you'll need to drive to most lodging, the trailheads in the mountains, rivers, and attractions.

ESSENTIALS

Visitor Information Heart of the Rockies Chamber of Commerce–Salida Chamber ✉ *406 W. Hwy. 50* ☎ *719/539–2068, 877/772–5432* ⊕ *www. salidachamber.org.*

SPORTS AND THE OUTDOORS

12

BIKING

Absolute Bikes. Absolute Bikes rents cruisers and mountain bikes for $10 for two hours or $50 a day, and provides repair service, maps, and good advice. ✉ *330 W. Sackett Ave.* ☎ *719/539–9295.*

DOWNHILL SKIING

Monarch. A small ski resort that tops out on the Continental Divide, Monarch has five chairlifts, 64 trails, 800 acres, and a 1,162-foot vertical drop. It's a family-friendly place with moderate pricing—one-day lift tickets cost $57. The resort also offers snow cat skiing on steep runs off the Divide, plus the 130 acres of extreme terrain in Mirkwood Basin. ✉ *22720 U.S. 50, 18 mi west of Salida* ☎ *719/530–5000, 888/996–7669* ⊕ *www.skimonarch.com* 🎫 *$57* ⊙ *Mid-Nov.–mid-Apr., daily 9–4.*

FISHING

The Arkansas River, as it spills out of the central Colorado Rockies on its course through the south-central part of the state, reputedly supports a brown-trout population exceeding 3,000 fish per mile. Some of the river's canyons are deep, and some of the best fishing locations are difficult to access, making a guide or outfitter a near necessity. See ⊕ *www.wildlife.state.co.us/fishing* for more information.

OUTFITTERS **ArkAnglers.** A good fly shop with an experienced staff, ArkAnglers offers guided float and wade trips, fly-fishing lessons, and equipment rentals. ✉ *7500 W. Hwy. 50* ☎ *719/539–4223* ⊕ *www.arkanglers.com.*

HORSEBACK RIDING

Mt. Princeton Hot Springs Stables. Mt. Princeton Hot Springs Stables offers trail rides along the dramatic Chalk Creek Cliffs. It's $35 per hour or $150 per day. ✉ *14582 County Rd. 162* ☎ *866/877–3630, 719/395–3630* ⊕ *www.mtprinceton.com.*

JEEP TOURS

High Country Jeep Tours. High Country Jeep Tours takes customers on four-wheel-drive trips to old mines, ghost towns, and mountain vistas. ✉ *410 U.S. Hwy. 24, Buena Vista* ☎ *719/395–6111, 866/458–6877* ⊕ *www.highcountryjeeptours.com.*

SNOWMOBILING

Monarch Snowmobile Tours. Monarch Snowmobile Tours takes customers on winter excursions around Monarch Park. Snowmobile rentals start at $75 for a one-hour rental and go up to $180 for six hours plus lunch. ✉ *22763 Hwy. 50, 18 mi west of Salida, Garfield* ☎ *719/539–2572, 800/539–2573* ⊕ *www.snowmobilemonarch.com.*

RAFTING

The Salida area is a magnet for rafting aficionados, and there are dozens of outfitters. Salida is constantly jockeying with Buena Vista for the title of "Colorado's White-Water Capital." *For outfitters, see the Buena Vista section.*

WHERE TO EAT

$
MEXICAN
⨉ **First Street Café.** This café in the historic district serves robust Mexican-American fare, sandwiches including an excellent Monte Cristo, burgers, and some vegetarian dishes. The restaurant has original brick walls, pews from an old church, and panel doors from an old stage at Denver's Red Rocks Amphitheatre. ✉ *137 E. 1st St.* ☎ *719/539–4759* ⊕ *www.firststreetcafesalida.com.*

$$
MODERN
AMERICAN
Fodor'sChoice
★
⨉ **Laughing Ladies.** Fine food is served in a relaxed atmosphere at a linen-covered table set on a century-old oak floor surrounded by exposed brick walls. Colorful oils, watercolors, and ceramics by local artists adorn the walls. The menu changes seasonally, but expect imaginative versions of classics, such as honey grilled pork chops with roasted sweet potatoes and candied bacon, or maple grilled salmon with crispy polenta. Laughing Ladies has an excellent wine selection. ✉ *128 W. 1st St.* ☎ *719/539–6209* ⊕ *www.laughingladiesrestaurant.com* ⟡ *Reservations essential* ⊙ *Closed Tues. and Wed.*

WHERE TO STAY

For expanded hotel reviews, visit Fodors.com.

$
B&B/INN
▦ **River Run Inn.** On the Arkansas River, this gracious 1842 Victorian home is a quiet and homey place to stay. **Pros:** convenient for fishing; terrific river and mountain views. **Cons:** 3 mi from downtown Salida; only open March through October; steps to climb. ✉ *8495 County Rd. 160* ☎ *719/539–3818, 800/385–6925* ⊕ *www.riverruninn.com* ⟿ *6 rooms, 1 dorm* ⟡ *In-room: no a/c, no TV. In-hotel: parking* ⊙ *Closed Sun. and Mon.* ❘⊙❘ *Breakfast.*

$
B&B/INN
▦ **Tudor Rose.** With beautiful furnishings and an idyllic setting, this Victorian B&B sits on a 37-acre spread of pine forest and mountain ridges. **Pros:** owners will stable horses in their barn. **Cons:** not for guests with young children; no pool. ✉ *6720 County Rd. 104* ☎ *719/539–2002, 800/379–0889* ⊕ *www.thetudorrose.com* ⟿ *4 rooms, 2 suites, 5 chalets* ⟡ *In-room: no a/c, no TV. In-hotel: parking, some age restrictions* ❘⊙❘ *Breakfast.*

¢
HOTEL
▦ **Woodland Motel.** Since 1975, Steve and Viva Borbas have run this impeccable mom-and-pop motel on the outskirts of downtown Salida. **Pros:** reliable; inexpensive rooms. **Cons:** a 12-minute walk to downtown; rooms can be noisy. ✉ *903 W. 1st St.* ☎ *719/539–4980, 800/488–0456* ⊕ *www.woodlandmotel.com* ⟿ *16 rooms, 2 condos* ⟡ *In-room: kitchen, Internet. In-hotel: parking, some pets allowed.*

THE ARTS

Salida Steam Plant Events Center. In a former power plant overlooking the Arkansas river, Salida Steam Plant Events Center has a theater that puts on several productions each summer, ranging from drama to comedy to music to cabaret. ✉ *Sackett St. and G St.* ☎ *719/530–0933* ⊕ *www.steamplant.org.*

SHOPPING

All Booked Up. All Booked Up has Native American art and jewelry, mixed media artwork, and more. ✉ *134 E. 1st St.* ☎ *719/539–2344.*

Culture Clash. Culture Clash has original artwork, glass, and intricately handcrafted jewelry. ✉ *101 N. F St.* ☎ *719/539–3118.*

Gallery 150. Gallery 150 has jewelry and wearable art, plus blown glass and fiber art. ✉ *150 W. 1st St.* ☎ *719/539–2971* ⊕ *www.gallery150.com.*

Rock Doc at Prospectors Village. At Prospectors Village, midway between Salida and Buena Vista, the Rock Doc is an enormous shop with gold-panning equipment, metal detectors, and rock art. The shop also gives gold-panning lessons. ✉ *17897 U.S. 285* ☎ *719/539–2019* ⊕ *www. therockdoc.net.*

Salida ArtWalk. First Street and F Street are home to many antiques shops and art galleries, including specialists in contemporary art, photography, and jewelry. The annual Salida ArtWalk takes place in late June. Ask the Chamber of Commerce for the *Art in Salida* or *Antique Dealers* brochures for information about the ArtWalk. ⊕ *www.salidaartwalk.org.*

Spirit Mountain, Antler & Design. Spirit Mountain, Antler & Design has stunning handcrafted tables inlaid with turquoise and other handmade furniture. ✉ *223 E. 1st St.* ☎ *719/539–1500.*

Sunlight Glassblowing Studios. Brice Turnbill's wonderful blown-glass creations are at Sunlight Studios. It helps that the studio is connected to the Reigning Wine Bar, making for a nice way to spend an hour. ✉ *1030 W. 1st St.* ☎ *719/539–5101* ⊕ *www.btglass.com.*

SOUTHEAST COLORADO

Pueblo is the biggest city along Interstate 25 between Colorado Springs and the New Mexico border. South of Pueblo, Trinidad is close to the state border, and there are a few small towns sprinkled around the region. West of Interstate 25 there's easy access to the mountains along picturesque routes such as the Highway of Legends, a scenic byway that runs through Cuchara Valley.

PUEBLO

40 mi east of Cañon City via U.S. 50; 42 mi south of Colorado Springs via I–25.

In 1842 El Pueblo trading post, on the bank of the Arkansas River, was a gathering place for trappers and traders. Today the trading post is an archaeological dig set in a pavilion next to the new El Pueblo History Museum. The thriving city of Pueblo surrounds the museum, and the Arkansas River runs through the city in a concrete channel, tamed by the Pueblo Dam.

To get a sense of the city and its offerings, start at the museum, stroll through the Union Avenue Historic District, and then take a ride on one of the tour boats leaving from the Historic Arkansas Riverwalk, an urban waterfront area that restored the Arkansas River channel to its original location. More than 110 parks, in addition to hiking and bicycling trails, help to define Pueblo as a sports and recreation center.

GETTING HERE AND AROUND

You can use the local bus system to move around during the day if you're staying near the Convention Center, but most of the buses you'll want stop running in the early evening. The local taxi is City Cab.

ESSENTIALS

Transportation Contacts City Cab ☎ 719/543–2525. **Pueblo Transit** ☎ 719/553–2727.

Visitor Information Pueblo Chamber of Commerce and Convention & Visitors Bureau ✉ 302 N. Santa Fe Ave. ☎ 719/542–1704, 800/233–3446 ⊕ www.pueblochamber.org.

EXPLORING

TOP ATTRACTIONS

El Pueblo History Museum. A nicely designed repository for the city's history, El Pueblo History Museum extends its scope to chronicle life on the plains since the prehistoric era. It tells of Pueblo's role as a cultural and geographic crossroads, beginning when it was a trading post in the 1840s. Remnants of the original trading post are now an archaeological dig enclosed in a pavilion next to the museum. ✉ 301 N. Union Ave. ☎ 719/583–0453 ▧ $4 ⊗ Tues.–Sat. 10–4.

Union Avenue Historic District. The century-old stores and warehouses of Union Avenue Historic District make for a commercial district filled with a mix of stores ranging from kitschy to good. Among the landmarks are the glorious 1889 sandstone-and-brick Union Avenue Depot and Mesa Junction. Pitkin Avenue, lined with fabulous gabled and turreted mansions, attests to the town's more prosperous times. Walking-tour brochures are available at the visitor bureau.

WORTH NOTING

♻ **City Park.** The fine City Park has fishing lakes, playgrounds, kiddie rides, tennis courts and a swimming pool.

Pueblo Zoo. In City Park, this biopark includes an eco-center with a tropical rain forest, black-footed penguins, ringtail lemurs, and pythons. Favorites here include the red kangaroos of the Australian Outback area and the annual holiday feature ElectriCritters, an evening light display that involves more than 250,000 lights, which runs from late November through the end of the year. ✉ 3455 Nuckolls Ave. ☎ 719/561–9664 ⊕ www.pueblozoo.org ▧ $8 ⊗ June–Aug., daily 9–5; call for winter hrs. ✉ Pueblo Blvd. and Goodnight Ave.

Historic Arkansas Riverwalk of Pueblo. The Historic Arkansas Riverwalk of Pueblo is a 26-acre urban waterfront park. Stroll on the paths or take to the water on a boat tour or in a paddleboat. Boat rides are available at 101 South Union. ☎ 719/595–1589 boat reservations ⊕ www.puebloharp.com.

Pueblo-Weisbrod Aircraft Museum. At the city's airport, the Pueblo-Weisbrod Aircraft Museum traces the development of American military aviation with more than two-dozen aircraft in mint condition, ranging from a Lockheed F-80 fighter plane to a Boeing B-29 Super Fortress of atomic-bomb fame. ✉ Pueblo Memorial Airport, 31001

CLOSE UP

The Pueblo Levee

12

In 1978 a group of University of Southern Colorado art students headed out in the cover of night, set up lookouts, and lowered themselves over the wall of the Pueblo Levee. Outfitted with makeshift rope-suspension devices and armed with buckets of paint, the students spent the wee hours crafting a large blue cod on the levee's concrete wall, watching for police as they mixed up their acrylics. Overnight, the waterway—which directs the Arkansas River through the center of town—became home to a public art project that would eventually capture the imagination of the Pueblo community, as well as the attention of the art world and the *Guinness Book of World Records*. Pueblo Levee is a fantastic, colorful vision field that sprawls over 175,000 square feet, stretches for a mile, and is recognized as the largest mural in the world.

Organizers estimate that more than 1,000 painters have contributed to the mural—everyone from self-taught father-and-son teams who come to paint on weekends to the members of fire precincts, to classically trained muralists and art students from New York and Chicago. From time to time, a teacher and students at the Schools for Arts and Sciences will refresh some of the older murals. Witty graffiti, comic illustrations, narrative scenes, and cartoons line the levee, which is visible to passengers zooming along Interstate 25. Today, you can take the walking or biking path along the levee to look at the murals, or even take a kayak lesson below it.

Magnuson Ave. ☎ *719/948–9219* ⊕ *www.pwam.org* 🖾 *$7* ⊙ *Weekdays 10–4, Sat. 10–2, Sun. 1–4.*

Rosemount Victorian Museum. Exquisite maple, oak, and mahogany woodwork gleams throughout this splendid 37-room mansion, with ivory glaze and gold-leaf trim. Italian marble fireplaces, Tiffany-glass fixtures, and frescoed ceilings complete the opulent look. The top floor—originally servants' quarters—features the odd Andrew McClelland Collection: objects of curiosity this eccentric philanthropist garnered on his worldwide travels, including an Egyptian mummy. ✉ *419 W. 14th St.* ☎ *719/545–5290* ⊕ *www.rosemount.org* 🖾 *$6* ⊙ *Tues.–Sat. 10–4; tours every half hr.*

☉ **Sangre de Cristo Arts Center.** Ranked among the best in the country, the Buell Children's Museum provides fun, interactive experiences for kids of all ages. The 12,000-square-foot facility has innovative exhibits on art, science, and history. It's in the same complex as the Sangre de Cristo Arts Center. ✉ *210 N. Santa Fe Ave.* ☎ *719/295–7200* ⊕ *www.sdc-arts. org/buellchildrensmuseum.html* 🖾 *$4* ⊙ *Tues.–Sat. 11–4.*

OFF THE BEATEN PATH

Bishop Castle. This elaborate creation, which resembles a medieval castle replete with turrets, buttresses, and ornamental iron, is the prodigious (some might say monomaniacal) one-man undertaking of Jim Bishop, a self-taught architect who began work in 1969. Once considered a blight on pastoral Highway 165, the castle is now a popular attraction. Not yet complete, it is three stories high with a nearly 165-foot tower.

Those who endeavor to climb into the structure must sign the guest book–cum–liability waiver. Bishop finances this enormous endeavor through donations and a gift shop. ⊠ *12705 Hwy. 165* ☎ *719/ 485–3040* ⊕ *www.bishopcastle.org* 🎫 *Free* ⊙ *Daily, hrs vary.*

SPORTS AND THE OUTDOORS

BIKING

Pueblo Bike Trail System. The extensive Pueblo Bike Trail System loops around the city, following the Arkansas River for part of the way before heading out to the reservoir. There are popular in-line skating routes along these trails, too. You can get trail maps at the Chamber of Commerce.

BOATING, KAYAKING, AND FISHING

Edge Ski, Paddle and Pack. Along the Arkansas River near the Pueblo Levee you'll notice a kayak course. The Edge Ski, Paddle and Pack rents kayaks and gives lessons. ⊠ *107 N. Union Ave.* ☎ *719/583–2021* ⊕ *www.edgeskiandpaddle.com.*

Lake Pueblo State Park. There's excellent camping and fishing at Lake Pueblo State Park, as well as many other outdoor activities.

South Shore Marina. In Lake Pueblo State Park, the South Shore Marina rents pontoon boats. ⊠ *Lake Pueblo State Park, off U.S. 50* ☎ *719/564–1043* ⊕ *www.thesouthshoremarina.com* ⊠ *Off U.S. 50* ☎ *719/561–9320* ⊕ *www.parks.state.co.us/parks/LakePueblo.*

GOLF

Walking Stick Golf Course. This challenging links-style course is named after the native cholla, the cacti in the rugged terrain and arroyos that surround the rolling green fairways. ⊠ *4301 Walking Stick Blvd.* ☎ *719/584–3400* ⊕ *www.pueblocitygolf.com* ⛳ *18 holes. Yards: 7147/5181. Par: 72/72. Green fee: $30–$32, plus $12 per person for cart.*

HIKING

Greenway and Nature Center. You can bicycle, hike, and canoe along the 35 mi in the river trail system that follows the Arkansas River. For more information, call the Greenway and Nature Center. A small interpretive center describes the flora and fauna unique to the area, and the Raptor Rehabilitation Center, part of the nature center, cares for injured birds of prey. ⊠ *5200 Nature Center Rd., off 11th St.* ☎ *719/549–2414* ⊕ *www.gncp.org.*

San Isabel National Forest. You can hike in relative solitude on many trails threading the San Isabel National Forest, 20 mi southwest of Pueblo. The Forest Service station in Pueblo is open 7:30 am–4:30 pm weekdays. Check in with them for backpacking and Christmas tree-cutting permits. ⊠ *2840 Kachina Dr.* ☎ *719/545–8737* ⊕ *www.fs.fed.us/r2/psicc.*

WORD OF MOUTH

"My favorite first-day trip is to drive through the San Isabel National Forest to Cottonwood Pass on the Continental Divide. On the way there and back there is the Denny Trail and a trail leading to Lake Ptarmigan." —mmcl

WHERE TO EAT

$$$
AMERICAN

✗ **dc's on b street.** There are two dining areas in this restaurant, housed in the historic redbrick Coors building across from the Union Depot. At lunch you can order sandwiches, salads, and other light fare in a room with simple tables, brick walls, and a tin ceiling. For dinner in the more-elegant dining room, try poulet cordon bleu, a spice-rubbed center pork chop with a pomegranate reduction, or a seared bistro steak. ⊠ *115 B St.* ☎ *719/584–3410.*

$$$
EUROPEAN

✗ **La Renaissance.** This converted church and parsonage is the most imposing and elegant space in town, and the impeccably attired, unfailingly courteous waitstaff completes the picture. Guests order five-course dinners (including sinful desserts), which are served with style. Standbys are prime rib, superb baby back ribs, and orange roughy. ⊠ *217 E. Routt Ave.* ☎ *719/543–6367* ⊕ *larenaissancerestaurant.com* ⊘ *Closed Sun.*

$$
AMERICAN

✗ **Shamrock Brewing Company.** This consistently jam-packed hot spot is a bar and grill with a good kitchen. With dishes like corned beef and cabbage, it's the place for authentic Irish pub grub. And of course they brew their own beer—six or seven varieties are usually on tap. It's especially popular with the after-work crowd. ⊠ *108 W. 3rd St.* ☎ *719/542–9974* ⊕ *www.shamrockbrewing.com.*

WHERE TO STAY

For expanded hotel reviews, visit Fodors.com.

$$
HOTEL

⊡ **Pueblo Convention Center Marriott.** A reliably good choice in downtown Pueblo, the Marriott offers excellent value and service. **Pros:** close to downtown destinations; concierge floor. **Cons:** not much nearby for tourists; because it's a convention hotel, your neighbors may be early risers. ⊠ *110 W. 1st St.* ☎ *719/542–3200, 888/238–6507* ⊕ *www.marriott.com* ⊸ *163 rooms* ☖ *In-room: Internet. In-hotel: restaurant, pool, gym, parking.*

NIGHTLIFE AND THE ARTS

THE ARTS

Broadway Theatre League. The Broadway Theatre League presents three touring shows a year, such as *A Chorus Line*, *The Wizard of Oz*, and *The Color Purple*. ⊠ *Memorial Hall, 1 City Hall Place* ☎ *719/295–7222.*

Pueblo Symphony. The Pueblo Symphony performs all types of music, from pop to classical. Concerts are held at the Hoag Recital Hall on the Colorado State University campus. ☎ *719/545–7967* ⊕ *www.pueblosymphony.com.*

Sangre de Cristo Arts Center. Rotating exhibits at the Sangre de Cristo Arts Center celebrate regional arts and crafts. The center also houses the superb Western art collection donated by Francis King and a theater with a performing-arts series that ranges from plays to ballets. ⊠ *210 N. Santa Fe Ave.* ☎ *719/295–7200* ⊕ *www.sdc-arts.org.*

NIGHTLIFE

Gus' Place. A legendary Pueblo dive bar, Gus' Place is a quintessential local hangout. ⊠ *1201 Elm St.* ☎ *719/542–0755.*

Shamrock Brewing Company. Popular with locals, the Shamrock Brewing Company is always hopping after the workday. ✉ *108 W. 3rd St.* ☎ *719/542–9974.*

SHOPPING

Union Avenue Historic District. Pueblo's beautifully restored Union Avenue Historic District has an eclectic mixture of shops selling everything from interesting gifts to inexpensive clothing. Around the Union Avenue Depot—an elegantly restored building—there are some art galleries, boutiques, and restaurants.

EN ROUTE

Rocky Ford. Leaving the Rockies far behind, U.S. 50 takes you toward the eastern plains, where rolling prairies give way to hardier desert blooms and the land is stubbled with sage and stunted pinyon pines. One fertile spot—50 mi along the highway—is the town of Rocky Ford, dubbed the "Melon Capital of the World" for its famously succulent cantaloupes.

LA JUNTA

60 mi east of Pueblo via U.S. 50; 105 mi southeast of Colorado Springs.

For an easy day trip from Pueblo into Colorado's past, head east to La Junta. The Koshare Indian Museum is in town, and Bent's Old Fort National Historic Site and the dinosaur tracks and ancient rock art of the canyonlands are nearby.

La Junta (which roughly translated from Spanish means "the meeting place") was founded as a trading post in the mid-19th century. It was a stop for the Santa Fe and Kansas Pacific railroads, and today is home to 7,600 residents.

GETTING HERE AND AROUND

Amtrak stops in La Junta but a private car is best to explore this remote area.

ESSENTIALS

Visitor Information La Junta Chamber of Commerce ✉ *110 Santa Fe Ave.* ☎ *719/384–7411* ⊕ *www.lajuntachamber.com.*

EXPLORING

★ **Bent's Old Fort National Historic Site.** About 8 mi east of La Junta, Bent's Old Fort National Historic Site painstakingly re-creates what life was like in this adobe fort. Founded in 1833 by trader William Bent, the fort anchored the commercially vital Santa Fe Trail, providing both protection and a meeting place for the soldiers, trappers, and traders of the era. The museum's interior reveals daily life at a trading post, providing looks at a smithy, barracks, and more. Guided tours are offered daily during the summer. ✉ *35110 Hwy. 194* ☎ *719/383–5010* ⊕ *www.nps.gov/beol* ✎ *$3* ☉ *June–Aug., daily 8–5:30; Sept.–May, daily 9–4.*

Koshare Indian Museum. With Navajo silver, Zuni pottery, and Shoshone buckskin clothing, the Koshare Indian Museum contains extensive holdings of Native American artifacts and crafts. It also displays pieces from Anglo artists, such as Remington, known for their depictions of Native

Americans. The Koshare Indian Dancers—actually a local Boy Scout troop—perform regularly. ✉ *115 W. 18th St.* ☎ *719/384–4411* ⊕ *www.koshare.org* ✉ *$5* ☺ *Daily noon–5.*

Boss Hogg's. For a quick bite, try this watering hole with a quirky personality. Boss Hogg's is a local institution. ✉ *808 E. 3rd St.* ☎ *719/384–7879.*

SPORTS AND THE OUTDOORS

Comanche National Grassland. Comanche National Grassland has a pair of canyon loops where there's a fair amount of rock art. Some of the largest documented sets of fossilized dinosaur tracks in the United States are in **Picket Wire Canyonlands,** a part of the grassland. There are tables for when you want an impromptu picnic. From La Junta, drive south on Highway 109 for 13 mi, west on County Road 802 for 8 mi, and south on County Road 25 for 6 mi. Turn left at Picket Wire Corrals onto Forest Service Road 500A and follow signs to Withers Canyon Trailhead. ✉ *Forest Service Rd. 500A* ☎ *719/384–2181* ⊕ *www.fs.fed.us/r2/psicc/coma.*

SANTA FE TRAIL

Southern Colorado played a major role in opening up the West, through the Mountain Branch of the Santa Fe Trail. Bent's Fort was the most important stop between the route's origin in Independence, Missouri, and its terminus in Santa Fe, New Mexico. U.S. 50 roughly follows its faded tracks from the Kansas border to La Junta, where U.S. 350 picks up the trail, traveling southwest to Trinidad. If you detour onto the quiet county roads, you can still discern its faint outline over the dip of arroyos, and with a little imagination, conjure up visions of the pioneers.

TRINIDAD

80 mi south of Pueblo via I–25, Trinidad is just across the border from New Mexico; 127 mi south of Colorado Springs.

If you're traveling on Interstate 25 and want to stop for a night in a historic town with character instead of a motel on the outskirts of a bigger city, check out Trinidad. Walk around Corazon de Trinidad, the downtown area where some of the streets still have the original bricks—instead of pavement—and visit a few of the town's four superb museums, a remarkably large number for a town of about 11,000 residents. Trinidad was founded in 1861 as a rest-and-repair station along the Santa Fe Trail. Starting in 1878 with the construction of the railroad and the development of the coal industry, the town grew and expanded during the period from 1880 to 1910. But the advent of natural gas, coupled with the Depression, ushered in a gradual decline in population. During the 1990s there was a modest increase in the population and a major interest in the upkeep of the city's rich cultural heritage. Although newcomers are moving in and Trinidad is coming to life again, with restaurants, cafés, and galleries, the streets in the heart of town are still paved with brick, keeping a sense of the town's history alive.

GETTING HERE AND AROUND

Amtrak stops here. You'll need a private car or you can take the Trinidad Trolley from the Welcome Center around the downtown area.

TOURS

From Memorial Day to Labor Day you can take the free Trinidad Trolley, and the driver will give you an informal history of Trinidad between the stops and at all of the museums.

ESSENTIALS

Visitor Information **Colorado Welcome Center** ⊠ *309 Nevada Ave.* ☎ *719/846–9512* ⊕ *www.colorado.com* ☉ *10–3.* **Trinidad & Las Animas Chamber of Commerce** ⊠ *136 W. Main* ☎ *719/846–9285* ⊕ *www. historictrinidad.com.*

EXPLORING

A.R. Mitchell Memorial Museum and Gallery. The A.R. Mitchell Memorial Museum and Gallery celebrates the life and work of the famous Western illustrator, whose distinctive oils, charcoal drawings, and watercolors graced the pages of pulp magazines and ranch romances. The museum is in an old historic building with the original tin ceiling. Also on display are photos by the Aultman family; dating from 1889, they offer a unique visual record of Trinidad. ⊠ *150 E. Main St.* ☎ *719/846–4224* ⊕ *www.armitchell.org* ⊠ *$3, free on Sun.* ☉ *May–Oct., Tues.–Sat. 10–4; call for off-season hrs.*

Corazon de Trinidad (*Heart of Trinidad*). Downtown Trinidad, called the Corazon de Trinidad, is a National Historic Landmark District, with the original brick-paved streets, several Victorian mansions, graceful churches, and the bright-red domes and turrets of Temple Aaron, Colorado's oldest continuously used Reform synagogue.

Louden-Henritze Archaeology Museum. On the other side of the Purgatoire River, the Louden-Henritze Archaeology Museum takes viewers back millions of years to examine the true origins of the region, including early geological formations, plant and marine-animal fossils, and prehistoric artifacts. ⊠ *Trinidad State Junior College, 600 Prospect St.* ☎ *719/846–5508* ⊠ *Free* ☉ *Jan.–Nov., Mon.–Thurs. 10–3.*

Trinidad History Museum. A complex with three separate museums and a garden, the Trinidad History Museum is a great way to learn about the town's history. The first museum is **Baca House**, the 1870s residence of Felipe Baca, a prominent Hispanic farmer and businessman. Displays convey a mix of Anglo (clothes, furniture) and Hispanic (santos, textiles) influences. Next door, the 1882 **Bloom Mansion** was built by Frank Bloom, who made his money through ranching and banking. He filled his ornate Second Empire–style Victorian with fine furnishings and fabrics brought from the East Coast and abroad. The adjacent **Santa Fe Trail Museum** is dedicated to the effect of the trail and railroad on the community. Inside are exhibits covering Trinidad's heyday as a commercial and cultural center. Finish up with a stop in the **Heritage Gardens**, filled with native plants and century-old grapevines similar to those tended by the pioneers. ⊠ *312 E. Main St.* ☎ *719/846–7217* ⊕ *www.coloradohistory.org* ⊠ *$8* ☉ *May–Sept., daily 10–4. Call for winter hrs.*

12

○ **Old Firehouse No. 1 Children's Museum.** The Old Firehouse No. 1 Children's Museum is in the delightful Old Firehouse Number 1, with displays of fire-fighting memorabilia, such as a 1936 American LaFrance fire truck (children love clanging the bell) and the city's original fire alarm system. Upstairs is a fine re-creation of an early 1900s schoolroom. This a favorite with the kids, but call ahead to make sure they're open—or to schedule a tour. Their regular open hours, in the summertime only, are sporadic. ⊠ *314 N. Commercial St.* ☎ *719/846–8220* 🎫 *Free* ⊙ *June–Aug., weekdays 11–3.*

SPORTS AND THE OUTDOORS

Trinidad Lake State Park. There's hiking, fishing, horseback riding, and camping in the Purgatoire River Valley at the Trinidad Lake State Park. ⊠ *Rte. 12, 3 mi west of Trinidad* ☎ *719/846–6951* ⊕ *parks.state.co.us/ parks/trinidadlake.*

GOLF

Cougar Canyon Golf Course. This Nicklaus Design course is a dramatic layout etched into arroyos and mesas, with views of the nearby Sangre de Cristo Mountains. ⊠ *3700 E. Main St.* ☎ *719/422–7015* ⊕ *www. cougarcanyonliving.com* ♣ *18 holes. Yards: 7669/5327. Par: 72. Green fee: $73–$83, plus $15 per person for cart.*

WHERE TO EAT AND STAY

For expanded hotel reviews, visit Fodors.com.

$ ✕ **The Café.** Set in a downtown historic building, this eatery serves imaginative and delicious sandwiches. Try the Stonewall Gap, which has honey-smoked ham and melted Brie slathered with chutney and served on a ciabatta roll. This spot is usually crowded at breakfast and lunch, but you order at the counter, so things move quickly. Drop in for a muffin or pecan sticky bun and a cup of strong coffee or chai tea if you don't want a full meal. The Café is inside Danielson Dry Goods, which you can explore while waiting for your food. ⊠ *135 E. Main St.* ☎ *719/846–7119* ⊙ *No dinner.*

CAFÉ

$ ✕ **Nana and Nano's Pasta House.** The aroma of garlic and tomato sauce saturates this tiny, unpretentious eatery. Pastas, including standards like homemade ravioli and rigatoni with luscious meatballs, are consistently excellent. If you don't have time for a sit-down lunch, stop at the deli counter for smashing heroes and sandwiches or takeouts of imported cheeses and olives. ⊠ *418 E. Main St.* ☎ *719/846–2696* ⊙ *Closed Sun.–Tues.*

ITALIAN

$ ☷ **Black Jack's Inn.** At this 1890s downtown building, where you can toss your peanut shells on the floor at the downstairs bar, there's atmosphere to spare. **Pros:** these rooms take you back to another era; in the center of the historic district. **Cons:** it's over a colorful and popular saloon; small rooms. ⊠ *225 W. Main St.* ☎ *719/846–9501* ⊕ *www.blackjackssaloon. com/inn.htm* ⇆ *5 rooms* ♿ *In-room: Wi-Fi* ⊙ *Restaurant closed Sun.* ¡Ol *Breakfast.*

B&B/INN

$ ☷ **Tarabino Inn.** This Italianate–Victorian B&B sits in the middle of the Corazon de Trinidad National Historic District. **Pros:** inn is filled with work by local artists; within walking distance of museums. **Cons:** feels like staying in someone's private home; no pets allowed. ⊠ *310*

B&B/INN

E. 2nd St. ☎ *719/846–2115, 866/846–8808* ⊕ *www.tarabinoinn.com* ➣ *2 suites, 2 rooms without bath* ⅍ *In-room: Internet* ⅋⦾⅋ *Breakfast.*

NIGHTLIFE

Choose from a variety of lagers and ales, with names like La Fiesta and Ghost Town Brown Ale or one of the other traditional brews, at the **Trinidad Brewing Company.** ⊠ *516 Elm St.* ☎ *719/846–7069* ⊕ *www.trinidadbrewingcompany.com.*

SHOPPING

Corazon Gallery. At artists' co-op, the Corazon Gallery has oil paintings, handwoven clothing, and mixed-media artwork. ⊠ *149 E. Main St.* ☎ *719/846–0207.*

Purgatoire River Trading Company. In the heart of the historic district there are some interesting shops. Purgatoire River Trading Company is the place to find authentic Navajo rugs, Native American pottery, Pima baskets, and old-pawn jewelry. ⊠ *113 E. Main St.* ☎ *719/845–0202.*

CUCHARA VALLEY

55 mi from Trinidad (to town of Cuchara) via Rte. 12; 117 mi south of Colorado Springs.

If you want a true mountain rural setting, head to Cuchara Valley. From here or La Veta you can go camping or hiking in the San Isabel National Forest, go horseback riding on trails through the woods, go fishing in streams, or play golf.

GETTING HERE AND AROUND

This is a tiny town along the Highway of Legends. You need a private car to get here and move around this region.

ESSENTIALS

Visitor Information Huerfano County Chamber of Commerce ⊠ *400 Main St., Walsenburg* ☎ *719/738–1065* ⊕ *www.huerfanocountychamberofcommerce. com.* **La Veta-Cuchara Chamber of Commerce.** ☎ *719/742–3676* ⊕ *www. lavetacucharachamber.com.*

TOP EXPERIENCE: HIGHWAY OF LEGENDS

Cokedale. This entire town is a National Historic Landmark District, and it's the most significant example of a turn-of-the-20th-century coal–coke camp in Colorado. As you drive through the area, note the telltale streaks of black in the sandstone and granite bluffs fronting the Purgatoire River and its tributaries, the unsightly slag heaps, and the spooky abandoned mining camps dotting the hillsides.

★ **Highway of Legends.** From Trinidad, the scenic Highway of Legends curls north through the Cuchara Valley. As it starts its climb, you'll pass a series of company towns built to house coal miners. The Highway of Legends, also known as Route 12, takes you through some of the wildest and most beautiful scenery in southern Colorado. You can start the drive in Trinidad or La Veta.

La Veta. The Highway of Legends passes through the tiny, laid-back resort town of La Veta before intersecting with Highway 160 and going on to Walsenburg, another settlement built on coal and the largest town between Pueblo and Trinidad. ⊠ *La Veta.*

San Isabel National Forest. As you approach Cuchara Pass, several switchbacks snake through rolling grasslands and dance in and out of spruce stands whose clearings afford views of Monument Lake. You can camp, fish, and hike throughout this tranquil part of the San Isabel National Forest, which in spring and summer is emblazoned with a color wheel of wildflowers. Four corkscrewing miles later you'll reach a dirt road that leads to Bear Lake and Blue Lake. The resort town of Cuchara is about 4 mi from the Highway 12 turnoff to the lakes. Nestled in a spoon valley (*cuchara* means "spoon"), the area became popular as a turn-of-the-20th-century camping getaway for Texans and Oklahomans because of its cool temperatures and stunning scenery.

Spanish Peaks. In the Cuchara Valley you'll see fantastic rock formations with equally fanciful names, such as Profile Rock, Devil's Staircase, and Giant's Spoon. With a little imagination you can devise your own legends about the names' origins. There are more than 400 of these upthrusts, which radiate like the spokes of a wheel from the valley's dominating landmark, the Spanish Peaks. In Spanish they are known as *Dos Hermanos,* or "Two Brothers." In Ute, their name *Huajatolla* means "breasts of the world." The haunting formations are considered to be a unique geologic phenomenon for their sheer abundance and variety of rock types.

SPORTS AND THE OUTDOORS
GOLF
Grandote Peaks Golf Club. This Weiskopf Morrish–designed course is an underutilized gem that sits close to the base of the Spanish Peaks. On weekends you need reservations to play the classic 18-hole mountain course, but you can sometimes get in at the last minute on weekdays. ⊠ *5540 Hwy. 12, La Veta* ☎ *719/742–3391, 800/457–9986* ⊕ *www. grandotepeaks.com* ⌘ *18 holes. Yards: 7085/5608. Par: 72/73. Green fee: $55/$75 plus $15 for cart.*

WHERE TO STAY
For expanded hotel reviews, visit Fodors.com.

$

B&B/INN

★

Inn at the Spanish Peaks Bed & Breakfast. This Southwestern-style B&B is set in an adobe-style home with open beams and high ceilings. **Pros:** mountain views; friendly owners; good breakfasts. **Cons:** you are really in the outback of Colorado; no air-conditioning. ⊠ *310 E. Francisco St., La Veta* ☎ *719/742–5313* ⊕ *www.innatthespanishpeaks.com* ⌘ *3 suites* ⌂ *In-room: no a/c, no TV* ▯◯▯ *Breakfast.*

$

B&B/INN

La Veta Inn. The shady courtyard, with its fireplace, is a selling point at this inn in the historic district of La Veta. **Pros:** next to galleries; a few blocks from Tom Weiskopf's Grandote Peaks Golf Course. **Cons:** not ideal for travelers who want a more urban atmosphere; closed January and February. ⊠ *103 W. Ryus Ave., La Veta* ☎ *719/742–3700, 888/806–4875 reservations* ⊕ *www.lavetainn.com* ⌘ *18 rooms* ⌂ *In-room: Wi-Fi. In-hotel: restaurant, bar, some pets allowed.*

THE SAN LUIS VALLEY

At 8,000 square mi, the San Luis Valley is considered to be the world's largest alpine valley, sprawling on a broad, flat, dry plain between the San Juan and La Garita mountains to the west and the Sangre de Cristo range to the east. But equally important is that the valley, like the Southwest, remains culturally rooted in the early Hispanic tradition rather than the northern European one that early prospectors and settlers brought to central and northern Colorado.

Despite its average elevation of 7,500 feet, the San Luis Valley's sheltering peaks help to create a relatively mild climate. The area is one of the state's major agricultural producers, with huge annual crops of potatoes, carrots, canola, barley, and lettuce. In many ways it's self-sufficient; in the 1950s local business owners threatened to secede to prove that the state couldn't get along without the valley and its valuable products. Half a century later, however, the reality is that the region is economically disadvantaged and contains two of the state's poorer counties. The large and sparsely populated valley contains some real oddities, including an alligator farm, a UFO-viewing tower, and the New Age town of Crestone, with its many spiritual centers.

This area was settled first by the Ute, then by the Spanish, who left their indelible imprint in the town names and architecture. The oldest town (San Luis), the oldest military post (Fort Garland), and the oldest church (Our Lady of Guadalupe in Conejos) in the state are in this valley.

GREAT SAND DUNES NATIONAL PARK AND PRESERVE

Created by winds that sweep the San Luis Valley floor, the enormous sand dunes that form the heart of Great Sand Dunes National Park and Preserve are an improbable, unforgettable sight. The dunes, as curvaceous as Rubens' nudes, stretch for more than 30 square mi. Because they're made of sand, the dunes' very existence seem tenuous, as if they might blow away before your eyes, yet they're solid enough to withstand 440,000 years of Mother Nature—and the modern stress of hikers and saucer-riding thrill-seekers.

GREAT SAND DUNES PLANNER
GETTING ORIENTED

The Great Sand Dunes Park and Preserve encompasses 150,000 acres (about 234 square mi) of land and mountains surrounding the dunes. Looking at the dunes from the west, your eye sweeps over the grassland and sand sheet, a vast expanse of smaller dunes and flatter sections of sand and knee-high brush. The Sangre de Cristo Mountains rear up in the east behind the dunes, forming a dramatic backdrop and creating a stunning juxtaposition of color and form.

Sand dunes. The 30-square-mi field of sand has no designated trails. The highest dune in the park—and, in fact, in North America—is 750-foot-high Star Dune.

Sangre de Cristo Mountains. Named the "Blood of Christ" Mountains by Spanish explorers because of their ruddy color—especially at sunrise and sunset—the range contains 10 of Colorado's 54 Fourteeners.

> **LODGING ALTERNATIVES**
>
> **Cuchara Cabins and Condos.** The rental of condominiums, homes, and cabins is handled by Cuchara Cabins and Condos. ☎ *719/742-3340* ⊕ *www.cucharacabinsandcondos.com.*

WHEN TO GO

About 300,000 visitors come to the park each year, most on summer weekends; they tend to congregate around the main parking area and Medano Creek. To avoid the crowds, hike away from the main area up to the High Dune. Or come in winter, when the park is a place for contemplation and repose—as well as skiing and sledding.

Fall and spring are the prettiest times to visit, with the surrounding mountains still capped with snow in May, and leaves on the aspen trees turning gold in September and early October. In summer, the surface temperature of the sand can climb to 140°F in the afternoon, so climbing the dunes is best in the morning or late afternoon. Since you're at a high altitude—about 8,200 feet at the visitor center—the air temperatures in the park itself remain in the 70s most of the summer.

GETTING HERE AND AROUND

Great Sand Dunes National Park and Preserve is about 240 mi from both Denver and Albuquerque, and roughly 180 mi from Colorado Springs and Santa Fe. The fastest route from the north is Interstate 25 south to U.S. 160, heading west to just past Blanca, to Highway 150 north, which goes right to the park's main entrance. For a more scenic route, take U.S. 285 over Kenosha, Red Hill, and Poncha Passes, turn onto Highway 17 just south of Villa Grove, then take County Lane 6 to the park (watch for signs just south of Hooper). When traveling from the south, go north on Interstate 25 to Santa Fe, then north on U.S. 285 to Alamosa, then U.S. 160 east to Highway 150. From the west, Highway 17 and County Lane 6 take you to the park. The park entrance station is about 3 mi from the park boundary, and it's about a mile from there to the visitor center; the main parking lot is about a mile farther.

PARK ESSENTIALS

PARK FEES AND PERMITS
Entrance fees are $3 per adult above age 16 and are valid for one week. Pick up camping permits ($14 per night per site at Pinyon Flats Campground) and backpacking permits (free) at the visitor center.

PARK HOURS
The park is open 24/7. It is in the mountain time zone.

CELL-PHONE RECEPTION
Cell-phone reception in the park is sporadic. Public telephones are at the visitor center, dunes parking lot, and at the Pinyon Flats campground—you need a calling card (these aren't coin-operated phones).

VISITOR INFORMATION

PARK CONTACT INFORMATION
Great Sand Dunes National Park and Preserve ✉ *11999 Hwy. 150, Mosca* ☎ *719/378-6399* ⊕ *www.nps.gov/grsa.*

VISITOR
CENTER

Great Sand Dunes Visitor Center. View exhibits and artwork, browse in the bookstore, and watch a 20-minute film with an overview of the dunes. Rangers are on hand to answer questions. Facilities include restrooms and a vending machine stocked with soft drinks and snacks spring, summer, and fall, but no other food. (The Great Sand Dunes Oasis, just outside the park boundary, has a café that is open generally late April through early October.) ⊠ *Near the park entrance* ☎ *719/378–6399* ⊙ *Late May–early Sept., daily 8:30–6:30; early Sept.–late May, daily 9–4:30 (sometimes until 5 in late spring and early fall—call ahead).*

EXPLORING
SCENIC DRIVES

★ **Medano Pass Primitive Road.** This 22-mi road connects Great Sand Dunes with the Wet Mountain Valley and Highway 69 on the east side of the Sangre de Cristo Mountains via a climb to Medano Pass (about 10,000 feet above sea level) and affords stunning views, especially in late September when the aspens change color. It also provides access to campsites in the national preserve. It is a four-wheel-drive-only road that is best driven by someone who already has good driving skills on rough, unpaved roads. (Your four-wheel-drive vehicle must have high clearance and be engineered to go over rough roads, and you may need to drop your tires' air pressure.) The road has sections of deep, loose sand, and it crosses Medano Creek nine times. Before you go, stop at the visitor center for a map and ask about current road conditions. Drive time pavement to pavement is 2½ to 3 hours.

SCENIC STOPS

★ **Dune Field.** The more than 30 square mi of big dunes in the heart of the park is the main attraction, although the surrounding sand sheet does have some smaller dunes. You can start putting your feet in the sand 3 mi past the main park entrance.

High Dune. This isn't the park's highest dune, but it's high enough in the dune field to provide a view of all the dunes from its summit. It's on the first ridge of dunes you see from the main parking area.

EDUCATIONAL OFFERINGS

PROGRAMS
AND TOURS
♻

Bison Tour. The Nature Conservancy, an international nonprofit conservation organization, owns a 103,000-acre ranch that includes a herd of roughly 2,500 bison in the 50,000-acre Medano Ranch section, in the southwest corner of the park. The conservancy offers a two-hour tour focused on the "Wild West" section of the park, where bison—along with coyotes, elk, deer, pronghorns, porcupines, and birds such as great horned owls and red-tailed hawks, roam in the grasslands and wetlands. Depending on the season, the tour will be led as a hayride or a four-wheel-drive vehicle drive. ⊠ *Tours begin at the Nature Conservancy's Zapata Ranch Headquarters, 5303 Hwy. 150, Mosca* ☎ *888/592–7282, 719/378–2356* ⊕ *www.zranch.org* ☞ *$50.*

RANGER
PROGRAMS

Interpretive Programs. Terrace talks and nature walks designed to help visitors learn more about the park are scheduled most days from late May through September, and sporadically in April and October. ⊠ *Programs begin at the visitor center* ☎ *719/378–6399* ☞ *Free.*

⟡ **Junior Ranger Programs.** In summer, children ages 3 through 12 can join age-appropriate activities to learn about plants, animals, and the park's ecology, and they can become Junior Rangers by working successfully through an activity booklet available at the visitor center. Youngsters can learn about the park prior to their trip via an interactive online program for kids at ⊕ *www.nps.gov/grsa/forkids/beajuniorranger.htm* ☎ *719/378–6399* ✉ *Free.*

SPORTS AND THE OUTDOORS
BIRD-WATCHING
The San Luis Valley is famous for its migratory birds, many of which make a stop in the park. Great Sand Dunes also has many permanent feathered residents. In the wetlands, you might see American white pelicans and the American avocet. On the forested sections of the mountains there are goshawks, northern harriers, gray jays, and Steller's jays. And in the alpine tundra there are golden eagles, hawks, horned larks, and white-tailed ptarmigan.

FISHING
Fly-fishermen can angle for Rio Grande cutthroat trout in the upper reaches of Medano Creek, which is accessible by four-wheel-drive vehicle. It's catch and release only, and a Colorado license is required. There's also fishing in Upper and Lower Sand Creek Lakes, but it's a long hike (3 or 4 mi from the Music Pass Trailhead, located on the far side of the park in the San Isabel National Forest).

HIKING
Visitors can walk just about anywhere on the sand dunes in the heart of the park. The best view of all the dunes is from the top of High Dune. There are no formal trails because the sand keeps shifting, but you don't really need them: There's no way you'd get lost out here.

■ **TIP→** Before taking any of the trails in the preserve, rangers recommend stopping at the visitor center and picking up the handout that lists the trails, including their degree of difficulty. The dunes can get very hot in summer, reaching up to 140°F in the afternoon. If you're hiking, carry plenty of water; if you're going into the backcountry to camp overnight, carry even more water and a water filtration system. A free permit is needed to backpack in the park. Also, watch for weather changes. If there's a thunderstorm and lightning, get off the dunes or trail immediately, and seek shelter. Before hiking, leave word with someone indicating where you're to hike and when you expect to be back. Tell that contact to call 911 if you don't show up when expected.

EASY **Hike to High Dune.** Get a panoramic view of all the surrounding dunes
⟡ from the top of High Dune. Since there's no formal path, the smartest approach is to zigzag up the dune ridgelines. High Dune is 650 feet high, and to get there and back takes about 1½ to 2 hours. It's 1.2 mi each way, but it can feel like a lot longer if there's been no rain for awhile and the sand is soft. If you add on the walk to Star Dune, which is another 1.5 mi there and back, plan on another two hours and a strenuous workout up and down the dunes. *Easy.* ✉ *Start from main dune field.*

CLOSE UP

Best Campgrounds in Great Sand Dunes

Great Sand Dunes has one campground that is open year-round. During weekends in the summer, it can fill up with RVs and tents by mid-afternoon. Black bears live in the preserve, so when camping there, keep your food, trash, and toiletries in the trunk of your car (or use bear-proof containers). There is one campground and RV park near the entrance to Great Sand Dunes, and several others in the area.

Pinyon Flats Campground. Set in a pine forest about a mile past the visitor center, this campground has a trail leading to the dunes. Sites are available on a first-come, first-served basis, although groups of 10 or more might be able to reserve in advance. RVs are allowed, but there are no hookups. ⊠ *On the main park road, near the visitor center* ☎ *719/378–6399.*

MODERATE

Fodor's Choice

★

Mosca Pass Trail. This moderately challenging trail follows the route laid out centuries ago by Native Americans, which became the Mosca Pass toll road used in the late 1800s and early 1900s. This is a good afternoon hike, because the trail rises through the trees and subalpine meadows, often following Mosca Creek. It is 3½ miles one way, with a 1,500-foot gain in elevation. Hiking time is two to three hours each way. *Moderate.* ⊠ *The lower end of the trail begins at the Montville Trailhead, just north of the visitor center.*

DIFFICULT

Music Pass Trail. This steep trail offers superb views of the glacially carved Upper Sand Creek Basin, ringed by several 13,000-foot peaks and the Wet Mountain Valley to the east. At the top of the pass you are about 11,000 feet above sea level and surrounded by yet higher mountain peaks. It's 3½ mi and a 2,000-foot elevation gain one way from the lower parking lot on the east side of the preserve, off Forest Service Road 119, and 1 mi from the upper parking lot (reachable only by four-wheel-drive). Depending on how fit you are and how often you stop, it can take six hours round-trip from the lower lot. *Difficult.* ⊠ *Trail begins on eastern side of park, reached via Hwy. 69, 4½ mi south of Westcliffe. Turn off Hwy. 69 to the west at the sign for Music Pass and South Colony Lakes Trails. At the "T" junction, turn left onto South Colony Rd. At the end of the ranch fence on the right you'll see another sign for Music Pass.*

ALAMOSA

35 mi southwest of Great Sand Dunes via U.S. 160 and Rte. 150; 163 mi southwest of Colorado Springs.

The San Luis Valley's major city is a casual, central base from which to explore the region and visit the Great Sand Dunes.

EXPLORING

Adams State College. Adams State College contains several superlative examples of 1930s WPA-commissioned murals in its administrative building. The college's **Luther Bean Museum and Art Gallery** displays European porcelain and furniture collections in a handsome, wood-panel 19th-century drawing room, and changing exhibits of regional arts and crafts. ☒ *Richardson Hall, Richardson and 3rd Sts.* ☎ *719/587–7151* ☒ *Free* ⊙ *mid-Aug.–mid-May, Tues.–Fri. 8–5; mid-May–mid-Aug., Tues.–Fri. 7:30–4:30.*

Alamosa National Wildlife Refuge. Less than an hour's drive southwest of Great Sand Dunes are two sanctuaries for songbirds, water birds, and raptors (they're also home to many other types of birds, along with mule deer, beavers, and coyotes). The smaller of the two is the Alamosa National Wildlife Refuge, comprising nearly 12,000 acres of natural and man-made wetlands bordering the Rio Grande. You can take a 2-mi hike along the river or a 3½-mi drive along the bluff overlook on the park's eastern side. The refuge office is staffed by volunteers sporadically from March through November and closed in winter—it's wise to call first. ☒ *9383 El Rancho La., off U.S. 160* ☎ *719/589–4021* ⊕ *www.fws.gov/alamosa* ☒ *Free* ⊙ *Daily sunrise–sunset.*

Monte Vista National Wildlife Refuge. Just west of the Alamosa wildlife refuge is its sister sanctuary, the Monte Vista National Wildlife Refuge, a 15,000-acre park that's a stopping point for up to 20,000 migrating cranes. It hosts an annual Crane Festival, held one weekend in mid-March in the nearby town of Monte Vista. You can see the sanctuary via a 4-mi driving tour. ☒ *6120 Hwy. 15, south off of U.S. 160/285, Monte Vista* ☎ *719/589–4021* ⊕ *www.fws.gov/alamosa* ☒ *Free* ⊙ *Daily sunrise–sunset.*

WHERE TO EAT AND STAY

For expanded hotel reviews, visit Fodors.com.

¢ | ASIAN ✕ **East West Grill.** Noodles and teriyaki top the menu at this casual, almost fast-food-style place with dine-in or carry-out options. The salads and bento boxes are great. ☒ *408 4th St.* ☎ *719/589–4600* ⊕ *www.east-westgrill.com.*

$$ | STEAKHOUSE ✕ **True Grits.** At this steak house, the cuts of beef are predictably good, but that's not the real draw. As the name implies, the restaurant is a shrine to John Wayne. His portraits hang everywhere: the Duke in action, the Duke in repose, the Duke lost in thought. ☒ *100 Santa Fe Ave.* ☎ *719/589–9954.*

$ | HOTEL 🏨 **Best Western Alamosa Inn.** This sprawling, well-maintained complex is your best bet for reasonably priced lodgings. **Pros:** reliable basic accommodations; easy to find. **Cons:** noisy street; nothing but fast food nearby. ☒ *2005 Main St.* ☎ *719/589–2567, 800/459–5123* ⊕ *www.bestwestern.com/alamosainn* ⤴ *52 rooms, 1 suite* ⚹ *In-room: Wi-Fi. In-hotel: pool, gym, laundry facilities, some pets allowed.*

$ | HOTEL ⊙ ★ 🏨 **Inn of the Rio Grande.** Alamosa's largest hotel is a pet-friendly property, with comfortable rooms and suites. **Pros:** great for families with children and/or pets (who stay free); close to restaurants and other amenities in town; sauna and hot tub. **Cons:** water park and gym area can get crowded; big property with the feel of a convention center. ⊠ *333 Santa Fe Dr.* ☎ *800/669–1658, 719/589–5833* ⊕ *www.innoftherio.com* ⇨ *120 rooms, 5 suites* ♿ *In-room: a/c, Wi-Fi. In-hotel: restaurant, bar, pool, gym, some pets allowed* ⑩ *Breakfast.*

SHOPPING

Rakhra Mushroom Farm. The San Luis Valley is noted for its produce. Mycophiles can take a tour of the Rakhra Mushroom Farm. Call ahead; mornings are preferred. ⊠ *10719 Rd. 5 S* ☎ *719/589–5882* ⊕ *www. rakhramushroom.com.*

MANASSA, SAN LUIS, AND FORT GARLAND LOOP

To get a real feel for this area, take an easy driving loop from Alamosa that includes Manassa, San Luis, and Fort Garland. In summer, take a few hours to ride one of the scenic railroads that take you into wilderness areas in this region.

TIMING

The driving distance for this loop, including a 7-mi jog down to Antonio if you want to take a ride on the Cumbres and Toltec Scenic Railroad, is about 100 mi. But, it's along secondary roads and goes through small towns, so don't expect to maintain highway speeds.

EXPLORING

⟳ **Cumbres & Toltec Scenic Railroad.** Take a day trip on the Cumbres & Toltec Scenic Railroad, an 1880s steam locomotive that chugs through portions of Colorado's and northern New Mexico's rugged mountains that you can't reach via roads. It's the country's longest and highest narrow-gauge railroad. The company offers two round-trip train routes—either Antonito to Osier or Chama, NM to Osier—plus several bus-and-train combinations and one-way trips. Cumbres & Toltec offers themed rides, including a special Christmastime train ride called "The Cinder Bear." ☎ *888/286–2737* ⊕ *www.cumbrestoltec.com* ⊠ *$75–$125, $165 for a seat in the adults–only parlor car* ◷ *Late May–late Oct.*

Fort Garland. One of Colorado's first military posts, Fort Garland was established in 1858 to protect settlers. It lies in the shadow of the Sangre de Cristo Mountains. The mountains were named for the "Blood of Christ" because of their ruddy color, especially at dawn. The legendary Kit Carson commanded the outfit, and five of the original adobe structures are still standing. The **Fort Garland State Museum** features a re-creation of the commandant's quarters and period military displays. The museum is 16 mi north of San Luis via Route 159 and 24 mi east of Alamosa via U.S. 160. ⊠ *U.S. 160 and Hwy. 159, Fort Garland* ☎ *719/379–3512* ⊠ *$5* ◷ *Apr.–Oct., daily 9–5; Nov.–Mar., Thurs.–Mon. 10–4.*

Manassa. The town of Manassa is about 23 mi from Alamosa, south on U.S. 285 and 3 mi east on Route 142.

Jack Dempsey Museum. Known as the "Manassa Mauler," one of the greatest heavyweight boxing champions of all time is honored in his hometown at the Jack Dempsey Museum. ⊠ *412 Main St., Manassa* ☎ *719/843–5207* ◷ *Memorial Day weekend–Labor Day weekend, Tues.–Sat. 10–5* ⊠ *Manassa.*

12

🐾 **Rio Grande Scenic Railroad.** This railroad carries passengers on excursions between Alamosa and La Veta or Monte Vista; also offered is a side trip from La Veta, via motor coach, to the Great Sand Dunes. Or you can catch a Rio Grande train to Antonito, where you'll connect with the Combres & Toltec train on its way to Osier or Chama. The Rio Grande also offers a round-trip "North Pole Express" train from Alamosa to La Veta several times in late November and December. ☎ 877/726–7245 ⊕ *www.riograndescenicrailroad.com* ✉ *$15–$90* ◷ *Late May–mid-Oct.*

San Luis. Founded in 1851, San Luis is the oldest incorporated town in Colorado. Murals depicting famous stories and legends of the area adorn several buildings in the town. A latter-day masterpiece is the **Stations of the Cross Shrine,** created by renowned local sculptor Huberto Maestas. The shrine is formally known as La Mesa de la Piedad y de la Misericordia (Hill of Piety and Mercy), and its 15 stations illustrate the last hours of Christ's life. The trail leads up to a chapel called Capilla de Todos Los Santos.

San Luis Museum & Cultural Center. San Luis's Hispanic heritage is celebrated in the San Luis Museum & Cultural Center. It has an extensive collection of artwork, *santos* (decorated figures of saints used for household devotions), *retablos* (religious paintings on wood), and *bultos* (carved religious figures). ⊠ *401 Church Pl., San Luis* ☎ *719/672–0999* ✉ *$2* ◷ *Summer, Mon.–Sat. 10–4, Sun. noon–4; winter, weekdays 10–4* ⊠ *San Luis.*

DEL NORTE

31 mi west of Alamosa via U.S. 160; 194 mi southwest of Colorado Springs.

Del Norte is a tiny town, but there's an excellent honey shop on the main street, a regional history museum, and good hiking in nearby Penitente Canyon.

EXPLORING

La Ventana Natural Arch. The beautiful La Garita Wilderness holds one of the region's marvels—the towering rock formation La Ventana Natural Arch.

Penitente Canyon. Just north of town is the gaping Penitente Canyon. Once a retreat and place of worship for a small, fervent sect of the Catholic Church known as Los Hermanos Penitente, it is now a haven for rock climbers, hikers, and mountain bikers. Follow Route 112 about 3 mi from Del Norte, then follow the signs to the canyon. ⊠ *Off Rte. 112.*

Rio Grande County Museum and Cultural Center. The Rio Grande County Museum and Cultural Center celebrates the region's multicultural heritage with displays of petroglyphs, mining artifacts, early Spanish relics, and rotating shows of contemporary art. ⊠ *580 Oak St.* ☎ *719/657–2847* ✉ *$1* ◷ *Tues.–Sat. 10–5.*

SPORTS AND THE OUTDOORS

FISHING

Rio Grande River. The Rio Grande River between Del Norte and South Fork teems with rainbows, browns, and cutthroats. The area is full of "gold medal" waters, designated as great fishing spots by the Colorado Wildlife Commission. ⊕ *www.wildlife.state.co.us/fishing*.

SHOPPING

Elk Ridge. Elk Ridge is the place for gourmet products and gift baskets overflowing with goodies. ⊠ *616 Grand Ave.* ☎ *719/657–2322*.

Travel Smart
Colorado

WORD OF MOUTH

"[To avoid altitude sickness, follow] these simple guidelines while traveling:
Stay below 7,000 feet the first day. . . . When sightseeing, work your way up to higher altitudes. Avoid strenuous exercise the first day. Drink more water than usual since your body will dehydrate more quickly. Reduce alcohol intake, which has a greater effect at this altitude. Avoid salty foods. Give your body time to adjust (there is a lot to see and do at the lower altitude levels). If you follow these simple suggestions, you are sure to enjoy each day of your vacation."

—DebitNM

GETTING HERE AND AROUND

Denver is Colorado's hub; the state's two major interstates, I–25 and I–70, intersect here, and most of the state's population lives within a one- or two-hour drive of the city. The high plains expand to the east from Denver, and the western edge of the metro area ends at the foothills of the Rocky Mountains. A corridor of cities along Interstate 25 parallels the foothills from Fort Collins to Pueblo, and most lonely stretches of highway are in the eastern portion of the state on the plains. Although scheduled air, rail, and bus service connects Denver to many smaller cities and towns, a car is the most practical way to explore the state.

▌ AIR TRAVEL

It takes about two hours to fly to Denver from Los Angeles, Chicago, or Dallas. From New York and Boston the flight is about 3½ hours. If you're traveling during snow season, allow extra time for the drive to the airport. If you'll be checking skis, arrive even earlier.

AIRPORTS

The major air gateway to the Colorado Rockies is Denver International Airport (DEN), usually referred to by its nickname, DIA. It's 30 mi northeast of downtown Denver and 45 mi from Boulder. Flights to smaller, resort-town airports generally connect through it. Inclement weather, fairly common in winter, occasionally delays or cancels flights. There are a few eateries in the airport, but no hotels. Most hotels are several miles away toward Denver.

Colorado Springs Airport (COS) has direct flights from many major cities and is slightly less subject to bad winter storms than Denver. The airport is sometimes still open when bad weather closes other airports (especially those in the ski towns). Some of the major airlines and their subsidiaries serve communities

WORD OF MOUTH

"My East Coast relatives still talk about their trip to Denver in 1993 for my wedding. Sept. 11, wedding day, sunny and 90 degrees. Sept. 13, a blizzard so bad most flights were cancelled. Then there was that Christmas Day where it was warmer in Denver than it was in Miami!"—tekwriter

around the state: Grand Junction (GJT), Durango (DRO), Steamboat Springs (HDN), Gunnison–Crested Butte (GUC), Montrose (MTJ), Telluride (TEX), Aspen (ASE), Vail (EGE). Some major airlines have scheduled service from points within the United States to Colorado Springs Airport (COS); the relatively mild weather in Colorado Springs means that its airport is sometimes still functional when bad weather farther north and west affects the state's other airports. Many ski towns increase their seasonal service, adding direct flights.

Airport Information Colorado Springs Airport (COS) ☎ 719/550–1972 ⊕ www.springsgov.com/airportindex.aspx. **Denver International Airport (DEN)** ☎ 800/247–2336 ⊕ www.flydenver.com.

GROUND TRANSPORTATION

If you are driving, the best route from Denver International Airport to Denver, the ski resorts, or the mountains is to drive west on Interstate 70. You can bypass some traffic by using the E–470 tollway, which you can access west of the airport. It connects to Interstate 25 both south and north of Denver. When flying into Colorado Springs, take Interstate 25 north and south. Vail, Aspen, Telluride, and the surrounding towns are accessible on Highway 24 without going through Denver.

RTD, the city's public transit, has frequent bus service to Denver and Boulder; visit their booth in the main terminal for destinations, times, and tickets. There are taxis and various private airport shuttles to cities along the Front Range from the airport, and some offer door-to-door service. Many hotels and ski resorts have their own buses; check with your lodging or ski resort to see if they offer service. The Ground Transportation Information Center is on the fifth level of the main terminal, and can direct travelers to companies' service counters. All services depart from and arrive on level five of the main terminal building.

FLIGHTS

Denver International Airport (DEN) has direct flights from most major U.S. cities, as well as quite a few smaller ones, especially in the West. A few international carriers serve Denver with nonstop flights from London, England; Frankfurt and Munich, Germany; as well as Canadian cities like Vancouver, Toronto, and Montréal. Frontier Airlines and United Airlines are Denver's largest carriers, with the most flights and the longest list of destinations. Colorado Springs is served by Allegiant Airlines as well as by most major domestic airlines. United Express and Great Lakes Airlines connect Denver with smaller cities and ski resorts within Colorado.

Airline Contacts Aero Mexico ☎ 800/237–639 ⊕ www.aeromexico.com. Air Canada ☎ 800/247–2262 ⊕ www.aircanada. om. Alaska Airlines ☎ 800/252–7522 ⊕ www.alaskaair.com. Allegiant Airlines ☎ 702/505–8888 ⊕ www.allegiantair.com. American Airlines ☎ 800/433–7300 ⊕ www. a.com. British Airways ☎ 800/247–9297 ⊕ www.britishairways.com. Continental Airlines ☎ 800/523–3273 ⊕ www.continental. om. Delta Airlines ☎ 800/221–1212 ⊕ www.delta.com. Frontier ☎ 800/432–1359 ⊕ www.frontierairlines.com. Great Lakes ☎ 800/554–5111 ⊕ www.flygreatlakes. om. jetBlue ☎ 800/538–2583 ⊕ www. jetblue.com. Lufthansa ☎ 800/399–5838 ⊕ www.lufthansa.com. Southwest Airlines ☎ 800/435–9792 ⊕ www.southwest.com. United Airlines ☎ 800/864–8331 ⊕ www.

united.com. USAirways ☎ 800/943–5436 ⊕ www.usairways.com.

■ BUS TRAVEL

Traveling by bus within the Denver–Boulder region is fairly easy with RTD, because the coverage of the area is dense and most routes are not too circuitous. The free 16th Street MallRide and the light-rail routes within Denver make travel to and from downtown attractions easy.

Mountain Metropolitan Transit serves the Colorado Springs area. Colorado Mountain Express offers both shared-ride shuttles and private-car airport services from Denver International Airport (DEN) and Eagle County Regional Airport.

Bus Information Colorado Mountain Express ☎ 800/525–6363, 970/926–9800 ⊕ www.coloradomountainexpress.com. Mountain Metropolitan Transit. Mountain Metropolitan Transit ☎ 719/385–7433 ⊕ www.springsgov.com. RTD ☎ 303/299–6000 ⊕ www.rtd-denver.com.

■ CAR TRAVEL

Colorado has the most mountainous terrain of the American Rockies, and the scenery can make driving a memorable—often breathtaking—adventure.

Car travel within the urban corridor north and south of Denver can be congested, particularly weekday mornings and afternoons. Weekends, too, can have quite a bit of traffic, particularly along I–70 between Denver and the high mountains. Heavy traffic is not limited to ski season or bad weather. It is nearly a matter of course now for eastbound I–70 to be heavily congested on Sunday afternoons. If you are returning to Denver International Airport for a Sunday-afternoon or evening flight, allow plenty of time to reach the airport.

GASOLINE
At this writing, gasoline costs between $3.50 and $4 a gallon. Gas prices in larger communities are comparable to those elsewhere in the country, but can be considerably higher in rural towns and mountain resorts. Although gas stations are plentiful in many areas, you can drive more than 100 mi in remote areas without finding gas.

LICENSE PLATE TOLL
Denver's Eastern Beltway, the E–470, is a toll road. You are automatically a License Plate Toll customer on E–470 if you're not an EXpressToll customer with a transponder. No advance registration is required, and customers drive nonstop through the tolls. Cameras photograph the license plates and a bill is sent one month later to the registered owner of the vehicle for tolls incurred during that period.

PARKING
On-street metered parking as well as by-the-hour garages and lots are fairly plentiful in larger cities. Meters take coins and, increasingly, credit cards.

ROAD CONDITIONS
Colorado offers some of the most spectacular vistas and challenging driving in the world. Roads range from multilane blacktop to barely graveled backcountry trails; from twisting switchbacks considerately marked with guardrails to primitive campgrounds with a lane so narrow that you must back up to the edge of a steep cliff to make a turn. Scenic routes and lookout points are clearly marked, enabling you to slow down and pull over to take in the views.

One of the more unpleasant sights along the highway is roadkill—animals struck by vehicles. Deer, elk, and even bears may try to get to the other side of a road just as you come along, so watch out for wildlife on the highways. Exercise caution both for the sake of the animal in danger and your car, which could be totaled in a collision.

FROM	TO	DRIVE TIME
Denver	Boulder	40–60 mins
Denver	Fort Collins	60 mins
Denver	Colorado Springs	60–75 mins
Denver	Estes Park	1½–2 hrs
Denver	Glenwood Springs	2½–3 hrs
Glenwood Springs	Aspen	1 hr
Glenwood Springs	Crested Butte	3 hrs
Denver	Grand Junction	4 hrs
Grand Junction	Telluride	2–3 hrs
Denver	Durango	6–7 hrs

Emergency Services **AAA of Colorado** ☎ *303/753–8800* ⊕ *www.colorado.aaa.com.* **Colorado State Patrol** ☎ *303/273–1875, *277 from a cell phone.*

License Plate Toll **EXpressToll** ☎ *303/537–3470, 888/946–3470* ⊕ *www.expresstoll.com.*

Road Condition Information **CO Trip** ☎ *303/639–1111* ⊕ *www.cotrip.org.*

For police or ambulance, dial 911.

RULES OF THE ROAD
You'll find highways and national parks crowded in summer, and almost deserted (and occasionally impassable) in winter. Follow the posted speed limit, drive defensively, and make sure your gas tank is full. The law requires that drivers and front-seat passengers wear seat belts.

Always strap children under age 5 or under 40 pounds into approved child-safety seats. You may turn right at a red light after stopping if there's no sign stating otherwise and no oncoming traffic. When in doubt, wait for the green.

If your vehicle breaks down, or you are involved in an accident, move your vehicle out of the traffic flow, if possible, and call for help: 911 for emergencies and *277 from a cell phone for the Colorado State Patrol.

The speed limit on U.S. interstates in Colorado is up to 75 mph in rural areas and between 55 mph and 65 mph in urban zones. Mountain stretches of I–70 have lower limits—between 55 mph and 70 mph.

WINTER DRIVING

Modern highways make mountain driving safe and generally trouble-free even in cold weather. Although winter driving can occasionally present real challenges, road maintenance is good and plowing is prompt. However, in mountain areas tire chains, studs, or snow tires are essential. If you're planning to drive into high elevations, be sure to check the weather forecast and call for road conditions beforehand. Even main highways can close. It's a good idea to carry an emergency kit and a cell phone, but be aware that the mountains can disrupt service. If you do get stalled by deep snow, do not leave your car. Wait for help, running the engine only if needed, and remember that assistance is never far away. Winter weather isn't confined to winter months in the high country (it's been known to snow in July), so be prepared year-round.

Automobile Association (AAA). ⊕ www.aaa. com.

CAR RENTAL

Rates in most major cities run about $40 to $60 a day and $180 to $300 a week for an economy car with air-conditioning, automatic transmission, and unlimited mileage. Rates can vary greatly from company to company, so it's worth comparing online. The above rates don't include tax or fees on car rentals,

which is as high as 24% in the Denver metro area. Keep in mind if you're venturing into the Rockies that you'll need a little oomph in your engine to get over the passes. If you plan to explore any back roads, an SUV is the best bet, because it will have higher clearance. Unless you plan to do much mountain exploring, a four-wheel drive is usually needed only in winter.

To rent a car in Colorado you must be at least 25 years old (or be willing to pay surcharges) and have a valid driver's license; most companies also require a major credit card. Some companies at certain locations set their minimum age at 21, and then add a daily surcharge. In Colorado, child-safety seats or booster seats are compulsory for children under 5 (with certain height and weight criteria).

You'll pay extra for child seats ($5–$12 a day), drivers under age 25 (at least $25 a day), and usually for additional drivers (about $10 per day). When returning your car to Denver International Airport, allow 15 minutes (30 minutes during busy weekends and around the holidays) to return the vehicle and to ride the shuttle bus to the terminal.

Major Rental Agencies Alamo
☎ 800/462–5266 ⊕ www.alamo.com. **Avis**
☎ 800/331–1212 ⊕ www.avis.com. **Budget**
☎ 800/527–0700 ⊕ www.budget.com. **Hertz**
☎ 800/654–3131 ⊕ www.hertz.com. **National Car Rental** ☎ 877/222–9058 ⊕ www.nationalcar.com.

▮ TRAIN TRAVEL

Amtrak connects several stations in Colorado to both coasts and major American cities. The *California Zephyr* and the *Southwest Chief* pass once per day with east- and west-bound trains that stop in Denver, Winter Park, Granby, Glenwood Springs, Grand Junction, and Trinidad. The Ski Train connects Denver's Union Station and the Winter Park ski resort during ski season and in summer. There are also several scenic narrow-gauge sightseeing railroads all over the state.

Information Amtrak ☎ 800/872-7245 ⊕ www.amtrak.com. **Cumbres & Toltec Scenic Railroad** ☎ 719/376-5483, 888/286-2737 ⊕ www.cumbrestoltec.com. **Durango & Silverton Narrow Gauge Railroad** ☎ 888/872-4607 ⊕ www.durangotrain. com. **Georgetown Loop Railroad** ☎ 888/456-6777 ⊕ www.georgetownlooprr. com. **Historic Royal Gorge Route Railroad** ☎ 719/276-4000 ⊕ www.royalgorgeroute. com. **Leadville, Co. & Southern Railroad Company** ☎ 719/486-3936, 866/386-3936 ⊕ www.leadville-train.com. **Rio Grande Scenic Railroad** ☎ 719/587-0520, 877/726-7245 ⊕ www.riograndescenicrailroad.com.

ESSENTIALS

■ ACCOMMODATIONS

Accommodations in Colorado vary from the posh ski resorts in Vail, Aspen, and Telluride to basic chain hotels and independent motels. Dude and guest ranches often require a one-week stay, and the cost is all-inclusive. Bed-and-breakfasts can be found throughout the state. Hotel rates peak during the height of the ski season, which generally runs from late November through March or April; although rates are high all season, they top out during Christmas week and in February and March. In summer months, a popular time for hiking and rafting, hotel rates are often half the winter price.

Properties are assigned price categories based on the cost of a standard double room during high season. Lodging taxes vary throughout the state.

Most hotels and other lodgings require you to give your credit-card details before they will confirm your reservation. However you book, get confirmation in writing and have a copy of it handy when you check in.

Be sure you understand the hotel's cancellation policy. Some places allow you to cancel without any kind of penalty—even if you prepaid to secure a discounted rate—if you cancel at least 24 hours in advance. Others require you to cancel a week in advance or penalize you the cost of one night. Small inns and B&Bs are most likely to require you to cancel far in advance. Most hotels allow children under a certain age to stay in their parents' room at no extra charge, but others charge them as extra adults; find out the cutoff age for discounts.

Hotels in Denver and Colorado Springs cater heavily to business travelers, often with facilities like restaurants, cocktail lounges, swimming pools, fitness centers, and meeting rooms. Many properties offer considerably lower rates on weekends,

particularly during the colder months. In resort towns hotels are decidedly more deluxe; rural areas generally offer simple, sometimes rustic accommodations.

Ski towns throughout Colorado are home to dozens of resorts in all price ranges; the activities lacking at any individual property can usually be found in the town itself—in summer as well as winter. Off the slopes, there are both wonderful rustic and luxurious resorts, particularly in out-of-the-way spots near Rocky Mountain National Park and other alpine areas.

General Information Colorado Hotel and Lodging Association ☎ *303/297-8335* ⊕ *www.coloradolodging.com.*

CATEGORY	COST
¢	under $80
$	$80–$120
$$	$121–$170
$$$	$171–230
$$$$	over $230

All prices are for a standard double room in high season and excluding tax and service charges.

APARTMENT AND HOUSE RENTALS

Rental accommodations are quite popular in Colorado's ski resorts and mountain towns. Condominiums and luxurious vacation homes dominate the Vail Valley and other ski-oriented areas, but there are scads of cabins in smaller, summer-oriented towns in the Rockies and the Western Slope. Many towns and resort areas have rental agencies.

With a direct home exchange you stay in someone else's home while they stay in yours. Some outfits also deal with vacation homes, so you're not actually staying in someone's full-time residence, just their vacant weekend place.

Exchange Clubs Forgetaway ⊕ *www. forgetaway.com.* **Home Away** ⊕ *www. homeaway.com.* **Home Exchange.com.** $99.95 for a one-year online listing. ☎ *800/877–8723* ⊕ *www.homeexchange.com.* **HomeLink International.** $115 yearly for Web-only membership, $175 includes Web access and two catalogs. ☎ *800/638–3841* ⊕ *www.homelink. org.* **Intervac U.S** ☎ *800/756–4663* ⊕ *www. intervacus.com.*

Local Rental Agencies Colorado Mountain Cabins & Vacation Home Rentals ☎ *719/636–5147, 866/425–4974* ⊕ *www. coloradomountaincabins.com.* **Colorado Vacation Directory** ☎ *303/499–9343, 888/222–4641* ⊕ *www.thecvd.com.*

BED-AND-BREAKFASTS

Charm is the long suit of these establishments, which often occupy a restored older building with some historical or architectural significance. They're generally small, with fewer than 20 rooms. Breakfast is usually included in the rates. The owners often also manage the B&B, and you'll likely meet them and get to know them a bit. Breakfasts are usually substantial, with hot beverages, cold fruit juices, and a hot entrée. Bed & Breakfast Innkeepers of Colorado prints a free annual directory of its members.

Reservation Services Bed & Breakfast.com ☎ *512/322–2710, 800/462–2632* ⊕ *www. bedandbreakfast.com.* **Bed & Breakfast Innkeepers of Colorado** ☎ *800/265–7696* ⊕ *www.innsofcolorado.org.* **Bed & Breakfast Inns Online** ☎ *310/280–4363, 800/215–7365* ⊕ *www.bbonline.com.* **BnB Finder.com** ☎ *888/469–6663* ⊕ *www.bnbfinder.com.*

GUEST RANCHES

If the thought of sitting around a campfire after a hard day on the range is your idea of a vacation, consider playing dude on a guest ranch. Wilderness-rimmed working ranches accept guests and encourage them to pitch in with chores and other ranch activities; you might even be able to participate in a cattle roundup. Most dude ranches don't require previous experience

with horses. Luxurious resorts on the fringes of small cities offer swimming pools, tennis courts, and a lively roster of horse-related activities such as breakfast rides, moonlight rides, and all-day trail rides. Rafting, fishing, tubing, and other activities are usually available at both types of ranches. In winter, cross-country skiing and snowshoeing keep you busy.

Lodgings can run the gamut from charmingly rustic cabins to the kind of deluxe quarters you expect at a first-class hotel. Meals may be sophisticated or plain but hearty. Be sure to check with the ranch for a list of items you might be expected to bring. If you plan to do much riding, a couple of pairs of sturdy pants, boots, a wide-brim hat to shield you from the sun, and outerwear that protects from rain and cold should be packed. Nearly all dude ranches in Colorado offer all-inclusive packages: meals, lodging, and generally all activities. Weeklong stays cost between $1,300 and $4,000 per adult, depending on the ranch's amenities and activities.

Information Colorado Dude and Guest Ranch Association ☎ *866/942–3472* ⊕ *www. coloradoranch.com.*

▌ BUSINESS SERVICES AND FACILITIES

Several cities throughout Colorado have business services where you can print photographs, photocopy documents, send a fax, and check your e-mail. The larger cities along the Interstate 25 corridor have more selection and locations. A few are locally owned, but most are franchises of FedEx Office.

Contacts FedEx Office ⊕ *www.fedex.com/ us/office.*

CHILDREN IN COLORADO

Colorado is tailor-made for family vacations, offering dude ranches, historic railroads, mining towns, rafting, and many outdoor activities. Places that are especially appealing to children are indicated by a rubber-duckie icon ⊙ in the margin.

Visitor centers and lodgings are often good at recommending places to spend time with children. The guides issued by the tourism office of Colorado have sections geared toward children. If you are renting a car, don't forget to arrange for a car seat when you reserve.

The free monthly magazine *Colorado Parent* is available online and in the lobbies of office buildings, hotels, and other businesses.

COMMUNICATIONS

INTERNET

Internet access is available throughout Colorado. Most lodgings have wireless access for laptops, and many have computers available for guests. Many cafés, coffee shops, and restaurants have Wi-Fi, though some charge a fee for access. Many municipal public libraries will allow patrons to use the Internet, either free or for a small fee. Cybercafes lists thousands of Internet cafés worldwide.

Contacts Cybercafes ⊕ *www.cybercafes.com.*

EATING OUT

Dining in Colorado is generally casual. Dinner hours are typically from 6 pm to 10 pm, but many small-town and rural eateries close by 9 pm. Authentic ethnic food is hard to find outside the big cities and major resort towns.

MEALS AND MEALTIMES

Unless otherwise noted, the restaurants listed in this guide are open daily for lunch and dinner.

Although you can find all types of cuisine in Colorado's major cities and resort towns, don't forget to try native dishes like trout, elk, and buffalo (the latter two have less fat than beef and are just as tasty). Steak is a mainstay in the Rocky Mountains. Chile verde, also known as green chile, is a popular menu item at Mexican restaurants in Colorado. Many restaurants serve vegetarian items, and some are exclusively vegetarian. Organic fruits and vegetables are also readily available.

CATEGORY	COST
¢	under $8
$	$8–12
$$	$13–18
$$$	$19–25
$$$$	$ over $25

All prices are per person for a main course at dinner.

ITEM	AVERAGE COST
Cup of Coffee	$1–$2
Glass of Wine	$5–$8
Glass of Beer	$4–$6
Sandwich	$6–$8
One-Mile Taxi Ride in Denver	$4.25
Museum Admission	$5–$8

RESERVATIONS AND DRESS

Regardless of where you are, it's a good idea to make a reservation if you can. In some places it's expected. We only mention them specifically when reservations are essential (there's no other way you'll ever get a table) or when they are not accepted. For popular restaurants, book as far ahead as you can (often 30 days), and reconfirm as soon as you arrive. Large parties should always call ahead to check the reservations policy. We mention dress only when men are required to wear a jacket or a jacket and tie—which is almost never in the Rockies.

SMOKING

Smoking is prohibited in Colorado's public places, including restaurants and bars.

WINES, BEER, AND SPIRITS

The legal drinking age in Colorado is 21. Colorado liquor laws do not allow anyone to bring their own alcohol to restaurants.

FOR INTERNATIONAL TRAVELERS

CURRENCY

The dollar is the basic unit of U.S. currency. It has 100 cents. Coins are the penny (1¢), nickel (5¢), dime (10¢), quarter (25¢), half-dollar (50¢), and the very rare golden $1 coin and even rarer silver $1. Bills are denominated $1, $5, $10, $20, $50, and $100, all mostly green and identical in size; designs and background tints vary. You may come across a $2 bill, but the chances are slim.

CUSTOMS

Information U.S. Customs and Border Protection ☎ *877/227–5511* ⊕ *www.cbp. gov.*

DRIVING

Driving in the United States is on the right. Speed limits are posted in miles per hour (usually between 55 mph and 75 mph). Watch for lower limits in small towns and on back roads (usually 30 mph to 40 mph). Most states require front-seat passengers to wear seat belts; many states require children to sit in the backseat and to wear seat belts. In major cities morning rush hour is between 7 and 10 am; afternoon rush hour is between 4 and 7 pm. To encourage carpooling, some freeways have special lanes, ordinarily marked with a diamond, for high-occupancy vehicles (HOV)—cars carrying two people or more.

Highways are well paved. Interstates—limited-access, multilane highways designated with an "I–" before the number—are fastest. Interstates with three-digit numbers circle urban areas, which may also have other limited-access expressways, freeways, and parkways. Tolls may be levied on limited-access highways. U.S. and state highways aren't necessarily limited-access, but may have several lanes.

Gas stations are plentiful. Most stay open late (24 hours along major highways and in big cities) except in rural areas, where Sunday hours are limited and where you may drive for long stretches without a refueling opportunity. Along larger highways, roadside stops with restrooms, fast-food restaurants, and sundries stores are well spaced. State police and tow trucks patrol major highways. If your car breaks down on an interstate, pull onto the shoulder and wait for help, or have your passengers wait while you walk to an emergency phone (available in most states). If you carry a cell phone, dial *277, noting your location on the small green roadside mileage marker.

ELECTRICITY

The U.S. standard is AC, 110 volts/60 cycles. Plugs have two flat pins set parallel to each other.

EMBASSIES

Contacts Australia ☎ *202/797–3000* ⊕ *www.austemb.org.* **Canada** ☎ *202/682–1740* ⊕ *www.canadianembassy.org.* **UK** ☎ *202/588–7800* ⊕ *www.britainusa.com.*

For police, fire, or ambulance, dial 911 (0 in rural areas).

HOLIDAYS

New Year's Day (Jan. 1); Martin Luther King Day (3rd Mon. in Jan.); Presidents' Day (3rd Mon. in Feb.); Memorial Day (last Mon. in May); Independence Day (July 4); Labor Day (1st Mon. in Sept.); Columbus Day (2nd Mon. in Oct.); Thanksgiving Day (4th Thurs. in Nov.); Christmas Eve and Christmas Day (Dec. 24 and 25); and New Year's Eve (Dec. 31).

MAIL
You can buy stamps and send letters and parcels in post offices. Stamp-dispensing machines can occasionally be found in airports, bus and train stations, office buildings, drugstores, convenience stores, and in ATMs. U.S. mailboxes are stout, dark-blue steel bins; pickup schedules are posted inside the bin (pull the handle). Mail parcels over a pound at a post office.

A first-class letter weighing 1 ounce or less costs 45¢; each additional ounce costs 20¢. Postcards cost 32¢. Postcards or 1-ounce airmail letters to most countries cost $1.05; postcards or 1-ounce letters to Canada and Mexico cost 85¢. To receive mail on the road, have it sent c/o General Delivery to your destination's main post office. You must pick up mail in person within 30 days with a driver's license or passport for identification.

Contacts DHL ☎ *800/225-5345* ⊕ *www.dhl. com.* **FedEx** ☎ *800/463-3339* ⊕ *www.fedex. com.* **Mail Boxes, Etc.** ☎ *800/789-4623* ⊕ *www.mbe.com.* **UPS** ☎ *800/742-5877* ⊕ *www.ups.com.* **USPS** ☎ *800/275-8777* ⊕ *www.usps.com.*

PASSPORTS AND VISAS
Visitor visas aren't necessary for citizens of Australia, Canada, the United Kingdom, or most citizens of EU countries coming for tourism and staying for under 90 days. A visa is $131, and waiting time can be substantial. Apply for a visa at the U.S. consulate in your place of residence.

Visa Information Destination USA ⊕ *www. travel.state.gov.*

PHONES
Numbers consist of a three-digit area code and a seven-digit local number. Within many local calling areas, dial just seven digits. In others, dial "1" first and all 10 digits; this is true for calling toll-free numbers—prefixed by "800," "888," "866," and "877." Dial "1" before

"900" numbers, too, but know that they're very expensive.

For international calls, dial "011," the country code, and the number. For help, dial "0" and ask for an overseas operator. Most phone books list country codes and U.S. area codes. The country code for Australia is 61, for New Zealand 64, for the United Kingdom 44. Calling Canada is the same as calling within the United States (country code: 1).

For operator assistance, dial "0." For directory assistance, call 555-1212 or 411 (free at many public phones). To call "collect" (reverse charges), dial "0" instead of "1" before the 10-digit number.

Instructions are generally posted on pay phones. Usually you insert coins in a slot (usually 25¢-50¢ for local calls) and wait for a steady tone before dialing. On long-distance calls the operator tells you how much to insert; prepaid phone cards, widely available, can be used from any phone. Follow the directions to activate the card, then dial your number.

CELL PHONES
The United States has several GSM (Global System for Mobile Communications) networks, so multiband mobiles from most countries (except for Japan) work here. It's almost impossible to buy just a pay-as-you-go mobile SIM card in the U.S.—needed to avoid roaming charges—but cell phones with pay-as-you-go plans are available for well under $100. AT&T (GoPhone) and Virgin Mobile have the cheapest with national coverage.

Contacts AT&T ☎ *800/331-0500* ⊕ *www.att.com.* **Virgin Mobile** ⊕ *www. virginmobileusa.com.*

You'll find renowned breweries throughout Colorado, including, of course, the nation's second-largest brewer: Miller-Coors. There are dozens of microbreweries in Denver, Colorado Springs, Boulder, and the resort towns—if you're a beer drinker, be sure to try some local brews. Although the region is not known for its wines, the wineries in the Grand Junction area and along the Front Range are earning increased acclaim.

▌ ECOTOURISM

Although neither the Bureau of Land Management (BLM) nor the National Park Service has designated any parts of Colorado as endangered ecosystems, many areas are open only to hikers; vehicles, mountain bikes, and horses are banned. It's wise to respect these closures, as well as the old adage **leave only footprints, take only pictures.** It is considered poor form to pick wildflowers while hiking, and it is illegal to pick columbine, the state flower of Colorado. Recycling is taken seriously throughout Colorado, and you will find yourself unpopular if you litter or fail to recycle your cans and bottles.

All archaeological artifacts, including rock etchings and paintings, are protected by federal law and must be left untouched and undisturbed.

Contacts National Park Reservation Service ☎ 877/444–6777 ⊕ www.recreation. gov. **U.S. Bureau of Land Management** ☎ 303/239–3600 ⊕ www.blm.gov/co.

▌ HEALTH

You may feel dizzy and weak and find yourself breathing heavily—signs that the thin mountain air isn't giving you your accustomed dose of oxygen. Take it easy, and rest often for a few days until you're acclimatized. Throughout your stay, drink plenty of water and watch your alcohol consumption. If you experience severe headaches and nausea, see a doctor. It's easy—especially in a state

where highways climb to 11,000 feet and higher—to go too high too fast. The remedy for altitude-related discomfort is to descend into heavier air.

▌ PACKING

For the most part, informality reigns in the Centennial State; jeans, sport shirts, and T-shirts fit in almost everywhere. If you plan to golf, a collared shirt may be required for men. No matter what your vacation plans are, don't forget to pack sunscreen, lip balm with SPF, sunglasses, and a cap or hat. The sunshine is intense at Colorado's altitude, and there are plenty of souvenirs available that you'll prefer over a sunburn.

If you plan to spend much time outdoors, and certainly if you go in winter, choose clothing appropriate for cold and wet weather. Cotton clothing, including denim, can be uncomfortable when it gets wet or when the weather's cold. Better choices are clothing made of wool or any of a number of synthetics that provide warmth without bulk and maintain their insulating properties when wet. It's not a bad idea to save your shopping for Colorado, where you'll find a huge selection of suitable clothing and gear.

In summer you'll probably want to wear shorts during the day. Because early morning and night can be cold, particularly in the mountains, pack a sweater and a light jacket, and perhaps a wool cap and gloves. For walks and hikes, you'll need sturdy footwear. Boots should have thick soles and plenty of ankle support; if your shoes are new and you plan to do a lot of hiking, break them in at home. Bring a day pack for short hikes, along with a canteen or water bottle, and don't forget rain gear, a hat, sunscreen, and insect repellent.

In winter, prepare for subzero temperatures with good boots, warm socks and liners, long johns, a well-insulated jacket, and a warm hat and mittens. Layers are the best preparation for fluctuating temperatures.

▌SAFETY

Although Colorado is considered to be generally safe, travelers should take ordinary precautions—unfortunate incidents can happen anywhere. At your hotel lock your valuables either in the hotel's safe or in the safe in your room, if one is available. Be aware of your surroundings, and keep your wallet and passport in a buttoned pocket, or keep your handbag in front of you where you can see it. At night, avoid dimly lighted areas and areas where there are few people. Consider a taxi ride to your hotel if it is a long walk or you are alone.

Regardless of the outdoor activity or your level of skill, safety must come first. When hiking or taking part in any other outdoor activity, it's best (and often more fun) to go in pairs or small groups. If you do hike, cycle, kayak, or backcountry ski alone, it is essential that you tell someone where you are going and when you plan to return, whether it's a park ranger or the host of your B&B. Let them know, of course, when you've returned safely.

Many trails are at high altitudes, where oxygen is scarce. They're also frequently desolate. Hikers and bikers should carry emergency supplies in their backpacks. Proper equipment includes a flashlight, a compass, waterproof matches, a first-aid kit, a knife, a space blanket, and a light plastic tarp for shelter. Backcountry skiers should add a repair kit, a blanket, an avalanche beacon, and a lightweight shovel to their lists. Always bring extra food and a canteen of water, as dehydration is a real danger at high altitudes. Never drink from streams or lakes, unless you boil the water first or purify it with tablets. Giardia, an intestinal parasite, may be present.

Although you may tan easily, the sun is intense even at mile-high elevations (which are relatively low for the state), and sunburn can develop in just a few hours of hiking or sightseeing. Coloradans slather on sunscreen as a matter of course. Be sure to pack plenty of it, and don't forget to put it on when skiing—there's nothing glamorous about a goggle tan. The state's dry climate and thin air can also dehydrate you quickly. Carry a couple of liters of water with you each day and sip frequently.

Flash floods can strike at any time and any place with little or no warning. The danger in mountainous terrain is heightened when distant rains are channeled into gullies and ravines, turning a quiet streamside campsite or wash into a rampaging torrent in seconds. Check weather reports before heading into the backcountry, and be prepared to head for higher ground if the weather turns severe.

One of the most wonderful parts of the Rockies is the abundant wildlife. And although a herd of grazing elk or a bighorn sheep high on a hillside is most certainly a Kodak moment, an encounter with a bear or mountain lion is not. To avoid such an unpleasant situation while hiking, make plenty of noise and keep dogs on leashes and small children between adults. While camping, be sure to store all food, utensils, and clothing with food odors far away from your tent, preferably high in a tree. If you do come across a bear or big cat, do not run. For bears, back away quietly; for lions, make yourself look as big as possible. In either case, be prepared to fend off the animal with loud noises, rocks, sticks, etc. And, as the saying goes, do not feed the bears—or any wild animals—whether they're dangerous or not.

When in any park, give all animals their space. If you want to take a photograph, use a long lens rather than a long sneak to approach closely. Approaching an animal can cause stress and affect its ability to survive the sometimes brutal climate. In all cases, remember that the animals have the right-of-way; this is their home, you are the visitor.

Safety Transportation Security Administration (*TSA;*). Transportation Security Administration ⊕ www.tsa.gov.

▌ SPORTS AND THE OUTDOORS

The Colorado Rockies are one of America's greatest playgrounds. Information about Colorado's recreational areas and activities is provided in each regional section; the following is general information.

Outfitter Listings Colorado Outfitters Association ☎ 970/824–2468 ⊕ www. coloradooutfitters.org.

GROUP TRIPS

Group sizes for organized trips vary considerably, depending on the organizer and the activity. Often, if you're planning a trip with a large group, trip organizers, or outfitters will offer discounts of 10% and more and are willing to customize trips. For example, if you're with a group interested in photography or in wildlife, trip organizers have been known to get professional photographers or naturalists to join the group.

One way to travel with a group is to join an organization before going. Conservation-minded travelers might want to contact the Sierra Club, a nonprofit organization, which offers both vacation and work trips. Hiking trails tend to be maintained by volunteers (this is more often done by local hiking clubs). Park or forest rangers are the best resource for information about groups involved in this sort of work.

Individuals or groups wanting to test their mettle can learn wilderness skills through "outdoor schools."

Contacts American Hiking Society ✉ 1422 Fenwick La., 20910, Silver Spring, Maryland ☎ 800/972–8608 ⊕ www.americanhiking.org. **Boulder Outdoor Survival School** 🏕 Box 1590, Boulder 80305 ☎ 303/444–9779, 800/335–7404 ⊕ www.boss-inc.com. **Sierra Club** ✉ 1536 Wynkoop St., 4th Fl., Denver 80202 ☎ 303/861–8819 ⊕ rmc.sierraclub.org.

▌ TAXES

Colorado's state sales tax is 2.9%, but after that it gets a little tricky, as there are additional city and county taxes that raise the total to between 7.5% and 8.5%. Lodging taxes also vary around the state, and can be as high as nearly 15% in Denver and less than 10% in other areas.

▌ TIME

All of Colorado is in the Mountain Time Zone. Mountain Time is two hours earlier than Eastern Time and one hour later than Pacific Time, so Colorado is two hours behind New York and one hour ahead of California.

Time Zones Timeanddate.com. Timeanddate.com can help you figure out the correct time anywhere. ⊕ www.timeanddate.com/worldclock.

▌ TIPPING

It's customary to tip 15% to 20% at restaurants in cities; in resort towns, 20% is increasingly the norm. For coat checks and bellmen, $1 per coat or bag is the minimum. Taxi drivers expect 10% to 15%. In resort towns, ski technicians, sandwich makers, coffee baristas, and the like also appreciate tips.

▌ TOURS

GUIDED TOURS

Tour Colorado offers a wide range of comprehensive tours statewide. Multi-day theme tours include train rides, scenic drives, wildlife spotting, adventure thrills, and shopping excursions.

Contacts Tour Colorado ☎ 888/311–8687 ⊕ www.tourcolorado.com.

SPECIAL-INTEREST TOURS

Colorado Wine Country Tours takes wine lovers on a sommelier-guided tour of Colorado wineries on the Front Range and the Western Slope. Culinary Connectors offers Denver-based culinary tours of the city's best restaurants as well as tours of ethnic, gourmet, and farmers' markets.

Field Guides takes birders on 10-day trips in search of Colorado's prairie chickens and grouse every April. OARS offers multiday rafting trips on the Yampa and Green rivers and hiking vacations in Chaco Canyon, Mesa Verde National Park, Ute Mountain Tribal Park, and National Bridges Monument. Victor Emanuel Nature Tours offers several Colorado-based birding tours in the spring and summer.

Contacts Colorado Wine Country Tours ☎ 303/777–9463 ⊕ www.coloradowinecountrytours.com. **Culinary Connectors** ☎ 303/495–5487 ⊕ www.culinaryconnectors.com. **Field Guides** ☎ 800/728–4953 ⊕ www.fieldguides.com. **OARS** ☎ 800/346–6277 ⊕ www.oars.com/colorado. **Victor Emanuel Nature Tours** ☎ 512/328–5221, 800/328–8368 ⊕ www.ventbird.com.

TRIP INSURANCE

Comprehensive trip insurance is valuable if you're booking a very expensive or complicated trip (particularly to an isolated region) or if you're reserving far in advance. Comprehensive policies typically cover trip-cancellation and interruption, letting you cancel or cut your trip short because of illness, or, in some cases, acts of terrorism in your destination. Such policies might also cover evacuation and medical care. (For trips abroad you should have at least medical-only coverage. *See Medical Insurance and Assistance under Health.*) Some also cover you for trip delays because of bad weather or mechanical problems as well as for lost or delayed luggage.

Another type of coverage to consider is financial default—that is, when your trip is disrupted because a tour operator, airline, or cruise line goes out of business. Generally you must buy this when you book your trip or shortly thereafter, and it's available to you only if your operator isn't on a list of excluded companies.

Always read the fine print of your policy to make sure that you're covered for the risks that most concern you. Compare several policies to be sure you're getting the best price and range of coverage available.

Comprehensive Insurers Access America ☎ 800/284–8300 ⊕ www.accessamerica.com. **AIG Travel Guard** ☎ 800/826–4919 ⊕ www.travelguard.com. **CSA Travel Protection** ☎ 800/873–9855 ⊕ www.csatravelprotection.com. **Travelex Insurance** ☎ 888/228–9792 ⊕ www.travelex-insurance.com. **Travel Insured International** ☎ 800/243–3174 ⊕ www.travelinsured.com.

Insurance Comparison Information Insure My Trip ☎ 800/487–4722 ⊕ www.insuremytrip.com. **Square Mouth** ☎ 800/240–0369 ⊕ www.squaremouth.com.

▌ VISITOR INFORMATION

Almost every town, county, and resort area has its own tourist office. Contact information is provided in the Essentials section at the start of each area.

Contact Colorado Tourism Office ☎ 800/265–6723 ⊕ www.colorado.com.

INDEX

PHOTO CREDITS

NOTES

NOTES

NOTES

NOTES

NOTES

NOTES

NOTES

NOTES

NOTES

ABOUT OUR WRITERS

Colorado native Ricardo Baca travels internationally each fall, from India to Australia, Laos to Nicaragua, China to Spain, Cambodia to Belize. He spends the rest of the year traveling across the United States, focusing on Colorado's delightfully varied terrain. When he's not on the road, he is the entertainment editor and lead music critic at *The Denver Post*.

Martha Schindler Connors is a freelance writer in Evergreen, CO, where she lives with her husband and two dogs. Her writing has appeared in many national and regional magazines. For this edition, Martha updated the Rocky Mountain National Park, Southwest Colorado, and Mesa Verde National Park chapters.

Jad Davenport, a freelance travel writer and photographer, grew up in Colorado where he lives with his wife and daughters. He enjoys backcountry skiing, ice climbing, white-water kayaking, and hiking. His work has appeared in *Outside, Islands,* and *Coastal Living* magazines. For this edition, Jad updated Summit County, Vail Valley, and Aspen.

Kyle Wagner wrote about restaurants and food in Denver for 12 years, first for the alternative weekly *Westword* and then for the *Denver Post*, before being named travel editor for the *Post* in 2005. Her work also has appeared in the *Rocky Mountain News* and *Sunset* magazine. She lives in Denver with her two teenage daughters, who had their passports stamped before they started kindergarten and prefer sushi to McDonald's. For this edition, Kyle updated Experience Colorado, Denver, the Rockies Near Denver, and Northwest Colorado and Steamboat Springs.